LANGUAGES AND CROSS-CULTURAL EXCHANGES
IN RENAISSANCE ITALY

LATE MEDIEVAL AND EARLY MODERN STUDIES

VOLUME 30

Editorial Board
Ian Moulton, Chair, *Arizona State University*
Frederick Kiefer, *University of Arizona*
Markus Cruse, *Arizona State University*
Catherine Kovesi, *University of Melbourne*
Charles Zika, *University of Melbourne*

Advisory Board
Susan Broomhall, *Australian Catholic University*
Megan Cassidy-Welch, *Australian Catholic University*
Albrecht Classen, *University of Arizona*
Robert W. Gaston, *University of Melbourne*
John Griffiths, *Monash University*
Anthony Gully, *Arizona State University*
Paul Salzman, *La Trobe University*
Anne Scott, *Northern Arizona University*
Juliann Vitullo, *Arizona State University*
Emil Volek, *Arizona State University*
Retha Warnicke, *Arizona State University*

Previously published volumes in this series
are listed at the back of the book.

Languages and Cross-Cultural Exchanges in Renaissance Italy

Edited by
ALESSANDRA PETROCCHI *and*
JOSHUA BROWN

BREPOLS

Cover image: Map of Europe from the *Cornaro Atlas* produced in *c.* 1489 for the Cornaro family, a patrician family of Venice. London, British Library, MS Egerton 73, fol. 36r. Image from doi.org/10.21250/pel01, issued under a CC 1.0 Universal Public Domain licence.

© 2023, Brepols Publishers n.v., Turnhout, Belgium.

All rights reserved. No part of this publication may be reproduced, stored in a retrieval system, or transmitted, in any form or by any means, electronic, mechanical, photocopying, recording, or otherwise without the prior permission of the publisher.

D/2023/0095/2
ISBN 978-2-503-60181-6
eISBN 978-2-503-60182-3
DOI 10.1484/M.LMEMS-EB.5.130905

ISSN 2406-5463
eISSN 2406-5471

Printed in the EU on acid-free paper.

Contents

Figures and Tables   7

Acknowledgements   9

Languages and Cross-Cultural Exchanges in Renaissance Italy
Alessandra PETROCCHI and Joshua BROWN   11

Part 1
The Italian Vernaculars

Multilingual Printing
Brian RICHARDSON   35

Communicating in Different Vernaculars
Italo-Romance Intercomprehension in Historical Perspective
Alessandro CARLUCCI   65

Untraced Polymorphy and Vernaculars in Contact in Renaissance Italy
Joshua BROWN   95

Medieval and Renaissance Venice
Language Contact at Home and Abroad
Ronnie FERGUSON   121

Latin, Sicilian, and the Adoption of Italian in Malta
Joseph M. BRINCAT   157

Trusting Vernacular Languages in the Italian Renaissance
Andrea RIZZI   185

Part 2
Linguistic and Cultural Exchanges with Europe

Language Contact between French and Italian in the Sixteenth Century
Evidence from the Diplomatic Letters of Georges d'Armagnac
Jenelle THOMAS 211

The Impact of Aragonese and Castilian Dominations on the Language and Literature of Sardinia
Immacolata PINTO 239

Libri alienigeni
Evidence of Anglo-Italian Language Contact from the Fifteenth-Century Port of Southampton
Megan TIDDEMAN 269

The Influence of French on Sixteenth-Century Italian
Thomas SCHARINGER 299

Part 3
Encounters with the East

Ethiopia and Ethiopian Languages in Renaissance Italy
Samantha KELLY 331

Ascanio Persio and the 'Greekness' of Italian
Han LAMERS 359

Hebrew Literature in Italy (1300–1600)
Fabrizio LELLI 389

Language Contacts and Contact Languages in Renaissance Naples
From the *moresche* to *Lo cunto de li cunti*
Carolina STROMBOLI 411

Figures and Tables

Figures

Figure 4.1.	Medieval population movements to, and within, the lagoons of north-eastern Italy. Copyright R. Ferguson.	127
Figure 4.2.	Venetian maritime trade routes. Copyright R. Ferguson.	132
Figure 6.1.	*Opera intitulata Aquila* (Naples: Ayolfus de Cantono, 1492), fol. Aiiv. Image reproduced from Biblioteca Europea di Informazione e Cultura under Creative Commons CC BY-SA 4.0.	191
Figure 6.2.	Ortensio Lando, *Commentario* (Venice, 1548). Reproduced under Google Books Creative Commons CC BY-SA 4.0.	194
Figure 6.3.	*L'Eneide di Virgilio* (Venice: Giunta, 1581). Reproduced under Google Books Creative Commons CC BY-SA 4.0.	198
Figure 7.1.	Number of letters written by year by Georges d'Armagnac, in French, Italian, and Latin.	223

Tables

Table 7.1.	Letters written by Georges d'Armagnac during his posts as ambassador to Venice and Rome.	224
Table 7.2.	Use of foreign-origin words by decade.	230
Table 9.1.	Frequency of the terms *naves* and *carrak* in Southampton sources (1371–1384) studied by Nicolini.	278
Table 10.1.	Number of Italianisms in French per century	300
Table 10.2.	Number of Gallicisms in Italian per century	300
Table 10.3.	Number of Italianisms in French per century	302
Table 10.4.	Number of Gallicisms in Italian per century	302
Table 10.5.	Number of French books printed in the 'Italian states' from 1501 to 1600 (*USTC*).	304

Acknowledgements

As editors, we would like to acknowledge those who have contributed to this project. We would like to thank the contributors of chapters that appear in the book for their willingness to submit their manuscripts, and for their careful attention to suggestions made by the editors to strengthen each paper.

All of the authors have tried their utmost to keep to our editorial deadlines, despite the major disruptions caused by the COVID-19 pandemic. We thank our authors for their patience and academic integrity while working on their chapters. Our deepest appreciation goes to Deborah A. Oosterhouse, our copyeditor, for her meticulous work. Finally our gratitude is due to our publishers, particularly Guy Carney, and to the editorial board of the series Late Medieval and Early Modern Studies, who supported the proposal and concept of the book from its inception with enthusiasm.

ALESSANDRA PETROCCHI AND
JOSHUA BROWN

Languages and Cross-Cultural Exchanges in Renaissance Italy

Few historical eras have attracted scholarly attention and elicited more discussion as the Renaissance. The Italian Renaissance remains a dynamic topic and continues to exercise a powerful hold on scholarly enquiry; ground-breaking new research, micro-studies of individual figures or aspects, and textual editions proliferate to this date.[1] The debate about the nature of, and explanation for, the Renaissance has raged for over a hundred years, since the publication of Jacob Burckhardt's *Civilization of the Renaissance in Italy*. Countless volumes have been written on various aspects of the Italian Renaissance, broadly understood as that unprecedented cultural and economic development of Italy which began in the fourteenth century and lasted until the seventeenth century.[2] Nonetheless, few have focused on language contact and multilingualism in Renaissance Italy in a way which brings scholars together with expertise in different world regions and research areas. The present volume aims to bridge this gap in literature by presenting a collection

---

[1] The body of recent literature on the Italian Renaissance is too vast to be mentioned, as are the scholarly debates about the nature of the Renaissance. In this regard, an excellent and recent historiographical overview is provided by Caferro, *Contesting the Renaissance*, see particularly chap. 1. The reader can refer to the studies mentioned in the bibliography at the end of this introduction and the essays collected here.

[2] The expression 'Italian Renaissance' has not gone unchallenged; its meaning and boundaries have aroused much controversy. Scholars arrange their period markers according to different criteria, and this volume makes no exception: periodization and definitions have differed according to the background of the author.

Alessandra Petrocchi (alessandra.petrocchi@ling-phil.ox.ac.uk) is a Research Fellow at the Faculty of Linguistics, Philology, and Phonetics at the University of Oxford. Her research areas include textual criticism, manuscript studies, language contact, and intellectual history.

Joshua Brown (joshua.j.brown@uwa.edu.au) is Senior Lecturer in Italian Studies at the University of Western Australia. His research interests include the history of the Italian language, dialect contact, and language change.

of micro-studies covering a variety of themes, ranging from language-related phenomena that took place in the Italian peninsula to those which occurred abroad but engaged with the people of Renaissance Italy.

In recent years, topics such as multilingualism and networks of knowledge across cultures have witnessed an unprecedented upsurge in interest. The emergence of this new trend has coincided with a radical departure from the Eurocentric focus of scholarship, seen as too limited to grasp and assess the multi-scalar interactions that defined the lives of communities in the Middle Ages and early modern period. Travel, language contact, and the circulation of ideas between East and West were vital aspects of medieval societies — yet it is only in recent decades that new frameworks and methodologies exploring the complex relations between local and global have fully emerged.[3] We are far from being alone in observing the fundamental importance of multilingualism in and with regard to Renaissance Italy, but we have tried to take its significance a step further. We bring diverse disciplinary perspectives together: literary scholars, historians, and linguists with different regional expertise. Our authors present a variety of case studies by often cross-fertilizing their approaches with other disciplinary lenses. Although much work has been done in the field of Renaissance studies, at present there is no book which offers a comparative overview of the linguistic interaction between Renaissance Italy and the wider world. The present volume is intended to fill this void. It tries to throw new light on old questions as well as address some issues for the first time and on a geographically wide perspective, which has required putting together scholars with different linguistic expertise.

This publication picks up on important current impulses within the study of language contact and global history, above all 'connectivity': in the Middle Ages boundaries were fluid, and people living in those centuries had global histories. Linguistic boundaries were easily crossed, connecting people for different purposes and giving rise to multilayered exchanges. Yet languages were signs of belonging, storehouses of literary traditions and cultural expressions. Responding to recent scholarly developments, the following collection of essays tries to avoid the temptation to draw straight lines from one time and place to another. We do not propose a single grand narrative; nor do we provide an exhaustive analysis of all aspects of Renaissance Italy over a three-hundred-year period. Instead, we argue for multilingualism and language contact *in* Renaissance Italy and *with respect to* Renaissance Italy as products of a period of dynamic change which cannot be fully grasped through a single framework or regional expertise. Our explorations rest upon chronological and geographical specificity, particularly in Parts 2 and 3 of the volume, where we do not begin from top-down theories about global processes and then seek regional case studies. Rather, we begin from regional expertise

---

3 This is testified by some developing scholarly subfields, such as comparative medieval literature and global medieval history.

and then try to link local situations to larger questions which transcend national boundaries. By addressing these objectives, we aim to generate questions, analyses, and theories that come from our understandings of the linguistic scenario in and in respect to Renaissance Italy, and which could offer new approaches to both later and earlier periods.

Medievalists and early modern historians working across a range of disciplines have increasingly sought to engage with the concept of 'Global Middle Ages'.[4] One of the earliest attempts at undertaking an analysis of global relations in the Middle Ages is Abu-Lughod's study of 'world system' (1989), which aims to redress a Eurocentric bias by emphasizing the role of Asia in the world economy of the thirteenth century. She proposes a system of sub-systems, dominated by nodal points — for instance Venice — and critical gateways between East and West, such as Baghdad and Peking. World-systems theory has provided new questions about the ways in which regions in the past and present were integrated with each other, and how the balance of economic power was constructed between them. Abu-Lughod argues for dynamism and adaptability being important components in these systems.[5]

What the essays presented here have in common is the way in which they make reference to Italy as a contact zone — a 'meeting point' whose languages, and therefore whose speakers, came into contact via some particular means, be they written or spoken. This approach to historical accounts of language finds parallels in subdisciplines immediately cognate to linguistics. Historical sociolinguistics has seen much focus on the development of standard languages, with only some of this focus aimed at non-standard language or marginalized groups. At the same time, new fields of endeavour in history have sought to broaden the purview of traditional chronological limits. Expressions such as 'Global Middle Ages' have arisen with a view to bringing medieval studies 'more visibly into conversation with other kinds of teaching and investigation in the twenty-first century academy'.[6] Vice versa, historians have also taken a more active role in sociolinguistics, arguing for languages as communities of speakers, and as forms of cultural translation in early modern Europe.[7] The

---

[4] Moore, 'A Global Middle Ages?'; Belich and others, eds, *The Prospect of Global History*. See also the exhaustive references to scholarly publications focusing on the Global Middle Ages mentioned by Holmes and Standen, 'Introduction: Towards a Global Middle Ages'.

[5] World-systems theory is a multidisciplinary approach to world history and social change which emphasizes the world-system (and not nation-states) as the primary (but not exclusive) unit of social analysis. World-systems theory emerged in the 1970s thanks to the work of Immanuel Wallerstein, an American sociologist and economic historian; see Wallerstein's highly influential, multi-volume opus *The Modern World-System*, one of this century's greatest works of social science.

[6] Heng, 'The Global Middle Ages', p. 206; Ramey and others, 'Revisioning the Global Middle Ages'.

[7] Burke, *Languages and Communities in Early Modern Europe*; Burke and Po-Chia Hsia, eds, *Cultural Translation in Early Modern Europe*; Busi and Greco, eds, *Rinascimento Plurale*; Campbell and Milner, eds, *Artistic Exchange and Cultural Translation*.

AHRC Project 'Defining the Global Middle Ages' (2012-2015), organized at the Universities of Oxford, Birmingham, and Newcastle, is among the latest and perhaps most comprehensive attempts to address theoretical issues and discuss methodologies relating to the concept of the 'Global Middle Ages', although almost exclusively from a historian's perspective.[8] The project leaders Catherine Holmes and Naomi Standen emphasize that 'Global Middle Ages' is 'an umbrella term for a collection of more specifically demarcated periodizations, with the exact chronological parameters of each depending on the global topic under consideration'.[9] The collection of essays edited by Holmes and Standen (2018) are innovative in the range of perspectives employed and global phenomena examined. Central to their understanding of the Global Middle Ages as both a period with identifiable characteristics and as an approach with its own themes and conceptual underpinnings is the idea of the Middle Ages as a time of great intensification of exchange, communication, and networks: a period characterized by increased economic activity, urbanization, social restructuring, multicentred politics, and new frameworks of ideas.

A conviction that informs newer methods today is the need to study societies from around the world in relation to one another and to move past short-sighted interpretations that consider civilizations as self-contained categories. For instance, the volume by Charles H. Parker, *Global Interactions in the Early Modern Age, 1400-1800* (2010), which explores encounters in the Early Modern Age and their influences on the development of world societies, employs a global perspective to demonstrate how new commercial networks, large-scale migration streams, and transfers of knowledge across oceans and continents wove together the major regions of the world. Language has much to do with political, military, and economic power. The volume edited by Albrecht Classen, *Multilingualism in the Middle Ages and Early Modern Age* (2016), presents a series of case studies focusing on important examples of multilingualism in medieval and early modern societies, that is, in linguistic and cultural contact zones, such as England, Spain, Hungary, the Holy Land, but also the lesser-known area of the New World. Our volume is thus to be situated within recent developments in linguistics, history, and the recent global turn in Renaissance studies.

Several interlocking themes are addressed in this project, and new textual corpora are examined for the first time. The rise of the vernacular, language contact, and multilingual spaces are three of the main themes explored. Although researchers have continued to investigate the language and cultural products

---

8 The project constituted a network of thirty-three UK-based scholars, each with different regional specialisms who could investigate a set of objectives under the banner question: 'What was global in the Middle Ages?' The group included those with expertise in Africa, the Americas, eastern Eurasia, and western Eurasia, thus breaking down traditional barriers between European medievalists and specialists in world regions beyond Europe.
9 Holmes and Standen, 'Introduction: Towards a Global Middle Ages', p. 20.

of the cultural elite, many fields of research have also turned attention towards sectors of society who have left traces in the archives, but whose stories are yet to be told. Italy provides ample material in the available sources. Recent studies have found Italy to be a fertile area of investigation for ways in which language choice can be explained among the cultural elite, or how language can be seen to articulate power throughout the Italian cities and courts.[10] The wealth of published and unpublished sources, archival sources, and now also digital editions and texts means that attention is also being paid to non-literary materials, whose potential is still yet to be explored. Oftentimes, we have barely scratched the surface of what is waiting to be exploited. Such materials contain language, stories, accounts, etc. of language(s) that are not and cannot be seen at the 'higher' levels of society. Thus, researchers of non-literary writing are continuing to explore the ways in which people of the past communicated, including but not limited to merchant writing, multilingual diplomatic writing, religious writing, women's writing, and others.[11] Indeed, even as recently as 2018, Murano noted that 'anche alcune donne di potere, letterate e religiose italiane hanno posseduto biblioteche ma, per lo più ignorate, queste collezioni attendono ancora in gran parte di essere identificate, indagate e ricostruite' (even some women of power, Italian literary writers, and religious women owned libraries but, mainly ignored, these collections are still waiting in large part to be identified, investigated, and reconstructed).[12] In short, to recall an old distinction from the Italian literary tradition, researchers are coming to see more and more value in *italiano dell'uso* as well as *italiano letterario*.[13] These new, interdisciplinary approaches to language and history provide one of the main motivations for the essays presented here. They give a broad picture of a composite amalgamation of influences, thriving intellectual culture, and networks of communication involving a variety of actors, such as intellectuals, officials, merchants, soldiers, slaves, and so forth.

Our goal was to bring together people working on related aspects of multilingualism but in scholarly spheres which had tended to remain rather separate.[14] We have assembled contributors from a range of backgrounds;

---

10   Del Soldato and Rizzi, eds, *City, Court, Academy* and Bornstein, Gaffuri, and Maxson, eds, *Languages of Power in Italy*, respectively.
11   On merchant writing, see Guidi Bruscoli, 'I mercanti italiani e le lingue straniere'; Wagner, Beinhoff, and Outhwaite, eds, *Merchants of Innovation*. On diplomatic writing, see Baglioni, 'Italoromanzo in caratteri arabi in un diploma magrebino del Trecento'; Fulton, '"Saluti da Londra"'. On religious writing, see Brown, 'Una memoria quattrocentesca in volgare lombardo'; Brown, 'Women's Literacy in a Late Medieval Religious Community'. On women's writing, see Plebani, *Le scritture delle donne in Europa*; Sanson, '"Io che donna indotta e minima sono"'.
12   Murano, 'Donne e libri nel Rinascimento italiano', p. 7.
13   For example, the title of the third volume of *Storia dell'italiano scritto*, edited by Antonelli, Motolese, and Tomasin, *Italiano dell'uso*, as well as the earlier *Storia della lingua italiana* volumes, edited by Serianni and Trifone, whose third instalment is entitled *Le altre lingue*.
14   Given the eclectic nature of the volume, we have decided not to include an index. While all authors have addressed the broad question of languages in Renaissance Italy, each chapter concerns a topic related to this question from the author's particular point of view and

although diverse in chronological and geographical dimensions, all the chapters are connected by the theme of language contact in and with Renaissance Italy. The essays here investigate the circumstances and extent of transfer of knowledge between dialects, languages, and cultures through linguistic/literary/historical means. The main questions which drive our project are the following: What were the characteristics of multilingualism in Renaissance Italy? What was the relationship between the spoken and the written word? How did different languages and language varieties coexist and interact in Italy? What were the registers involved? What was the relationship outside the Italian peninsula between Italian and other languages? How can linguistic analysis help to illuminate the circumstances of global networks of knowledge between Renaissance Italy and the wider world? In addressing these research questions, the volume's main objectives are to establish a linguistic overview of Renaissance Italy in a comparative, interdisciplinary, and wider perspective which includes Italian, its sister dialects, and European and Eastern languages; to analyse primary sources and cultural contexts which have been so far neglected or treated in isolation; and to employ comparative linguistic and textual analysis to shed light on knowledge transfer across cultures and cross-fertilization of ideas.

In one sense, any descriptor, whether linguistic, geographical, or chronological, can be seen to be an artificial segmentation of time and space. Authors have been free to interpret these limits as they wish, and in this regard, the volume finds a place in the tradition of earlier collections which take Italy and the question of 'languages in contact' as their foci.[15] The chronological limits, from 1300 to 1600, also help to problematize the question of precisely what we mean by 'Italian' here. Trifone has noted that the syntagm *lingua italiana* is a 'Renaissance neologism', which became popular following Gian Giorgio Trissino's use of it in the title of his *Epistola de le lettere nuovamente aggiunte ne la lingua italiana*.[16] Benedetto Varchi's *Ercolano* also posed the question whether *la lingua volgare* should be called 'italiana o toscana o fiorentina'. It is significant that, precisely around the year 1500, one finds the term *lingua italiana* (actually spelled *taliana*) on the cover of an instruction booklet designed to learn foreign languages: *Questo si è uno libro utilissimo a chi se dileta de intendere todescho dechiarando in lingua taliana* (Venice: Giovanni Battista Sessa, 1500).

One reason for the narrow focus on individual standard varieties may be due to nationalism's identification and mapping with a single language. The

---

expertise. Therefore, readers interested in the specific topic of language in Sardinia or Anglo-Norman, say, will be able to find the appropriate chapter dealing with these subjects from the table of contents.

15 Filipponio and Seidl, eds, *Le lingue d'Italia e le altre*; Lepschy, *Varietà linguistiche e pluralità di codici nel Rinascimento*; Lepschy and Tosi, eds, *Multilingualism in Italy*; Lepschy and Tosi, eds, *Rethinking Languages in Contact*.

16 Trifone, 'L'affermazione del concetto di una "lingua italiana"', p. 105.

concept of the nation is a particularly European idea. It develops clearly from the eighteenth century onwards.[17] The idea that a nation closely identifies with one particular language is even more restricted, and little more than two centuries old. For individual nations, 'the potential for a shared first language can facilitate greater economic and political cooperation between citizens'.[18] Multilingual states were seen by emergent ethnic and national elites as barriers to progress. The concept of 'one nation, one language' throughout Europe was heavily influenced by the French case, 'where the common language was promoted by the revolutionary state as a means of achieving democracy and equality'. Ruzza has observed that nationalism's attitude towards language was 'one of minimizing internal linguistic difference in the community in question, formalizing language in a way that would empower intellectual classes, and emphasizing external linguistic difference'.[19] How do these elements, then, influence the way we should investigate situations of multilingual contact? These movements provide the broader context within which we must see language and the circulation of forms in the past. In short, the main focus so far has shown little attempt to consider mixed varieties of language as forming part of official histories of standard languages. Italy is one 'place' where a teleological tradition of language history is also present.[20]

Ever since the publication of Bruno Migliorini's *Storia della lingua italiana* in 1960, language histories have taken standard Italian as their starting point, and then retraced its steps, so to speak, to arrive at the formation of the modern variety.[21] These histories 'from above' lend weight to the forms of literary language produced throughout the history of Italy, beginning with fourteenth- and fifteenth-century writers, notably the 'Three Crowns' of Florence (Dante, Petrarch, and Boccaccio). A more recent historiography has sought to 'uncover' the various Italian(s) written and spoken not just throughout the peninsula, but also abroad. Since it is people who use languages, the personal networks of transcontinental travellers reveal illuminating cases about historical multilingualism. Given that any language history should attempt at least in part to be an accurate portrayal of the people who used such languages, language contact is an essential part of the story. Personal networks of an international nature therefore have much to tell us about how

---

17 Barbour, 'Nationalism, Language, Europe', p. 14.
18 Barbour, 'Nationalism, Language, Europe', p. 15. See also Gamberini and Lazzarini, *The Italian Renaissance State* and Wyatt, ed., *The Cambridge Companion to the Italian Renaissance*.
19 Ruzza, 'Language and Nationalism in Italy', p. 173.
20 See, for example, the insightful comments by Mattheier, 'Is There a European Language History?', pp. 353–54: 'the concept of a "national language history" has dominated the view of what historical linguistics should be concerned with in relation to virtually all European languages, and continues to do so today. The theoretical starting point of this view — which at the very least needs to be seriously questioned — is that the "standard" language is the genuine teleological goal of any historical language development'.
21 To quote one example for the many, Cella, *Storia dell'italiano*.

languages 'travel'. They continue right through the early modern period up to and including the presence of Italian in colonial settlements of the nineteenth century, which is only recently being uncovered.[22]

Language is a useful lens through which human contact and exchange can be seen to be part of both global and local circulation. Since all languages are to some extent contact languages (in that all standard languages of modern nation-states contain lexemes deriving from 'outside' sources), this collection of essays simply aims to reveal various aspects of these sources which are yet to be told, or which have so far been ignored. This may be because, until now, these sources have been hidden from view, or because researchers have not been looking for them.[23] Scholars have only recently come to appreciate the multilingual origins of standard languages.[24] As Vincent has noted, the 'standard view' has led to the imposition of the so-called 'pyramid metaphor' familiar from sociolinguistics.[25] At the top, there is Latin. The intermediate, local written standards (*scriptae*) have been estimated to be as many as seven hundred according to Muljačić.[26] Historical grammars have also allowed a more nuanced picture to emerge of the linguistic variation characteristic of its origins.[27] This influence could already be discerned in the first half of the fourteenth century. Reassessments of these early stages of Italian allow us to understand the variation at the base of what is commonly thought of as a single entity, whether it be 'standard', 'Florentine', 'Italian', whatever.

There is a further rationale for the volume. Although some previous scholarship has dealt with issues of languages in contact in Italy, the topic has not yet received a proper treatment, even if attention to historical multilingualism seems to have proliferated in studies of other nations. For example, a cursory glance at some recent literature shows a steady stream of publications dealing with various aspects of multilingualism in medieval Britain, and the various ways in which languages were distributed across society or used for literary affect.[28] Several volumes have recently been published drawing together individual micro-studies in an effort to explore

---

22 Gallagher, 'The Italian London of John North'; Colombo and Kinder, 'Italian as a Language of Communication in Nineteenth Century Italy and Abroad', p. 119.
23 Cf. Tamburelli, 'Uncovering the "Hidden" Multilingualism of Europe'.
24 Wright, ed., *The Multilingual Origins of Standard English*; Brown, 'Language History from Below'.
25 Vincent, 'Languages in Contact in Medieval Italy', p. 15.
26 Muljačić, 'The Relationship between the Dialects and the Standard Language', p. 390. For a useful overview of this debate, as well as a fresh insight into the available evidence, see Carlucci, 'Opinions about Perceived Linguistic Intelligibility'.
27 Unlike its English counterpart, a 'dialect' in the Italian context is a daughter language of Latin, such that 'Italian dialects' are brothers and sisters, not daughters of 'Italian'. See Maiden and Parry, eds, *The Dialects of Italy*, p. 2.
28 Trotter, ed., *Multilingualism in Later Medieval Britain*; Kleinhenz and Busby, eds, *Medieval Multilingualism*; Tyler, ed., *Conceptualizing Multilingualism in England*; Jefferson, Putter, and Hopkins, eds, *Multilingualism in Medieval Britain*, to name a few.

topics such as multilingualism, networks of knowledge, and language contact. Our interest in the very same issues is obviously a facet of a larger concern. For instance, the essays collected by Brownlee and Gondicas in *Renaissance Encounters Greek East and Latin West* (2013) explore an interrelated nexus of topics that illuminate our understanding of the cultural transactions (social, political, economic, religious, and artistic) between the Greek East and Latin West, unexpected cultural appropriations and forms of resistance, continuity and change, and the construction and hybridization of traditions in a wide expanse of the eastern Mediterranean. Christopher Kleinhenz and Keith Busby's *Medieval Multilingualism: The Francophone World and its Neighbours* (2010) contains essays on various aspects of multilingualism in medieval France, Italy, England, and the Low Countries. The fourteen contributions discuss the use of the vernaculars and Latin in both literary and non-literary contexts, showing how cultural and social factors determined the choice of language for a particular purpose or type of text. Judith A. Jefferson, Ad Putter, and Amanda Hopkins's *Multilingualism in Medieval Britain (c. 1066–1520): Sources and Analysis*, a volume devoted to the study of multilingual Britain in the later medieval period, brings together experts from different disciplines (mainly history, linguistics, and literature) in a joint effort to recover the complexities of spoken and written communication in the Middle Ages. As Tyler says in the introduction to her volume, questions of historical multilingualism are often tied to language politics of contemporary time periods. In this sense, the 'symbolic value' which she argues for takes on a particular significance in connecting the past and the present. Such an approach 'ensures that Anglophone scholars have become more conscious that the monolingual present of much of England does not reflect its medieval past'.[29] While we are acutely aware that parallels with traditions of other nation-states must be avoided, Tyler's observation can be equally applied to the Italian case. The attention that England has so far received, and which is only now being applied to Italy, may be partly due to a heightened recognition that Italy has always been, and still is now, very much part of a linguistic plurality. In part this can be seen to be due to the obvious presence of contemporary dialects in addition to standard Italian which pervade the peninsula, but also the prevalence of Latin in medieval and early modern contexts. In short, the history of multilingualism in Italy, one that takes into account the plurality of *all* varieties of language, is yet to be written.

The editors of the present volume invited the authors to bring out arguments for the themes proposed from the sources at hand, without imposing a predetermined methodological framework. These essays, each from their own perspectives, demonstrate how circulation and the crossing of geographical, linguistic, cultural, and religious boundaries have been a tremendous creative force, spurring centuries of literary innovation. This

---

29   Tyler, ed., *Conceptualizing Multilingualism in England*, p. 7.

volume attempts to transcend the boundaries of different fields and provide a variety of approaches to understand the role played by Italian and its sister dialects in and outside Italy. In doing so, it introduces current debates in relation to the topics of multilingualism and the global movement of ideas in the Middle Ages through three particular lenses reflecting the specialization of the contributors: the linguistic, the literary, and the historical-cultural. The volume is articulated into three sections: (1) The Italian Vernaculars, (2) Linguistic and Cultural Exchanges with Europe, and (3) Encounters with the East. Any treatment of language in Italy and particularly in historical accounts must perforce begin from a premise that Italy is, and always has been, a multilingual place.[30] Hence, our insistence that *languages* be plural in the title. In this way, we aimed to avoid any descriptor which may have potentially limited authors' fields of interests and their contributions. At the same time, we hope the volume's focus provides an adequate 'red thread' which holds the various chapters together. We have made no attempt at comprehensiveness in the volume, but we *have* sought to provide a broad representation of the remarkable diversity characteristic of Renaissance Italy. Naturally, any volume must be selective. Albanian, for example, which has a long historical presence in Italy, is not included. Nor are other varieties, such as Cimbrian or Griko. We were not able to include others still, such as German, Slovene, Croatian, the language of the Romani, and many of the so-called 'linguistic minorities' which are still very much thriving in contemporary Italy. The chapters which we *have* been able to include, we hope, present state-of-the-art essays that deal with a range of issues, from multilingual printing to the presence of Italian in Ethiopia. The thematic divisions referred to above, therefore, also have geographical limits, with both 'internal' contact (between vernaculars of Italy) but also contact with 'external' varieties (varieties not descendent from Latin, such as Greek or Gəʿəz).[31] Our intent was *not* to produce a history of multilingualism in Italy (although this remains a desideratum of the field), but to offer a panorama of the different comparative methods, cross-linguistic research, and interdisciplinary topics which researchers have employed to investigate language in late medieval and early modern Italy.

A brief overview of the key findings of the fourteen papers contained in this volume is presented here, underlying their connections to more general themes. The title of the book represents the main objective of the volume and its focal point: we do not speak only of the languages of Italians in the age of

---

30 It is worth recalling Maiden's observation that 'the extent and depth of historical "multilingualism" within Italy is a matter of perspective. If we were prepared to limit our view to relatively elevated domains (for example, the language of the law, chronicles, science, medicine, religion and much literature), and to the small minority of the population that could read and write, then Italy could be said to have enjoyed centuries of virtually unbroken linguistic unity': Maiden, 'The Definition of Multilingualism', p. 34.

31 We regret that the author who had agreed to deliver a chapter on Arabic had suddenly to drop out because of personal circumstances.

the Renaissance within the Italian peninsula, but also of the languages which came into contact with those used by Italians, for written or spoken purposes, beyond the Alps. The authors have explored literary and non-literary sources to provide multifaceted insights into the variety of languages, communities, and contexts crossing geographical, religious, and political boundaries. This volume follows knowledge, things, and people as they move within the East and the West, and especially between these phenomena; the circulation of knowledge was also the circulation of languages, things, and people. The confluence of languages and cultures is the book's thematic coherence. Each author demonstrates by example what careful analysis can reveal about the nature of multilingualism and about attitudes to the different living languages in the Renaissance period. By addressing a wide range of spoken and written languages (Latin, French, Spanish, Catalan, Sardinian, Florentine and its sister dialects, Hebrew, Greek, and Gəʿəz), this collection reveals the linguistic situation of the period in its true diversity and shows the resourcefulness employed by different types of actors when faced with the need to communicate. The ability to move between languages opened up a wealth of possibilities.

The first part of the volume looks at various aspects of the Italian vernaculars. It begins with Brian Richardson's chapter, who shows how printing in Renaissance Italy was a multilingual business in three major respects. First, groups of individuals came together to prepare, produce, and sell printed texts, from different parts of the peninsula or from beyond it. Richardson demonstrates how the languages of communication might have involved two or more of the Italian dialects descended from Latin, but could also involve German, French, Spanish, Catalan, or modern Greek. Second, printed texts were composed in diverse languages, both ancient — chiefly Latin, Greek, Hebrew, and Arabic — but also modern European vernaculars. Third, texts in one vernacular language might be marketed to readers who spoke another vernacular for their daily business. Richardson examines different aspects of multilingual printing in Renaissance Italy, from the personnel involved in printing and how the printed text might be affected by linguistic habits and tastes, to the wide range of languages that were found in printed books, which were sometimes juxtaposed with one or more other languages. Printing provided new opportunities for combining two or more languages to assist the study of an unfamiliar language, and sometimes to assist comparative scholarship. This was the case, for example, with a work printed frequently from 1480 onwards such as the *Vocabulista ecclesiastico* of the Augustinian friar Giovanni Bernardo Forte, which gave Italian equivalents of Latin from the Bible. Richardson provides numerous other examples, including evidence from polyglot dictionaries as well as school texts. Through this multifaceted account of multilingual printing, Richardson highlights a nuanced picture of languages and interlingual relationships which were created throughout Renaissance Italy.

Alessandro Carlucci returns to the fascinating question of Italo-Romance intercomprehension across different vernaculars. He examines the vicissitudes of this question from the point of view of the major scholars in the past century up until today, showing how recent assessments have moved away from the consensus formed during the second half of the twentieth century, when it was generally believed that Italo-Romance varieties were as incommunicable yesterday as they are today, to paraphrase Dionisotti's words. Carlucci questions the conventional notion of a widespread lack of intelligibility between varieties in medieval and early modern Italy. By contrasting the dominant view against alternative and more recent proposals, the author is able to show how the potential for mutual comprehension between Italo-Romance speakers from different areas was greater than has been traditionally estimated. Carlucci surveys a range of historical evidence, from metalinguistic comments and literary representations to vocabulary and grammar. Although phonological differences are remarked upon more often than morphological and syntactic differences, Carlucci finds that there is little indication that phonology was perceived to be a significant obstacle to intercomprehension. An important finding from this chapter highlights how problems of comprehensibility were mentioned also for an increasingly prestigious and widespread variety such as Tuscan, suggesting that no variety was immune to such problems.

Joshua Brown's chapter considers variation at the origin of Italian, and how histories of the language have (re)presented such variation. Using historical grammars as well as the currently available descriptions of polymorphy in Renaissance Italy, the aim is to highlight the extent to which variation existed and quantitatively assess how such variation played out up until codification, fixing this date at the publication of Pietro Bembo's *Prose della volgar lingua* in 1525. Brown uses the latest databases for investigations into historical Italian, arguing that the current historiography pays insufficient attention to variation in the history of Italian. In particular, contact between historical varieties, within and between Tuscan vernaculars, is shown to be an instrumental factor in the formation of the standard. The author shows how what is often considered a monolithic, homogeneous entity, referred to variously as Florentine, the standard, or even just Italian, is in fact a variety which at its base has multiple origins. Although previous scholars have assessed those elements which can be said to be 'non-Florentine' in the past, the chapter demonstrates the extent to which these elements were prevalent in Renaissance Italy, thereby uncovering the 'hidden' plurality of Italian. A similar approach is taken in Thomas's chapter (see below), who also considers forms of communication often disregarded by scholars due to its lack of literary interest. In much the same way, looking at hitherto ignored processes of language contact allows us to reconsider bilingual speakers in the past as agents of contact-influenced language change.

The chapter by Ronnie Ferguson considers the unique city state of Venice in 1500, that is, at the pinnacle of its power and prestige. This chapter documents and evaluates the remarkable range of language-contact dynamics of which Venice was the focal point in the Middle Ages and Renaissance. Ferguson is able to shed light on the contact interactions which characterized various periods throughout the linguistic history of Venice. These include the complex long-term processes of koineization which forged a lagoon language with high-register stability by the 1300s, multiple contact pressure points from the Italian mainland post-1300, as well as the idiosyncratic configuration of adstratum vocabulary absorbed into the Venetian lexicon from Germanic, Byzantine, Islamic, and French sources. Moving beyond Venice, the chapter also considers Venetian language impact throughout the Renaissance, when the city exercised profound superstratum contact pressure on the north-eastern mainland of Italy and along the eastern Adriatic. At the same time, it transmitted to Italian a body of words unmatched by any other dialect of Italy. Through a series of case studies, Ferguson shows the complexity and potential overlap of societal phenomena which were at play during contact situations, including migratory movements, colonial expansion, commercial outreach and production, civilizational prestige, cultural pressure, and literary influence. Overall, the chapter provides a fascinating insight into the way in which Venice can be seen as a nexus of long-term contact dynamics, from multiple viewpoints. Similarly, language contact is also the focus of Tiddeman's contribution (see below), which looks at Anglo-Italian trade in the late 1300s and 1400s. This chapter also considers lexical borrowing in three sets of account books, showing how a series of loanwords can be seen to be functionally distributed. Both Ferguson's and Tiddeman's chapters therefore shed light on different historical contexts through a prism of language contact.

Joseph Brincat's chapter deals with multilingual contact in and around Malta, considering Latin, Sicilian, and the adoption of Italian on the island during the period 1300–1550. After providing the necessary historical context, he shows how different varieties were used in different domains. For example, in the domain of administration, Latin was adopted by the Normans from the mid-twelfth century onwards, but Sicilian came to be increasingly used from the mid- to late 1300s, as Latin became more reserved for regal and international correspondence. Brincat shows how Sicilian was strictly administrative in nature, with documents ranging from minutes of council meetings, petitions, inventories, to authorizations of payments and notarial deeds. Later, Tuscan was introduced by the Knights Hospitallers of the Order of St John. Tuscan was spread by 'agents' such as preachers and especially religious orders who modelled their language on Umbrian sermons. The author also raises the interesting question of the use of Tuscan as a spoken variety. Particular attention is paid to the Knights of Malta and their use of Tuscan in official documentation. Brincat draws attention to the important processes of demunicipalization occurring in administrative circles and chanceries, demonstrating how terminology and style were adopted and adapted to more local varieties. What emerges is a sophisticated account of the multilingual nature of Malta during the Renaissance.

The final chapter in this section by Andrea Rizzi explores the question of trust-signalling of Italian Renaissance translators and editors working in the vernacular. By considering four examples of commercially successful vernacular texts that were first published in the late fifteenth or early to mid-sixteenth centuries, the chapter shows how trust-signalling practices addressed readers on matters of trustworthiness in prefaces, letters of dedication, and other accompanying materials. In turn, this influenced the perceived trustworthiness of the particular vernacular language chosen for the translation or edition. Rizzi demonstrates how introductory statements composed by early modern authors, editors, and translators tended to invoke the trustworthiness of the ancient and authoritative authors whose work they had relied upon. These declarations encode a culturally and historically typical set of assumptions about trust and the nature of the translations which are being created. Rizzi illustrates how trust is a historical product informed by a complex web of rhetorical, emotional, and attitudinal factors. The chapter then turns to the question of trustworthiness of early modern Italian vernaculars themselves, and how the perceived reliability of such vernaculars was, in certain cases, advanced by the attribution of translations to influential and authoritative humanists. Rizzi also highlights examples of inconsistent trust-signalling in translation, showing how one author and pseudo-translator uses Latin and Tuscan to both conceal and unmask his identity. In doing so, he is able to sharpen his anti-papist and anti-Roman agenda, using inconsistent trust-signalling as a strategy to encourage the reader's vigilance in bestowing trust. Finally, the question of translating and ventriloquizing mutual trust in the Italian vernacular is discussed. The chapter provides a fascinating account of the editorial strategies used by early modern translators, editors, and printers involved in processes of trust and distrust, all aimed at convincing readers of vernacular books' usefulness and enjoyment.

The second part of the volume looks at language contact and the interaction between Italian and its dialects and other European languages. It begins with the chapter by Jenelle Thomas, who takes the letters of Georges d'Armagnac, cardinal and diplomat who held one ambassadorial post in Venice and two in Rome during the period from 1530 to 1560, as a case study of diplomatic correspondence from Frenchmen in Italy. The author demonstrates the value of epistolary communication as a source for tracing language contact and the importance of investigating the daily communication of bilingual speakers present in a foreign country as a mechanism for the early stages of contact-influenced lexical innovation. This type of communication, often disregarded by scholars because of its lack of literary interest, provides a unique perspective on cultural and linguistic contacts between France and Italy; it sheds light on processes of linguistic contact and lexical borrowing as well as sociocultural questions of language choice. Thomas's study, in line with work in contact linguistics, elucidates the bilingual speaker as the agent of contact-influenced language change. She focuses on the lexical innovations in evidence in d'Armagnac's French-language correspondence and argues that the sociocultural relationship between populations speaking different linguistic varieties is a determining factor in the linguistic effects of contact. Thomas illustrates that there was a clear sphere of use of each language for practical purposes according to location and recipient: Italian was not used between French speakers for diplomatic communication; the messages that d'Armagnac composed in Italian were, in fact, sent almost exclusively to Italian recipients. D'Armagnac's diplomatic letters also illuminate the process of lexical borrowing taking place during the period. It is noteworthy that the contact effects which Thomas has analysed are attributable to his time in Venice in the 1530s. Thomas contends that the time period of increased contact effects on his lexicon also corresponds to a time period in which he sent numerous letters in Italian, confirming that social and linguistic integration facilitates the incorporation of lexical items from one language to the other.

The chapter by Immacolata Pinto shows that multilingualism has long been the norm in Sardinia. For almost four centuries, Sardinia was part of the Kingdom of Aragon and the Crown of Castile. The Aragonese-Castilian period was characterized by the simultaneous presence of at least five languages: Catalan, Spanish, Sardinian, Latin, and Italian. Spanish became the dominant language from the second half of the seventeenth century onwards and the only one used, besides Latin, in the classroom during the period. Notwithstanding the prominent role of Spanish, each of the other four languages did retain some high functions within the written and spoken repertoire. By analysing late medieval and early modern sources, Pinto sheds light on the effects that the Iberian-Romance superstratum had on the development of the Sardinian language. The selected corpus consists of the following four groups of texts: texts written in Sardinian with borrowings from Latin, Catalan, Spanish, and Italian; mixed works written in Spanish with some parts in Catalan or Sardinian; monolingual but coeval texts written in either Latin, Spanish, Catalan, Sardinian, or Italian; and texts in which contextual factors, such as users and audience, account for language choice. The author demonstrates that the high productivity of four emblematic word-formation processes in contemporary Sardinian is largely related to four centuries of Catalan-Castilian domination. Pinto focuses on these four processes (N-*eri*, (*i*)*s*-, N-*dora*, and V → N-*u*) because of their morphological productivity, mostly caused by the vast number of Catalan and Spanish borrowings. The author also elucidates the morphological analysis of contemporary Sardinian in light of the evidence provided by sources of the early modern period and by taking into account the nature of multilingualism in Sardinia, particularly code-switching and mixed-language accounts.

Megan Tiddeman's chapter looks at evidence for Anglo-Italian language contact from the fifteenth-century port of Southampton. This port played a key role in Anglo-Italian trade in the late 1300s and 1400s. Extant documentation from the city archives contains numerous instances of Italian lexical borrowings. By focusing on three sets of account books from the fifteenth century, Tiddeman traces the maritime and mercantile Italianisms in this corpus to a Genoese or Venetian origin. In many instances these loanwords are explored for the first time here through a series of loanword case studies. These loanwords are further categorized into 'common loanwords', 'rarer loanwords', and 'hapaxes in the Southampton Stewards' Books', allowing the reader to grasp some detail about the distribution of these particular lexemes. Further, the selected corpora are placed in their proper sociolinguistic contexts, allowing for a more comprehensive picture to emerge of the various linguistic and non-linguistic contact that was ongoing in Southampton. Tiddeman identifies the matrix language of the sources she has investigated, the earlier of which are noted as being Anglo-French (also known as Anglo-Norman or insular French). Following the Norman Conquest in 1066, this distinct dialect of medieval French flourished particularly in bureaucratic and literary material in the British Isles up until the 1500s. These sources prove very useful in shedding further light on medieval Anglo-Italian language contact, which up until now has been largely overlooked.

The influence of French on Italian is explored by Thomas Scharinger, who investigates cultural and linguistic contact between these two varieties in the sixteenth century. Scharinger examines literary *loci* of language contact, the production of French prints in the peninsula, and the use of French in multilingual literary texts. The author also analyses translations of French texts into Italian and letters written by Italian ambassadors and intellectuals who spent some time in France. Scharinger argues that these migrating individuals played a more important role in introducing Gallicisms into Italian than the circulation of French books and translations did. The author demonstrates that translations from French are an important *locus* of language contact, especially translations of non-literary texts, which often abound with unknown Gallicisms and sometimes even contain new first attestations of known loanwords. Scharinger's exploratory study of letters and memoirs written by Italian ambassadors and courtiers who had resided in France for a long time suggests that such migrating individuals played a significant role in promoting Gallicisms after their return to Italy. Apart from exotic loans, there are numerous first attestations of Gallicisms that eventually became established in Italian.

The third part of the volume deals with linguistic and cultural exchanges between Italian and the East, from a variety of perspectives. Samantha Kelly looks at the major role played by Italy in Ethiopian–European contacts in the Renaissance. Italy was the region most commonly visited by Ethiopian ambassadors before 1500 and, through the papacy, retained an important role in diplomatic exchange in the sixteenth century. It was also the primary destination of Ethiopian pilgrims throughout the period. The author demonstrates that these relations provide an opportunity to approach the question of Ethiopian languages in Italy from a social-cultural perspective by addressing the interests that undergirded contact, the occasions and methods of knowledge transfer, and the individuals and networks involved. Before the sixteenth century and despite a long-standing interest in the Ethiopian Church, Italians evinced virtually no interest in Gəʿəz, an ancient language belonging to the Semitic family. Gəʿəz was the language of the Ethiopian Church, of royal chronicles and administrative documents, and of all Christian Ethiopian writing through the sixteenth century. Without recourse to it before the Cinquecento, Italians and Ethiopians communicated rather through a many-sided vernacular multilingualism utilized by the great Italian courts and centres of learning. This practice, which continued into the sixteenth century, included the use of an intermediate idiom, Arabic, as well as limited European acquisition of spoken Ethiopian languages (and the reverse as well). The vernacular multilingualism of both Ethiopians and Italians (for whom Arabic was at best a second or third language) thus made communication possible. Only among a rather small group of humanist scholars did Gəʿəz eventually attract attention. The results of their and their Ethiopian collaborators' efforts were landmarks in the burgeoning field of European 'oriental' language study: the first editions of Gəʿəz texts and scholarly studies of the Gəʿəz language.

Han Lamers explores the connection between Greek humanism and Italian vernacular culture. He demonstrates that the Renaissance rediscovery of ancient Greek language and literature encouraged people to abandon well-trodden paths and explore new ones. One of those new paths that lastingly changed Europe's cultural landscape was the further emancipation of the vernaculars from the dominance of Latin. Lamers argues that scholars have explored humanist Hellenism and the *questione della lingua* largely in isolation, while the importance of Greek in the Italian language question, and the unfolding of humanist vernacular culture more generally, has been acknowledged in the scholarship. The author explores how individual humanists, through their study of Greek letters, opened themselves up to the vernacular tongues and eventually embraced them as languages in their own right. He looks at how they enhanced the cultural significance of their languages by identifying affinities with the sounds, expressions, and structures of ancient Greek. The chapter investigates the argument about the 'Greekness' of Italian which Ascanio Persio (1554–1610) formulated in his *Discourse on the Conformity of the Italian Language with the Most Noble Ancient Languages, and Greek in Particular*, first published in Italian in 1592. Persio proposed the creation of a standard variety of written Italian that would also incorporate speech varieties different from the dominant Tuscan. He also wanted to reaffirm the superiority of a newly modelled, common Italian over the other emerging languages of culture in Europe — French in particular — by enhancing the 'Greekness' of its lexicon, syntax, phonetics, and phraseology. In addition to exploring Persio's argument with a special interest in the role of Greek, Lamers also considers how his argument both responded to European debates over the cultural significance of the vernaculars and creatively intervened in the Italian language question.

In his chapter, Fabrizio Lelli investigates the contacts between Hebrew and Italian literature from the fourteenth to the seventeenth centuries. Although the vast Hebrew production of the Italian Jews (for the most part still unpublished) is often considered by scholars as poorly related to Italian literature, the various Hebrew corpora composed in the Mediterranean peninsula show many affinities, in terms of both style and content, with the contemporary works written in the various Italian vernaculars. The interferences between the two productions are numerous and much more significant than might be expected. In most cases, Jewish Italian authors were able to use Hebrew and Romance languages for their scripts. Lelli argues that Italian Jewish communities developed specific linguistic and stylistic patterns that allowed them to follow in the footsteps of their own internal traditions, while borrowing elements from the outside. In his analysis, the author sheds light on the main parallels between the Hebrew productions of the Italian Jews and those of their non-Jewish contemporaries. He focuses on the linguistic contacts between the two communities and surveys four main cases. Lelli shows that by borrowing 'external' styles and contents and by adapting them to Hebrew productions, Italian Jews supplemented their 'internal' literary creativity, shaped after biblical and post-biblical models, and made it consonant to the intellectual agenda of their non-Jewish contemporaries. Analogous were the patterns of integration of Hebrew and non-Hebrew languages among Italian Jews. Likewise, the general trend of Italian Jewish communities to translate best-sellers into Hebrew (or into any local Judaeo-language) not only was aimed at the broader circulation of those productions among Jews, but also boosted their own identity.

Carolina Stromboli examines literary evidence to investigate the presence in Renaissance Naples of a contact language similar to the coeval Mediterranean lingua franca, which commonly refers to a Romance-based language characterized by a restricted lexicon and simplified grammar, documented in the Mediterranean basin from the sixteenth to the nineteenth centuries. Capital of the Spanish Viceroyalty in southern Italy, Naples was a multicultural and multilingual city where Italian, Neapolitan and other Italo-Romance varieties, the Spanish of the ruling class, and other foreign languages existed side by side. Stromboli describes the contact language used in Renaissance literary Neapolitan texts representing black slaves and sheds light on some aspects of a well-established Neapolitan tradition in the representation of black slaves and their language which starts with the *moresche*, a genre of Neapolitan musical poetry that developed in the sixteenth century. The author analyses the language used by a black female slave character in two stories of *Lo cunto de li cunti* (1634–1636), a collection of fairy tales written in Neapolitan dialect, highlighting literary traces of the dance called *catubba* and street performances named *luciate*: in both, the main character is the black slave Lucia, whose linguistic repertoire is similar to the one employed by the slave in *Lo cunto*. The author also investigates Neapolitan *moresche* and analyses the term *bernagualla*, which is a hallmark of the language used by Neapolitan black people and could be considered as an example of a word of African origin. Stromboli demonstrates that the language used by the slave in *Lo cunto* and *luciate* and the language used in the *moresche* are based on Neapolitan and have some common features, despite not being exactly the same.

Works Cited

Abu-Lughod, Janet L., *Before European Hegegomy: The World System A.D. 1250–1350* (New York: Oxford University Press, 1989)

Antonelli, Giuseppe, Matteo Motolese, and Lorenzo Tomasin, eds, *Storia dell'italiano scritto*, III: *Italiano dell'uso* (Rome: Carocci, 2014)

Baglioni, Daniele, 'Italoromanzo in caratteri arabi in un diploma magrebino del Trecento', *Filologie medievali e moderne*, 9 (2015), 177–95

Barbour, Stephen, 'Nationalism, Language, Europe', in *Language and Nationalism in Europe*, ed. by Stephen Barbour and Cathie Carmichael (Oxford: Oxford University Press, 2000), pp. 1–17

Belich, James, John Darwin, Margret Frenz, and Chris Wickham, eds, *The Prospect of Global History* (Oxford: Oxford University Press, 2016)

Bornstein, Daniel, Laura Gaffuri, and Brian J. Maxson, eds, *Languages of Power in Italy (1300–1600)* (Turnhout: Brepols, 2017)

Brown, Joshua, 'Language History from Below: Standardization and Koineization in Renaissance Italy', *Journal of Historical Sociolinguistics*, 6.1 (2020), <https://doi.org/10.1515/jhsl-2018-0017>

——, 'Una memoria quattrocentesca in volgare lombardo', *La lingua italiana: Storia, strutture, testi*, 15 (2019), 57–73, <https://doi.org/10.19272/201904301004>

——, 'Women's Literacy in a Late Medieval Religious Community: Organisation and Memorialisation at Santa Marta in Milan, 1405–1454', *Journal of Religious History*, 45 (2021), 435–54

Brownlee, Marina, and Dimitri Gondicas, eds, *Renaissance Encounters: Greek East and Latin West* (Leiden: Brill, 2013)

Burckhardt, Jacob, *Die Kultur der Renaissance in Italien* (Leipzig, 1860)

Burke, Peter, *Languages and Communities in Early Modern Europe* (Cambridge: Cambridge University Press, 2004)

Burke, Peter, and R. Po-Chia Hsia, eds, *Cultural Translation in Early Modern Europe* (Cambridge: Cambridge University Press, 2007)

Busi, Giulio, and Silvana Greco, eds, *Rinascimento Plurale: Ibridazioni linguistiche e socioculturali tra Quattro e Cinquecento* (Castiglione delle Stiviere: Fondazione Palazzo Bondoni Pastorio, 2021)

Caferro, William, *Contesting the Renaissance* (Malden, MA: Wiley-Blackwell, 2011)

Campbell, Stephen J., and Stephen J. Milner, eds, *Artistic Exchange and Cultural Translation in the Italian Renaissance City* (Cambridge: Cambridge University Press, 2004)

Carlucci, Alessandro, 'Opinions about Perceived Linguistic Intelligibility in Late-Medieval Italy', *Revue Romane*, 55 (2020), 140–65, <https://doi.org/10.1075/rro.19013.car>

Cella, Roberta, *Storia dell'italiano* (Bologna: Il Mulino, 2015)

Classen, Albrecht, ed., *Multilingualism in the Middle Ages and Early Modern Age: Communication and Miscommunication in the Premodern World* (Berlin: De Gruyter, 2016)

Colombo, Michele, and John J. Kinder, 'Italian as a Language of Communication in Nineteenth Century Italy and Abroad', *Italica*, 89 (2012), 109–21

Del Soldato, Eva, and Andrea Rizzi, eds, *City, Court, Academy: Language Choice in Early Modern Italy* (London: Routledge, 2018)

Filipponio, Lorenzo, and Christian Seidl, eds, *Le lingue d'Italia e le altre: Contatti, sostrati e superstrati nella storia linguistica della Penisola* (Milan: Franco Angeli, 2015)

Fulton, Helen, '"Saluti da Londra": Italian Merchants in the City of London in the Late Fourteenth and Early Fifteenth Centuries', in *Anglo-Italian Cultural Relations in the Later Middle Ages*, ed. by Michele Campopiano and Helen Fulton (York: York University Press, 2018), pp. 103–27

Gallagher, John, 'The Italian London of John North: Cultural Contact and Linguistic Encounter in Early Modern England', *Renaissance Quarterly*, 70 (2017), 88–131

Gamberini, Andrea, and Isabella Lazzarini, *The Italian Renaissance State* (Cambridge: Cambridge University Press, 2012)

Guidi Bruscoli, Francesco, 'I mercanti italiani e le lingue straniere', in *Comunicare nel Medioevo: La conoscenza e l'uso delle lingue nei secoli XII–XV*, ed. by Isa Lori Sanfilippo and Giuliano Pinto (Rome: Istituto storico italiano per il Medioevo, 2015), pp. 103–31

Heng, Geraldine, 'The Global Middle Ages: An Experiment in Collaborative Humanities, or Imagining the World, 500–1500 C.E.', *English Language Notes*, 47 (2019), 205–16

Holmes, Catherine, and Naomi Standen, 'Introduction: Towards a Global Middle Ages', *Past & Present*, 238 (2018), 1-44

Jefferson, Judith A., Ad Putter, and Amanda Hopkins, eds, *Multilingualism in Medieval Britain (c. 1066–1520): Sources and Analysis* (Turnhout: Brepols, 2013)

Kleinhenz, Christopher, and Keith Busby, eds, *Medieval Multilingualism: The Francophone World and its Neighbours*, Medieval Texts and Cultures of Northern Europe, 20 (Turnhout: Brepols, 2010)

Lepschy, Anna Laura, *Varietà linguistiche e pluralità di codici nel Rinascimento* (Florence: Olschki, 1996)

Lepschy, Anna Laura, and Arturo Tosi, eds, *Multilingualism in Italy: Past and Present*, Studies in Linguistics, 1 (Oxford: Legenda, 2002)

——, eds, *Rethinking Languages in Contact: The Case of Italian* (London: Legenda, 2006)

Maiden, Martin, 'The Definition of Multilingualism in Historical Perspective', in *Multilingualism in Italy: Past and Present*, ed. by Anna Laura Lepschy and Arturo Tosi, Studies in Linguistics, 1 (Oxford: Legenda, 2002), pp. 31–46

Maiden, Martin, and Mair M. Parry, eds, *The Dialects of Italy* (London: Routledge, 1997)

Mattheier, Klaus J., 'Is There a European Language History?', *Multilingua: Journal of Cross-Cultural and Interlanguage Communication*, 29 (2010), 353–60

Migliorini, Bruno, *Storia della lingua italiana* (Florence: Sansoni, 1960)

Moore, Robert I., 'A Global Middle Ages?', in *The Prospect of Global History*, ed. by James Belich, John Darwin, Margret Frenz, and Chris Wickham (Oxford: Oxford University Press, 2016), pp. 80–92

Muljačić, Žarko, 'The Relationship between the Dialects and the Standard Language', in *The Dialects of Italy*, ed. by Martin Maiden and Mair M. Parry (London: Routledge, 1997), pp. 387–93

Murano, Giovanna, 'Donne e libri nel Rinascimento italiano: Tra committenze, matronage e biblioteche', *Pecia: Livres manuscrits et mécénat du Moyen Âge à la Renaissance*, 21 (2018), 7–50

Parker, Charles H., *Global Interactions in the Early Modern Age, 1400-1800* (Cambridge: Cambridge University Press, 2010)

Plebani, Tiziana, *Le scritture delle donne in Europa: Pratiche quotidiane e ambizioni letterarie (secoli XIII–XX)* (Rome: Carocci, 2019)

Ramey, Lynn, David Neville, Sahar Amer, Jonathan deHaan, Maxime Durand, Brandon Essary, Rob Howland, Mubbasir Kapadia, Felix Kronenberg, Brett E. Shelton, and Barbara Vance, 'Revisioning the Global Middle Ages: Immersive Environments for Teaching Medieval Languages and Culture', *Digital Philology*, 8 (2019), 86–104

Ruzza, Carlo, 'Language and Nationalism in Italy: Language as a Weak Marker of Identity', in *Language and Nationalism in Europe*, ed. by Stephen Barbour and Cathie Carmichael (Oxford: Oxford University Press, 2000), pp. 168–82

Sanson, Helena, '"Io che donna indotta e minima sono": Women, Translation and Classical Languages in Early Modern Italy', *Women Language Literature in Italy*, 3 (2021), 29–51

Serianni, Luca, and Pietro Trifone, eds, *Storia della lingua italiana*, III: *Le altre lingue* (Turin: Einaudi, 1993)

Tamburelli, Marco, 'Uncovering the "Hidden" Multilingualism of Europe: An Italian Case Study', *Journal of Multilingual and Multicultural Development*, 35 (2014), 252–70

Trifone, Pietro, 'L'affermazione del concetto di una "lingua italiana" come lingua di cultura e lingua comune degli Italiani', in *Pre-sentimenti dell'Unità d'Italia nella tradizione culturale dal Due all'Ottocento*, ed. by Claudio Gigante and Emilio Russo (Rome: Salerno, 2012), pp. 105–16

Trotter, David, ed., *Multilingualism in Later Medieval Britain* (Cambridge: D. S. Brewer, 2000)

Tyler, Elizabeth M., ed., *Conceptualizing Multilingualism in England, c. 800–c. 1250* (Turnhout: Brepols, 2012)

Vincent, Nigel, 'Languages in Contact in Medieval Italy', in *Rethinking Languages in Contact: The Case of Italian*, ed. by Anna Laura Lepschy and Arturo Tosi (London: Legenda, 2006), pp. 12–27

Wagner, Esther-Miriam, Bettina Beinhoff, and Ben Outhwaite, eds, *Merchants of Innovation: The Languages of Traders*, Studies in Language Change, 15 (Berlin: De Gruyter Mouton, 2017)

Wallerstein, Immanuel, *The Modern World-System* (New York: Academic Press; Berkeley: University of California Press, 1974)

Wright, Laura, ed., *The Multilingual Origins of Standard English* (Berlin: De Gruyter, 2020)

Wyatt, Michael, ed., *The Cambridge Companion to the Italian Renaissance* (Cambridge: Cambridge University Press, 2014)

Part 1

The Italian Vernaculars

BRIAN RICHARDSON

Multilingual Printing

Printing in Renaissance Italy was a multilingual business in three major respects. First, the groups of individuals who worked together to prepare, produce, and sell printed texts often came from different parts of the peninsula or from beyond it. The languages in which they communicated might thus involve two or more of the Italian dialects descended from Latin, or a foreign language such as German, French, Spanish, Catalan, or modern Greek. Second, the texts that they printed were composed in diverse languages, both ancient — chiefly Latin, Greek, Hebrew, and Arabic, each requiring their own founts of type — and modern European vernaculars that used the Roman alphabet. Third, texts in one vernacular language might be marketed to readers who spoke another tongue in their daily lives. This was the case even within Italy, since versions of the literary Italian vernacular were based to a greater or lesser extent on a dialect from the past, fourteenth-century Florentine, that was no longer spoken in precisely the same form, even in Florence. This essay will begin with a look at the geographical origins of the personnel involved in printing and at how the printed text might be affected by their linguistic habits and tastes, as well as by the tastes that they anticipated in their readers. It will then survey the wide range of languages that were found in printed books, usually on their own but sometimes juxtaposed with one or more other languages.

Printers and Editors

The businesses of printing and bookselling during the Renaissance were characterized by mobility: those involved in them very often needed to travel in order to find employment or to find markets for books. The art of printing with movable type was developed in Mainz around 1450, and its invention is traditionally ascribed to Johann Gutenberg. After it had spread to two other German cities, Bamberg and Strassburg (now Strasbourg), it was brought

---

Brian Richardson (b.f.richardson@leeds.ac.uk) is Emeritus Professor of Italian Language at the University of Leeds.

Languages and Cross-Cultural Exchanges in Renaissance Italy, ed. by Alessandra Petrocchi and Joshua Brown, LMEMS 30 (Turnhout: Brepols, 2023), pp. 35–64
BREPOLS ❧ PUBLISHERS   10.1484/M.LMEMS-EB.5.131427

over the Alps to Italy. The establishment of presses in the peninsula was led initially by the expertise of northern Europeans allied with the financial support and the editorial advice of Italians. The earliest securely datable press in the peninsula was set up by Conrad Sweynheym and Arnold Pannartz, who came perhaps from Mainz and Prague respectively, in the Benedictine monastery of Subiaco in Lazio. Here they produced four editions between 1465 and 1467. The pair then printed in Rome with support from local merchants until 1473, after when Pannartz printed for a while on his own. Presses in Rome during the rest of the fifteenth century were operated by Germans, apart from two run by Italians and two run by Frenchmen. A survey carried out by Armando Petrucci shows that, of ninety-six printers active in Italy in the period 1465–1474, sixty-four came from other countries: fifty-two Germans, seven French, three from what is now Belgium, one Dutchman, and one Swiss.[1] A German, John of Speyer, introduced printing to Venice in 1469, and his typographic material passed after his death to his brother Wendelin and then to other Germans. Nicolas Jenson, born in Sommevoire (Haute-Marne) in France, began printing in Venice in 1470; three years later, he set up an influential company with two merchants from Frankfurt, Johann Rauchfass and Peter Ugelheimer, and in 1480 he started to work with a former rival, John of Cologne.[2] The nomadic Henricus de Colonia printed in at least seven places in northern and central Italy from 1474 onwards: Brescia, Bologna, Modena, Siena, Lucca, Nozzano, and Urbino. In Naples, the first three printers were the German Sixtus Riessinger, Arnaldus de Bruxella, and Mathias Moravus. Milan and Florence were among the few large centres in which printing was introduced by Italians, but these men were soon joined by printers of German origin.

In the sixteenth century, when presses came to be operated mainly by Italians, leading foreign printers included Étienne Guillery, from Lunéville in Lorraine, who produced nearly 140 editions in Rome in 1506–1524; Giovanni Angelo Scinzenzeler, who followed his Bavarian father Ulrich as a printer in Milan in 1500–1526; the Germans Sigismund Mayr and Ioanne Sultzbach in Naples in the first half of the century; Antonio Gardano, a musician from a French family (Gardane) who around 1538 introduced to Venice a new system of printing musical notation; Vincent Vaugris (Vincenzo Valgrisi), from Charly near Lyon, who printed in Venice from 1540; Laurens Leenaertsz van der Beke (Lorenzo Torrentino), from Brabant, appointed as ducal printer first in Florence in 1547 and then in Mondovì in 1562; and Georges Marescot (Giorgio Marescotti), who printed in Florence from 1563 and introduced printing in musical notation to this city. Another polyglot press was that

---

1 Petrucci, 'Pouvoir de l'écriture', pp. 828–31. For an overview of printing in Renaissance Italy, see Harris, 'The History of the Book in Italy', pp. 420–33.
2 Scholderer, 'Printing at Venice to the End of 1481'; Lowry, *Nicholas Jenson and the Rise of Venetian Publishing*, pp. 97, 113–15, 163–65.

of Daniel Bomberg, a specialist in Hebrew printing working in Venice, to whom we shall return. Bomberg himself came from Antwerp, and those he employed included Jacob ben Hayyim, a refugee from Tunis, and the Frenchman Guillaume Le Bé, who cut his Hebrew founts.

From time to time, Italian printers might employ men born outside Italy. A young man called Jacob Levi, from the province of Tarragona in Spain, worked (perhaps as a compositor) for Estellina Conat when she printed Jedaiah Hapenini's *Iggeret Behinar ha' olam* (Treatise on the Contemplation of the World) in Mantua in 1474.[3] A young black African worked as an apprentice on the production of an edition of a Latin treatise on the reform of the calendar written by Paul of Middelburg when it was printed in Fossombrone in the Marche in 1513. A local scholar, Girolamo Postumo, who was employed by the author to carry out corrections on the printed text, explained in a note to the reader that this youth was partly to blame for typographical errors in the edition:

> Si qua, lector candidissime, in hoc opere errata offendes, ea correctori non adscribas velim, sed chalcographis: qui cum docti non sint, saepenumero literas invertant, dictiones pro dictionibus, et subsultantes syllabas reponant necesse est. Insuper ne nescius omnium existas, scire debes Ioannem Baptistam aethiopem adulescentulum imberbem excusoriae artis tyrocinium in hoc opere exercuisse.
>
>> (Honest reader, if you find any errors in this work, please do not lay them to the account of the corrector, but to that of the printers. Since they are not learned, it is inevitable that they often turn letters upside down, replace one word with another, and have to replace the syllables that jump about. Further, so that you may be apprised of the facts, you should know that Giovanni Battista, an Ethiopian and a beardless youth, served his apprenticeship as a compositor on this work.)[4]

Arnoldo Arlenio, a scholarly compatriot of Torrentino's who assisted him as an editor, is probably the 'Arnaldo' who was employed in the early 1560s to correct proofs of Greek texts for the Florentine printer Iacopo Giunti.[5]

Italians who ran or worked for presses had often migrated from elsewhere in the peninsula, and thus printing houses were places where one would regularly hear spoken the varieties of Italian vernacular that in this period came to be termed dialects.[6] Venice, which in the sixteenth century became the leading printing centre of Europe, was an especially attractive point of

---

3 De Rossi, *Annales Hebraeo-typographici*, p. 111; Offenberg, 'The Chronology of Hebrew Printing at Mantua', pp. 301, 307.
4 Paul of Middelburg, *Paulina de recta Paschae celebratione*, fol. GG4ᵛ; Grafton, *The Culture of Correction*, pp. 85–87. On the presence of Africans in Italy, see Lowe, 'Visible Lives'.
5 Pettas, *The Giunti of Florence*, p. 129.
6 See especially Trovato, '"Dialetto" e sinonimi'.

immigration.[7] Aldo Manuzio and Gabriele Giolito, the two greatest printers working in the city in this period, were born respectively in the small town of Bassiano, south-east of Rome, and in Trino in Piedmont. Editors and proofreaders of vernacular texts, who were ultimately responsible for their linguistic form in print, did not necessarily share a text's region of origin. For example, non-Tuscans were predominant among early editors of the three most prestigious Tuscan vernacular authors of the fourteenth century. They included, for Dante's *Commedia*, Colombino Veronese, Cristoforo Berardi of Pesaro, and Pietro Bembo of Venice; for the *Canzoniere* and *Triumphi* of Petrarch (Francesco Petrarca), Nicolò Peranzone of Montecassiano in the Marche, Bembo, Lodovico Dolce of Venice, and Girolamo Ruscelli of Viterbo; and for works by Giovanni Boccaccio, Gerolamo Squarzafico of Alessandria in Piedmont, Lucio Paolo Rosello of Padua, Tizzone Gaetano of Pofi, near Frosinone, Dolce, and Ruscelli. These men had varying degrees of expertise in fourteenth-century Tuscan and varying respect for its specificities.

When the native vernacular of a compositor was different from that of the work he was setting, there was the risk that his linguistic habits would creep unintentionally into the printed text. Ruscelli commented on such interference in his annotations at the end of a poetic anthology that he edited in 1558, as an aside when he was criticizing the use, by Northern Italians (whom he generically calls Lombards) of the first-person plural conjunctive pronoun *si* where Tuscan would have *ci*:

> Questo vitio di metter sempre SI, in vece di Ci, è proprio della lingua Lombarda, et di tutti questi paesi d'attorno. Onde perché i Lavoranti delle stamperie sono la più parte di questi tali, quando lavorano (che essi dicono comporre) se ben l'Autore ha scritto bene, et Toscanamente, essi prendendo, o tutto o mezo, il verso a memoria, se lo ricordano secondo che loro lo detta la nativa et continuata favella loro, et non come una volta sola l'habbiano veduto così incorso nello scritto dell'Autore. Et poi quei che correggono, o sono di quei medesimi ancor'essi, et non lo hanno et non lo conoscono per errore, o è come impossibile, che possano in una volta sola vedere, et corregger tutti gli errori, che in gran copia ne sono spesso nelle stampe, che si danno a correggere, essendo questo pessimo uso fra gli stampatori di qui, che una sola volta danno a corregger la stampa.[8]
>
> (This bad habit of always putting *si* instead of *ci* is typical of the language of Lombardy and surrounding areas. Hence, because the workers in printing houses are mostly such people, when they are working, or composing as they call it, even when the author has written correctly and in a Tuscan manner, they memorize all or half the line

---

7 Salzberg, *Ephemeral City*, pp. 51–52, 73–76.
8 *I fiori delle rime*, fol. PP7ʳ. On the contemporary sense of 'Lombardia', see Machiavelli, *Discorso intorno alla nostra lingua*, pp. 9–10.

and remember it as their native and continuously used tongue speaks it to them, and not as they may have seen it just once when coming across it in the author's written text. And then either proof correctors also belong to this category, and do not consider and recognize it as an error, or it is well-nigh impossible for them to see and correct in just one occasion all the many errors often found in the printed texts given for correction; for it is a very bad habit among printers here to give what is printed to be corrected just once.)

These factors probably lie behind cases in which a printed text introduces some linguistic features that are not characteristic of the author and do not all result from attempts to make the text conform with literary Tuscan. The collection of fifty short stories called the *Novellino*, composed by a southern author, Masuccio Salernitano (*c.* 1410–1475), was first printed in Naples in 1476. No copy of this edition survives, but on it were based two editions printed independently in Milan in 1483 and in Venice in 1484. While the Milanese text contains southern dialect forms that must come from its source, the Venetian version contains both some Tuscanizing forms that are probably due to an editor and some northern forms that may derive from the habits of the compositor or compositors, such as 'zudìo', 'cargo', 'giesa', and 'zò' where the Milanese edition has 'giudìo', 'carrico', 'chiesa', and 'ciò'.[9] Even canonical Tuscan works such as Petrarch's *Canzoniere* might be infiltrated by northern forms such as *fiolo* for *figliuolo*; on the other hand, there was also the possibility that a compositor who was aware that northern dialects have single intervocalic consonants where Tuscan has double consonants might introduce a hypercorrect form such as *fratte* for *frate*.[10] Pierfrancesco Giambullari's grammar of contemporary Florentine, printed in Florence around 1552, contains some forms that do not conform with Florentine phonology, such as 'aggionto', 'longo', 'mandarebbe', and 'divideno' rather than 'aggiunto', 'lungo', 'manderebbe', and 'dividono', and these forms could well be due to compositors.[11]

Ancient Languages

The first editions printed in Subiaco contained texts in classical Latin, and Latin texts continued to dominate the market for several decades. Data from the *Incunabula Short Title Catalogue* suggest that some 75 per cent of books

---

9 Trovato, *Con ogni diligenza corretto*, pp. 112–13.
10 Trovato, *Con ogni diligenza corretto*, pp. 125–28, 221.
11 Giambullari, *Regole della lingua fiorentina*, p. xxvi. The first edition is *De la lingua che si parla et scrive in Firenze* (Florence: [Lorenzo Torrentino, 1552?]). For examples of the different habits of two compositors setting Latin texts in the same printing house, see Boorman, *Ottaviano Petrucci*, pp. 169–70.

printed in Italy in the fifteenth century were in Latin.[12] Thereafter, the demand for Latin texts of all kinds — classical literature, religious texts (the Scriptures, liturgical, devotional, and theological works), and neo-Latin humanistic texts — remained high but was accompanied by a growing demand for texts in other languages. The database of sixteenth-century Italian editions held mainly in Italian libraries shows that the proportion of editions in Latin fell to just under 47 per cent over this period. Translations, often composed especially for print, made much of classical literature more accessible to those people, including women, who were unable to read the original texts easily. It is striking, however, that nearly two-thirds of the Latin editions of the Cinquecento were produced in the second half of the century.[13] This development seems to reflect a decline in reading in the vernacular in the age of the Counter-Reformation, whether for entertainment or for the purposes of religious devotion. Indexes of Prohibited Books issued from 1559 onwards forbade vernacularizations of the Scriptures without permission. No complete Bible in Italian was printed in Italy between 1567 and 1769–1781, when the translation of Antonio Martini was published.[14]

Diacritic markings were sometimes added to Latin texts in print, as they had already been in manuscript texts, in order to aid comprehension and pronunciation. They are found chiefly in roman founts, and then in italic founts after their introduction from 1501 onwards, but sometimes also in gothic founts. Acute accents were used to indicate stressed vowels in a guide to the pronunciation of Church Latin, the *Casselina, sive Compendiolum sacrae scripturae*, composed by an anonymous Franciscan friar, printed first in Venice by Bernardo di Morano in 1487 and several times in the sixteenth century. (The author explains that he chose the work's title 'quia cassat barbarismos', because it destroys barbarisms.) Diacritics were first used in a humanistic text in 1496 by a trio of men working in Venice: the author Pietro Bembo, the printer Aldo Manuzio, and his punch cutter Francesco Griffo of Bologna. Their edition of Bembo's dialogue *De Aetna* used acute, grave, and circumflex accents to indicate some stressed vowels (as in 'pérbene'), long vowels (as in 'cratêres'), and the presence of enclitics (as in 'nósque'), and to distinguish adverbs or conjunctions from inflected forms (as in 'ferè' or 'aliâs'). They also used most of the punctuation signs to which we are now accustomed: full stop, comma, colon, semicolon, question mark, apostrophe, parentheses.[15]

While Latin was studied intensively in the school syllabus, there were fewer opportunities to learn ancient Greek and hence there was a much smaller market for printed texts in this language. Moreover, technical problems needed

---

12   <https://data.cerl.org/istc> [accessed 11 March 2020].
13   Censimento nazionale delle edizioni italiane del XVI secolo, <edit16.iccu.sbn.it> [accessed 11 March 2020].
14   Fragnito, *La Bibbia al rogo*, pp. 75–109; Fragnito, *Proibito capire*.
15   Richardson, 'Dalla metà del Quattrocento', pp. 107–09.

to be overcome because Greek texts were conventionally accompanied by several diacritic markings — accents, breathings, and the iota subscript. Both émigré Greeks and Italians played crucial roles in facing these challenges. The scribe Demetrius Damilas, born in Crete of Milanese parents, financed the first edition of a Greek grammar by Constantinus Lascaris (Milan, 1476), and designed its type, using as a model the handwriting of his compatriot Michael Apostolis.[16] His type matrices were used in the preparation of other editions produced in Milan and Florence, most important among them the imposing first edition of the works of Homer, printed in Florence in 1488 and overseen by Demetrius Chalcondyles of Athens.[17] A short-lived but influential collaboration took place in Milan between the scholar-printer Bonaccorso da Pisa (Bonus Accursius) and Giovanni Crastone, born near Piacenza. From around 1478 to 1481 they oversaw the publication of four editions intended to promote Greek studies: a Greek–Latin lexicon and a Latin–Greek lexicon, both compiled by Crastone; Lascaris's grammar, with a new Latin translation by Crastone; and the first printed edition of the Psalms in Greek with nine canticles, also with a Latin translation by Crastone.[18] Janus Lascaris of Constantinople designed the type used to print the *Anthologia Graeca Planudea* and other texts in Florence in 1494.[19] The scribe Zacharias Callierges, of Cretan origin, designed and probably cut a Greek fount with which he printed four editions in Venice in 1499 and 1500 with the support of a Cretan stationer, Nicolaus Blastos.[20] Major impetus was given to Greek printing by Aldo Manuzio in Venice between 1495 and 1514, using founts cut by Griffo, all based on the hands of contemporary scribes.[21] In order to promote knowledge of the language and its literature, Aldo published texts including the first editions of works by Aristotle and other classical authors, grammars, and further aids to the study of the language. He also served devotion among Greek exiles by printing a Greek Psalter and two little Books of Hours.

After Aldo's death in 1515, the press that he had established continued to produce many Greek-language editions. Among them was the first edition of the complete Bible in Greek, issued in 1518, which combined the Septuagint

---

16 Barker, *Aldus Manutius and the Development of Greek Script and Type*, pp. 19, 29–31; Speranzi, 'Prima di Aldo'. For overviews, see Layton, *The Sixteenth Century Greek Book*, pp. 3–264; Jones, *Printing the Classical Text*, pp. 143–94.
17 Barker, *Aldus Manutius and the Development of Greek Script and Type*, pp. 37–38; Megna, 'Per la storia della princeps di Omero'.
18 On this last work, see Linde, 'Johannes Crastonus's 1481 Edition of the Psalms'.
19 On Chalcondyles and Janus Lascaris, see Wilson, *From Byzantium to Italy*, pp. 95–100, and on Lascaris, see Barker, *Aldus Manutius and the Development of Greek Script and Type*, pp. 15–16, 39–42.
20 Barker, *Aldus Manutius and the Development of Greek Script and Type*, pp. 69–75; Layton, *The Sixteenth Century Greek Book*, pp. 318–33; Staikos, 'The Printing Shop of Nikolaos Vlastos and Zacharias Kallierges'.
21 Barker, *Aldus Manutius and the Development of Greek Script and Type*, pp. 43–63; Layton, *The Sixteenth Century Greek Book*, pp. 381–87.

with Erasmus's text of the New Testament, first printed by Johann Froben in Basel in 1516. Many Greek editions were produced by two men who had honed their skills in the Aldine press, Giovanni Antonio Nicolini, from Sabbio Chiese in Lombardy, and his younger brother Stefano.[22] They set up a press in Venice around 1521 with financial support from two other immigrants, the Greek merchant Andreas Kounadis and his Dalmatian son-in-law Damiano di Santa Maria, who paid a young Greek, Dimitrios Zinos, to correct proofs. Stefano went on to run his own press in Venice. In 1542 he moved to Rome to take on a senior role in the short-lived Greek press set up by the learned Pope Marcellus II, which in 1542 published the first volume of Eustathius's commentary on Homer and Theophylact's commentary on the Gospels.[23] A landmark edition printed in Rome by Francesco Zanetti in 1587 was the Greek Old Testament, prepared by Cardinal Antonio Carafa and a group of scholars.[24]

Printers working in Italy established themselves as European leaders in the printing of Hebrew.[25] The first dated edition in this language, Rashi's commentary on the Pentateuch, was produced in Reggio di Calabria in 1475. Gerolamo (Gershom) Soncino began to print books in Hebrew in 1488 in the town of Soncino, in Lombardy, before continuing his activity in Brescia and elsewhere.[26] Aldo Manuzio used Hebrew type in a tiny *Introductio utilissima hebraice discere cupientibus* (Very useful introduction for those wishing to learn Hebrew), which he published first on its own around 1500 and then as an appendix to Greek and Latin grammars. Soncino printed this work in Pesaro in 1510, claiming that it was his and that Aldo, in his ignorance of Hebrew, had introduced errors.[27] The first printer in Venice who specialized in Hebrew texts was a Christian, Daniel Bomberg, working in collaboration with a converted Jew, the Augustinian friar Felice da Prato.[28] In 1515–1518 the Venetian senate granted them book-privileges in connection with their plans for editions 'in Hebrew letters', and the Jewish compositors to be employed by them were permitted to wear black skullcaps instead of the usual yellow ones. With this support from the state, they embarked on a very ambitious programme that included the Rabbinic Bible — the Hebrew text of the Old Testament with the *targums* (Aramaic paraphrases) and rabbinic commentaries — in 1517, dedicated by fra Felice to Pope Leo X, and in 1524–1525 a revised edition of the same work that was taken as a model by later editions.[29] Between these

---

22 Layton, *The Sixteenth Century Greek Book*, pp. 402–20; Sandal, ed., *Il mestier de le stamperie de i libri*.
23 Sachet, *Publishing for the Popes*, pp. 66–90.
24 Hall, 'Biblical Scholarship', pp. 58–59.
25 For overviews, see Amram, *The Makers of Hebrew Books in Italy*; Tamani, 'Edizioni ebraiche veneziane'.
26 Veneziani, *La tipografia a Brescia*, pp. 106–08; Pellegrini, 'Soncino, Gerolamo'.
27 Davies, *Aldus Manutius*, pp. 52, 55.
28 Cioni, 'Bomberg, Daniel'; Nielsen, 'Daniel van Bombergen'; Penkower, 'The First Books'.
29 Hall, 'Biblical Scholarship', pp. 52–53; Stern, 'The Rabbinic Bible'.

two editions, in 1519–1523, Bomberg printed the Talmud, the book of Jewish law. Several texts in Hebrew were produced from around the middle of the century by two Venetian patricians, Marcantonio Giustinian and Alvise Bragadin, who became rivals of each other.[30] Among Bragadin's books were bilingual editions of prayers in Spanish and Hebrew, such as the *Orden de oraciones segundo el uso ebreo en lengua ebraica y vulgar espanol* (1550–1551). However, antisemitism was growing on the part of the Church and of the Venetian state. In 1553, Pope Julius III ordered the burning of all copies of the Talmud, and many more Hebrew books were destroyed in Venice in 1568.[31] In 1570, a priest denounced Giustinian for allegedly trafficking in Hebrew books and even of setting up a clandestine press with the help of a German punch cutter, in defiance of the authority of Venice.

Editions of texts in Arabic were produced in Italy primarily for export to the Middle East, where there was a lack of presses capable of printing with movable type. Some of these books were to be read by Arabs who were already Christian. This was the case with the first Arabic edition, a Book of Hours intended for Melchite Christians in Syria, dated 1514 and printed probably in Venice by Gregorio de' Gregori.[32] Around 1537–1538, however, a remarkable edition was produced for Muslims, a Qur'ān printed in Venice by Paganino and Alessandro Paganini. It was doubtless unwelcome in the East because it had originated among 'infidels', and just one copy survives.[33] Later in the century, presses in Rome produced Arabic texts for the purpose of making converts to Christianity. A Jesuit press, the Tipografia del Collegio Romano, operated from 1555 to 1617, using Arabic and Hebrew types to print books to be used by Jesuit missionaries in the Eastern world.[34] The Typographia Medicea Orientale, founded in 1584 by Cardinal Ferdinando de' Medici, also produced books for proselytization as well as for scholarly study. It was directed by the Oriental scholar Giovanni Battista Raimondi, whose bold ambition was to print, in Arabic, books including the Bible, for Christian Arabs, and other texts that would make Muslims aware of their 'errors' and the truth of Christianity.[35] The press used Roman, Greek, Hebrew, Syriac, Arabic, Persian, Turkish, and Coptic types, cut by specialists such as the elderly Frenchman

---

30 Antonucci, 'Giustinian, Marcantonio'; Cioni, 'Bragadin, Alvise'.
31 Grendler, 'The Destruction of Hebrew Books'.
32 Vercellin, 'Venezia e le origini della stampa', p. 54; Roper, 'Printed in Europe, Consumed in Ottoman Lands', pp. 272–73. See also Roper, 'The History of the Book in the Muslim World'.
33 Nuovo, 'A Lost Arabic Koran Rediscovered'. Nuovo points out that Venetian presses had previously issued a few texts in Cyrillic and Armenian scripts (p. 283). See also Roper, 'Printed in Europe, Consumed in Ottoman Lands', p. 273.
34 Roper, 'Printed in Europe, Consumed in Ottoman Lands', pp. 274–75.
35 Tinto, *La Tipografia Medicea Orientale*, p. 94. See also Fani and Farina, eds, *Le vie delle lettere*; Barbarics-Hermanik, 'European Books for the Ottoman Market', pp. 401–05; and, on Raimondi, Jones, *Learning Arabic in Renaissance Europe*, especially pp. 66–68, 126–43, 175–249.

Robert Granjon.[36] Pope Gregory XIII, who commissioned Granjon's work, was anxious that these foreign types should not fall into Protestant hands and be used to propagate anything perceived as contrary to the Roman Catholic faith.[37] An outstanding Arabic edition of 1590 from this press contained the Gospels with elaborate woodcut illustrations, in two issues, each with a large number of copies, 1500 of the Arabic text alone and 3500 of a version that combined the Arabic text with an interlinear Latin translation.[38]

Another culturally and technically complex undertaking was Teseo Ambrogio degli Albonesi's extraordinary *Introductio in Chaldaicam linguam, Syriacam, atque Armenicam, et decem alias linguas. Characterum differentium alphabeta, circiter quadraginta, et eorundem invicem conformatio*, published in Pavia by Giovanni Maria Simonetta in 1539, at the author's expense, which must have been considerable. The project involved printing in specially cut types and in red ink as well as black; however, blank spaces were left so that the symbols of some languages, such as Arabic, Ethiopic, and Coptic, could be filled in by hand.[39]

Venice pioneered the printing of books in Church Slavonic in Glagolitic characters. A missal dated 1483/84 is attributed to a Venetian press. A Glagolitic breviary was printed in 1492 in a fount probably created by the versatile Griffo. The editor and one of the compositors was a Franciscan born in Bosnia, known as fra Matteo da Zara. The contract envisaged a print run of at least one thousand, but the sale of copies was blocked because of the death of the main sponsor of the enterprise. Perhaps taking advantage of this opportunity, Andrea Torresani printed another Glagolitic breviary in 1493.[40] The same printer issued in 1527 an alphabet with prayers in Church Slavonic using Glagolitic characters, entitled *Alphabeticum et preces Illyricae*.[41] Venetian presses also published Church Slavonic texts in roman characters, such as a Book of Hours from around 1495 and a Roman missal issued by Francesco Bindoni and Maffeo Pasini in 1528.[42]

Vernaculars of Italy

Texts in Italian vernaculars began to be printed about 1470, some five years after those in Latin. Among the earliest were the great literary verse and prose

---

36 Tinto, *La Tipografia Medicea Orientale*, pp. 22–56.
37 Roper, 'Printed in Europe, Consumed in Ottoman Lands', p. 275.
38 Harris, 'Printing the Gospels in Arabic'.
39 Levi della Vida, 'Albonesi, Teseo Ambrogio degli'; Wilkinson, *Orientalism, Aramaic, and Kabbalah in the Catholic Reformation*, pp. 11–27. Albonesi considered 'Chaldaic' equivalent to Syriac.
40 Pelusi, 'Il libro liturgico veneziano', p. 44; Fattori, 'Venezia culla della stampa glagolitica'.
41 Dyneley Prince, 'A Rare Old Slavonic Religious Manual'.
42 Dondi, *Printed Books of Hours*, no. 38, pp. 359–60; Pelusi, 'Il libro liturgico veneziano', p. 45.

works of the Tuscan Trecento, including Petrarch's *Canzoniere* and *Triumphi* (Venice, 1470), Boccaccio's *Decameron* (editions printed probably in Naples around 1470 and in Venice, 1471) and Dante's *Commedia* (three editions of 1472 from Foligno, Mantua, and Venice or Iesi). At the same time, presses produced texts in other forms of Italian. For instance, an edition of 1470 contained the *Consegli della salute del peccatore* addressed to the citizens of Sansepolcro in Tuscany by the renowned Franciscan preacher Antonio da Vercelli. As this extract from the opening lines illustrates, the friar's language was a koinè or interregional language, based on Tuscan with northern inflections (for instance, single intervocalic consonants where Tuscan would have double consonants, *de* and *ve* rather than *di* and *vi*, *alguni* rather than *alcuni*) and occasional Latinisms:

> Avendo io facto alguni sermoni in forma de predicacione nella terra vostra, fra gli altri sermoni m'è singularmente accaduto de far alcuni sermoni chiamati sermoni de li consigli de la salute del peccatore; li quali per divina gratia essendo sumamente piazuti a tuto lo populo, pregato io da la magiore parte de li citadini principali che io per opera de caritade et etiam *quam maxime* per utilitade e salute de le anime me dignasse de volere soto breve e picolo compendio in sermone volgare insiema componere et scrivere li prediti consigli de salute e così fare che per ogne modo voi gli avesti, io como sitibondo et desideroxo de satisfare a ogne vostra iusta, santa, et onesta peticione et domanda, a ziò in tuto deliberato de volervi consolare, avixandovi che molto maggiore cosa sarebe et intendo de fare per quella nobile et benedeta et venerabile comunità, tredici consigli ve dechiarai.[43]

> (Since I wrote some sermons in the form of exhortation in your town, among other sermons I happened to write some called sermons of advice on the sinner's salvation. By God's grace they pleased the whole populace, and I was asked by most of the leading citizens, as a work of charity and also especially for the benefit and salvation of souls, to kindly gather together and write down this advice on salvation in a brief summary in the vernacular, and to ensure you would have them. Since I am eager and desirous to fulfil any just, holy, and honourable appeal and request of yours, I decided to satisfy you completely in this matter. While informing you that I intend to do something that would be of much greater importance for that noble, blessed, and venerable community, I declared to you thirteen pieces of advice.)

For the rest of the fifteenth century, those working in presses, and presumably also readers, were largely willing to accept texts in regional varieties of the vernacular. In Naples, for example, the language of the version of the *Aesopus moralisatus* made by a local writer, Francesco Del Tuppo, and printed for him

---

43 Antonio da Vercelli, *Consegli della salute del peccatore*, fol. [1]1ʳ.

in 1485, has southern features such as *capilli* ('capelli'), *quisti denare* ('questi denari'), *menazo* ('minaccio'), and *siti* ('siete'). The first page of an edition of Paolo Varisco's translation of the *Chirurgia* of Guido de Cauliaco printed in Venice in 1493 contains northern forms such as *medega* ('medica'), *a mi* ('a me'), *la rason* ('la ragione'), and *nui siemo puti* ('noi siamo ragazzi'). Even a Tuscan press might print a text with a strong non-Tuscan colouring: the *Fiore novello estratto della Bibbia*, printed in Lucca in about 1477 by a man born in that city, Bartolomeo Civitali, preserved northern forms such as *oldire* ('udire'), *mi* as a first-person subject pronoun, *digando* ('dicendo'), and *vogliando* or *voiando* ('volendo'). In a remarkable edition of the fourteenth-century *Laude* of Jacopone da Todi printed in Florence in 1490, the anonymous editor, perhaps Giorgio Antonio Vespucci, treated the poet's Umbrian dialect with great respect, stating in his proem that he has kept 'la simplicità e purità anticha secondo quel paese di Todi' (its simplicity and ancient purity according to that town of Todi), changing nothing.[44] An edition of the late fourteenth-century *Carta de Logu* — the legal code of Sardinia, written in Sardinian — was probably produced on the island around 1480 by an itinerant printer summoned from Spain for this purpose by the Aragonese authorities.[45]

However, copies of texts in print usually needed to be sold to a broad and often interregional public, who might well prefer not to encounter unfamiliar forms of language. We can infer that most readers came to expect texts, especially literary ones, to conform with what was currently conceived as correct usage, because towards the end of the fifteenth century, and increasingly in the sixteenth, those responsible for printed texts tended to eliminate linguistic features not found in the canonical vernacular works of the Tuscan fourteenth century, or to reduce their frequency. Their main targets were linguistic traits derived from areas outside Florence, or traits typical of contemporary rather than fourteenth-century Florentine, such as the masculine singular definite article *el* rather than *il*, or Latinizing spellings and lexical items, such as *dicto* ('detto') or *excubie* ('guardie'). Authors themselves might undertake a revision of their works: a well-known case is that of Ludovico Ariosto's rewriting of his chivalric romance *Orlando Furioso* for its third edition, which he oversaw himself in Ferrara in 1532.[46] Alternatively, they might turn for advice on language and punctuation to a professional editor or a trusted friend. Pietro Aretino wrote to Lodovico Dolce on 1 September 1541, asking for help in this respect and explaining bluntly that his motivation was both aesthetic and financial:

> Veramente una opra bene scritta e ben puntata è simile a una sposa bene adorna e ben polita. Onde coloro che la debbono imprimere, nel vederla sì fatta, ne hanno quel piacere che si prova mentre si vagheggia il polito

---

44 Jacopone da Todi, *Laude*, fol. A1ᵛ. See Barbieri, 'Le *Laudi* di Francesco Bonaccorsi'.
45 Balsamo, *La stampa in Sardegna*, pp. 34–35; Veneziani, 'Note su tre incunabuli "spagnoli"', pp. 62–67.
46 Fahy, *L'"Orlando furioso" del 1532*.

e lo adorno de la donna predetta. [...] Or perché l'amore ch'io porto a cotali fatiche mi sforzono a riguardare più tosto al profitto de l'utile, che al dovere de l'onesto, vi mando il libro, con arbitrio però che ci potiate e aggiugnere e scemare né più né meno che a l'altezza del vostro fedel giudizio parrà e di scemarci e di aggiugnerci.[47]

> (In truth, a work that is well written and well punctuated is like a well-adorned and well-embellished bride. Thus, when those who have to print it see it prepared in this way, they derive the same pleasure as one feels when one gazes on the embellishment and the adornment of such a woman. [...] Now, since my love for such labours obliges me to consider the benefit of profit rather than the duty of what is honourable, I am sending you the book, allowing you freedom to prune, and to add and remove no more or less than the loftiness of your faithful judgement sees fit to remove from it and add to it.)

Bernardo Tasso took his time before sending a manuscript of his romance *Amadigi* and his lyric verse to the press, as he explained in a letter of 1557 to Girolamo Ruscelli, another man of letters who worked as a professional editor: 'non potrò darlo alla stampa per alcuni mesi, volendo prima rivederlo da me [...]; dopoi rivederlo con M. Sperone [Speroni] e con altri amici miei, fra' quali uno sarete voi' (I will not be able to send it to press for some months, since I first wish to revise it by myself [...]; then to revise it with Sperone and other friends of mine, one of whom will be you).[48] Editors were often employed by printers to prepare their copy-text, especially in the case of literary works; this process had the effect of standardizing many aspects of the formal written language, from spelling, phonology, and morphology to lexis, but it often made the 'corrected' text less authentic in respect of what its author had intended.[49]

There was also a market for printings of texts that made humorous use of rustic or popular language, and these naturally preserved at least some original forms: to standardize them would have removed an essential part of their appeal. In the fifteenth century, such editions were not numerous. One that was probably printed in Venice by Filippo Pincio in about 1492 contains three Paduan *mariazi* (nuptial dialogues), the first entitled *El mariazo da Pava* (of Padua).[50] The language of a *Frottola nuova de uno Caligaro, con una del Conzalavezo, cosa da ridere e da recettare in maschera* (New frottola about a cobbler with one about the tinker, funny and performable on stage)

---

47 Aretino, *Lettere*, IV, pp. 318–19.
48 Tasso, *Lettere inedite*, p. 148.
49 For an overview, see Trovato, *Con ogni diligenza corretto*, and Richardson, *Print Culture*.
50 On this and later editions, see *Antichi testi di letteratura pavana*, ed. by Lovarini, pp. lii–lviii, 89–143; Lommatzsch, *Beiträge zur älteren italienischen Volksdichtung*, pp. 83–87; Milani, 'Le origini della poesia pavana', pp. 371–72. On the printing of dialect texts, see also Richardson, 'Dialects and Standard Language'.

printed by the brothers Giovanni and Gregorio de' Gregori in Venice around 1485 has been described as broadly that of the Veneto with just a few traces of Bergamask.[51] Five anonymous tailed sonnets containing laments addressed by a Bergamask peasant to his beloved Togna were included in a short collection of performable courtly poetry, the *Strambotti d'ogni sorte et Sonetti alla bergamasca gentilissimi da cantare insù liuti e variati stormenti* that was published in three editions, probably Roman, about or after 1500, and three *Strambotti alla bergamasca* precede a *Contrasto* (alternating dialogue) between a Florentine and a Bergamask in two editions of *Le malitie de vilani*, datable to around the second or third decades of the sixteenth century.[52] This type of juxtaposition of poems in Tuscan and in another dialect, and thus of linguistic registers, is also found in the *Opera nuova de Vincentio Calmeta, Lorenzo Carbone, Orpheo Mantuano, et Venturino da Pesaro, et altri auctori. Sonetti. Dialogi ala vilanesca. Capitoli. Epistole. Stramboti*, printed in Venice in 1507, and in a very successful *Compendio de cose nove de Vicenzo Calmeta et altri auctori, cioè sonetti capitoli epistole egloghe pastorale strambotti barzelette et una predica d'amore*, printed seven times in the same city between 1507 and 1517. These editions include a collection of tailed sonnets, composed by different authors in the late fifteenth century, that depict peasant dialogues in Ferrarese dialect. In the first sonnet, for instance, a doctor wants to treat an old man, who offers a copious urine sample. It begins:

> 'Barba Guiozo, a' ve lasè haver male'.
> 'Oimè, tasì ch'a' me sento morire!
> Pensai ch'ò perso el magnare e 'l dormire,
> ma son può fatto gaiardo al bocale'.[53]

> > ('Uncle Guiozo, you're letting yourself fall ill'. 'Alas, be quiet, for I feel I'm dying! I thought I could no longer eat and sleep, but then I've been in fine form with the jug'.)

Texts, such as these, that used regional language for comic effect might still be subject to the levelling tendency of print: in cases in which printed editions can be compared with manuscripts of the same or similar material, the language of the former tends to be more hybrid and less authentic.[54] *La Nencia da Barberino*, a love poem addressed by a male peasant to a peasant girl in a parody of the language of the Mugello, was printed in several Florentine

---

51 Paccagnella, '"Insir fuora de la so buona lengua"', p. 121. Paccagnella provides a list of fifteenth- and sixteenth-century editions that use Bergamask in his *Il fasto delle lingue*, p. 219, n. 119.
52 Corti, '"Strambotti a la bergamasca"', pp. 275–76; Ciociola, 'Attestazioni antiche del bergamasco letterario', pp. 166–70. A tailed sonnet has, after the first fourteen lines, one or more three-line codas made up of a *settenario* and two hendecasyllables.
53 Milani, 'Sonetti ferraresi', pp. 304–22 (the passage quoted is on p. 307); Milani, 'Le origini della poesia pavana', pp. 371–73; Largaiolli, *La Predica d'Amore*, pp. 228–38.
54 See, for example, Milani, 'Sonetti ferraresi', pp. 317–18.

editions between the early 1490s and 1622, and they all contain not the A version, attributable to Lorenzo de' Medici, which is probably the earliest and whose language is the most deliberately rustic, but the vulgate version, which excluded, for instance, the characteristic forms with *-gghi-* for *-gli-*, as in *tagghiare* for *tagliare*.[55]

From about the second decade of the sixteenth century, there was a gradual but marked expansion of the printing of works that were written in dialect or that juxtaposed or blended two or more different types of Italian vernacular. This development appears to have been in part a reaction against the tendency of authors and editors to adopt Trecento Tuscan as a model in printed literary texts: the process of standardization on the basis of a written language of the past, sometimes at the expense of textual authenticity, increased the sense of the distinctiveness and vitality of the everyday tongues of contemporary Italy and allowed an independent space for them. Such editions appeared especially in Venice, the most polyglot city of the peninsula. The tongues preferred for imitation were the most outlandish and exotic, those of outsiders and immigrants of various kinds. Some texts featured the dialect of Bergamask porters or servants, deemed nearly impenetrable to outsiders; others gave voices to peasants from the countryside around Padua, Ferrara, Milan, Florence, or Siena. An early example of a caricature of the vernacular spoken by Slavonian traders is the *Canzon alla schiavonescha* that opens the *Strambotti de Misser Rado e de Madonna Margarita: cosa nova* ([Venice, 1525?]). An epic poem by Antonio Molino, *I fatti e le prodezze di Manoli Blessi strathioto*, written in the language of the cavalrymen known as stradiots — Venetian dialect with an admixture of elements of Istrian, Dalmatian, and modern Greek — was printed in 1561 by the most prestigious Venetian press of the period, that of Gabriele Giolito. The bookseller Stefano Alessi, born in Asola and working in Venice between 1551 and 1561, specialized in publishing the dialectal and plurilingual plays of Angelo Beolco, known as Ruzante, and Andrea Calmo.[56] An edition of *Tutte le opere del famosissimo Ruzante* was printed in Vicenza by Giorgio Greco in 1584; as Luca D'Onghia has shown, the editor or editors, who perhaps included the dialect poet Giovan Battista Maganza, known as Magagnò, aimed at a language that was more regular by making it more rustic in some respects but more 'Italian' in others.[57]

The artificial language of macaronic verse — Latin infiltrated by colloquial vernacular and northern dialect terms and forms — had a learned readership and thus lent itself naturally to print. Its chief pioneer was Michele (known as Tifi) Odasi, whose family moved from the Bergamo region to the university city of Padua, and his *La Macaronea* was printed in at least six editions from about 1485 to about 1500. *Boazana*, an anonymous macaronic poem set in

---

55 *La Nencia da Barberino*, pp. 134–35; Tavoni, *Storia della lingua italiana*, pp. 142–45.
56 Rhodes, 'Ruzzante e il suo primo editore'.
57 D'Onghia, 'Primordi della filologia dialettale', pp. 319–22.

the University of Bologna, was printed in this city around 1495.[58] There were many editions of the macaronic works of Teofilo Folengo of Mantua, writing under the pseudonym Merlin Cocai. They were published in four authorial redactions in Venice (1517), Toscolano (1521, an edition in which the author made numerous corrections during the printing process), the fictitious 'Cipada' (but perhaps Venice, c. 1535), and posthumously again in Venice (1552).[59] Further Venetian editions appeared up to 1585. Giovan Giorgio Alione's *Opera iocunda metro macharronico materno et Gallico composita*, printed in the author's native Asti in 1521, drew on macaronic Latin, French ('lingua galica'), and *astigiano* dialect, which Alione distinguished from the cultured 'bon vulgar', and it mocked the speech of Genoa and Florence.[60]

Occasionally, dialect might be used out of a sense of local pride together with resentment of the fact that the spoken languages of Italy could normally no longer influence the written language at any but the lowest levels. When authors wished to champion the use of their own tongue in literature, they used print to give the greatest possible publicity to their case. An early example is found in Mario Podiani's prose comedy *I megliacci*, printed in Perugia in 1530. The title, referring to a popular dish of blood pudding, is used as a metaphor for the manner of the play, rooted in local tradition and avoiding affectation: Podiani writes 'in suono tosco Peroscino' as he puts it in his prologue, in a language with a Tuscan base but coloured by the refined dialect of Perugia.[61] There was no such compromise, however, in the *Rime diverse in lengua zeneise: di nuoevo stampé, e misse in luxe*, collected by Cristoforo Zabata, first printed in Genoa by Marcantonio Bellone in 1575 and republished in several editions.[62] An edition printed by Paolo Gottardo Da Ponte in Milan in 1589 collected dialect verse by Giovanni Paolo Lomazzo and fellow-members of an academy of this city that purported to belong to a remote Alpine valley: *Rabisch dra Academiglia dor compà Zavargna, nabad dra vall d' Bregn, ed tucch i sù fidigl' soghit, con rà ricenciglia dra Valada* (Arabesques of the academy of brother Zavargna, abbot of the Valle di Blenio, and of all his faithful subjects, with the permission of the Valley).[63]

Printing promoted the use of punctuation signs and diacritic accents in the literary vernacular to elucidate meaning and to indicate pronunciation. Reform was initiated by the editions of Petrarch (1501) and Dante (1502) printed by Aldo Manuzio in italic type cut by Griffo, and edited by Pietro Bembo — the trio who, as we saw, had produced the *De Aetna* of 1496. As well as the range of punctuation mentioned above, Bembo used the apostrophe to mark elision and aphaeresis, as in 'quand'era' and 'e 'l pentirsi' respectively,

---

58 Soltész, 'Ein bologneser Frühwerk'.
59 Folengo, *Macaronee minori*, pp. 555–609.
60 Chiesa, 'La questione della lingua in Asti e Giovan Giorgio Alione'.
61 Podiani, *I megliacci*, fol. A5ʳ. See Mattesini, 'L'Umbria', pp. 544–45.
62 Beniscelli, Coletti, and Còveri, 'La Liguria', pp. 54–55; Còveri, 'La Liguria', pp. 76–77.
63 Lomazzo, *Rabisch*.

and he introduced a few grave and acute accents to disambiguate words such as the verbs è (as opposed to the conjunction *e*) and *empiè* (past historic, as opposed to the adjective *empie*) and to indicate the stress accent in *piéta*. In view of the evident usefulness of these innovations and of the prestige of the texts established by Bembo, other presses gradually adopted the marks used in the Aldine editions and extended the use of accentuation, making it more systematic. Roman type lagged somewhat behind italic in this respect, and Giovanni Domenico Lega felt it necessary to note the lack of accents in the edition of his *Rime* printed in roman type in Naples by Mattia Cancer and Ioanne Sultzbach in 1535: 'Vi mancano anchora molti, anzi assai più di molti accenti, i quali non vi sono stati posti per lo stampatore non gli havere havuti in questa lettera' (There are still lacking many, indeed very much more than many, accents, which have not been added because the printer does not have them in this fount).[64]

Vernaculars from beyond the Peninsula

Modern foreign languages did not appear on the Renaissance school syllabus, but a knowledge of at least some of them was expected of educated people. An aristocratic character in Baldesar Castiglione's dialogue *Il libro del Cortegiano*, published in 1528, considered '[il] saper diverse lingue' (knowing various languages) to be a very praiseworthy accomplishment of the ideal courtier,

> e massimamente la spagnola e la franzese, perché il commerzio dell'una e dell'altra nazion è molto frequente in Italia e con noi sono queste due più conformi che alcuna dell'altre; e que' dui prìncipi, per esser potentissimi nella guerra e splendidissimi nella pace, sempre hanno la corte piena di nobili cavalieri, che per tutto 'l mondo si spargono; ed a noi pur bisogna conversar con loro. (II. 37)
>
>> (especially as regards French and Spanish, since in Italy we have very frequent dealings with both countries and their ways conform more with ours than any others, and their rulers (who are powerful in war and splendid in peace) keep their courts full of fine gentlemen who then travel the world; and we are obliged to converse with them.)[65]

Among the texts printed in Italy in a foreign vernacular, those in Spanish were most prominent, above all in the second half of the sixteenth century. They would have been sought after by some cultured Italians and by the Spaniards who were present in the peninsula, mostly in Rome and in the mainland states that they ruled, those of Naples and, from 1535, Milan. The main centre of

---

64 Cited in Trovato, *L'ordine dei tipografi*, p. 216.
65 Castiglione, *Il libro del cortegiano*, pp. 248–49; Castiglione, *The Book of the Courtier*, p. 147.

production was Venice — where the bookseller-publisher Giovanni Battista Pederzano in the 1530s and Gabriele Giolito for a few years in the 1550s were among those who specialized in Spanish texts — followed by Rome, Milan, and Naples. Editions of literary texts included the *Tragicomedia de Calisto y Melibea* (*La Celestina*) by Fernando de Rojas, the *Propalladia* by Bartholomé de Torres Naharro, and the prose narratives *Cárcel de amor* by Diego de San Pedro and *Primaleón*. The play *Retrato de la Loçana andaluza*, written in Rome in 1524 by Francisco Delicado (Delgado) and set in that city, was printed around 1528–1530 in Venice, to where the author had moved.[66] The notes on Spanish pronunciation that Delicado provided for Venetian editions of *La Celestina* and *Primaleón* in the 1530s indicate that at least some readers were not from Spain. In Rome, the bookseller-publisher Antonio Salamanca commissioned editions of the romance *Amadís de Gaula* (1519), Antonio de Guevara's *Libro áureo de Marco Aurelio emperador* (1531), and poetry by Juan Boscan and Garcilaso de la Vega (1547). Spanish pilgrims to the Holy City could purchase versions of the medieval guidebook known as *Mirabilia Urbis Romae*, with titles such as *Las yglesias y indulgentias de Roma en vulgar castellano* or *Las cosas maravillosas de la santa ciudad de Roma*. Grammars of Spanish began to appear later in the century. Giovanni Mario Alessandri pointed out similarities and differences between Tuscan and Castilian in his *Il paragone della lingua toscana e castigliana*, printed just once, in 1560, by Mattia Cancer in Naples, and Lorenzo Franciosini claimed that his *Gramatica spagnola e italiana* (Venice: Giacomo Sarzina, 1624) was intended for those learning either language. It is probable, however, that both these works were most useful for those who already knew literary Tuscan.[67] Juan Miranda's *Osservationi della lingua castigliana* was widely used: it was printed in Venice in ten editions between 1566 and 1595 by the Giolito press, for which Miranda worked as an editor and translator.

The first printed Spanish version of Hebrew Scripture, the influential *Biblia en lengua española traduzida palabra por palabra dela verdad hebrayca por muy excelentes letrados*, was printed in Ferrara in 1553 by Abraham Usque (Olschki), a Jew of Portuguese origin. It was intended mainly for Jewish readers driven out of Spain by the Inquisition; there were many of them in Ferrara, some eventually moving on to Venice and Ancona.[68] Usque also printed two works in Portuguese, Samuel Usque's *Consolaçam as tribulacoens de Ysrael* in

---

66 Delicado, *Retrato de la Loçana andaluza*. On Venice, see Pallotta, 'Venetian Printers and Spanish Literature'.
67 Polo, *La tradición gramatical del español en Italia*; Mattarucco, 'Grammatiche per stranieri', pp. 156–57.
68 Roth, 'The Marrano Press at Ferrara', pp. 309–11; Rypins, 'The Ferrara Bible at Press'; Wilson, 'Spanish Versions', p. 127. On Jewish migrants in Ferrara from the Iberian peninsula, see Ioly Zorattini, 'Sephardic Settlement in Ferrara', and Di Leone Leoni, *La nazione ebraica spagnola e portoghese di Ferrara*.

1553 and Bernardim Ribeiro's pastoral romance *Menina e Moça* in 1554.[69] Two earlier and isolated Portuguese editions contained the translations made by the humanist Damião de Góis of Ecclesiastes (*Ecclesiastes de Salamam, con algunas annotaçones neçessarias*) and of Cicero's *De senectute* (*Livro de Marco Tullio Ciçeram chamado Catam maior, ou Da velhiçe*). They were printed by Stefano Nicolini (Venice, 1538), probably at the instance of Góis, who at that time was studying in Padua.[70] A work in Catalan (the language of the ruling elite in Sardinia), a translation of the *Expositio missae, seu Speculum ecclesiae* of Hugh of Saint-Cher, was, according to its colophon, printed in Cagliari in 1493.[71] Printing in Sardinia began again in 1566 with a press that the priest Nicolò Canelles set up in his house in Cagliari at his own expense, and this produced several editions in Spanish and Catalan as well as texts in Latin and a poem in Sardinian (Girolamo Araolla, *Sa vida, su martirio, et morte dessos gloriosos martires Gavinu, Brothu et Gianuari*, 1582).[72]

French texts were printed far less frequently than those in Spanish, even though Castiglione judged the two languages to be of similar cultural and political importance. Presses in Turin produced French translations of Guevara's *Libro áureo de Marco Aurelio* (1535) and of a selection of tragic tales by Matteo Bandello (*XVIII histoires tragiques mises en langue françoise*, 1569–1571 and 1582). Francophone pilgrims could visit Rome with the aid of locally printed editions of *Les Maravilles de Rome* (1519) or *Les Merveilles de Rome* (1536).

Printing in German was largely limited to devotional and liturgical works, such as guidebooks to the churches of Rome, a translation of the fifteen prayers attributed to St Birgitta of Sweden, or a breviary. The *Geschichte des zu Trient ermordeten Christenkinde* (Trento: Albrecht Kunne, 1475) and the *Gedicht von dem getöteten Knaben Simon von Trient* ([Santorso?]: Johannes de Reno, 1475) recounted the murder of a little boy in Trento, an event that was blamed on the Jewish community and retained its power as a piece of antisemitic propaganda throughout the Renaissance.[73]

Liturgical and devotional editions in Serbo-Croat intended for Christians were published in Venice.[74] Giorgio Rusconi printed two Offices in Bosnian Cyrillic in 1512, at the expense of Franjo Ratković, a merchant of the republic of Ragusa (modern Dubrovnik).[75] In 1519, Božidar Vuković, from Podgorica

---

69 Roth, 'The Marrano Press at Ferrara', pp. 313–15; Ioly Zorattini, 'Sephardic Settlement in Ferrara', p. 9.
70 Earle, '*Ecclesiastes de Salamam*'; Góis, *O livro de Eclesiastes*; Sandal, ed., *Il mestier de le stamperie de i libri*, p. 194; Earle, 'Damião de Góis's Translation and Commentary'.
71 Balsamo, *La stampa in Sardegna*, pp. 35–39, 118.
72 Balsamo, *La stampa in Sardegna*, pp. 50–59, 121–61.
73 Studies include Donati, *L'inizio della stampa a Trento*; Kristeller, 'The Alleged Ritual Murder of Simon of Trent', pp. 131, 133; Po-Chia Hsia, *Trent 1475*; Teter, *Blood Libel*, pp. 43–151.
74 Pesenti, 'Stampatori e letterati', p. 105.
75 Pelusi, 'Il libro liturgico veneziano', p. 46; Gasperoni, *Gli annali di Giorgio Rusconi*, pp. xxiv–xxvi, 57.

in modern-day Montenegro, set up a press whose first Slavonic book was an Office, and this printing house continued to operate under his son into the second half of the century.[76] Other presses produced some literary texts in Serbo-Croat, by authors such as Marin Držić and Dominko Zlatarić. The best-selling catechism composed by the Spanish Jesuit Diego de Ledesma, the *Dottrina christiana*, was published in a translation into Croatian, termed 'lingua schiava' (Venice, 1578), and in a translation into Albanian (Rome, 1592). The former edition was probably intended for use by Christians within the Venetian state, while the second was perhaps to be used by Christian missionaries as well as by Christians. Šime Budinić, from Zadar, published a *Breve instruttione per imparare il carattere serviano, et la lingua illyrica* in 1597.

Two Roman Catholics who had left Wales for Italy during the reign of Elizabeth I concerned themselves with the printing of texts in Welsh. Gruffydd Robert, a priest and confessor to Carlo Borromeo in Milan, published the first part of his grammar of this language in Milan in 1567. The grammar's printer, probably Vincenzo Girardoni, had to contend with typographic difficulties such as the letter *y*, for which Greek characters had to serve. In the following year, Robert oversaw publication of his uncle Morys Clynnog's Welsh adaptation of Ledesma's *Dottrina christiana* (*Athrawaeth Gristnogawl*), doubtless intended to promote Catholicism among his compatriots.[77] Throughout the 1570s, Clynnog tried to win papal support for the printing in Italy of Welsh translations of Catholic Reformation literature that were to be smuggled into Wales as an 'antidote' to Protestant publications.[78] A Jesuit born in Dublin, Robert Corbington, translated a Latin text on the Holy House of Loreto into Welsh, English, and Scots, and his versions were published in Loreto as broadsheets by Francesco Serafini in 1634–1635.[79]

Languages in Parallel

Printing provided new opportunities for combining two or more languages to assist the study of an unfamiliar language and sometimes to assist comparative scholarship. The range of bilingual dictionaries grew. Giovanni Crastone's Greek–Latin and Latin–Greek lexicons have already been mentioned. A work

---

76 Pelusi, 'Il libro liturgico veneziano', pp. 46–48, 49–50; Mitric, 'The First Slavonic Book Printed by Božidar Vuković'; Barbarics-Hermanik, 'European Books for the Ottoman Market', pp. 395–96.
77 Griffith, 'Robert, Gruffydd'. I am grateful to Dr Paul Bryant-Quinn for information on Robert.
78 Price, 'Welsh Humanism after 1536', p. 189.
79 *Dechreuad a rhyfedhus esmudiad eglwys yr arglwdhes Fair o Loreto*; *The Miraculous Origin and Translation of the Church of our B. Lady of Loreto*; *The Wondrus Flittinge of the Kirk of Our B. Ledy of Loreto*. An Irish version was printed in Rome in 1707. See Davidson, 'Perceptions of the British Isles and Ireland among the Catholic Exiles', p. 318.

printed frequently from 1480 onwards was the *Vocabulista ecclesiastico* of the Augustinian friar Giovanni Bernardo Forte, which gave Italian equivalents of Latin from the Bible. From 1561 onwards there appeared many editions of a work that aided translation from the vernacular into Latin, Filippo Venuti's *Dittionario volgare, et latino: nel quale si contiene, come i vocaboli italiani si possano dire, et esprimere latinamente*. A popular bilingual dictionary of a modern language was the *Vocabulario de las dos lenguas toscana y castellana* of Cristobal de las Casas, printed for the first time in 1576 by Egidio Regazzola at the instance of Damiano Zenaro, bookseller in Venice. Some works had a practical orientation. A bilingual Italian–German dictionary containing wordlists arranged by topics was printed many times, under different titles, from 1477 until the mid-sixteenth century. The first edition ([Venice]: Adam de Rottweil, 1477) begins: 'Questo libro el quale si chiama introito e porta de quele che voleno imparare e comprender todescho a latino cioè taliano el quale è utilissimo per quele che vadeno a pratichando per el mundo el sia todescho o taliano' (This book which is called entrance and door of those who wish to learn and understand German from Latin, that is Italian, which is very useful for those who travel and deal around the world, whether German or Italian). In the gothic type of this edition, a small *e* is placed above vowels where modern German would use umlaut marks.[80] Short phrasebooks provided equivalent terms in languages that traders might use, as in the *Opera chi se delettasse de saper domandar ciascheduna cosa in turchesco* of around 1530 and the *Opera nova de vocaboli turcheschi et gregheschi li quali sono dechiarati in lingua italiana* of around 1580. Gerolamo Bartoli appears to have printed the first edition (of which no copy survives) of a Milanese–Italian dictionary by Giovanni Capis, the *Varon milanes de la lengua da Milan*, revised and printed in 1606 by Gian Giacomo Como, together with a phonological description of Milanese by Giovanni Ambrogio Biffi.[81]

Polyglot dictionaries also grew in number and scope during the sixteenth century. In 1510 there appeared an *Introductio quaedam utilissima sive vocabularius quattuor linguarum Latinae Italicae Gallicae et Alamannicae per mundum versari cupientibus summe utilis* (very useful for those wishing to engage in business across the world). To the four languages covered here, Spanish was added in 1526 (*Quinque linguarum utilissimus vocabulista Latine, Tusche, Gallice, Hyspane et Alemanice*) and English in 1541 (*Sex linguarum, Latinae, Gallicae, Hispanicae, Italicae, Anglicae, et Teutonice, dilucidissimus dictionarius*). One of the many undertakings of the brothers Giovanni Antonio and Stefano Nicolini in Venice was an *Introduttorio nuovo intitolato Corona preciosa, per imparare, legere, scrivere, parlare, et intendere la lingua greca volgare et literale, et*

---

80 Rossebastiano Bart, *Vocabolari veneto-tedeschi*, and Rossebastiano Bart, *Antichi vocabolari plurilingui d'uso popolare*. Studies of bilingual dictionaries include Tancke, *Die italienischen Wörterbücher*, pp. 41–88, and Marello, *Dizionari bilingui*.
81 Lepschy, 'Una fonologia del 1606'.

la lingua latina, et il volgare italico con molta facilità e prestezza sanza precettore, printed in 1527. This provided parallel wordlists in Italian, Latin, modern Greek, and ancient Greek, and, as Stefano pointed out, it enabled Greeks and all who knew Latin — 'come sono Francesi, Tedeschi, Spagnuoli, Inglesi, Flamenghi, Onghari, et Polacchi et di qualonche altra natione' (such as the French, Germans, Spanish, English, Flemish, Hungarians, Poles, and any other nation) — to learn the other languages.[82] From 1574 onwards, a *Vocabulario nuovo, con il quale da se stessi, si può benissimo imparare diversi linguaggi, cioè, Italiano e Greco, Italiano e Turco, et Italiano e Todesco* provided Italians with a means of learning independently three other languages, each paired with their own. The *Colloquia et dictionariolum septem linguarum, Belgicae, Anglicae, Teutonicae; Latinae, Italicae, Hispanicae, Gallicae* (Padua: Paolo Meietti, 1592), offered parallel short dialogues, a dictionary, and verb paradigms.

The juxtaposition of texts in different languages, as found in the dialogues of this last volume, was a long-standing method of study, and innovative use was made of it in print. We have already seen other examples such as the bilingual Greek and Latin texts printed by Bonaccorso da Pisa in Milan in the years around 1480 and the edition of the Gospels in Arabic and Latin of 1590. One of the standard school texts for learning Latin, Aesop's *Fables* in Latin translation, was printed several times with Italian versions by Accio Zucco (1479 onwards) and by Francesco Del Tuppo (1485 onwards). New methods of juxtaposing Greek and Latin versions of a text were developed by Aldo Manuzio. In 1495, he published a short version of the Greek grammar by Constantinus Lascaris with a Latin translation on the facing page, rather than placing the versions in two columns on the same page, as Bonaccorso da Pisa had done. Within the next couple of years, Aldo began to print Greek texts and their Latin translations in separate gatherings (which, like most books of the period, would have been sold unbound), so that readers could either detach them or interleave them.[83] In about 1501, Aldo planned an edition of the Bible with the Hebrew, Greek, and Latin texts side by side, but only a pair of proof sheets survives.[84] A polyglot *Psalterium Hebraeum, Graecum, Arabicum, et Chaldaeum*, intended for scholars, was printed in Genoa in 1516 and dedicated to Leo X.[85] The text is set in seven columns across facing pages; from left to right: a version marked 'Hebrea', its Latin equivalent ('Latina respondens Hebree'), the Latin Vulgate ('Latina communis'), the Greek Septuagint ('Greca'), the Arabic equivalent ('Arabica'), a Chaldean Aramaic version using Hebrew characters ('Paraphrasis Chaldea'), and a Latin equivalent of the Chaldean ('Latina respondens Chaldee'), together with blocks of

---

[82] Nicolini, *Introduttorio nuovo*, fol. A2ʳ. See Layton, *The Sixteenth Century Greek Book*, pp. 404–05; Sandal, ed., *Il mestier de le stamperie de i libri*, p. 150.
[83] Richardson, 'Aldo Manuzio and the Uses of Translation', pp. 153–62.
[84] Scapecchi, 'Aldo alle origini della Bibbia poliglotta'; Davies, *Aldus Manutius*, pp. 52, 57.
[85] Nuovo, 'A Lost Arabic Koran Rediscovered', p. 284.

'Scholia' (explanatory notes) in Latin. The *Flores italici, ac latini idiomatis* of Orazio Toscanella (Venice: Grazioso Percacino, 1568) added Italian versions to the Latin dialogues that had been created for schoolchildren earlier in the century by the Spaniard Juan Luis Vives. Toscanella hoped to benefit not only students of Latin but also, as the title pages of the work implied from the first edition onwards, foreigners learning Italian ('in gratiam [...] praecipue Exterarum Nationum').[86]

Bilingual and polyglot editions such as these constituted the most obvious of the means through which print played a major part in cross-cultural exchanges during the Italian Renaissance. We have seen, however, that interlingual relationships were created in other ways, not only through contacts between the artisans, merchants, and scholars of diverse provenance who were brought together by the book trade, but also because of the collaborations and accommodations that were needed in order to prepare, print, and sell books that were to be used for many purposes, within Italy and abroad, in an ever-widening range of languages, as distant from each other as Arabic and Welsh. Although there were episodes of intolerance shown towards books in Hebrew in the 1550s and 1560s, printing in this language is just one instance of the productive interaction that print publication could inspire among individuals from different cultures and ethnicities.

Works Cited

Primary Sources

Antichi testi di letteratura pavana, ed. by Emilio Lovarini (Bologna: Romagnoli, 1894)

Antonio da Vercelli, *Consegli della salute del peccatore* ([Italy: Printer of Sallustius, 'Opera' (H 14196)], 1470)

Aretino, Pietro, *Lettere*, ed. by Paolo Procaccioli, 6 vols (Rome: Salerno Editrice, 1997–2002)

Castiglione, Baldesar, *The Book of the Courtier*, trans. by George Bull (Harmondsworth: Penguin, 1976)

——, *Il libro del cortegiano con una scelta delle opere minori*, ed. by Bruno Maier, 2nd edn (Turin: UTET, 1964)

Delicado, Francisco, *Retrato de la Loçana andaluza*, ed. by Rocío Díaz Bravo (Cambridge: MHRA, 2019)

I fiori delle rime de' poeti illustri, nuovamente raccolti et ordinati da Girolamo Ruscelli (Venice: Giovanni Battista and Melchiorre Sessa, 1558)

---

86 On the use of conversation manuals such as this, see Gallagher, *Learning Languages in Early Modern England*, pp. 55–100.

Folengo, Teofilo, *Macaronee minori: Zanitonella, Moscheide, Epigrammi*, ed. by Massimo Zaggia (Turin: Einaudi, 1987)
Giambullari, Pierfrancesco, *Regole della lingua fiorentina*, ed. by Ilaria Bonomi (Florence: Accademia della Crusca, 1986)
Góis, Damião de, *O livro de Eclesiastes: reprodução em fac-símile da edição de Stevão Sabio (Veneza, 1538)*, ed. by T. F. Earle (Lisbon: Fundação Calouste Gulbenkian, 2002)
Jacopone da Todi, *Laude* (Florence: Francesco Bonaccorsi, 1490)
Lomazzo, Giovan Paolo, *Rabisch: Giovan Paolo Lomazzo e i Facchini della Val di Blenio*, ed. by Dante Isella (Turin: Einaudi, 1993)
Machiavelli, Niccolò, *Discorso intorno alla nostra lingua*, ed. by Paolo Trovato (Padua: Antenore, 1982)
La Nencia da Barberino, ed. by Rossella Bessi (Rome: Salerno Editrice, 1982)
Nicolini da Sabbio, Stefano, *Introduttorio nuovo intitolato Corona preciosa, per imparare, legere, scrivere, parlare, et intendere la lingua greca volgare et literale, et la lingua latina, et il volgare italico con molta facilità e prestezza sanza precettore* (Venice: Giovanni Antonio Nicolini da Sabbio and brothers at the expense of Andrea Torresani, 1527)
Paul of Middelburg, *Paulina de recta Paschae celebratione* (Fossombrone: Ottaviano Petrucci, 1513)
Podiani, Mario, *I megliacci* (Perugia: Girolamo Cartolari, 1530)
Tasso, Bernardo, *Lettere inedite*, ed. by Giuseppe Campori (Bologna: Romagnoli, 1869)

Secondary Studies

Amram, David W., *The Makers of Hebrew Books in Italy: Being Chapters in the History of the Hebrew Printing Press* (Philadelphia: Greenstone, 1909)
Antonucci, Laura, 'Giustinian, Marcantonio', *Dizionario biografico degli Italiani*, vol. LVII (Rome: Istituto della Enciclopedia Italiana, 2001), pp. 255–57
Balsamo, Luigi, *La stampa in Sardegna nei secoli XV e XVI* (Florence: Olschki, 1968)
Barbarics-Hermanik, Zsuzsa, 'European Books for the Ottoman Market', in *Specialist Markets in the Early Modern Book World*, ed. by Richard Kirwan and Sophie Mullins (Leiden: Brill, 2015), pp. 389–405
Barbieri, Edoardo, 'Le *Laudi* di Francesco Bonaccorsi (1490): Profilo di un'edizione', in *La vita e l'opera di Iacopone da Todi: Atti del Convegno di studio, Todi, 3–7 dicembre 2006*, ed. by Enrico Menestò (Spoleto: Fondazione Centro italiano di studi sull'alto medioevo, 2007), pp. 639–82
Barker, Nicolas, *Aldus Manutius and the Development of Greek Script and Type in the Fifteenth Century*, 2nd edn (New York: Fordham University Press, 1992)
Beniscelli, Alberto, Vittorio Coletti, and Lorenzo Còveri, 'La Liguria', in *L'italiano nelle regioni: Lingua nazionale e identità regionali*, ed. by Francesco Bruni (Turin: UTET, 1992), pp. 45–83
Boorman, Stanley, *Ottaviano Petrucci: A Catalogue Raisonné* (New York: Oxford University Press, 2006)

Chiesa, Mario, 'La questione della lingua in Asti e Giovan Giorgio Alione', in *Omaggio a Gianfranco Folena*, 3 vols (Padua: Editoriale Programma, 1993), II, pp. 971–84

Ciociola, Claudio, 'Attestazioni antiche del bergamasco letterario: Disegno bibliografico', *Rivista di letteratura italiana*, 4 (1986), 141–74

Cioni, Alfredo, 'Bomberg, Daniel', *Dizionario biografico degli Italiani*, vol. XI (Rome: Istituto della Enciclopedia Italiana, 1969), pp. 382–87

——, 'Bragadin, Alvise', *Dizionario biografico degli Italiani*, vol. XIII (Rome: Istituto della Enciclopedia Italiana, 1971), pp. 659–61

Corti, Maria, '"Strambotti a la bergamasca" inediti del secolo XV: Per una storia della codificazione rusticale nel Nord', in *Storia della lingua e storia dei testi* (Milan: Ricciardi, 1989), pp. 273–91

Còveri, Lorenzo, 'La Liguria', in *L'italiano nelle regioni: Testi e documenti*, ed. by Francesco Bruni (Turin: UTET, 1994), pp. 55–100

Davidson, Peter, 'Perceptions of the British Isles and Ireland among the Catholic Exiles: The Case of Robert Corbington SJ', in *British and Irish Emigrants and Exiles in Europe, 1603–1688*, ed. by David Worthington (Leiden: Brill, 2010), pp. 315–22

Davies, Martin, *Aldus Manutius: Printer and Publisher of Renaissance Venice* (Tempe: Arizona Center for Medieval and Renaissance Studies, 1999)

De Rossi, Giovanni Bernardo, *Annales Hebraeo-typographici sec. XV* (Parma: ex Regio typographeo, 1795; repr. Amsterdam: Philo Press, 1969)

Di Leone Leoni, Aron, *La nazione ebraica spagnola e portoghese di Ferrara (1492–1559)*, ed. by Laura Graziani Secchieri (Florence: Olschki, 2011)

Donati, Lamberto, *L'inizio della stampa a Trento ed il beato Simone* (Trento: Centro culturale 'Fratelli Bronzetti', 1968)

Dondi, Cristina, *Printed Books of Hours from Fifteenth-Century Italy: The Texts, the Books, and the Survival of a Long-Lasting Genre* (Florence: Olschki, 2016)

D'Onghia, Luca, 'Primordi della filologia dialettale', in *La filologia in Italia nel Rinascimento*, ed. by Carlo Caruso and Emilio Russo (Rome: Edizioni di Storia e Letteratura, 2018), pp. 311–25

Dyneley Prince, J., 'A Rare Old Slavonic Religious Manual', *Proceedings of the American Philosophical Society*, 55 (1916), 357–62

Earle, T. F., '*Ecclesiastes de Salamam*: An Unknown Biblical Translation by Damião de Góis', *Portuguese Studies*, 17 (2001), 42–63

Earle, Thomas F., 'Damião de Góis's Translation and Commentary on Cicero's *De Senectute*', in *Medieval and Renaissance Spain and Portugal: Studies in Honor of Arthur L.-F. Askins*, ed. by Martha E. Schaffer and Antonio Cortijo Ocaña (Woodbridge: Tamesis, 2006), pp. 144–57

Fahy, Conor, *L'"Orlando furioso" del 1532: Profilo di una edizione* (Milan: Vita e Pensiero, 1989)

Fani, Sara, and Margherita Farina, eds, *Le vie delle lettere: La Tipografia Medicea tra Roma e l'Oriente* (Florence: Mandragora, 2012)

Fattori, Daniela, 'Venezia culla della stampa glagolitica: L'editio princeps del Breviario (1492)', *Gutenberg-Jahrbuch*, 77 (2002), 110–23

Fragnito, Gigliola, *La Bibbia al rogo: La censura ecclesiastica e i volgarizzamenti della Scrittura (1471–1605)* (Bologna: Il Mulino, 1997)

——, *Proibito capire: La Chiesa e il volgare nella prima età moderna* (Bologna: Il Mulino, 2005)

Gallagher, John, *Learning Languages in Early Modern England* (Oxford: Oxford University Press, 2019)

Gasperoni, Lucia, *Gli annali di Giorgio Rusconi (1500–1522)* (Manziana: Vecchiarelli, 2009)

Grafton, Anthony, *The Culture of Correction in Renaissance Europe* (London: British Library, 2011)

Grendler, Paul F., 'The Destruction of Hebrew Books in Venice, 1568', *Proceedings of the American Academy for Jewish Research*, 45 (1978), 103–30

Griffith, T. Gwynfor, 'Robert, Gruffydd [Griffith Roberts]', *Oxford Dictionary of National Biography* <https://doi.org/10.1093/ref:odnb/23752> [accessed 1 April 2020]

Hall, Basil, 'Biblical Scholarship: Editions and Commentaries', in *The Cambridge History of the Bible: The West from the Reformation to the Present Day*, ed. by S. L. Greenslade (Cambridge: Cambridge University Press, 1963), pp. 38–93

Harris, Neil, 'The History of the Book in Italy', in *The Book: A Global History*, ed. by Michael F. Suarez and H. R. Woudhuysen (Oxford: Oxford University Press, 2013), pp. 420–40

——, 'Printing the Gospels in Arabic in Rome in 1590', in *A Concise Companion to the Study of Manuscripts, Printed Books, and the Production of Early Modern Texts: A Festschrift for Gordon Campbell*, ed. by Edward Jones (Chichester: Wiley-Blackwell, 2015), pp. 131–49

Ioly Zorattini, Pier Cesare, 'Sephardic Settlement in Ferrara under the House of Este', in *New Horizons in Sephardic Studies*, ed. by Yedida K. Stillman and George K. Zucker (Albany: State University of New York Press, 1993), pp. 5–13

Jones, Howard, *Printing the Classical Text* (Utrecht: HES & De Graaf, 2004)

Jones, Robert, *Learning Arabic in Renaissance Europe (1505–1624)* (Leiden: Brill, 2020)

Kristeller, Paul Oskar, 'The Alleged Ritual Murder of Simon of Trent (1475) and its Literary Repercussions: A Bibliographical Study', *Proceedings of the American Academy for Jewish Research*, 59 (1993), 103–35

Largaiolli, Matteo, *La Predica d'Amore: Indagine su un genere parodistico quattro-cinquecentesco con edizione critica dei testi* (Trento: Università degli Studi di Trento, 2019)

Layton, Evro, *The Sixteenth Century Greek Book in Italy: Printers and Publishers for the Greek World* (Venice: Istituto Ellenico di Studi Bizantini e Postbizantini di Venezia, 1994)

Lepschy, Giulio, 'Una fonologia del 1606: Il *Prissian da Milan della parnonzia Milanesa*', in *Saggi di linguistica italiana* (Bologna: Il Mulino, 1978), pp. 177–215

Levi della Vida, Giorgio, 'Albonesi, Teseo Ambrogio degli', *Dizionario biografico degli Italiani*, vol. II (Rome: Istituto della Enciclopedia Italiana, 1960), pp. 39–42

Linde, Cornelia, 'Johannes Crastonus's 1481 Edition of the Psalms', *The Library*, 7th ser., 13 (2012), 147–63

Lommatzsch, Erhard, *Beiträge zur älteren italienischen Volksdichtung*, I: *Die Wolfenbütteler Sammelbände* (Berlin: Akademie-Verlag, 1950)

Lowe, Kate, 'Visible Lives: Black Gondoliers and Other Black Africans in Renaissance Venice', *Renaissance Quarterly*, 66 (2013), 412–52

Lowry, Martin, *Nicholas Jenson and the Rise of Venetian Publishing in Renaissance Europe* (Oxford: Blackwell, 1991)

Marello, Carla, *Dizionari bilingui* (Bologna: Zanichelli, 1989)

Mattarucco, Giada, 'Grammatiche per stranieri', in *Storia dell'italiano scritto*, ed. by Giuseppe Antonelli, Matteo Motolese, and Lorenzo Tomasin, 4 vols (Rome: Carocci, 2014–2018), IV: *Grammatiche*, pp. 141–68

Mattesini, Enzo, 'L'Umbria', in *L'italiano nelle regioni: Testi e documenti*, ed. by Francesco Bruni (Turin: UTET, 1994), pp. 517–56

Megna, Paola, 'Per la storia della princeps di Omero: Demetrio Calcondila e il *De Homero* dello pseudo Plutarco', *Studi medievali e umanistici*, 5–6 (2007–2008), 217–78

Milani, Marisa, 'Le origini della poesia pavana e l'immagine della cultura e della vita contadina', in *Storia della cultura veneta*, vol. III: *Dal primo Quattrocento al Concilio di Trento*, ed. by Girolamo Arnaldi and Manlio Pastore Stocchi, pt 1 (Vicenza: Neri Pozza, 1980), pp. 369–412

——, 'Sonetti ferraresi del '400 in una raccolta di poeti cortigiani', *Giornale storico della letteratura italiana*, 150 (1973), 292–322

Mitric, Olimpia, 'The First Slavonic Book Printed by Božidar Vuković in Venice from the Collections of the Dragomirna Monastery (Bukovina, Romania)', *Slavonic and East European Review*, 90 (2012), 482–88

Nielsen, Bruce, 'Daniel van Bomberghen, a Bookman of Two Worlds', in *The Hebrew Book in Early Modern Italy*, ed. by Joseph R. Hacker and Adam Shear (Philadelphia: University of Pennsylvania Press, 2011), pp. 56–75

Nuovo, Angela, 'A Lost Arabic Koran Rediscovered', *The Library*, 6th ser., 12 (1990), 273–92

Offenberg, Adri K., 'The Chronology of Hebrew Printing at Mantua in the Fifteenth Century: A Re-examination', *The Library*, 6th ser., 16 (1994), 298–315

Paccagnella, Ivano, *Il fasto delle lingue: Plurilinguismo letterario nel Cinquecento* (Rome: Bulzoni, 1984)

——, '"Insir fuora de la so buona lengua": Il bergamasco di Ruzzante', in *Ruzzante*, Filologia veneta, 1 (Padua: Editoriale Programma, 1988), pp. 107–212

Pallotta, Augustus, 'Venetian Printers and Spanish Literature in Sixteenth-Century Italy', *Comparative Literature*, 43 (1991), 20–42

Pellegrini, Paolo, 'Soncino, Gerolamo', *Dizionario biografico degli Italiani*, vol. XCIII (Rome: Istituto della Enciclopedia Italiana, 2018), pp. 270–72

Pelusi, Simonetta, 'Il libro liturgico veneziano per serbi e croati fra Quattro e Cinquecento', in *Le civiltà del Libro e la stampa a Venezia: Testi sacri ebraici, cristiani, islamici dal Quattrocento al Settecento*, ed. by Simonetta Pelusi (Padua: Il Poligrafo, 2000), pp. 43–52

Penkower, Jordan S., 'The First Books Published by Daniel Bomberg', *La Bibliofilía*, 123 (2021), 303–28

Pesenti, Tiziana, 'Stampatori e letterati nell'industria editoriale a Venezia e in Terraferma', in *Storia della cultura veneta*, vol. IV: *Il Seicento*, ed. by Girolamo Arnaldi and Manlio Pastore Stocchi, pt 1 (Vicenza: Neri Pozza, 1983), pp. 93–129

Petrucci, Armando, 'Pouvoir de l'écriture, pouvoir sur l'écriture dans la Renaissance italienne', *Annales: Économies, Sociétés, Civilisations*, 43 (1988), 823–47

Pettas, William A., *The Giunti of Florence: Merchant Publishers of the Sixteenth Century* (San Francisco: Rosenthal, 1980)

Po-Chia Hsia, Ronnie, *Trent 1475: Stories of a Ritual Murder Trial* (New Haven: Yale University Press, 1992)

Polo, Anna, *La tradición gramatical del español en Italia: 'Il paragone della lingua toscana et castigliana' di Giovanni Mario Alessandri d'Urbino. Estudio y edición crítica* (Padua: CLEUP, 2017)

Price, Angharad, 'Welsh Humanism after 1536', in *The Cambridge History of Welsh Literature*, ed. by Geraint Evans and Helen Fulton (Cambridge: Cambridge University Press, 2019), pp. 176–93

Rhodes, Dennis E., 'Ruzzante e il suo primo editore, Stefano di Alessi', in *Ruzzante*, Filologia veneta, 1 (Padua: Editoriale Programma, 1988), pp. 1–13

Richardson, Brian, 'Aldo Manuzio and the Uses of Translation', in *Collectanea Manutiana: Studi critici su Aldo Manuzio*, ed. by Pier Davide Accendere and Stefano U. Baldassarri (Florence: Le Lettere, 2017), pp. 145–69

——, 'Dalla metà del Quattrocento alla metà del Cinquecento', in *Storia della punteggiatura in Europa*, ed. by Bice Mortara Garavelli (Bari: Laterza, 2008), pp. 99–121

——, 'Dialects and Standard Language in Renaissance Printing and Editing', in *Italian Dialects and Literature: From the Renaissance to the Present*, ed. by Emmanuela Tandello and Diego Zancani, *Journal of the Institute of Romance Studies*, Supplement 1 (London: Institute of Romance Studies, 1996), pp. 7–22

——, *Print Culture in Renaissance Italy: The Editor and the Vernacular Text, 1470–1600* (Cambridge: Cambridge University Press, 1994)

Roper, Geoffrey, 'The History of the Book in the Muslim World', in *The Book: A Global History*, ed. by Michael F. Suarez and H. R. Woudhuysen (Oxford: Oxford University Press, 2013), pp. 524–52

——, 'Printed in Europe, Consumed in Ottoman Lands: European Books in the Middle East', in *Books in Motion in Early Modern Europe: Beyond Production, Circulation and Consumption*, ed. by Daniel Bellingradt, Paul Nelles, and Jeroen Salman (Cham: Palgrave Macmillan, 2017), pp. 267–88

Rossebastiano Bart, Alda, *Antichi vocabolari plurilingui d'uso popolare: La tradizione del 'Solenissimo Vochabuolista'* (Alessandria: Edizioni dell'Orso, 1984)

——, *Vocabolari veneto-tedeschi del secolo XV*, 3 vols (Savigliano: Edizioni l'Artistica, 1983)

Roth, Cecil, 'The Marrano Press at Ferrara, 1552–1555', *Modern Language Review*, 38 (1943), 307–17

Rypins, Stanley, 'The Ferrara Bible at Press', *The Library*, 5th ser., 10 (1955), 244–69

Sachet, Paolo, *Publishing for the Popes: The Roman Curia and the Use of Printing (1527–1555)* (Leiden: Brill, 2020)

Salzberg, Rosa, *Ephemeral City: Cheap Print and Urban Culture in Renaissance Venice* (Manchester: Manchester University Press, 2014)

Sandal, Ennio, ed., *Il mestier de le stamperie de i libri: Le vicende e i percorsi dei tipografi di Sabbio Chiese tra Cinque e Seicento e l'opera dei Nicolini*, essays by Ennio Sandal and Cristina Stevanoni, bibliography ed. by Lorenzo Carpané (Brescia: Grafo, 2002)

Scapecchi, Piero, 'Aldo alle origini della Bibbia poliglotta', in *Le civiltà del Libro e la stampa a Venezia: Testi sacri ebraici, cristiani, islamici dal Quattrocento al Settecento*, ed. by Simonetta Pelusi (Padua: Il Poligrafo, 2000), pp. 77–82

Scholderer, Victor, 'Printing at Venice to the End of 1481', in *Fifty Essays in Fifteenth- and Sixteenth-Century Bibliography*, ed. by Dennis E. Rhodes (Amsterdam: Hertzberger, 1966), pp. 74–89

Soltész, Elisabeth, 'Ein bologneser Frühwerk der maccaronischen Dichtung', *Gutenberg-Jahrbuch*, 41 (1966), 105–11

Speranzi, David, 'Prima di Aldo: Demetrio Damilas disegnatore di caratteri', in *Manuciana Tergestina et Veronensia*, ed. by Francesco Donadi, Stefano Pagliaroli, and Andrea Tessier (Trieste: EUT, 2015), pp. 143–61

Staikos, Konstantinos Sp., 'The Printing Shop of Nikolaos Vlastos and Zacharias Kallierges: 500 Years from the Establishment of the First Greek Printing Press', *La Bibliofilía*, 102 (2000), 11–32

Stern, David, 'The Rabbinic Bible in its Sixteenth-Century Context', in *The Hebrew Book in Early Modern Italy*, ed. by Joseph R. Hacker and Adam Shear (Philadelphia: University of Pennsylvania Press, 2011), pp. 76–108

Tamani, Giuliano, 'Edizioni ebraiche veneziane dei secoli XVI–XVIII', in *Le civiltà del Libro e la stampa a Venezia: Testi sacri ebraici, cristiani, islamici dal Quattrocento al Settecento*, ed. by Simonetta Pelusi (Padua: Il Poligrafo, 2000), pp. 29–36

Tancke, Gunnar, *Die italienischen Wörterbücher von den Anfängen bis zum Erscheinen des 'Vocabolario degli Accademici della Crusca' (1612): Bestandsaufnahme und Analyse* (Tübingen: Niemeyer, 1984)

Tavoni, Mirko, *Storia della lingua italiana: Il Quattrocento* (Bologna: Il Mulino, 1992)

Teter, Magda, *Blood Libel: On the Trail of an Antisemitic Myth* (Cambridge, MA: Harvard University Press, 2020)

Tinto, Alberto, *La Tipografia Medicea Orientale* (Lucca: Pacini Fazzi, 1987)

Trovato, Paolo, *Con ogni diligenza corretto: La stampa e le revisioni editoriali dei testi letterari italiani (1470–1570)* (Bologna: Il Mulino, 1991)

——, '"Dialetto" e sinonimi ("idioma", "proprietà", "lingua") nella terminologia linguistica quattro- e cinquecentesca', *Rivista di letteratura italiana*, 2 (1984), 205–36

——, *L'ordine dei tipografi: Lettori, stampatori, correttori tra Quattro e Cinquecento* (Rome: Bulzoni, 1998)

Veneziani, Paolo, 'Note su tre incunabuli "spagnoli"', *La Bibliofilía*, 80 (1978), 57–72
——, *La tipografia a Brescia nel XV secolo* (Florence: Olschki, 1986)
Vercellin, Giorgio, 'Venezia e le origini della stampa in caratteri arabi', in *Le civiltà del Libro e la stampa a Venezia: Testi sacri ebraici, cristiani, islamici dal Quattrocento al Settecento*, ed. by Simonetta Pelusi (Padua: Il Poligrafo, 2000), pp. 53–64
Wilkinson, Robert J., *Orientalism, Aramaic, and Kabbalah in the Catholic Reformation: The First Printing of the Syriac New Testament*, Studies in the History of Christian Traditions, 137 (Leiden: Brill, 2007)
Wilson, E. M., 'Spanish Versions', in *The Cambridge History of the Bible: The West from the Reformation to the Present Day*, ed. by S. L. Greenslade (Cambridge: Cambridge University Press, 1963), pp. 125–29
Wilson, Nigel G., *From Byzantium to Italy: Greek Studies in the Italian Renaissance* (Baltimore: Johns Hopkins University Press, 1992)

ALESSANDRO CARLUCCI

Communicating in Different Vernaculars

Italo-Romance Intercomprehension in Historical Perspective

In a 2015 collective volume on Dante, Mirko Tavoni suggested that comprehension across Italy's different vernaculars was historically 'greater than we today consider possible'.[1] Two other Italian linguists, Alvise Andreose and Lorenzo Renzi, have speculated not only about the degree, but also the actual mechanisms, of medieval and early modern Italo-Romance intercomprehension:

> Sembra [...] che il rapporto orizzontale (cioè in sostanza paritetico) tra i diversi volgari (e poi tra i dialetti) non creasse particolari problemi. Probabilmente chi parlava adattava parzialmente la propria lingua ad alcuni tratti di quella d'arrivo, ma soprattutto chi ascoltava trasformava mentalmente alcuni fonemi e morfemi in quelli propri, come facevano, *mutatis mutandis*, i copisti che, per es., copiando un manoscritto siciliano in toscano, lo toscanizzavano, o, copiando dal fiorentino al veneziano, lo venezianizzavano. I rapporti tra i volgari, in altre parole, non erano conflittuali, e i parlanti erano portati a diminuirne le differenze.[2]
>
> (It seems that the horizontal (that is to say, essentially equal) relationship between different vernaculars (and, later, dialects) did not create particular problems. Those who spoke probably adapted their language to certain features of the target language, and, above all, those who listened mentally transformed some phonemes and morphemes into their own phonemes and morphemes. This was similar to what copyists did when, for instance, they used Tuscan to copy a Sicilian manuscript, and in doing so they Tuscanized it, or when they inserted

---

I wish to thank Marcello Barbato, Luciano Giannelli, and Pär Larson for their suggestions and encouragement. I am also grateful to the anonymous reviewer and the editors of this collective volume.

1 Tavoni, 'Linguistic Italy', p. 251.
2 Andreose and Renzi, 'Volgari medievali', p. 1593.

Alessandro Carlucci (Alessandro.Carlucci@uib.no) is a postdoctoral research fellow in Italian linguistics at the University of Bergen.

Venetian features while copying from Florentine into Venetian. In other words, the relationship between vernaculars was not a conflictual one, and speakers were disposed to minimize differences.)

As we shall see, these proposals mark a significant departure from the consensus which implicitly dominated Italian studies during the second half of the twentieth century, when it was generally believed that Italo-Romance varieties were 'incomunicabili ieri come oggi da un capo all'altro d'Italia' (as incommunicable yesterday as they are today, from one end of Italy to the other).[3] However, proposals such as those put forward by Tavoni and by Andreose and Renzi are essentially speculative, in the sense that these authors do not produce specific historical evidence supporting their claims. In previous works I have begun to assemble and discuss surviving evidence from late medieval Italy,[4] including metalinguistic comments by medieval speakers,[5] which may either prove or disprove the hypothesis of relatively good levels of Italo-Romance intercomprehension. In the present chapter I move further in this direction by adding more evidence and by offering a preliminary, tentative assessment of the relative impact that different structural modules (phonology, morphology, syntax, and lexicon) had on intercomprehension.[6] When discussing phonological and morphological differences, I will also try to substantiate Andreose and Renzi's hypothesis in general theoretical terms by referring to the notion of 'conversion formula'.[7] Medieval and early modern Italo-Romance intercomprehension can be compared not only to other historical cases,[8] but also to multilingual communication between speakers of present-day Romance varieties or other groups of genetically related varieties. In their research on this type of multilingual communication, scholars in contact and applied linguistics often refer to conversion formulae,[9] which are 'consciously or unconsciously' followed by speakers 'and have the form "Your language has *x* where my language has *y*"'.[10] In the particular case of medieval and early modern Italy, conversion formulae could help speakers

---

3   Dionisotti, *Geografia e storia della letteratura italiana*, p. 79. See also Kristeller, 'The Origin and Development of the Language of Italian Prose', pp. 480–81.
4   See Carlucci, 'How Did Italians Communicate When There Was No Italian?'.
5   Carlucci, 'Opinions about Perceived Linguistic Intelligibility'.
6   In this chapter I do not focus on the difficulties caused by different handwriting habits (often involving the use of mercantile scripts), which I discussed in 'Opinions about Perceived Linguistic Intelligibility in Late-Medieval Italy'.
7   Weinreich, *Languages in Contact*, p. 2.
8   See Wright, 'Early Medieval Pan-Romance Comprehension', Blanche-Benveniste, 'Comment retrouver l'expérience des anciens voyageurs en terres de langues romanes?', and Lodge, 'Jacques-Louis Ménétra and his Experience of the *langue d'oc*'. See also Braunmüller, 'Receptive Multilingualism in Northern Europe in the Middle Ages'.
9   Also known as *correspondances inter-langues* (cross-linguistic correspondences) (Meissner, 'Introduction à la didactique de l'eurocompréhension', p. 130), or *correspondence rules* (Thomason, *Language Contact*, p. 144).
10   Thomason, *Language Contact*, p. 144.

to adapt a text from a different area to the features of their own variety, or, conversely, to adapt their own speech to that of other areas, and to do this not only in reading or writing, but also orally.

In the first three of the following sections, I define the topic and its research context, and I summarize the conflicting opinions which have been expressed about it. As I do so, I also clarify the terminology used in this chapter. Three other sections follow which constitute the central part of the chapter, where I present relevant historical evidence. I start with metalinguistic comments by medieval and early modern speakers, which reveal their expectations and perceptions about the comprehensibility of different Italo-Romance vernaculars. I then devote two sections to the role played by lexical and grammatical differences, respectively, in favouring or hindering cross-vernacular communication. Finally, a short concluding section pulls together the various threads discussed in this chapter and proposes some questions for future research.

The Problem

By asking how Dante would 'communicate with ordinary people, from different parts of Italy', Anna Laura and Giulio Lepschy have pointed out a crucial, problematic aspect of the linguistic situation in medieval Italy: 'The degree of our ignorance is especially worrying if we try to take into account not only literate people (who would have known Latin, perhaps together with vernacular literary traditions) but also illiterate speakers of local varieties'.[11] Our uncertainty about how Dante talked to ordinary folk — for instance during his exile, or on other occasions 'when he was not in Florence, but in Bologna, Ravenna, Padua, Verona, Venice'[12] — is remarkable not simply because of the fame of the speaker in question, but more precisely because of 'the extraordinary amount of erudition that has been devoted to clarifying every detail of Dante's life and works'.[13] However, the same problem applies 'to most situations of the past, not just to Dante'.[14]

Our ability to answer this kind of question seems to be inversely proportional to the chronological distance from the present, and directly proportional to the sociocultural level of the speakers involved. Had Dante lived in the second half of the twentieth century, he would obviously have used Italian (perhaps with regional Tuscan features) in order to communicate with people from other parts of Italy. The answer to the question raised by the Lepschys already becomes less straightforward if we go back to the period between Italy's

---

11   Lepschy and Lepschy, 'Dante as a Native Speaker', p. 313.
12   Lepschy, 'Mother Tongues in the Middle Ages and Dante', p. 19.
13   Lepschy and Lepschy, 'Dante as a Native Speaker', p. 313.
14   Lepschy, 'Mother Tongues in the Middle Ages and Dante', p. 19.

unification (1861) and the Second World War, when Italian would probably have enabled Dante to talk only to a minority of literate and well-educated people, while the rest of the population, especially in rural areas, still had difficulties in using and understanding Italian. The dominant views among linguists are that, when Italy became a unified country, nine-tenths of its population only spoke local varieties different from Italian,[15] and that these varieties (also known as 'dialects' — see below) 'are very different from each other, and mostly unintelligible to speakers of other dialects'.[16]

The number of people who confidently controlled Italian was even smaller between the sixteenth and the nineteenth centuries, when its use was mostly confined to literature and official communication. During the fifteenth century, convergence on Latin or Tuscan models and avoidance of the most idiosyncratic local features had led to the emergence of regionally shared vernacular varieties (also known as 'koine languages'), which were used in particular domains and especially in written texts, such as chancery documents. We also know that, further back in time, educated elites could communicate by using Latin among themselves, and some of their members (especially those who had literary inclinations) had already begun to be exposed to the prestige of Tuscan, which they were perhaps able to understand, even if they could not actively use it. Our uncertainty, however, reaches its peak if we focus on this early period, especially if we try to consider wider sections of the population.

This chapter is aimed at reducing this uncertainty by considering precisely the period which goes from the earliest available evidence to roughly the mid-fifteenth century.[17] Especially during this period, Italy offers a particularly relevant case for the historical study of how speakers manage, or fail, to establish mutual comprehension between closely related languages, given that most local communities used Italo-Romance varieties descended from Latin. These varieties are traditionally called *volgari* (vernaculars) with reference to the period considered in this chapter (i.e. before the codification of the old Florentine used by Dante, Petrarch, and Boccaccio). With reference to the period following the adoption of Florentine-based literary Italian throughout the entire peninsula, the same varieties are called *dialetti* (dialects). This terminological distinction is quite common especially among Italian scholars.[18]

---

15 See De Mauro, *Storia linguistica dell'Italia unita*, and Castellani, 'Quanti erano gl'italofoni nel 1861?'. See also Carlucci, 'How Did Italians Communicate When There Was No Italian?', for discussion and further bibliographical references.
16 Lepschy, 'How Popular Is Italian?', p. 64.
17 On the political, technological, and cultural transformations which took place during the fifteenth century and which increased the need for linguistic uniformity, especially in the second half of the century, see Migliorini, *The Italian Language*, pp. 159–60, Maraschio and Manni, 'Il plurilinguismo italiano', and Maraschio, 'Il plurilinguismo italiano quattrocentesco e l'Alberti'.
18 See Marazzini, *La lingua italiana*, p. 76.

However, in order to facilitate the inclusion of definitions and quotations from a wider range of authors, in this chapter I use 'vernacular' and 'dialect' as synonyms for the more neutral term 'variety'.

My research is linked to scholarship in Italian linguistics, particularly to the works of specialists who have begun to question the conventional idea of a widespread lack of intelligibility between different Italo-Romance varieties in medieval and early modern Italy. However, the material gathered in this chapter and the arguments I put forward are relevant to a broader set of research themes and approaches. As already mentioned, the illustrious case of Dante is but one example. Ignazio Baldelli asked the following question about Saint Francis of Assisi:

> Quale lingua avrà usato Francesco a Bologna nel 1222 per farsi capire dal popolo di Bologna e da uomini di diversa origine regionale e nazionale come Federico Visconti da Pisa e Tommaso da Spalato? Non certo il suo volgare assisano, non comprensibile appunto dai popolani di Bologna o da gente come Tommaso da Spalato. Eppure il tono e lo stesso svolgimento della predica, pur se da lasciare ammirati i dotti, erano appunto 'popolari'.[19]

> (What language did Francis use in Bologna in 1222 in order to be understood by the locals and by men of different regional and national origins such as Federico Visconti of Pisa and Thomas of Split? Certainly not his Assisi vernacular, which was incomprehensible to the ordinary people of Bologna or to people such as Thomas of Split. Nonetheless, the tone and the actual delivery of his sermon were indeed 'popular', even though they also impressed the educated.)

Similar questions have long been posed with regard to merchants, too. Although their letters showed signs of koineization,[20] they remained noticeably different according to the area of provenance of each correspondent, and yet communication among merchants from different parts of Italy did take place on a regular basis.[21] More recently, the question of Italo-Romance intercomprehension has occasionally been mentioned in connection with burgeoning research on topics such as the reception and dissemination of Dante's *Commedia* beyond Florence,[22] the diplomatic relations between the different states in pre-unification Italy,[23] and, more generally, the interactions

---

19 Baldelli, *Conti, glosse e riscritture*, p. 127.
20 See e.g. Brown, 'Language Variation in Fifteenth-Century Milan' and Brown, 'Language History from Below'.
21 See Casapullo, *Il Medioevo*, pp. 68–75.
22 See Armour, 'The *Comedy* as a Text for Performance', pp. 18–21, and Barański, 'Early Reception', p. 523. See also Armour, 'Comedy and the Origins of Italian Theatre around the Time of Dante', Armour, 'Exile and Disgrace', Ahern, 'Singing the Book', Franceschini, *Tra secolare commento e storia della lingua*, and Havely, '*Un grido di sì alto suono*'.
23 See Lazzarini, 'Orality and Writing in Diplomatic Interactions', pp. 99–100. By this same author, see also 'Patterns of Translation' and *Communication and Conflict*.

between writing and orality in the cultural and artistic life of the late Middle Ages and the Renaissance.[24]

The Dominant View

The view that ever since the Middle Ages Italians had been trapped within mutually unintelligible dialects and unable to communicate beyond their local area, unless they knew Latin or other languages of wider circulation, has deep roots in Italian culture. In the eighteenth century, the Venetian playwright Carlo Goldoni claimed that, in Italy, linguistic variation was greater than in other countries, so much so that different regional groups 'parlano diversamente [...] e molti fra di loro non si capiscono' (speak differently, and many of them do not understand each other).[25] In the early nineteenth century, the poet and literary historian Ugo Foscolo similarly stated that:

> se niun dialetto provinciale può scriversi facilmente per tutta una nazione, l'impresa riesce in Italia impossibile, dove dodici uomini di diverse province che conversassero fra di loro, ciascuno ostinandosi a usare il dialetto suo proprio, si partirebbero senza saperti dire di che parlavano.[26]

> (while no regional dialect can easily be written by an entire nation, this task would be impossible in Italy, where twelve men from different regions who insist on using their own dialects while talking to each other will leave without being able to tell you what they were talking about.)

During the nineteenth and early twentieth centuries, the difficulties experienced by many speakers seemed to vindicate these negative views. Various aspects of modern life — especially military conscription and mass migration — created new contacts and a sudden need to communicate between speakers of different Italo-Romance varieties, which often exacerbated the perception of mutual incomprehension.[27] Linguists, too, would eventually uphold similar views. According to Alberto Mioni and Anna Maria Arnuzzo-Lanszweert, 'mutual intelligibility [is] generally impossible in Italy between people speaking

---

24 On this topic, which is currently at the centre of much historical research in Italian studies, see Dall'Aglio and others, eds, 'Oral Culture in Early Modern Italy', and Degl'Innocenti, Richardson, and Sbordoni, eds, *Interactions between Orality and Writing in Early Modern Italian Culture*.
25 Goldoni, 'I rusteghi', p. 619.
26 Foscolo, 'Discorso storico sul testo del Decamerone', p. 337.
27 See e.g. De Mauro's reference to migrants to the United States switching to a 'rozzo gergo anglicizzante' (basic Anglicized jargon) as a way of overcoming 'la barriera delle diversità dialettali' (the barrier of dialectal diversity): *Storia linguistica dell'Italia unita*, p. 42. See Carlucci, 'How Did Italians Communicate When There Was No Italian?', for other examples and bibliographical references.

dialects of two non-adjoining regions'.[28] Lepschy once recalled a conversation he overheard in Venice, his hometown, between two speakers of 'the dialect of Roseto, a town in the province of Teramo, in the Southern Abruzzi'. He tried 'to understand what they were saying: not a single word was intelligible'.[29]

Modern perceptions and concepts have often been projected back onto the Middle Ages.[30] The resulting 'standard view' (as Nigel Vincent calls it) is that, in Italy, 'around the end of the first millennium AD there were [...] a myriad of local vernaculars, perhaps as many as 700 according to Muljačić, each with a high degree of autonomy and mutual unintelligibility with respect to other surrounding dialects'.[31] The number of varieties differs according to different estimates, and a reduction is usually factored in for later periods, due to convergence between local varieties and especially to the spread of prestigious linguistic features from the varieties of culturally, politically, and economically prominent cities.[32] In any case, it is still widely believed that the medieval situation did not significantly change until the twentieth century, when Italo-Romance dialects began to be replaced by regional varieties of Italian in all domains of use.

Alternative Views and Recent Proposals

The dominant views outlined in the previous section have been questioned by Martin Maiden, Alberto Varvaro, and Vincent, who have called for an alternative interpretation of the modern, and especially the medieval, situation. As we shall see, by combining the arguments of these linguists we can formulate the hypothesis that the potential for mutual comprehension between Italo-Romance speakers from different areas was higher than traditionally thought. This hypothesis should not be confused with the far more obvious supposition that Italo-Romance varieties of adjacent localities must have been mutually intelligible (as they are today, unless they are separated by a bundle of isoglosses). Nor should it be confused with unrealistic

---

28 Mioni and Arnuzzo-Lanszweert, 'Sociolinguistics in Italy', p. 83.
29 Lepschy, 'How Popular Is Italian?', p. 63. See also Pellegrini, 'La classificazione delle lingue romanze e i dialetti italiani' and Pellegrini, *Saggi di linguistica italiana*, pp. 63–65; Tosi, *Language and Society in a Changing Italy*, who writes that 'dialect diversity is still so marked in Italy that it usually prevents intelligibility' (p. 21); Ledgeway, 'Understanding Dialect'; and the experimental study by Tamburelli, 'Uncovering the "Hidden" Multilingualism of Europe'.
30 For a representative example, see Serianni's comments on *Decameron*, II, 9 ('Lingua e dialetti d'Italia nella percezione dei viaggiatori sette-ottocenteschi', pp. 56–57). According to this author, real medieval speakers would not perceive different Italo-Romance varieties 'come sparse membra d'un organismo comune' (as separate parts of the same organism), as Boccaccio's characters instead seem to do.
31 Vincent, 'Languages in Contact in Medieval Italy', p. 15. Cf. Muljačić, 'The Relationship between the Dialects and the Standard Language'.
32 See Muljačić, 'The Relationship between the Dialects and the Standard Language', p. 391.

expectations of intelligibility for non-Romance varieties (such as those used by the Germanic- and Slav-speaking minorities who have settled in various parts of Italy since the Middle Ages).

In fact, the view that Italo-Romance intercomprehension is not an exceptional experience has a long history itself. It seems possible to find it already expressed by Machiavelli during the Renaissance period, as he claims that the languages of different parts of Italy are 'differenti […] ma non tanto che le non s'intendino' (different, but not so much that they would not be understood).[33] Foscolo, too, realized that his above-mentioned comments about radical linguistic fragmentation are difficult to reconcile with historical information about the economic and cultural exchanges between different parts of pre-unification Italy, which involved various sectors of the population and not just intellectual elites. Foscolo would seem to have considered the possibility that incomprehension might be overcome by developing passive competence in another dialect. For example, 'un Bolognese e un Milanese' (someone from Bologna and someone from Milan) would at first be unable to understand each other, but this might change 'dopo parecchi giorni di mutuo insegnamento' (after several days of mutual teaching).[34] Elsewhere, however, he opted for a partly different solution to the problem of intercomprehension, suggesting that, already in the Middle Ages, communication between speakers of different varieties might have been facilitated by a rudimentary knowledge of Italian. He spoke of a 'lingua comune' (common language), 'un linguaggio comune, tal quale tanto da farsi intendere, e che potrebbe chiamarsi mercantile ed itinerario' (a common way of speaking, sufficient for being understood, which could be called mercantile or itinerant).[35]

These early intuitions are similar to the arguments which have been put forward in more recent years. In a series of papers, Varvaro has suggested that the emergence of Tuscan-based Italian as a 'roof language' for the entire peninsula was possible because a sense of linguistic unity already existed in medieval Italy.[36] The perception of linguistic fragmentation was countered by the realization that local varieties were part of regional groups consisting of fundamentally similar varieties, and that these regional groups were in turn part of a pan-Italian linguistic entity, different from other Romance languages. According to Dante (*De vulgari eloquentia*, Book 1), the varieties of Friuli and Sardinia could also be associated with this pan-Italian entity.[37]

---

33 Machiavelli, *Discorso intorno alla nostra lingua*, pp. 16–17; see Sbordoni, 'Theories on Linguistic Variety in Renaissance Italy', p. 117, for English translation and discussion.
34 Foscolo, 'Epoche della lingua italiana', p. 153.
35 Foscolo, 'Epoche della lingua italiana', p. 153 and p. 211. See also Foscolo, 'Discorso storico sul testo del Decamerone', p. 337.
36 See Varvaro, 'La tendenza all'unificazione'.
37 See also Varvaro, '"La tua loquela ti fa manifesto"' and Varvaro, 'Per lo studio dei dialetti medievali'.

Drawing on the terminology used by medieval philosophers who discussed these topics (most notably Roger Bacon and Aquinas), and essentially following Dante's *De vulgari eloquentia*, Varvaro claims that the linguistic differences between the Italian, the Occitan, the French, and the other Romance areas were perceived as 'substantial', whereas the internal variations within each area were defined as more superficial distinctions of 'accident' (Latin *accidens*, as opposed to *substantia*). This perception was not exclusive to philosophers and other intellectuals, but was shared by ordinary speakers — to a greater or lesser degree, depending on how broad their cultural horizons and experience of the world were. When faced with the need to communicate with someone from a different locality, Italo-Romance speakers instinctively avoided local features which made their speech impenetrable.[38] In doing so, they probably relied on their familiarity with interdialectal equivalences — from equivalences between local and regional variants, to more extensive equivalences such as Tuscan *-aio* = non-Tuscan *-aro*, as in the type *notaio/notaro* 'notary',[39] or northern intervocalic *voiced* consonants = Tuscan and southern intervocalic *voiceless* consonants, as in *saver/sapere* 'to know, knowledge'.[40] Conceivably, similar equivalences also aided comprehension at the other end, that is, on the part of the listener.[41]

Varvaro's proposal is compatible with the arguments put forward by Maiden and Vincent. Vincent argues that different dialects had 'sufficient structure in common to enable speakers to move more or less freely between them, or at least while having active competence in one to acquire without problems passive competence in one or more of the others'.[42] According to Maiden, grammatical differences would not cause major difficulties of comprehension between two varieties (X and Y) as long as 'a speaker of dialect X [could] recognize the lexicon of dialect Y'.[43] These arguments can be treated as forming

---

38 See Varvaro, 'La tendenza all'unificazione', pp. 125–26, and Varvaro, 'Per lo studio dei dialetti medievali', pp. 165–68.
39 The presence of *-aro* became 'the hallmark of a non-Tuscan origin' (Maiden, *A Linguistic History of Italian*, p. 55). On the use of *-ar(o)* in northern Italy during the Middle Ages, also in areas where -ARIU(M) yields *-e(r)* in the local dialects, see Sanga, 'La lingua lombarda'. However, the history and geographical distribution of the Tuscan allomorph (which is characterized by the distinctively Tuscan sound change [rj] > [j]) should not be oversimplified: Tuscany itself probably went through three stages of development (sg.: *notaio* vs. pl.: *notari* > sg.: *notaro* vs. pl.: *notari* > sg.: *notaio* vs. pl.: *notai*); moreover, medieval and early modern evidence suggests that *-aio* was originally used in Umbria, in parts of the Marche, and in the north of Latium (Castellani, *Grammatica storica della lingua italiana*, p. 263), and it was also borrowed into Sardinian varieties (Wagner, *La lingua sarda*, pp. 354–55; Pisano, 'Language Contact in Sardinian between the Middle and the Early Modern Ages').
40 Both forms became part of the language of poetry and were used by Dante and Petrarch (see Manni, *Il Trecento toscano*, pp. 147–48, 202–03).
41 As suggested by Andreose and Renzi, 'Volgari medievali'.
42 Vincent, 'Languages in Contact in Medieval Italy', p. 20.
43 Maiden, 'The Definition of Multilingualism', p. 42.

one global hypothesis, namely that Italo-Romance intercomprehension was not as difficult as traditionally assumed. As already mentioned, in previous contributions I began to test this hypothesis against historical records which contain relevant information about speakers' responses to linguistic diversity and problems of communication. This move seemed essential, given that not only Maiden and Vincent, whose arguments are essentially structural (or 'internalist'), but also Varvaro do not actually produce a comprehensive speaker-oriented account, despite the evident relevance of the speakers' perspective in substantiating or disproving their views.

In the present chapter, however, I shall take into account also the main differences between the views of these scholars. In particular, Vincent argues for 'a greater degree of geographical intelligibility [...] than is usually supposed' on the basis of 'syntactic uniformity across medieval dialects',[44] whereas Maiden believes that the lexicon (including 'recurrent grammatical morphemes'), rather than syntax, is what essentially matters when it comes to intelligibility: 'It is often the case that a very high degree of intelligibility can be acquired if just the lexicon can be recognized'.[45] On this point Maiden is in agreement with Roger Wright, who, in his study of the comprehensibility of the Strasbourg Oaths, had deemed syntax to be of 'almost no practical importance'.[46] By contrast, Adam Ledgeway views morphosyntax as the main barrier to intercomprehension, the morphosyntactic features of Italy's dialects being 'so exotic from a typological perspective that they [...] erect major barriers to intelligibility even when the individual lexemes are otherwise recognisable'.[47] It is worth noting that Ledgeway's predictions, too, are based on language-oriented comparisons of grammatical structures — not on the actual behaviour of speakers (including their strategies to overcome comprehension problems) during real communicative acts involving the use of different Italo-Romance varieties.

One last aspect of existing scholarship should be recalled before proceeding to our discussion of historical evidence. Recent research has also revived the idea that the spread of Tuscan models helped to create some kind of common language — still embryonic and uneven, but nonetheless available also to speakers who had limited familiarity with the literary language of thirteenth- and early fourteenth-century Florence.[48] If not at pan-Italian level, in the

---

44 Vincent, 'Language, Geography and History in Medieval Italy', p. 46 and p. 57. See Vincent, 'Languages in Contact in Medieval Italy', pp. 15–21, on how his views partly differ from Varvaro's on the question of koineization.
45 Maiden, 'The Definition of Multilingualism', pp. 41–42.
46 Wright, 'Early Medieval Pan-Romance Comprehension', p. 186.
47 Ledgeway, 'Understanding Dialect', p. 105 (see also pp. 107–08).
48 On Tuscanization, see Sgrilli, 'L'espansione del toscano nel Trecento', and Brown, *Early Evidence for Tuscanisation*. Works such as D'Achille, 'L'italiano dei semicolti', Bianconi, '"La nostra lingua italiana comune"', Bruni, 'Per la vitalità dell'italiano preunitario fuori d'Italia', and Testa, *L'italiano nascosto* point towards practical use of Italian in earlier periods and

Middle Ages convergence between different varieties took place at regional level and eventually gave rise to those koine languages which philologists and language historians have abundantly discussed. The issue of koineization in Italy's linguistic history has generated considerable disagreement on the exact diachronic and geographic extent of the resulting koinai and their degree of stability and homogeneity, and also on whether Tuscan models really prevailed over Latin, or purely regional, models. Disagreement has also emerged on whether the notion of koineization should be stretched to include occasional subconscious accommodation, or should instead be reserved for situations in which speakers consciously imitate the language of groups with which they wish to be identified.[49] Finally, it is not clear if medieval koineization was limited to written communication or, as suggested by Nicoletta Maraschio, also affected oral speech.[50]

In any case, the idea of koineization does not contradict — but in fact implies — our hypothesis about intercomprehension. Although certain linguistic changes have been attributed to convergence between, for instance, Germanic and Romance languages (as in the controversial case of the spread of uvular trills across Europe), koine languages normally emerge from the mixing and levelling of 'mutually intelligible varieties',[51] as confirmed both by general definitions of koineization, and by historical research on medieval cases.[52] It is therefore interesting to ask if, and to what extent, intelligibility already existed in medieval Italy, as a precondition for the increasing levels of koineization and 'pre-standardizzazione' (pre-standardization) which characterize fifteenth-century Italy.[53]

General Comments and Literary Representations

Only a few comments have come down to us which refer to the ability of speakers of an Italo-Romance variety to understand other Italo-Romance varieties used in different parts of Italy. Two of these comments refer to the particular variety (or group of local varieties) which was to become the basis of Italian, that is, Tuscan. In an early vernacular translation of the Bible, which I

---

lower sociocultural sections of the population, compared to the dominant view summarized above. See also Colombo and Kinder, 'Italian as a Language of Communication in Nineteenth Century Italy and Abroad' and references therein.

49 See the various contributions in Sanga, ed., *Koinè in Italia dalle origini al Cinquecento* (esp. Baldelli's chapter).
50 See Maraschio, 'Il plurilinguismo italiano quattrocentesco e l'Alberti', p. 620.
51 Tuten, 'Koineization', p. 185.
52 See Hinskens, Auer, and Kerswill, 'The Study of Dialect Convergence and Divergence', p. 46, and Tuten, *Koineization in Medieval Spanish*.
53 I borrow the term 'pre-standardization' from Maraschio and Manni, 'Il plurilinguismo italiano'. See also Brown, 'Language History from Below'.

shall quote from a fourteenth-century manuscript,[54] the anonymous translator — perhaps a Tuscan — explains that he has opted for 'uno chomune parlare toscano però che è il più intero e il più aperto e il più apto chomunemente di tutta Ytalia e il più piacevole e il più intendevole di ogni lingua' (a common Tuscan speech, since it is the most complete, the most open, and the most commonly suitable in all Italy, the most pleasant and most intelligible of all languages).[55] The other comment is from the first half of the fourteenth century, when the Paduan judge and poet Antonio Da Tempo claimed that 'Lingua tuscia magis apta est ad literam sive literaturam quam aliae linguae, et ideo est magis comunis et intelligibilis' (The Tuscan language is more suitable for writing or literature than other languages, and is therefore more common and intelligible).[56] Attitudes and other related factors, however, need to be considered when interpreting these judgements. The perceived intelligibility of Tuscan may have been favoured by its growing prestige. At the same time, our anonymous translator — and, even more likely, an intellectual such as Da Tempo[57] — may have more or less consciously wished to promote the role of Tuscan, rather than simply describe it in neutral terms.

Comments referring to a lack of intercomprehension between speakers of different Italo-Romance varieties are more numerous. One such comment can be extracted from a letter written by the Tuscan literary scholar Zanobi da Strada, who worked as an adviser to Niccolò Acciaioli following the latter's appointment as Grand Seneschal at the Angevin court in Naples. The letter in question was written in Naples on 25 May 1354 and is addressed to another member of the powerful Acciaioli family, Jacopo, who had remained in Tuscany. With regard to the young generations who were growing up in Naples, Zanobi writes that Sismonda (Francesco Acciaioli's daughter) 'è fatta sì napoletana' (has become so Neapolitan) that Jacopo's wife 'non la intenderebbe' (would not understand her).[58] Neapolitan influence on Sismonda's speech must have been quite strong and, according to Zanobi, capable of disorientating Tuscan-based members of the family.

Nine years before Zanobi's remarks, the Sienese merchant Francesco Bartolomei had written a letter which contains some references to the

---

54 See the catalogue Leonardi, Menichetti, and Natale, eds, *Le traduzioni italiane della Bibbia nel Medioevo*, pp. 49–51.
55 Florence, Biblioteca Medicea Laurenziana, MS Palatino 3, fol. 1ʳ. English translation from Richardson, 'The Concept of a *lingua comune* in Renaissance Italy', pp. 12–13, with adaptations. Richardson assigns this vernacular translation of the Gospels to the fifteenth century. Bruni, *La città divisa*, pp. 242–43, seems to consider the translation — or, perhaps, the choice of Tuscan as the target variety by the person who copied it — even more recent. But see Asperti, 'I Vangeli in volgare italiano', for a study of the manuscript tradition of this translation.
56 Da Tempo, *Summa artis rithmici vulgaris dictaminis*, p. 99.
57 See Brugnolo, 'I toscani nel Veneto e le cerchie toscaneggianti', pp. 383–85.
58 I quote from Sabatini, *Napoli angioina*, p. 103.

reading difficulties of a friar called Pacino.[59] Francesco wrote from Crete (on 27 October 1345) to Pignol Zucchello, another Tuscan merchant who originally came from Pisa but was based in Venice. Some scholars have interpreted this episode as an example of the difficulties which a Venetian would encounter when trying to understand a letter written in Tuscan.[60] While the interpretation of this particular source is in fact uncertain,[61] other sources similarly point towards limited intelligibility of Tuscan varieties in north-eastern regions. Lexical barriers to communication emerge from a letter of the Florentine Dominican Giovanni Dominici of 28 January 1401. Writing from Florence to the members of a Venetian nunnery, Dominici expresses his frustration at having forgotten the meaning of 'pesteruole' — probably meat choppers of a particular type — and adds that those around him were unable to understand this word.[62] Interestingly, this letter points towards mutual difficulties: 'Dimenticato ho che sien pesteruole e non è chi m'intenda; penso che sieno pestelli e voi de' vocaboli miei avete la fedele interprete madre mia' (I have forgotten what *pesteruole* are and nobody understands me; I think they are pestles, and you have my mother as a faithful interpreter of my words).[63] Dominici expected his own lexicon to be potentially obscure, hence the reference to the help that could be provided by his mother (who lived in Venice). Later, when Tuscan models had already acquired a dominant role not only in literature but in a wide range of communicative domains, the Friulian priest Pietro Edo still regarded 'la toschana lengua' (the Tuscan language) as 'troppo oscura' (too obscure). In 1484 he claimed to have written one of his works in a variety from the Veneto region because it was 'intelligibile da tutti' (intelligible by all), particularly by the geographically contiguous 'populi furlani' (Friulian peoples).[64] However, it has been observed that his language contained Tuscan

---

59 *Lettere di mercanti a Pignol Zucchello*, pp. 45–46.
60 See Stussi, 'Appunti su una raccolta di testi antichi', and especially Poggi Salani, 'La Toscana', p. 416.
61 See Carlucci, 'Opinions about Perceived Linguistic Intelligibility'. The interpretation of the following apologetic passage, which the Prato-born but Genoa-based Piero Benintendi included in a letter to the famous Tuscan merchant Francesco Datini, is also somewhat problematic: 'Ogni genovese me reputa e tene genovese e nato sia in Genova, perché vegni a Genova de agni VI in VII, e aparai a Genova la letera, ed è che a Genova sono agni XXXXIII, e pertanto, se no scripvo intendevele et a vostro modo, dimando perdono' (Every Genoese thinks that I am also Genoese and believes that I was born in Genoa, because I came to Genoa when I was between six and seven years old, I learned how to write in Genoa, and I have been in Genoa for forty-three years. So, if I do not write intelligibly or in your way, I beg your pardon): Is this a form of *captatio benevolentiae* which overstates real communication problems? To what extent is Benintendi referring to linguistic differences, and to what extent to different writing styles? The passage can be read in Piattoli, 'Lettere di Piero Benintendi mercante del Trecento', p. 62.
62 Cf. the entry *Pestarula* in the glossary at the end of *Testi padovani del Trecento*, ed. by Tomasin, and *Pestaruola* in the GDLI.
63 Dominici, *Lettere spirituali*, p. 148.
64 See *Costituzioni della patria del Friuli nel volgarizzamento di Pietro Capretto del 1484 e nell'edizione latina del 1565*, p. 104.

features.⁶⁵ Moreover, in the space of a few years Pietro would seem to have changed his mind: in the preface to another work, he explained that this time 'he had chosen to blend Tuscan and Lombard vernaculars, while giving the spoken Tuscan language preference', insofar as it was not 'oscuro o poco usato' (obscure or little used).⁶⁶ This further suggests that the metalinguistic comments contained in late medieval and early modern sources need to be taken with a pinch of salt.

The distance between Friulian and Tuscan was reciprocally noticed by the Florentine politician and businessman Franco Sacchetti, who was born in Dubrovnik and was well acquainted with northern Italy and the regions on the northern Adriatic coast. Allusions to Friulian as a distinctive and potentially obscure language appear in Sacchetti's fourteenth-century collection of novellas, *Le trecento novelle*.⁶⁷ For instance, the demonstrative *cest* 'this' used by a Friulian character is jokingly linked to *canestre* 'baskets', presumably because of its similarity to Tuscan *cesto* 'basket' (*Trecento novelle*, XCII, 9).⁶⁸ Although introduced for comic purposes, this confusion is realistic in that it closely resembles the mistakes that scribes made when copying texts written in varieties different from their own (we shall return to these lexical misunderstandings in the following section).

The mid fourteenth-century *Dittamondo* — a poem by the Tuscan Fazio Degli Uberti, in which the protagonist-poet recounts a series of journeys through Europe, Asia, and Africa — contains a particularly resolute statement about the difficulty of understanding Sardinians and being understood by them:

> Io vidi, che mi parve maraviglia,
> una gente che niuno non la intende
> né essi sanno quel ch'altri pispiglia.⁶⁹
>
> (I saw with astonishment a people that nobody understands, and they do not know what others are talking about.)

Sardinian had similarly appeared in a poem by the Provençal troubadour Raimbaut de Vaqueiras, *Domna, tant vos ai preiada*, which is often referred to as the earliest example of Italian vernacular literature. As Fazio was to do, Raimbaut had spent part of his life in northern Italy. In *Domna, tant vos ai preiada* he has a Genoese woman turn down the advances of an Occitan-speaking minstrel by saying: 'No t'entend plui d'un Toesco | O Sardo o

---

65 See Migliorini, *The Italian Language*, p. 175, and Trovato, *Con ogni diligenza corretto*, p. 115.
66 See Del Soldato and Rizzi's introduction to Del Soldato and Rizzi, eds, *City, Court, Academy*, p. 1.
67 See Cadorini, 'Friulano, veneto e toscano nella storia del Friuli', who discusses the presence of Venetan and Tuscan varieties in medieval Friuli, including the difficulties in understanding the latter on the part of the locals.
68 In his *De vulgari eloquentia* (I, XI, 6) Dante had already singled out initial [tʃ] (< [kw]) as a distinctively Friulian feature.
69 Fazio Degli Uberti, *Il Dittamondo e le Rime*, I, p. 218.

Barbarì' (I don't understand you any more than I do a German or Sardinian or Berber).[70] Literary works thus seem to confirm that Sardinian was widely perceived as incomprehensible. In a sense, this might not be particularly surprising, if we bear in mind that many linguists have proposed to classify Sardinian (excluding Gallurese) as an autonomous group of Romance varieties, separate from Italo-Romance.

On the whole, however, literary works point to good levels of mutual intelligibility. Sacchetti himself recounted several, seemingly unhindered, conversations between speakers from different localities and sociocultural backgrounds, and so did many other authors within the novella tradition and other genres.[71] In the *Decameron*, natives of different parts of Italy — merchants, in particular — travel widely and do not have problems communicating with other Italo-Romance speakers.[72] The ninth novella of the second day begins with a conversation between Italian merchants in Paris, which results in Ambrogiuolo da Piacenza questioning the conjugal fidelity of the wife of the Genoese Bernabò Lomellin. This conversation will eventually have dramatic consequences for the unjustly vilified woman. Bernabò's wife is forced to quit Genoa and move to several places, including the port of Acre (today an Israeli city), where she spends time with 'molti mercatanti e ciciliani e pisani e genovesi e viniziani e altri italiani' (many Sicilian, Pisan, Genoese, Venetian, and other Italian merchants) (*Decameron*, II, 9, 47).[73] In the early fifteenth-century collection of novellas attributed to Gentile Sermini da Siena, a woman and her lover move from Perugia to Milan, where the woman learns the local vernacular, and when back in Perugia she pretends to be Milanese by virtue of her way of speaking (*Novelle*, I, 47–52).[74] The difference between the two varieties is there, but with no indication of significant communication problems. By contrast, problems of communication do emerge when the characters of Boccaccio's novellas have recently reached Italy from the Muslim world (most notably in *Decameron*, II, 7, but see also X, 9), which further confirms the attention to linguistic diversity within this realistic narrative genre.

---

70 Text and English translation from *The Poems of the Troubadour Raimbaut de Vaqueiras*, pp. 98–107.
71 See Varvaro, '"La tua loquela ti fa manifesto"', and Bruni, 'Fra Lombardi, Tusci e Apuli'.
72 For a recent discussion of geography and travels in Boccaccio's masterpiece, see Bolpagni, *La geografia del Decameron*.
73 This episode is particularly at odds with modern perceptions, so much so that Serianni has questioned its closeness to historical reality (see note 30, above).
74 On the author's attention to linguistic differences, including his particularly accurate representation of *diphthongization* and *metaphony* in the variety of Perugia, see Stussi, *Lingua, dialetto e letteratura*, p. 146, and Marchi, 'Le novelle dello Pseudo-Sermini'.

Vocabulary

As we have already seen in the previous section, lexical differences between different Italo-Romance vernaculars had the potential to disorientate and mislead speakers. Even literate speakers sometimes fell into lexical pitfalls, as shown for instance by a Sicilian version of the *Aeneid*, based on a Tuscan version: the Sicilian version has *matrimoniu* 'marriage' instead of *legnaio* 'pyre', which was probably confused with *lignaiu* 'lineage, descent', and also *sochira* 'mother-in-law' instead of *serocchia* 'sister'.[75] Similarly, Guglielmo Maramauro's commentary on Dante's *Inferno* reveals how Florentine *arnie* 'beehives' had misled early readers, who had mistaken it for the place name 'Nargnie' (nowadays Narni, Umbria).[76] Lexical equivalences were often provided in order to avoid such misunderstandings. In his thirteenth-century chronicle, Salimbene de Adam does so with reference to a vessel of wine, 'quod illi de Tuscia *flasconem* dicunt, Lombardi vero *botacium*' (which Tuscans call *flasco* and Lombards *botacium*).[77] Similar efforts to facilitate comprehension appear in literary texts, such as the *Novellino*: 'In Lombardia e nella Marca si chiamano le pentole, "ole"' (in Lombardy *pentole* [pots] are called *ole*).[78] An instance of this kind of lexical clarification also appears in a dialogue in one of Masuccio Salernitano's fifteenth-century novellas, when a Milanese gentleman asks for mustard in Naples: 'io vorrei un poco di salsa del sinapo, che vui la nominate mostarda, senza la quale non porrei mangiare lo rosto stamane' (I would like a little bit of *sinapo* [mustard] sauce, which you call *mostarda*, without which I could not eat my roast this morning).[79]

In a few cases, the need to provide Italo-Romance lexical equivalences goes beyond individual words and results in more comprehensive lists aimed at clarifying the vocabulary used for a certain topic or in a particular text. A topic-oriented example is to be found in the mid-fourteenth-century trade handbook by the Florentine businessman and politician Francesco Balducci Pegolotti. At the beginning of the manuscript that preserves this text (Florence, Biblioteca Riccardiana, MS Riccardiano 2441) we find lists of equivalents for various technical terms and other words used in the rest of the handbook. Many of the equivalents listed are from the languages of England, France, Provence, Spain, North Africa, Persia, and Armenia; others, however, belong to Italo-Romance varieties. For instance, according to Balducci Pegolotti the meaning 'toll' is signified by *gabella* in Tuscany, by *spedicamento* or *pedaggio* in Genoa, by *dazio* in Venice, by *doana* in Naples, by *doana, piazza, fondaco*, or *bindanaio* in Apulia and Sicily, and by *munda* in Friuli.[80]

---

75 See Paccagnella, 'Uso letterario dei dialetti', p. 510.
76 Maramauro, *Expositione sopra l'Inferno*, p. 279.
77 Salimbene de Adam, *Cronica*, p. 308.
78 *Il novellino*, p. 143.
79 Masuccio Salernitano, *Il Novellino*, p. 128.
80 Balducci Pegolotti, *La pratica della mercatura*, p. 15.

What is particularly worth noticing is that the adaptation of the lexicon from a source to a target variety was consciously carried out also in the case of texts which were, at least to some extent, publicly performed orally. In this respect, relevant evidence seems to be provided by a 1438 copy of the *laude* of the Umbrian friar Jacopone da Todi (MS Plut. 90 inf. 27) kept at the Biblioteca Medicea Laurenziana in Florence. This manuscript was probably prepared for circulation and recitation in northern Italy.[81] The introduction (fols 1^r–3^v) repeatedly mentions the lexicon as a potential obstacle to the comprehension of Jacopone's religious poems: these poems contain 'vocabula quae [...] non bene intelliguntur' (words which are not well understood) by someone from northern Italy, and appropriate support is needed in case he finds 'aliquod vocabulum [...] non intelligibile secundum linguam suam' (a word that is not intelligible in his own language) (fol. 3^v). This support is provided in the form of a bilingual wordlist or glossary (fols 3^v–5^v), which immediately follows the introduction. In this period, bilingual dictionaries were still relatively rare and usually comprised Latin or French in combination with an Italo-Romance variety. Here, instead, the two varieties are indicated as 'Spoletanum', literally the variety of the Umbrian town of Spoleto, and 'Longobardus', which arguably stands for 'northern Italo-Romance'; that is, they are two Italo-Romance varieties. We find entries such as *Hogi = Anchoy* 'today', *Loto = Fango* 'mud', *Moglie = Muyere* 'wife', etc.[82] Furthermore, the need to carry out lexical substitutions was explicitly mentioned by outstanding communicators, who successfully crossed geolinguistic boundaries in their preaching. In his 1427 *Prediche volgari sul Campo di Siena*, Saint Bernardino explains:

> Io ti prometto ch'io non direi in Lombardia queste parole per buona cosa. Quando io vo predicando di terra in terra, quando io giogno in uno paese, io m'ingegno di parlare sempre sicondo i vocaboli loro; io avevo imparato e so parlare al lor modo molte cose. El 'mattone' viene a dire el fanciullo, e la 'mattona' la fanciulla, etc.[83]

---

81   See Tenneroni, 'Antico glossarietto umbro-lombardo', Bruni, 'Fra Lombardi, Tusci e Apuli', pp. 21–22, and Leonardi, 'Per il problema ecdotico del Laudario di Jacopone'. On the long-lasting role of shared reading (or 'aurality'), memorization, and singing in the circulation of Jacopone's poetry, see also Tavoni, *Il Quattrocento*, pp. 44–45.

82   Incidentally, the alphabetical order generally followed in this list is also noteworthy, compared to other medieval glossaries or proto-dictionaries. See Rossebastiano Bart, 'Alle origini della lessicografia italiana'.

83   Bernardino da Siena, *Prediche volgari sul Campo di Siena*, pp. 672–73. *Mattone* and *mattona* belong to a lexical type which is found in Lombard and Piedmontese varieties (see p. 673, n. 155). Its presence in Piedmontese dialects (cf. Gribaudo, Seglie, and Seglie, *Dissionari piemontèis*, s.v. *mat*) does not necessarily suggest a different geographic distribution in comparison with Bernardino's reference to Lombardy, given that this toponym probably designated northern Italy in general (as shown by Zancani, 'The Notion of "Lombard" and "Lombardy" in the Middle Ages').

(I can tell you that in Lombardy I certainly would not use these words. When I travel to preach, when I arrive in a place, I always try to speak according to their own words; and I had learned and know how to say many things in their way. 'Mattone' means boy, 'mattona' means girl, and so on.)

Likewise, speaking in Padua in 1460, Giacomo della Marca says that Bernardino himself, when he was a child, lived with 'una sua *cia*, al modo de Toscana, ma a lo modo di qua vegniria chiamata *ameda*' (one of his aunts — *zia* in Tuscany, but here she would be called *ameda*), and then sticks to the latter term in the rest of his sermon.[84] These remarks are interesting also because of the particular source language involved, namely Tuscan. They can be linked back to Maramauro's fourteenth-century comments on Dante's *Commedia*. With reference to the passage from *Inferno* where *arnie* occurs, Maramauro also explained another word which appears in the same lines (*Inf.* XVI, 1–6): 'Primo è da sapere che cossa è rimbombo. E dico che "rimbombo" in toscano è a dir "risono" d'alcuna cossa che cade d'alto in basso e risona' (First of all, one needs to know what *rimbombo* means. This Tuscan word refers to the noise that an object makes when it falls down and resonates).[85] Clearly, although Tuscan was sometimes mentioned as a most intelligible variety, this opinion was likely to conceal various degrees of incomprehension.

Grammar

Writers from medieval and early modern Italy did not normally identify the grammatical information encoded in the form of words, and/or in their position within a sentence, as a source of misunderstanding. To an extent, this is also true of phonological differences — which are remarked on more often than morphological and syntactic differences are, but usually without any clear indication that phonology was perceived as a significant obstacle to intercomprehension. The already mentioned Salimbene de Adam expressed his preference for certain vernaculars (Florentine, most notably) over others, and in doing so he referred to phonological features. For instance, he condemned 'Siculi et Apuli' because they speak 'in gutture' (in the throat) and, 'quando volunt dicere: "Quid vis?", dicunt: "Ke boli?"' (when they want to say *What do you want?* they say *Ke boli?*).[86] This example reflects the confusion between [b] and [v] (here in continuants of Latin VOLO) — a widely present phenomenon in southern Italy, known as 'betacism' in modern linguistics. Yet, this well-travelled Franciscan friar from Parma does not

---

84 Quoted and discussed by Bruni, *La città divisa*, pp. 172–73.
85 Maramauro, *Expositione sopra l'Inferno*, p. 279.
86 Salimbene de Adam, *Cronica*, p. 1002.

argue that phonological differences make vernaculars incomprehensible.[87] Weakening of intervocalic consonants is used to characterize northerners in various literary works — including Dante's *Commedia* (*figo* 'fig', *Inf.* XXXIII, 120), Boccaccio's *Decameron* (*marido* 'husband', IV, 2), Sacchetti's *Trecento novelle* (*medego* 'doctor' and *avrite* 'open.IMP.2pl.', CLXXIII, *luvo* 'wolf', CLXXVII, *levada* 'taken off', CLXXVIII), the *Motti e facezie del Piovano Arlotto* (*miego* 'with me', 69),[88] as well as the already mentioned novellas whose unidentified author goes by the name of Gentile Sermini. In one of these novellas (IV), we encounter a mayor ('podestà') who is not from Pisa, where the novella is set, but from the northern town of Mantua (in late medieval Italy, local authorities were typically led by non-native men, who constituted one of several geographically mobile groups, alongside merchants, diplomats, and political exiles, including their families and servants). This character communicates with characters from other parts of Italy, despite the fact that dialectal features clearly and copiously appear in his direct speech. He says, for instance, 'voi savi' quel che porta rason, fasilo pur che mi non ne vo' affanno, né 'npazo negun' (you know what should reasonably be done, so do it as I do not want any burden or nuisance),[89] where we notice the voiced fricative [v] in intervocalic position in *savi'* (instead of the [p] in the Tuscan equivalent *sapete*).

The equivalence between voiceless [k] and voiced [g] seems to crop up also in the wordlist contained in the *laudario* of the Biblioteca Laurenziana, where we find *Coco = Cogo* 'I burn'. However, it is difficult to imagine how such a small difference could prevent comprehension. More likely, this pairing is part of a number of entries in which the person who compiled this glossary exemplified recurrent phonological correspondences between central Italy (including Tuscany) and northern Italy, with the aim of helping the audience of Jacopone's poetry to overcome linguistic obstacles. This aim is explicitly declared in the introduction to the poems with reference to another wide-ranging correspondence, which had arisen from the diachronic development of [lj]. In much of central and southern Italy, this sequence of sounds had led to the emergence of long palatal sonorants ([ʎː], [jː], and other variants), indicated by the graphic sequence *gl(i)*; whereas in northern Italy it had yielded [j] or [ʤ],[90] which here seem to be represented by *i* (also *y* in the glossary) and *g* respectively. In the introduction we read: 'ubicumque invenies istas sillabas *gli, glo, gla, gle*, longobardus dicit et scribit *li, io, ia*, vel

---

87 This point holds true for Dante, too. In *De vulgari eloquentia*, Dante provides an outline of the differences between Italo-Romance varieties (focusing especially on phonological and lexical variation) but 'never condemns any of them on grounds of unintelligibility': Maiden, 'The Definition of Multilingualism', p. 44. That betacism did not prevent intercomprehension is posited also by Baldelli, *Conti, glosse e riscritture*, pp. 102–03.
88 See Folena's edition of *Motti e facezie del Piovano Arlotto*, and cf. Rohlfs, *Morfologia*, p. 139.
89 Pseudo Gentile Sermini, *Novelle*, p. 155.
90 See Rohlfs, *Fonetica*, pp. 396–97, and Stussi, *Introduzione agli studi di filologia italiana*, p. 81.

ga, ie, vel *ge*, sive ipse sillabe sint sole sive ipse sillabe composite cum aliis' (wherever you find the syllables *gli, glo, gla, gle*, Lombards say and write *li, io, ia* or *ga, ie* or *ge*, irrespective of whether these syllables appear on their own or in combination with others). We then find the relevant correspondence in several entries listed in the glossary, such as *Famiglia* = *Fameya* 'family', *Battaglia* = *Battaia* 'battle', *Paglia* = *Paya* 'straw', etc. On the one hand, this source may thus lend support to Andreose and Renzi's supposition that speakers from different parts of Italy communicated by adapting their language to that of their interlocutors, and, above all, by mentally converting their interlocutors' phonological units into their own. More precisely, we can refer to Weinreich's notion of conversion formulae which typically emerge 'among genetically related systems';[91] as shown by later research, such formulae provide speakers with a crucial aid to cross-dialectal accommodation and comprehensibility.[92] On the other hand, however, the fact that explicit instructions were provided for those who wished to appreciate Jacopone's *laude* suggests that the ability to apply conversion formulae was not immediately available to all speakers. This ability must have varied depending on the vernaculars involved and the degree of familiarity which speakers enjoyed with the particular vernacular they wished to understand.

This glossary also exemplifies some systematic differences in the formation of the future indicative (*Serayo* = *Saroe* 'I will be') and especially the present conditional (*Conueria* = *Conuengnereue* 'it would be necessary').[93] In other sources, a largely stereotypical morphosyntactic feature, namely the subject pronoun *mi*,[94] is used in order to imitate the speech of northerners. We have seen this feature in the direct speech of the Mantuan character in the novellas by the pseudonymous author Gentile Sermini ('mi non ne vo' affanno'). In a dialogue which Saint Bernardino recited in front of fellow Tuscans, as part of his already mentioned sermons, the same subject pronoun *mi* appears in the speech of a character from Milan:

> uno [...] va per camino, e truova un altro, il quale nol vidde mai più. L'uno non sa chi sia l'altro, né l'altro l'uno, né donde è. L'uno di costoro per sapere qualche cosa di lui, dice: Donde se', compagnone? — So' da Milani, mi.[95]
>
> (someone comes across a person he has never seen before. Neither knows who the other is or where he comes from. In order to obtain information about the other, one of them says: Where are you from, my friend? — I am from Milan.)

---

91 Weinreich, *Languages in Contact*, p. 2.
92 See Trudgill, *Dialects in Contact*, pp. 1–81, and Bahtina and Ten Thije, 'Receptive Multilingualism'.
93 See Carlucci, 'Opinions about Perceived Linguistic Intelligibility'.
94 See Rohlfs, *Morfologia*, p. 131.
95 Bernardino da Siena, *Prediche volgari sul Campo di Siena*, p. 190.

Bernardino's linguistic characterization of the Milanese interlocutor rests on the equivalence between Tuscan *io* and northern *mi* 'I'. The fact that Tuscan has *mi* as an unstressed non-subject form does not seem to have created problems, at least not in these contexts. In general, syntactic differences would seem to have gone largely unnoticed as potential barriers to Italo-Romance intercomprehension.

Again, overt opinions and metalinguistic comments (or lack thereof) probably conceal some subtler difficulties involved in understanding different Italo-Romance varieties. Faced with a verb form from the variety of Todi, the 3pl. *o* 'they have', one of the scribes who copied Jacopone's *laude* probably took it to mean 'I have', while in other cases he changed it to a 3sg. form *à*.[96] Later, the inflected infinitives of old Neapolitan — one of the typologically exotic features which Ledgeway deems likely to create 'insurmountable problems of intelligibility'[97] — disorientated some of those who discussed and reproduced the text of Jacopo Sannazaro's *Arcadia*.[98] Verb inflection is not the only domain of morphology where similar instances of partial incomprehension can be detected. With regard to nouns, in his Milanese-Florentine glossary the Florentine Benedetto Dei would seem to have failed to understand the metaphonic plural *ticc* [titʃ] 'roofs' (vs. *tecc* [tɛtʃ] 'roof') — hence the headword *ticcio* 'roof', with the *-i-* of the plural extended to the singular.[99] Prefixes and suffixes also created comprehension problems — not only the Milanese plural marker *-an*,[100] which Dei included in the erroneous headword *tosana* 'girl' (instead of *tosa*), but also the more widespread *ar-* 'again', as in *arprovo* 'I experience again', which still created problems for early sixteenth-century editors of Jacopone's *laude*.[101]

Provisional Conclusions

Medieval and early modern speakers of different Italo-Romance vernaculars were faced with various intercomprehension problems. Unless they were able to use Latin or other languages of wider circulation, it is reasonable to argue that they could not communicate as easily and effectively as modern Italians can thanks to the post-unification spread of Italian as an increasingly common

---

96 Ravesi, 'Sondaggi sulla lingua del laudario oliveriano', pp. 621–22 (I have cited the verb forms as transcribed by this author).
97 Ledgeway, 'Understanding Dialect', p. 106.
98 See Loporcaro, 'L'infinito coniugato nell'Italia centromeridionale', esp. pp. 196–97 and p. 214, and the philological commentary in Sannazaro, *Opere volgari*, p. 433.
99 See Folena, 'Vocaboli e sonetti milanesi di Benedetto Dei', p. 26. Cf. Cherubini, *Vocabolario milanese-italiano*.
100 See Rohlfs, *Morfologia*, p. 42, Tekavčić, *Morfosintassi*, p. 84, and Sanga, 'Lombardy', p. 255.
101 See Richardson, 'The First Edition of Jacopone's *Laude* (Florence, 1490) and the Development of Vernacular Philology', p. 38, n. 30.

language.[102] The fact that problems of comprehensibility were mentioned also for an increasingly prestigious and widespread variety such as Tuscan suggests that no variety was immune to them. Those problems could sometimes result in particular varieties being perceived as unintelligible; but in most cases, intercomprehension problems were probably not as radical or insurmountable as a certain *idée reçue* about the linguistic situation in pre-unification Italy would lead us to expect. As we have seen, those speakers who wished to communicate devised means of doing so (except, perhaps, when Sardinian was one of the varieties involved) thanks to skills and resources which are typical of language contact situations involving closely related varieties. All in all, the evidence reviewed in this chapter thus seems to disprove the assumption that medieval and early modern Italo-Romance intercomprehension was 'quasi impossibile' (almost impossible).[103]

Sources such as the *laudario* of the Biblioteca Medicea Laurenziana also confirm that speakers clearly identified the lexicon as a potential barrier to cross-vernacular communication, and that phonological, and to a lesser extent also morphological, differences were occasionally perceived as potential sources of misunderstanding. This finding seems to contrast with Ledgeway's identification of morphosyntax as the main obstacle to intercomprehension within the Italo-Romance domain, whereas it is compatible both with Maiden's hypothesis that grammatical differences did not cause major difficulties of comprehension, as long as speakers of different varieties could mutually recognize lexical items, and with Vincent's claim that intercomprehension was relatively easy thanks to the syntactic uniformity across Italy's vernaculars. Further research is needed, though, in order to decide whether morphosyntactic patterns really created fewer problems, or if lexical and phonological items were simply more salient because they are more accessible to speakers' observation and conscious control.

Works Cited

Manuscripts and Archival Sources

Florence, Biblioteca Medicea Laurenziana, MS Palatino 3
Florence, Biblioteca Medicea Laurenziana, MS Plut. 90 inf. 27

---

102   That said, from a linguistic point of view communication is not always smooth in today's Italy either, due to differences between regional varieties of Italian. In Tuscany, for instance, differences in intonation and other phonological processes can occasionally lead to local speakers misunderstanding and even reacting negatively to requests by northern speakers, as in the case of polite (3sg.) *va via?* 'are you leaving, Sir?' (northern pronunciation: [va via], Tuscan pronunciation: [va v:ia]) being interpreted as a rather impolite (2sg.) *va' via* 'go away'. See Lapucci, 'Introduzione'.
103   Serianni, 'Lingua e dialetti d'Italia nella percezione dei viaggiatori sette-ottocenteschi', p. 57.

Primary Sources

Balducci Pegolotti, Francesco, *La pratica della mercatura*, ed. by A. Evans (Cambridge, MA: Mediaeval Academy of America, 1936)

Bernardino da Siena, *Prediche volgari sul Campo di Siena (1427)*, ed. by C. Delcorno (Milan: Rusconi, 1989)

Costituzioni della patria del Friuli nel volgarizzamento di Pietro Capretto del 1484 e nell'edizione latina del 1565, ed. by A. Gobessi and E. Orlando (Rome: Viella, 1998)

Da Tempo, Antonio, *Summa artis rithmici vulgaris dictaminis*, ed. by R. Andrews (Bologna: Commissione per i testi di lingua, 1977)

Dominici, Giovanni, *Lettere spirituali*, ed. by M. T. Casella and G. Pozzi (Fribourg: Edizioni universitarie, 1969)

Fazio Degli Uberti, *Il Dittamondo e le Rime*, ed. by G. Corsi (Bari: Laterza, 1952)

Folena, Gianfranco, 'Vocaboli e sonetti milanesi di Benedetto Dei', in *Il linguaggio del caos: Studi sul plurilinguismo rinascimentale* (Turin: Bollati Boringhieri, 1991), pp. 18–68

Foscolo, Ugo, 'Discorso storico sul testo del Decamerone', in *Opere*, X: *Saggi e discorsi critici (1821–1826)*, ed. by C. Foligno (Florence: Le Monnier, 1953), pp. 304–75

―――, 'Epoche della lingua italiana', in *Opere*, XI.1: *Saggi di letteratura italiana*, ed. by C. Foligno (Florence: Le Monnier, 1958)

Goldoni, Carlo, 'I rusteghi', in *Tutte le opere*, ed. by G. Ortolani, vol. VII: *Commedie* (Milan: Mondadori, 1946), pp. 617–96

Lettere di mercanti a Pignol Zucchello, 1336–1350, ed. by R. Morozzo della Rocca (Venice: Comitato per la pubblicazione delle fonti relative alla storia di Venezia, 1957)

Machiavelli, Niccolò, *Discorso intorno alla nostra lingua*, ed. by P. Trovato (Padua: Antenore, 1992)

Maramauro, Guglielmo, *Expositione sopra l'Inferno di Dante Alligieri*, ed. by P. G. Pisoni and S. Bellomo (Padua: Antenore, 1998)

Masuccio Salernitano, *Il Novellino*, ed. by G. Petrocchi (Florence: Sansoni, 1957)

Motti e facezie del Piovano Arlotto, ed. by G. Folena (Milan: Ricciardi, 1953)

Il novellino, ed. by A. Conte (Rome: Salerno, 2001)

Piattoli, Renato, 'Lettere di Piero Benintendi mercante del Trecento (1392–1409)', *Atti della Società Ligure di Storia Patria*, 60.1 (1932), 1–174

The Poems of the Troubadour Raimbaut de Vaqueiras, ed. by J. Linskill (The Hague: Mouton, 1964)

Pseudo Gentile Sermini, *Novelle*, ed. by M. Marchi (Pisa: ETS, 2012)

Salimbene de Adam, *Cronica*, ed. by G. Scalia (Parma: Monte Università Parma, 2007)

Sannazaro, Iacobo, *Opere volgari*, ed. by A. Mauro (Bari: Laterza, 1961)

Tenneroni, Annibale, 'Antico glossarietto umbro-lombardo', *Rivista critica della letteratura italiana*, 5 (1888), 28–30

Testi padovani del Trecento, ed. by L. Tomasin (Padua: Esedra, 2004)

Secondary Studies

Ahern, John, 'Singing the Book: Orality in the Reception of Dante's Comedy', in *Dante: Contemporary Perspectives*, ed. by A. Iannucci (Toronto: University of Toronto Press, 1997), pp. 214–39

Andreose, Alvise, and Lorenzo Renzi, 'Volgari medievali', in *Enciclopedia dell'italiano*, ed. by Raffaele Simone, vol. II (Rome: Istituto dell'Enciclopedia Italiana Treccani, 2011), pp. 1592–97

Armour, Peter, 'Comedy and the Origins of Italian Theatre around the Time of Dante', in *Writers and Performers in Italian Drama from the Time of Dante to Pirandello*, ed. by J. R. Dashwood and J. E. Everson (Lewiston, NY: Edwin Mellen Press, 1991), pp. 1–31

—— , 'The *Comedy* as a Text for Performance', in *Dante on View: The Reception of Dante in the Visual and Performing Arts*, ed. by A. Braida and L. Calè (London: Ashgate, 2007), pp. 17–22

—— , 'Exile and Disgrace', in *Dante in Oxford: The Paget Toynbee Lectures*, ed. by T. Kay, M. McLaughlin, and M. Zaccarello (Oxford: Legenda, 2011), pp. 39–68

Asperti, Stefano, 'I Vangeli in volgare italiano', in *La Bibbia in italiano tra Medioevo e Rinascimento: Atti del convegno internazionale (Firenze, Certosa del Galluzzo, 8–9 novembre 1996)*, ed. by L. Leonardi (Florence: Edizioni del Galluzzo, 1998), pp. 119–44

Bahtina, Daria, and Jan D. Ten Thije, 'Receptive Multilingualism', in *The Encyclopedia of Applied Linguistics*, ed. by C. A. Chapelle (Oxford: Blackwell, 2012), pp. 4899–4904

Baldelli, Ignazio, *Conti, glosse e riscritture: Dal secolo XI al secolo XX* (Naples: Morano, 1988)

Barański, Zygmunt, 'Early Reception', in *Dante in Context*, ed. by Z. Barański and L. Pertile (Cambridge: Cambridge University Press, 2015), pp. 518–37

Bianconi, Sandro, '"La nostra lingua italiana comune". Ovvero: La strana questione dell'italofonia preunitaria', in *Italiano: Strana lingua?*, ed. by G. Marcato (Padova: Unipress, 2003), pp. 5–16

Blanche-Benveniste, Claire, 'Comment retrouver l'expérience des anciens voyageurs en terres de langues romanes?', in *S'entendre entre langues voisines: Vers l'intercompréhension*, ed. by V. Conti and F. Grin (Chêne-Bourg: Georg, 2008), pp. 33–51

Bolpagni, Marcello, *La geografia del Decameron* (Novate Milanese: Prospero, 2016)

Braunmüller, Kurt, 'Receptive Multilingualism in Northern Europe in the Middle Ages', in *Receptive Multilingualism: Linguistic Analyses, Language Policies and Didactic Concepts*, ed. by J. D. Ten Thije and L. Zeevaert (Amsterdam: Benjamins, 2007), pp. 25–47

Brown, Joshua, *Early Evidence for Tuscanisation in the Letters of Milanese Merchants in the Datini Archive, Prato, 1396–1402* (Milan: Istituto Lombardo, Accademia di Scienze e Lettere, 2017)

—— , 'Language History from Below: Standardization and Koineization in Renaissance Italy', *Journal of Historical Sociolinguistics*, 6.1 (2020), <https://doi.org/10.1515/jhsl-2018-0017>

———, 'Language Variation in Fifteenth-Century Milan: Evidence of Koineization in the Letters (1397–1402) of the Milanese Merchant Giovanni da Pessano', *Italian Studies*, 68.1 (2013), 57–77

Brugnolo, Furio, 'I toscani nel Veneto e le cerchie toscaneggianti', in *Storia della cultura veneta*, ed. by Girolamo Arnaldi and Manlio Pastore Stocchi, vol. II: *Il Trecento* (Vicenza: Neri Pozza, 1976), pp. 369–439

Bruni, Francesco, *La città divisa: Le parti e il bene comune da Dante a Guicciardini* (Bologna: Il Mulino, 2003)

———, 'Fra Lombardi, Tusci e Apuli: Osservazioni sulle aree linguistico-culturali', in *Testi e chierici del medioevo* (Genoa: Marietti, 1991), pp. 11–41

———, 'Per la vitalità dell'italiano preunitario fuori d'Italia', *Lingua e stile*, 42 (2007), 189–242

Cadorini, Giorgio, 'Friulano, veneto e toscano nella storia del Friuli', in *Manuale di linguistica friulana*, ed. by S. Heinemann and L. Melchior (Berlin: De Gruyter, 2015), pp. 317–37

Carlucci, Alessandro, 'How Did Italians Communicate When There Was No Italian? Italo-Romance Intercomprehension in the Late Middle Ages', *The Italianist*, 40.1 (2020), 19–43

———, 'Opinions about Perceived Linguistic Intelligibility in Late-Medieval Italy', *Revue Romane*, 57 (2022), 140–65, <https://doi.org/10.1075/rro.19013.car>

Casapullo, Rosa, *Il Medioevo*, Storia della lingua italiana (Bologna: Il Mulino, 1999)

Castellani, Arrigo, *Grammatica storica della lingua italiana* (Bologna: Il Mulino, 2000)

———, 'Quanti erano gl'italofoni nel 1861?', *Studi Linguistici Italiani*, 8 (1982), 3–26

Cherubini, Francesco, *Vocabolario milanese-italiano* (Milan: Regia stamperia, 1839–1843)

Colombo, Michele, and John J. Kinder, 'Italian as a Language of Communication in Nineteenth Century Italy and Abroad', *Italica*, 89 (2012), 109–21

D'Achille, Paolo, 'L'italiano dei semicolti', in *Storia della lingua italiana*, ed. by Luca Serianni and Pietro Trifone (Turin: Einaudi, 1993–1994), vol. II: *Scritto e parlato*, pp. 41–79

Dall'Aglio, Stefano, Luca Degl'Innocenti, Brian Richardson, Massimo Rospocher, and Chiara Sbordoni, eds, 'Oral Culture in Early Modern Italy: Performance, Language, Religion', special issue, *The Italianist*, 34.3 (2014)

Degl'Innocenti, Luca, Brian Richardson, and Chiara Sbordoni, eds, *Interactions between Orality and Writing in Early Modern Italian Culture* (London: Routledge, 2016)

Del Soldato, Eva, and Andrea Rizzi, eds, *City, Court, Academy: Language Choice in Early Modern Italy* (London: Routledge, 2017)

De Mauro, Tullio, *Storia linguistica dell'Italia unita* (Bari: Laterza, 1963)

Dionisotti, Carlo, *Geografia e storia della letteratura italiana* (Turin: Einaudi, 1967)

Franceschini, Fabrizio, *Tra secolare commento e storia della lingua: Studi sulla Commedia e le antiche glosse* (Florence: Cesati, 2008)

GDLI = Battaglia, Salvatore, and Giorgio Barberi Squarotti, *Grande dizionario della lingua italiana*, 21 vols (Turin: UTET, 1961–2002)

Gribaudo, Gianfranco, Pinin Seglie, and Sergio Seglie, *Dissionari piemontèis* (Turin: Ij Brandé, 1972)

Havely, Nick, '*Un grido di sì alto suono*: Voicing the *Commedia*', in *Dante beyond Borders: Contexts and Reception*, ed. by N. Havely, J. Katz, and R. Cooper (Oxford: Legenda, 2021), pp. 119–31

Hinskens, Frans, Peter Auer, and Paul Kerswill, 'The Study of Dialect Convergence and Divergence: Conceptual and Methodological Considerations', in *Dialect Change: Convergence and Divergence in European Languages*, ed. by Peter Auer, Frans Hinskens, and Paul Kerswill (Cambridge: Cambridge University Press, 2005), pp. 1–48

Kristeller, Paul Oskar, 'The Origin and Development of the Language of Italian Prose', in *Studies in Renaissance Thought and Letters* (Rome: Edizioni di Storia e Letteratura, 1956), pp. 473–93

Lapucci, Carlo, 'Introduzione', in V. Camaiti, *La lingua fiorentina: Dizionario* (Florence: Libreria S.P. 44, 1991), pp. 1–12

Lazzarini, Isabella, *Communication and Conflict: Italian Diplomacy in the Early Renaissance, 1350–1520* (Oxford: Oxford University Press, 2015)

——, 'Orality and Writing in Diplomatic Interactions in Fifteenth-Century Italy', in *Voices and Texts in Early Modern Italian Society*, ed. by S. Dall'Aglio, B. Richardson, and M. Rospocher (London: Routledge, 2017), pp. 97–109

——, 'Patterns of Translation: Contacts and Linguistic Variety in Italian Late Medieval Diplomacy', in *Translators, Interpreters, and Cultural Negotiators: Mediating and Communicating Power from the Middle Ages to the Modern Era*, ed. by F. Federici and D. Tessicini (London: Palgrave, 2014), pp. 29–47

Ledgeway, Adam, 'Understanding Dialect: Some Neapolitan Examples', in *Didattica della lingua italiana: Testo e contesto*, ed. by A. Ledgeway and A. L. Lepschy (Perugia: Guerra, 2008), pp. 99–111

Leonardi, Lino, 'Per il problema ecdotico del Laudario di Jacopone: Il manoscritto di Napoli', *Studi di filologia italiana*, 46 (1988), pp. 13–85

Leonardi, Lino, Caterina Menichetti, and Sara Natale, eds, *Le traduzioni italiane della Bibbia nel Medioevo: Catalogo dei manoscritti (secoli XIII–XV)* (Florence: Galluzzo, 2018)

Lepschy, Giulio, 'How Popular Is Italian?', in *Culture and Conflict in Postwar Italy*, ed. by Z. Baranski and R. Lumley (London: Macmillan, 1990), pp. 63–75

——, 'Mother Tongues in the Middle Ages and Dante', in *Dante's Plurilingualism: Authority, Knowledge, Subjectivity*, ed. by S. Fortuna, M. Gragnolati, and J. Trabant (Oxford: Legenda, 2010), pp. 16–23

Lepschy, Giulio, and Laura Lepschy, 'Dante as a Native Speaker', in *'Legato con amore in un volume': Essays in Honour of John A. Scott*, ed. by J. J. Kinder and D. Glenn (Florence: Olschki, 2013), pp. 309–19

Lodge, Anthony, 'Jacques-Louis Ménétra and his Experience of the *langue d'oc*', in *Norms and Usage in Language History, 1600–1900: A Sociolinguistic and Comparative Perspective*, ed. by G. J. Rutten, R. Vosters, and W. Vandenbussche (Amsterdam: Benjamins, 2014), pp. 201–22

Loporcaro, Michele, 'L'infinito coniugato nell'Italia centromeridionale: Ipotesi genetica e ricostruzione storica', *L'Italia dialettale*, 49 (1986), 173–240

Maiden, Martin, 'The Definition of Multilingualism in Historical Perspective', in *Multilingualism in Italy: Past and Present*, ed. by Anna Laura Lepschy and Arturo Tosi, Studies in Linguistics, 1 (Oxford: Legenda, 2002), pp. 31–46

———, *A Linguistic History of Italian*, Longman Linguistics Library (London: Longman, 1995)

Manni, Paola, *Il Trecento toscano: La lingua di Dante, Petrarca e Boccaccio*, Storia della lingua italiana (Bologna: Il Mulino, 2003)

Maraschio, Nicoletta, 'Il plurilinguismo italiano quattrocentesco e l'Alberti', in *Alberti e la cultura del Quattrocento: Atti del convegno internazionale del Comitato Nazionale VI Centenario della nascita di Leon Battista Alberti, 16–17–18 dicembre 2004*, ed. by R. Cardini and M. Regoliosi (Florence: Polistampa, 2007), pp. 611–28

Maraschio, Nicoletta, and Paola Manni, 'Il plurilinguismo italiano (secc. xiv–xv): Realtà, percezione, rappresentazione', in *L'Italia alla fine del Medioevo: I caratteri originali nel quadro europeo*, ed. by F. Salvestrini and F. Cengarle (Florence: Firenze University Press, 2006), ii, pp. 239–67

Marazzini, Claudio, *La lingua italiana: Profilo storico*, 3rd edn (Bologna: Il Mulino, 2002)

Marchi, Monica, 'Le novelle dello Pseudo-Sermini: Un novelliere senese?', *Studi di grammatica italiana*, 29–30 (2010–2011), 53–90

Meissner, Franz-Joseph, 'Introduction à la didactique de l'eurocompréhension', in *EuroComRom — Les sept tamis: Lire les langues romanes dès le départ*, ed. by F. J. Meissner, C. Meissner, H. G. Klein, and T. D. Stegmann (Aachen: Shaker, 2004), pp. 7–140

Migliorini, Bruno, *The Italian Language*, abridged, recast, and revised by T. Gwynfor Griffith (London: Faber, 1984)

Mioni, Alberto, and Anna Maria Arnuzzo-Lanszweert, 'Sociolinguistics in Italy', *International Journal of the Sociology of Language*, 21 (1979), 81–107

Muljačić, Zarko, 'The Relationship between the Dialects and the Standard Language', in *The Dialects of Italy*, ed. by Martin Maiden and Mair M. Parry (London: Routledge, 1997), pp. 387–93

Paccagnella, Ivano, 'Uso letterario dei dialetti', in *Storia della lingua italiana*, ed. by Luca Serianni and Pietro Trifone (Turin: Einaudi, 1993–1994), vol. iii: *Le altre lingue*, pp. 495–539

Pellegrini, Giovan Battista, 'La classificazione delle lingue romanze e i dialetti italiani', *Forum Italicum*, 4 (1970), 211–37

———, *Saggi di linguistica italiana* (Turin: Boringhieri, 1975)

Pisano, Simone, 'Language Contact in Sardinian between the Middle and the Early Modern Ages', in 'Language Contact in the Mediterranean in the Middle Ages and in Early Modern Times (with special focus on loanword lexicography)', ed. by Francesco Crifò, Elton Prifti, and Wolfgang Schweickard, thematic part of *Lexicographica: International Annual for Lexicography*, 33 (2017), 225–54

Poggi Salani, Teresa, 'La Toscana', in *L'italiano nelle regioni: Lingua nazionale e identità regionali*, ed. by Francesco Bruni (Turin: UTET, 1992), pp. 402–61

Ravesi, Marcello, 'Sondaggi sulla lingua del laudario oliveriano', in *La vita e l'opera di Iacopone da Todi: Atti del Convegno di studio, Todi, 3–7 dicembre 2006*, ed. by Enrico Menestò (Spoleto: Fondazione Centro italiano di studi sull'alto medioevo, 2007), pp. 603–24

Richardson, Brian, 'The Concept of a *lingua comune* in Renaissance Italy', in *The Languages of Italy: Histories and Dictionaries*, ed. by A. L. Lepschy and A. Tosi (Ravenna: Longo, 2007), pp. 11–28

——, 'The First Edition of Jacopone's *Laude* (Florence, 1490) and the Development of Vernacular Philology', *Italian Studies*, 47 (1992), 26–40

Rohlfs, Gerhard, *Fonetica*, vol. I of *Grammatica storica della lingua italiana e dei suoi dialetti* (Turin: Einaudi, 1966)

——, *Morfologia*, vol. II of *Grammatica storica della lingua italiana e dei suoi dialetti* (Turin: Einaudi, 1968)

Rossebastiano Bart, Alda, 'Alle origini della lessicografia italiana', in *La lexicographie au Moyen Age*, ed. by C. Buridant (Lille: Presses Universitaires de Lille, 1986), pp. 113–56

Sabatini, Francesco, *Napoli angioina: Cultura e società* (Naples: Edizioni scientifiche italiane, 1975)

Sanga, Glauco, ed., *Koinè in Italia dalle origini al Cinquecento: Atti del Convegno di Milano e Pavia (25–26 settembre 1987)* (Bergamo: Lubrina 1990)

——, 'La lingua lombarda: Dalla koinè alto-italiana delle Origini alla lingua cortigiana', in *Koinè in Italia dalle origini al Cinquecento: Atti del Convegno di Milano e Pavia (25–26 settembre 1987)*, ed. by Glauco Sanga (Bergamo: Lubrina 1990), pp. 79–163

——, 'Lombardy', in *The Dialects of Italy*, ed. by Martin Maiden and Mair M. Parry (London: Routledge, 1997), pp. 253–59

Sbordoni, Chiara, 'Theories on Linguistic Variety in Renaissance Italy: Between Regional Identities and Oral Performance', in *Interactions between Orality and Writing in Early Modern Italian Culture*, ed. by Luca Degl'Innocenti, Brian Richardson, and Chiara Sbordoni (London: Routledge, 2016), pp. 113–26

Serianni, Luca, 'Lingua e dialetti d'Italia nella percezione dei viaggiatori sette-ottocenteschi', in *Viaggiatori, musicisti, poeti: Saggi di storia della lingua italiana* (Milan: Garzanti, 2002), pp. 55–88

Sgrilli, Paola, 'L'espansione del toscano nel Trecento', in *La Toscana nel Secolo XIV: Caratteri di una civiltà regionale*, ed. by Sergio Gensini (Pisa: Pacini, 1988), pp. 425–64

Stussi, Alfredo, 'Appunti su una raccolta di testi antichi', *L'Italia dialettale*, 26 (1963), 146–50

——, *Introduzione agli studi di filologia italiana* (Bologna: Il Mulino, 1994)

——, *Lingua, dialetto e letteratura* (Turin: Einaudi, 1993)

Tamburelli, Marco, 'Uncovering the "Hidden" Multilingualism of Europe: An Italian Case Study', *Journal of Multilingual and Multicultural Development*, 35 (2014), 252–70

Tavoni, Mirko, 'Linguistic Italy', in *Dante in Context*, ed. by Z. Barański and L. Pertile (Cambridge: Cambridge University Press, 2015), pp. 243–59

———, *Il Quattrocento*, Storia della lingua italiana (Bologna: Il Mulino, 1992)

Tekavčić, Pavao, *Morfosintassi*, vol. II of *Grammatica storica dell'italiano*, 2nd edn (Bologna: Il Mulino, 1980)

Testa, Enrico, *L'italiano nascosto: Una storia linguistica e culturale* (Turin: Einaudi, 2014)

Thomason, Sarah, *Language Contact: An Introduction* (Edinburgh: Edinburgh University Press, 2001)

Tosi, Arturo, *Language and Society in a Changing Italy* (Clevedon: Multilingual Matters, 2001)

Trovato, Paolo, *Con ogni diligenza corretto: La stampa e le revisioni editoriali dei testi letterari italiani (1470–1570)* (Bologna: Il Mulino, 1991)

Trudgill, Peter, *Dialects in Contact* (Oxford: Blackwell, 1986)

Tuten, Donald, 'Koineization', in *The Routledge Companion to Sociolinguistics*, ed. by C. Llamas, L. Mullany, and P. Stockwell (London: Routledge, 2007), pp. 185–91

———, *Koineization in Medieval Spanish* (Berlin: De Gruyter, 2003)

Varvaro, Alberto, 'Per lo studio dei dialetti medievali', in *Storia della lingua italiana e dialettologia*, ed. by G. Ruffino and M. D'Agostino (Palermo: Centro di studi filologici e linguistici siciliani, 2010), pp. 161–71

———, 'La tendenza all'unificazione dalle origini alla formazione di un italiano standard' (1989), in *Identità linguistiche e letterarie nell'Europa romanza* (Rome: Salerno, 2004), pp. 109–26

———, '"La tua loquela ti fa manifesto": Lingue e identità nella letteratura medievale' (2002), in *Identità linguistiche e letterarie nell'Europa romanza* (Rome: Salerno, 2004), pp. 227–42

Vincent, Nigel, 'Language, Geography and History in Medieval Italy', in 'Ciò che potea la lingua nostra: Lectures and Essays in Memory of Clara Florio Cooper', ed. by V. De Gasperin, supplement 2 to *The Italianist*, 30 (2010), 44–60

———, 'Languages in Contact in Medieval Italy', in *Rethinking Languages in Contact: The Case of Italian*, ed. by Anna Laura Lepschy and Arturo Tosi (Oxford: Legenda, 2006), pp. 12–27

Wagner, Max Leopold, *La lingua sarda: Storia, spirito e forma* (Bern: Francke, 1951)

Weinreich, Uriel, *Languages in Contact: Findings and Problems*, 2nd edn (The Hague: Mouton, 1964)

Wright, Roger, 'Early Medieval Pan-Romance Comprehension', in *A Sociophilological Study of Late Latin* (Turnhout: Brepols, 2002), pp. 175–90

Zancani, Diego, 'The Notion of "Lombard" and "Lombardy" in the Middle Ages', in *Medieval Europeans: Studies in Ethnic Identity and National Perspectives in Medieval Europe*, ed. by A. P. Smyth (London: Palgrave-Macmillan, 1998), pp. 217–32

JOSHUA BROWN

Untraced Polymorphy and Vernaculars in Contact in Renaissance Italy

Introduction

Historical sociolinguistics, a relatively new subdiscipline of linguistics, has gone some way in recovering forms of language that have not traditionally been the main domains of linguistic investigation. Within this research paradigm, processes of standardization 'make up a particularly strong strand in historical research'.[1] Part of the reason for this focus has been the direct connection to the present, where researchers are often able to trace contemporary standard forms through a well-attested written historical record, adopting a teleological approach. Recently, scholars have attempted to 'recover' the multilingual origins of various European standards and non-standards. Part of the aim of these approaches has emerged precisely from historical sociolinguistics, and the possibility of revealing the sometimes 'hidden' multilingualism and variation that is inherent of all linguistic varieties.[2] This chapter is situated in this vein. It proposes a new taxonomy of the 'birth' of Italian by situating its origin within a picture of variation. I argue that insufficient attention has been paid to non-literary forms of writing, in particular merchant and religious texts, and that by considering this low-register writing, a different picture for the history of Italian can emerge.[3]

One milestone recorded by language histories in the codification of Italian is the publication of Pietro Bembo's *Prose della volgar lingua* in 1525. This four-volume grammar provided an authoritative guide for subsequent writers

---

1 Nevalainen, 'What Are Historical Sociolinguistics?', p. 246.
2 For example, see Wright, ed., *The Multilingual Origins of Standard English*; Tamburelli, 'Uncovering the "Hidden" Multilingualism of Europe'.
3 Unless otherwise stated, I use the term 'Italian' to refer to the modern standard as used in contemporary Italy, and the histories which trace this particular variety.

Joshua Brown (joshua.j.brown@uwa.edu.au) is Senior Lecturer in Italian Studies at the University of Western Australia. His research interests include the history of the Italian language, dialect contact, and language change.

Languages and Cross-Cultural Exchanges in Renaissance Italy, ed. by Alessandra Petrocchi and Joshua Brown, LMEMS 30 (Turnhout: Brepols, 2023), pp. 95–120

to model their language on, and essentially resolved the evolving debates about whether Italy should adopt a vernacular or Latin as a national language, and if vernacular, which one it should be. These debates are known as the *Questione della lingua*. In a brief comparison to Italy, Ayres-Bennett, referring to Padley's study, notes that 'France did not have a "classical" vernacular literature of the eminence of that represented in the works of Dante, Petrarch and Boccaccio', pointing out the lack of centralized authority in Renaissance Italy.[4] She asks the question: 'Why did the lack of political unity and independence apparently not impede the codification process in Italy?'.[5] While this question is important, it is not the focus of this essay. Rather, I aim to concentrate on the multiple origins of Italian itself, and quantitatively assess untraced polymorphy in the history of Italian with a focus on the verb. The aim will be to look at those processes of linguistic accommodation and convergence 'from below', that is, in non-literary writing and specifically in merchant texts.[6] At the same time as a standard was becoming established, broader social and linguistic processes in the north of Italy led to the development of a regional koine.[7] Given that koineization is but one type of language change when dialects are brought into contact, this essay forms part of a broader research agenda surrounding the role of standard varieties of language and dialect convergence, as articulated by Hinskens, Auer, and Kerswill.[8]

Similar to other language histories, the traditional historiography of Italian has taken a teleological approach in accounting for its vicissitudes. This approach, which has left an entire period of language history unexplored, is best captured by Mattheier:

> the concept of a 'national language history' has dominated the view of what historical linguistics should be concerned with in relation to virtually all European languages, and continues to do so today. The theoretical starting point of this view — which at the very least needs to be seriously questioned — is that the 'standard' language is the genuine teleological goal of any historical language development.[9]

---

4 Ayres-Bennett, 'Codification and Prescription in Linguistic Standardization', p. 100; Padley, *Grammatical Theory in Western Europe*.
5 Ayres-Bennett, 'Codification and Prescription in Linguistic Standardization', p. 100.
6 Brown, 'Language History from Below'. On the role of literature in the standardization of Italian, see Maraschio and Matarrese, 'The Role of Literature in Language Standardization'.
7 For example, during the 1300s and 1400s, increased mobility and contact between people of the northern city states and the rapid expansion of certain centres of power with new political structures, such as courts and chanceries, led to the formation of a pan-Lombard, supra-regional koine. Increased contact between the vernaculars of individual city states led to a process in which the most local linguistic features of these vernaculars were abandoned in favour of a process of demunicipalization. For further details, see Brown, 'Language Variation in Fifteenth-Century Milan'.
8 Hinskens, Auer, and Kerswill, 'The Study of Dialect Convergence and Divergence'.
9 Mattheier, 'Is There a European Language History?', pp. 353–54.

Standardization is one area of sociolinguistics that is now receiving increased attention, following the pioneering work of Haugen, Milroy and Milroy, and others.[10] For example, Ayres-Bennett has recently looked at codification and prescription in the history of French, noting how 'the simple dichotomy descriptive ~ prescriptive becomes untenable'.[11] Armstrong and Mackenzie list seven characteristics they deem to be 'essential features of standard languages', such as the standard as an ideology, the socially dominant variety, the synecdochic variety, and others.[12] Recent research suggests that the concept of standardization itself has more in common with variation, including with concepts related to koineization, than what has previously been understood. As Kabatek has said, 'there are obviously no instances of conscious, institutional language planning, such as are found in modern times, in the Middle Ages'.[13] But he also recognizes that Haugen's criteria for standardization referenced above are, at least to some degree, implicitly present in Renaissance convergence processes as well.

One characteristic of the history of Italian is the presence of polymorphy — the existence of multiple forms at the base of fourteenth-century Florentine, the vernacular chosen to form the standard. I have shown elsewhere that this vernacular was itself a mixed variety.[14] It evinces a greater degree of heterogeneity than what is usually assigned to it in histories of Italian. By and large, the traditional histories of the language take this variety to be a homogeneous entity, often using the terms 'Florentine', 'Tuscan', or 'Italian' synonymously, and taking as their starting point the literary variety of the language used by Dante, Petrarch, and Boccaccio.[15] Recent work has continued in this vein, aiming to trace the evolution of the norm during the sixteenth century, that is, while standardization was in progress.[16]

This chapter is partly motivated by a recently revived interest in overabundance in Italian verb morphology and its interactions with other non-canonical phenomena. Thornton, for example, has shown how a relatively large set of overabundant cells in Italian verb paradigms is still present in contemporary Italian, using the *Corpus e Lessico di Frequenza dell'Italiano Scritto* (*COLFIS*) as well as the newspaper *Repubblica* from 1985 to 2000.[17] Other studies by

---

10 Haugen, 'Dialect, Language, Nation'; Milroy and Milroy, *Authority in Language*; Milroy, 'Language Ideologies'.
11 Ayres-Bennett, 'Codification and Prescription in Linguistic Standardization', p. 124.
12 Armstrong and Mackenzie, *Standardization, Ideology and Linguistics*, p. 5.
13 Kabatek, '*Koinés* and *scriptae*', p. 148.
14 Brown, 'Language Variation in Fifteenth-Century Milan'; see also Nencioni, 'Fra grammatica e retorica'; De Mauro, *Storia linguistica dell'Italia unita*, pp. 29–30.
15 Durante, *Dal latino all'italiano moderno*; Gensini, *Elementi di storia linguistica italiana*; Coletti, *Storia dell'italiano letterario*; Tesi, *Storia dell'italiano*; Morgana, *Capitoli di storia linguistica italiana*; Kinder, *CLIC*; Cella, *Storia dell'italiano*; Patota, *La Quarta Corona*.
16 See, e.g., Miesse and Valenti, eds, '*Modello, regola, ordine*'.
17 Thornton, 'Overabundance'. See also Thornton, 'Reduction and Maintenance of Overabundance'.

Maiden and by Pirrelli and Battista have considered stem allomorphy in the Italian verb, but not from a historical stance, and not from a sociolinguistic viewpoint.[18] The purpose of this chapter is to provide these extra pieces of the puzzle for select phenomena as a case study, showing how such variants can be seen to represent the broader tendencies occurring in the language while a standard was developing. It is also hoped that, by supplementing these earlier studies with further data and theoretical explanation, a more complete picture of the sociolinguistic nature of Renaissance Italy can be provided.

The chapter begins by looking at how previous scholars have characterized the origins of Italian, and provides some detail about what authors mean when they use the terms 'Italian', 'Florentine', or 'standard'. It then considers some aspects of verb polymorphy in the major databases for historical research in Italian, the *Opera del vocabolario italiano* and *Morfologia dell'italiano in diacronia*. Results and discussion of select verb polymorphy are provided, before considering how effects of vernaculars in contact are evident in a corpus of merchant writing from the late fourteenth century. A brief conclusion and implications of the study are offered at the end.

The Multiple Origins at the Base of Italian

Italian is a language which is particularly rich in doublets due to historical reasons.[19] This situation of polymorphy has been stressed as early as De Mauro, in a paragraph worth quoting in full:

> Allorché una stessa forma flessionale si presentava in due varianti, queste venivano entrambe conservate per secoli nella tradizione italiana, nella quale non potevano intervenire le tendenze selettive, economiche, operanti in lingue sottoposte a un uso più largo. E se talora il pur esiguo uso scritto ha differenziato almeno stilisticamente gli elementi polimorfi, facendo d'una forma quella canonica nella versificazione e d'un'altra quella propria della prosa (è il caso, per fare qualche esempio, di *esto* e *questo*, *gito* e *andato*, *alma* e *anima*, *augello* e *uccello*), più spesso tale differenziazione, ancora a metà Ottocento, mancava: così in *fo* e *faccio*, *vo* e *vado*, *devo* e *debbo* ('poetico' era *deggio*), *dovuto* e *debito*, *dette diede* e *dié*, *visto* e *veduto*, *apparisco* e *appaio* ecc.

---

18 Maiden, 'When Lexemes Become Allomorphs'; Maiden, 'Morphological Autonomy and Diachrony'; Pirrelli and Battista, 'The Paradigmatic Dimension of Stem Allomorphy'.
19 Thornton, 'Overabundance in Italian Verb Morphology', p. 254. See also Cappellaro, 'Overabundance in Diachrony', who investigates Italian third-person pronouns in a corpus of texts dating from the sixteenth century to the twentieth century, as well as Cappellaro, 'Genesis and Diachronic Persistence of Overabundance'. For a similar approach, see Formentin, 'Forme verbali doppie negli antichi volgari italiani'; Sornicola, 'A Diachronic Perspective on Polymorphism, Overabundance, and Polyfunctionalism'.

(When the same inflected form appeared as two variants, these were both retained for centuries in the Italian tradition, in which the selective, economical tendencies at work in more widely used languages could not operate. And if sometimes written usage, however scant, has differentiated the polymorphous items at least at the stylistic level, making one form canonical in verse and another one in prose (this is the case, for example, of *esto* and *questo*, *gito* and *andato*, *alma* and *anima*, *augello* and *uccello*), more often this differentiation was still lacking by the middle of the 19th century: this was the case for *fo* and *faccio*, *vo* and *vado*, *devo* and *debbo* (*deggio* was 'poetic'), *dovuto* and *debito*, *dette diede* and *diè*, *visto* and *veduto*, *apparisco* and *appaio*, etc.)[20]

A limited number of studies have sought to trace the variation at the base of the standard. Maiden, for example, notes that 'already in the fifteenth century a literary language was gaining ground throughout Italy whose basis was undoubtedly Florentine, but which had acquired general characteristics which could be said to be "Italian", but were *not* typical of Florence, and which on occasion were capable of opposing and ousting features exclusive to Florence'.[21] Among such features, the following are recorded as likely contenders: the change from the type *lo mi dà* 'he gives it to me', to *me lo dà*; the triumph of the structure *non facendolo* 'not doing it' over *non lo facendo*; the establishment of the type *presero* 'they took' over *presono*; and other phenomena.[22] As further evidence, Maiden points to Weinapple's research, which investigates variation in clitic pronouns during the Renaissance.[23] The persistence of variation in these cases is but one example of the 'fuzziness' of the standard.[24] Consistency is identified as an 'important advantage' of standard varieties by Pountain.[25] The lack of consistency referenced above would seem to point, instead, to the necessary (but not sufficient) conditions for dialect contact, which brings several varieties together.

Authors have so far paid insufficient attention to the multiple origins at the base of Italian. Given the cultural and, to some extent, political and literary dominance of Tuscan during later centuries, catch-all terms such as *italiano* and

---

20 This quotation and translation are taken from Thornton, 'Overabundance in Italian Verb Morphology', pp. 254–55.
21 Maiden, *A Linguistic History of Italian*, pp. 7–8.
22 See Aski and Russi, *Iconicity and Analogy in Language Change*, pp. 168–71, on the question of whether borrowing from Tuscan vernaculars can be seen to motivate the change from the accusative-dative order of double object clitic clusters to dative-accusative in Florentine. While there is insufficient room to enter into this argument here, the authors note that 'borrowing due to contact cannot be excluded as possible source of the DAT-ACC order in Florentine' (p. 171), but that current scholarship does not provide enough detail for this hypothesis to be proven either way.
23 Weinapple, 'La clisi nel linguaggio comico'.
24 On this concept, see Ammon, 'On the Social Forces that Determine What Is Standard'.
25 Pountain, 'Standardization', p. 634.

toscano are used to refer to a variety which would become standard, but which during the thirteenth and fourteenth centuries still evinced much variation.[26] Nevertheless, certain authors have been able to provide some detail on the linguistic variation in Tuscany during these centuries, even if the focus of some of this work has been on the transfer of variants to literary Italian.[27] Manni, for example, provides a useful overview of fifteenth-century Florentine and its phonetic and morphological traits.[28] In a later chapter, she refers to a 'mine of documents' from Tuscany, profiling both the traditions and descriptions of the vernacular. Rossi's chapter on 'Fiorentino e italiano' highlights how, due to a complex series of historical, cultural, and literary reasons, contemporary Italian is formed on the base of fourteenth-century Florentine. He lists a series of phenomena, pointing to those that were common to Tuscany, unique to Florentine, and others shared across central Italy.[29] Marazzini, too, highlights the question of variation in the period immediately preceding codification:

> prima della codificazione definitiva della lingua letteraria, ci sono casi di multilinguismo molto accentuato, in settori diversi, dalla predicazione, alla prosa narrativa, alla scrittura cancelleresca, e di *koinè*.[30]

> (before the final codification of the literary language, there are very accentuated cases of multilingualism, across different sectors, from preaching, to prose narrative, to chancery writing, and koine writing.)

A distinctive feature of this characterization is its specification of the different domains, literary and non-literary, where such multilingualism exists. Although not concerned with varieties other than Italo-Romance, this chapter builds upon these studies which highlight the multilingual and variational situation characteristic of some early texts in the history of Italian.

Verb Polymorphy in Old Italian

The pioneering work of Nencioni, De Mauro, and Castellani showed how verb polymorphy has existed throughout the linguistic history of Italy, including

---

26 Here it is worth recalling Rossi's comments that 'nel secolo XII, anzi, l'importanza di Firenze era marginale rispetto a quella di altre città, specialmente Pisa, che conobbe straordinaria vigoria come Repubblica marinara' (in the twelfth century, the importance of Florence was marginal compared to other cities, especially Pisa, which had extraordinary strength as a maritime Republic) (Rossi, 'Fiorentino e italiano', p. 73).
27 See, for example, Manni, 'Dal toscano all'italiano letterario'.
28 Manni, 'Ricerche sui tratti fonetici e morfologici'; Manni, 'La situazione linguistica'.
29 Rossi, 'Fiorentino e italiano', pp. 70–90. I return to some of these phenomena below.
30 Marazzini, *La lingua italiana*, p. 134.

at its origins in thirteenth-century writing.[31] When it comes to the question of codification during the Renaissance, Vanvolsem has recently advanced the hypothesis that the Tuscan grammarians of the sixteenth century, while prolific writers, were largely absent during the debates on the *Questione della lingua*.[32] In part, this was due to the fact that Bembo's *Prose* was not published until 1549 in Florence, and by a printer originally from the Netherlands. Vanvolsem maintains that the variation in Florentine was one reason why the variety encountered 'un grand obstacle à la diffusion du modèle' (a large obstacle for the model's diffusion). Castellani's historical grammar furthers our understanding of the variation at the base of what is commonly thought of as a single entity, whether it be the 'standard', 'Florentine', or 'Italian'. In a magisterial chapter outlining the major dialectal divisions within Tuscany during the Renaissance, he provides us with a detailed picture of competing varieties.[33] This study allows us to see how Florentine was just a 'face in the crowd' in the panorama of several Tuscan varieties, and was far from being homogeneous itself. In particular, western Tuscan dialects exercised a strong influence over Florentine. Rossi notes that it was in the late fourteenth and fifteenth centuries that Florentine absorbed new changes, many of which entered into the language from western Tuscan dialects following Florence's conquests of Pistoia in 1295, Prato in 1351, and especially Pisa in 1406.[34] These influences could already be discerned in the first half of the fourteenth century.[35]

---

31 Nencioni, 'Fra grammatica e retorica'; De Mauro, *Storia linguistica dell'Italia unita*; Castellani, *Grammatica storica della lingua italiana*. For contemporary studies of what has been called 'overabundance' (multiple forms realizing the same cell), and attempts to introduce multiple variants along a 'canonicity cline', see Thornton, 'Overabundance'.

32 Vanvolsem, 'La standardisation en italien', p. 327. Linguistic variation of writers, including Dante, was recognized but ultimately evaluated as inappropriate to be adopted for a standard during the series of debates on language during the late fifteenth and early sixteenth centuries, known later as the *Questione della lingua*. As Baldissone, 'History of Literary Criticism', p. 1058, has noted: 'Petrarch and Boccaccio were chosen as archetypes of stylistic perfection in poetry and prose, with the significant omission of Dante, considered ill-suited owing to the multilingual choices he adopted in the *Comedia*'.

33 Castellani, *Grammatica storica della lingua italiana*, pp. 253–365, identifies the following seven varieties in his chapter: (1) Tuscan dialects, (2) western Tuscan dialects, (3) transitional dialects, (4) Sienese, (5) Montieri, (6) Grosseto, and (7) eastern Tuscan dialects.

34 Rossi, 'Fiorentino e italiano', p. 77. Among the various phenomena he describes, the following relate to verb morphology: *dia* and *stia* replacing *dea* and *stea*; *arò* and *arei* are introduced as variants alongside *avrò* and *avrei*; *fusti* and *fussi* alongside *fosti* and *fossi*; *missi* with *misi*; *lavamo* with *lavammo*; *lavorono/lavorno* with *lavarono*. Certain verb forms in the 6th person in *-eno* are introduced alongside those already present (*vedeno* 'vedono') and in strong perfects (*disseno* 'dissero').

35 Castellani, *Grammatica storica della lingua italiana*, p. 253, notes that 'i dialetti contermini, per parte loro, specie quelli delle zone poste a occidente di Firenze, hanno esercitato un forte influsso sul fiorentino; influsso già percepibile prima della metà del Trecento' (the coterminous dialects, for their part, especially those in the areas west of Florence, exerted a strong influence on Florentine; an influence that is already perceptible before the mid-fourteenth century) and that there is, therefore 'un'altra componente della nostra

The polymorphy identified by these previous studies concerns variants at all linguistic levels. These include lexical (*desiderio – desio* 'desire'), morphological (*farei – faria* 'I would do / make'; *facevo – faceva* 'I used to do / make'; *devo – debbo – deggio* 'I must'), and even semantic, with conjunctions such as *tuttavia* 'however' also taking on the meaning of an adversative. While an investigation of all variants would lead to an enormous number of forms, this chapter focuses only on the following (finite) variants of verb morphology:
1. *farei – faria* 'I would do / make' (1sg. present conditional of FARE)
2. *facevo – faceva* 'I used to do / make' (1sg. imperfect indicative of FARE)
3. *devo – debbo – deggio* 'I must' (1sg. present indicative of DOVERE)

The reasons for looking at these particular variants are several. First, while verb polymorphy can be said to be a characteristic of many varieties used historically within Italy, the above forms are all Tuscan. Therefore, they provide a good basis for comparison with a homogeneous region, and within one particular variety with a long written tradition. Secondly, Castellani's *Grammatica storica* contains sufficient detail about the provenance of linguistic forms, as well as the isoglosses characteristic of historical Italian, to allow a comprehensive examination and to trace each form's propagation in its diatopic and diachronic evolution.[36] Third, all forms listed above are common verbs in terms of frequency, allowing for a high degree of tokens to emerge from the databases used for analysis and described below. Fourth, in the case that one sees more than two variants emerge, such as with the variants listed for 1sg. present indicative of DOVERE, a more complete picture will be able to be shown when writers incorporated, or rejected, more than two competing variants for the same morphology. Fifth, verb morphology is one area where there are significant differences between early vernaculars in Tuscany, including between the major varieties identified by Castellani such as those from Pisa and Lucca.[37] Such variation allows us to gauge retrospectively which variant 'wins out' over the other two and, more importantly, to track their linguistic fate in writing that is understudied.

The method I have adopted to search for these variants includes two sources of data. The first is the *Opera del vocabolario italiano* (*OVI*). This textual database is the largest corpus available for research into historical Italian. It is

---

lingua [...] di cui va tenuto conto, la componente toscana non fiorentina' (another component of our language [...] that must be taken into consideration, that is, the non-Florentine Tuscan component).

36 While Castellani provides detailed description of the linguistic situation in Tuscany, a further reason for looking at these verbs here is their lack of treatment in his work. See, for example, *Grammatica storica della lingua italiana*, pp. 352–53, where in the section '22. Singoli verbi', only a few examples are provided of finite forms and none in the conditional.

37 Castellani, *Grammatica storica della lingua italiana*, p. 320, even though 'il lucchese si dimostra in genere più conservativo del pisano' (generally speaking, the vernacular of Lucca is more conservative than the vernacular of Pisa).

located in Florence, at the Accademia della Crusca, and is updated with new texts quarterly. As of February 2022, it contained 3261 texts with approximately twenty-nine million words. While the database is not restricted to Florentine or to Tuscan texts, the majority do come from this region. Indeed, this provides a further reason for selecting the forms listed above, since the *OVI* database is likely to record a large number of Tuscan forms over non-Tuscan variants.[38]

The second database is *Morfologia dell'italiano in diacronia* (*MIDIA*). This diachronic corpus contains over 7.5 million words from eight hundred Italian texts from the thirteenth century to the first half of the twentieth century. Texts are divided into five time periods:

1) 1200–1375, the formation of Tuscan-centred Old Italian
2) 1376–1532, the affirmation of Italian outside Tuscany
3) 1533–1691, standardization of Italian in the late Renaissance
4) 1692–1840, the birth of modern Italian
5) 1841–1947, the language of Italian political unification

Since the purpose of this chapter is to trace verb polymorphy at the origins of Italian, I list only those forms in the first category, that is, the category containing texts from 'Old Italian'. The search tool provided allows an easy extraction of the data, particularly for the study of word-formation, and means that data can be filtered in a relatively easy way. The database also provides useful frequency tables for search results, frequency lists, graphs for temporal evolution of phenomena, and several other tools. Finally, texts have been tagged in the database according to seven genres, thereby already suggesting a social continuum.[39] For each genre, twenty-five texts are included so that each section has a total of eight thousand tokens. These genres are expository prose, literary prose, normative and juridical prose, personal prose, scientific prose, poetry, and spoken language mimesis.[40]

Data referred to in later sections of the chapter are taken from studies of Old Italian, and specifically of merchant texts housed in the voluminous Datini Archive in the Archivio di Stato di Prato. These sources are discussed in further detail below.

---

38 For further details on the creation of the *OVI* database, see Dupont, 'The Opera del Vocabolario Italiano Database'.
39 In certain cases, the *MIDIA* corpus appears to have tagged certain phenomena incorrectly. For example, a search for infinitivals ending in *-ari* produces 299 occurrences, but includes ten noun forms: *cassari, colari, Emendari, emendari* (twice), *exemplari, Morgari, operari, Pesari, i ragionari*. Forms which have been incorrectly tagged have been eliminated from the data presented below.
40 For further details on the design of the *MIDIA* corpus, as well as the ability to incorporate PoS (part-of-speech) tagging, see Iacobini, De Rosa, and Schirato, 'Part-of-Speech Tagging Strategy'. Brown, 'Towards the Elaboration of a Diastratic Model', has recently provided an analysis of one particular type of dialect contact (known as 'koineization') in a framework of social variation.

Evidence of Verb Polymorphy from Electronic Corpora

I present the results for these forms below, in addition to the discussion and commentary, before providing a brief conclusion. Forms are quantitatively assessed, and a description of the text types in which they appear is also provided, in order to highlight the variation inherent in non-literary writing.

farei – faria

The various diachronic and synchronic variants of the 1sg. present conditional of FARE in Old Italian have been amply documented. Rohlfs notes that the conditional in *-ìa* is formed from the infinitive and the imperfect of the verb *avere* and that, given the 'Italian phonetic development' (HABEBAM > *aveva*), one expects an ending in *-eva* or *-ea*.[41] Conditionals of this kind were found in Aretine poets (*darea* 'darebbe') in Guittone, as well as further afield in Liguria and Piedmontese (*porea*, and modern Ligure *bevreiva*, etc.).[42] With regard to endings in *-ei*, composed with HABUI, the Tuscan endings (*-ei, -esti, -ebbe*, etc.) correspond exactly with the perfect forms of 'avere'. Further, Old Italian also had *-ebbi* in the first person, such as in Guittone *ardirebbi, vivrebbi*.[43] Manni had noted that the penetration of conditionals in *-ia* into Florentine is due, in the main, to literary influences. She notes that this innovation may have derived from the southern Tuscan *contado*, and that forms before the fifteenth and sixteenth centuries are very rare.[44]

The *OVI* shows there to be 234 occurrences of *farei*, with the earliest dating from 1265. The first occurrence appears in a letter from Andrea de' Tolomei da Tresi to messer Tolo e agli altri compagni de' Tolomei, in Siena.[45] In total, only sixteen forms of *farei* appear from the thirteenth century, including in works from Florence, such as *Vita nuova* (*farei parlando innamorar la gente*). These data clearly outnumber forms of *faria*, with 157 occurrences. However, *faria* first appears in a text from c. 1190, in the poem *Domna, tant vos ai priada* by Raimbaut de Vaqueiras. With regard to distribution in the thirteenth century, there are more occurrences, with fifty instances of *faria* if we include cases in the writing of Cecco Angiolieri. This uneven distribution of forms points already to the variation inherent in the earliest Italian texts, but both are widely present in the corpus.

A similar distribution is also found in the *MIDIA* corpus, although with fewer occurrences of both forms. This corpus provides seventeen instances of *farei* from the period 1200–1375. Of these, the majority are found in literary

---

41 Rohlfs, *Morfologia*, § 593.
42 The hypothesis of whether the *-ìa* desinence can be said to have come from central-northern Tuscany was first put forward by Schiaffini, 'Influssi dei dialetti centro-settentrionali sul toscano e sulla lingua letteraria'.
43 Rohlfs, *Morfologia*, § 593. For recent overviews of the formation of the conditional in Romance, see Vincent, 'Compositionality and Change'.
44 Manni, 'Ricerche sui tratti fonetici e morfologici', p. 155.
45 See Castellani, *La prosa italiana delle origini*, pp. 401–07.

texts: poetry (9), literary prose (4), theatre and mimesis (2). They are also a feature of non-literary texts as well. There are cases also in expository (1) and personal texts (1). The one instance in personal text is from Saint Catherine of Siena, writing in the second half of the fourteenth century (Letter 2: *piuttosto farei in effetto che con parole*), while the expository example is from the late thirteenth century in *Lo Diretano Bando* written by an anonymous author (§ 47: *E così farei, bella dolcissima amica, se voi mi volessi […]*). In terms of *faria*, the corpus contains twelve examples, all in literary texts (11 poetry and 1 prose).

In short, what we see in the corpus data is a situation of fluidity and multiple competing forms. Even at the earliest stages, both *farei* and *faria* are present, including in some of the earliest texts from Tuscany. Although variants of *farei* outnumber those of *faria*, they show a similar distribution and persistence in the following centuries. These data are confirmed by both the *OVI* and *MIDIA* corpora, and although the latter shows fewer instances, one cannot discount that this is due to the construction of the corpus itself. Both forms are present in literary and non-literary texts alike.

faceva – facevo

The 1sg. imperfect indicative desinence and alternation between -*a* and -*o* vowels (not just of FARE) is well known. In Tuscan, previous studies have shown that a wide variety of outcomes were present for first conjugation -ARE verbs, such as -*ea*, -*ava*, -*o*.[46] Even though -*o* came to distinguish the 1sg. in standard Italian, this ending is lacking in the language of Dante, Petrarch, and Boccaccio. Migliorini pointed to the possibility of external borrowing for the source of this desinence. Rohlfs notes that it may have in fact 'irradiated' from Siena and Lucca, and that it is found in Jacopone da Todi, and then in the writing of Saint Catherine and in the language of the *Fioretti*. After, it became adopted in literary writing during the Renaissance by authors such as Luigi Pulci, Francesco Berni, Benvenuto Cellini, and Galileo Galilei, although non-Tuscans remained 'faithful' to endings in -*a*. In a well-known episode of Italian linguistic history, it was only following Alessandro Manzoni, who transformed all -*a* endings into -*o* endings, that this variant entered into the literary standard.[47] The only reflexes of 1sg. FARE in Trolli's study are *faceva* and *feva*.

---

46 These desinences are documented, for example, in Serianni, *Testi pratesi*; Rohlfs, *Morfologia*, § 550; Manni, 'La situazione linguistica', p. 39; Castellani, 'Italiano e fiorentino argenteo', pp. 33–34; Trolli, 'La lingua di Giovanni Morelli', p. 92. Trolli notes that 'l'imperfetto indicativo esce costantemente in -*a* alla prima persona singolare, con quattro eccezioni: *ero* 502, 506, 507; *aspettavo* 508' (the imperfect indicative ending is consistently -*a* in the first person singular, with four exceptions).

47 Rohlfs, *Morfologia*, § 550. In this same paragraph, Rohlfs also notes while the *Cento novelle antiche* regularly use *dovea*, *volea*, *rispondea*, Dante uses both -*iva* and -*ia* endings, as well as a clear prevalence of -*ea* over -*eva* in the *Divine Comedy*. The -*ea* desinence is still common in contemporary Tuscan varieties, particularly in the provinces of Lucca, Pistoia, Florence, Siena, and Livorno.

The *OVI* provides a surprising distribution of forms. While the philological studies cited above might lead one to expect a complementary distribution in Tuscany, there are only seven occurrences available of *facevo*. Of these, five are in the *Libro della divina dottrina* of Saint Catherine of Siena (1378), one is found in *Le lettere del beato Gio. Colombini da Siena* of 1376, and one is in *Lo Diretano Bando*, also from the fourteenth century. In terms of *feva*,[48] there are 267 occurrences across a wide variety of texts — nevertheless, the earliest occurrences in Italian writing appear to all be northern. Indeed the earliest, from 1274, is found in the writing of Pietro da Bescapè. The other occurrences show *feva* to be a widely distributed northern form, present in texts from early Venetian writing from 1321 (such as in the *Legenda da Santo Stady*), to Bologna (Jacopo della Lana) and the *Rime* of Francesco di Vannozzo, written in Tosco-Venetian, from the fourteenth century. On the other hand, *faceva* presents 1699 instances across a wide variety of texts.[49] Searching for all instances of *faceva* preceded by the subject pronoun *io* returns thirteen results (the earliest from 1315/21), and with the subject pronoun *i'* returns nine results (the earliest from 1313). There are no occurrences of *feva* in texts from any period later than the fourteenth century. In short, these results point to a wide geographical distribution of forms, with a clear predominance of *feva* over *facevo* and mainly in literary texts.

In the *MIDIA* corpus, there is one occurrence of 1sg. *faceva* for the period 1200–1375 and no occurrences of *facevo*.[50] This single occurrence is in Boccaccio's *Amorosa visione* (1342–1343) and clearly shows the penetration of this form into literary Tuscan: *Il dir ch'io le **faceva**: – Un poco aspetta – non mi valeva, per ch'io mi voltai verso la terza faccia a man diretta* (ll. 49–51).

What these data from both corpora demonstrate is the widespread presence of both forms at the origin of Italian, and their strong resistance to encode the grammaticality of person and number as 1sg. variants. In the literary standard, this competition endures right up until at least the nineteenth century. In non-literary vernaculars, this variation is characteristic of dialects even in contemporary Tuscany. In this sense, 'the idea often put forward in the literature, that overabundance will eventually inevitably be eliminated in all cases, is not fully supported by the data.'[51] While these comments could reasonably be applied as well to the early centuries of the formation of Italian, they seem to support also the examples presented above.

---

48   There are no instances of *fevo*.
49   I have not been able to cross-check every form to distinguish between 1sg. and 3sg. forms at this stage of the research, but would simply note that the earliest presence of *faceva* (1271/75) in the *Fiori e vita di filosafi e d'altri savi e d'imperadori*, written by an anonymous author, is in the 3sg.: *Questo imperadore, per lo male che faceva* (This emperor, due to the evil he was doing).
50   There are thirty-four occurrences of *faceva* in total, of which one is 1sg. and thirty-three are 3sg. There are five occurrences for the period 1376–1532, which I do not deal with here.
51   Thornton, 'Reduction and Maintenance of Overabundance', p. 183.

devo – debbo – deggio

The allophonic variation present in 1sg. reflexes of the stem of DOVERE are also characteristic of the earliest written attestations of Italian. The form *deggio* is part of a broader subset of Tuscan verbs showing palatalization of the final consonant in the verb root (Rohlfs suggests that this is due to *j* < *-eo* and *-io* producing palatalization). Early Tuscan would have had *debeo, facio, taceo, jaceo*, etc., which produced *deggio, faccio, taccio, giaccio*.[52] Forms such as *debbo* and old Tuscan *abbo* 'ho' may have lost *i* thanks to a process of analogy with other cells in the paradigm of *essere*. Similarly, the root *dev-* also appears in some of the earliest literary writing from Tuscany as a modal.[53] Although I discuss only these particular verb stems here, Castellani highlights a much more variegated picture, noting how the forms *dea* or *dia*, *deano* or *dieno* in the sense of 'deve' / 'debbono' (s/he must / they must) 'sembrano essere una caratteristica dei soli dialetti toscani orientali in fase antica' (seem to be a characteristic only of eastern Tuscan dialects in an old stage).[54] The earliest Florentine texts, the *Frammenti d'un libro di conti di banchieri fiorentini* of 1211, show *die, diono* < DĒ(B)ET, *DĒ(B)UNT (with closed 'e' > 'i' due to hiatus).[55]

Similarly to the other forms discussed above, the *OVI* shows a varied patterning. Surprisingly, only two instances of *devo* are recorded. Much more widespread are occurrences of *debbo* (757 instances) and *deggio* (152 occurrences). Instances of *debbo* show a wide distribution across text types and genres. The earliest is from Brunetto Latini's *Retorica* of *c.* 1260–1261, although the variant is also present right up until the fourteenth century, in *La Bibbia volgare secondo la rara edizione del I di ottobre MCCCCLXXI*. In the case of *deggio*, the oldest forms are found in the poetry of Giacomo da Lentini from *c.* 1230/50 and are denominated simply 'Tuscany', while other occurrences of this form are more localized, such as in Bonagiunta Orbicciani da Lucca's *Rime*. All forms of *deggio* show the literary nature which

---

52 Rohlfs, *Morfologia*, § 534.
53 Migliorini, *Storia della lingua italiana*, p. 212, notes that 'notevoli gli usi modali di *dovere, venire, volere*' (the modal uses of *dovere* [to have to], *venire* [to come], *volere* [to want] are notable) quoting Boccaccio, *Decamerone*, VII, 9: *Pirro adunque cominci ad aspettare quello che far dovesse la gentil donna* (Piero therefore began to expect what the noble lady should do). Castellani, *Grammatica storica della lingua italiana*, p. 360, records particular forms of *dovere* such as 2sg. *diei* (by way of analogy on 3sg. *die*, pronounced *diè*), as well as 3pl. *deono* as being present in Sienese. On p. 441, he notes that 3pl. *deano, dieno* appear alongside the 'rarer types' *de, debe, debbono*. In non-literary writing from Arezzo, *dia* appears more common, although he counts sixteen instances of *debbe* and one of *debe* (p. 441, n. 327). For additional detail on these forms in Arezzo, see Serianni, 'Ricerche sul dialetto aretino'. On the question of when *dia, stia* entered into competition with *dea, stea* in fifteenth-century Florentine, see Manni, 'Ricerche sui tratti fonetici e morfologici', pp. 142–43.
54 Castellani, *Grammatica storica della lingua italiana*, p. 445.
55 Castellani, *Grammatica storica della lingua italiana*, p. 446.

it progressively acquired, and almost all occurrences are in language from Tuscan writers. These data can be seen to be instances of forms occupying the same cell, showing how such variation was not levelled for centuries and in fact typifies some of the earliest Italian writing. Used in both literary and non-literary genres, this heterogeneity of forms provides further evidence of verb polymorphy in Old Italian.

The *MIDIA* corpus shows one occurrence of *devo* for the period 1200–1375, thirty-two occurrences of *debbo*, and fourteen occurrences of *deggio*. The one instance of *devo* is in the *Libro di ragioni*, by an anonymous author, from the early fourteenth century.[56] With regard to *debbo*, occurrences appear distributed across the various genres of the corpus (5 *espositivi*; 2 *giuridici*; 1 *personali*; 4 *poesia*; 12 *prosa*; 5 *scientifici*; 3 *teatro*). The one occurrence in personal writing is in the letters of Saint Catherine of Siena, while the occurrences in texts classified as *espositivi* all appear in *Lo Diretano Bando* (2) or in the *Specchio di vera penitenza* by Jacopo Passavanti from the fourteenth century. The occurrences of *deggio* appear more restricted in their distribution. All appear in the genre 'poetry', except for one occurrence in the *Tristano riccardiano* (classified under 'prosa' in the *MIDIA* corpus). All instances of *deggio* are literary, possibly alluding to the early classification of the form in particular domains of linguistic usage at a high register.

Having seen some instances of verb polymorphy in late medieval Tuscany and their distribution across various Tuscan vernaculars, let us turn our attention to how these forms appear in texts which show evidence of vernaculars in contact. The differences between Tuscan vernaculars and the forms discussed above (that is, conditional mood, imperfect endings, and 1sg. persons of *dovere*) show significant differences between Tuscan and other dialectal regions. Mixed-language texts can offer evidence of the effects which occur when different vernaculars come into contact and which characterize some of the earliest writing in the history of Italian.

Vernaculars in Contact: Tuscan / Genoese and Tuscan / Milanese in Early Merchant Writing

A clear characteristic of the earliest recorded forms of 'Italian' is the variation present not just in Tuscany, but across the peninsula. Scholars have shown how the major dialectal differences of Tuscan dialects present during the thirteenth century were progressively abandoned in favour of supra-regional

---

56 For a recent critical edition and linguistic analysis of the language of this manuscript, see Bocchi, 'Un libro d'abaco pisano'. While highlighting particular aspects of the morphology present in this manuscript on pp. 192–201, *devo* does not appear to be mentioned here.

forms that continued to evolve during the fourteenth and fifteenth centuries.[57] What is less clear is how particular forms continued to evolve for those writers who were far removed from the standard, and who were not from Tuscany. Merchants were a new, middle class of people with little education but who produced an extraordinary range of written material, including letters, bills of exchange, financial receipts, lists of goods and inventories, and other types of writing. While some merchants remained in fixed locations, there is evidence that others travelled around vast geographical distances and, in doing so, brought different vernaculars into contact in a process of accommodation. The way in which the particular verb forms discussed above were levelled in their writing has not yet been fully discussed. A comparison between the verb forms discussed above, limited to Tuscan writing, and merchant writing from other areas around Italy can help to show the extraordinary range of verb polymorphy that continued to exist parallel to the ongoing evolution of the standard.[58]

The first example considered here looks at a situation of language contact between Tuscan and Genoese. The thirty-two letters of the Tuscan merchant Piero Giusto Benintendi show a *scripta* which progressively incorporates Tuscan elements into his writing, following his transfer from Tuscany to Genoa when he was either six or seven years of age.[59] Of the thirty-two items of correspondence currently housed in the Datini Archive, thirty were sent from Genoa to Florence. One item was sent from Recco to Florence, while another was sent from Genoa to Prato. Benintendi was born in Tobbiana in either 1342 or 1343 and corresponded with various members of the Datini company over the life of its existence.[60] His correspondence shows his linguistic and non-linguistic integration into Genoese society and a communicative competency which belies his place of origin:[61]

> Ogni genovese me reputa e tene genovese e nato sia in Genova, perché vegni a Genova de agni VI in VII, e aparai a Genova la letera, ed è che a

---

57 Castellani, *Grammatica storica della lingua italiana*; Manni, 'Toscana'; Serianni, ed., *La lingua nella Storia d'Italia*, pp. 70–90.
58 For other examples of vernaculars in contact in merchant writing throughout Romània, see Tomasin, 'Sul contatto linguistico nella Romània medievale' and Tomasin, 'Testi in italiano antico'. Brown, 'Una memoria quattrocentesca in volgare lombardo', presents a critical edition of a semi-religious nun, whose language shows evidence of various northern vernaculars in contact as well as Tuscan.
59 These letters were first published in Piattoli, 'Lettere di Piero Benintendi mercante del Trecento'.
60 Elsewhere Benintendi is mentioned in Barker, *That Most Precious Merchandise*, p. 176 (who appears to mistake him as Venetian), and Cassandro, 'Aspects of the Life and Character of Francesco di Marco Datini', p. 15.
61 Stella, 'Liguria', p. 140, also comments on the mixed nature of Benintendi's writing. He notes the presence of Tuscan, Genoese, and mixed forms, but highlights how *lunesdì* (Monday) and *martesdì* (Tuesday) are unmistakeably Ligurian lexemes.

Genova sono agni XXXXIII, e pertanto, se no scripvo intendevele et a vostro modo, dimando perdono.[62]

(Every Genoese believes me and holds me to be Genoese and born in Genoa, because I came to Genoa at six or seven years old and I learnt to read and write in Genoa, and I have been in Genoa for forty-three years, and therefore even if I do not write intelligibly and in your way, I ask forgiveness.)

The variants discussed above present the following outcomes. I have highlighted in bold the specific variants and reflexes of FARE and DOVERE discussed above, particularly when these forms show allophones in the stem (for example, between *dev-* and *deb-*). I also provide reflexes of other verbs in each linguistic category to show the more general pattern which emerges for each in Piero's writing.

Conditional: In general, Tuscan forms are present, although one sees also a slight presence of northern *-ev* endings as well as loss of *-v-*: *avere'-la*; **farei**; *arei, vorei, metere'-mi; porei; serebe; vorebe; revocherebe; basterebe; serebono; potrebono; darebono; vorebono; sereboro; sereva-ne; averea; raxonerea; sentirea; serea;* **farea**.

Imperfect indicative: *avvevi; credevate; avavate; dovavate; dovevate; potavate; erono; erano.*

Present indicative: 1pl.: *dubitiamo;* **debiamo**; *abiamo; sapiamo; stiamo* but *semo; siamo; seamo; portamose; aspetamo; pensamo; speramo; posamo; concludemo; atendemo*. For 2pl.: *mostrate; avete; sete; potetegi;* **devete**; *salutatimelo; guardè; savei*. For the 3pl.: *voihono;* **debono**; *vegnono; possono* and *posseno; ocideno; vegeno* and *voihano; vorano; restono; soperchono; èno*.

Although he moved to Genoa at a young age, the forms presented above of Benintendi's language show a mixed variety of linguistic forms, between Tuscan and Genoese, that are typical of situations of language contact. The language presents a heterogeneous variety, without impeding communicative competency. While clear Tuscan outcomes can be seen in forms such as *farei* and other *-ei* endings in the conditional, northern allophones are also present. The imperfect indicative generally shows Tuscan forms, although occurrences of *-ono* show evidence of the infiltration from Genoese. In terms of the present indicative, there is much variety in both stems and endings of all reflexes,

---

62 Reported in Stella, 'Liguria', p. 138. This letter is dated 24 September 1392 and is currently housed in the Archivio di Stato di Prato, Fondo Datini, busta 1091, inserto 28, codice 134825. For further commentary on this passage, see Carlucci, 'Opinions about Perceived Linguistic Intelligibility'.

including in reflexes of DOVERE. Overall, this variation points to a situation of highly fluid linguistic contact in late medieval mercantile documents and a wide exchange of forms. Benintendi's mixed language is one example of vernaculars in contact, and of a native Tuscan who migrated from Tuscany in his youth to relocate to an area with a typologically different vernacular than the one he had learnt as a child.

The second case study presented here provides evidence of the linguistic outcomes between Tuscan and Milanese.[63] The commercial letters by the Milanese merchant Giovanni da Pessano were written between 30 August 1397 and 17 December 1402, and all were sent from Milan. These letters are held in the Archivio di Stato di Prato in the Datini Archive and have been previously published by Frangioni.[64] The analysis which follows is based on a sample of sixty-eight letters by Giovanni out of the seventy-two letters included in Frangioni's corpus. In aiming to create the most homogeneous corpus possible, I have excluded four items from the analysis below: two items which are *estratti conto* (receipts), and two items which are not in Giovanni's hand.[65] Although Giovanni da Pessano was based in Milan, his correspondence is all addressed to Tuscan merchants working for the Datini company and who were all Tuscan.

As with Piero Benintendi's letters discussed above, I have highlighted in bold all reflexes of FARE and DOVERE. I have provided additional variants to show the more general pattern which emerges for each form in Giovanni's writing.[66]

---

63 In total, there are over 810 letters from Milan in the Datini Archive. Of these, 526 were written by Datini's business associates, all Tuscan (who travelled to Milan on business errands and to meet with their Milanese correspondents), and are thus in Tuscan. Of the remaining 284 letters, 70 were written by other Tuscans or merchants from a Tuscan family or by merchants whose provenance I have been unable to establish, 9 pieces of correspondence are not letters, 4 are in Latin, and one letter was sent by an anonymous merchant. Out of the remaining 200 letters, there are 72 from one of Datini's main Milanese correspondents, Giovannino da Pessano. Studies which make use of material in the Datini Archive as evidence for the early diffusion of Tuscan are Brown, *Early Evidence for Tuscanisation*, and Brown, 'Testimonianze di una precoce toscanizzazione'.

64 Frangioni, ed., *Milano fine Trecento*. For an account of so-called 'foreign' languages present in this archive as recorded by the online database of the Archivio Datini, see Brown, 'Multilingual Merchants'. A similar process is found to be present also in religious writing from Milan in the fifteenth century; see Brown, 'Il contatto linguistico' and Brown, 'The Influence of Milan on the Development of the Lombard Koiné'.

65 The two items not in Giovanni's hand but which appear in Frangioni's corpus are letter 697 (pp. 500–501) and letter 758 (p. 531). Letter 697 is written by one of Giovanni's cousins. Letter 758 is 'lettera non firmata di mano di Giovanni da Pessano' (not a letter signed in the hand of Giovanni da Pessano).

66 In addition to lexical forms, I also provide the frequency counts of each form in round brackets immediately following the citation, using data from Brown, *Early Evidence for Tuscanisation*.

Conditional: the 1sg., 1st conjug. has Tuscan -*ebe* (10) and only one case of northern -*eve*. The 2nd conjug. only has -*ebe* (3), and there are no forms for the 3rd conjug. Irregulars show a variety of Tuscan and Lombard forms: northern **derisavo** 'dovrei' (1), Tuscan *farebe* (2), *poterebe* (2) but northern *potisavo* (1) and *poterisavo* (2), *saperebe* (1), *togliarebe* (1). There are no plural forms. There are no 2sg. forms. For the 2pl., only northern forms are present. 1st conjug.: -*isavo* (1), -*issavo* (1) and for the 2nd conjug., -*isavo* (1), -*essevo* (1). There are no forms for the 3rd conjug. The only irregulars present the northern forms **farisavo** (1) and *voresche* (1).

Imperfect indicative: Almost all forms for the imperfect indicative are common to both Tuscan and Lombard. For the 1sg., the 1st conjug., has -*ava* (5) and -*avo* (3), both common to Tuscan and Lombard. The 2nd conjug. has -*eva* (7), -*eo* (1), and -*ivo* (1). There are no forms for any persons for the 3rd conjug. Irregulars: *dicevo* (1), **deveva** (3), *voleva* (3). The only 2pl. form is *devavitti* (2). For the 3sg., the 1st conjug. has -*ava* (9). The 2nd conjug. has -*eva* (6) and -*iva* (2). Irregulars are *diceva* (2), **deveva** (3), **faceva** (2) and northern *feva* (2), *poteva* (4), *veneva* (2), *voreva* (1). The 3pl. has -*ano* (1) for the 1st conjug. The 2nd conjug. has -*evano* (4), -*ivano* (1), and -*iveno* (1). Irregulars: *potevano* (1).

Present indicative: Although there are no occurrences of *devo* / *debbo* / *deggio* in Giovanni da Pessano's letters, I note here that most forms in the 1sg. present indicative present a Tuscan ending, with 116 cases of -*o*, 7 with -*e* ending, and none with a (northern) consonant ending. For completeness, I also present instances of the other reflexes of DOVERE in cells other than the 1sg. These are 2pl. **devatti** 'dovete' (1), **debiati** (1), **devitti** (1); 3pl. **debeno** (1), **debono** (1), **deno** (1), and **denno** (1).

Similarly to Benintendi's language, the variants present in Giovanni da Pessano's letters show instances of similar forms 'occupying the same cell'. In some cases, this variation can be explained by the different desinences of particular reflexes, while in others there is clear allophonic variation in the stem, between *dev*-, *deb*-, and *den*- while forms such as *deno* show a particularly northern variant in a particularly contracted form.[67] The language of this letter, and all of Giovanni's writing, is heterogeneous, with Latin, Tuscan, and Lombard elements distributed in an uneven way. With regard to the Lombard items, it is clear that Giovanni has a range of forms from which to choose. There exists, so to speak, a continuum between the low-register forms found in the writing of a fourteenth-century nun from Lombardy, Margherita Lambertenghi,

---

67 For a systematic overview of the verb morphology and reflexes at the origins of Milanese, see Domokos, 'La morfologia verbale' and Domokos, 'Analytic and Synthetic Structures in Medieval Milanese'.

and the high-register forms of the chancery.[68] Giovanni appears to be using linguistic items heavily slanted towards the latter and is avoiding the most local forms of the vernacular from Milan in favour of the Lombard koine. The koine was not solely confined to high-register writing, but it was also being used in low-register texts such as letters sent by merchant writers. They are, therefore, evidence of language contact between Milanese and Tuscan, and can be seen as a form of accommodation to Giovanni's interlocutors.[69] In short, these forms are the expected result when vernaculars of typologically different varieties come into contact.[70]

Conclusion

This chapter has investigated verb polymorphy at the basis of Italian, paying particular attention to vernaculars in contact in late medieval and Renaissance Italy. I have attempted to situate these findings within a discourse of historical sociolinguistics. While previous studies had documented the presence of these forms and the variants that preceded codification of Italian, no study has presented a quantitative analysis of the multivariation inherent in verb morphology in Old Italian. Many authors either dismiss the question of variation altogether, or tend to use terms such as *italiano*, *toscano*, and *standard* in a synonymous way. When this variation is alluded to, oftentimes readers are simply presented with a series of phenomena in list form, without being able to grasp anything about the distribution of these variants, their geographical diffusion, or the particular text types in which they appeared. The history of the literary standard has been well documented. However, even recent assessments have sought to frame their analyses of the major literary writers through a prism of variation and/or plurilingualism.[71] Part of this research trajectory has been to recover the multilingualism and variation latent in historical writing. Such text types have traditionally been neglected by historians of the language, either because they were not looking for it, or because variation was seen to be an impediment to a teleological approach in tracing the standard.[72]

---

68 Brown, 'Women's Literacy in a Late Medieval Religious Community'.
69 For further details on the mixed nature of Giovanni's writing, see Brown, 'Language Variation in Fifteenth-Century Milan'.
70 In her chapter on semi-literary writing, Fresu reports that the agrammaticality of such writing can be reduced to two principal mechanisms. The first is contact with the underlying dialectal reality, and the second are processes of restructuring, particularly in terms of linguistic simplification. For further details and examples, see Fresu, 'Scritture dei Semicolti'; Schulte, 'Romance in Contact with Romance'. On the question of 'borrowed morphology' more generally, see Gardani, Arkadiev, and Amiridze, 'Borrowed Morphology'.
71 See for example Webb, 'Language'; Tomasin, 'Dante e l'idea di lingua italiana'.
72 On recent efforts to counter this trend, see Tomasin, 'Urban Multilingualism'.

This chapter has focused on a subset of verb reflexes to highlight a situation of polymorphy in Old Italian. However, the full extent of the variation present at the origins of Italian is yet to be written. Although Renaissance grammarians were also aware of the different forms which authors adopted in their writings, be they literary or non-literary, scholars have questioned whether variation may have impeded the late development of a standard emerging during the early modern period or could even have constituted an obstacle for the diffusion of a model to become adopted. Using the major databases currently available for research in historical Italian has allowed a more nuanced picture to emerge. Certain databases, such as the *Opera del vocabolario italiano*, currently comprise the largest textual source for scholars to search, in a relatively quick way, the various types of morphological variation characteristic of the oldest texts deemed to be Italian. More recent databases such as the *Morfologia dell'italiano in diacronia*, while comprising a smaller corpus, provide new ways of classifying data either chronologically or according to text type. Making use of the tools available and integrating a variety of sources, both electronic and philological, allows for a richer understanding of what Italian looked like from its very beginnings. The importance of providing an accurate linguistic description of the variation in late medieval and early modern Italy also has implications for broader questions, such as the degree of intelligibility and communicative competence between speakers of different regions in the past.[73]

At its origin, then, Italian evinces a wide variety of forms as recorded in both electronic corpora, historical grammars, and philological editions. This variety was so great that one can even find multiple forms for the same verb and, in certain cases, even for the same cell within Tuscany and particular areas of Tuscany. In a situation of vernaculars in contact, as in the merchant letters of Piero Benintendi and Giovanni da Pessano, the variation which emerges is even greater. This variation needs to be recovered in order to show the full extent of the multiregional and multivariate patterning of Italian of the earliest texts. The forms of linguistic exchange and contact that are the social conditions which incarnate this variation have traditionally been overlooked in scholarly description of the origins of Italian. Oftentimes the precise delimitations of the variety under discussion are not clear, especially when a term like *Italian* can be taken to mean a particular variety or even varieties of *fiorentino, toscano*. It is precisely this variety which historical sociolinguistics can help to bring into focus. This new subdiscipline of linguistics can also help us to reinterrogate the histories that have been told so far. The implications of rediscovering this 'hidden' variation raise important questions for scholars of language contact, but also for historical sociolinguists who wish to understand the fate of forms which did not standardize and how particular forms enter the standard through the complicated processes of language selection and

---

73 For an excellent assessment of these arguments and associated historiography of the debate, see Carlucci, 'How Did Italians Communicate When There Was No Italian?'.

codification. While it is not the place to enter into a discussion of the merits of this approach here, it is clearly part of a broader research paradigm that scholars of particular languages are developing at the same time as the tools and methods from new fields, such as historical sociolinguistics, are also beginning to emerge.

Works Cited

Ammon, Ulrich, 'On the Social Forces that Determine What Is Standard in a Language and on Conditions of Successful Implementation', *Sociolinguistica*, 17 (2003), 1–10

Armstrong, Nigel, and Ian E. Mackenzie, *Standardization, Ideology and Linguistics* (Basingstoke: Palgrave Macmillan, 2013)

Aski, Janice, and Cinzia Russi, *Iconicity and Analogy in Language Change: The Development of Double Object Clitic Clusters from Medieval Florentine to Modern Italian*, Studies in Language Change, 13 (Berlin: De Gruyter Mouton, 2015)

Ayres-Bennett, Wendy, 'Codification and Prescription in Linguistic Standardization: Myths and Models', in *Constructing Languages: Norms, Myths and Emotions*, ed. by Josep Maria Nadal and Francesc Feliu (Amsterdam: Benjamins, 2016), pp. 99–129

Baldissone, Giuseppina, 'History of Literary Criticism', in *Encyclopedia of Italian Literary Studies*, ed. by Gaetana Marrone (Florence: Taylor and Francis, 2006), pp. 1058–64

Barker, Hannah, *That Most Precious Merchandise: The Mediterranean Trade in Black Sea Slaves, 1260–1500*, The Middle Ages Series (Philadelphia: University of Pennsylvania Press, 2019)

Bocchi, Andrea, 'Un libro d'abaco pisano del primo Trecento', *Studi Linguistici Italiani*, 32 (2006), 15–209

Brown, Joshua, 'Il contatto linguistico nel medioevo lombardo', *Revista de Filología Románica*, 35 (2018), 103–18

———, *Early Evidence for Tuscanisation in the Letters of Milanese Merchants in the Datini Archive, Prato, 1396–1402* (Milan: Istituto Lombardo, Accademia di Scienze e Lettere, 2017)

———, 'The Influence of Milan on the Development of the Lombard Koiné in Fifteenth-Century Italy: The Letters of Elisabetta of Pavia', *Quaderni d'Italianistica*, 38.1 (2017), 131–51

———, 'Language History from Below: Standardization and Koineization in Renaissance Italy', *Journal of Historical Sociolinguistics*, 6.1 (2020), <https://doi.org/10.1515/jhsl-2018-0017>

———, 'Language Variation in Fifteenth-Century Milan: Evidence of Koineization in the Letters (1397–1402) of the Milanese Merchant Giovanni da Pessano', *Italian Studies*, 68.1 (2013), 57–77

———, 'Una memoria quattrocentesca in volgare lombardo', *La lingua italiana: Storia, strutture, testi*, 15 (2019), 57–73

——, 'Multilingual Merchants: The Trade Network of the 14th Century Tuscan Merchant Francesco di Marco Datini', in *Merchants of Innovation: The Languages of Traders*, ed. by Esther-Miriam Wagner, Bettina Beinhoff, and Ben Outhwaite, Studies in Language Change, 15 (Berlin: De Gruyter Mouton, 2017), pp. 235–51

——, 'Testimonianze di una precoce toscanizzazione nelle lettere commerciali del mercante milanese Francesco Tanso (?–1398), Archivio Datini, Prato', *Forum Italicum*, 49 (2015), 683–714

——, 'Towards the Elaboration of a Diastratic Model in Historical Analyses of Koineization', *Sociolinguistic Studies*, 14.4 (2020), 505–29

——, 'Women's Literacy in a Late Medieval Religious Community: Organisation and Memorialisation at Santa Marta in Milan, 1405–1454', *Journal of Religious History*, 45 (2021), 435–54

Cappellaro, Chiara, 'Genesis and Diachronic Persistence of Overabundance: Data from Romance Languages', in *Reorganising Grammatical Variation: Diachronic Studies in the Retention, Redistribution and Refunctionalisation of Linguistic Variants*, ed. by Antje Dammel, Matthias Eitelmann, and Mirjam Schmuck (Amsterdam: John Benjamins, 2018), pp. 119–48

——, 'Overabundance in Diachrony: A Case Study', in *The Boundaries of Pure Morphology: Diachronic and Synchronic Perspectives*, ed. by Silvio Cruschina, Martin Maiden, and John Charles Smith (Oxford: Oxford University Press, 2013), pp. 209–20

Carlucci, Alessandro, 'How Did Italians Communicate When There Was No Italian? Italo-Romance Intercomprehension in the Late Middle Ages', *The Italianist*, 40.1 (2020), 19–43

——, 'Opinions about Perceived Linguistic Intelligibility in Late-Medieval Italy', *Revue Romane*, 55 (2020), 140–65, <https://doi.org/10.1075/rro.19013.car>

Cassandro, Michele, 'Aspects of the Life and Character of Francesco di Marco Datini', in *Francesco di Marco Datini: The Man, the Merchant*, ed. by Giampiero Nigro (Florence: Firenze University Press, 2010), pp. 3–52

Castellani, Arrigo, *Grammatica storica della lingua italiana*, I: *Introduzione* (Bologna: Il Mulino, 2000)

——, 'Italiano e fiorentino argenteo', in *Saggi di linguistica e filologia italiana e romanza (1946–1976)*, ed. by Arrigo Castellani (Rome: Salerno Editrice, 1967), pp. 17–35

——, *La prosa italiana delle origini*, I: *Testi toscani di carattere pratico* (Bologna: Patron, 1982)

Cella, Roberta, *Storia dell'italiano* (Bologna: Il Mulino, 2015)

Coletti, Vittorio, *Storia dell'italiano letterario* (Turin: Einaudi, 1993)

De Mauro, Tullio, *Storia linguistica dell'Italia unita* (Bari: Editori Laterza, 1970)

Domokos, György, 'Analytic and Synthetic Structures in Medieval Milanese', in *Language and Language-Processing*, ed. by Pawel Karnowski and Imre Szigeti (Frankfurt am Main: Lang, 2006), pp. 21–29

——, 'La morfologia verbale del milanese antico di Bonvesin dra Riva', *Verbum*, 9.2 (2007), 261–77

Dupont, Christian, 'The Opera del Vocabolario Italiano Database: Full-Text Searching Early Italian Vernacular Sources on the Web', *Italica*, 78 (2001), 526–39

Durante, Marcello, *Dal latino all'italiano moderno: Saggio di storia linguistica e culturale* (Bologna: Zanichelli, 1981)

Formentin, Vittorio, 'Forme verbali doppie negli antichi volgari italiani: Frammenti di una "Stellungsregel" italoromanza', *Lingua e stile*, 55 (2020), 183–228

Frangioni, Luciana, ed., *Milano fine Trecento: Il carteggio milanese dell'Archivio Datini di Prato*, 2 vols (Florence: Opus Libri, 1994)

Fresu, Rita, 'Scritture dei Semicolti', in *Storia dell'italiano scritto*, III: *Italiano dell'uso*, ed. by Giuseppe Antonelli, Matteo Motolese, and Lorenzo Tomasin (Rome: Carocci, 2015), pp. 195–223

Gardani, Francesco, Peter Arkadiev, and Nino Amiridze, 'Borrowed Morphology: An Overview', in *Borrowed Morphology* ed. by Francesco Gardani, Peter Arkadiev, and Nino Amiridze (Berlin: De Gruyter, 2015), pp. 1–23

Gensini, Stefano, *Elementi di storia linguistica italiana* (Bergamo: Minerva Italica, 1982)

Haugen, Einar, 'Dialect, Language, Nation', *American Anthropologist*, 68.4 (1966), 922–35

Hinskens, Frans, Peter Auer, and Paul Kerswill, 'The Study of Dialect Convergence and Divergence: Conceptual and Methodological Considerations', in *Dialect Change: Convergence and Divergence in European Languages* ed. by Peter Auer, Frans Hinskens, and Paul Kerswill (Cambridge: Cambridge University Press, 2005), pp. 1–48

Iacobini, Claudio, Aurelio De Rosa, and Giovanna Schirato, 'Part-of-Speech Tagging Strategy for MIDIA: A Diachronic Corpus of the Italian Language', in *Proceedings of the First Italian Conference on Computational Linguistics CLiC-it*, ed. by Roberto Basili, Alessandro Lenci, and Bernardo Magnini (Pisa: Pisa University Press, 2014), pp. 213–18

Kabatek, Johannes, '*Koinés* and *scriptae*', in *The Cambridge History of the Romance Languages*, II: *Contexts*, ed. by Martin Maiden, John Charles Smith, and Adam Ledgeway (Cambridge: Cambridge University Press, 2013), pp. 143–86

Kinder, John J., *CLIC: Culture and Language of Italy on CD-ROM/Cultura e Lingua d'Italia in CD-ROM* (Interlinea: Novara, 2008)

Maiden, Martin, *A Linguistic History of Italian*, Longman Linguistics Library (London: Longman, 1995)

―――, 'Morphological Autonomy and Diachrony', in *Yearbook of Morphology 2004*, ed. by Gert Booij and Jaap van Marle (Dordrecht: Springer, 2005), pp. 137–75

―――, 'When Lexemes Become Allomorphs: On the Genesis of Suppletion', *Folia Linguistica*, 38.3/4 (2004), 227–56

Manni, Paola, 'Dal toscano all'italiano letterario', in *Storia della lingua italiana*, II: *Scritto e parlato*, ed. by Luca Serianni and Pietro Trifone (Turin: Einaudi, 1994), pp. 321–42

——, 'Ricerche sui tratti fonetici e morfologici del fiorentino quattrocentesco', *Studi di grammatica italiana*, 8 (1979), 115–71
——, 'La situazione linguistica: Profilo fonomorfologico delle varietà toscane', in Manni, *Il Trecento toscano: La lingua di Dante, Petrarca e Boccaccio*, Storia della lingua italiana (Bologna: Il Mulino, 2003), pp. 33–60
——, 'Toscana', in *Storia della lingua italiana*, III: *Le altre lingue*, ed. by Luca Serianni and Pietro Trifone (Turin: Einaudi, 1994), pp. 294–329
——, *Il Trecento toscano: La lingua di Dante, Petrarca e Boccaccio*, Storia della lingua italiana (Bologna: Il Mulino, 2003)
Maraschio, Nicoletta, and Tina Matarrese, 'The Role of Literature in Language Standardization', in *The Cambridge Handbook of Language Standardization* ed. by Wendy Ayres-Bennett and John Bellamy (Cambridge: Cambridge University Press, 2021), pp. 313–46
Marazzini, Claudio, *La Lingua italiana: Profilo storico* (Bologna: Il Mulino, 1994)
Mattheier, Klaus J., 'Is There a European Language History?', *Multilingua: Journal of Cross-Cultural and Interlanguage Communication*, 29 (2010), 353–60
Miesse, Hélène, and Gianluca Valenti, eds, *'Modello, regola, ordine': Parcours normatifs dans l'Italie du Cinquecento* (Rennes: Presses universitaires de Rennes, 2018)
Migliorini, Bruno, *Storia della lingua italiana* (Florence: Sansoni, 1960)
Milroy, James, 'Language Ideologies and the Consequences of Standardization', *Journal of Sociolinguistics*, 5.4 (2001), 530–55
Milroy, James, and Lesley Milroy, *Authority in Language: Investigating Language Prescription and Standardisation* (London: Routledge, 1991)
Morgana, Silvia, *Capitoli di storia linguistica italiana* (Milan: LED, 2003)
Nencioni, Giovanni, 'Fra grammatica e retorica: Un caso di polimorfia della lingua letteraria dal secolo XIII al XVI', *Atti e memorie dell'Accademia toscana di scienze e lettere 'La Colombaria'*, 18 (1953), 213–59
Nevalainen, Terttu, 'What Are Historical Sociolinguistics?', *Journal of Historical Sociolinguistics*, 1.2 (2015), 243–69
OVI = *Opera del Vocabolario Italiano: Corpus OVI dell'Italiano antico*, <http://gattoweb.ovi.cnr.it>
Padley, G. Arthur, *Grammatical Theory in Western Europe, 1500–1700: Trends in Vernacular Grammar II* (Cambridge: Cambridge University Press, 1988)
Patota, Giuseppe, *La Quarta Corona: Pietro Bembo e la codificazione dell'italiano scritto* (Bologna: Il Mulino, 2017)
Piattoli, Renato, 'Lettere di Piero Benintendi mercante del Trecento (1392–1409)', *Atti della Società Ligure di Storia Patria*, 60.1 (1932), 1–174
Pirrelli, Vito, and Marco Battista, 'The Paradigmatic Dimension of Stem Allomorphy in Italian Verb Inflection', *Rivista di Linguistica*, 12.2 (2000), 307–80
Pountain, Christopher J., 'Standardization', in *The Oxford Guide to the Romance Languages*, ed. by Adam Ledgeway and Martin Maiden (Oxford: Oxford University Press, 2016), pp. 634–43

Rohlfs, Gerhard, *Morfologia*, vol. II of *Grammatica storica della lingua italiana e dei suoi dialetti* (Turin: Einaudi, 1968)

Rossi, Leonardo, 'Fiorentino e italiano', in *La lingua nella Storia d'Italia*, ed. by Luca Serianni, 2nd edn (Rome: Società Dante Alighieri; Milan: Libri Scheiwiller, 2002), pp. 70–90

Schiaffini, Alfredo, 'Influssi dei dialetti centro-settentrionali sul toscano e sulla lingua letteraria. II. L'imperfetto e condizionale in *-ia*', *L'Italia dialettale*, 5 (1929), 1–31

Schulte, Kim, 'Romance in Contact with Romance', in *Manual of Romance Sociolinguistics*, ed. by Wendy Ayres-Bennett and Janice Carruthers (Berlin: De Gruyter, 2018), pp. 595–626

Serianni, Luca, ed., *La lingua nella Storia d'Italia*, 2nd edn (Rome: Società Dante Alighieri; Milan: Libri Scheiwiller, 2002)

———, 'Ricerche sul dialetto aretino nei secoli XIII e XIV', *Studi di filologia italiana*, 30 (1972), 59–191

———, *Testi pratesi della fine del Dugento e dei primi del Trecento* (Florence: L'Accademia della Crusca, 1977)

Sornicola, Rosanna, 'A Diachronic Perspective on Polymorphism, Overabundance, and Polyfunctionalism', in *Periphrasis and Inflexion in Diachrony: A View from Romance*, ed. by Adam Ledgeway, John Charles Smith, and Nigel Vincent (Oxford: Oxford University Press, 2022), pp. 305–32

Stella, Angelo, 'Liguria', in *Storia della lingua italiana*, III: *Le altre lingue*, ed. by Luca Serianni and Paolo Trifone (Turin: Einaudi, 1994), pp. 105–53

Tamburelli, Marco, 'Uncovering the "Hidden" Multilingualism of Europe: An Italian Case Study', *Journal of Multilingual and Multicultural Development*, 35 (2014), 252–70

Tesi, Riccardo, *Storia dell'italiano: La lingua moderna e contemporanea* (Bologna: Zanichelli, 2005)

Thornton, Anna M., 'Overabundance in Italian Verb Morphology and its Interactions with Other Non-canonical Phenomena', in *Irregularity in Morphology (and Beyond)*, ed. by Thomas Stolz, Hitomi Otsuka, Aina Urdze, and Johan Van der Auwera (Berlin: Akademie Verlak, 2012), pp. 251–70

———, 'Overabundance (Multiple Forms Realizing the Same Cell): A Non-canonical Phenomenon in Italian Verb Morphology', in *Morphological Autonomy: Perspectives from Romance Inflectional Morphology*, ed. by Martin Maiden, John Charles Smith, Maria Goldbach, and Marc-Olivier Hinzelin (Oxford: Oxford University Press, 2011), pp. 358–81

———, 'Reduction and Maintenance of Overabundance: A Case Study on Italian Verb Paradigms', *Word Structure*, 5.2 (2012), 183–207

Tomasin, Lorenzo, 'Dante e l'idea di lingua italiana', in *Dante e la lingua italiana*, ed. by Mirko Tavoni, Letture classensi, 41 (Ravenna: Longo Editore, 2013), pp. 29–46

———, 'Sul contatto linguistico nella Romània medievale: Le lettere di Bartolo de Cavalli alias Bartol de Savalls. Prima parte', *Estudis Romànics*, 41 (2019), 267–90

———, 'Testi in italiano antico di scriventi provenzali e catalani (secoli xiv–xv)', *Annali della Scuola Normale Superiore di Pisa: Classe di Lettere e Filosofia*, 9.2 (2017), 391–422

———, 'Urban Multilingualism: The Languages of Non-Venetians in Venice during the Middle Ages', in *Mittelalterliche Stadtsprachen*, ed. by Maria Selig and Susanne Ehrich (Regensburg: Schnell & Steiner, 2016), pp. 61–73

Trolli, Domizia, 'La lingua di Giovanni Morelli', *Studi di grammatica italiana*, 2 (1972), 51–153

Vanvolsem, Serge, 'La standardisation en italien: Les grammairiens et le problème de la norme au xvie siècle', in *The Dawn of the Written Vernacular in Western Europe* ed. by Michèle Goyens and Werner Verbeke (Leuven: Leuven University Press, 2003), pp. 323–36

Vincent, Nigel, 'Compositionality and Change in Conditionals and Counterfactuals in Romance', in *The Boundaries of Pure Morphology: Diachronic and Synchronic Perspectives*, ed. by Silvio Cruschina, Martin Maiden, and John Charles Smith (Oxford: Oxford University Press, 2013), pp. 117–37

Webb, Heather, 'Language', in *The Oxford Handbook of Dante* ed. by Manuele Gragnolati, Elena Lombardi, and Francesca Southerden (Oxford: Oxford University Press, 2021), pp. 464–79

Weinapple, Fiorenza, 'La clisi nel linguaggio comico del Cinquecento', *Studi di grammatica italiana*, 12 (1983), 5–106

Wright, Laura, ed., *The Multilingual Origins of Standard English* (Berlin: De Gruyter, 2020)

RONNIE FERGUSON

Medieval and Renaissance Venice

Language Contact at Home and Abroad

Introduction

The aim of the present essay is to document and evaluate the remarkable range of language-contact dynamics — internal and external — of which Venice was the focal point in the Middle Ages and Renaissance.[1] It begins by exploring the contact interactions which profoundly shaped Early Venetian itself,[2] both structurally and lexically, in this period. These are the complex long-term processes of koineization that arguably forged a lagoon language with high-register stability by the 1300s; the multiple contact pressure points from the Italian mainland post-1300 that influenced the subsequent selection of competing residual variants from within the new system; and the idiosyncratic configuration of adstratum vocabulary absorbed into the Venetian lexicon from Germanic, Byzantine, Islamic, and French sources. The survey goes on to touch on aspects of Venetian language impact beyond the lagoon in the

---

[1] The foundational study on contact linguistics is Weinreich, *Languages in Contact*, and its most influential theoretical elaboration is Thomason and Kaufman, *Language Contact, Creolization, and Genetic Linguistics*. Romance contact is surveyed in Sala, 'Contact and Borrowing'. For an Italian focus, see Lepschy and Tosi, eds, *Rethinking Languages in Contact*, particularly Vincent, 'Languages in Contact in Medieval Italy'.

[2] The chronology of Venetian employed in the present essay is Early Venetian (EV) *c.* 1200–*c.* 1500, Middle Venetian (MidV) *c.* 1500–*c.* 1800, Modern Venetian (ModV) *c.* 1800–*c.* 1950, Contemporary Venetian (CV) *c.* 1950–the present. Each boundary marks a watershed moment where societal or cultural events with linguistic repercussions altered the status and/or structure of Venetian. The year 1200 conventionally represents the appearance of *venexian* in written texts. Around 1500 Tuscan was achieving consensus status among Italy's elites and interfering with unmarked written Venetian. The grammatical codification of Tuscan → Italian that introduced writing-speech bilingualism to Venice was also imminent at that point.

Ronnie Ferguson (rgf@st-andrews.ac.uk) is Emeritus Professor of Italian at the University of St Andrews, Cavaliere della Stella d'Italia, and Fellow of the Ateneo Veneto and of the Accademia Galileiana. His research interests include the language and culture of Venice, historical linguistics, medieval epigraphy, and Renaissance comedy.

Languages and Cross-Cultural Exchanges in Renaissance Italy, ed. by Alessandra Petrocchi and Joshua Brown, LMEMS 30 (Turnhout: Brepols, 2023), pp. 121–156

long Renaissance, when the city exercised pervasive superstratum contact pressure on the north-eastern mainland of Italy and along the eastern Adriatic, while at the same time transmitting to Italian a body of words unmatched by any other dialect of Italy. It considers in particular the extent and nature of Venice's lexical exports to Early Modern English, an instance of significant but little-appreciated Venetian adstratum influence. Our investigation of Venice as a nexus of long-term contact dynamics has intertwined historical, cultural, and linguistic implications which are not negligible.[3] *Venexian* is arguably the most important European language never to have undergone formal codification and standardization. This surprising absence explains both the variant features and structural drift, within a complex diasystem, disclosed by the historical evidence. The rich documentation of written Venetian from *c.* 1250 onwards, which has received intense philological attention in recent times,[4] therefore provides the linguist and historian with exceptional insights into long-term processes of language contact and language change which may remain hidden or obscured in spoken dialects, on the one hand, and in standard languages on the other.[5]

Venice in 1500 was at the pinnacle of its power and prestige. Politically, commercially, and territorially it was a unique city state in the European context, with a singular geography and topography that were already legendary. It was an outlier, too, in terms of settlement and language origins. The lagoon metropolis was the only major Italian centre without a direct Roman urban past. It had its ultimate demographic and linguistic roots in intersecting population movements from the *terraferma*, and over more than half a millennium had refashioned these diverse migratory currents into a new and hybrid stability. Culturally too it was highly distinctive. With a mainland and overseas empire, ascendancy over the shipping lanes in the eastern Mediterranean, consistent interchange with the Islamic world — latterly with the Mamluk and Ottoman sultanates — and a past as dominion then dominator of Byzantium it had evolved sui generis cultural traditions combining Western and Eastern influence. This was at its most visible in the city's palimpsestic architecture, integrating Byzantine, Moorish, Gothic, and Renaissance elements, which reached its syncretic apotheosis on St Mark's Basilica. It was inevitable that Venetian, the polity's new and distinctive Italo-Romance vernacular, should

---

3   On the interwoven nature of language and culture, see Terracini, *Lingua libera e libertà linguistica*, pp. 124–65. On the importance of Venetian for historical studies, see Ferguson, 'Between the Lines'.

4   Bibliographies of studies of Venetian are in Holtus and Metzeltin, 'I dialetti veneti'; Zamboni, 'Venezien/Veneto'; Stussi, 'La lingua'; Eufe, *'Sta lengua ha un privilegio tanto grando'*; Ferguson, 'Alle origini del veneziano'; Ferguson, *A Linguistic History of Venice*; Ferguson, *Saggi di lingua e cultura veneta*; and, more recently, the *VEV*, pp. 13–29. Bibliographical details on the EV textual tradition are in Ferguson, 'La formazione del veneziano'.

5   On processes of long-term change in Venetian, see Ferguson, 'Dinamiche contrastive'.

also have been strongly inflected by such eclecticism in its grammar and vocabulary. The early written evidence reveals a dialect of Latin, of the Veneto type, exhibiting both Western and Eastern Romance features, with a striking level of structural variability compared to other Italo-Romance varieties, including those from the Veneto mainland, and a lexis enriched by multiple external contact sources.

In 1500 language contact remained a lived reality in a capital of far-flung business interests that was at one and the same time a teeming cosmopolitan emporium — with settled Tuscan, Lombard, German, Albanian, Dalmatian, Greek, and Armenian communities — and an ongoing absorber of immigration from its own hinterland.[6] We know for certain that Venetian-German language teaching was offered near the Rialto in the early fifteenth century. The bilingual glossaries and dialogues it employed circulated widely in manuscript throughout the century, suggesting long-term demand for tuition.[7] A school that taught reading and writing in Arabic ('una scola che insegna lezer e scriver in moresco') would soon operate in the great retail artery of the *Marzaria*.[8] As the main port of embarkation and organizer of logistics for the lucrative pilgrimage traffic to the Holy Land the city had long experienced and managed intense language contact with travellers from all over Europe,[9] providing pilgrims with interpreter-guides known as *tolomazi*.[10] Multilingualism, interpreting, and translating went hand in hand not only with commercial and treaty negotiations and diplomatic exchange but also

---

6 See Ravid, 'Venice and its Minorities'.

7 Rossebastiano Bart, *I 'Dialoghi' di Giorgio da Norimberga*; Rossebastiano Bart, *Vocabolari veneto-tedeschi*. For context and detail, see Braunstein, *Les Allemands à Venise*, pp. 460–86.

8 Reported as an eye-witness by Marin Sanudo in 1517. Sanuto, *I diarii*, XXV, col. 20. One suspects, though, that this was indeed, as Sanudo put it, 'cossa notanda', for in 1511 the Venetian merchant Martin Merlini complained of being unable to find Turkish or Arabic teaching in the city for his nephew who was due to go overseas. Dalla Santa, 'Commerci', p. 1571, n. 1. It seems likely that Venetians gained their proficiency in Eastern languages essentially in situ. The Arabic of Marco Zorzi, the commercial agent in Alexandria of the entrepreneur Michiel Foscari, was certainly good enough for him to translate and forward to Foscari in Venice in 1503 a Mamluk memorandum on Asian spices and prices. ASV, Procuratori di S. Marco, *Misti*, busta 42, *fasc.* 23. In Venice itself translating (*tra(n)slatar*) or interpreting (*interpretar*) for diplomatic exchange in Arabic, French, German, Greek, Spanish, and Turkish were carried out ad hoc by chancery secretaries with relevant expertise, although a specific expert in Turkish languages and Greek, Hironimo Zivran, was appointed in 1515. ASV, Consiglio dei Dieci, *Misti*, reg. 30, fol. 7ᵛ.

9 Jacoby, 'Pèlerinage médiéval'.

10 The earliest reference to them is to a Simeon *teutonicum tolomacium* in an appeal of 1329 from the merchant consuls of the Fontego dei Todeschi to the Venetian authorities (Simonsfeld, *Der Fondaco dei Tedeschi*, I, p. 29). The first vernacular attestation (*tholomazi*), in ASV, Ufficiali al Cattaver, busta 2, reg. IV, fol. 99, is from 1442. The term appears to be adapted from Middle High German *tolmetsche* 'interpreter', itself via south-east European languages. The distribution and chronology of European attestations coincides with Ottoman expansion, and the original etymon is plausibly northern Turkish *tilmaç* 'interpreter'. The early history of the Venetian forms is in Lepschy, 'Tholomacii non Tholomarii'.

with the administration of Venice's overseas outposts and colonies.[11] It is little wonder that curiosity and familiarity with the speech of its neighbours and minorities surfaced on stage in the lively strand of multilingual comedy that characterized Venice's theatre in the sixteenth century.[12]

With a beguiling visual identity — increasingly sublimated by its elites as the embodiment of Venetian exceptionalism — the city compelled contemporary visitors to admiration. Cartographic representations rapidly disseminated the fascinating otherness of the city in print, materially reinforcing its idealized conception of itself as the enduring seat of republican stability, justice, and freedom and as an entity, unlike any other, suspended between land and sea. Outstanding among these figurations with international resonance was Jacopo de' Barbari's view of 1500. Combining realism and subtle symbolism the huge perspective plan poised the meticulously observed offshore conurbation, simultaneously open and enclosed, on an axis between Alps and Adriatic. It thus created an iconic image of Venice at a pivotal moment in its history that was to become an indispensable reference point for subsequent depictions of the Serenissima.[13] The most neglected, but not the least important, aspect of de' Barbari's woodcut cityscape is its discreet inked captioning of buildings, landmarks, and islands: occasionally in Latin but mainly in fully realized Venetian.[14] Indeed, the joint prestige of Venice and Venetian at this point was such that Albrecht Dürer, during his second extended stay in the city (1505–1507), interspersed his letters in Nuremburg German to his patron Willibald Pirckheimer with Venetianisms as well as with novel artistic coinages influenced by *venexian*.[15] Only recently identified and studied, these adapted contact borrowings are significant both culturally and linguistically.[16]

As is well known, management from above of the city's self-image was recalibrated in the later fifteenth and early sixteenth centuries. This reflected a change of outlook in the direction of what can conveniently be called Renaissance

---

11 On Venetian-Greek language interaction in colonial Greece and Byzantium, see Thiriet, *La Romanie vénitienne*, pp. 217–19; Jacoby, 'Multilingualism'. On Greek as the language of diplomatic exchange between Venice and the Ottomans in our period, see Vatin, 'L'emploi du grec comme langue diplomatique'. On official Venetian translations of diplomatic correspondence in Arabic, see Wansbrough, 'A Mamluk Letter'. The commonest EV term for 'interpreter, translator' was *turziman, turciman, truciman*, or *truziman* 'truchman' < Ar. *turğumān* 'interpreter'. The origins of this cluster of borrowings, including *tolomazi*, point to the pioneering role of Islamic states in the practice of interpreting. Venetian merchants made use, notably, of the interpreting service (EV *truzimanaria, turcimanaria, turzimanaria*) provided by the Mamluk *dīwāns* in Egypt and Syria (Wansbrough, 'Venice and Florence').

12 Andrews, *Scripts and Scenarios*, pp. 144–54.

13 See Schulz, 'Jacopo de' Barbari's View of Venice'.

14 Ferguson, *Venetian Inscriptions*, inscriptions 82–91.

15 *Venexian* (Italian, *veneziano*) is historically the commonest native spelling of Venetian, with the variants *venezian* and *venes(s)ian*. It is currently pronounced [veneˈsjaŋ]. The city has called itself *Venexia* (with early variants *Veniexia, Ven(i)esia*, and *Veniesa*) since the later medieval period, the current pronunciation being [veˈnɛsja]. *Venexia* is a reflex of Latin VENETIA.

16 See Ferguson, 'Dinamiche contrastive', pp. 213–14 n. 39; Ashcroft, 'Albrecht Dürers *Venexian*'.

norms. Venice belatedly began to fall into line with the classicizing trends of humanism already overwhelmingly adopted by the intellectual and ruling classes elsewhere in Italy, just as its own aristocracy increasingly preferred land investment to seaborne entrepreneurship. In so doing it arguably turned away from the fluid, eclectic vernacular traditions which for centuries had shaped its art, architecture, and language. A sequence of traumatic events hastened the shift towards mainland Italy of Venice's perspective. In quick succession around 1500 the city lost its near monopoly of the highly lucrative East–West spice trade, suffered a major banking collapse, relinquished to the Ottomans the key Ionian fortresses of Modon and Coron which it had held for three centuries, and faced an existential threat to its territorial integrity and very existence in the War of the League of Cambrai (1509–1517).

In the wake of these setbacks, during the more settled climate of the early-to-mid 1520s, the city sealed its recovery with a conclusive Renaissance paradigm shift. Two dates are particularly significant: the first political, the second linguistic. In 1523 Andrea Gritti, a hero of the recent war, was elected doge. During his autocratic and culturally ambitious reign the classical tendencies present in Venice since the mid-fifteenth century were definitively entrenched. This was most visible in public architecture, with the medieval St Mark's Square and Rialto as depicted by de' Barbari radically reshaped. The city no longer aspired to be the heir to Constantinople, as it had in the great period of its medieval ascendancy when it was the Comun de Ven(i)exia. The Serenissima Signoria de Venetia wished instead to be the new Rome. In 1525 Pietro Bembo's *Prose della volgar lingua* was published in the city.[17] The appearance of this influential volume emblematically marked the moment when the archaizing Trecento variety of Tuscan modelled on Petrarch and Boccaccio in particular, which the Venetian cardinal canonized, became the basis of the written 'Italian' rapidly adopted by the educated throughout the peninsula, including Venice. In the fourteenth and fifteenth centuries the city's native Venetian had increasingly penetrated written documentation of all types — legal, administrative, statutory, historical, and epigraphic — albeit with an increasing Tuscan patina from the later Quattrocento. After the decisive cultural turn it was rapidly reduced in status to a 'dialect', in writing at least.[18] However, it would remain until the modern period the spoken idiom of the

---

17 Bembo, *Prose*.
18 The term 'dialect' (*dialetto*) first appeared in Italy in the mid-1540s, and from Italian spread to other European languages, occurring in French in 1550 and English in 1579. It was calqued, by scholars interested in the related topical issues of language codification and divergent varieties within a national territory, on the Greek διάλεκτος 'discourse, conversation, language, language of a country or district', especially applied to regional variations in Classical Greek. On the concept and evolution of 'dialect' in the Renaissance, see Alinei, 'Dialetto'; Trovato, '"Dialetto" e sinonimi'. On its application to Venice/Venetian, see Ferguson, 'Lo status storico del veneziano'. On Venice's unusual indifference to language policy and on its written-spoken bilingualism post-1500, see Ferguson, *A Linguistic History of Venice*, pp. 209–18.

city and its overseas possessions at all levels of society and continue to exert, via cultural-cum-language contact, its prestige influence in Italy and abroad.

Contact Origins of Venetian: The Formation of a Stable Lagoon Koine

The future city of Venice was born around the ninth century as a coalescence of small communities on a series of tidal islands and mudflats in the middle of a lagoon in the upper Adriatic. Lying between the mouths of the Rivers Adige and Piave, the present lagoon within which the city stands is only the central remnant of a much more extensive lagunar system which in Late Antiquity stretched some one hundred kilometres along the Adriatic shoreline, from the Po delta to beyond Grado. Traffic transited in Late Antiquity through its sheltered waters and, with hunting, fishing, and salt-panning, provided a living for a modest population. Substantial settlement of the lagoons is broadly attributable to the traumatic historical events which drove populations from the profoundly Romanized province of Venetia et Histria (the Augustinian X Regio) in north-eastern Italy to the refuge of their port outlets on the islands and sandspits off the coast (Figure 4.1). Urban and rural migration from the arc of Roman towns in the region in the fifth and, especially, the sixth and seventh centuries was triggered by successive waves of foreign incursion: by Huns, Ostrogoths, and Longobards. In particular, the Longobard invasion and occupation of Italy, starting in 568 provoked the permanent coastward evacuation of the main cities from the early seventh century onwards, and led to the formation of a new entity: a Venetian lagunar confederation, the *ducatus venetus* (→ Dogado) owing allegiance to Byzantium. This duchy gradually asserted its economic and political autonomy from the Eastern Empire. After a series of internal power struggles linked to factions favouring either the Frankish Empire or Byzantium, and its own conquest of the waters of the Gulf of Venice, and following the permanent transfer of the lagoon capital to the central archipelago of Rivus altus → Rivoalto → Riolto/Rialto, the embryonic Venice emerged. Known from *c.* 900 as the Civitas rivoalti, the statelet grew in power and in its self-awareness of being a new, maritime, Venetia: by the twelfth century it was calling itself the Civitas or Commune Venetiarum/Veneciarum. As the island communities fused and grew around the central archipelago, the city and its shortened name took final shape: Venetiae, Venetia, or Venecia in Latin, Ven(i)esia ~ Ven(i)exia in EV.[19]

The synergy of linguistics, philology, and history has in recent years clarified our understanding of how Venice and Venetian were formed in tandem. This

---

19 On the origins of Venice, see Cessi, *Venezia ducale*; Carile and Fedalto, *Le origini di Venezia*; Dorigo, *Venezia origini*. On lagoon settlement, see Forlati Tamaro and others, eds, *Da Aquileia a Venezia*.

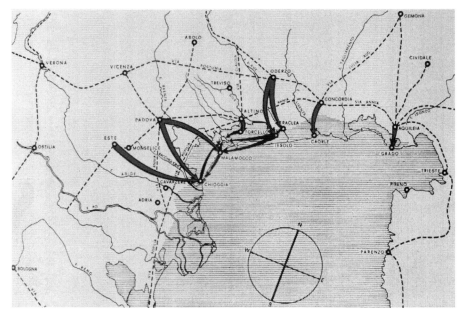

Figure 4.1. Medieval population movements to, and within, the lagoons of north-eastern Italy. Copyright R. Ferguson.

research advance has confirmed that the city had language contact inscribed in its DNA. Our knowledge of the population movements which eventually generated a major urban settlement in the lagoon had previously relied on the patriotic, apparently semi-legendary, narratives of the Venetian medieval and Renaissance chronicle tradition, supplemented by scanty archaeological evidence. The tools of historical linguistics and dialectology — and particularly our increased grasp of the processes of koineization which lead to stable new language varieties in the wake of the convergence of different population streams speaking related dialects — have sharpened our perceptions of these demographics. Alongside theoretical work on koine formation,[20] the research foundation for my own work on EV as a koine was laid by the concrete case-studies of the formation of Greek, Spanish, and Parisian French.[21] These demonstrated how the detailed scrutiny of language patterns over time can be used to illuminate large-scale historical shifts. The starting point for applying such lessons to Venice was to employ language data in order to put to the test existing theories about the formation of Venice and about its likely

---

20 Trudgill, *Dialects in Contact*; Siegel, 'Dialect Contact and Koineization'; Kerswill, 'Koineization and Accommodation'.
21 Bubenik, 'Dialect Contact and Koineization'; Penny, *Variation and Change in Spanish*; Lodge, 'Convergence and Divergence'.

demographic origins. The process involved confronting and comprehending the linguistic unevenness of the earliest Venetian textual evidence compared to the linguistically much more stable contemporaneous documents in other Italian vernaculars. This surprising internal variability of EV was imputed, traditionally, to factors such as multiple scribal origins, although some studies had suggested that the geographical provenance of early lagoon settlers might be involved.[22] The conceptual parameters of koine studies, applied to databases extracted from philologically accurate editions of early texts from Venice and from strategic Veneto mainland centres, have allowed the isolation and chronological comparison across textual areas of key language marker-traits. From this data it has been possible to marry language with history in order to evaluate more accurately the relative weight of settler movement from the north-eastern (preponderant) and central-southern Veneto in the populating of the Rialto nucleus. Simultaneously, it has been possible to clarify the processes of community and identity formation in Venice from 1000 to 1350, by which time Venice's informal language norms were largely stabilized.[23]

The contact cross-currents sketched in above are bound to have had profound linguistic consequences. A probably modest indigenous population and new relatively autonomous communities of Veneto migrants from various parts of the mainland — followed by subsequent waves of migration from both north and south within the lagoon — interacted gradually, in an initial phase, then rapidly merged. Such a fluid situation is bound to have favoured complex processes of koineization between speakers of closely related but not identical dialects: first at the micro-level then at the macro-level. Consequently, it is a persuasive hypothesis, backed up by considerable concrete evidence, that the disconcerting variability endemic in the phonology and morphology of Venetian vernacular writing up to at least 1300 reflects an ongoing koineization process at the macro-level, in the very period when the urban nuclei of Venice were definitively coalescing. If this were indeed the case, one would expect to find evidence in higher-register texts from the fourteenth and fifteenth centuries of a linguistic situation stabilized by acts of accommodation, with new supra-local norms. One should anticipate being able to localize elements in the new koine directly connectable to the north-eastern and south-western contributory streams, as well as interdialect forms originally present in neither. It would not be surprising to detect in the lower-register writing of this subsequent period evidence of stratification in *venexian*, with structures from the original melting pot reallocated diastratically and/or diatopically.

This is precisely what is observable in the documentation. Two striking interdialect phenomena, which eventually imposed themselves in higher-register

---

22 Notably Tuttle, 'Profilo linguistico del Veneto'.
23 Ferguson, *A Linguistic History of Venice*, pp. 161–91, and, on the formation and consolidation of the city's intertwined demography/topography, Crouzet-Pavan, *Le Moyen Âge de Venise*.

EV writing post-1300 after a long period of flux, are symptomatic: the elimination of metaphony in plural forms of nouns and adjectives and the intermediacy of apocope on final -*e* and -*o* on singular nouns and adjectives. Metaphony or anticipatory internal vowel raising (caused by final /i/) altered /e/ and /o/ to /i/ and /u/ respectively in north-eastern and south-western Veneto dialects, although with /o/ > /u/ less prevalent in the former. Typical were mainland forms such as sg. *pero*, pl. *piri* ('pear, pears'), sg. *mese*, pl. *misi* ('month, months') and sg. *bon*, pl. *buni* ('good') from PĬRUM, MENSEM, and BŎNUM respectively. These outcomes contrast with Venetian which, from the fourteenth century to the present, has simplified the pattern to *pero-peri*, *mese-mesi*, and *bon-boni*. Again, strong final-vowel retention on singular nouns and adjectives was the norm in south-western Veneto, with only a vowel (other than /a/) following the sonorant consonant /n/ eliminated — and even there not on geminate reflexes — while the north-east manifested final vowel apocope (other than on /a/) in almost all contexts. Venetian settled, instead, on a compromise system found nowhere on the mainland. On singular nouns and adjectives it deleted, and continues to delete, final /e/ and /o/ after the sonorants /n/ and /l/ on original paroxytones, but not on derivatives of original geminates, for example, *pan* 'bread' < PĀNEM, *san* 'healthy' < SĀNUM, *man* 'hand' < MĂNUS vs *ano* 'year' < ANNUM; *canal* 'canal' < CĂNĀLEM vs *cal(l)e* 'street' < CALLEM; *frutar(i)ol* 'fruiterer' < *FRUCTAREOLUM vs *cavalo* 'horse' < CĂBALLUM. Final /e/ is also deleted after the sonorant /r/, but again not on geminate reflexes or after -TR-, for example, *cuor* 'heart' < COREM (CL CŎR) vs *tore* 'tower' < TURREM and *mar* 'sea' < MĂRE vs *mare* 'mother' < MĀTREM. Final /o/ is, however, retained after /r/, for example, *caro* 'dear' < CĀRUM alongside *caro* 'cart' < CARRUM.

External Contact and its Words: Germanic, Greek, Islamic, and French Borrowings in Venetian up to c. 1525

The Venetian lexicon exhibits a high degree of distinctiveness within the northern Italian, Italo-Romance, and Romance contexts.[24] This specificity applies to the forms and semantics of its inherited Latin vocabulary. It is also true of its legacy of phonologically adapted loanwords characterized by an exceptional input of Byzantine Hellenisms, a conspicuous presence of Arabisms, a sizeable contribution of Gallicisms, and an unexpected stock

---

24 ModV forms are employed for headwords in bold in the present section. Here and elsewhere in the essay ModV spellings are derived for the most part from Boerio, *Dizionario del dialetto veneziano*. Etyma are based on my judgement of the documentary evidence — including that of archival sources, the *OVI*, standard dialect dictionaries, and relevant national and regional linguistic atlases, particularly the *AIS* — evaluated against the etymologies proposed in the *DEI*, *DELI*, *GDLI*, *LEI*, *OED*, *REW*, *VEV*, in Prati, *Etimologie venete*, Marcato, *Ricerche etimologiche*, Sallach, *Studien*, and in studies cited by footnote.

of Germanisms.[25] Such a salient profile of borrowings was generated by the overlapping contact factors — geographical, historical, commercial, and cultural — which moulded the city and its language.

It is received wisdom that Venice was shielded from the important body of superstratum Germanisms in Italo-Romance, especially from Longobardic.[26] This is not borne out by the lexical evidence.[27] It is certainly true that a few common Germanic borrowings established on the Veneto mainland only partly crossed the lagoon to Venice or failed to penetrate at all. The Veneto names for 'starling' (*striolo, storlo, storlin* < Longob. diminutive *storilo from Germ. **stor-* 'starling'), concentrated in the central-southern area of the region,[28] did not replace in Venice the traditional *storno* (< STŬRNUM) and its diminutive *stornelo*. The widespread Veneto term *magon* 'stomach' < Germ. **mag-* never ousted *stomego* < STŎMĂCHUM, tending instead to be confined in EV to the specialized sense of bird's gizzard. A mainland Germanism that partially penetrated the lagoon barrier only to retreat later is EV/early MidV *sunda, sonda* 'slice', a noun derivative from Germ. *sundar 'separate, apart, split'. However, these are exceptions. By and large Venice shares the Germanisms found on the Veneto mainland. Typical are a quartet of Longobardic craft terms shared by the *terraferma*, Venice, and Tuscany: *stanga* 'bar, pole' < *stanga 'bar', *spranga* 'wooden or metal door-bolt' (< *spanga 'rod' with intrusive /r/), *stringa* 'a lace for clothes or shoes' < *stringa 'line, cord, thread', and *(s)biaca* (~ EV *blac(h)a*) 'lead white' < *blaih 'bleached, pale'. A pair of Gothic craft borrowings are also characteristic: *strica* 'strip, stripe, streak' < *striks* 'line, stroke' and *fodra* (Tuscan/Italian *fodera*) 'lining' < *fodr* 'sheath'. Our examination of the demographic and linguistic evidence for how the city was populated and for how its Romance dialect emerged predicts the presence of such Germanic influence by contact that predated Venice. The population streams from the north-eastern and central-southern Veneto, where Gothic and especially Longobardic settlement had been considerable, were bound to carry a substantial body of assimilated Germanic loanwords to the evolving Venetian word-stock. The variegated nature of these words, going beyond military, legal, or prestige terms associated with the Germanic elites, suggests population intermingling at lower social levels, with varying degrees of bilingualism involved.

Within this indirect inheritance a number of loanwords linked to the Germanic way of life and experience are particularly interesting in terms of their subsequent semantic development in Venetian. *Albergo* < Goth. *haribergo

---

25 For a discussion of lexical loan mechanisms, see Minervini, 'Lexical Contact in the Mediterranean'.

26 See Pfister, 'Le superstrat germanique', pp. 69–70.

27 On Germanisms in the Italo-Romance dialects, see Gamillscheg, *Romania Germanica*; Rohlfs, *Germanisches Spracherbe in der Romania*; Arcamone, 'L'elemento germanico'; Morlicchio, *Lessico etimologico italiano: Germanismi*.

28 *AIS*, III, map 500 'Starling'.

'military shelter' could mean 'hostel, lodging(s), residence, quarters, shelter' or even 'storeroom' in the early Italo-Romance vernaculars, including Venetian. Only in Venice, though, did it take on the specialized sense of 'meeting room or hall of confraternities', those essential institutions in the social and religious fabric of the lagoon city in the Middle Ages and Renaissance. Similarly, Longob. *gastald 'administrator of royal property' became *gastaldo*, initially '(ducal) steward' but eventually the 'alderman of a Venetian guild or confraternity'. Longob. *balko 'beam' gave the augmentative *balcon* (~ EV *balchion*), meaning first 'ornate window, French window, shutter, shop front', then simply 'window' in Venice rather than 'balcony' (ModV *pozol* or *pergolo*).[29] Shared by Italian are the semantically amplified *guera* 'war' (EV *verra* ~ *guer(r)a*) < *werra from Germ. *werz- 'strife', *schinco* (Ital. *stinco*) 'shin' < Longob. *skinko 'tibia', and even, with the horse still present in medieval Venice, *stafa* 'stirrup' < Germ. *staf- 'bar, stave, support'. Unknown to Italian are Venetian *strucar* 'to squeeze, press' < Germ. *strūk- 'to stroke, rub', and the adjective *fiapo* 'limp' < Longob. *flap- 'flap, flop'. A number of names of birds reached Venice via Germanic contact in the northern Veneto, notably *finco* 'chaffinch' < Germ. *fink- 'finch' and *tacola* 'jackdaw' < Longob. *takhala, a diminutive of *takha 'jackdaw'. With them came *schito* 'bird dropping' and *schitar* 'to shit (of animals)' < Goth. *skeitan 'to shit(e)'. Among landscape features Longob. *melm- 'fine sand' (Goth. *malma* 'sand' is attested), the source of Ital. *melma* 'mud', developed a semantic twist in Venice with the dissimilated *velma* 'lagoon mud flat'.

In the wake of the ousting of the *regnum Longobardorum*, the last wave of Germanisms in Italy, from the late eighth to the tenth centuries, came from Frankish, a western Germanic language (or grouping of related varieties) that, like Longobardic, was never written down. In Venetian there are two sources of Frankish borrowings: direct contact between Venice and the transalpine aristocracy, officialdom, and ecclesiastical network of the Carolingian Italian kingdom, involving ownership, endowment and exchange, religious and business interests, and administrative and legal customs; and the influence of written texts emanating from northern then southern France. In the case of direct contact, Frankish words may possibly have been filtered (at least semantically) through early Gallo-Romance, although their phonology does not exclude oral exposure to Germanic forms themselves.[30] Otherwise they were Latinized. Frankish loanwords tend in Venetian towards the military/ judicial or agricultural spheres. Notable are **graspo** 'bunch (of grapes)', in full *graspo de ua*, a derivative of *graspa* 'stripped grape bunch' < Frank. *krappa

---

29 *Fenestra* (~ EV *fanestra*) is a more technical synonym. It was originally employed for a small, high barred window.
30 In this context it is worth remembering that alongside the Frankish officials and appointees from Francia, who were probably bilingual, there were native High-German speakers, especially of Alemannic. On the complex issue of the routes by which Frankish borrowings penetrated Italy, see Cella, *I gallicismi nei testi dell'italiano antico*, pp. 39–67.

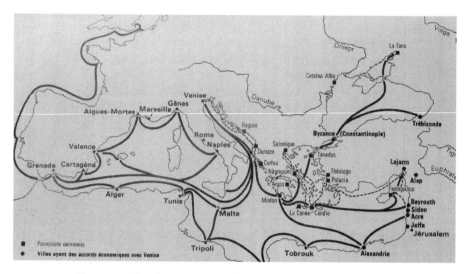

Figure 4.2. Venetian maritime trade routes. Copyright R. Ferguson.

'hook' x EV *raspo* 'bunch of grapes'; **guanto** ~ **vanto** 'glove' (EV/MidV *vanto*, first recorded in tenth-century sworn oaths within contracts between Frankish-controlled mainland Venetia and Venice) < Frank. **want* 'gauntlet'; **roba** 'stuff, possessions, goods' < Frank. **rauba* 'armour, jacket' then 'booty'; **robar** 'to rob, pillage, despoil' < Frank. **rauba* 'booty'; **spiron** ~ **speron** (~ EV *sporon*) 'spur' < Frank. **sporo* 'spur' (via Carolingian Lat. *sporonus*); **trapola** 'trap, snare' < Frank. **trappa* 'trap'; **vardar** 'to look at, guard from' < Frank. **wardon* 'to guard, keep watch, beware'. Important evidence of Frankish economic impact are **guadagnar** (EV/MidV *vadagnar*) 'to earn' < Frank. **waidanjan* 'to hunt, graze, forage' from **waid* 'meadow', and **sparagnar** 'to save, spare' < Germ. **spar-* 'save' x morphological influence of **waidanjan/ vadagnar*. The Germanic W was usually rendered as /v/ in EV/MidV, but Tuscan-influenced forms in /gw/ generally prevailed in ModV.

Venice was born under the aegis of the Byzantine Roman Empire with its Greek language and culture, surrounded by important Hellenic centres in the upper Adriatic: Grado, Istria, and Dalmatia to the north-east and Ravenna/Classe and the Pentapolis to the south-west. Until the end of the eleventh century the city remained nominally subject to Byzantium and underwent its influence governmentally, ecclesiastically, commercially, and artistically. The latter is most clearly visible in medieval church architecture and mosaics in Venice and in the iconography and style of its early painting. From *c*. 1100 Venice became a competitive and sometimes antagonistic ally, obtaining exceptional trading privileges and duty exemptions from the emperors in Constantinople in return for military support. Venetians were soon resident in numbers there and elsewhere in the empire. Inevitably, such direct contact at all levels with a mature and prestigious culture had a linguistic influence on an expanding Venice. Intense commerce with Byzantium and Byzantine centres in the Adriatic meant that the lexical impact of Greek was not restricted in this early period to high-register borrowing but penetrated, at a popular level, into many semantic areas, particularly the vocabulary of building, ships/boats, the sea, and nature. Its impact during the formative period of Venice was undoubtedly facilitated by the prestige and substantial structural stability of the Byzantine Greek diasystem in a context of Romance vernacular fragmentation and increasing distance from Latin. The contact and exchange that came with the Crusades and the partial annexation of Constantinople after 1204 led not only to the plunder of relics, *spolia*, and Greek works of art but to a further wave of loanwords. This lexical diffusion was bolstered by Venice's centuries-long occupation from 1200 onwards of major Greek-speaking colonies: in the Peloponnese, the Aegean, and Crete which it ruled for some four hundred and fifty years (Figure 4.2). The fall of the empire to the Turks in 1453 triggered a cultural and physical diaspora towards Venice, where a substantial Greek colony was established. Ecclesiastical words, but also plebeian and slang expressions, were consequently taken up into Venetian, and in the early sixteenth-century pidgin Greek was one of the favoured languages of Venice's characteristic polyglot theatre.

The selection of Hellenisms below, all still 'active' in the ModV period, illustrates the exceptionally eclectic Byzantine Greek penetration of the Venetian lexicon whose reach probably even moulded the unique EV ending in -*brio* of months from September to December on the basis of the equivalent Greek suffix in -βριος.[31] I omit some historically important but now obsolete loanwords such as *angaria* 'Greek-peasant corvée on Venetian estates' (and, by extension, 'vexation'), *arzipelago* 'the Aegean archipelago', *colfo* 'gulf (of Venice), Adriatic sea', and *(i)perpero* 'hyperper', the Byzantine gold coin.[32] Of the close to three hundred Byzantinisms in Venetian some, such as *liagò ~ diagò* and *sandalo*, have remained essentially confined to Venice. Others, like *musina*, have a wide circulation in the Veneto and probably radiated out from Venetian itself. Some, such as *anguria*, also penetrated early into the other Greek-influenced north-eastern regions of Italy and have become pan-northern and even Italian. Still others, such as *gondola* and *scampi*, have been spread much further afield by the prestige of Venetian. In many cases the semantics of the borrowed word have remained similar or identical to the source, but sometimes they show radical alteration.

---

31 This development was doubtless consolidated by Venetian administrative maintenance in the Middle Ages of the Byzantine indiction system for dating.
32 On Byzantine Greek loanwords in Venetian, see Cortelazzo, *L'influsso linguistico greco*; Kahane and Kahane, 'On Venetian Byzantinisms'; Ferguson, 'Passeri e rondini nel Veneto'; Ferguson, 'L'etimologia del tipo veneto *cocal* "gabbiano"'. On Greek borrowings in Italian varieties, see Crifò, 'Popular Lexicon of Greek Origin'. On the history of Western Byzantinisms, see Kahane and Kahane, 'Byzantium's Impact on the West'.

Ancona 'devotional image, altar painting' < Gk. εἰκών (or acc. εἰκώνα) 'sacred image'. ***Anguria*** (~ EV/MidV *languria*) 'watermelon' < ἀγγούρια, pl. of ἀγγούριον 'cucumber'. ***Armizar*** 'to moor' (with initial /a/ by analogy with *armiçar/armizar* 'to combat' and *armar* 'to arm, equip') < ὁρμίζω 'to moor'. ***Astese*** 'lobster' < ἀστακός 'lobster'. ***Baracocolo*** 'yellow plum [*Prunus domestica italica*]' and, residually, 'apricot [*Prunus armeniaca*]' < βερικόκκιον, a diminutive of βερίκοκκον 'apricot', ultimately from Lat. PRAECOQUUM 'ripe early'; in its original sense of 'apricot' *baracocolo* has been in competition since EV/MidV with *armelin* 'apricot' < *armeninum (pomum)* 'Armenian fruit';[33] the encroachment of *armelin*, which accelerated through ModV/CV, has led to *baracocolo* being largely reassigned. ***Basegò*** 'basil' (Ital. *basilico*) < βασιλικός 'royal'. ***Bombaso*** (EV *bombaxo, banbasi, banbaxio, banbacio, banbaso, bambasio, bambas(s)o*) 'cotton (wool)' < βαμβάκι(ον) 'cotton (wool)', a diminutive of βάμβαξ; the first syllable of *bombaso* was probably influenced by medieval Venetian Latin *bombix* 'cotton' and by the Venetian word series in *bomb-* 'swollen, puffed'. ***Botarga*** 'salted fish eggs' < αὐγοτάραχα 'salt egg' x EV *bota* 'barrel'; in EV/MidV often in pl. *botarg(h)e*; *bottarga*, the roe of tuna or grey mullet dried and cured in salt, was shipped to Venice from the Black Sea. ***Calafatar*** 'to caulk' < καλαφατίζω 'to caulk'. ***Catastico*** 'register of public and private possessions for tax purposes' < κατάστιχον 'business register', literally '(register) by line'. ***Celega*** ['seega] (EV *çelega*, MidV *zelega*) 'sparrow' (the passerine par excellence in the Veneto) < χελιδών 'swallow' (the archetypal small bird of the Greeks). ***Cisila*** [si'zia] (EV *çisila, çes(s)ila*, MidV *zisila, sizeta*) 'swallow' < κύψελος 'sand martin'. ***Cocal*** 'seagull' < (ὄρνις) κροκάλης 'shore-bird', with original reflex *crocal* → *cocal* by attraction to *coca* 'simpleton, gull'; first recorded in EV on a caption of Fra Mauro's *mappamundi* (*c.* 1448–1460); however, the detailed distribution of the original *crocal* type, along the arc of the upper Adriatic, suggests the tantalizing possibility that it reached those shores before the fall of Ravenna and the Exarchate in 751. ***Dragoman*** 'interpreter, translator' (often in the context of countries where Turkish, Arabic, or Persian were spoken) < δραγούμανος 'interpreter' from Ar. *turğumān* 'truchman'; *dragoman* came to the fore (superseding the previously dominant Arabic-derived *turciman* and variants) in early MidV in the context of Venice's intensified diplomatic relations with the Porte; the prominence of Greek interpreter-translators there from *c.* 1500, with diplomatic exchange between Venice and the Ottomans conducted via Greek, may not be unconnected to the shift.[34] ***Fanò*** 'lighthouse, ship's sternlight' < φανός 'torch, lantern'. ***Galia*** 'galley' < γαλία '(shark-shaped)

---

[33] This is confirmed by the German botanist Georg Matthias von Martens writing in 1844 (Martens, *Italien*, p. 215): 'heißt die Aprikose in Venedig Armellin und Baracòcolo'. *AIS*, VII, map 1276 'Apricot' has no data for Venice. It is not unlikely that the progress of *armelin* 'apricot' was in part impeded in EV/MidV by the presence of the homograph/homophone *armelin* 'ermine' < *armeninus (mus)* 'Armenian (rat)'. The generic Venetian term for 'plum' [*Prunus domestica*] is ModV *susin* (EV *susina*), lit. 'fruit from Susa in Persia'.

[34] For concrete examples, see Sanuto, *I diarii*, XIV, col. 411 and XXV, col. 52.

Byzantine war ship'. ***Ganassa*** 'jaw' < γνάδος 'jaw'. ***Gazeta*** 'small Venetian coin' then, by extension, the name given to Venetian 'gazettes' from the original price of these first periodical news sheets; a diminutive of early MidV *carzia* ~ *garzia* < Gk. χάρξια 'copper coin of low value'; Venice minted the *carzia* for circulation in Cyprus from 1515 onwards; already by 1518 it was called the *garzia* by Marin Sanudo.³⁵ ***Go*** 'goby, small lagoon fish [*Gobius niger*]' < γάδος 'type of fish'. ***Gondola*** 'gondola', possibly from κώντουρος or κονθούρα 'short-tailed (craft)'; the earliest unequivocal attestation of *gondola* in Venetian that I have located is from *c.* 1270.³⁶ ***Inghistera*** (~ EV/MidV *ingistera, angastera, angestera, anghestera, anghistera*) 'spherical-shaped bottle or flask with long narrow neck' < ἡ γαστέρα '(the) earthenware pot'. ***Liagò*** ~ ***diagò*** 'roofed sun terrace on Venetian house' < λιακός or λιακό 'balcony'. ***Magari*** 'if only!, God willing!, maybe' < μακάρι 'if only!'. ***Malvasia*** 'Malmsey, sweet Greek wine', from Malvasia, the vernacular Venetian name of the fortress of Μονεμβασία (colloquially Μονοβασία, rendered as *Monovasia* in the Venetian Latin documentation) on the southern tip of the Peloponnese; the internationally renowned wine was originally produced on its hinterland and shipped from its port; however, Venetian Crete would become from the fourteenth century its main production and export source; the once numerous *malvasie* 'wine shops serving Malmsey' have left a street-name imprint in Venice. ***Maroele*** 'haemorrhoids' < αἱμορροΐδες 'haemorrhoids'. ***Mastelo*** 'tub, pail' < μαστός 'breast-shaped cup'. ***Musina*** 'money-box, piggy-bank' < ἐλεημοσύνη 'alms'. ***Pampalugo*** 'simpleton' < πομφόλυγα 'bubble, bladder, windbag'. ***Pantegana*** 'rat' < (μυς) ποντικός '(mouse) from Pontus, rat' x EV *pantan(o)* 'bog, marsh' or *pança* 'belly'. ***Pestachio*** (EV/MidV *pistachio*) 'pistachio' < πιστάκιον 'pistachio'. ***Piron*** 'fork' < πειρούνι or πιρούνι 'fork', with back-formation giving a new singular in Venetian. ***Piter*** 'flower-pot' and, jocularly, 'chamber-pot' < πιθάριον 'small wine amphora'. ***Pitima*** 'poultice' and, metaphorically, 'pain-in-the-neck' < ἐπίθεμα 'poultice'. ***Proto*** 'craft master, foreman of works, building-project superintendent' < πρωτο(μάγιστρος) 'first (master)'. ***Sandolo*** 'light rowing boat of the Venetian lagoon' < σάνδαλις 'type of boat'. ***Scafa*** 'sink' < σκάφη 'trough, tub'. ***Scagio*** (EV/early MidV *scaio*) 'armpit' < μασχάλιον 'basket of palm leaves', a diminutive of μασχάλη 'palm branch, armpit'. ***Scampo*** 'scampi' < κάμπη 'caterpillar'; the original singular form is likely to have been *scampi*, with *scampo* created by back-formation; introduction of initial /s/ may have been influenced by *scampo* 'flight', *scampar* 'to flee'. ***Scuger*** [sku'ʤer] (EV/early MidV *cusl(i)er, cusulier*, MidV/early ModV *sculier*) 'spoon' < κοχλιάριον 'measure'. ***Seleno*** 'celery' < σέλινον 'celery'. ***Squero*** 'boatyard for repairing gondolas and small craft' < ἐσχάριον 'building yard'>. ***Zago*** (~ EV *çago*) 'deacon, altarboy' < διάκος 'deacon'.

---

35 Sanuto, *I diarii*, XXVI, col. 152.
36 *Remi de barcha et de gondola* 'boat and gondola oars'. In the *Racione de Alexandria*, an unpublished Venetian merchant handbook of Mediterranean weights and measures in BNM, MS It. XI 87 (= 7535), fol. 7ʳ.

The medieval Islamic world translated into Arabic the ancient Greek medical, scientific, and mathematical traditions, and continued them with its own empirical speculation. This fundamental corpus of knowledge was then recovered by the West through Latin translation. Like the other Romance languages, Venetian therefore absorbed Arabic terms which became Italian or European, such as *zero* 'zero', *zifra* 'cipher, code', *siropo* 'syrup', and *archimia* 'alchemy'. In addition, a dominant and sophisticated Islamic urban civilization directly impacted on a rapidly developing Europe between the ninth and sixteenth centuries. Contact influence stemmed, on the one hand, from the religious, political, and economic expansion of Islam: from Asia to Iberia, via the Middle East, Sicily, the Maghreb, and the Balearics. On the other hand, after the fiscal and territorial concessions accorded to Venice in Alexis I Comnenus's imperial chrysobull of 1082 the lagoon city extended its commercial activity in the eastern Mediterranean and beyond, and its major trading partners became Latin and Islamic as well as Greek. Venice rapidly built up a substantial presence of merchant communities and officials in Levantine ports, where it obtained a string of self-governing enclaves, and in its *funduqs* in Alexandria, Aleppo, and Damascus. The earliest dated vernacular documents in Venetian are, in fact, translated treaties with the Sultanate of Aleppo from the early thirteenth century,[37] although Venice's commercial contact with Syria and Egypt long predated them. Unsurprisingly, Venice is the only European city with an indigenous Arabic name, *al-Bunduqiyya*, linked to EV *venedego* < VENETICUS 'Venetian'.

The city's unrivalled business success and the stupendous wealth that it generated were founded, above all, on a Levant trade that only faltered after 1500 with the irruption of the Ottomans and the Portuguese discovery of the sea route to India. Venice became the great gateway between the Islamic and Christian worlds, transiting goods, fashions, artistic styles, and the prestigious or distinctive Islamic words connected with them. One need only peruse the fourteenth-century Venetian merchant manual, the *Zibaldone da Canal*, the correspondence of Venetian merchants in this period, and the treaties entered into with the Mamluks to gauge the lexical impact — on the nomenclature of merchandise, weights, measures, and officialdom — made on the Venetian trading community through to the Renaissance by daily contact with Levantine vocabulary.[38] Inevitably, many such terms were ephemeral while others are now obsolete. However, a substantial body survived into ModV — augmented during the Early Modern period by loans such as *bagigi* 'tiger nuts' [*Cyperus esculentus*] and now 'peanuts' (< Ar. *habb* 'berry' + *aziz* 'precious'), *papuzze* 'slippers', and *zensamin* 'jasmine' — with some of it passed by Venetian to other European languages including English. Below is a selection of loans, with commerce and its infrastructure strongly represented. Distinctively

---

37 Pozza, ed., *I trattati con Aleppo*.
38 Stussi, ed., *Zibaldone da Canal*; Morozzo della Rocca, ed., *Lettere di mercanti*.

Venetian in form, their semantics sometimes reveal interesting restriction/ extension of meaning.[39]

Amiragio ~ asmiragio (EV *armiraio, armiraglo, amiraio, amirallo*) 'naval commander, admiral, executive director of the Arsenal' and, following Arab Levant usage, 'lagoon-port chief customs officer/harbour master' < Ar. *amīr* 'commander'; the *-aio/-agio* suffix (*-aglus/-alius*) in the thirteenth-century Venetian Latin equivalents *amiraglus, ameraglus, armiralius*) may be a residue of genitive constructions with *amīr* followed by the Arabic article *al*, that is, *amir al-* 'commander of'. ***Arsenal*** (EV *arsenà, arsanà*, with the occasional hypercorrected forms *arsenada, arsanada*)[40] 'state shipyard of Venice' (in EV also 'private waterfront timber yard') < Ar. *dār aṣ-ṣinā'a* or *dār aṣ-ṣanā'a* 'house of work/skills, factory'; *arsenal* with final /l/ predominated from late EV until CV, by analogy with a Venetian word-series including *canal* and *feral* 'lantern'. ***Artichioco*** (Ital. *carciofo*) 'artichoke' < Ar. *al ḫaršūf* 'artichoke'. ***Azuro*** (~ EV *laçuro, lazuro, açuro*) 'blue' < Ar.-Pers. *lāžward* 'lapis lazuli, blue'; lapis lazuli (ModV *lapislazaro, lapislazolo*), a luxury ore, was imported to Venice in small quantities from Afghanistan via the Levant; it was ground and processed in Venice to make ultramarine blue (EV/MidV *azuro oltramarin*), the vibrant pigment made famous by Titian. ***Bazaro*** 'rough-and-ready calculation or agreement' (EV/MidV 'bazaar, agreement, deal') < Pers. *bāzār* 'market' via Turkish. ***Boraso*** (~ EV *boraxo, boraço*) 'borax' < Ar. *baurak, būrak* from Pers. *būrāh*, a native salt, imported via the Silk Road, used in Venetian glassmaking, goldsmithery, textile cleansing, and medicine. ***Cafetan*** (~ MidV *caftan*) 'caftan' < Turk. *kaftan* or Ar. *qaftān* 'caftan'. ***Caravana*** (~ EV *carevana*) 'company of merchants, travellers or pilgrims' and, by analogy, 'convoy of merchant ships' < Ar. *qayrawān* or *qayruwān* from Pers. *kārwān* 'group of travellers or camels'. ***Coton*** (~ EV/MidV *got(h)on*, often in pl. *got(h)oni*) 'cotton' < Ar. *quṭun* 'cotton'; the biannual convoy, the *muda de/di gotoni de Soria*, transported cargoes of cotton to Venice from Syria in licensed or regulated cogs. ***Cremese*** (EV *cremexe*) or ***cremesin*** (EV *cremexin*) 'crimson' < Ar. *qirmizī* 'crimson' from *qirmiz*, the female kermes beetle which provided the costly crimson dyestuff that from the fifteenth century was crucial to luxury silk production, including velvet and brocade, in Venice. ***Doana*** 'customs (house)' < Ar. *dīwān* 'book for registering goods in transit' then 'customs house'. ***Dulipan*** (~ MidV *tulipan*) 'turban', and later, 'tulip' < Turk./Pers. *dul(i)band* 'turban'. ***Fontego*** (Ital. *fondaco*) 'trading complex with warehousing and lodgings, originally in the Arab Levant' < Ar. *funduq* 'warehouse, merchant quarters, inn, hotel', itself from Gk. πάνδοκος

---

39 On Arabisms in Venetian and other Italo-Romance dialects, see Cortelazzo, 'Arabismi di Pisa e arabismi di Venezia'; Pellegrini, *Gli arabismi nelle lingue neolatine*; Mancini, 'Voci orientali'; Schweickard, 'Italian and Arabic'.

40 *Arzanà*, familiarized by Dante (*Inferno* XXI, 7) in his vivid description of the world's first assembly-line shipyard, is not recorded in EV.

'lodging, hostel, inn'; the Venetians partly mirrored the *funduq* formula in the Fontego dei Todeschi; *fontego*, with *doana* and *zeca*, is, unsurprisingly, one of the earliest Arabisms recorded in Venetian. **Limon** [i'moŋ] 'lemon' < Ar. *leimūn* or Pers. *līmū(n)*. **Magazen** (EV *magaçen*) 'warehouse, storeroom, cellar' < Ar. *maḫāzin* 'depots'. **Marzapan** [marsa'paŋ] 'marzipan' < Ar. *marṭabān* 'porcelain pot from the city of Mataban in the Bay of Bengal'; by metonymy the name of the pot (and, subsequently, of wooden containers) for the almond and sugar paste was applied to marzipan itself x *pan* 'bread'; the earliest Venetian vernacular attestation is from *c.* 1483 (3 *marzapani* '3 marchpanes'),[41] while the subsequent records suggest that marzipan cake rapidly became Venice's favourite sweetmeat. **Naranza** (EV *narança*) 'orange' < Ar.-Pers. *nārang* 'bitter orange'. **Recamar** 'to embroider' < Ar. *raqama* 'to embroider' from *raqm* 'drawing, sign, embroidery', with *ra-* → *re-* as if a prefix; it may have entered Venetian and other Italo-Romance dialects via Sicilian *raccamari*, propelled by the prestige of the school of embroidery, employing Islamic craftworkers, at the Norman court in Palermo. **Risego ~ risigo** 'risk' (and EV/MidV *risegar* or *tuor risego* 'to risk'), possibly from Ar. *rizq* 'payment in kind to occupying troops' via Gk. ριζικό 'fate, fortune'. **Senser ~ sanser** 'broker, go-between' < Ar. *simsār* 'go-between'; the state-appointed *sanseri* were the official middlemen for all legitimate business done in the Fontego dei Todeschi and sometimes also acted as translators. **Soldan** 'sultan' < Ar. *sulṭān* 'king, sovereign'. **Tarifa** 'tarif, price list' and in EV also 'schedule of customs duties for the use of merchants' < Ar. *ta'rīf* 'publication, notification'. **Zafaran** (EV *çaf(a)ran, çaforan, zafran*) 'saffron' < Ar. *za'farān* or Turk. *çafrān* 'saffron'. **Zeca** (EV *çec(h)a*) 'the mint in Venice' < Ar. (*dār as-*) *sikka* 'mint', lit. 'house of coin/striking'. **Zechin** [se'kiŋ] 'Venetian gold ducat', from EV/MidV *ducato de zec(h)a* 'minted ducat' (< Ar. *sikka* 'coin, minting die') as opposed to the *ducato* as money of account. **Zucaro** ['sukaro] (EV *çuc(h)aro, zuc(h)aro*) 'sugar' < Ar. *sukkar* 'sugar'.

French was the first Romance language to make its presence felt on EV, exerting important cultural-cum-lexical pressure between *c.* 1000 and *c.* 1400. The growing political, military, religious, and economic power of France in the later medieval period — with Norman rule in Sicily in the eleventh and twelfth centuries, Angevin rule in Naples and Sicily in the thirteenth century, and the removal of the papacy to Avignon in the fourteenth — added weight to the early vernacular emergence of the *langue d'oïl*. It strengthened the impact of French both as language of civilization and as medium of an immensely prestigious literature. The multiple and overlapping pathways of French influence left an exceptionally diverse lexical imprint, ranging from feudal terminology to key concepts related to dining, travel, and language, and to abstractions like thought, worry, and manner. Occasionally, even adjectives, verbs, and adverbs entered *venexian*, while on the structural level productive

---

41 Sanudo, *Itinerario*, p. 282.

suffixes developed from Old French -*aige* and -*ier*.[42] All loans were assimilated to Venetian phonology, most conspicuously with the Old French voiced palatal /dʒ/ or /ʒ/, as in *jardin*, rendered in EV/early MidV as the voiced affricate /dz/ which in ModV became the sibilant /z/. Semantics remain generally close to the original referent, apart from a few cases like *barbacan*, *missier*, and *soaza* which developed a specific slant within Venetian culture.

Venetian merchants were active in the fairs of northern France from at least the thirteenth century. Furthermore, the Veneto was one of the most receptive areas of Italy to literature in the *langue d'oïl*: from the *chansons de geste*, via the Arthurian romances of the *matière de Bretagne*, to the *Roman de la Rose*. Such was its impact that a particular form of Franco-Veneto hybridized literary language evolved as a vehicle for Carolingian narrative-poem reworkings, especially in the thirteenth and fourteenth centuries. The prestige of French, the vernacular with the widest European circulation among the educated, made it so compelling that the Venetian chronicler Martin da Canal opted for it in his *Estoires de Venise* (*c.* 1267–*c.* 1275). Important, too, was direct contact with overseas French in the Crusader statelets established in the eastern Mediterranean from the late eleventh until the late thirteenth centuries.[43] The numerous Venetian trading communities in the Christian Levant — notably at Acre, the main port of the Kingdom of Jerusalem — as well as Venice's administrators and settlers in colonial Greece, were in constant contact with the 'Frankish' kingdoms where French was the common language of the nobility and of their chivalric and courtly literature. To French influence proper should be added that of the *langue d'oc*, in the Levant and especially via troubadour verse — the first vernacular European lyric tradition and one which exercised considerable influence on early Italo-Romance poetry — and via the presence of troubadours themselves in the courts and cities of northern Italy from the end of the twelfth century. Old Provençalisms in Venetian can sometimes be identified with certainty, but when *oc* influence is present it may often be assumed to complement that of French. Some of the many medieval Gallicisms in EV, especially those connected with chivalry and courtly love, for example, *servente* 'servant', *drueria* 'gallantry', and *dolçor* 'sweetness', have died out, as have *mason* 'house, palace', *çanbra* 'room', *partison* 'dividing wall', the adverb *ensembre* 'together', and even the once-common adjective/pronoun *plux(i)or*, *plusor*, *ploxor* 'several'. The selection below illustrates the sweep — and enduring imprint on high-level civilizational concepts — of French influence.

Barbacan 'corbel, jetty, overhang on a building supporting a floor extension' < O.Fr. *barbacan(e)* 'rampart, bulwark, outer defence or support of a city/castle wall'; imported from the Crusader states — with their fortified citadels — into

---

[42] On Gallicisms in Italo-Romance, see Hope, *Lexical Borrowing in the Romance Languages*; Morgana, 'L'influsso francese'; Cella, *I gallicismi nei testi dell'italiano antico*.

[43] See Folena, 'La Romània d'oltremare'; Minervini, 'Le français dans l'Orient latin'; Minervini, 'Veneziano e francese nell'Oriente latino'.

the Romance languages, its martial semantics were altered in unfortified Venice, becoming a characteristic feature of the city's civil architecture; of disputed origin but plausibly < Ar.-Pers. *bāb (al-)khānah* 'towered gateway'. **Baron** 'baron' (~ MidV/ModV 'ruffian, villain') < O.Fr. *baron* 'baron' from Frank. *baro 'freeman, warrior'. **Cavalier** (~ EV *c(h)avaler*, EV/MidV *kavalier*) 'knight, nobleman, gentleman' < O.Prov. *cavallier* 'horseman, knight'. **Confalon** 'banner' < O.Fr. *confanon, confalon, gonfalon* 'banner' from Frank. *gundfano 'combat flag'. **Consegier** (~ EV *conseiero*, EV/early MidV *c(h)onseier, consier*) 'councillor, adviser' < O.Fr. *conseillier* 'adviser'. **Cotola** 'underskirt' < O.Fr. *cotte* 'tunic, dress'. **Disnar** 'to dine' < O.Fr. *disner*, O.Prov. *disnar* 'to dine'. **Formagio** (EV *formaio, fromaio, formazo*, MidV *formazo*) 'cheese' < O.Fr. *formage*, O.Prov. *formatge* from *FORMATICUM 'cheese from a mould'; the native EV term was *caso/caxo* < CĀSĔUM. **Garantir** ~ **varentar** (EV *varentar(e), guarentar, gaurentir*; MidV *varentar*) 'to warrant, protect from harm' < O.Fr. *guarenter, warantir, g(u)arantir* 'to warrant'. **Lenguagio** (EV *lenguaç(i)o*, MidV *lenguaz(i)o*) 'language' < O.Fr. *lang(u)age*, with ab initio *lengua* restricted to 'tongue, native language'. **Lezier** (EV *leçier, liçer*) 'light (weight)' < O.Fr. *legier* 'light'. **Magnar** (EV/early MidV *mançar, manzar*) 'to eat' < O.Fr. *mangier* 'to eat'; *magnar*, the dominant mainland Veneto form, ousted *manzar* after early MidV. **Maniera** (~ EV *manera, magnera, mainera*) 'manner' < O.Fr. *maniere* 'manner'. **Mestier** 'trade, profession' (~ 'necessity' in EV) < O.Fr. *mestier* 'office, service, profession, need'. **Missier** (EV *mis(i)er, mes(i)er*) 'Sir, Mr' ('father-in-law' in later MidV/ModV) < O.Prov. *meser* 'my Lord'. **Parlar** 'to speak' < O.Fr. *parler* 'to speak' from ecclesiastical Lat. PARABŎLARE 'to talk in parables, discuss'; *parlar* overcame *favelar, favolar* 'to speak' (< FĀBŬLARI) in the course of EV. **Penelo** 'confraternity banner' < O.Fr. *penel* 'pennant'. **Pensier** 'thought, worry' < O.Prov. *pensier* 'thought, worry, sorrow'. **Piezo** 'pledge, surety, guarantor' and **piezar** 'to pledge' (~ EV *pleço/pleçaria* and *pleçar*) < O.Fr. *ple(i)ge, ple(i)g(i)er, ple(i)gerie* 'pledge, guarantee' from Frank. *plegan 'to vouch for'. **Ruga** 'shop-lined street' (and, formerly, also 'house-lined street'), a probable adaptation of O.Fr. *rue* 'street' via the Italo-Romance borrowed form *rua* 'street' (< RŪGAM 'fold, wrinkle'); *ruga*, with insertion of /g/ to cover vowel hiatus,[44] appears to be an independent Venetian vernacular development, although the issue is complicated by its first appearing in Latin documents;[45] it came to prominence in Frankish Levant cities to designate the commercial thoroughfare of a Westerners' quarter and sometimes, by metonymy, the entire quarter itself. Its likely prototype was Venice's seminal *ruga* in Acre whose concession in 1111 is confirmed in the

---

44 See Ferguson, 'Passeri e rondini nel Veneto', pp. 248–49.
45 For medieval attestations (in Latin documentation) of *rua* in the Venetian lagoon, see Formentin, *Baruffe muranesi*, p. 106. As early as 819 a boundary-marking channel with the vernacular name *Ruga* is recorded in a Venetian document couched in Latin (ASV, S. Gregorio, *busta* 8, Liber sextus, fols 10^r–11^v).

Pactum Warmundi of 1123;[46] the term spread back widely to Italian cities and is differentiated from *calle* 'street' in fourteenth-century Venetian vernacular documentation; Ruga Rialto, Ruga dei Oresi, and Ruga Giuffa are the best known in contemporary Venice. **Sentier** 'path' < O.Fr. *sent(i)er* 'path'. **Soaza** 'picture frame' < O.Fr. *suage* 'border or edging on porcelain dishes or pewter plates' < *SOCA 'rope'; the *marangon da soaze* 'picture frame carpenter/maker' is a traditional Venetian craftsman. **Sparavier** (EV *sparv(i)er(o), sparvier*; MidV *sparvier, sparavier*) 'sparrowhawk' < O.Prov. *esparvier* 'sparrowhawk', itself from Frank. **sparwari*, lit. 'sparrow eagle', attested as *sparuarius* in the *Lex Salica*. **Viazo ~ viagio** (EV *viaço, viazo*) 'journey' (in EV also 'voyage' or 'seasonal galley convoy') < O.Prov. *viatge*, O.Fr. *ve(i)age* 'journey' from VĬĀTĬCUM 'necessary supplies for a journey'. **Zalo** (~ EV *çalo*) 'yellow' < O.Fr. *jalne* 'yellow'. **Zardin** (EV *çardin*) 'garden' < O.Fr. *jardin* 'cultivated enclosure'; a high-register word originally designating a flower garden in Venice and an orchard in the Levant; kitchen garden remained *orto* < HORTUM. **Zentilomo** (EV *çentil(h)omo, çintil(h)omo*) 'patrician' < O.Fr. *gentilz hom* 'nobleman'. **Zogia** (EV *çoia*) 'jewel' < O.Fr. *joie*/O.Prov. *joia* 'jewel'. **Zorno** (EV *çorno*) 'day' < DIURNUM via (or reinforced by) O.Fr. *jor(n)*/O.Prov. *jorn* 'day(light)'; *zorno* progressively confined original *dì* (< DĬEM) to fixed expressions.

Contact Pressure from Mainland Italy on Early Venetian Variant Forms

By *c.* 1350 EV appeared as a stable koine containing tell-tale evidence of residual forms recycled as diastratic or diatopic variants. However, this delicate systemic equilibrium was short-lived. Pressure on its variant-form choices began immediately to be exerted in the fourteenth and fifteenth centuries by contact influence from the Italian mainland. This led to the strengthening or eventual predominance of some originally minority variants and to the surprising marginalization of formerly dominant elements in the system. Three different sources of pressure can be identified as affecting preferences in Venice from within a series of phonological, morphological, and lexical pairs: face-to-face contact across Venice with immigrants from the city's nearby mainland territories; the effects on educated Venetians of the prestigious compromise *scripta* of the northern Italian chanceries; and the roofing influence on the same class of literary Florentine/Tuscan, supplemented arguably by educational contact and even by direct interaction with Tuscans at home and abroad.

---

46 Tafel and Thomas, eds, *Urkunden*, pp. 85–91. *Rua* and *ruga* appear side by side in the vernacular-influenced Latin toponymy of Paolino da Venezia's early Trecento map of Acre. Jacoby, 'L'évolution urbaine', pp. 98–99.

Venice expanded decisively onto its hinterland in the early fifteenth century. By 1450 it had acquired a Stato *da terra* that stretched east to Friuli, south towards Ferrara, and above all, west almost to the gates of Milan. Among the consequences of this expansion was a steady flow of economic migrants, the best known in the Renaissance period being porters from the valleys near Bergamo, stonemasons from Lake Como, and domestics from Friuli. Probably predominant over time were rural workers originating in those south-western and north-eastern Veneto territories from the confluence of whose population streams Venetian had actually originated. A number of alterations in the balance of choice between the components of variant pairs in EV and MidV — sometimes extending into ModV and therefore constituting true language change — seem to be down to selective reinforcing of a form that happened to coincide with mainland preferences.

Two high-profile cases, one morphonological, one lexical, illustrate the point. The final-stem segment indicating the future and conditional tenses in first and second conjugation verbs in ModV/CV is /ar/, for example, *andarò* 'I will go', *andaria* 'I would go'; *vendarò* 'I will sell', *vendaria* 'I would sell'. This contrasts with the corresponding morph in EV texts which was, predominantly, /er/. Although /er/ persisted strongly through MidV and even into early ModV, it was increasingly challenged by /ar/. This form of the segment started as very much a minority diastratic and diatopic variant within the city but appears to have been increasingly reinforced by the identical /ar/ realization, common in the central, western, and southern parts of the Veneto and carried into the city by lower-class migration. The second case involves common lexical items which have plausibly been nudged in the direction of originally minority Venetian variants by such pressures from the Renaissance onwards. Most obvious are the gradual ousting of the traditional nouns for 'boy' and 'girl' and of the adverb for 'too (much)'. In EV/MidV the former were overwhelmingly *puto, puta*, flanked by the diminutives *putelo, putela*. The latter was *tropo*. The minority variants, respectively *toso, tosa* and *massa*, seemed destined for elimination. Instead, they were bolstered by the constant influx of such forms from the Veneto mainland and Lombardy, to such an extent that they became the exclusive outcomes in ModV/CV, with only the diminutives *putelo, putela* (= [puˈtɛo], [puˈtɛa]) 'little boy, little girl' of the formerly dominant lexemes surviving.

One of the most intriguing cases of variant-pair persistence across the history of Venetian involves two aspectually identical but competing forms of conditional ending, *-ave* versus *-ia*: the former from the Latin perfect of HABĒRE 'to have', the latter from the imperfect of HABĒRE, for example, *darave* 'I would give' < DĂRE + HĂBUI vs *daria* 'I would give' < DĂRE + HĂBĒBAM.[47] The *-ave* type was undoubtedly the commoner mainland form, with *-ia* appearing

---

47 The fundamental examination of the origin and distribution of these two conditional forms in Italo-Romance is Parkinson, 'A Diachronic Study'.

as a north-eastern Veneto variant. Both show up in the earliest Venetian texts in an apparently random way. By the stabilization and consolidation phase of EV, in the Trecento and especially the Quattrocento, the *-ia* ending had become predominant in higher-register texts and looked to be on the way to supremacy. It is not unreasonable to assume that this edge was, in part at least, the result of its coinciding with the favoured choice in northern Italian chancery writing practice. It was, therefore, prestigious and familiar in the eyes of the Venetian professional classes who would have exerted pressure 'from above' in its favour. The competing morph *-ave* predominated at this point only in lower-register writing and therefore appeared vulnerable to marginalization. That this failed to happen can be imputed to the pressure exerted in its support by immigration from the mainland carrying the *-ave* form. The *-ave* conditional type suddenly appeared massively in Venetian 'spoken' theatrical texts of the Cinquecento, and in fact its place in writing alongside *-ia* was consolidated from the sixteenth until the nineteenth century, in an apparent equilibrium that would be difficult to conceive of in a codified or standardized language. Only after that point did *-ia* reassert itself decisively and finally, radiating out from Venice and establishing its dominance even on the mainland.

Between 1350 and 1500 there is unmistakable, and perhaps surprising at that date, evidence of Tuscan/Italian contact pressure on spoken and written Venetian phonology and morphology. It also tended to operate seamlessly via the reinforcement of originally minority variants in EV, so that distinctive and potentially marked Venetian features aligned themselves with Tuscan, thereby eliminating some once dominant and characteristic elements of the Venetian system. In phonology the two most striking examples, affecting both the written and spoken domains, are the removal from Venetian grammar of the tendency to raise /a/ before a nasal (best known in the case of *sen* and *senta* 'saint' which predominated until the fourteenth century over *san* and *santa*) and to raise /al/, if followed by a dental consonant, to /ol/ (e.g. *Riolto* dominated *Rialto* until the fourteenth century). In morphology the most notable examples are the shift in the adverbial suffix from the idiosyncratic *-mentre*, dominant until the mid-fourteenth century, to minority *-mente* which coincided with Tuscan, and the realignment of the first person singular of the future tense from original *-è* to *-ò*, the latter coinciding with Tuscan.[48]

The first of the three contact factors which may have combined to produce such shifts is face-to-face interaction. Medieval and Renaissance Venice was home to substantial communities of Tuscans, particularly from Florence and Lucca, involved in trade and manufacture. There was a good deal of structural and lexical commonality between early Tuscan varieties

---

48 In Venetian high-register writing in the later Quattrocento there is also a tendency to align to some other Tuscan paradigms, most notably the disambiguation of third singular/plural tense forms which in Venetian are identical.

and EV, so it is likely that code-switching and code-mixing were common on the part of the immigrants and, to a certain extent, their interlocutors. There is compelling evidence of this from two sources. The first is the vernacular correspondence (1336–1350) addressed to the Tuscan merchant Pignol Zucchello, resident in Venice, by his Venetian and Tuscan agents abroad. Observable in the letters are the linguistic effects on individuals of operating overseas alongside speakers of other Italian varieties, as well as the conscious or unconscious effort they make to accommodate to their recipient's native or adopted code.[49] The second is a unique last will and testament in inscriptional form on two marble plaques from Murano. It was carved in 1340 at the behest of the Tuscan Angelo Piarini, resident in Murano and married to a local woman, to function as an exact copy — for public viewing in perpetuity — of his legacy instructions. His text is a remarkable *Sprachmischung*, unselfconsciously combining Tuscan, Venetian, and even local Muranese features of phonology, morphology, and lexis.[50]

External face-to-face contact between Venetians and Tuscans is also very much a possibility in a city where some 20 per cent of the adult male population resided abroad for long periods, often in direct contact with other Italians. However, change 'from above', interacting with direct internal and external contact, may well have been the decisive factor. Between 1300 and 1500 school texts in Venice were increasingly in a Tuscanizing vernacular,[51] and post-1300 there was a succession of Tuscan teachers operating in Venetian schools.[52] In addition, Tuscan literary models had high prestige, to the extent that from the fifteenth century they conditioned the linguistic preferences of the nascent printing industry in Venice and also, occasionally, of public writing. A conspicuous case of the latter is the inscription carved on the dedication plaque of 1505 over a gateway into almshouse properties in Cannaregio owned by the Scuola Grande della Misericordia, one of the great lay brotherhoods of medieval and Renaissance Venice.[53] It is plausible, therefore, that phonological and morphological convergence with Tuscan infiltrated the written, then spoken, Venetian of social elites by these channels, then percolated down to

---

49 Morozzo della Rocca, ed., *Lettere di mercanti*. Originally Pisan, Zucchello moved first to Venetian Crete then settled in Venice before 1328, becoming a Venetian citizen *de intus et de extra* and running an emporium at the Rialto. The majority of letters, memorandums, and price-lists in the collection are addressed to him by his contacts operating from the Adriatic to the Black Sea. Forty-seven letters employ a form of Tuscan, while seventeen documents have Venetian. Despite the philological shortcomings of the edition, language mixing and accommodation are clearly detectable, most strikingly in the letter (pp. 120–23) from the Florentine Vannino Fecini to Zucchello's Venetian widow in January 1348 (= 1349). See Tomasin, 'Urban Multilingualism'; Rinaldin, 'Il veneziano dei mercanti', pp. 33–40.
50 Transcribed, translated, and analysed for the first time in Ferguson, *Venetian Inscriptions*, pp. 89–95.
51 Bertanza and Dalla Santa, *Maestri, scuole e scolari in Venezia*.
52 Rossi, 'Maestri e scuole a Venezia', p. 775.
53 See Ferguson, *Venetian Inscriptions*, pp. 338–42.

other groups. The prose of Marin Sanudo around 1500 in his indispensable diaries embodies the contact fluidity of Renaissance Venice, with its impasto of Venetian, Tuscan, and northern Italian *scripta* norms.

Venetian Prestige Contact at Home and Abroad

Far from being stigmatized in any way by the overwhelming encroachment of written Italian, spoken Venetian paradoxically reached its apogee of internal and external influence in the MidV period. This is the time of the expansion and consolidation of *venexian* in north-eastern Italy, when the prestige spoken language of Venice became the pole of attraction for the upwardly mobile throughout the dominions of the Venetian state, *da terra* and *da mar*. Venetian radically restructured the urban dialects of the Veneto from the fifteenth century onwards, especially those of Padua, Vicenza, and Treviso.[54] It Venetianized the Lombard dialects of the contiguous Trentino region, ousted Friulan from several major urban centres in Friuli and eventually erased the Ladin speech of Trieste. The lasting genetic imprint of 'colonial' Venetian along the eastern Adriatic seaboard has no parallel in Europe, and almost completely absorbed the original Romance idioms of the Gulf of Venice, 'Istriot' and 'Dalmatian' in their various guises. This was also the time of the greatest diffusion of Venetian lexical items both within and outside Italy. EV/MidV left an imprint on Balkan Slav, Albanian, and Greek, and influenced maritime terminology across the Mediterranean.[55] We have secure and detailed information about the Venetian impact on Cyprus, which in the Quattrocento developed a Franco-Venetian *scripta*,[56] while the cities of Dalmatia, particularly Ragusa (Dubrovnik) and Zara (Zadar), also evolved Venetian-influenced *scriptae* which have now been studied.[57] Between c. 1500 and c. 1600 Venetian even exported to Italian some two dozen lexical items connected with Venice's institutions, way of life, commerce, and administration.[58]

---

54 On the linguistic configuration of the Veneto in the twentieth century and how it was moulded by Venetian, see Ferguson, *A Linguistic History of Venice*, pp. 64–68; Ferguson, 'La formazione del veneziano', pp. 22–26.
55 A bibliography of Venetian linguistic influence in the Adriatic and beyond is in Ferguson, 'Lo status storico del veneziano', pp. 150–51 nn. 37–39. For a detailed study of Venetian structural impact on an Istrian Slav dialect, see Kalsbeek, 'Contact-Induced Innovations'. On 'colonial' Venetian, see Bidwell, 'Colonial Venetian'; Cortelazzo, 'Il veneziano coloniale'. On Venetian maritime loanwords exported across the Mediterranean, see Tomasin, 'Sulla diffusione del lessico marinaresco italiano'; Tomasin, 'Non solo Levante'. The two fundamental overviews of Venetian language contact overseas are Cortelazzo, *Venezia, il Levante e il mare*; Folena, 'Introduzione al veneziano *de là da mar*'. More recent is Baglioni, ed., *Il veneziano 'de là da mar'*.
56 Baglioni, *La scripta italoromanza*.
57 Dotto, *'Scriptae' venezianeggianti*; Vuletić, 'Volgare venezianeggiante'.
58 Ferguson, 'Lo status storico del veneziano', pp. 167–70.

Less well known, but no less indicative of the intertwined prestige of Venice and Venetian from the late EV period until the seventeenth century, is language contact on English unmatched by any other Italian idiom. Direct contact with England began when a Venetian convoy first put up in the deep-water port of Southampton in 1314. From the later fourteenth century until 1532 the annual state-sponsored Venetian Flanders galleys (EV/MidV *galie de Fiandra*), part of the city's great network of seasonal armed convoys,[59] brought exotic spices and other luxury goods, shipping metals, cloth, and wool out of England in return.[60] As well as generating considerable profits, Venetian business interchange in English customs ports unsurprisingly led to the early language contact discussed in the present volume by Megan Tiddeman.

As Venetian seaborne trade with northern Europe declined post-1500, English naval and mercantile power strengthened, so that by the second half of the sixteenth century English merchants were intruding on routes and markets once the preserve of Venice, while an increasingly prosperous and expanding England acquired a new self-confidence in its own language and literature. However, in spite of serial disruptions to its traditional trading patterns, and despite the rise in naval power of England, Holland, and Spain, Venice partially renewed itself as a commercial and manufacturing centre in this period and, although diminished, was still an important player in East–West trade. Around 1600 its cultural-civilizational resonance was, in fact, at its zenith. More than any other European power of the time England became fascinated by the mythical status of its great maritime predecessor, seeing it as a model of wealth, sophistication, art, luxury, political cunning, and efficient government.[61] Knowledge of Venice's history and institutions increased sharply among the educated thanks to the availability in English of Gasparo Contarini's fundamental Latin text, published posthumously in 1543, on Venetian governance.[62] Lewes Lewkenor's accurate translation of 1599, based in part on the anonymous 1544 Italian version of Contarini, also made available practical material on Venice from Francesco Sansovino's best-selling guidebook of 1581.[63] It soon became *de rigueur* for serious Elizabethan and Jacobean travellers to visit Venice. This is precisely the point at which the

---

59 Known as *le mude*, plausibly from EV/MidV sg. *muda* 'turn around, switch over' < MŪTARE 'to move, alter, change'. A uniquely Venetian term, *muda* also designated the period when business was transacted while the galleys from Venice were in foreign ports. Here its semantics may have been influenced by Ar. *mudda* 'period'.

60 The galley mariners left their Venetian linguistic imprint on a splendid inscribed ledgerstone dated 1491 in a Southampton church: Ferguson, *Venetian Inscriptions*, p. 26, n. 10.

61 An exhaustive account is Hammerton, 'English Impressions of Venice'.

62 Contarini, *De magistratibus et republica Venetorum*. Sir Politick (*Volpone* IV, 1) proudly states that 'I had read Contarene', as if it were a household name among his class, and Coryate in the *Epistle Dedicatorie* to the *Crudities* acknowledges the authority of 'Cardinall Contarens Commonwealth of Venice'.

63 Lewkenor, *The Commonwealth and Government of Venice*; Sansovino, *Venetia città nobilissima et singolare*.

city, as a site of fascination in the English imagination, appears in the theatre of Shakespeare and Jonson.

The English captivation with Venice around 1600 is reflected in the peak reception of Venetian loanwords in the fifteen years either side of this date. As I have shown elsewhere, it is also emblematically present in three influential texts of the period which display a combined and unprecedented focus on the Serenissima and its language.[64] Ben Jonson's *Volpone* (1607), set in Venice, contains numerous and accurate Venetianisms related to institutions and lifestyle. The extended section on Venice in Thomas Coryate's *Crudities* (1611), based on the author's first-hand experience, provided the liveliest description 'ever done before in our English tongue' — interspersed with Venetianisms — of 'that most glorious, renowned and Virgin Citie of Venice'.[65] John Florio's Italian–English dictionary published in 1598 and expanded in 1611 is remarkable for its wealth of synonyms, absence of linguistic purism, breadth of written sources, and inclusion of Italian regionalisms.[66] As well as recording numerous first lexical attestations in English, it is a largely unexplored treasure-house of Venetianisms.

The very recent appreciation of the extent of lexical diffusion from Venetian is correcting our understanding of the chronology, weight, and origin of Italianisms in English.[67] I list below the Venetian loanwords — some in their original guise, others in various stages of adaptation — which I have traced, in full or in part, to EV/MidV provenance. This corpus, including recycled Arabisms, has in large part survived into Modern English and is a not insignificant historical document of the Renaissance civilization of Venice and of the image that it projected. The main areas of semantic impact are toponyms and onomastics, institutions and practices, ships/boats, coinage, exotic products, Venice-specific cultural objects, entertainment, and public health provision. The date of first attestation in English is taken from the *OED*,[68] as is the modern form of the headwords listed in chronological order. I provide the EV/MidV etymon unless cited already.

Ducat [c. 1387] < EV *duc(h)ato* from the legend DUCAT(VS) (VENETVS) 'duchy (of Venice)' on the coin; first minted in 1285, the Venetian ducat was for centuries the 'gold standard' in the Mediterranean, although largely as a money of account (→ *zechin* [1572], *chequin* [1587], *sequin* [1617]). **Arsenal** [1511] 'naval shipyard in Venice' < MidV *arsenal* (→ *arsenal* [1572]). **Artichoke** [1531] < MidV *artichioco*. **Armada** [1533] 'fleet of war ships' < MidV *armada* 'fleet, navy'. **Contraband** [c. 1540] 'illegal traffic, smuggling' < MidV *contrabando*

---

64 Ferguson, 'Primi influssi culturali italo-veneti sull'inglese'.
65 Coryate, *Coryats Crudities*, I, p. 2.
66 Florio, *A Worlde of Wordes*; Florio, *Queen Anna's New World of Words*.
67 On Italianisms in English, see Pinnavaia, *The Italian Borrowings*; Lepschy and Lepschy, 'From *antipasto* to *zabaglione*'; Stammerjohann and others, eds, *Dizionario*; Dietz, 'Die frühen italienischen Lehnwörter'.
68 Except for *ghetto*, first recorded by Florio in 1598 not by Coryate in 1611.

'illegal traffic', from *contra* 'against' and *bando* 'decree, law'; Venice operated a contraband office from 1281. **Marzipan** [1542] < MidV *marzapan*. **Ballot** [1549] 'voting ball, ballot' < MidV *balota* 'ball used in Venetian government elections, ballot'. **Doge** [1549] < MidV *doxe* ~ *dose* in Tuscanized form, from DŬCEM 'leader'. **Gondola** [1549] < MidV *gondola*. **Lazaretto** [1549] 'house for the reception of the diseased poor, especially lepers, in Venice' < MidV *lazareto*, from S. Maria de Nazaret(o) (= Nazareth), the original name of the leper island-hospital in the lagoon x MidV *lazaro* 'pauper, leper' from the beggar Lazarus in the Gospel of Luke (→ *lazaretto* [1607]); Venice's first quarantine hospital ('lazareto over nazareto') was founded in 1423 while the 'new' *lazaretto* dated from 1468. **Mountebank** [1566] 'itinerant vendor of medicines' < MidV *montimbanco* from *montar* 'mount' and *banco* 'boards, bench'. **Arsenal** [1572] 'government establishment where weapons and ammunition are stored or made'. **Zechin** [1572] 'Venetian ducat' (→ *chequin* [1587], *sequin* [1617]). **Magnifico** (hist.) [1573] 'magnate of Venice' < MidV *magnifico*. **Rebuff** [1582] < EV/MidV *rebuf(f)o* 'insult, rebuff', onomatopoeic. **Buffoon** [1584] 'clown, jester' < MidV *buf(f)on* 'clown', onomatopoeic. **Madrigal** [1584] < MidV *madregal* ~ *madrigal* 'simple love poem, part-song for several voices', of uncertain etymology. **Chequin** (obs.) [c. 1587] 'Venetian ducat' (→ *sequin* [1617]). **Zany** [1588] 'clown's assistant, professional jester, buffoon' < MidV *Z(u)an(e)* (John), the Bergamask porter in Venetian polyglot comedy then in commedia dell'arte. **Balloon** (hist.) [c. 1591] 'game played with large inflated ball' (→ *balloon* [1598]). **Pantaloon** [1592] 'character of the *senex* in commedia dell'arte' < MidV *Pantalon*, a characteristic Venetian saint's name, from Gk. Πανταλέων (→ *pantaloons* [1661]). **Balloon** (hist.) [1598] 'ball used in the game of balloon' < MidV *bal(l)on* 'ball'. **Ghetto** [1598] 'Jewish quarter of Venice' < MidV *g(h)et(t)o*, from *geto de rame* 'copper foundry', that is, the former munitions-casting district with copper-smelting furnaces at S. Girolamo in Cannaregio where the Jewish quarter was established in 1516; *geto/gheto* is a derivative of EV/MidV *getar/gitar* ~ EV *ghetar(e)/ghitar(e)* 'to cast, pour, throw, throw up, engender, produce, amount to', with ab origine velar /g/ confirmed by fourteenth- and fifteenth-century documentation;[69] this pronunciation is still preserved on the verb and its noun derivatives in some archaic Veneto dialects and, combined with a semantic range unique to Venetian, suggests as etymon Germ. **get-* 'beget' influenced by IACTARE 'to throw'. **Mocenigo** (obs.) [1598] 'Venetian silver coin current in the Renaissance' < MidV *mocenigo*, from doge Piero Mocenigo (1474–1476) who introduced the coin. **Pistachio** [1598] < MidV *pistachio*. **Sestiere** [1599] 'one of the six districts of Venice' < MidV *sestier* from SEXTĀRĬUS 'sixth part'. **Soldo** (obs.) [1599] 'Venetian coin' < MidV *soldo*. **Rialto** [1600]. **Gondolier** [1603] < MidV *gondolier*. **Gazet(t)** (obs.) [1607] 'Venetian coin of small value' < MidV *gaz(z)eta*. **Gazette** [1607] 'news-sheet,

---

69 Zille, 'Il *ghetto* in un documento veneziano'. On the exceptional use of /g/ on *getar/gitar*, see Alinei, 'La grafia veneziana', p. 245.

periodical, gazette' < MidV *gaz(z)eta* 'news-sheet', from its cost-price; the first gazettes in Europe appeared in Venice c. 1550. **Lazaret(t)o** [1607] 'quarantine building'. **Terra firma** [1607] 'territories on the Italian mainland subject to the state of Venice' < MidV *terra ferma*. **Bucentaur** (hist.) [1612] 'the state barge of Venice' < MidV *bucentoro ~ bucintoro*, of uncertain origin. **Caviar** [c. 1612] < MidV *caviaro*; Venice was a major importer of caviar into Europe, in particular via its emporium enclave of Tana in the Don delta on the Sea of Azov. **Regatta** [1613] 'annual boat-race on the Grand Canal' < MidV *regata* from EV/MidV *regatar* 'to compete'; first depicted and captioned in De Barbari's view of 1500. **Sequin** (obs.) [1617] 'Venetian ducat' < MidV *zechin* 'gold ducat'. **Ditto** [1625] 'said, aforesaid' < EV/MidV *dit(t)o* 'aforementioned, ditto' used in commercial inventories. **Malvasia** (hist.) [1640] 'Malmsey wine' < MidV *malvasia*. **Pantaloons** [1661] 'men's loose breeches', from the garment of the Pantaloon character in commedia dell'arte. **Lagoon** [1673] 'the lagoon of Venice' < MidV *laguna* from LĀCŪNA 'pool'. **Lido** [1673] 'lagoon sandspit of Venice' < MidV *lido ~ lio* 'sandbank, shore' < LĪTUS 'sea-shore'.

Conclusion

The case studies in the present essay have evoked the range, complexity, and overlap of societal phenomena that came into play in the push and pull of language-contact situations involving Venice in the Middle Ages and Renaissance. These include migratory movements, colonial expansion, commercial outreach and production, civilizational prestige, cultural pressure, and literary influence. Sociolinguistic and psycholinguistic factors provided the triggers that mediated such contact into the concrete outcomes of language exchange within and outside Venice that we have explored and illustrated: from the import and export of words in various forms of adaptation to restructuring on the phonological and morphological levels.

It goes without saying that these outcomes are exceptional, if underused, historical documents. In the first place we observed the flux then stabilization of Early Venetian, conditioned by the city's multiple internal contact interchanges. We also scrutinized the subsequent emergence between 1350 and 1500 of a series of unexpected structural preferences favoured by contact pressure points from mainland Italy. Our analysis and synthesis of both long-term processes provided compelling evidence of the melting-pot formation and migration-driven co-development of Venetian demography and language. Our selective interrogation of the unusual inheritance of loanwords in *venexian* revealed distinctive moments and patterns of civilizational influence exerted on Venice from sources stretching from Europe to the Levant and beyond. Although only partial, our commented word inventories add vivid detail to the broad-brush picture of Venetian contact that can be inferred from chronicles, diaries, and treaties. They also suggest that the study of the timescale and pathways of penetration of this culture-rich verbal information, at the micro and macro levels, is a potentially formidable research tool for scholars of Venice. Finally, on the external front, our fine-grained investigation of Venetian lexical infiltration of English in the Renaissance exemplified how new perspectives on the nature, extent, and chronology of the Serenissima's overseas impact can be achieved by incorporating the language dimension.

Works Cited

Primary Sources

ASV = Archivio di Stato di Venezia
Bembo, Pietro, *Prose […] nelle quali si ragiona della volgar lingua* (Venice: Tacuino, 1525)
BNM = Biblioteca Nazionale Marciana, Venice
Contarini, Gasparo, *De magistratibus et republica Venetorum* (Paris: Vacosani, 1543)
Coryate, Thomas, *Coryats Crudities*, 2 vols (London: W.S., 1611)
Florio, John, *Queen Anna's New World of Words* (London: Bradwood, 1611)
——, *A Worlde of Wordes* (London: Arnold Hatfield, 1589)
Jonson, Ben, *Volpone or The Foxe* (London: Thomas Thorppe, 1607)
Lewkenor, Lewes, *The Commonwealth and Government of Venice* (London: John Windet, 1599)
Sansovino, Francesco, *Venetia città nobilissima et singolare* (Venice: Iacomo Sansovino, 1581)

Secondary Studies

AIS = *Sprach- und Sachatlas Italiens und der Südschweiz*, ed. by Karl Jaberg and Jakob Jud, 8 vols (Zofingen: Ringier, 1928–1940)
Alinei, Mario, 'Dialetto: Un concetto rinascimentale fiorentino', *Quaderni di Semantica*, 2 (1981), 147–73
——, 'La grafia veneziana delle origini', in Mario Alinei, *Lingua e dialetti: Struttura, storia e geografia* (Bologna: Il Mulino, 1984), pp. 225–56
Andrews, Richard, *Scripts and Scenarios: The Performance of Comedy in Renaissance Italy* (Cambridge: Cambridge University Press, 1993)
Arcamone, Maria Giovanna, 'L'elemento germanico antico, medievale e moderno (con esclusione dell'inglese)', in *Storia della lingua italiana*, III: *Le altre lingue*, ed. by Luca Serianni and Pietro Trifone (Turin: Einaudi, 1994), pp. 751–90
Ashcroft, Jeffrey, 'Albrecht Dürers *Venexian*: Zu seinen venezianischen Sprachkenntnissen und zur Ausformen seiner Lexik der Kunst', *Beiträge zur Geschichte der deutschen Sprache und Literatur*, 141.3 (2019), 360–94
Baglioni, Daniele, *La scripta italoromanza del regno di Cipro: Edizione e commento di testi di scriventi ciprioti del Quattrocento* (Rome: Aracne, 2006)
——, ed., *Il veneziano 'de là da mar': Contesti, testi, dinamiche del contatto linguistico e culturale* (Berlin: De Gruyter, 2020)

Bertanza, Enrico, and Giuseppe Dalla Santa, *Maestri, scuole e scolari in Venezia fino al 1500* (Venice: Neri Pozza, 1993)

Bidwell, Charles E., 'Colonial Venetian and Serbo-Croat in the Eastern Adriatic: A Case Study of Languages in Contact', *General Linguistics*, 7 (1967), 13–30

Boerio, Giuseppe, *Dizionario del dialetto veneziano* (Venice: Santini, 1829 / Venice: Cecchini, 1865)

Braunstein, Philippe, *Les Allemands à Venise (1380–1520)* (Rome: École Française de Rome, 2016)

Bubenik, Vit, 'Dialect Contact and Koineization: The Case of Hellenistic Greek', *International Journal of the Sociology of Language*, 99 (1993), 9–23

Carile, Antonio, and Giorgio Fedalto, *Le origini di Venezia* (Bologna: Pàtron, 1978)

Cella, Roberta, *I gallicismi nei testi dell'italiano antico: Dalle origini alla fine del sec. XIV* (Florence: Accademia della Crusca, 2003)

Cessi, Roberto, *Venezia ducale* (Venice: Deputazione di Storia Patria per le Venezie, 1963)

Cortelazzo, Manlio, 'Arabismi di Pisa e arabismi di Venezia', *Lingua Nostra*, 18.4 (1957), 95–97

——, *L'influsso linguistico greco a Venezia* (Bologna: Pàtron, 1970)

——, *Venezia, il Levante e il mare* (Pisa: Pacini, 1989)

——, 'Il veneziano coloniale: Documentazione e interpretazione', in *Processi di convergenza e differenziazione nelle lingue dell'Europa medievale e moderna*, ed. by Fabiana Fusco, Vincenzo Orioles, and Alice Parmeggiani (Udine: Forum, 2000), pp. 317–26

Crifò, Francesco, 'Popular Lexicon of Greek Origin in Italian Varieties', in 'Language Contact in the Mediterranean in the Middle Ages and in Early Modern Times (with special focus on loanword lexicography)', ed. by Francesco Crifò, Elton Prifti, and Wolfgang Schweickard, thematic part of *Lexicographica: International Annual for Lexicography*, 33 (2017), 95–120

Crouzet-Pavan, Élisabeth, *Le Moyen Âge de Venise: Des eaux salées au miracle de pierres* (Paris: Albin Michel, 2015)

Dalla Santa, Giuseppe, 'Commerci, vita privata e notizie politiche dei giorni della lega di Cambrai', *Atti del Reale Istituto Veneto di Scienze, Lettere ed Arti*, 76.2 (1916–1917), 1547–1605

DEI = Battisti, Carlo, and Giovanni Alessio, *Dizionario etimologico italiano*, 5 vols (Florence: Barbera, 1950–1957)

DELI = Cortelazzo, Manlio, and Paolo Zolli, *Dizionario etimologico della lingua italiana*, 5 vols (Bologna: Zanichelli, 1979–1988)

Dietz, Klaus, 'Die frühen italienischen Lehnwörter des Englischen', *Anglia: Zeitschrift für englische Philologie*, 123.4 (2006), 573–631

Dorigo, Wladimiro, *Venezia origini: Fondamenti, ipotesi, metodi* (Milan: Electa, 1983)

Dotto, Diego, *'Scriptae' venezianeggianti a Ragusa nel XIV secolo* (Rome: Viella, 2008)

Eufe, Rembert, *'Sta lengua ha un privilegio tanto grando': Status und Gebrauch des Venezianischen in der Republik Venedig* (Frankfurt: Peter Lang, 2006)

Ferguson, Ronnie, 'Alle origini del veneziano: Una koiné lagunare?', *Zeitschrift für romanische Philologie*, 121.3 (2005), 476–509
——, 'Between the Lines: Language Dimensions in Venetian History', *News on the Rialto*, 33 (2014), 22–26
——, 'Dinamiche contrastive di mutamento linguistico in veneziano', in Ronnie Ferguson, *Saggi di lingua e cultura veneta* (Padua: Cleup, 2013), pp. 197–236
——, 'L'etimologia del tipo veneto *cocal* "gabbiano"', in Ronnie Ferguson, *Saggi di lingua e cultura veneta* (Padua: Cleup, 2013), pp. 255–77
——, 'La formazione del veneziano', in Ronnie Ferguson, *Saggi di lingua e cultura veneta* (Padua: Cleup, 2013), pp. 13–65
——, *A Linguistic History of Venice* (Florence: Olschki, 2007)
——, 'Passeri e rondini nel Veneto: La storia intrecciata di *selega* e *sisila*', in Ronnie Ferguson, *Saggi di lingua e cultura veneta* (Padua: Cleup, 2013), pp. 237–54
——, 'Primi influssi culturali italo-veneti sull'inglese: I venezianismi in Florio, Coryate e Jonson', *Quaderni Veneti*, 1 (2012), 57–82
——, *Saggi di lingua e cultura veneta* (Padua: Cleup, 2013)
——, 'Lo status storico del veneziano: Lingua o dialetto?', in Ronnie Ferguson, *Saggi di lingua e cultura veneta* (Padua: Cleup, 2013), pp. 135–86
——, *Venetian Inscriptions: Vernacular Writing for Public Display in Medieval and Renaissance Venice* (Cambridge: Legenda, 2021)
Folena, Gianfranco, 'Introduzione al veneziano *de là da mar*', in Gianfranco Folena, *Culture e lingue nel Veneto medievale* (Padova: Programma, 1990), pp. 227–68
——, 'La Romània d'oltremare: Francese e veneziano nel Levante', in Gianfranco Folena, *Culture e lingue nel Veneto medievale* (Padova: Programma, 1990), pp. 269–86
Forlati Tamaro, Bruna, and others, eds, *Da Aquileia a Venezia: Una mediazione tra l'Europa e l'Oriente dal II secolo a.C. al VI secolo d.C.* (Milan: Garzanti/Scheiwiller, 1986)
Formentin, Vittorio, *Baruffe muranesi: Una fonte giudiziaria medievale tra letteratura e storia della lingua* (Rome: Edizioni di Storia e Letteratura, 2017)
Gamillscheg, Ernst, *Romania Germanica: Sprach- und Siedlungsgeschichte der Germanen auf dem Boden des alten Römerreiches* (Berlin: De Gruyter, 1935)
GDLI = Battaglia, Salvatore, *Grande dizionario della lingua italiana*, 21 vols (Turin: UTET, 1961–2002)
Hammerton, Rachel Joan, 'English Impressions of Venice up to the Early Seventeenth Century' (unpublished doctoral thesis, University of St Andrews, 1987)
Holtus, Günter, and Michael Metzeltin, 'I dialetti veneti nella ricerca recente', in *Linguistica e dialettologia veneta: Studi offerti a Manlio Cortelazzo*, ed. by Günter Holtus and Michael Metzeltin (Tübingen: Narr, 1983), pp. 1–38
Hope, T. E., *Lexical Borrowing in the Romance Languages: A Critical Study of Italianisms in French and Gallicisms in Italian from 1100 to 1900*, 2 vols, Language and Style Series, 10 (Oxford: Blackwell, 1971)

Jacoby, David, 'L'évolution urbaine et la fonction méditerranéenne d'Acre à l'époque des croisades', in *Città portuali del Mediterraneo: Storia e archeologia*, ed. by Ennio Poleggi (Genoa: Sagep, 1989), pp. 95–109
——, 'Multilingualism and Institutional Patterns of Communication in Latin Romania (Thirteenth–Fourteenth Centuries)', in *Diplomatics in the Eastern Mediterranean, 1000–1500*, ed. by Alexander Beihammer, Maria Parani, and Christopher Schabel (Leiden: Brill, 2008), pp. 27–48
——, 'Pèlerinage médiéval et sanctuaires de Terre Sainte: La perspective vénitienne', *Ateneo Veneto*, 24 (1986), 27–58
Kahane, Henry, and Renée Kahane, 'Byzantium's Impact on the West: The Linguistic Evidence', *Illinois Classical Papers*, 6.2 (1981), 389–415
——, 'On Venetian Byzantinisms', *Romance Philology*, 27.3 (1974), 356–67
Kalsbeek, Janneke, 'Contact-Induced Innovations in Istrian Čakavian Dialects', in *Language Contact in Times of Globalization*, ed. by Cornelius Hasselblatt, Peter Houtzagers, and Remco van Pareren (Amsterdam: Rodopi, 2011), pp. 61–76
Kerswill, Paul, 'Koineization and Accommodation', in *The Handbook of Language Variation and Change*, ed. by J. K. Chambers, Peter Trudgill, and Natalie Schilling-Estes (Malden: Blackwell, 2002), pp. 669–701
LEI = *Lessico etimologico italiano*, ed. by Max Pfister, Wolfgang Schweickard, and Elton Prifti (Wiesbaden: Reichert, 1979–)
Lepschy, Anna Laura, 'Tholomacii non Tholomarii', *Italian Studies*, 25 (1970), 79–80
Lepschy, Anna Laura, and Giulio Lepschy, 'From *antipasto* to *zabaglione*: Italianisms in the *Concise Oxford Dictionary*', in *Sguardi sull'Italia: Miscellania dedicata a Francesco Villari dalla Society for Italian Studies*, ed. by Gino Bedani and others (Leeds: Society for Italian Studies, 1997), pp. 242–59
Lepschy, Anna Laura, and Arturo Tosi, eds, *Rethinking Languages in Contact: The Case of Italian* (Oxford: Legenda, 2006)
Lodge, Anthony, 'Convergence and Divergence in the Development of the Paris Urban Vernacular', *Sociolinguistica*, 13 (1999), 51–68
Mancini, Marco, 'Voci orientali ed esotiche nella lingua italiana', in *Storia della lingua italiana*, III: *Le altre lingue*, ed. by Luca Serianni and Pietro Trifone (Turin: Einaudi, 1994), pp. 825–79
Marcato, Carla, *Ricerche etimologiche sul lessico veneto* (Padua: Cleup, 1982)
Martens, Georg Matthias von, *Italien*, vol. II (Stuttgart: Scheible, Rieger and Sattler, 1844)
Minervini, Laura, 'Le français dans l'Orient latin (XIIIe–XIVe siècles): Éléments pour la caractérisation d'une *scripta* du Levant', *Revue de Linguistique Romane*, 74 (2010), 119–98
——, 'Lexical Contact in the Mediterranean in the Middle Ages and Early Modern Times: French', in 'Language Contact in the Mediterranean in the Middle Ages and in Early Modern Times (with special focus on loanword lexicography)', ed. by Francesco Crifò, Elton Prifti, and Wolfgang Schweickard, thematic part of *Lexicographica: International Annual for Lexicography*, 33 (2017), 255–76

———, 'Veneziano e francese nell'Oriente latino', in *Il veneziano 'de là da mar': Contesti, testi, dinamiche del contatto linguistico e culturale*, ed. by Daniele Baglioni (Berlin: De Gruyter, 2020), pp. 177–200

Morgana, Silvia, 'L'influsso francese', in *Storia della lingua italiana*, III: *Le altre lingue*, ed. by Luca Serianni and Pietro Trifone (Turin: Einaudi, 1994), pp. 671–719

Morlicchio, Elda, *Lessico etimologico italiano: Germanismi* (Wiesbaden: Reichert, 2000–)

Morozzo della Rocca, Raimondo, ed., *Lettere di mercanti a Pignol Zucchello* (Venice: Il Comitato Editore, 1957)

OED = *Oxford English Dictionary*, <http://www.oed.com/>

OVI = *Opera del Vocabolario Italiano: Corpus OVI dell'Italiano antico*, <http://gattoweb.ovi.cnr.it>

Parkinson, Jennie, 'A Diachronic Study into the Distribution of Two Italo-Romance Synthetic Conditional Forms' (unpublished doctoral thesis, University of St Andrews, 2009)

Pellegrini, Giovan Battista, *Gli arabismi nelle lingue neolatine con speciale riguardo all'Italia* (Brescia: Peideia, 1972)

Penny, Ralph, *Variation and Change in Spanish* (Cambridge: Cambridge University Press, 2000)

Pfister, Max, 'Le superstrat germanique dans les langues romanes', in *XIV Congresso internazionale di linguistica e filologia romanza*, ed. by Alberto Varvaro (Amsterdam: Benjamins, 1978), pp. 48–97

Pinnavaia, Laura, *The Italian Borrowings in the 'Oxford English Dictionary': A Lexicographical, Linguistic, and Cultural Analysis* (Rome: Bulzoni, 2001)

Pozza, Marco, ed., *I trattati con Aleppo, 1207–1254* (Venice: Il Cardo, 1990)

Prati, Angelico, *Etimologie venete* (Venice: Istituto per la Collaborazione Culturale, 1968)

Ravid, Benjamin, 'Venice and its Minorities', in *A Companion to Venetian History, 1400–1797*, ed. by Eric Dursteler (Leiden: Brill, 2013), pp. 449–85

REW = *Romanisches etymologisches Wörterbuch*, ed. by Wilhelm Meyer-Lübke (Heidelberg: Winter, 1911)

Rinaldin, Anna, 'Il veneziano dei mercanti in Oltremare', in *Il veneziano 'de là da mar': Contesti, testi, dinamiche del contatto linguistico e culturale*, ed. by Daniele Baglioni (Berlin: De Gruyter, 2020), pp. 27–48

Rohlfs, Gerhard, *Germanisches Spracherbe in der Romania* (Munich: Bayerisches Akademie der Wissenschaften, 1947)

Rossebastiano Bart, Alda, *I 'Dialoghi' di Giorgio da Norimberga: Redazione veneziana, versione toscana, adattamento padovano* (Savigliano: L'Artistica, 1984)

———, *Vocabolari veneto-tedeschi del secolo XV*, 3 vols (Savigliano: L'Artistica, 1983)

Rossi, Vittorio, 'Maestri e scuole a Venezia verso la fine del Medioevo', *Rendiconti del Reale Istituto Lombardo di Scienze e Lettere*, 40 (1907), 765–81

Sala, Marius, 'Contact and Borrowing', in *The Cambridge History of the Romance Languages*, II: *Contexts*, ed. by Martin Maiden, John Charles Smith, and Adam Ledgeway (Cambridge: Cambridge University Press, 2013), pp. 187–236

Sallach, Elke, *Studien zum venezianischen Wortschatz des 15. und 16. Jahrhunderts* (Tübingen: Niemeyer, 1993)

Sanudo, Marino, *Itinerario per la Terraferma veneziana*, ed. by Gian Maria Varanini (Rome: Viella, 2014)

Sanuto, Marino, *I diarii*, ed. by Rinaldo Fulin and others, 58 vols (Venice: Visentini, 1879–1903)

Schulz, Juergen, 'Jacopo de' Barbari's View of Venice: Map Making, City Views, and Moralized Geography before the Year 1500', *Art Bulletin*, 60 (1978), 425–74

Schweickard, Wolfgang, 'Italian and Arabic', in 'Language Contact in the Mediterranean in the Middle Ages and in Early Modern Times (with special focus on loanword lexicography)', ed. by Francesco Crifò, Elton Prifti, and Wolfgang Schweickard, thematic part of *Lexicographica: International Annual for Lexicography*, 33 (2017), 121–84

Siegel, Jeff, 'Dialect Contact and Koineization', *International Journal of the Sociology of Language*, 99 (1993), 105–21

Simonsfeld, Henry, *Der Fondaco dei Tedeschi in Venedig und die deutsch-venetianischen Handelsbeziehungen*, 2 vols (Stuttgart: Cotta, 1887)

Stammerjohann, Harro, and others, eds, *Dizionario di italianismi in francese, inglese, tedesco* (Florence: Accademia della Crusca, 2008)

Stussi, Alfredo, 'La lingua', in *Storia di Venezia dalle Origini alla caduta della Serenissima*, ed. by Giorgio Cracco and Gherardo Ortalli, 8 vols (Rome: Istituto della Enciclopedia Italiana, 1992–1998), II, pp. 783–801, III, pp. 911–32

——, ed., *Zibaldone da Canal* (Venice: Il Comitato Editore, 1967)

Tafel, Gottlieb, and Georg Thomas, eds, *Urkunden zur ältern Handels- und Staatsgeschichte der Republik Venedig* (Vienna: Hof- und Staatsbucherai, 1856)

Terracini, Benvenuto, *Lingua libera e libertà linguistica: Introduzione alla linguistica storica* (Turin: Einaudi, 1963)

Thiriet, Freddy, *La Romanie vénitienne au Moyen Âge* (Paris: De Boccard, 1959)

Thomason, Sarah G., and Terrence Kaufman, *Language Contact, Creolization, and Genetic Linguistics* (Berkeley: University of California Press, 1988)

Tomasin, Lorenzo, 'Non solo Levante: Venezia e le lingue del Mediterraneo occidentale', *Autografo*, 63 (2020), 13–24

——, 'Sulla diffusione del lessico marinaresco italiano', *Studi Linguistici Italiani*, 36 (2010), 263–92

——, 'Urban Multilingualism: The Languages of Non-Venetians in Venice during the Middle Ages', in *Mittelalterliche Stadtsprachen*, ed. by Maria Selig and Susanne Ehrich (Regensburg: Schnell & Steiner, 2016), pp. 61–73

Trovato, Paolo, '"Dialetto" e sinonimi ("idioma", "proprietà", "lingua") nella terminologia linguistica quattro- e cinquecentesca', *Rivista di letteratura italiana*, 2 (1984), 205–36

Trudgill, Peter, *Dialects in Contact* (Oxford: Blackwell, 1986)

Tuttle, Edward, 'Profilo linguistico del Veneto', in *La linguistica italiana fuori d'Italia*, ed. by Lorenzo Renzi and Michele Cortelazzo (Rome: Bulzoni, 1997), pp. 125–59

Vatin, Nicolas, 'L'emploi du grec comme langue diplomatique par les Ottomans (fin du xve – début du xvie siècle)', in *Istanbul et les langues orientales*, ed. by Frédéric Hitzel (Paris: L'Harmattan, 1997), pp. 41–48

VEV = Tomasin, Lorenzo, and Luca D'Onghia, *Vocabolario storico-etimologico del veneziano*, <http://vev.ovi.cnr.it>

Vincent, Nigel, 'Languages in Contact in Medieval Italy', in *Rethinking Languages in Contact: The Case of Italian*, ed. by Anna Laura Lepschy and Arturo Tosi (Oxford: Legenda, 2006), pp. 12–27

Vuletić, Nikola, 'Volgare venezianeggiante a Zara nel xiv secolo', in *Il veneziano 'de là da mar': Contesti, testi, dinamiche del contatto linguistico e culturale*, ed. by Daniele Baglioni (Berlin: De Gruyter, 2020), pp. 75–102

Wansbrough, John, 'A Mamluk Letter of 877/1473', *Bulletin of the School of Oriental and African Studies*, 24.2 (1961), 200–13

——, 'Venice and Florence in the Mamluk Commercial Privileges', *Bulletin of the School of Oriental and African Studies*, 28.3 (1965), 483–523

Weinreich, Uriel, *Languages in Contact: Findings and Problems* (New York: Linguistic Circle of New York, 1953)

Zamboni, Alberto, 'Venezien/Veneto', in *Lexikon der romanistischen Linguistik*, ed. by Günter Holtus, Michael Metzeltin, and Christian Schmitt, vol. iv (Tübingen: Niemeyer, 1988), pp. 517–38

Zille, Ester, 'Il *ghetto* in un documento veneziano', *Archivio Veneto*, 124 (1985), 101–14

JOSEPH M. BRINCAT

Latin, Sicilian, and the Adoption of Italian in Malta

France, England, and Spain achieved early national status under strong monarchies in the first centuries of the second millennium and slowly established a unitary language for administration and culture, but Italy remained politically fragmented into medium-sized and small states up to 1861. This hampered the adoption of a standardized literary and administrative language for the whole peninsula, despite heartfelt appeals by Dante, Petrarch, and Machiavelli. It was only in the mid-sixteenth century that consensus was reached, thanks to the hotly debated *Questione della lingua*, for the codification and standardization of the Florentine *volgare* that would establish it as the literary language for the culturally minded persons of all Italy. When Pietro Bembo provided grammatical guidelines based mainly on the writings of Dante, Petrarch, and Boccaccio, he had understood the needs of writers from different regions who were doing their best to imitate the language of the *Tre corone*. Bembo's *Prose della volgar lingua* in 1525, Fortunio's earlier but less successful attempt, and especially the many grammatical descriptions that were printed in the second half of the sixteenth century satisfied those needs, together with the *Vocabolario degli Accademici della Crusca* in 1612, and so a polished and Latinized variety of Florentine became the literary language of all Italian writers. Before that, the attempts of Matteo Maria Boiardo in the North (Ferrara, the *Orlando Innamorato* in 1483–1504) and Jacopo Sannazaro in the South (Naples, the *Arcadia* in 1480–1504), whose early drafts had very strong local features, can be taken as symptomatic of the difficulties that non-Tuscan authors faced when writing for a public outside their region. So did Ludovico Ariosto in the mid-1500s, who not only produced three drafts of his *Orlando Furioso* (1516, 1521, and 1532), but also submitted the third redaction to Bembo himself for revision. One may add here that this problem haunted many non-Tuscan authors for centuries, up to Alessandro Manzoni who wrote his *Promessi Sposi*

> **Professor Joseph M. Brincat** (joseph.m.brincat@um.edu.mt) teaches Italian Linguistics at the University of Malta. His areas of research include Italian philology, the linguistic history of Malta, onomastics, and the dubbing of English films into Italian.

three times between 1821 and 1840. The adoption of Italian in Malta needs to be seen against this background.

Sicily and Malta, 1300–1550

After the Norman conquest in the eleventh century, Sicily was governed by the Swabians, the Angevins, the Aragonese, and then by Charles V's Spain. In the thirteenth century a group of writers at the court of Frederick II developed a polished, literary variety of Sicilian to express the thoughts and feelings of Provençal courtly love in sonnets and *canzoni*. The poets of the *Scuola siciliana* were admired by Dante (in *De vulgari eloquentia*), but their poems came to be known in the Tuscan adaptation made at the court of Lorenzo de' Medici. In their time they conferred prestige on a Sicilian koine which became the language of administration in the island and its dependencies in the fourteenth and fifteenth centuries. On the literary level Sicilian writers kept up a steady stream of works in their own variety from the fourteenth century onwards: religious works (a translation of the *Dialogues* of Saint Gregory in 1315, and of the Gospel according to Matthew in 1373 'in vulgari nostro siculo', and the anonymous *Libru di li vitii et di li virtuti* in 1360–1380), translations from Latin (Valerius Maximus's *Memorable Deeds and Sayings* in 1320; Virgil's *Aeneid* by Angilu di Capua in 1315, from Tuscan), historical accounts like the *Lamento di parte siciliana* (*c.* 1350), and also scientific works (Arnaldo da Villanova's *Thesaurus pauperum*, and others). Original works began in the fifteenth century in the form of love poems inspired by Petrarch and continued in the following centuries, despite the growing importance in the use of Tuscan.

In the domain of administration Latin was adopted by the Normans from the mid-twelfth century onwards, but the local *volgare* was introduced in the fourteenth (the earliest known documents in Sicilian are the *Capitoli* of 1320 and 1341) and its use increased from 1398 onwards, with Latin being reserved for regal and international correspondence. Worthy of note is the fact that Antonio de Nebrija's proposal in 1492 to introduce Castilian as the instrument of the Spanish Empire, which would have included Sicily and Malta, was not effected. It was blocked by the Sicilians' preference to align themselves with the Tuscanization process that was then spreading all over Italy.[1]

Malta, like Sicily, was under Muslim rule from 870 to 1091 and had to be reconquered by Roger II in 1127, but no Maltese documents in Arabic survived. When Frederick II expelled the Muslims from both islands, partly in 1224 and definitively in 1246, the language lost its prestige and kept on being spoken and written only by a small Jewish community up to their expulsion in 1492. From the mid-thirteenth century onwards Maghrebin Arabic died out in Sicily but survived in Malta where it developed under its own steam

---

1 Alfieri, 'La Sicilia', pp. 801–12.

in a long, slow process of Romanization. The first known document in Latin that reached Malta was sent by Queen Constance in 1198, together with an Arabic translation, addressed to all the Maltese, both Christians and Muslims.[2] Henry VI and his successors ceded Malta as a fief to Genoese counts from 1194 to 1285, with a spell around 1240 under Sicilian governors, and later to the Florentine Acciaioli family from 1358 to 1391. One can only surmise Sicilian, Genoese, and Florentine being spoken among the governors and their followers and by the garrison and their families, who must have interacted with locals living near the Castle-by-the-Sea in the respective periods, but all documents continued to be written in Latin.

A remarkable exception was the composition of two or three *cansos-sirventes* in Provençal by Peire Vidal who was hosted by the Genoese count Enrico Pescatore in 1204/05. One of them says:

> Ar ai conquist sojorn e banh
> a Mauta, on sui albergatz
> ab lo comt'Enric.
>
> > (Now I have gained pleasure and bliss
> > in Malta, where I am hosted
> > by Count Henry.)[3]

This is the only reference to cultural activity in the island in late medieval times, preceding by 270 years a reference to 'Petri de Caxaro philosophi poete et oratoris' who wrote in Latin and possibly Sicilian but has left only a *Cantilena* in Maltese datable to c. 1470.[4] The first evidence of the use of Latin in Malta after the Norman conquest is a document signed by notary Daniele De Danielis in 1271: 'In presentia Ruberti de Ebulo et Stephani de Natho judicum subscriptorum Castri malte notarij danielis de danielis puplici insularum maltij et Gaudicii notari et testium subscriptorum ad hoc specialiter vocatorum [...]' (In the presence of the undersigned Rubertus de Ebulo and Stephanius de Natho, judges of the Castle of Malta, of the notary Daniel de Danielis, public notary of the islands of Malta and Gozo, and of the undersigned witnesses called specifically for this purpose [...]).[5] A significant factor in the Romanization of the local variety of Arabic is the presence of Romance speakers who increased steadily as time went by, occasionally in groups, like the rebellious inhabitants of Celano (in the Abruzzi) who were deported to Malta by Frederick II in 1224 to fill the gap left by the expelled Muslims. Punitive deportations to Malta were not rare: in 1450 a whole family was sent from Scicli, and in 1485 forty persons were exiled to Malta. Moreover, the majority of notaries working in Malta came from Sicily, and their integration

---

2 Jamil and Johns, 'A New Latin-Arabic Document'.
3 Brincat, 'Le poesie "maltesi" di Peire Vidal'.
4 Wettinger and Fsadni, *Peter Caxaro's Cantilena*; Brincat, 'The *Cantilena*'.
5 Luttrell, 'Christian Slaves at Malta', pp. 382–83.

in local circles was facilitated by the ordinance that no foreigner was eligible to hold public office in Malta and Gozo unless he was married to a Maltese and had been resident for at least five years. Like the clergy, notaries were constantly in touch with ordinary citizens, and this necessarily generated linguistic contact, hence Romanization.

In the fourteenth and fifteenth centuries Malta was ruled from Sicily, but it had a municipal government, the *Universitas*, which left abundant records written from 1434 to around 1550 (with attached documents dating back to 1410). The *jurati* were generally members of the Siculo-Catalan noble families and local professionals, mainly notaries, but they also comprised two *giudici idioti*, illiterate representatives of the people. The minutes of the council meetings were either totally in Latin, or in Latin (the formal introductory and conclusive sentences) and Sicilian (the main paragraphs). The debates must have been carried out in Sicilian, but the presence of the unschooled members would have necessitated the use of Maltese too, otherwise the latter would not have been able to follow what was going on. An explicit statement that discussions were also held in Maltese is found in the minutes of the meeting held on 14 December 1592, a relatively late date which, however, does not exclude that it was practiced before. Anyway, Maltese words do appear here and there, especially with reference to place names and ordinary objects whose Latin equivalent was not known. It is therefore clear that educated locally born persons were trilingual: they had learnt Latin, were conversant with Sicilian administrators, landowners, merchants, and artisans, and spoke Maltese with family, friends, and fellow-countrymen.

The variety of Sicilian that was written in Malta was strictly administrative in nature. Literary works are unknown, and the documents consist of minutes of council sittings, *capitula* (petitions), *mandati* (authorizations of payments), inventories, and notarial deeds. The vocabulary varies, obviously, according to the subject matter, from highly formal to down-to-earth. This high variety, also called Chancery Sicilian, has been defined as 'sopraregionale' and marked by 'deregionalizzazione',[6] which means showing a strong tendency to distance itself from low local varieties by reducing regional features. Its heavy dependence on Latin in the creation of bureaucratic formulas is also evident. The most important registers of the council sittings at Mdina (Notabile, the old capital) are the manuscripts marked BNM, Università 11, whose contents have been published by Godfrey Wettinger, and BNM, Università 12 published by Stanley Fiorini.[7] These registers contain the minutes concerning a wide range of activities, especially revenues, expenditure, salaries, victuals, defence, and various events and affairs affecting the islands of Malta and Gozo.

---

6 Alfieri, 'La Sicilia', pp. 810–11.
7 *Acta juratorum et consilii civitatis et insulae Maltae (1450–1499)*; DSMH, III.3: *Acta juratorum et consilii civitatis et insulae Maltae II, 1512–1531*.

The earliest surviving document written in Sicilian is a petition presented to Martin I of Aragon, king of Sicily, at Lentini on 31 May 1398 by Francesco Gatto, a Maltese fiefholder, and Antoni Budara of Catania in the name of the castellan and his men who were besieged in the castle: 'Martinus dei gracia, [...] Quisti su li capituli facti per mi Antoni Vitellu, Castellanu di lu Castellu di Mari di Malta, et quisti su li graczi li quali eu adimandu alu serenissumu signuri Re'.[8] A document sent from Catania in 1345 attests that Sicilian was understood at least fifty years earlier because although the text is in Latin the goods that are to be sold in Malta are listed in Sicilian (*sagulj, spacu, aurupellj, cartj, scupi, inchensu, candelj di sivu pinti*, etc.). However, all the letters sent to Malta by the royal or vice-royal chanceries in Palermo or Catania from 1360 to 1400 are in Latin, and only seven are in Sicilian out of 293, dated 1393–1399. The first one was sent on 10 July 1393: 'Richiputa per nuy la vostra lictera et tractandu delu spacxamentu per mandarj pristu a Malta di quo nj scriviristiriu, vinni Jza Urlandu di Castru lu qualj he prumptu ad exequirj tuctu quillu kj prumissi'.[9] After 1400 Sicilian is used more often. Documents received in Malta from the royal and vice-royal chanceries in Palermo, Catania, or Messina between 1405 and 1542 are mostly in Sicilian, only 22 out of 136 being in Latin, and eleven in Spanish (one sent in 1488, one in 1509, and the others between 1513 and 1535). The first one in Sicilian is dated 1405, sent by King Martin from Catania: 'Comu ben sapiti per la nostra excellentia et maturu consiglu e statu provistu la construccioni di li galey ki fachimu fari in la Nobili nostra chitati di Missina per lu saluti et beneficiu universali di quistu regnu'.[10] It abounds in words ending in -*u*, unlike documents written a hundred years later, where Sicilian features seem to be limited to spelling and occasional words ending in -*i* in the singular:

> Per la qual cosa dicto magnifico jurato et ambaxiatori ut supra ni ha supplicato che li fachissimo exequiri et observari li preinserti provisioni; nuy intesa sua supplicatione como justa volendo rendirini conformi con li mandati di lo Illustrissimo [Signuri] presidenti di quisto regno havimo provisto et per la presenti vi dicimo et comandamo expresse che quanto ad nui et al nostro officio specta digiati exequiri, compliri et observari et fari per quos decet exequiri compliri et observari la forma continenti et tenuri di li preinserti provisioni senza aspectari altro nostro comandamento ne consulta sub pena in preinsertis provisionibus contenta fisco regio applicanda.[11]

> (For this reason the aforementioned honourable council member and ambassador asked that we should execute and apply the attached

---

8 *DSMH*, III.2: *The Capitula of Malta and Gozo*, p. 3; also *DSMH*, II.1: *Cancelleria Regia*, p. 269.
9 *DSMH*, II.1: *Cancelleria Regia*, p. 187.
10 *DSMH*, III.1: *Cathedral Museum, Mdina*, p. 2.
11 *DSMH*, III.1: *Cathedral Museum, Mdina*, p. 193.

decisions; having considered his request as a just one, and wishing to conform with the decisions of the honourable president of this kingdom, we have decided and, by the present we inform and command you expressly that, as it is our duty to execute, complete, and apply and do what is necessary to execute, complete, and apply the formal contents and tenure of the attached decisions without expecting any other order or consultation from us, to apply sub poena the contents of the royal tax system.)[12]

This document was sent from Palermo in 1542, but apparently the typical endings in *-u* had already been avoided or reduced for some years: 'sensa aviri danno alchono et se ale S. V. pari che ad tanto populo sia alchono danno nexiri lu prezo de quilli pensati quanto danno e amme solo et dela chasa mia che non a altra chosa al mondo' (Messina, 1521); 'lo quondam magnifico Joanni de Givara olim secreto et al presenti in potiri di so figlo pro certo precio carta gratie reddimendi' (Palermo, 1528).[13] The will to move away from local features and approach Tuscan is evident after 1500.

The registers in the Notarial Archives are another valuable source of information concerning life in Malta, including linguistic orientation, from 1467 to 1530. As in Sicily, in Malta most acts were drawn up in Latin, but the use of Sicilian increased, as the following quotation, dated 13 February 1495, shows: 'Testamur quod eu notaru Jacobu Sabara regiu publicu notaru dj lj Jnsolj, chitati et terra dj Malta e Gozu scrjvu lu Jnfrascriptu assecuramentu. Pro nomu et arte di honorabilj Vicenciu Bestardes Cathalanu et di raxuni di lo dicto Vicencio oy di altri [...]'.[14] Giacomo Sabara (or Zabbara) left registers with acts covering the years 1486–1488 and 1494–1497, and the one of 1495 quoted above seems to be the first notarial contract drawn up entirely in Sicilian, but this koine appears in phrases and paragraphs before 1495. The same Sabara in proceedings dated 30 October 1486 inserted whole passages in Sicilian reporting the declarations of witnesses: 'Item dixit quod [...] foru facti li pedamenti et incomenczaru a murari lu dictu muru alargandulu di lu antiquu pedamentu per forma prout occulatim videri potest et apparet ky veni ad obturari la dicta antiqua fenestra di lu dictu Cataldu'.[15]

However, documents in the curia of the Archbishop of Malta show the earlier use of Sicilian: an act dated 2 July 1453 transcribes a will that was drawn up the year before, on 23 June 1452:

> Eu Anthoni Vagnolo miles essendo sano et la mia memoria de mia manu scrivo lo meu presenti testamentu, et voglo ke omni mei autri testamenti,

---

12 All the translations are my own.
13 *DSMH*, III.1: *Cathedral Museum, Mdina*, p. 147 (1521), p. 179 (1528).
14 *DSMH*, I.2: *Notary Giacomo Zabbara R494*, p. 84.
15 *DSMH*, I.3: *Notary Paulo Bonello; Notary Giacomo Zabbara*, p. 226.

codicilli et autri mei voluntati siano cassi et non haiano nullu valuri, ma voglo che lo mio presente testamento sulamenti haia valuri in ogni cossa, etc.[16]

> (I, Anthoni Vagnolo, knight, being in a good state of health and memory write down the present will and testament, and I wish that all the other wills and testaments, codicils, and other wishes of mine be cancelled and have no validity at all, but I want that only the present will and testament will be valid for all matters, etc.)

The language in this will is intriguing because although Sicilian forms are not lacking (*manu, testamentu, autri, voluntati, haianu, nullu valuri, sulamenti*), words ending in *-o* are many and reveal a desire to approach Tuscan in Malta too (*essendo sano, haiano, scrivo, voglo, testamento*). A short phrase in Tuscan is found in a document written in Latin in 1487: 'Jn quolibet festo pasce resurreccionis dominice prout morjs est Melite videlicet *la prima annata si paga*.'[17] The italicized words may be simply an overlap between high Sicilian and Tuscan, but it indicates how the process of de-regionalization facilitated the shift which would take place in a few decades.

The Church obviously produced its documents mainly in Latin. The only register of the Maltese curia that has been published contains ninety-seven Latin documents of which one attaches the will in Sicilian dated 1452 quoted above. Sicilian phrases, usually very short, sometimes found their way into the Latin texts, almost as slips of the pen: 'in li faudi di la montagna' in doc. 76 (1532), 'de lino Lixandrino' in doc. 82 (1537), and a couple of paragraphs in docs. 66 (1533) and 67 (1519).[18] An earlier document called the *Rollo* of 1436 lists all the ecclesiastical benefices in Malta that were subject to taxation imposed by the papacy, and although the text is in Latin, the benefices are mostly in Sicilian: 'lo Animagio di la muglieri di Notaro Paulu'; 'la Petia di lu Ciantratu'; 'la putiga di Donna Margarita'; 'la cappella di lu Burgu'; 'lo animagio di Misser Brancato'. These definitions appear Italianized in seventeenth-century copies, but Abela copied them as quoted here in 1647.[19] One can add here that the *Rollo* of 1459 was drawn up in Latin. In the sixteenth century the Maltese diocese was a truly multinational institution: from 1501 to 1614 the bishops, most of whom were not resident, hailed from Noto, Rome, Genoa, Palermo, Pisa, Asti, and also from Spain and Germany. The diocesan clergy were mainly Maltese, but a good number of surnames indicate recent Sicilian or Italian descent. There were foreigners too, who came mostly from Sicily, but some were Spaniards, Florentines, Venetians, and a few were French.[20]

---

16 *DSMH*, v.1: *The Registrum Fundationum Beneficiorum Insulae Gaudisii*, p. 54.
17 *DSMH*, I.1: *Notary Giacomo Zabbara R494/1(1)*, p. 219.
18 *DSMH*, v.1: *The Registrum Fundationum Beneficiorum Insulae Gaudisii*, pp. 95–98, 109, 116.
19 Abela, *Descrittione di Malta*, pp. 313–16; Borg, *The Maltese Diocese and the Sicilian Environment*, pp. 737–48.
20 Borg, *The Maltese Diocese during the Sixteenth Century*, pp. 89–456.

Although the importance of the written use of Sicilian in Malta cannot be overestimated, the influence of the Sicilian dialect on the local language was significant too. This came about mainly through perennial commercial contacts, because Malta depended heavily on the importation of wheat, barley, and legumes from Licata, Syracuse, and Scicli, and even more through Sicilian craftsmen and labourers who worked here, a good number of whom married local girls and settled down. Proof of this is borne by the Maltese language itself which absorbed thousands of Sicilian technical terms regarding the arts and crafts (particularly carpentry, fishing, and building), apart from the more obvious learned terms pertaining to law, administration, religion, medicine, and education. Immigration is also substantiated by the numerous Sicilian surnames that are common in Malta.[21] Suffice it to remark, here, that the population of Malta rose from about 10,000 persons in 1241 to over 20,000 in 1530, and then up to 100,000 in 1797 (520,000 in 2022), and that in the lexicon of common usage words of Arabic origin are now only 22.5 per cent (but they enjoy the highest frequency) whereas those of Sicilian and Italian origin are more numerous (61.6%, mainly advanced and specialized terms), with a fair sprinkling of English words that are rapidly increasing.[22]

The Use of Tuscan in Malta before the Knights

The formal and consistent use of Tuscan was introduced by the Knights Hospitallers of the Order of St John from 1530 onwards, but there is sporadic evidence that it was known before that. There had been links between Malta and Tuscany during the Middle Ages, including an intriguing hypothesis: in 1268, during the preparations for the Battle of Tagliacozzo, sixteen-year-old Conradin, the last descendant of the glorious Swabian dynasty, signed an agreement with the Ghibelline government of Pisa offering the castle of Malta in exchange for Pisa's naval support of his campaign. Conradin's dream dissolved in a bloodbath, therefore Tuscan did not become the official language of Malta in the thirteenth century. Documents occasionally mention the presence of persons from Tuscany: the merchant Bonaccurso Saullo from Lucca is named in notarial deeds of 1274–1276, and so is notary Leone de Puntetremulo who wrote a will in 1299. However, if the latter hailed from Pontremoli, he would not have spoken Tuscan because the area known as Lunigiana has its own dialect, but his education and profession may have taken him to Florence. In 1314 the Bardi bankers of Florence had a fondaco here, and there was also a hypothetical Florentine ruler: Niccolò Acciaioli was given the title Count

---

21 Brincat, 'I cognomi a Malta'; Cassar, 'Maltese Surnames'.
22 Brincat, *Maltese and Other Languages*, pp. 222–26, 344–46, 409–19; Brincat, 'Maltese: Blending'.

of Malta by Queen Joan of Naples in 1357, but apparently he never set foot on the island although he kept his title till his death and passed it on to his son Angelo, who still bore it in 1391.

In Sicily the Church was one of the first agents of Tuscanization, and Varvaro reports that preachers, especially the members of the religious orders, were nurtured on Tuscan and Umbrian model sermons, and therefore brought Tuscan elements into circles where literature was unknown before the sixteenth century.[23] In Malta, the local convents belonged to the Sicilian province, most of the members of the religious orders were Sicilian, and Maltese youths were trained for the priesthood in Sicily, but there may have been Tuscan monks in the various orders that founded monasteries and built churches between 1371 and 1452 (Benedictines in 1371, Franciscans in 1372, Augustinians in 1413, Carmelites in 1418, the Benedictine sisters and the Dominicans in 1452), but there is no evidence of Tuscan texts in administrative circles in Malta before the arrival of the Knights of St John.

Local lay circles comprised the legal system and education, and Latin dominated in both sectors; however, one would expect that in the fifteenth century Sicilian notaries and teachers would have read works by Dante, Petrarch, and Boccaccio at least, and the passive use of Tuscan in this sense may have been picked up by local practitioners. An indirect reference to local culture is reported by Giacomo Bosio: on his first visit to the old capital of Malta in 1530, Grand Master Philippe Villiers de L'Isle Adam, who was French, was introduced to the nobles and other important people and found out that 'some of them are quite learned, and loved literature'. He enjoyed their company and spoke to them for a long time, but we do not know whether they conversed in Latin, French, Tuscan, or Sicilian because the author did not specify.[24] The Maltese nobles' welcoming speech pronounced by the First Jurat on handing the capital's keys to the Grand Master, or according to one source an official letter sent on 13 November 1530, has come down to us in Tuscan:

> Ser.mo Signore. Essendosi degnata S. O. M. sublimare V.A.S. al Principato di quest'isola di Malta e Gozo, e dovendo oggi felicemente prendere il possesso, io ed i miei colleghi, come Giurati di questa città Notabile ed Isola di Malta, riverentemente supplichiamo V.A.S. giurare sopra l'abito della Sua Gran Croce come fecero li ser.mi suoi Predecessori d'osservare, e comandare che siano osservati, tutti li Privilegi, usanze e franchigie dell'Isola concessi dall'Invittissimi Regi d'Aragona e di Sicilia e da' Magnanimi Principi. Consegno le chiavi di Città Notabile a V.A.S. en segno di Vassallaggio, fedeltà e servitù, e Dio lo conservi con ogni prosperità per lunghi e felicissimi anni. Amen.[25]

---

23 Varvaro, 'Bilancio degli studi sulla storia linguistica meridionale', p. 34.
24 Bosio, Dell'Istoria della Sacra Religione, III, p. 90.
25 BNM, MS Libr. 255.

(Honourable Gentleman. Having His Majesty deigned to raise Your Most Serene Highness to the Principality of this island of Malta and Gozo, of which you are happily taking possession today, my colleagues and I, as Council members of this town of Notabile and the Island of Malta, respectfully supplicate your Most Serene Highness to swear by the habit of your Grand Cross, as your predecessors have done, to apply and order that they be applied all the Privileges, Customs, and franchises of the island conceded by the Invincible Kings of Aragon and Sicily and by the Magnanimous Princes. I hand over the keys of the Town of Notabile to Your Serene Highness as a token of Allegiance, loyalty, and servitude, and may God grant you prosperity for many long and happy years. Amen.)

The plea to keep the privileges guaranteed by the Order of St John's predecessors would witness the first formal use of Tuscan by Maltese citizens, but unfortunately, it has survived only in two later copies, wherefore one cannot rule out its being a translation of the original in Latin or Sicilian.

In the fifteenth century, education was badly organized, teachers were few and badly paid, and no syllabi have survived. The capital city's school is first mentioned in 1461 and had a Sicilian teacher in 1471–1472 and the first Maltese teacher in 1479 (Don Giulius di Lia). Traces of some knowledge of Italian literary works are very few and appear mainly in legal and ecclesiastical documents that belong to the sixteenth century. Davide Basaldella traced quotations from Petrarch dated 1531 in a register of notary Giacomo Bondino ('da man destra ove gli occhi in prima porsi | la bella donna avea Cesare e Scipio' — *Triumphus Famae*, vv. 22–23), from Ariosto ('Magnianimo s(ignor) ogni vostro atto | l'ho sempre co(n) ragion lodato e laudo' — *Orlando Furioso*, canto XVI, vv. 1–2), and from an anonymous sixteenth-century villotta (*Battaglia amorosa*: 'All'arma, all'arma affin di miei pensieri | Correte tutti in guardia del mio core | perché s'avicina il mio inimico'), dated 1575 in a register of notary De Bonetiis.[26] Although written on rough manuscript pages among other scribblings, they show that Maltese literati were somewhat familiar with Italian literature. It is worth noting that notary Bondino was also the schoolteacher at the old capital town from 1519 to 1525 and from 1528 to 1531, wrote epigrams in Latin, and collaborated with Neapolitan scholars on the 1526 edition of the medieval *Cronaca di Partenope*. A bit more informative is the strambotto of Leonardo Giustinian (1388–1446), *Se li Arbori sapessero parlare*, declaimed by Marino Micallef, an Augustinian, at a friars' informal event. It was copied in a note dated 1598, unattributed and wrongly defined as 'una cansone in siciliana'. The anecdote was written at the close of the century, but it suggests that the custom of reading poems for entertainment was well established:

---

26 Basaldella, 'Testimonianze primocinquecentesche', p. 123.

È costume fra noi altri frati tre o quattro volte l'anno in certe feste solenne con licentia de superiori pigliare alc.e recreat.e et spassi. Et ultimam.te quindici dì fa inc.a con occ.ne che allogiava nel d.o mon.o un n.ro visitatore mandato dal provinciale et p. dargli un poco di recreatione, il mio priore mi pregò che cantassi una cansone in siciliana la q.ale comincia così.[27]

> (It is the custom among us friars that three or four times a year on certain solemn festivities, with the permission of our superiors, we enjoy some form of entertainment. Lately, about fifteen days ago, on the occasion of the stay with us of a visitor sent by the provincial, and to entertain him, my prior asked me to sing a Sicilian song that begins with these words.)

The first record of verses written by a Maltese author in Tuscan is an *Inno alla Vittoria* by Gregorio Xerri written between 1565 and 1625. This is an unusual composition of thirteen unequal lines, a religious and patriotic celebration of the Great Siege of 1565, with consonance in lines 1–2 and 8–9, and a rhyming couplet at the end. Considering that the author died sixty years after the siege, and that it is signed 'Barone di Cicciano', a title he inherited in 1581, it was probably a later commemoration of the event, perhaps intended to be sung in church:

Dio Signor degli Eserciti, noi vincemmo.
Dio Signor onnipotente, noi trionfammo.
Nostra è la vittoria, a Voi sia sempre gloria.
Gloria al Padre, al Figlio, allo Spirito Santo.
Donzelle Maltesi venite al Tempio,
Venite in bianca veste,
Venite per lodare e benedire il Signore.
Nel nostro giubilo
Ti lodiamo, o nostro Publio.
Fanciulli, giovani e vecchi
Correte, correte al Tempio,
Gettate rose e viole per vera allegria
All'altare di Maria.[28]

> (God, Lord of hosts, we won.
> God, Lord Almighty, we triumphed.
> Victory is ours, glory be to You.
> Glory be to the Father, the Son, and the Holy Spirit.
> Girls of Malta come to the Temple.
> Come wearing white,
> Come to praise and bless the Lord.

---

27 AIM, Proc. Crim. MS 16A, Case 30, fol. 241ʳ.
28 Bonello, 'Gregorio Xerri's Poem'.

In our joy
We praise you, our Publius.
Children, youths, and old people
Run, run to the Temple,
Throw roses and violets to express your sincere joy
At the altar of Mary.)

Spoken Italian

As for the spoken level, the earliest sentence in Tuscan was written in the minutes of the Universitas dated 15 November 1453. Although the document is in Latin, the sentences uttered by Fiderico Calavà, a Maltese notary who was a member of the council, are one in Tuscan and one in Sicilian: 'fuit facta presens nota in presenti quaterno juratorum per me notarium Petrum [de Caxaro] predictum tamquot notarium juratorum cui notarius Fidericus respondit "Portatemi nota et diarii et farrovi la protesta" intelligendo pro protestacione requisita ut supra "Nentiminu se voglu primu maniari et poy farrovi la protesta"'.[29] Speech was sometimes quoted in legal documents when the witnesses' words were reported verbatim, but in most cases testimony was paraphrased.

An idea of the way people spoke can be conjectured on the basis of the less formal, practical documents, like wills, contracts of sale, insurance instruments, inventories, *capitula*, and *mandati*. One of the earliest examples of the transition from Sicilian to Tuscan is a marine insurance policy of 1536 in the records of notary De Agatiis, who worked in Malta but was from Marsala: 'Al nome de Dio et di bon salvamento si fa assecurare lo no. Gabrieli Martino. Fachendosi assecurare tanto p. sì q.nto et p. nome di soi compagni in solidum di loro ragione supra certa quantitati di sacch. di cuttone filate di Cattara dedichotto'. On analysing its language, Davide Basaldella notes that Sicilian features are still present, but it also shows the tendency to Tuscanize.[30] A legal document at the Mdina Cathedral Museum dated 22 August 1550 written in Latin also carries parts which show an effort to write Tuscan:

> have lassato a la ditta Ysabella figla del ditto mro damiano unzi quatro [...] si deviano pagare in questo modo vz li tre unzi per li ditti heredi et l'una per lo ditto Cola Schachapani suo marito deloq.e legato le ditti heredi hanno avuto et tenino plena notitia et hanno visto lo testamento de la ditta donna Agnesa et se haviano consentito bonamenti ditti unzi quatro pagar a la donna Ysabella.[31]

---

29 *Acta juratorum et consilii civitatis et insulae Maltae*, doc. 38.
30 Basaldella, 'Testimonianze primocinquecentesche', pp. 123–24.
31 CEM, MS 30, *Acta Originalia*, anno 1550, fol. 9ʳ.

(he left four ounces for the said Isabella, daughter of the aforementioned Master Damiano […] which have to be paid as follows: three ounces for the said heirs and one for the said Cola Schachapani her husband, of whose legacy the said heirs have been notified and are fully aware, and they have seen the will and testament of the said Lady Agnesa, and they have willingly approved that the said four ounces be paid to Lady Isabella.)

In these documents the words spoken by the witnesses are usually recorded in Sicilian, which was probably how they were uttered during the proceedings, but the above passage shows a mixed medium where Latin, Tuscan, and Sicilian elements merge. Other useful scraps of information on the changing linguistic situation can be found in documents of the Dominican order. These were examined by Fr. Michael Fsadni who states that before 1565 novices learned Latin and Italian, though he admits that this is not attested in documents. He also reproduced a marble inscription which commemorated the construction of the refectory in the monastery dedicated to the Annunciation at Borgo which said 'Li magnifici Francesco et Dionisia Mego han fatto fare questo refettorio per la celebratione perpetua delli misse chi li convento è obbligato, 1556'. Unfortunately, this plaque was discovered among the war ruins in 1952 but is now considered lost. Fr. Fsadni also found a reference to the private notebook of a Dominican friar called Pasquale Vassallo who wrote poems in Italian and in Maltese, but his manuscripts were burned on account of their author's homosexual and paedophile sentiments. They had been written around 1584, and the disciplinary entry quotes the manuscript's *incipit* which has no Sicilian features. It began 'Questo quinterno è mio, Pasquale Vassallo' and ended 'et fa lo disegno che vuoi tu'.[32] At present this anecdote is the earliest reference we have to poems written in Italian and, considering that Vassallo's works were mentioned only because they were censored, one can surmise that there were earlier attempts which nobody bothered to record.

The linguistic medium that linked the people with the authorities were the *bandi* or proclamations, because these were read out in the squares and streets of the various towns and villages. The proclamations of the fifteenth century were in Sicilian, as the following shows (4 October 1469): 'Emissum fuit proclama et bannum puplicum […] ki nixunu piscaturi et venditori di pixi oy di canna sia oy di xabica oy per qualsivoglia maynera si pigli lu pixi et portasi a vindiri digia vindiri li pixi si non a lu locu solitu di la piscaria'.[33] The collection of *bandi* enacted during the seventeenth and eighteenth centuries are all written in Italian, but they were probably not read out as they were written. Since they were meant to be obeyed by the whole population that was mainly monolingual, they must have been interpreted or explained in Maltese.

---

32 Fsadni, *Id-Dumnikani*, pp. 110–11.
33 *Acta juratorum et consilii civitatis et insulae Maltae*, p. 368.

Regarding the books that were read in Malta, only one reference has turned up. An inventory listing the possessions notary Brandano de Caxaro left to family and friends on his demise in 1565 mentions some books, but only one title is given, 'uno libro chiamato li capituli dilo regno', which can be identified as the *Capitula et Constitutiones Regni Siciliae* printed at Messina in 1497.[34] Other books have been mentioned only thanks to religious censure: witnesses testifying at the proceedings of the Inquisition in 1543–1545 said that they read Terence, Ovid, Cicero, Virgil, Horace, and other Latin writers, but do not mention any Italian authors. However, their evidence is recorded in Italian, calling their teachers 'maestro di scola di Gramatica', or 'mio precettore di Gramatica'.[35] Witnesses in 1560 mention notaries and schoolteachers who read prohibited books by Luther and the *Colloquii* of Erasmus, presumably in Latin, and one witness reported that these books were also read in the schools.[36] Among the books, mostly of a religious or Protestant nature in Latin, French, English, or Italian, burned at the Main Square of Vittoriosa by order of Inquisitor Evangelista Carbonese on 5 May 1609 one finds Machiavelli, but 'in lingua gallica'.[37] Not surprisingly, the only Italian literary work mentioned is Boccaccio's. In a letter dated 13 September 1577 the General Inquisitor in Rome congratulates Inquisitor Raynaldo Corso for having burned prohibited books like those of Erasmus and the *Decamerone*.[38]

The shift from Sicilian to Italian at the Mdina local council may have taken place when a knight was appointed governor of Mdina, Gonzalo Cervantes in 1534. But the use of Sicilian in local administration did not die out so soon because records show documents in Sicilian written in 1539, 1543, 1557, and 1561. The *mandati* of the Universitas and of the Mdina cathedral kept on being written in Sicilian up to 1539. When the Order of St John settled in Malta in 1530 the jurats of the local Universitas continued writing in Sicilian even when addressing the Grand Master, as the petitions presented in 1530, 1531, and 1532 (quoted below) show:

> In primis, per quando che la dicta Universita teni certi introyti patrimoniali super certi gabelli dicti dila intrata di lo porto et di la xisa, separati di altro patrimonio ab antiquo ordinati ad opu et servicio di dicta Universita et non ab re et sine causa ma comu utili et necessari ad effectu che dicta Universita in soi bisogni et necessita si recurri et subveni supra dicti introyti, li quali introyti Vostra Illustrissima et Reverendissima S. havi impedito in gravi discommodo, preiudicio et mancamento di dicta Universita, pertanto li plaza relaxari dicti introyti ala dicta Universita eo modo et forma che innanti erano per la causa et effecto supradicto.

---

34 Abela, 'Don Brandano Caxario', p. 29.
35 AIM, Processi, II, MS 14, fol. 1ᵛ; MS III xv, fol. 5ᵛ; MS IV 30, fol. 8ʳ. Borg, *The Maltese Diocese during the Sixteenth Century*, pp. 54–55.
36 Cassar, 'The Reformation in Sixteenth Century Malta', pp. 61–62.
37 Cassar, *Witchcraft, Sorcery and the Inquisition*, p. 95.
38 Cassar, *Witchcraft, Sorcery and the Inquisition*, p. 61.

(First of all, regarding the property earnings of the said Council from certain land rents described as harbour dues and excise duties, separate from other property which have been long ago assigned for the good and service of the said Council, and not from themselves and without cause, but they are useful and necessary for the said Council's needs and necessities and it relies on their return, which earnings Your Illustrious and Reverend Lordship has held back, causing serious discomfort, prejudice, and scarcity to the said Council, therefore may you be pleased to release these earnings to the said Council in the same manner that was used formerly for the causes and effects mentioned above.)

In this plea, as in other documents written in Sicily at the time, the avoidance of the typical ending in -*u* is evidently an attempt to approach Tuscan. It is also significant that the reply they obtained from Grand Master L'Isle Adam, penned by Vice-Chancellor Thomas De Bosio on 15 June 1532, is in Tuscan:

Molto Magnifici Signori,
L'altro giorno poi havessi trattato piu volte sopra li capitoli et cose delle S. V. et questa Universita Mons.or R.mo et suo Ven.do Consiglio discusso il negocio et declarata quasi lor volonta sopra le partite sequente, commessero et accordarono che tutto quello saria fatto sopra cio dalli R.di S.ri et Prior nostro Della Chiesa et Baglio di Manoasc l'haverieno per bene et terrieno per fatto. Quali S.ri Priore et Baglio, essendo io presente, conclusero.[39]

(Very reverend Gentlemen
The other day, having discussed many times the chapters and affairs of Your Lordship and this Council, the Most Reverend Monsignor and his Venerable Council discussed the business and declared their wish on the following matter, they decided and agreed that all shall be done by the Most Reverend Gentlemen and our Prior of the Church and Bailiff of Manoasc which they approve and take as done. In my presence the said Gentlemen, Prior, and Bailiff concluded the matter.)

The above is the first document in Tuscan received by the jurats of the Maltese Universitas, and it started a process that took a few decades during which Chancery Sicilian was slowly abandoned and Tuscan adopted not only in dealing with the Order but also among the Maltese, in both administration and culture. An early example of this shift is a legal document written in 1536 by notary De Agatiis that has been analysed in detail by Davide Basaldella who carefully discussed its Sicilian and Tuscan features.[40]

---

39 *DSMH*, III.2: *The Capitula of Malta and Gozo*, pp. 337 and 341–42.
40 Basaldella, 'Testimonianze primocinquecentesche', pp. 122–24.

The Knights and Malta

The Knights of St John had already used Tuscan occasionally in the mid-fifteenth century in Rhodes. Parts of the proceedings of the Chapters General held there in 1454, 1475, 1495, and 1501 are written in Tuscan. The Chapter General was the highest legislative and administrative organ of the Order of St John. There are also translations of statutes and regulations from Latin in a fifteenth-century manuscript,[41] as well as instructions to non-Italian knights and privileges granted to Turkish merchants in the *Liber Bullarum*.[42] The influence of Latin and Venetian is evident, but on the whole the language can be defined as Italian. Since its foundation, the Order of St John used French as its official language because the majority of its members came from France, but in 1357 the need was felt to produce a Latin version of the statutes to guarantee textual precision, and Latin remained the high language of the Order till its expulsion from Malta in 1798. However, in 1446, since the cultural level of the knights was not very high, a simplified form of Latin was adopted. Giacomo de Soris wrote:

> Nunc de Regula et Statutis apud urbem romanam in sancta congregatione ad ipsius augmentum et Religionis confirmacionem factis, verba faciemus in quo humili stilo et materno quasi sermone utimur ut, cum ipsi milites magis ferro quam litteris apti sint, ad interpretanda varia rerum vocabula laborare non cogantur.[43]
>
>> (Now having confirmed the Regulations and Statute at the city of Rome for the holy congregation and for its improvement and for the confirmation of the Order, we wrote in humble and almost native words so that, as the knights are better at using the sword than letters, they will not find it difficult to understand the text.)

De Soris's 'materno sermone' was obviously Tuscan, since he belonged to the Langue of Italy.[44] In Bartolomeo Del Pozzo's *Ruolo Generale* (1738), he is listed under the surname Sorij with the title of Commendatore of Bologna, but his priory is not specified and so his region is not known.

In Malta the Order of St John immediately adopted Italian in some of its official organs, as can be seen in the minutes of the first Chapter General held in Malta under Grand Master Philippe Villiers de L'Isle Adam on

---

41 BNM, MS Arch. 1700, written in 1467. Stefano Rapisarda traced another, almost identical version, BNM, MS 501, and surprisingly a Sicilian version, BNM, MS Libr. 461, written in 1433. Rapisarda, 'Il volgarizzamento siciliano'.
42 BNM, MS Arch. 363 for the years 1451–1452.
43 BNM, MS Arch. 1698, fol. 14[r].
44 For administrative purposes the Order of St John grouped the knights in eight Langues, roughly corresponding to the languages they spoke: France, Provence, Auvergne, Castille and Leon, Aragon, Italy, Germany, and England. See note 52, below.

9 February 1532 ab. inc. [1533].[45] The following passage in Italian forms part of a document of fifty-six articles:

> De triremibus XXVII Item post varias confabulationes sine directione statu et armamento triremis seu Gallearum, Rev.di D. xvi Capitolares statuerunt et decreverunt in modum qui sequitur E primo
> Che 'l venerando Capitano e patroni de gallere se debiano constituire et ponere in l'officio per doi anni bene faciendo.
> Item che sopra cadauna gallera non si debia portare più de ottanta scapuli boni et sufficienti et portandone davantagio che sia sopra el capitano et patroni, et cossì medemo che ogni gallera non possa portare più de sei gallioti ultra el numero delli remi.
>
>> (About the triremes. XXVII Again after a long and inconclusive dicussion about the state and armaments of the galleys, the sixteen Reverend members of the Chapter decree and establish in the following manner. Firstly
>> That the venerable Captain and the skippers of the galleys shall be nominated and appointed for two years and work well.
>> Also that on every galley there should not be more than eighty good worthy sailors and, if there are more, that will be the responsibility of the captain and the skipper, and in the same way on every galley there should not be more than six galley-slaves above the number of oars.)

The choice was not dictated solely by the island's geographical proximity (93 km south of Sicily), but also because the Knights' settlement in Malta coincided with the spread of Tuscan in Italy itself. In comparison to the variety used in Rhodes, it is not surprising to note that the language written in Malta took on a southern character.[46] Considering the international set-up of the Order, the adoption of Tuscan seems to have been rather precocious. In fact before the unification of Italy the first state to introduce Tuscan in judicial proceedings, in official reports, and in notarial deeds was the kingdom of Piedmont in 1560–1561. However, the process of de-municipalization and Tuscanization had already started in the second half of the fifteenth century in the more important regional courts and in high-level writings.[47] The use of the local varieties became frequent after 1400, but Latin was still dominant. In Florence a decree of 1414 introduced the *volgare* in writings concerning commercial lawsuits, and in Siena Bartolomeo Carli Piccolomini, chancellor of the Siena *comune* from 1527 to 1529, wrote a treatise about the ideal chancellor (*Trattato del perfetto cancelliere*) where he stated that 'ogni città usa il [vulgare] particular suo'; he called writing in Latin 'usanza antica' and declared that

---

45 BNM, MS Arch. 286, *Sacra Capitula Generalia* for the years 1526, 1532, 1538. The quoted passage is on fol. LIX^v.
46 Brincat, 'L'uso del volgare', pp. 384–88.
47 Tavoni, *Storia della lingua italiana*, p. 13.

this habit was by then 'molto diminuita'.[48] In Sicily the first document that shows the use of Tuscan in administrative circles is an official letter sent by the municipal officers of Monterosso (near Ragusa) to those of nearby Buscemi on 3 April 1524 in a language that has been defined by Varvaro as 'containing slight imperfections but showing only one partial Sicilian feature and a rather heavy syntax'.[49]

The highest degree of de-municipalization was achieved in administrative circles, especially in the chanceries, because in public administration and law the principal model was Latin, whose terminology and style were adopted and adapted to the local varieties, giving them automatically a uniform patina in that specific domain. Latin and the local variety were used side by side in the chanceries of Italy, but the use of Latin gradually decreased. In the scenario of the small states of Italy, the Order of St John should occupy a significant, though peripheral, position. Historians of the Italian language have generally ignored its role, but its importance is not inferior to that of the other Renaissance courts of Italy. Being a supranational order, its administrative structure necessarily gave Latin a privileged status. Therefore, the use of Tuscan in its official documents is all the more worthy of note, especially certain parts of the records of the Chapters General of 1454, 1475, 1495, and 1501 held in Rhodes. The records of those held in Malta from 1533 onwards were written in Latin and Tuscan. Even the council registers, which were always drawn up in Latin, contain attached documents in Tuscan from 1549 onwards, and the *Liber Conciliorum* no. 88 (years 1548–1553) shows one passage in Spanish and at least five in Tuscan. The testimonies collected in 1566 by the Bishop of Malta, Mgr Domenico Cubelles, in the defence of Padre Roberto Novella da Eboli are all in Tuscan,[50] including that of the French Jean Parisot de Valette.[51]

It is known that around 1560 the chancery employed a secretary for each of four languages, Latin, French, Spanish, and Italian. Unfortunately no documents reveal the language spoken during the debates of the Chapter General's meetings: it could have been strictly Classical or approximative Latin, or else each member would have used his own language relying on interpreters or explanations by others. There could have been agreement on the acceptability of a restricted number of languages, say Latin, French, and Spanish, but it is quite plausible that Tuscan could have been a convenient overall solution. Tuscan was certainly spoken in the Italian Langue, considering that their *Albergia* accommodated under one roof the members of the seven priories that represented Italy (Lombardy, Rome, Venice, Pisa, Capua, Barletta, and Messina).[52] Their feeling of *italianità* was stressed by

---

48 Trovato, *Storia della lingua italiana*, p. 71.
49 Varvaro, 'Note per la storia', p. 180.
50 ACM, Acta Orig., MS 46, fols 70–75ᵛ.
51 AOM, Liber Bullarum, MS 430, fol. 271ᵛ.
52 Every Langue had its *Auberge*, the building which housed the offices on the ground floor and the residential quarters of the majority of their knights on the upper floors.

the fact that the Langue's escutcheon did not feature the usual emblems of heraldry, like all the others, but just the word ITALIA diagonally in letters of gold on a black background. This must have predisposed the Italian knights to the use of a common variety. The early choice of Tuscan was due to its well-known characteristics: its literary prestige, its similarity to Latin, and its being easily comprehensible to speakers of the various regional dialects of Italy. Moreover, in the sixteenth century its codification made it easier to learn. The same qualities determined its choice for communication between members of the various Langues who did not speak one another's language, despite the fact that the French Knights, with three Langues, were the most numerous. A report for 1630 lists 2050 knights of whom 455 were French, 359 Provençal, and 181 Auvergnats (totalling 955), whereas the Italians were 584, the Iberians (Aragon and Castille) 414, the Germans 55, and the English only two.[53] Figures for the sixteenth century would have been similar because the knights' numbers were fairly consistent throughout the Maltese period.

The fact that Tuscan was spoken by members of various nationalities is described by a Tuscan knight, Onofrio Acciaioli, who commissioned Paolo Del Rosso to write the Tuscan version of the Order's statutes. The *Statuti della Religione de' Cavalieri Gierosolimitani tradotti di latino in lingua Toscana* was published in Florence in 1567, and Acciaioli explained his decision with the following words:

> essendo che la maggior parte delle persone de' nostri tempi hanno poca notizia della Latina, la quale ordinariamente non si usa, et che questa nostra non solamente in Italia, ma ancor in ogni altra Provincia è conosciuta, et si intende, et si parla ancora più che ogni altra lingua, in cotesta isola di Malta dove è la nostra residenza.[54]

> (as nowadays most people do not know Latin well, since this language is not used in everyday matters, and that our [language] is known not only in Italy but also in many other Provinces, and is understood, and spoken more than any other language here in Malta where we reside.)

This means that towards the mid-sixteenth century Tuscan was spoken more than any other language in Malta, but there must have been a distinction between the way it was spoken by the Italian knights, on the one hand, and the way it was spoken by the other members of the Order in ordinary conversation, on the other. Alfieri also notes a tendency to Italianize Sicilian words as reflected in Thezan's dictionary.[55] The earnestness with which the Knights resolved to learn the Tuscan *volgare* is proved by the fact that copies of all the grammars published in the sixteenth century are found at the National Library of Malta, starting with the first edition of Pietro Bembo's *Prose della*

---

53   *Lo Stato dell'Ordine di Malta 1630*, pp. 62, 102–77.
54   Del Rosso, *Statuti della Religione*, pp. 1–2.
55   Alfieri, 'Il siciliano come dialetto di contatto', p. 246.

volgar lingua, as well as those of Fortunio, *Regole grammaticali della volgar lingua,* 1516; Claudio Tolomei, *Polito,* 1525, and *Il cesano,* 1555; Giangiorgio Trissino, *Il castellano. Grammatichetta* and *Dubbii grammaticali,* 1529; Jacomo Gabriele, *Regole grammaticali,* Venice 1545; Rinaldo Corso, *Fondamenti del parlar toscano,* Venice 1549; Lodovico Dolce, *Osservationi nella volgar lingua,* Venice 1550; Pierfrancesco Giambullari, *De la lingua che si parla e scrive in Firenze,* Florence 1552; Leonardo Salviati, *Orazione in lode della fiorentina lingua,* 1564, and *Degli Avvertimenti della lingua sopra 'l Decameron,* Venice 1584, Florence 1586; A. Acarisio, *Vocabolario, grammatica et orthographia della lingua volgare,* Cento 1543; F. Alunno, *Le osservazioni sopra il Petrarca,* Venice 1543, and *La Fabbrica del mondo,* Venice 1546–1548; G. Pergamini, *Il Memoriale della lingua volgare,* Venice 1601; Girolamo Muzio, *Battaglie in diffesa dell'italica lingua,* Venice 1582.[56]

The Order's adoption of Italian as its most frequently used language in writing is confirmed by the manuscripts and volumes conserved at the Malta National Library in Valletta. The knights were obliged to bequeath all their books to the Order after their death, so that they could be used by the other members of the Order and by educated Maltese persons. As a consequence, the library's collection is very rich and includes the most significant works that were published in Europe between the sixteenth and the eighteenth century. Of the 362,000 titles, two-thirds are in Italian, a number that reflects its importance for the Order and places Malta in the forefront of the spread of Italian not only outside Italy but even among the peninsula's many states. This is quite surprising when one considers that of the twenty-eight Grand Masters twelve were French, eight were Aragonese, three Portuguese, one German, and only four were Italian, of whom only Gregorio Carafa reigned for ten years; the other three had little time to leave their mark, dying after one or two years. This fact shows that the decision in favour of Italian was not political but practical, because the various princes did not identify the Order with one of the large European monarchies, nor with Italy itself. The choice could also have been a sort of diplomatic compromise. The books and manuscripts at the library treat every subject under the sun, and the Order's archives consist of seven thousand volumes, divided into seventeen sections, covering every sphere of activity of the Knights (e.g. council meetings, the hospital, the navy, the church, etc.).[57]

The Malta National Library catalogue also shows manuscripts and books of a cultural nature: countless celebratory poems, written about the famous

---

[56] Although nowadays we call 'Italian' all literary works since the thirteenth century, it must be noted that the above-mentioned grammars speak of *volgar lingua, parlar toscano, fiorentina lingua,* and *italica lingua*. Migliorini points out that *italiano* was also used with these terms 'promiscuamente e quasi indifferentemente', adding that it was preferred when compared to other living languages (*Storia della lingua italiana,* p. 244).

[57] *Catalogues of the Records of the Order of St. John of Jerusalem in the Royal Malta Library* are published by the Malta University Press.

victory over the Turks in the Great Siege of 1565, about battles at sea, speeches, and laments in verse for the death of Grand Masters, and also poems, songs, and plays performed at events honouring Grand Masters on their election or anniversaries, as well as narratives written by knights in prose (Fabrizio Cagliola) or verse (Ciro di Pers). The use of Tuscan by non-Italian members of the Order in the sixteenth century, when the Knights had barely settled on the island in their first turbulent forty years, is exemplified by the report sent by the Spanish engineer Scipione Campi to the French Grand Master La Cassière in 1576 and the answer he obtained, both in Italian.[58] Of particular significance are the laws of Malta published in Italian under the Portuguese Grand Master Antonio Manoel De Vilhena in 1724 (*Leggi e Costituzioni Prammaticali*) and the French Grand Master De Rohan in 1784 (*Diritto Municipale di Malta*).

The Knights brought Malta out of the conditions that it previously shared with Pantelleria and Lampedusa and raised it to the prestigious status of an average-sized European city, endowed with impressive fortifications, Baroque palaces and churches, the splendid conventual church of St John, a hospital which enjoyed an international reputation, a college, a theatre, a university, and other institutions which were previously unimaginable. These were made possible thanks to the huge funds that came from abroad. Malta's commercial, social, and artistic activities brought it up to date with events in the best European cities, and this is witnessed by the presence of artists like Caravaggio and Mattia Preti; architects like Bartolomeo Genga, Francesco Laparelli, and Pietro Floriani; and a host of cultured knights who lived here for many years and created an environment where Maltese citizens could obtain their basic education on the island and further it abroad, and thus develop sound artistic tastes and talents that would help them to become scholars, artists, and writers in their own right who flourished in the seventeenth and eighteenth centuries.

Special mention is deserved by the archaeologist Antonio Bosio (1575–1629), the architects Girolamo Cassar (1520–1592) and his son Vittorio (1550–1607), the architect and sculptor Lorenzo Cafà (1639–1703), the historian Gian Francesco Abela (1582–1655), the writer, traveller, and naturalist Giovan Francesco Buonamico (1639–1680), the playwright Carlo Magri (1617?–1693) and his brother Domenico Magri (1604–1672), authors of a highly successful encyclopaedic dictionary of religious terms, the *Hierolexicon*, that had nineteen editions in Italian and in Latin from 1644 to 1751 and grew from 1600 to over 8000 entries, the men of letters Enrico Magi (born in 1630) and Giacomo Farrugia (1641–1716), the historian Count Gian Antonio Ciantar (1696–1778), the scholar Gian Francesco Agius De Soldanis (1712–1770) who became the Order's librarian, the preacher Ignazio Saverio Mifsud (1722–1773), the surgeon Michel Angelo Grima (1723–1798), the musician Niccolò Isouard (1775–1818),

---

58 Mallia-Milanes, 'Scipione Campi's Report', pp. 284–90, and 281–82 respectively.

and the linguist and patriot Michel Antonio Vassalli (1764–1829). All these obtained recognition abroad, and their example was followed by a host of amateurs who did not produce high-quality contributions but kept culture alive on the island. They all wrote in Latin and in Italian and considered the latter as their language of culture.

Spoken Italian and Maltese

Although the transition from Sicilian to Italian was rapid in writing, on the spoken level the change was gradual. Highly educated Maltese people spoke correct Italian, albeit inevitably marked by local pronunciation and intonation, whereas illiterate people did not speak Italian at all, or at best they had only a very superficial knowledge of some useful words and colloquial phrases, unless they were employed in Italian-speaking homes or other establishments, like port workers and seamen. However, members of the middle class, especially shopkeepers, tailors, and other craftsmen who lived in the city and were in daily contact with foreigners, must have conversed with them in Italian, broken or not, since they did not know the various languages spoken by the knights and their followers. On the informal level, direct speech is sometimes reported in the proceedings of the Inquisition which was set up as a Tribunal in 1546 and more formally in 1561, where the evidence given by witnesses is mostly in Italian and sometimes even in Maltese. On the formal level as well, Italian became common as shown by its use in titles: in the 1540s Fra Francesco Gesualdo, a Calabrian teacher, had founded La Confraternita dei Buoni Cristiani practising Lutheran beliefs, and in 1562 the offices of the Tribunal were named Promotore fiscale, Depositario, Capitano, Erario, Cursore, and Aromatario familiare. Even more important is the fact that the Apostolic Visitor Mgr Pietro Dusina (born in Brescia) wrote his letters to the Cardinal of Pisa and the detailed report on ecclesiastical affairs in Malta in 1574 in Italian.[59]

It is interesting to note that the statute of the diocesan seminary, founded in 1591, and the Jesuits' *Collegium Melitense*, opened in 1593, specified: 'Si parlerà sempre in latino eccetto il Giovedì e la Domenica, che si potrà parlare volgare toscano o maltese'; however, their Italian was apparently marked by strong Sicilian interference. As late as 1726 the Grand Master wrote to the Order's ambassador in Rome and expressed the people's wish in the following terms: 'che siccome i detti Padri tengono le scuole, desidera ardentemente questo Popolo possano fare imparare agli scolari la buona Lingua Italiana, per togliere una volta la corruttela di quella di Sicilia'.[60] The Grand Master's rebuke coincided with a caricature written four years later, confirming that many Maltese people still spoke Italian

---

59 Vella, 'La missione di Pietro Dusina a Malta', pp. 174–84; Cassar, 'The Enemy Within', pp. 172–74.
60 Borg, 'The Teaching of Philosophy', p. 144.

in a very Sicilianate way in the eighteenth century. Mgr Boccadifuoco, a priest from Palermo, came to Malta in 1730 to be invested as *cappellano* of the Order and was so amused by the way Italian was spoken, especially by women, that he wrote an *Intermezzo*.[61] The humorous nature of this short play exaggerates the unorthodox linguistic features, but the words spoken by Vittoria, the Maltese woman, may be considered representative of a widespread habit. The plot is simple: Pantalone, an Italian gentleman, courts Vittoria, a Maltese middle-class housewife who rejects his advances. Pantalone speaks perfect Italian, but Vittoria, who apparently has never had formal instruction in Italian, answers in a mixed medium which contains many Sicilian phonetic and morphological elements. Her vocabulary mixes three types: Sicilian words, Sicilian or Italian words that have been adopted in Maltese with phonetic and semantic modifications, and Maltese words of Arabic origin.

Having been written and spoken for about four hundred years, Sicilian had embedded itself in the Maltese language as a superstratum by the adoption of a large number of words and the assimilation of its five-vowel system and some consonant changes, to which all new Italian words were, and still are, automatically subjected. At this point it is important to note that the 'corruption' of the language concerned only the spoken register, because most Maltese authors wrote very good Italian, and their style was practically indistinguishable from that of contemporary Italian writers. The fact that students at the Jesuits' college were expected to speak Latin all the time except on Thursdays and Sundays, when they could speak Tuscan or Maltese, means that they did know Italian, but they must have read Italian literature in class too because in the early years only grammar (Latin) and *Litterae Humaniores* were taught, and some lessons may have been delivered in Italian. The rule that 'il venerdì s'interpreteranno li testi delle letioni passate e ciaschuno tradurrà una parte d'un'epistola di Cicerone'[62] implies that Italian was used for the interpretation and translation of Latin texts. And, of course, these same statutes and regulations, *Statuti et ordini da osservarsi dalli figluoli del Nostro Seminario*, drawn up in 1629, were written in Italian, unlike the *Constitutiones* of 1591 which were in Latin. In the eighteenth century the study of Italian increased, as shown by academic programmes, grammars reprinted in Malta, textbooks treating many subjects in Italian, and cultural events.

The quality of spoken Italian reached a very high standard among those who not only studied it at school but also spoke it often, at work or at home, and more so if they had spent some years in Italy to further their studies. This was the case of Ignazio Saverio Mifsud, esteemed as a preacher in both Italian and Maltese, who studied for his priesthood in Tivoli, near Rome, where he celebrated his first Mass. One day the director of the missions school where he was lodging complimented him for speaking excellent Italian, and the

---

61 Cassola, *L'italiano di Malta*, p. 74.
62 Fiorini, 'The *Collegium Melitense* and the *Universitas Studiorum*', p. 39.

young novice explained that in Malta he had many opportunities to speak Italian with the Knights and other foreigners:

> venne il Direttore a discorrere, voleva saper cose di Malta, e sentendomi parlar così sciolto, franco e lesto, si maravigliò che i Maltesi discorrono meglio che un Romano nella pronuncia, [...] non è gran fatta che si discorre bene in Italiano dai Maltesi, per la continua conversazione de' Cavalieri, che in Malta vi sono sì de' Italiani, e benesi che di tutte l'altre Nazioni.[63]
>
> (The Director came to speak to me and wanted to know things about Malta, and hearing me speak so fluently, frankly, and quickly he was surprised to see that the Maltese speak better than a Roman, as regards pronunciation [and I explained] that it is not surprising that the Maltese speak Italian well, because they interact continually with the Knights because there are Italian [knights] in Malta, as well as knights of all the other Nations.)

Besides introducing Italian, the Knights left a lasting influence on the linguistic situation in Malta by creating the right conditions for the enrichment of the local tongue. The Order's supranational character, guaranteed by the fact that the office of Grand Master was filled by men of different nationalities, also ensured the survival of the Maltese language. In fact the Grand Masters never conceived the idea of changing the people's language, as was happening in those times in larger countries like France and Spain which spread the national language on the written and on the spoken levels. On the other hand, the progressive increase of the Romance element helped the Maltese to communicate with their rulers or foreign superiors because it facilitated at least a passive competence, depending on the individual's exposure to Italian. The foundation of the city of Valletta around 1600, on a previously uninhabited hilly promontory between two harbours, promoted the development of a new community and a new spoken variety. The Knights at first settled in the small borgo behind the Castle-by-the-Sea, but after the Great Siege, fearing a second onslaught, they built Valletta as a strongly fortified city. This necessitated the importation of hundreds of labourers and all sorts of craftsmen from Sicily and elsewhere who, together with the Knights and their followers, about three thousand in all, took up residence in the area. The new opportunities also attracted Maltese workers from all over the island, and so the demographic shift towards the new harbour towns made the area the meeting place for foreign settlers and a large part of the Maltese population that reached the figure of 42 per cent of the total in 1740. The locals tended to shed their local linguistic peculiarities and absorbed innovative vocabulary from the foreigners, and so this new variety became the basis for standard Maltese. A few Knights were the first to take an interest in the local language, even by learning how to speak it: Luc D'Argens, Deguast

---

63 BNM, MS Libr. 1, p. 433.

Junior, Joseph Turgot, Laberivière, Victor Belmont, the Bailiff de Neveu, and de Tournon. These and others produced or inspired the first grammars and glossaries like that of Thezan, c. 1650,[64] and even a few specific conversation manuals, like instructions for soldiers on how to use firearms, and for sailors employed by the Order. The codification of the Maltese language began in this humble way and gained momentum in the seventeenth and eighteenth centuries, and thanks to the increasing production of literary works raised its prestige, preparing the way for its official recognition in the early twentieth century. Some credit for this is also due to the Knights of the Order of St John.

Works Cited

Abbreviations

ACM, Archives of the Cathedral of Malta, Mdina
AIM, Archives of the Inquisition of Malta, Mdina
AOM, Archives of the Order of Malta, Valletta
BNM, Bibljoteka Nazzjonali ta' Malta (National Library of Malta), Valletta
CEM, Curia Episcopalis Melitensis
DSMH, Documentary Sources of Maltese History

Manuscripts and Archival Sources

ACM, Acta Orig., MS 46
AIM, Proc. Crim., MS 16A, Case 30
AOM, Liber Bullarum, MS 430
BNM, MS Arch. 286
BNM, MS Arch. 363
BNM, MS Arch. 1698
BNM, MS Arch. 1700
BNM, MS Libr. 1
BNM, MS Libr. 255
CEM, MS 30, *Acta Originalia*, anno 1550

Primary Sources

Acta juratorum et consilii civitatis et insulae Maltae, ed. by Godfrey Wettinger (Palermo: Centro Studi Filologici e Linguistici Siciliani, 1993)
Catalogues of the Records of the Order of St. John of Jerusalem in the Royal Malta Library, comp. by Anton Zammit Gabarretta and Joseph Mizzi, vols I–XIII (Malta: Malta University Press, 1964–2004)

---

64 Cassola, *The Biblioteca Vallicelliana 'Regole'*.

Del Pozzo, Bartolomeo, *Ruolo generale de' Cavalieri Gierosolimitani della Veneranda Lingua d'Italia* (Messina, 1738)

Del Rosso, Paolo, *Statuti della Religione de' Cavalieri Gierosolimitani tradotti di latino in lingua Toscana*, preface by Onofrio Acciaioli (Florence, 1567)

DSMH, I: *Notarial Documents*, pt 1: *Notary Giacomo Zabbara R494/1(I): 1486–1488*, ed. by Stanley Fiorini (Malta: Malta University Press, 1990)

DSMH, I: *Notarial Documents*, pt 2: *Notary Giacomo Zabbara R494 (II–IV): 1494–1497*, ed. by Stanley Fiorini (Malta: Malta University Press, 1999)

DSMH, I: *Notarial Documents*, pt 3: *Notary Paulo Bonello MS 588: 1467–1517; Notary Giacomo Zabbara MS 1132: 1471–1500*, ed. by Stanley Fiorini (Malta: Malta University Press, 2005)

DSMH, II: *Documents in the State Archives, Palermo*, pt 1: *Cancelleria Regia: 1259–1400*, ed. by Stanley Fiorini (Malta: Malta University Press, 1999)

DSMH, III: *Documents of the Maltese Universitas*, pt 1: *Cathedral Museum, Mdina Archivum Cathedralis Melitae Miscellanea 33: 1405–1542*, ed. by Stanley Fiorini (Malta: Malta University Press, 2001)

DSMH, III: *Documents of the Maltese Universitas*, pt 2: *The Capitula of Malta and Gozo: 1398–1532*, ed. by Stanley Fiorini (Malta: Malta University Press, 2014)

DSMH, III: *Documents of the Maltese Universitas*, pt 3: *Acta juratorum et consilii civitatis et insulae Maltae II, 1512–1531*, ed. by Stanley Fiorini (Malta: Malta University Press, 2016)

DSMH, v: *Documents in the Curia of the Archbishop of Malta*, pt 1: *The Registrum Fundationum Beneficiorum Insulae Gaudisii, 1435–1545*, transcribed by Joseph Busuttil, ed. by Stanley Fiorini (Malta: Malta University Press, 2006)

Lo Stato dell'Ordine di Malta 1630, ed. by Victor Mallia-Milanes (Taranto: Ecumenica Editrice, 2017)

Secondary Studies

Abela, Giovan Francesco, *Della descrittione di Malta, isola nel mare siciliano con le sue antichità, ed altre notitie* (Malta: Paolo Bonacota, 1647; facsimile edn, Malta: Midsea Books, 1984)

Abela, Joan, 'Don Brandano Caxario u l-għejun primarji – xi punti ta' riflessjoni' (Don Brandano Caxario e le sue fonti primarie – alcuni punti di riflessione), *Il-Malti: Rivista tal-Akkademja tal-Malti*, 87 (2014), 3–38

Alfieri, Gabriella, 'La Sicilia', in *L'italiano nelle regioni: Lingua nazionale e identità regionali*, ed. by Francesco Bruni (Turin: UTET, 1992), pp. 798–860

——, 'Il siciliano come dialetto di contatto tra le "Lingue" nazionali dei cavalieri di Malta nel Sei-Settecento', in *Dialetti e lingue nazionali*, ed. by Maria Teresa Romanello and Immacolata Tempesta (Rome: Bulzoni, 1995), pp. 241–74

Basaldella, Davide, 'Testimonianze primocinquecentesche del toscano a Malta', in *Migrazioni della lingua: Nuovi studi sull'italiano fuori d'Italia*, ed. by Francesca Malagnini (Florence: Cesati, 2018), pp. 119–34

Bonello, Giovanni, 'Gregorio Xerri's Poem for the Great Siege of 1565', *Sunday Times of Malta*, 23 March 2014, pp. 36–37

Borg, Vincenzo, *The Maltese Diocese and the Sicilian Environment from the Norman Period till 1500 AD*, Melita Sacra, 1.2 (Malta: V. Borg, 2008)
——, *The Maltese Diocese during the Sixteenth Century*, Melita Sacra, 2 (Malta: V. Borg, 2009)
——, 'The Teaching of Philosophy at the Jesuit Collegium Melitense', in *Veterum Exempla* (Malta: Faculty of Theology of the University of Malta, 1991), pp. 137–68
Bosio, Giacomo, *Dell'Istoria della Sacra Religione et Ill.ma Militia di San Giovanni Gierosolimitano*, 3 vols (Rome, 1594–1602)
Brincat, Giuseppe, 'I cognomi a Malta', *Rivista Italiana di Onomastica*, 14.2 (2008), 379–90
—— 'Le poesie "maltesi" di Peire Vidal (1204–1205)', *Melita Historica*, 7.1 (1976), 65–89
——, 'L'uso del volgare nei documenti ufficiali dei Cavalieri di San Giovanni a Rodi e a Malta tra Quattrocento e Cinquecento', in *Italia linguistica anno Mille: Italia linguistica anno Duemila*, ed. by Nicoletta Maraschio and Teresa Poggi Salani (Rome: Bulzoni, 2003), pp. 376–91
Brincat, Joseph M., 'The *Cantilena*: Vintura. Why? Who?', in *Karissime Gotifride*, ed. by Paul Xuereb (Malta: University of Malta Press, 1999), pp. 177–83
——, *Maltese and Other Languages: A Linguistic History of Malta* (Malta: Midsea Books, 2011; 2nd edn, 2021)
——, 'Maltese: Blending Semitic, Romance and Germanic Lexemes', in 'Language Contact in the Mediterranean in the Middle Ages and in Early Modern Times (with special focus on loanword lexicography)', ed. by Francesco Crifò, Elton Prifti, and Wolfgang Schweickard, thematic part of *Lexicographica: International Annual for Lexicography*, 33 (2017), 207–23
Cassar, Carmel, 'The Enemy Within: The Roman Inquisition and the Control of Protestant Practices in Malta 1561–1575', in *Ecclesiastical Archives in Malta: Crossroads of Cultures and Religions 1968–2018*, ed. by Stanley Fiorini and William Zammit (Malta: The Cathedral Archives, 2018), pp. 171–95
——, 'The Reformation in Sixteenth Century Malta', *Melita Historica*, 10.1 (1988), 51–68
——, *Witchcraft, Sorcery and the Inquisition* (Malta: Mireva Publications, 1996)
Cassar, Mario, 'Maltese Surnames: A Historical Perspective', *Bollettino del Centro di studi filologici e linguistici siciliani*, 27 (2016), 149–66
Cassola, Arnold, *The Biblioteca Vallicelliana 'Regole per la Lingua Maltese'* (Malta: Said International, 1992)
——, *L'italiano di Malta: Storia, testi e documenti* (Malta: Malta University Press, 1998)
Fiorini, Stanley, 'The *Collegium Melitense* and the *Universitas Studiorum* to 1798', in *Yesterday's Schools*, ed. by Ronald G. Sultana (Malta: PEG, 2001), pp. 31–58
——, 'The Notary in Maltese Late Medieval Society', in 'Essays on the Cantilena', ed. by Bernard Micallef, special issue, *Journal of Maltese Studies*, 28 (2014), 29–74
Fsadni, Michael, *Id-Dumnikani fir-Rabat u fil-Birgu sal-1652* (Malta: Stamperija Il-Ħajja, 1974)

Jamil, Nadia, and Jeremy Johns, 'A New Latin-Arabic Document from Norman Sicily (November 595 H/1198 CE)', in *The Heritage of Arabo-Islamic Learning: Studies Presented to Wadad Kadi*, ed. by Maurice A. Pomerantz and Aram Shahin (Leiden: Brill, 2016), pp. 111–66

Luttrell, Anthony, 'Christian Slaves at Malta: 1271', *Melita Historica*, 9.4 (1981), 381–83

Mallia-Milanes, Victor, 'Scipione Campi's Report on the Fortifications of Valletta, 1576', *Melita Historica*, 8.4 (1983), 275–98

Migliorini, Bruno, *Storia della lingua italiana*, introduction by Ghino Ghinassi (Florence: Sansoni Editore, 1988)

Rapisarda, Stefano, 'Il volgarizzamento siciliano della "Regola" dei Cavalieri di Malta', *Medioevo letterario d'Italia*, 5 (2008), 169–80

Tavoni, Mirko, *Storia della lingua italiana: Il Quattrocento* (Bologna: Il Mulino, 1992)

Trovato, Paolo, *Storia della lingua italiana: Il primo Cinquecento* (Bologna: Il Mulino, 1994)

Varvaro, Alberto, 'Bilancio degli studi sulla storia linguistica meridionale', in *Cultura meridionale e letteratura italiana: I modelli narrativi dell'età moderna*, ed. by P. Giannantonio (Naples: Loffredo, 1985), pp. 25–37

———, 'Note per la storia degli usi linguistici in Sicilia', in *La parola nel tempo*, ed. by Alberto Varvaro (Bologna: Il Mulino, 1984), pp. 175–85

Vella, Andrew, 'La missione di Pietro Dusina a Malta nel 1574 con la trascrizione del MS Vat Lat 134111', *Melita Historica*, 5.2 (1969), 165–84

Wettinger, G., and M. Fsadni, *Peter Caxaro's Cantilena* (Malta: Lux Press, 1968)

ANDREA RIZZI

Trusting Vernacular Languages in the Italian Renaissance

This chapter explores the trust-signalling of Italian Renaissance translators and editors working in the vernacular, through analysis of four revealing examples of commercially successful vernacular texts that were first published in Italy in the late fifteenth or early to mid-sixteenth centuries. It is especially concerned with the trust-signalling practices evidenced in prefaces, letters of dedication, and other accompanying materials, through which the translators, printers, or editors variously addressed their readers on matters of trustworthiness, and the perceived trustworthiness of the particular vernacular language chosen for the translation or edition.

The topic is premised on an interpretive shift from over-reliance on tropes concerning the 'fidelity' or 'faithfulness' of early modern translators, authors, and editors to an investigation of their textual trust-signalling — the rhetorical means through which they sought to stimulate an affective looping of trust from their intended readers. The argument put forward here is that what made the early modern vernacular texts a worthy investment for their readers was not their alleged or perceived 'faithfulness' to an earlier source, nor was it the notion of what a good and reliable text might have been, but the dispositional trustworthiness of a text's translator, printer, or editor.[1]

The broader picture informing the present chapter is an understanding of trust as 'a historical product rather than a phenomenon whose variation we can explain without reference to history'.[2] Detailed and empirical research is necessary to understand how and why past individuals or people believed in the reliability or capacity of someone or something. Such empirical research also promises to shed light on the specific ways in which trustworthiness

---

1 Trustworthiness does not need to be demonstrated or put into practice for the truster to be convinced. Hence the use of 'dispositional'. See Jones, 'Trustworthiness'.
2 Tilly, *Trust and Rule*, p. 26.

Andrea Rizzi (arizzi@unimelb.edu.au) is Associate Professor in Italian Studies, School of Languages and Linguistics, University of Melbourne.

Languages and Cross-Cultural Exchanges in Renaissance Italy, ed. by Alessandra Petrocchi and Joshua Brown, LMEMS 30 (Turnhout: Brepols, 2023), pp. 185–207
BREPOLS ❧ PUBLISHERS   10.1484/M.LMEMS-EB.5.131432

is produced through cultural and linguistic mediation. It is surprising that trust — a key sociocultural aim and ambition for cultural mediation — has received very little attention in translation.[3]

Scholars of scribal and printed cultures of early modern Europe have variously explored the marketing strategies adopted by authors, translators, editors, and printers to promote their work among their intended readers. A key aim of publications in early modern Western cultures was to 'provide a better opportunity for more people, from a wider spectrum society, to enjoy the benefits of reading, by deriving from the written word their own personal usefulness and pleasure'.[4] Thanks to literary and social historians, and to the broadening influence of the history of the book as a field of study, we are coming to appreciate in greater detail exactly which and what kinds of books early modern readers enjoyed purchasing and owning or sharing.[5]

Yet there is still much to be learnt about how early modern readers selected their books and libraries, why they preferred some editions over others, and how the marketing strategies adopted by printing houses and authors influenced readers' choices. As an important correlate, there is a need to closely investigate the strategies used by authors, translators, and editors to promote the trustworthiness of their texts, and thus sell their work and increase their reputation. Of course, countless prefaces by fifteenth- and sixteenth-century Italian authors, editors, and translators working in the vernacular contain stylized statements about their trustworthiness, which include assurances of their sincere commitment to their patrons or intended readers. In his preface to his account of the life of Charlemagne, Donato Acciaiuoli (1429–1478) reveals to the dedicatee, King Louis XI of France (r. 1461–1483), his trust of and devotion to the monarch ('che dimostrassi la fede et devozione mia verso el tuo felicissimo nome'). At the same time, Acciaiuoli is keen to reassure the king and readers that his narrative contains facts that are trustworthy and worth remembering ('degnie di fede e di memoria').[6] The author's aim, as outlined by Brian Richardson in the passage quoted above, is to provide useful and enjoyable knowledge: 'acciò che tutti quelli che vogliono ben possino la vita

---

3 Rizzi, Lang, and Pym, *What Is Translation History?*, pp. 4–12.
4 Richardson, *Printing, Writers and Readers in Renaissance Italy*, p. 157. See also Sebastiani and Ricketts, 'Froben Press Editions'.
5 Representative and influential studies from this scholarship are (in chronological order) Cornell, 'Books and their Owners'; Bec, *Les Livres des Florentins*; Richardson, *Printing, Writers and Readers in Renaissance Italy*; Biow, *Doctors, Ambassadors, Secretaries*; Zorzi, 'Le biblioteche veneziane'; Pettegree, *The Book in the Renaissance*; Nuovo, *The Book Trade in the Italian Renaissance*; Maxson, *The Humanist World of Renaissance Florence*; and Ross, *Everyday Renaissances*.
6 Donato Acciaiuoli, *Vita Caroli Magni* (Life of Charlemagne), c. 1465. Acciaiuoli wrote the text in Latin first then self-translated the resultant work into Tuscan. The copy consulted and quoted from here is BNC, II, II, 32, fols 46^r–92^r; here fol. 47^r. On Acciaiuoli's text, see Gatti, *La Vita Caroli di Donato Acciaiuoli*. On Acciaiuoli's visit to the French court in January 1462 and the presentation copy of his life of Charlemagne, see Margolis, 'The "Gallic Crowd"'.

di Charlo Magnio con piacere ["voluptate" in the Latin version of Acciaiuoli's text] vedere' (so that everyone who wishes and is truly able to enjoy reading Charlemagne's life).[7]

In the introductory statements they composed to accompany their works, early modern authors, editors, and translators also tended to invoke the trustworthiness of the ancient and authoritative authors whose work they had relied upon. Take, for instance, Pier Candido Decembrio's 1438 translation from Latin into vernacular of the *Historiae Alexandri Magni* (*Histories of Alexander the Great*) by Quintus Curtius Rufus. In his preface to Duke Filippo Maria Visconti, Decembrio assures his dedicatee that, in his translation, he did not swerve from the trustworthy writing of the notable and true authors ('pieghando mai niente di meno la penna dalla fede de' notabili et veri auctori').[8]

At play in such declarations is a culturally and historically typical set of assumptions about relationships of trust; namely, that trustworthy ancient authors are best translated by trustworthy vernacular translators in a trustworthy fashion. In order to compensate for lacunae he found in Curtius Rufus's text, Decembrio had recourse to an account of the life of Alexander the Great by the Greek historian Plutarch. Such an addition to his translation of the ancient text prompted Decembrio to reassure the dedicatee that his translation of extracts from Plutarch was based on a trustworthy Latin version of the Greek text: specifically, a translation that he himself had made: 'P. Candido [Decembrio] ricercata quella nelle lettere grece la ritrovo ne' libri di Plutarcho et fedelmente quella ha trasferita in latino questo modo' (Pier Candido [Decembrio] searched [the true account] in the Greek words and found it in Plutarch's work, which he then translated reliably into Latin).[9]

As in countless other examples of such first-person statements, here Decembrio makes a forceful case that the trustworthiness of ancient, authoritative authors and texts needs to be matched by the trustworthiness of the early modern translator who is working in the vernacular. Lippo Brandolini's translation of Pliny's *Panegirico di Caio Plinio Secondo in laude di Traiano* (*c.* 1478) is another case in point. In his preface to the translation, Brandolini writes to Ferrante I, King of Naples, apologizing for having tried, with all his skills and diligence, to retain Pliny's elegance and dignity of language.[10] Brandolini informs the king that translation always brings loss of dignity and elegance. Even so, Brandolini represents himself as a philologist

---

7   BNC, II, II, 32, fol. 47[r–v].
8   BNC, Magliab. XXIII, 44, fol. 248[v].
9   Quote from BML, Conv. Soppr. 165, fol. 74[r]. See also fol. 172[r].
10 BnF, MS Ital. 129, fol. 7[v]: 'con ogni mia industria et diligentia quella oratione tradutta, nella quale traductione non ho potuto sì la elegantia sì la dignità de la pliniana lingua ritenere'. On Brandolini, see *Dizionario biografico degli italiani*, 'Brandolini, Lippo Aurelio', and Tissoni Benvenuti, 'La ricezione delle Silvae di Stazio'; also Mayer, *Un umanista italiano alla corte di Mattia Corvino*.

dedicated to the restoration of the Latin text: he informs his readers that his copy of Pliny's oration contains several passages that are 'mendosi e depravati' (corrupted and wrong). Brandolini adds that he managed to overcome the inevitable difficulties associated with his task of translating into the vernacular. The translation meant losing some of the eloquence and dignity of the Latin language, but offered an opportunity to restore the Latin text to its original perfection.

Brandolini and other vernacular translators of his time claimed to be restoring ancient texts to their original perfection on the basis that they employed diligence and trustworthiness in their translation. Thus, in his preface Brandolini assures the readers that with 'più diligentia et fede che ho potuto tradutta finalmente la oration di Plinio' (utmost diligence and trustworthiness I have finally translated Pliny's oration).[11] Translators working in the vernacular approached their translative work as an opportunity to stabilize ancient or medieval texts that they considered corrupted, or lacking in the style and clarity that a new readership was understood to expect. Ultimately, as we see below, Italian Renaissance translators promoted readers' confidence in the benefit and enjoyment of their chosen reading by signalling the mutual trustworthiness of the ancient or earlier source and the patron or dedicatee, as well as that of translator and the vernacular language of the translation.

Trust and Trustworthiness

Trust concerns counting on someone to respond to being counted on.[12] It is a circular or looping process in which both trust-signalling and trust feed each other. The examples discussed here evidence Italian Renaissance vernacular editors' and translators' basic confidence that their patrons and readers will trust their work. In their prefaces, they signal a complex range of attitudes, from optimism to distrust, that their reader's response will be positive; indeed, that it will be appreciative, alive to the usefulness, pleasure, and trustworthiness of their work. By the same token, the readers will trust the translators' work by having an attitude of optimism that the translators will fulfil the readers' interest and needs by means of competence and responsiveness.

From this perspective, prefaces accompanying early modern translations (and authored texts, too) were an opportunity to signal an attitude of optimism in the hope that this would trigger a favourable affective reaction on the part of readers. Even if several such texts tend to contain stylized and overblown statements, the first-person approach was clearly intended to encourage an affective response of trust. Broadly, the exchange of knowledge was informed by a reciprocal, affective attitude of trust. Likewise, reciprocal trustworthiness

---

11 BnF, MS Ital. 129, fol. 8ʳ.
12 Jones, 'Trust, Distrust, and Affective Looping', p. 957.

was a key element for the trading of commercial and cultural goods. For seventeenth-century Sephardic merchants — as for eleventh-century Maghribi traders — to trade across Europe and the East, an effective reputation-based system was essential. Cultural and commercial agents had to be deemed trustworthy, and accepted as such.[13] With reference to the early modern printed book, trust-based cultural transactions were fostered by three key factors: the reputation of the agent (author, translator, interpreter), the role of the particular combination of languages involved (Latin and vernacular, as discussed here), and the leap of trust of the client (patron, reader, leader, or audience) who chose to invest resources and expectations into the cultural exchange.

Lorenzo Valla (c. 1406–1457) understood the importance of the material quality of the medium: an illuminated book had strong sensual appeal to an illustrious reader such as Pope Nicholas V. It is not by accident that, in the preface to his Latin translation of Thucydides, Valla compares the translator to the merchant. Both make available to buyers useful and precious goods.[14] Thus he represented the culture of ancient Greece as having both monetary and spiritual value. Translation of ancient knowledge allowed the trade (*commercium*) of spirituality in the same way as the Christian Mass is a 'commerce' with God.[15] Valla's translation deftly transformed the ancient text into a medium for learning and knowledge that was advantageous to his eminent patron and readers.

Clearly, trust is a historical product informed by a complex web of rhetorical, emotional, and attitudinal factors: signalling or promise making, sincerity; also, the receptivity of readers and audiences to texts and agents of culture. Not always a functional and rational practice, as Niklas Luhmann has observed, 'trust is a solution to a specific problem of risk'.[16] What risks did vernacular translators in Renaissance Italy actively seek to forfend? As we can infer from Richardson's quote above, poor (and poorly rewarded) translation impeded access to the desirably useful and pleasurable knowledge that early modern readers and patrons expected from their books. With reference to the intended recipient or audience for a published translation, patrons, intended readers, and book buyers implicitly accepted the risk that the text offered by a translator might not be trustworthy — and which might, therefore, prove of little or no use and enjoyment.

---

13   On Sephardic traders, see Trivellato, *The Familiarity of Strangers*. On Maghribi merchants, see Greif, 'Reputation and Coalitions in Medieval Trade', and, by the same author, 'The Maghribi Traders', especially at pp. 465–69.
14   Grafton, *Commerce with the Classics*, pp. 14–15. On Valla's preface to his translation of Thucydides, see Camporeale, *Christianity, Latinity, and Culture*, pp. 281–86.
15   As noted by Grafton, 'commercium' has an ecclesiastic usage: communion with God. See Grafton, *Commerce with the Classics*, p. 15.
16   Luhmann, 'Familiarity, Confidence, Trust', p. 95.

Trustworthiness of Early Modern Italian Vernaculars

Especially among well-educated readers of early modern Italian vernaculars, the perceived reliability of vernacular languages was, in some cases, advanced by the attribution of translations to influential and authoritative humanists. Such attribution allowed translators, editors, and printers to extend the affective looping of trust. This is the case for the *Aquila volante*, actually a fourteenth-century collection of texts, which comprised Filippo Ceffi's translation of Ovid's *Heroides*, Guido da Pisa's *Fiorita* (especially when quoting and commenting on passages from Dante's *Commedia*), and a universal history from the beginning of the world to the life of Pope Boniface VIII, an assemblage from medieval chronicles such as those written by Martinus Polonus and Orosius.[17] The *Aquila volante* was aimed at promoting the Da Ceccano and Prefetti di Vico families.

The preface accompanying all the known versions and printed editions of the *Aquila volante* conveys that the work is a translation into vernacular of various Latin sources: 'Intendo de translatare de latino in vulgare certi memoriali ditti & fatti dell'antichi' (My aim is to translate from Latin into the vernacular certain deeds and narratives from the ancients).[18] The earliest version is a late fourteenth-century manuscript written in a southern-Lazio vernacular. The second oldest example is from Naples, a manuscript copied in 1447.[19] The first printed version was published in Naples in 1492 by Aiolfo de Cantona, and reprinted numerous times between the end of the fifteenth century and throughout the sixteenth (1494, 1495, 1497, 1506, 1508, 1508*, 1517, 1531, 1535, 1539, 1549, 1563, and 1565). In the first printed edition, a decorated woodcut (Fig. 6.1) adorns the frontispiece; a flying eagle sports a crown and a banner engraved with the following message: 'Opera intitulata la Aquila composta per missere Leonardo Aretino' (Work entitled the Eagle written by messer

---

17 Vaccaro, 'Storia e geografia di un centone di volgarizzamenti'. See also Blasio and Vaccaro, *Il libro dell'Aquila, sec. XIV*.
18 I quote from *Opera intitulata Aquila*, 1492 (ISTC ib01231000), fol. Aii[v].
19 The 1447 copy is in Paris, BnF, MS Ital. 438. The manuscript belonged to the Aragonese court of Naples. This copy bears no title page or author. The title can be inferred from the preface that opens with 'Incipit prologus Liber delaquileda' (fol. 1[r]). In this version, a section of the life of Boniface VIII is missing. The language is Neapolitan, thus suggesting that its author or translator was from southern Italy. The 1492 edition by Aiolfo de Cantona contains a short addition by a Allegrettus Salensis (ISTC ib01231000); Pellegrino de' Pasquali printed a 1494 edition in Venice, also containing the addition by Allegrettus (ISTC ib01232000); Antonio Zarotti printed an edition in 1495 in Milan (with Allegrettus's addition, see ISTC ib01233000); Teodoro Ragazzoni printed another edition in 1497, in Venice, also with Allegrettus's addition (ISTC ib01233100). All sixteenth-century editions are listed here: Edizioni Italiane del XVI Secolo, <https://edit16.iccu.sbn.it/web/edit-16/resultset-titoli?mo nocampo=aquila+volante#1664119061676>.

Figure 6.1. *Opera intitulata Aquila* (Naples: Ayolfus de Cantono, 1492), fol. Aiiv. Image reproduced from Biblioteca Europea di Informazione e Cultura under Creative Commons CC BY-SA 4.0.

Leonardo Aretino [Leonardo Bruni from Arezzo, or Aretino, 1370–1444]).[20] The text's colophon provides further details regarding authorship:

> Qui finisse [...] la excellente & delectabile opera intitulata Laquila composta per lo magnifico & doctissimo homo miser Leonardo Aretino & da ipso curiosamente translata da latino in vulgare sermone.
>
> (Here ends [...] the excellent and enjoyable work named The Eagle written by the illustrious and most learned man messer Leonardo Aretino, who also, unusually, translated it from Latin into the vernacular language.)[21]

---

20 The border of the beautiful woodcut decorating the title page of this 1492 edition was made by a Jewish artist, Moses ben Isaac, and the same decoration appears in Hebrew books also printed in Naples: Rashi's *Perush ha-Torah* (Soncino, 1487) and the editio princeps of the Hebrew Bible (Soncino, 1488). See Heller, *Further Studies*, pp. 3–20.

21 *Opera intitulata Aquila*, 1492, fol. x4r. I follow the Biblioteca Casanatese, Rome (Inc. 44) copy of the 1494 edition. In this chapter, all translations into English are mine unless otherwise indicated.

This attribution of the fourteenth-century collection to the fifteenth-century Tuscan humanist and statesman Leonardo Bruni is noteworthy. Since neither of the two known manuscripts mention his name as the author, it can be supposed that the Neapolitan printer Aiolfo de Cantona first conceived of the marketing strategy to attribute this work to Bruni, who was renowned as perhaps the most distinguished and best-selling Latin humanist of the Quattrocento. The Neapolitan printer, and the printers after him, exploited Bruni's reputation as an influential Latin author and translator, also a writer of *canzoni*, a sonnet, orations, and lives in the Florentine vernacular; they did this to dehistoricize and delocalize a quintessentially Trecento text. The language of the printed version is transmuted from its Roman and Neapolitan flavours, and the claimed authorship promotes the compatibility of Latin and vernacular cultures. This is affirmed by the description of the *Aquila volante* in the colophon quoted above: Bruni wrote this work in Latin first before self-translating it into the vernacular.[22]

Later editions emphasize Bruni's role as vernacular translator by placing this detail on the title page: Melchiorre Sessa's 1531, 1535, and 1539 editions state on the frontispiece that this work is 'LIBRO INTITO / lato Aquila Volante, di latino in volgar lingua dal Magnifico et eloquentissimo messer Leonardo Aretino tradotto' (BOOK ENTIT / led the Flying Eagle translated from Latin to the vernacular by the Magnificent and most eloquent messer Leonardo Aretino).[23] Sessa's choice, from 1531, to hide the earlier attribution of the Latin version but not the name of the vernacular translator shifts and oversimplifies Bruni's contribution: rather than esteemed author and self-translator, the Aretine humanist is figured solely as the vernacular translator of an unattributed Latin work. The decision to blur the attribution of the Latin version of the *Aquila volante* was most likely motivated by strong suspicion that such a work could truly have been written by the early fifteenth-century scholar.

The generalized authority and trustworthiness that humanist culture had come to associate with a Latin-language source prompted the publishers to bolster the cultural value of this work, and persuade readers on this basis to purchase the text. In the 1506 and 1508 editions printed by Pietro Quarengi, a prefatory poem immediately follows the book's title:

> Che se dilecta de scriptura antica
> Et pigliasse piacere de ogni storia
> Questa opereta se la faza amica
> [...].

---

22 Bruni wrote in the Florentine vernacular two *canzoni* (1424), one sonnet, the *Difesa del popolo di Firenze nella impresa di Lucca* (1431), the orations for Niccolò Tolentino (1433) and for the Guelf party, three letters to the city of Volterra (1431), Pope Eugene IV (1435), and Francesco Sforza (1439) respectively, the *Novella di Antioco* (1437), the *Lives of Dante and Petrarch* (1436), and the *Risposta agli ambasciadori del Re d'Aragona* (1443). See Hankins, 'Humanism in the Vernacular'; Celenza, *The Lost Italian Renaissance*.
23 USTC 802575, USTC 802681, and USTC 800671, fol. 1ʳ.

> Legi questa opera senza tua pigricia
> Che troverai quel che voi vedere
> Et si la compri non usar avaritia
> Si alo fine non te voi pentere
> Quanto piu dinari te costa & amicitia
> Tanto piu cara la potrai tenere.
>
>> (Who enjoys the ancient writings
>> and revels in all histories
>> should make friends with this little work
>> [...].
>> Read this work without delay
>> as you will find what you are looking for
>> and if you buy it do not be close-fisted
>> you will not regret it
>> the more you spend
>> the more dear the friendship will be.)[24]

This passage openly expresses optimism that the translator and printer have indeed fulfilled readers' interest and needs by making available narratives and deeds from Antiquity. The use of the second-person pronouns in the vernacular poem encourages an affective loop of trust that has its origins in Bruni's alleged Latin sources, and encompasses his trustworthy vernacular translation. Indeed, his translation has made the 'ancient writings' and 'histories' as accessible as a new friend for the book's avid sixteenth-century friend and reader. The end result is a useful and enjoyable text whose trustworthiness hinged on the authority presumed of its content, author, translator, and the vernacular language in which it was commercially available to many.

Inconsistent Trust-Signalling in Translation

In the following example we see the author and pseudo-translator use Latin and Tuscan languages to both conceal and unmask his identity, as well as his sharp anti-papist and anti-Roman agenda. In this case, the apparently inconsistent trust-signalling is a strategy intended to encourage the reader's vigilance in bestowing trust, and to downplay and deflect from a particular individual's responsibility for a parlous work. In his 1548 *Commentario delle più notabili et mostruose cose d'Italia, et altri luoghi: di lingua Aramea in Italiana tradotto* (Commentary on the most notable and monstrous things in Italy and elsewhere: translated into Italian from the Aramaic), Ortensio Lando (*c.* 1510–1558) uses the literary device of the foreign traveller exploring the

---

24   *Libro intitulato aquila volante*, 1506 (USTC 800008), fol. A. The same poem, with minor variations, is also found in Sessa's editions.

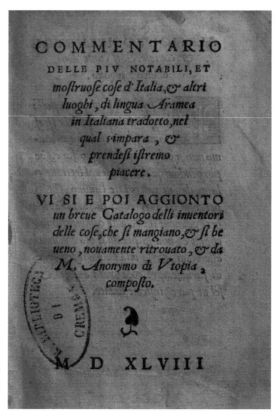

Figure 6.2. Ortensio Lando, *Commentario* (Venice, 1548). Reproduced under Google Books Creative Commons CC BY-SA 4.0.

author's country to expose the debauchery and corruption of his time.[25] This expedient is taken from Thomas More's *Utopia*, which Lando had translated anonymously into Tuscan in the same year, 1548. Lando explicitly connects his translation of More's *Utopia* and the *Commentario* in the 1548 edition (Fig. 6.2) by presenting the latter as a translation by 'Messer Anonymo di Utopia' (Sir Anonymous from Utopia).[26] Later editions of the *Commentario* (1553, 1554, and 1559) abandon this detail but still avoid naming the author on the frontispiece.

Such a refusal to reveal the authorship of the *Commentario prima facie* can be explained by the anti-papal views expressed in the vernacular throughout. This work presents the Roman court in highly ironic and irreverent terms; Lando freely turns the names of well-known cardinals into jokes:

---

25 On Ortensio Lando, see *Dizionario biografico degli italiani, ad vocem*. There are several editions of this text: 1548, most likely printed in Venice (USTC 837267); Venice: Bartolomeo Cesano, 1553 (USTC 837287); Venice: Giovanni Padovano, 1554 (USTC 837289), and Giovanni Bariletti, 1569 (USTC 837296).

26 Lando, *Commentario*, 1548, p. xxii. This is the modern edition used at this point and in the next quote from Lando's text.

vidi un canuto Gambero sedere a concistoro, vidi un Cardinale che aveva tre volti et uno che aveva tre denti, et uno ne conobbi il quale per quella parte mandava fuori il pane patito per la quale intromesso l'haveva; trovai in Roma beccari li quali non scorticarno mai ne' vitella, ne' vaccina.

(I saw an old Prawn take part in a meeting of cardinals; I also saw a Cardinal with three faces and one with three teeth. I also encountered one who would expel the bread from the same orifice from which he had ingested it; I found in Rome butchers who never skin veal or beef.)

These puns by Lando are generally explained by means of printed annotations in the margins, which are likewise in the vernacular. By these, the reader learns that the prawn or 'gambero' stands for the Cardinal of Gambara, the one with three faces stands for Cardinal Trivulzio, the one with three teeth is Cardinal Tridente, and the bread joke refers to Cardinal De Cesis ('Il Cecis'). Finally, the butchers are 'Casa Beccari'.

Lando's translation of several Lutheran works before 1529 and the ongoing deliberations of the Council of Trent, which opened only three years before the *Commentario* was written, both help to explain the omission of his name from the frontispiece. In the *Commentario*, Lando uses the expedient of the pseudo-translation (see Fig. 6.2) to veil the origins of — and deflect responsibility for — the acerbic wit found in the work. Yet this concealment of the text's authorship and translatorship on the frontispiece proves only temporary, as we see shortly. In the opening of the *Commentario*, Lando recounts that the anonymous Armenian author had decided to travel to Italy to see if all the ancient histories he had read — and his grandfather — were correct in praising Italy as the richest, most beautiful, and most civil country in the world.[27] The anonymous Armenian author happened to meet a Florentine merchant, who was sailing back to Italy from the island of Utopia, carrying carrots. The Florentine man was called Tetigio (quite possibly a pun from the past tense 'tetigi', the perfect indicative form of the Latin verb 'tango'). The Armenian asked Tetigio to take him on a journey across Italy, and the Florentine man agreed. The strongest criticism in this work is directed towards the Kingdom of Naples, Rome, and Lombardy, which are described as oppressed by an infinite number of small tyrants ('infinito numero di Tirannetti').[28]

The concealment of authorship is eventually lifted by means of another concealment. At the end of the *Commentario* per se, before the second section dedicated to a list of food and drinks found in Italy, there is a postface by a Nicolò Morra: a further disguise adopted by Lando. The postface is addressed to the

---

27 'Avendo più fiate avendo letto nelle antiche storie tante maravigliose cose dalli italiani virilmente oprate, et essendomi da mio avolo molte volte detto esser l'Italia la più bella parte, la più ricca, & la più civile che ritrovar si possi': Lando, *Commentario*, ed. by Salvatori and Salvatori, p. 2.
28 Lando, *Commentario*, 1548, fol. 4.

readers. In this section, Lando reveals the full paternity of the *Commentario*, 'nato del costantissimo cervello di M. O. L. [Messer Ortensio Lando]' (born from the very reliable mind of M. O. L.), and warns his readers that they will not be able to enjoy the full version of the text, as the author eliminated certain sections out of respect, suspicion, and spite.[29] Lando then expresses concern that the text will be received by readers as a mere 'favola' (fiction), whereas in fact the author's intention is to expose the fakery and corruption of the Church. Lando is keen to expose the corruption of truth and trustworthiness associated with the Church and its hierarchy by affirming his own trustworthiness. He seeks his readers' understanding, and apologizes for being at times too harsh ('mordace, et furioso'), and for not using the Tuscan language 'come hoggidì molti si sforzano di fare' (as many today try to use it).[30] He proceeds to beg forgiveness for the 'rozza e vile mano che lo scrisse' (coarse hand of the author) and any mistake or negligence on the part of the printer and editor.[31] Thus Lando calls before the reader all contributors to the production of this work: the author and his masks (pseudo-author, pseudo-translator, and the pseudo-author of the postface, Nicolò Morra), together with the editor and printer. In other words, Lando's intricate layering of trust-signalling in the *Commentario* does not prevent him from progressively revealing his authorial responsibility for the work's provocative content and tone as the reader moves from one section of the book to the next.

The final instance where the truth of Lando's authorship is deliberately confused is found at the end of a 'Catalogo degl'inventori delle cose che si mangiano et delle bevande ch'oggidì s'usano' (Catalogue of the inventors of the things that are eaten and the drinks that are commonly drunk today).[32] This section is accompanied by yet another postface, which has the heading 'Brieve apologia di M. Ortensio Lando, per l'autore del presente Cathalogo' (Brief apology by M. Ortensio Lando written in support of the author of the present catalogue).[33] Lando endorses the work of his alter ego Nicolò Morra, the alleged author of the 'Catalogo degl'inventori'. Lando guards him from the accusation that his compilation is mostly 'finto' (fake). To demonstrate the validity and veracity of this catalogue, Lando lists the sources used by Morra and pens a flamboyant praise of his alter ego: he is a man of 'miserabile fortuna' (miserable fortune), but he also owned the library of the emperor Gordian, has seen the libraries of Pergamon, and inherited the libraries owned by Tyrannion and Triphon (first-century CE grammarians). To conclude, Lando invites the readers to pray that God give Morra a long life.

The game of disguise played throughout this work here reaches its finale, with boastful praise of Morra becoming praise of and by Lando himself. The

---

29 Lando, *Commentario*, 1548, fol. 48^v. See Fahy, 'The Two "Neapolitan" Editions of Ortensio Lando's *Forcianae Questions*', p. 140.
30 Lando, *Commentario*, 1548, fol. 48^v.
31 Lando, *Commentario*, 1548, fol. 48^v.
32 Lando, *Commentario*, 1548, fols 50^r–70^r.
33 Lando, *Commentario*, 1548, fol. 69^v.

author of the catalogue and the author of the *Commentario* will not write less than the stoic Chrysippus, or Servius Sulpitius, or Atteus Capitonus. All of these ancient philosophers were extremely prolific: Chrysippus alone wrote more than 750 books.[34] As the successive parts of his *Commentario* unfold on the page, Lando therefore takes his self-representation full circle: from total concealment of his identity on the frontispiece to the self-promotional screeds at the end of the work. He exploits all the roles available to him as a Cinquecento polygraph to defuse and diffuse his reputation and skills as author. But the hide-and-seek he plays as pseudo-author and pseudo-translator is also, of course, a game of language. Tuscan and Latin are used to unleash his wit and confuse or reveal the targets of his satire. The plurality of roles performed by Lando on the page (author, commentator, translator) is supported by an alternation of languages, Latin and Tuscan. Thus, for instance, at folios 30ᵛ–31ʳ the reader encounters the description of the Venetian Marcantonio da Mula enjoying the company of a 'porcello' (little pig). The reader immediately learns from the gloss printed next to the main body of text that the little pig is captain Orlando Porcello. In the same gloss the captain is described in Latin ironically as 'comito inexpectando' (an unusual companion), thus setting forth a compelling counterpoint that might be described as a visual impression of courtly repartee.

One language endorses and signals the pertinence and changing credibility of the other. Hence the game played by Lando involves generating an affective loop of distrust (signalled by means of anonymity and pseudonymity) progressing towards trust and identification. Lando seeks to create an affective response on the part of the reader who is asked to trust him while distrusting the debauched and corrupted subjects exposed by his work. Ultimately, Lando enacts the fundamental instability of text per se by showing up the instability (even the vacuity) of defending the 'ultimate' or unassailable authority of published texts.

Translating and Ventriloquizing Mutual Trust in the Italian Vernacular

By the mid-sixteenth century, and following the progressive establishment of a standardized Tuscan literary vernacular, western European intellectuals tended towards freely displacing ancient Latin sources in favour of elegant Tuscan versions, which were excessively ornate at times. This is well demonstrated by the vernacular translation of Virgil's *Aeneid* made (*c.* 1564) by Annibale Caro (1507–1566), which was printed posthumously in Venice by Bernardo Giunta in 1581. The book's frontispiece (Fig. 6.3) shows the prominence given to the translator's role, in that it accords him authorial status. In the title of this edition, Virgil's *Aeneid* is unequivocally attributed to Caro: '*L'Eneide di*

---

34 Gould, *The Philosophy of Chrysippus*, p. 8.

Figure 6.3. *L'Eneide di Virgilio* (Venice: Giunta, 1581). Reproduced under Google Books Creative Commons CC BY-SA 4.0.

Virgilio, del Commendatore Annibal Caro' (*The Aeneid of Virgil*, by the Grand Officer Annibale Caro).[35] In this formulation, the translator is far from a subservient mediator between the source text and the target audience; Caro is presented as the new author of the epic poem, while the first author has become an extension of the title. As a result, '*The Aeneid of Virgil*' describes the Latin text used by Caro to produce his 'Eneide'.

The preface addressed to Caro's patron, Alessandro Farnese III, duke of Parma and Piacenza, reinforces the translator's authority and trust-signalling. Written by Lepido Caro, nephew of Annibale, it presents the translation through the use of the common metaphor of clothes:

> Ma perché questo Poema esce in Theatro con habiti diversi da quelli che da Virgilio li furono lasciati, et può agevolmente haver bisogno et

---

35 The 1581 edition of *L'Eneide di Virgilio* is USTC 862861.

d'introduttione et di difesa, acciò non fosse repudiato come non vero et legitimo figliuolo del suo antico et honoratissimo padre.

> (But because this poem comes out on the stage with different costumes from the ones Virgil had left, and for this reason could easily require both an introduction and defence, so that this version is not rejected as inauthentic and illegitimate son of his ancient and illustrious father.)[36]

This statement betrays a certain level of anxiety on the part of Lepido Caro, the editor of this translation. Whereas the frontispiece asserts the translator as the new and legitimate author — or father — of the *Aeneid*, the editor feels compelled to recognize the paternity of Virgil, and to pre-empt any criticism on the readers' part that the text has been modified so radically that its original guise is unrecognizable. The confident appeal for the support of Annibale Caro's dedicatee and former patron is calculated to dispel this potential criticism, and the frontispiece seals the authority of the 'new' garments in which Annibale Caro clothed the Virgilian poem.

On a broader level, Lepido Caro's preface to his uncle's translation presents the act of printing as 'staging', with the phrase 'esce in Theatro'. Lepido Caro had already relied on this expression some ten years before the publication of *L'Eneide di Virgilio*, in his edition of his uncle's *Lettere familiari*. Published in two volumes by Aldo Manuzio II between 1574 and 1575, the second volume of the letters is dedicated to the Cardinal of Como. In his preface to this dedicatee, Lepido Caro invokes the trustworthiness of the text and the praise of its author, his uncle. This text, says Lepido, 'potrà uscire in Theatro con molta utilità del mondo, & parimente con non poca laude de l'Autore' (will come out on stage and will be of much use for the world and will bring much praise for the author).[37] The evocation of performance in promotional language like that of an impresario underscores the significance of his editorship in the publication and endorsement of his uncle's work. The roles of the authoritative translator and the editor are spelled out clearly in Lepido Caro's preface to the *Lettere familiari*. In 1581, Bernardo Giunta republished the two volumes of the *Lettere familiari* with the same prefaces by Lepido Caro, in the hope of rekindling interest in the work of his uncle Annibale Caro.[38]

This collaboration across time between the two members of the Caro family reveals a key aspect in the Cinquecento publication of vernacular translations in Italy: a habit of signalling, in prefatory materials, mutual trust and collaboration between the translator, their employer and patron, editor, and author. In the case of Annibale Caro's translation of the *Aeneid*, Lepido Caro's posthumous editing of the text reactivated Annibale Caro's connection with his former distinguished patron Alessandro Farnese, while

---

36 *L'Eneide di Virgilio*, fol. III.
37 Caro, *De le lettere familiari*, 1574–1575, fol. 2ᵛ.
38 With the same title, the 1581 Giunti edition is USTC 819052.

also asserting the prestige and authority of the translator who had clothed Virgil with vernacular garments in view of a new appearance. The numerous later editions of Annibale Caro's vernacular translation demonstrate that the new staging of the Aeneid with new clothes and a 'new' language proved extremely successful.

Another work by Ortensio Lando shows this singular humanist engage in a game of vernacular ventriloquism, mutual trust, and collaboration in order to promote himself and his circle of friends and encourage a favourable affective reaction on the part of readers. Titled *Lettere di molte valorose donne*, and first published in 1548, this collection of letters is conspicuously attributed to noblewomen from the Veneto region. In this work, Lando, the editor and, as discussed below, the author, conceals his name.[39] Neither the frontispiece nor the preface to the book — addressed to the ambassador of Henry VIII, Edmund Harwel (Sigismondo Rovello) — reveal the name of the editor who had 'ridotto molte lettere da vari luoghi raccolte et da savie donne scritte' (gathered from various places several letters by wise women).[40]

The editor's identity is made clear only at the end of the work, where the reader also finds poems by a community of prolific scholars from the Venetian literary circle who were gravitating around the Giolito press. This community included polygraphs such as Lodovico Dolce and Lando, who, at a time of popularizing printing presses, sought to live by their writing — a matter also of managing their reputations (thus the threat of social marginalization) as much as any controversy arising from their projects and published works.[41] Following the final letter, the *Lettere di molte valorose donne* includes a message from Bartolomeo Pestalozzi of Chiavenna ('Rhetus'), addressed to the reader. The message is in Latin and reveals at last that 'Hortensius Lando' had gathered the letters, and Ottaviano Raverta, bishop of Terracina, had turned this collection into a volume.[42]

Raverta was a close friend of Lando's and part of the Venetian circle to which Lando, Dolce, Pietro Aretino, and Giuseppe Betussi belonged. This connection is made evident by a dialogue published in 1544 by Gabriel Giolito and titled *Il Raverta, Dialogo di Messer Giuseppe Betussi, nel quale si ragiona d'amore, e degli effetti suoi*.[43] The dialogue shows Ottaviano Raverta in conversation with the Venetian courtesan Francesca Baffa about the nature of love, thus portraying him within the ranks of Venice's vibrant community of authors, printers, and editors. In this dialogue Raverta supports Baffa's

---

39 On this work by Lando, see Simonetta, 'Il dissidente segretario delle valorose donne', especially the relevant bibliography given on p. 554. See also Jordan, *Renaissance Feminism*, pp. 138–43; Ray, *Writing Gender in Women's Letter Collections*, pp. 45–80, and, by the same author, 'Textual Collaboration and Spiritual Partnership'.
40 Lando, *Lettere di molte valorose donne*, fol. Aii.
41 For an account of 'poligrafi' in sixteenth-century Italy, see Terpening, *Lodovico Dolce*.
42 Lando, *Lettere di molte valorose donne*, fol. 161ᵛ.
43 Betussi, *Il Raverta*.

independence as a woman. Unsurprisingly, then, in the *Lettere di molte valorose donne* Pestalozzi presents Raverta and Lando as collaborators in this edition of letters, and also strong supporters of the cause of women. Such emphasis on the collaborative nature of this book — a work purportedly written by several women, gathered by Lando, and finally edited by Pestalozzi — is indicative of ways in which early modern printed texts were often the product of close and creatively dynamic relationships between intellectuals, editors, and printers. The temporary concealment of Lando's name on the frontispiece is a strategy to defuse responsibility for a project that would have been considered controversial by contemporary readers.

If Pestalozzi's postface affirms the collaborative nature of the book project, Lodovico Dolce asserts the authorial role for Lando. In a sonnet addressed to women, Dolce calls for them to thank Lando, since his 'vago stil de le sue dotte carte' (the elegant style of his learned pages) honours the women's virtue.[44] Lando is therefore evoked for his questionable achievement of having ventriloquized educated women of his time. His eloquence praises and elevates the reputation of women: the use of the possessive pronoun in the sentence above ('his learned pages') leaves little doubt that Lando has composed most, if not all, of the letters that Lando himself attributes to women. Dolce's sonnet retrospectively casts a completely different light on the absence of Lando's name enacted on the frontispiece. If, as Dolce suggests, the letters are indeed written by Lando to celebrate the virtues of women, the withholding of the real author's name is essential to mask a clear contradiction underpinning this editorial enterprise: the letters by noblewomen that are published to demonstrate their virtues are, in fact, composed by an author who fabricated letters that were never written by the women he set out to praise.

The tables are turned yet again in the sonnet that follows, by Girolamo Parabosco. After asserting that the work is the fruit of collaboration between the female authors and the two editors, and after naming Lando as the sole author, Parabosco presents Lando as he who

> Ecco chi vi torrà donne gentili
> Quel biasmo, che vi dan le false lingue
> Del vulgo sciocco, che mai non destingue.
>
>> (will lift, my sweet ladies
>> the scorn coming from the lying tongues
>> of the ignorant populace.)[45]

Only a year earlier, Parabosco had published the second edition of his collection of *Lettere amorose*, a series of templates for writing love letters and

---

44 'Non tanto e così vivo obligo havete: | Quanto al buon LANDO; ch'ogni rara parte | Di voi consacra (onde chiare vivrete) | Nel vago stil de le sue dotte carte': Lando, *Lettere di molte valorose donne*, fol. 162ʳ.
45 Lando, *Lettere di molte valorose donne*, fol. 162ʳ.

proffered for the benefit of readers.[46] In this sonnet for the *Lettere di molte valorose donne*, Parabosco does not indicate the authorship of the letters published in Lando's edition. This ambiguity is probably intentional, as the following passage suggests:

> Lo stile, e i bei concetti alti, e virili,
> [...]
> Vi faranno a i piu saggi esser simili.
>
> > (The style, the beautiful, lofty, and virile concepts
> > [...]
> > will make you look like the most wise men.)[47]

The next sonnet, one by Pietro Aretino, shifts the focus back on the editor, while also finally dispelling any ambiguity regarding the authorship of the letters:

> Hortensio lampa a le piu dotte scole,
> Et chiaro Heroe de le scienze invitte,
> Le carte illustri l'una a l'altra scritte
> Ha posto in luce del lor proprio sole:
> [...]
> Ma perche voi non sareste immortali
> Se la nobil di lui pietosa cura
> Non raccoglieva de i vostri spiriti i Sali
> [...]
> Dateli loda.
>
> > (Ortensio, the splendour of the most learned schools, and shining hero of the deathless arts, has placed the illustrious letters written by one woman to another in the light of their own sun. [...] However, seeing that you would not be immortal if he had not, through his worthy and devoted efforts, gathered together the clever wit of your spirits [...] give him praise.)[48]

Here the women are indicated as the authors of the letters published in this collection, but as part of an exhortation to them — it is only thanks to Lando's efforts that these authors will be read and praised. In this new literary scenario, Aretino suddenly declares that the compiler is more important than the authors. Aretino's statement might be called, at one level, a key concluding instance of trust-signalling in the volume, one which briskly seeks to return a binary-gendered 'order' to the representation of intellectual

---

46 Parabosco, *Lettere amorose di M. Girolamo Parabosco*, published in Venice by Gabriele Giolito de' Ferrari, 1547 (USTC 762674); the first edition of Parabosco's *Lettere* was published in 1545, also by Giolito.
47 Lando, *Lettere di molte valorose donne*, fol. 162^r.
48 Lando, *Lettere di molte valorose donne*, fol. 162^v. This English translation is by Christopher Nissen, in his study *Kissing the Wild Woman*, p. 66.

authority.[49] Aretino invokes here a collaboration that is very different from that described by Pestalozzi in which the editor shines light on the work of women who would have been otherwise ignored. For this reason, Aretino's poem encourages women to give the compiler praise. Such a twist in designations of merit and expressing acclaim puts the women that Lando tried to praise in a lower position: this contrasts stridently with the frontispiece of the same work, in which the women who authored the letters published in this collection are presented as not being inferior to men in the art of writing.[50] The last encomiastic postfaces are addressed to Lando (a sonnet by Francesco Sansovino) and to women (a poem by Niccolò degli Alberti from Bormio).

These different readings of the collected letters *or* letter collection underpin the signalling of shared trustworthiness between author, editor, and printer. The concealment of the editor's or authors' names in the title and main body of the text is compounded by deliberately ambiguous statements in which the feminist stance of the work, and the self-presentation and promotion of the authors and their close circle of friends and colleagues, all coexist and wrangle.

Conclusion

In his *Prince*, Niccolò Machiavelli (1469–1527) describes some of the leadership qualities that are worthy of reward by means of 'vigilant trust', not blind faith.[51] He calls for cautious and conditional trust and invites citizens to identify signs and qualities in their leaders that can inspire a vigilant trust. The trust-signalling and editorial strategies employed by early modern authors, translators, editors, and printers aimed to stimulate confidence in the readers and patrons that the cultural product they had been offered or bought would bring the knowledge and enjoyment they hoped to achieve. But clearly the premise for such confidence was vigilant trust on the part of the readers and patrons. The examples discussed in this chapter provide an opportunity to witness translators, editors, and printers experimenting in their pursuit of personal, cultural, and commercial reward for their work. This was part of seeking to reach and foster new trustworthy readerships for material that pre-print humanist culture, with its close appreciation of the differences and complementarities between Latin and vernacular languages, had defended as highly appealing.

The editorial strategies discussed here show that the games of authorial disguise and language shifting played by early modern translators, editors, and printers involved a complex and affective process of trust or distrust aimed at convincing

---

49 See LaFleur, Raskolnikov, and Klosowska, *Trans Historical* and DeVun, *The Shape of Sex*.
50 'Lettere di molte valorose donne, nella quali chiaramente appare non esser né di eloquenza né di dottrina alli huomini inferiori'.
51 Benner, 'Natural Suspicion and Reasonable Trust', p. 70.

readers of the vernacular books' usefulness and enjoyment. The early modern editorial and commercial enterprises examined here offer a unique vantage point from which to observe the production of trustworthy secular written culture through communication strategies and marketing tools. They also offer insight into how the readers' vigilant trust was stimulated by translators' and editors' games of disguise performed in the margins of texts (prefaces, glosses, dedications, etc.).

Clearly, vernacular editors and translators of early modern Italy were crucial agents of cultural trust. Studying the ways in which they signalled the trustworthiness of their editions and translations sheds light on the 'infrastructures of trustworthiness' that their contemporaries understood, accepted, or rejected.[52]

Works Cited

Manuscripts and Archival Sources

Florence, Biblioteca Medicea Laurenziana, Conv. Soppr. 165
Florence, Biblioteca Nazionale Centrale, II, II, 32
Florence, Biblioteca Nazionale Centrale, Magliab. XXIII, 44
Paris, Bibliothèque nationale de France, MS Ital. 129
Paris, Bibliothèque nationale de France, MS Ital. 438

Primary Sources

Betussi, Giuseppe, *Il Raverta, Dialogo di Messer Giuseppe Betussi, nel quale si ragiona d'amore, e degli effetti suoi* (Venice: Gabriele Giolito de' Ferrari, 1544) [USTC 814328]
Caro, Annibale, *De le lettere familiari del commendatore Annibal Caro Volume primo [-secondo]* (Venice: Aldo Manuzio, 1574–1575) [USTC 819046]
——, *De le lettere familiari del commendatore Annibal Caro Volume primo [-secondo]* (Venice: Bernardo Giunti and brothers, 1581) [USTC 819052]
L'Eneide di Virgilio, del Commendatore Annibal Caro (Venice: Bernardo Giunta and brothers, 1581) [USTC 862861]
Lando, Ortensio, *Commentario delle piu notabili, et mostruose cose d'Italia, et altri luoghi, di lingua aramea in italiana tradotto, nel qual s'impara, et prendesi istremo piacere. Vi si è poi aggionto un breue catalogo delli inuentori delle cose, che si mangiano, et si beueno, nouamente ritrouato, et da m. Anonymo di vtopia, composto* (Venice: [n.pub.], 1548) [USTC 837267]
——, *Commentario delle più notabili et mostruose cose d'Italia, et altri luoghi: Di lingua Aramea in Italiana tradotto*, ed. by Guido Salvatori and Paola Salvatori (Bologna: Pendragon, 1994)

---

52 Miller, *Trust in Texts*, p. 8. See also Rizzi, 'Signs of Trust'.

———, *Lettere di molte valorose donne* (Venice: Giolito, 1548) [USTC 837270]
Libro intitulato aquila volante (Venice: Pietro Quarengi, 1506) [USTC 800008]
Libro intitolato Aquila volante. Di Latino nella volgar lingua dal magnifico Leonardo Aretino tradotto (Venice: Melchiorre Sessa, 1531) [USTC 802575]
Libro intitolato Aquila volante. Di Latino nella volgar lingua dal magnifico Leonardo Aretino tradotto (Venice: Melchiorre Sessa, 1535) [USTC 802681]
Libro intitolato Aquila volante. Di Latino nella volgar lingua dal magnifico et eloquentissimo Leonardo Aretino tradotto (Venice: Melchiorre Sessa, 1539) [USTC 800671]
Opera intitulata Aquila (Naples: Ayolfus de Cantono, 1492) [ISTC ib01231000]
Opera intitulata Aquila (Venice: Peregrinus de Pasqualibus, Bononiensis, 1494) [ISTC ib01232000]
Opera intitulata Aquila (Milan: Antonius Zarotus, 1495) [ISTC ib01233000]
Opera intitulata Aquila (Venice: Theodorus de Ragazonibus, 1497) [ISTC ib01233100]
Parabosco, Girolamo, *Lettere amorose di M. Girolamo Parabosco, con alcune altre di nuovo aggiunte* (Venice: Gabriele Giolito de' Ferrari, 1547) [USTC 762674]

Secondary Studies

Bec, Christian, *Les Livres des Florentins (1413–1608)* (Florence: L. S. Olschki, 1984)
Benner, Erica, 'Natural Suspicion and Reasonable Trust: Machiavelli on Trust in Politics', in *Trust and Happiness in the History of European Political Thought*, ed. by László Kontler and Mark Somos (Leiden: Brill, 2017), pp. 53–75
Biow, Douglas, *Doctors, Ambassadors, Secretaries: Humanism and Professions in Renaissance Italy* (Chicago: University of Chicago Press, 2002)
Blasio, Maria Grazia, and Giulio Vaccaro, *Il libro dell'Aquila, sec. XIV: Cultura dantesca in area romano-laziale* (Rome: Roma nel Rinascimento, 2018)
Camporeale, Salvatore, *Christianity, Latinity, and Culture. Two Studies on Lorenzo Valla*, trans. and ed. by Patrick Baker and Christopher Celenza (Leiden: Brill, 2013)
Celenza, Christopher S., *The Lost Italian Renaissance: Humanists, Historians, and Latin's Legacy* (Baltimore: Johns Hopkins University Press, 2004)
Cornell, Susan, 'Books and their Owners in Venice, 1345–1480', *Journal of the Warburg and Courtauld Institutes*, 35 (1972), 163–86
DeVun, Leah, *The Shape of Sex: Nonbinary Gender from Genesis to the Renaissance* (New York: Columbia University Press, 2021)
Dizionario biografico degli italiani, 85 vols (Rome: Istituto della Enciclopedia Italiana, 1960–2018)
Fahy, Conor, 'The Two "Neapolitan" Editions of Ortensio Lando's *Forcianae Questions*', in *Collected Essays on Italian Language & Literature Presented to Kathleen Speight*, ed. by Giovanni Aquilecchia, Stephen N. Cristea, and Sheila Ralphs (Manchester: Manchester University Press, 1971), pp. 123–42
Gatti, Daniela, *La Vita Caroli di Donato Acciaiuoli: La leggenda di Carlo Magno in funzione di una historia di gesta* (Bologna: Pàtron, 1981)
Gould, Josiah B., *The Philosophy of Chrysippus* (Leiden: Brill, 1970)

Grafton, Anthony, *Commerce with the Classics: Ancient Books and Renaissance Readers* (Ann Arbor: University of Michigan Press, 1997)

Greif, Avner, 'The Maghribi Traders: A Reappraisal?', *Economic History Review*, 65.2 (2012), 445–69

——, 'Reputation and Coalitions in Medieval Trade: Evidence on the Maghribi Traders', *Journal of Economic History*, 49.4 (1989), 857–83

Hankins, James, 'Humanism in the Vernacular: The Case of Leonardo Bruni', in *Humanism and Creativity in the Renaissance: Essays in Honor of Ronald G. Witt*, ed. by Christopher S. Celenza and Kenneth Gouwens (Leiden: Brill, 2006), pp. 11–29

Heller, Marvin J., *Further Studies in the Making of the Early Hebrew Book* (Leiden: Brill, 2013), pp. 3–20

Jones, Karen, 'Trust, Distrust, and Affective Looping', *Philosophical Studies*, 176.4 (2019), 955–68

——, 'Trustworthiness', *Ethics*, 123.1 (2012), 61–85

Jordan, Constance, *Renaissance Feminism: Literary Texts and Political Models* (Ithaca, NY: Cornell University Press, 1990)

LaFleur, Greta, Masha Raskolnikov, and Anna Klosowska, *Trans Historical: Gender Plurality before the Modern* (Ithaca, NY: Cornell University Press)

Luhmann, Niklas, 'Familiarity, Confidence, Trust: Problems and Alternatives', in *Trust Making and Breaking: Cooperative Relations*, ed. by Diego Gambetta (New York: Blackwell, 1988), pp. 94–107

Margolis, Oren J., 'The "Gallic Crowd" at the "Aragonese Doors": Donato Acciaiuoli's *Vita Caroli Magni* and the Workshop of Vespasiano da Bisticci', *I Tatti Studies in the Italian Renaissance*, 17.2 (2014), 241–82

Maxson, Brian, *The Humanist World of Renaissance Florence* (Cambridge: Cambridge University Press, 2014)

Mayer, Elisabetta, *Un umanista italiano alla corte di Mattia Corvino: Aurelio Brandolini Lippo*, Biblioteca dell'Accademia d'Ungheria di Roma, 14 (Rome: [n.pub.], 1938)

Miller, Susan, *Trust in Texts: A Different History of Rhetoric* (Carbondale: Southern Illinois University Press, 2008)

Nissen, Christopher, *Kissing the Wild Woman: Art, Beauty, and the Reformation of the Italian Prose Romance in Giulia Bigolina's 'Urania'* (Toronto: University of Toronto Press, 2011)

Nuovo, Angela, *The Book Trade in the Italian Renaissance*, trans. by Lydia Cochrane (Leiden: Brill, 2013)

Pettegree, Andrew, *The Book in the Renaissance* (New Haven: Yale University Press, 2010)

Ray, Meredith K., 'Textual Collaboration and Spiritual Partnership in Sixteenth-Century Italy: The Case of Ortensio Lando and Lucrezia Gonzaga', *Renaissance Quarterly*, 62 (2009), 694–747

——, *Writing Gender in Women's Letter Collections of the Italian Renaissance* (Toronto: University of Toronto Press, 2009)

Richardson, Brian, *Printing, Writers and Readers in Renaissance Italy* (Cambridge: Cambridge University Press, 1999)

Rizzi, Andrea, 'Signs of Trust in the Italian Renaissance', *I Tatti Studies in the Italian Renaissance*, 22.2 (2019), 335–43

Rizzi, Andrea, Birgit Lang, and Anthony Pym, *What Is Translation History? A Trust-Based Approach* (Cham: Palgrave, 2019)

Ross, Sarah Gwyneth, *Everyday Renaissances: The Quest for Cultural Legitimacy in Venice* (Cambridge, MA: Harvard University Press, 2016)

Sebastiani, Valentina, and Wendell Ricketts, 'Froben Press Editions (1505–1559) in the Holdings of the Centre for Reformation and Renaissance Studies Library: A Brief Survey', *Renaissance and Reformation / Renaissance et Réforme*, 37.3 (2014), 213–34

Simonetta, Elisabetta, 'Il dissidente segretario delle valorose donne: Ortensio Lando tra camouflage epistolare e retorica del paradosso', *Bruniana & Campanelliana*, 22.2 (2016), 553–63

Terpening, Richard H., *Lodovico Dolce, Renaissance Man of Letters* (Toronto: University of Toronto Press, 1997)

Tilly, Charles, *Trust and Rule* (Cambridge: Cambridge University Press, 2005)

Tissoni Benvenuti, Antonia, 'La ricezione delle Silvae di Stazio e la poesia all'improvviso nel Rinascimento', in *Gli antichi e i moderni: Studi in onore di Roberto Cardini*, ed. by Lucia Bertolini and Donatella Coppini, 3 vols (Florence: Polistampa, 2010), III, pp. 1283–1324

Trivellato, Francesca, *The Familiarity of Strangers: The Sephardic Diaspora, Livorno, and Cross-Cultural Trade in the Early Modern Period* (New Haven: Yale University Press, 2009)

Vaccaro, Giulio, 'Storia e geografia di un centone di volgarizzamenti: Il Libro dell'Aquila', in *Storia sacra e profana nei volgarizzamenti medioevali: Rilievi di lingua e di cultura*, ed. by Michele Colombo, Paolo Pellegrini, and Simone Pregnolato (Berlin: De Gruyter), pp. 273–98

Zorzi, Marino, 'Le biblioteche veneziane, espressione di una singolare civiltà', in *The Books of Venice / Il libro veneziano*, ed. by Lisa Pon and Craig Kallendorf (Venice: La Musa Talìa and Oak Knoll Press, 2007), pp. 1–31

Part 2

Linguistic and Cultural Exchanges with Europe

JENELLE THOMAS

Language Contact between French and Italian in the Sixteenth Century

Evidence from the Diplomatic Letters of Georges d'Armagnac

There is a long historical tradition of contact and cultural interchange between the Italian peninsula and its northern French neighbour. Some interchange was the by-product of commercial, diplomatic, religious, or military activity, while other exchanges resulted from the pursuit of education, cultural enrichment, artistic and literary inspiration, or tourism on the part of the elite. Although significant movements of people, money, and ideas throughout the transalpine network date from at least the Middle Ages, during the sixteenth century we can identify 'the opening of a new phase of closer, more fruitful contact' between the two regions.[1]

All these cultural, political, and commercial contacts had the potential to initiate or spread contact-induced changes, including lexical innovations, in the linguistic varieties spoken by the individuals involved. However, discussion of the linguistic effects, and particularly the 'Italianization' of the French language and culture taking place during the sixteenth century, is often centred on literary texts and the trends of the court. This chapter, in contrast, will focus on the role played by speakers who spent a great deal of time in Italy. Work in contact linguistics has long held that the bilingual speaker is the agent of contact-influenced language change, and that the sociocultural relationship between populations speaking different linguistic varieties is a determining factor in the linguistic effects of contact.[2] Evidence of the day-to-day behaviour of bilingual speakers is available in correspondence composed by those with close ties to both languages, including diplomats tasked with

---

1 Hope, *Lexical Borrowing in the Romance Languages*, p. 229.
2 Weinreich, *Languages in Contact*; Thomason, 'Social and Linguistic Factors as Predictors of Contact-Induced Change'.

> **Jenelle Thomas** (jenelle.thomas@berkeley.edu) is a historical sociolinguist interested in the history of Romance varieties in contact. She has published on a variety of topics including historical multilingualism in epistolary and legal texts.

Languages and Cross-Cultural Exchanges in Renaissance Italy, ed. by Alessandra Petrocchi and Joshua Brown, LMEMS 30 (Turnhout: Brepols, 2023), pp. 211–237

being the intermediary between the various power brokers on both sides of the Alps. This type of communication is not known for its stylistic creativity nor performative Italophilia in the way other genres from the time might be, and it therefore provides a unique perspective on cultural and linguistic contacts between France and Italy.

I will take as a case study of diplomatic correspondence the letters of Georges d'Armagnac, who held one ambassadorial post in Venice and two in Rome during the period from 1530 to 1560. I begin by outlining the nature and historical development of the cultural and linguistic contacts between Italy and France during the sixteenth century and the value of epistolary communication as a source for tracing language contact. In the rest of the chapter, I focus on the lexical innovations in evidence in d'Armagnac's French-language correspondence.

Transalpine Connections: Historical and Cultural Links between France and Italy

The sixteenth century should not be taken as a monolith, and in fact most traditional conceptions break it into halves or thirds, with the intensity and frequency of contact varying over time and in each area of activity. The periods of the most intense French contact with Italy — political and military as well as sociocultural — took place in the middle of the century, coinciding with the reign of François I (1515–1547) and the ensuing three-decade-long period marked by the influence of Caterina de' Medici as queen, regent, and queen mother. While the personal influence of these royals as patrons of the arts, models of courtly manners, and wielders of political, military, economic, and commercial power cannot be denied, it is also true that the extent and effects of contact between France and Italy reach far beyond these individuals.

Our narrative of sixteenth-century contact begins with the invasion of Naples by Charles VIII in 1494. This event marks the starting point of the Italian Wars and a half century of French military presence in the Italian peninsula. A series of skirmishes would punctuate this period, but after the 1529 Treaty of Cambrai the influence of France began to diminish in relation to that of other European powers, and direct intervention became increasingly rare. In striking opposition to the interventionist tendencies of a hundred years before, the last decades of the sixteenth century were characterized by French political disengagement from Italian affairs.[3]

The effects of French military intervention went far beyond political investment and boots on the ground; the fight for territory bred a new familiarity with and passion for Italian culture, architecture, literature, and art. In this new spirit of French Italophilia, wealthy patrons induced Italian artists to

---

3 Hope, *Lexical Borrowing in the Romance Languages*, pp. 229–33, 265–66.

visit France, chateaux were rebuilt to imitate Italian architecture, and demand increased for translation of Italian literary works. Meanwhile, although the wars made existing internal politics within the Italian city states even more complicated, with concomitant changes in prevailing attitudes towards France, 'plenty of historical evidence is available to confirm that Italians at this time were almost as interested in French affairs as the French were in those of their neighbours. Even when there was a political rift between the two countries cultural exchanges continued'.[4] In fact, other types of contact did not follow the same declining pattern over the century as direct military intervention did, though of course cultural and even commercial interchange was never entirely independent from the changing political winds.

In contrast to the political sphere, where the last few decades of the century were distinguished by French political disinterest and disengagement in the affairs of the Italian city states, there was during this period an increase in cultural exchange and especially tourism. The European elite's interest in foreign lands for reasons beyond commercial gain — and particularly Italy — increased from the sixteenth century through the early modern period. Trips to the peninsula such as the one taken by Montaigne (recorded as his *Voyage*, 1580–1581) were seen as de rigueur for the cultured and are early examples of the phenomenon of the Grand Tour and related genre of travel literature which would flourish in the following centuries.[5] Italy was seen as a site for intellectual as well as cultural development; throughout the sixteenth century French universities welcomed Italian professors, and Francophone students flocked to Italian universities in Pavia, Ferrara, and Padua. Once there, they mainly studied law, with a few more choosing medicine or theology. Those seeking military or courtly skills such as riding or fencing attended the Academies in Naples, Bologna, or Padua.[6]

On the other hand, this current of Italophilia in sixteenth-century French society was matched by a strong backlash against it. This anti-Italian reaction, which gained in strength in the last decades of the century, has been pinned in part on the influence of Caterina de' Medici and her favouritism towards Italians, but in fact was indicative of a more widespread shift in public sentiment. This was a period of primacy and influence of a small Italian elite in multiple aspects of French society — the Church, the court, banking and trade, literature and the arts — but also a period of decreasing profitability of French investments in the peninsula and of religious wars in France, specifically the 1527 St Bartholomew's Day Massacre. Thus the

---

4 Melani, '*Di qua' e 'di là da' monti*', pp. 523–24; Hope, *Lexical Borrowing in the Romance Languages*, pp. 229, 272.

5 Wind, *Les mots italiens introduits en français au XVI*^{e} *siècle*, pp. 27–29; Balsamo, 'Le voyage d'Italie et la formation des élites françaises'; Cro, 'Montaigne's Italian Voyage', p. 154; Tosi, *Language and the Grand Tour*.

6 Bingen, *Aux escholles d'outre-monts*; Picot, *Les Italiens en France au* XVIe *siècle*, p. 279; Balsamo, 'Le voyage d'Italie et la formation des élites françaises'.

backlash against Italians and Italianism can also be read as a rejection of a specific ethnic and religious identity, one which had the effect of defining a new sense of state-centred national identity in the early modern period.[7] This evolution of policies, attitudes, and relationships makes the sixteenth century a particularly interesting period for the study of contact and interchange.

Language Use and Contact

The effects of this sustained contact were linguistic as well as cultural. In the streets of the border regions and even in several cities farther removed on both sides of the Alps, varieties of both Italo- and Gallo-Romance could be heard. The States of Savoy, for example, boasted official multilingualism from the medieval period right through to the nineteenth century.[8] One sphere in which Italian — although far from a codified variety — appears to have occupied a special place even amongst foreigners is in the commercial sphere. Merchants and traders communicated in a mix of languages, but Paré argues that 'par son rayonnement transfrontalier, la langue italienne se construit justement comme le code emblématique de la diversité méditerranéenne' (due to its transborder influence, the Italian language became a code emblematic of Mediterranean diversity).[9] It was learned as a tool of the trade by travelling merchants throughout the Mediterranean who viewed the peninsula as being at the centre of a zone of economic interest extending well beyond its borders.[10] The Italians themselves were also vehicles for transmission of their language; the merchants who settled in France — by and large with a view to their stay being temporary, though families often remained for generations — nonetheless retained very strong ties to their regions of origin, including linguistic and cultural traditions.[11] Reports from Lyon speak of a 'semi-Italianization' of its language and culture, unsurprising given the size of the Italian population there.[12] The southern region of France arguably acted as a linguistic 'filter' for Italianisms entering French through the spoken language.[13] In the Parisian court, the influence of Caterina de' Medici and her compatriots was clear, and though she communicated with her countrymen in Italian, she did in fact often speak French with Frenchmen. In fact, the French court and the salons continued to be home to conversations in both languages into the seventeenth

---

7 Heller, *Anti-Italianism in Sixteenth-Century France*; Hope, *Lexical Borrowing in the Romance Languages*, p. 231.
8 See Aimerito, 'Aspects of Legal Multilingualism in the States of Savoy', for discussion.
9 Paré, 'L'impact sur l'Italie des débats français sur la langue au milieu du XVIe siècle', p. 61.
10 Paré, 'L'impact sur l'Italie des débats français sur la langue au milieu du XVIe siècle', p. 60; Cremona, 'Italian-Based Lingua Francas around the Mediterranean'.
11 Dubost, *La France italienne*, pp. 121, 127.
12 Boucher, *Présence italienne à Lyon*.
13 Sampson, 'The Loss of French Prosthesis and the Problem of Italianisms'.

century, and Italians could arrive and thrive in the Hexagon with no prior knowledge of French.[14] Of course, this Italianization of culture and language was also parodied and criticized, for example by Henri Estienne in his *Deux dialogues du nouveau langage françois italianizé, et aultrement desguizé* (1578).[15] Thus we see many routes of transmission for Italianisms into French, from merchants to multilingual populations to the language of the court.

On the Italian side, French had a strong tradition in the arts; across the north, a set of linguistic varieties known as 'franco-italiano', 'franco-veneto', or 'franco-lombardo' were popular in literary-minded social groups in the fourteenth and fifteenth centuries,[16] and Italian scribes of musical texts demonstrated a familiarity with French until at least the mid-fifteenth century.[17] With the rising power and cultural prestige of the Italian Renaissance, however, there was a dip in the general knowledge and prestige of the French language on the Italian peninsula between the fifteenth and seventeenth centuries — after the great artistic influence cited above but before the rise of French as a global diplomatic language. This is corroborated by the dates of publication of educational materials: manuals to teach Italian to Frenchmen appeared from 1510,[18] alongside grammars of Italian published in French, but the first Italian-language grammar of French was not published until 1625,[19] perhaps indicative of a lack of widespread desire to learn that language.

The period of most intense influence of French on Italian has in fact been identified as beginning in the seventeenth century, with the rise of the global status of the latter in the early modern period.[20] Hope, however, cautions us against believing either that there was an abrupt surge of Gallomania at the end of the seventeenth century or that the previous periods were woefully lacking in borrowings from French despite the imbalance in borrowed words. In fact, his assessment of the sixteenth century is that the influence of French on Italian was at a sort of baseline level, that is, 'moderately intimate contact; but no sign of uncritical enthusiasm, of unwarranted or uncontrolled psychological attitudes towards particular social groups or their way of life; no wholesale drift of ideas, no "transfusions de civilisation", in Marcel Cohen's phrase'.[21] French and other foreign languages seem to have been necessary for trade and taken as the unmarked case, so much so that language acquisition

---

14 Dubost, *La France italienne*, p. 124.
15 Heller, *Anti-Italianism in Sixteenth-Century France*; Dubost, *La France italienne*.
16 Benincà, Parry, and Pescarini, 'The Dialects of Northern Italy', p. 187; Brown, 'Language Variation in Fifteenth-Century Milan', p. 59.
17 Fallows, 'French as a Courtly Language in Fifteenth-Century Italy'.
18 Bingen, *Le Maître italien (1510–1660)*.
19 Pellandra, 'Toward a Bibliography of Manuals for the Instruction of French in Italy'; Minerva, *Manuels, maîtres, méthodes*.
20 Cella, *I gallicismi nei testi dell'italiano antico*, p. vii; Tosi, *Language and the Grand Tour*, p. 215.
21 Hope, *Lexical Borrowing in the Romance Languages*, p. 273.

or language competence are not specifically mentioned in sources from the period.[22]

In contrast to this baseline level of influence of French on Italian, the influence of Italian on French — claimed by Wind to be the greatest external influence in the history of the French language — arguably reached its peak in the sixteenth century. For example, Hope shows that six and a half times more Italian words were borrowed into French than vice versa, though the list of Gallicisms in Italian is not inconsiderable.[23] Its impact has also endured; Wind notes that the majority of words introduced in the sixteenth century are still present in the language.[24] The story told by lexical borrowing seems to correspond with sociohistorical accounts in dividing the sixteenth century into three parts. The highest level of borrowing took place in the 1540s and 1550s, though large numbers of words continued to be borrowed in the second half of the century.[25] While some of these coincide with events and sociocultural and demographic trends (for example, the large numbers of Italian immigrants arriving in the middle of the century),[26] they also indicate that cultural contact, and especially commercial activity, did not end abruptly after 1560. It is also true that despite the unequal numbers of borrowed words, borrowings into both French and Italian appear to have occurred in largely the same semantic fields, leading Hope to argue that 'in no century can the two opposite French and Italian influences be compared and contrasted so profitably as in the sixteenth'.[27]

The sixteenth century is an especially interesting period in the history of French and Italian in contact for another reason as well; the intensity of cultural contact detailed above coincides with linguistic debates becoming more prevalent on both sides of the border. These debates centred around the status of the vernacular in relation to Latin: for example, Sperone Speroni (1542) and Joachim du Bellay (1549) each published defences of the vernacular during this period (the latter modelled on the former). The second element of the debate was concerned with what form each vernacular might take. Ayres-Bennett calls the sixteenth century a 'key period in the history of French, [when] concerted efforts are made not only to codify but also to "enrich" the language'.[28] In Italy, meanwhile, the so-called Questione della Lingua was the subject of active debate, with the publication of Pietro Bembo's *Prose della volgar lingua* (1525) marking a particularly important milestone. This selection and codification process is often described in ways that are teleological or generalizing, obscuring the endemic and enduring

---

22 Brown, 'Multilingual Merchants', p. 239.
23 Hope, *Lexical Borrowing in the Romance Languages*, p. 272.
24 Wind, *Les mots italiens introduits en français au XVIe siècle*, p. 207.
25 Hope, *Lexical Borrowing in the Romance Languages*, p. 237.
26 Scharinger, 'Les lettres de Catherine de Médicis', p. 42.
27 Hope, *Lexical Borrowing in the Romance Languages*, p. 271.
28 Ayres-Bennett, *A History of the French Language through Texts*, p. 140.

variability as well as the multiple processes of dialect mixing and koineization occurring at the same time as more top-down prescriptive and codification processes.[29] It is important to emphasize that despite increasing koineization and standardization, diversity and variation was still the order of the day during the Renaissance period, and neither were these the only two varieties in the mix — Latin and Provençal, to name only two, were also present in the region.[30] To speak of French and Italian in contact is in fact a question of contact between the multiple varieties spoken in the relevant regions as well as the role of new or second-language speakers.

Foreign speakers thus entered into the linguistic ecology of the Italian peninsula as L2 learners, but this ecology was already characterized by a number of 'new speakers': speakers of other Italo-Romance dialects. The proportion of Italians capable of speaking the form that would become standard Italian was probably no more than 10 per cent even at the time of unification;[31] it cannot have been even that high two centuries earlier. Serra highlights the role of these speakers in the developing literary standard, with non-Tuscans but also Florentines and other Tuscans learning the archaic variety. This language was native to no one, but by general agreement was becoming the prestige language, the literary variety, and a 'roof' language for local varieties.[32] In some ways this is akin to the koineization processes which had taken place earlier within the peninsula.[33] This leads us to ask whether foreigners had access to or engaged in the linguistic diversity of the Italian peninsula. What variety might they have learned either from Italians in France or during their time spent across the Alps, and what did they then pass on? It seems that on both sides of the border, this would most commonly have been the literary form of the language. For those foreigners visiting or even studying in Italy, it is not clear that speakers would have had a great deal of access to local dialect features. Although some travellers were interested in dialectal variation, there are surprisingly few instances of words taken from local dialects, apart from Venetian. This is likely a combination of the characteristics of travel — foreigners were less likely to encounter social spaces where dialects were spoken most frequently — and an accommodation effect on the part of native Italians, who believed it more polite to use a form of Italian foreigners would already be accustomed to. Of course, in practice and especially in oral contexts, there was likely a range

---

29 Brown, 'Language History from Below'; Lodge, 'Standardisation, koinéisation et l'historiographie du français'; see also Joseph, Rutten, and Vosters, 'Dialect, Language, Nation' for a discussion of Haugen's standardization framework.
30 Paré, 'L'impact sur l'Italie des débats français sur la langue au milieu du XVIe siècle', p. 60.
31 Maiden, 'The Definition of Multilingualism', p. 31.
32 Serra, 'New Speaker Paradigm and Historical Sociolinguistics'; Maiden, 'The Definition of Multilingualism', p. 35.
33 Brown, 'Language History from Below'.

of intermediary forms of the language used by both educated Italians and the foreigners who interacted with them.[34]

The written communication of Italians living in France, particularly the elites, is composed in 'une langue fort proche de l'italien classique' (a language very close to Classic Italian), even if there are a few dialectal features here and there.[35] Grammars and dictionaries of Italian available to foreigners at the time, such as de Mesmes's *La Grammaire italienne* (1548), were based for the most part on the rules elaborated by Bembo and deriving from Trecento literary Tuscan.[36] Evidence also comes from Frenchmen who produced texts in Italian or a mix of French and Italian;[37] Montaigne's *Voyage* is one of the more famous examples of a mixed text. Estimates show that 29 per cent of the text is written in Italian, in a register which 'recalls the oral' and shows Tuscan influences, though his (considerable) knowledge of Italian was likely literary.[38] Even the words cited in Estienne's *Dialogues*, arguably containing as many nonce borrowings or inventions for comedic effect as words in widespread use, were likely taken from the literary variety and writings of prestigious Italian authors or conceivably the speech of the highly educated elite.[39]

Documenting Language Contact: Renaissance Diplomatic Letters as Linguistic Bridges

One aspect that has not been adequately treated, despite attention paid to cultural contacts, is the source of this Italian influence on French, that is, the activity of individual speakers. One source of diffusion of features was certainly Frenchmen putting on Italian-inspired airs; as Wind puts it, 'On aimait faire entendre qu'on avait fait son petit voyage d'Italie; même ceux qui n'y avaient pas été se plaisaient à faire croire qu'ils avaient passé les Alpes et italianisaient pour paraître' (One liked to be understood to have undertaken one's little trip to Italy; even those who had not been there enjoyed giving the impression that they had crossed the Alps and Italianized [their speech] to appear to have done so).[40] However, as Scharinger notes, the prevailing assumption that there is a large contrast between French speakers who were infusing Italian features into their speech, and Italian immigrants in France — present in

---

34 Tosi, *Language and the Grand Tour*, p. 218.
35 Dubost, *La France italienne*, p. 123.
36 Richardson, 'The Italian of Renaissance Elites in Italy and Europe', pp. 18–19.
37 Picot, *Des Français que ont écrit en italien au XVIe siècle*.
38 Cro, 'Montaigne's Italian Voyage', p. 156, and citing Rigolot, 'Introduction', p. xiii; Picot, *Des Français que ont écrit en italien au XVIe siècle*, p. 2.
39 Sampson, 'Henri Estienne and Vowel Prosthesis', p. 338.
40 Wind, *Les mots italiens introduits en français au XVIe siècle*, p. 30.

large numbers — who were assimilating as quickly as possible, is incorrect.[41] It is clear that change must have come from a variety of sources, and we should look to both Frenchmen and Italians, on both sides of the Alps and in multiple roles, as agents of change in introducing and spreading contact features. Tosi argues that travellers are 'natural innovators and conduits of language contact',[42] and Hope mentions the letters of Rabelais as illustrative of 'the actual mechanism of borrowing in its early stages';[43] his trips to the peninsula appear to have provided some number of the Italianate vocabulary items for which he is famous. We will therefore be focusing on the written evidence from Frenchmen who spent a significant amount of time on the peninsula: diplomatic correspondence.

During the sixteenth century, letters were shipped back and forth along a communicative network connecting a variety of people and places in France and Italy, as well as other European countries. Letters were exchanged between nobles, artists, and intellectuals: one example is that of Marguerite d'Angoulême, who exchanged letters in Italian with the artist Vittoria Colonna.[44] Another is the correspondence exchanged between the musician Orlando di Lasso and his patron Wilhelm, Duke of Bavaria, described as 'a wonderful mix of languages, mainly French, Latin (liturgical in flavour), Italian (with traces of Venetian) and German, spiced with puns, deliberate mistakes and a few words of Spanish'. Burke characterizes this correspondence as 'a form of clowning, an extension into the domain of the private letter of the polyglot comedy, the *commedia dell'arte* with which Lasso was associated at the court'.[45] This type of 'clowning' which recalls the literary does not appear to be a common occurrence, although some amount of code-switching was not unusual in European correspondence at this time.[46]

Diplomatic letters from Frenchmen in Italy are physical evidence of cultural and political links between France and Italy. In addition to political and military matters, they often contain matters of a more personal nature. For example, Marguerite d'Angoulême's request for copies of Vittoria Colonna's work was relayed through letters to the French ambassador Georges d'Armagnac, and the manuscripts then perhaps reached her via the Ferrarese ambassador.[47] These letters between France and Italy were written in multiple languages, as Picot describes:

---

41 Scharinger, 'Les lettres de Catherine de Médicis'; Paré, 'L'impact sur l'Italie des débats français sur la langue au milieu du XVIe siècle', pp. 60–61.
42 Tosi, *Language and the Grand Tour*, p. 216.
43 Hope, *Lexical Borrowing in the Romance Languages*, p. 244.
44 Brundin, 'Vittoria Colonna and the Virgin Mary'.
45 Burke, *Languages and Communities in Early Modern Europe*, p. 137.
46 Nurmi and Pahta, 'Social Stratification and Patterns of Code-Switching in Early English Letters'.
47 Brundin, 'Vittoria Colonna and the Virgin Mary', p. 61 The connection between the two women may also have been made via Renée de Navarre, see p. 63, n. 5.

> La plupart de nos diplomates, au XVIe siècle, entendaient l'italien et l'écrivaient au besoin. Les agents, d'origine génoise ou milanaise qui servaient François Ier, imposaient parfois leur langue à leurs collègues français. C'est ainsi que nous voyons, en 1529, l'évêque d'Avranches, Jehan de Langeac, signer, avec Gio. Gioacchino da Passano, des lettres italiennes adressées au roi. Rien d'étonnant à ce qu'Antonio Rincon, qui est Espagnol, écrive tantôt en français, tantôt en italien. Au fond, la langue de ces correspondances n'a qu'une importance secondaire. Celui qui les signe peut fort bien emprunter la plume et le style d'un secrétaire. Nous possédons pourtant, surtout à l'époque de la Ligue, d'assez nombreuses lettres qui paraissent avoir été réellement écrites en italien par des Français; mais il ne faut pas les citer comme des modèles de style.[48]

> (The majority of our [French] diplomats in the sixteenth century understood Italian and used it in writing when necessary. Agents of Genoese or Milanese origin who served François I sometimes imposed their language on their French colleagues. Thus we see that in 1529 the bishop of Avranches, Jehan de Langeac, along with Gio. Gioacchino da Passano, sign letters in Italian addressed to the king. It is unsurprising that Antonio Rincon, who is Spanish, writes sometimes in French and sometimes in Italian. At its core, the language of these letters is of only secondary importance. The person whose signature appears could very well have made use of a secretary's quill and style. However, we do have, especially during the era of the [Italic] League, a decent number of letters which seem to really have been written in Italian by Frenchmen; but these should not be cited as models of style.)

I would argue that, far from being of only 'secondary importance', the language of these letters is in fact very revealing for the linguistic ecology of this time and place. The dynamics described by Picot — of Italian agents serving the French king, and 'imposing' their language on day-to-day operations, including the practice of correspondence — provide information about the ways that individuals negotiated multilingual situations in the service of diplomacy. The language of official or trade correspondence can be revealing of the language competencies and preferences of the persons interacting in a multilingual space, in addition to the social dynamics at play.[49] These letters may also showcase linguistic contact, since words and structures are transferred along with cultural and political information. Much of the seminal work on sixteenth-century contact, specifically lexical borrowing, has been focused on dictionaries, glossaries, and literary texts, with admirable forays into lesser-known and non-literary works by scholars such as Hope. However, as we know from

---

48 Picot, *Des Français que ont écrit en italien au XVIe siècle*, p. 2.
49 Brown, 'Multilingual Merchants'; Lazzarini, *Communication and Conflict*; Thomas, 'L'espagnol, une langue administrative?'.

recent work on ego-documents, non-published works can be as informative, if not more, regarding the processes of language contact and contact-induced change.[50] The value of epistolary texts, and ego-documents more broadly, for historical sociolinguistic analysis has been well documented.[51] Studying letters lets us access forms written by a variety of (non-elite) speakers: that is, language history 'from below' as well as 'from above'; it also allows access to a particular type of communication which differs from literary or other published works in its style and communicative goals.[52] Like conversations, letters are inherently dialogic: they are written with a particular recipient in mind, and because in most cases they are not meant for publication, may showcase a less studied form of the language. Most letters are written in cases of physical distance between interlocutors, by their very nature creating cultural links for personal or official purposes. Moreover, the linguistic value of autograph letters is different from — but not necessarily superior to — that of letters composed by scribes, and the latter cannot be summarily dismissed when discussing either the linguistic landscape and social context of sixteenth-century Italy or the particular linguistic traits appearing in epistolary texts. The additional context about style may also be relevant, although Picot is dismissive of it. These were not literary works planned out ahead for greatest effect, but rather official missives with the goal of 'informing' and therefore often appear quite rigid in their adherence to genre conventions.[53] Their characteristics and vocabulary will therefore differ from those of the literary works of the era which are often mined for information about neologisms and Italianisms, for example the works of Rabelais. A comprehensive account of contact and lexical borrowing must take into account the linguistic behaviour exhibited in this type of everyday composition.

Language in the Letters of Georges d'Armagnac

This chapter will focus on the letters of one particular diplomat, Georges d'Armagnac, an ambassador posted in Venice (1536–1539) and Rome (1547–1550 and 1554–1555). D'Armagnac, like a large percentage of the diplomatic corps in the sixteenth century, was also a member of the Church. Born the illegitimate son of a count around 1500, he rose to be Bishop and Archbishop of Toulouse, was made cardinal in 1544, and died in his seat in Avignon in 1585. He was a

---

50 Schneider, 'Investigating Variation and Change in Written Documents'; van der Wal and Rutten, 'Ego-Documents in a Historical-Sociolinguistic Perspective'.
51 Elspass, 'The Use of Private Letters and Diaries in Sociolinguistic Investigation'; van der Wal and Rutten, 'Ego-Documents in a Historical-Sociolinguistic Perspective'; Watts, 'Setting the Scene'.
52 Koch and Oesterreicher, 'Langage Parlé et Langage Écrit'; Bergs, 'Letters'.
53 See, for example, Amatuzzi's discussion of letters from seventeenth-century Savoy. Amatuzzi, 'La valeur linguistique des correspondances diplomatiques du XVIIe siècle'.

fervent Catholic, a learned man, a humanist and protector of men of letters.[54] As a long-serving ambassador whose tenure in Venice and Rome coincides with the most intense period of French–Italian contact during the middle third of the sixteenth century, his writings will provide insight into the character of diplomatic correspondence and to what extent it served as a medium for the transfer of lexical items from one language to another.

D'Armagnac's correspondence (1530–1560) is reproduced in an unedited collection compiled by Charles Samaran and Nicole Lemaître, historically contextualized with editor's notes and a comprehensive biographical dictionary.[55] D'Armagnac was a prolific correspondent over the course of these thirty years; the 312 letters reproduced in the collection include 247 letters sent and 65 received. Samaran and Lemaître also include notes about an additional 71 letters which we know existed from historical context but are now lost or inaccessible.[56]

For the present analysis, I have used the reproductions in this volume. Nevertheless, the materiality of the original letters is important and may contain clues to questions such as the role of scribes in epistolary composition.[57] The use of scribes was very common for a person like d'Armagnac during this time; even private letters began to be written by scribes at a very early date, with d'Armagnac likely adding a closing, signature, and perhaps a postscript himself. By 1545, his secretaries were copying even his signature, likely with his blessing. The exact role of scribes is debatable and perhaps unknowable if the only evidence is the final drafts of correspondence, but it seems clear that they influenced the final product at the level of content as well as perhaps the linguistic one. It will be particularly relevant here to know that the secretaries used by d'Armagnac appear to have been different according to the language: in Venice, the most famous of his secretaries, a man named Philandrier, wrote in French and Latin, but a different secretary, Antonio Bucelli, took over the Italian missives fairly quickly.[58] D'Armagnac's handwriting and signatures also evolve over the years; Lemaître attests changes in the latter around 1555, occurring first in the French and then the Italian letters, then another change towards the end of the 1560s, first in the Italian letters.

---

54 Burns, 'Cleric-Diplomats and the Sixteenth-Century French State'.
55 D'Armagnac, *Correspondance*. The letters were to be presented in three volumes; to my knowledge only the first, 1530–1560, was ever published and will form the basis of the analysis here.
56 I have excluded four texts from this count; one speech, one receipt, one text written and signed by a man named Clausonne when d'Armagnac was ill, and one text which was duplicated exactly and sent to an additional addressee.
57 For a discussion of the linguistic effects of scribes, see also e.g. Bergs, 'Linguistic Fingerprints of Authors and Scribes'; Dossena, 'The Study of Correspondence'.
58 D'Armagnac, *Correspondance*, p. lvi.

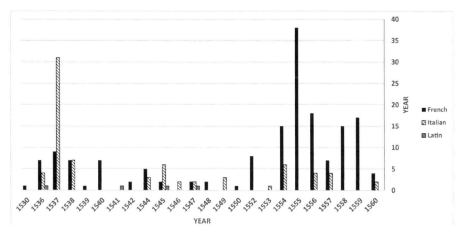

Figure 7.1. Number of letters written by year by Georges d'Armagnac, in French, Italian, and Latin.

Language Choice

I will first discuss the choice of language to determine if it is possible to discern macro-patterns in the use of each language over time. Language choice is conditioned by a variety of factors but gives us an overall idea of the amount that d'Armagnac was communicating in each language at a given time. For example, we might expect the relative proportions of letters sent and received to fluctuate according to the political situation and whether he was currently stationed in Italy as well as according to recipient and topic.

Of the 247 letters sent by d'Armagnac, four were composed in Latin, seventy-five in Italian, and 168 in French. That is, about 70 per cent of the letters sent over this thirty-year period from 1530 to 1560 were in French. The letters written in Latin were addressed to the pope; to Ercole II d'Este, Duke of Ferrara; and to Giovanni Giustiniani, a poet and translator. The letters in Italian are addressed to Italian nobles, government officials, and cardinals. These are spread unevenly over time, as seen in Figure 7.1, with Italian letters forming a larger proportion of d'Armagnac's correspondence during his time in Venice (1536–1539) than in subsequent years. Though the later peaks do not correspond exactly with his appointments as ambassador in Rome (1547–1550, 1554–1555), they do align with times he was present in Italy, as only five of the letters in Italian were written from France.

More fine-grained quantitative measures are unlikely to give more than an overall impression given the variable numbers of letters that survive from each year; however, we may compare the years of d'Armagnac's ambassadorship in Venice to the two subsequent appointments in Rome (Table 7.1). In the Venetian years, over 60 per cent of his compositions were written in Italian, whereas only about 16 per cent of those written during his two stints in Rome were in that language.

Table 7.1. Letters written by Georges d'Armagnac during his posts as ambassador to Venice and Rome.

Years (post)	Letters in French	Letters in Italian	Letters in Latin	Total
1536–1539 (Venice)	24 (35.8%)	42 (62.7%)	1 (1.5%)	67
1547–1550 (Rome)	5 (45.5%)	5 (45.5%)	1 (9.1%)	11
1554–1555 (Rome)	53 (89.8%)	6 (10.2%)	0	59

This perhaps runs counter to our expectations of an increasing 'Italianization' effect in his correspondence; although d'Armagnac and his scribes appear to have been perfectly comfortable using Italian as well as French for multiple purposes, his use of Italian decreases over time. This is conceivably due to some or all of the following factors: his change in location from Venice to Rome, his rising seniority, the evolving sociopolitical relationship between France and the peninsula, or changes in his communication network.

Overall, the letters written in French are for the most part addressed to correspondents in France, including King Henri II (and his son François I); the constable of France, Anne de Montmorency; and fellow officials of the Church and ambassadors such as Jean du Bellay. Notable amongst this group is also the queen, Caterina de' Medici, further confirming the idea that she tended to speak French with Frenchmen. Other noblewomen — the Duchess of Ferrara (Renée de France) and Marguerite, Duchess of Parma — also received letters in French, although d'Armagnac wrote to their husbands in Italian. The choice of French for the former seems logical as she was born in France and indeed responded in the same language, but the latter is perhaps more puzzling. The small number of women represented in this collection makes it difficult to say, but perhaps d'Armagnac preferred to write to women in French.[59] It seems that even if Italian was being used at court among the fashionable set, it was not necessarily preferred among the higher classes for written correspondence outside of Paris.

It seems that language-choice patterns vary consistently according to addressee, with the exception of the Duke of Ferrara. D'Armagnac addressed letters to this recipient in Italian (1536–1538, except one letter composed in Latin in 1536), then French (1539–1547), Italian (1549), and finally French (1555–1559). Interestingly, the letters sent to d'Armagnac from the Duke of Ferrara (five from 1554 and one from 1559) were written in Italian. The changes in language we see in d'Armagnac's compositions therefore do not appear

---

59 This may not have been a reciprocal arrangement; although he wrote to Marguerite de Navarre and her husband (both in 1558) in French, she alternated between French (1542) and Italian (1545) in her letters to d'Armagnac.

to be in response to letters received. Although of course we may be missing correspondence, the effect seems to be quite the opposite, that rather than accommodating to the interlocutor, each was writing in his own language during the period from 1554 to 1559.

The changes seen over time may thus be said to be due to changes in location and correspondence network, but these are in turn dependent on the political climate as well as the changing nature of d'Armagnac's position and possibly personal relationships. This overview gives us an idea of the periods where d'Armagnac was using Italian more frequently as well as the evolving nature of his diplomatic work.

Lexical Borrowing: Italianisms in French

We may now investigate the lexical choices of Georges d'Armagnac. This study is based on an examination of the vocabulary of the French-language letters signed by d'Armagnac. These lexical items have been cross-referenced with etymological information drawn from the *Trésor de la Langue Française informatisé* (*TLFi*) and with Hope's work.[60] References to individual letters follows the system used in Samaran and Lemaître's edition according to its date of composition, for example letter 55 03 16 is dated 16 March 1555. Where words are attested multiple times in the letter collection, I have cited the first occurrence. I have retained the original orthography.

Although d'Armagnac wrote (or at least signed) letters in three languages, there are very few instances of code-switching. Foreign items are limited to short phrases and are for the most part adapted to French orthography and phonology. Examples of this can be seen in place names; French versions in wide circulation like *Venize* (55 03 16), *Ferrare* (40 11 29), and *Corsse* (56 02 01) appear alongside forms which have been adapted from their Italian version: for example, *Grotheferracte, Crotteferrate* to refer to Grottaferrata (40 07 29), *Corsique* (60 08 01). This last example indicates that instead of reaching for the French word, he worked backwards from the Italian name for Corsica. There are, however, a few examples of non-adapted names as well, sometimes alternating with adapted forms: *Civitavecchia* (55 04 30) / *Civitavechhe* (55 11 18); *Padova* (59 08 10) / *Padoue* (38 10 13); *Pesaro* (37 09 19); *Gradisca* (38 04 05); *Vicovaro* (57 02 17). Also of note is the adjective *bolognois* (from Bologna; 60 03 21) which makes use of the productive suffix *-ois* to derive a French demonym, although according to the *TLFi* the first attestation in French is 1807. In addition, there are occasional examples of Latin phrases, for example, *de nepote et reditu, item de recuperandis numinis hispaniae* (about his nephew and my return, likewise about recovering power over Spain; 56 05 20); *inter spem et metum* (between hope and fear; 56 07 01). The only non-adapted form from Italian appears in the title *seignora Victoria* (40 07 29). This may be surprising

---

60 *TLFi*; Hope, *Lexical Borrowing in the Romance Languages*.

given the overall multilingual nature of the corpus, but showcases a broader tendency toward adherence to a single matrix language and adaptation of foreign items to French orthography and phonology.

There are a number of innovative lexical items, which can be divided into the following categories:
a) French material: attestations of neologisms which predate those listed in the *TLFi* as well as very recent borrowings, defined as words with first attestations in 1500 or later;
b) Latinate calques and very recent borrowings;
c) Italian calques and very recent borrowings; and
d) borrowings or calques from other languages.

The date of 1500 for 'very recent' was selected as a convenient cut-off coinciding with both the turn of the century and d'Armagnac's birth; thus these are words which came into common French usage during his lifetime, although they may be circulating long before they are first attested, especially if that first attestation is in literary works. Calques and attestations predating those previously recorded by lexicographers are clearer indications of contact effects; these words are being borrowed in adapted form, and may be not yet used or not yet widespread in French. I shall begin with a short discussion of (a) and (d) and then focus more in depth on items belonging to categories (b) and (c).

It is possible to point to a few factors which would lead us to believe that d'Armagnac's lexicon is somewhat conservative, as we might expect in the genre of diplomatic correspondence. One is the lack of code-switching, contrasting with, for example, Orlando di Lasso's correspondence described above. Another is the use of older French terms such as *exercite* (army; 36 09 19) alongside the newer *armée* (36 08 20; attested from the fourteenth century), or *souldars* (soldier; 36 07 31) alongside *soldat* (37 07 31; attested from 1475 and common in the sixteenth century). This may be simple variability between competing and synonymous lexical items as we see both *exercite* and *armée* appear throughout the thirty years of correspondence, even in close proximity to each other: *mectre son armée en mer* (put his army on the sea) is followed in the next line by *son exercite de terre* (his army on land; 37 04 27). However, for 'soldier' there may be a change in progress, as *souldars* is only attested once, very early. In one sense, this increasing frequency of *soldat* in d'Armagnac's correspondence appears to mirror a larger trend in the language, but it may also be worth noting that this change took place during his first ambassadorship in Venice and so its use could be reinforced by the existence of the Italian *soldato*. French neologisms, whether very recent or predating existing attestations, are outnumbered by words with Latin or French origins and mostly consist of derivation or semantic extension, for example, *colloquer* (40 12 06; attested in 1530 with the meaning of placing (a young woman) by marriage); *arremens* (act of putting down a deposit, derived from *arrher*; 56 01 16; first attested 1577). Borrowings from other languages are rare and come from a variety of sources, including Provençal, Greek, and Turkish. One example of the latter, *cahuz* (37 02 09), messengers of the Sultan, is noted by Samaran and Lemaître as being influenced by Italian orthography in the initial <c>; the French term is more commonly spelled and pronounced *tchaouche*.[61]

The greatest amount of foreign material in d'Armagnac's letters comes from Latin and Italian. The use of Latinate vocabulary 'trahit l'humaniste' (reveals the humanist in him) and may also be reliably attributed to his status as a clergyman who also communicated in Latin.[62] It is also unsurprising given the larger sixteenth-century context, where extensive use was being made of Latinate resources to enrich the French lexicon. Several of the recently borrowed Latinisms are in fact religious in nature: *dataire* (officer of the Roman curia; 40 11 29; first attested 1533); *monialles* (monk; 42 08 19; first attested 1530); *rotte* (Rota, a Catholic tribunal; 57 06 18; first attested 1526); *schismatique* (schismatic; 58 10 16; first attested 1549, 1562 with the meaning of 'Protestant'). Others include *dupplicata* (duplicate; 37 03 15; first attested 1528), *cappitulations* (treaties; 37 07 15; attested before 1528), *pretexte* (pretext; 40 12 08; first attested 1530), *republique* (republic; 55 09 07; first attested 1520). There are also a number of Latinate calques or words whose use in the d'Armagnac letters predates the first attestation in the *TLFi* and Hope's work: *simulté* (enmity; 36 07 31; first attestation 1552); *delation/dilation* (denunciation; 37 03 07; first attestation 1549); *pronostiq* (prognostic; 37 04 27; first attestation 1552); *decanat* (deanship; 55 11 28; first attestation 1650).

Very recent borrowings from Italian include *nunce* (papal nuncio, messenger; 40 07 29; first attestation 1521), *collonelz* (colonel; 44 05 05; first attestation 1534), *fanteryees* (infantry; 36 09 19; first attestation c. 1500 as *enfenterye*; *fanterie* in 1547). The former is in keeping with the ecclesiastical vocabulary used by d'Armagnac, while the other two fit with the general trend of Italianisms in the military sphere. Also attested are *a l'improviste* (unexpectedly, suddenly; 37 07 16; first attestation 1528), *disgrâce* (misfortune; 54 09 10; first attested 1539), *garbouge* (tumult; 40 11 29; first attestation 1528), *gondole* (gondola; 59 08 10; first attested with a specific meaning of a Venetian gondola in 1549), and *bust* (bust; 55 04 30; first attestation 1549 meaning the torso; the sculptural meaning here is not attested until 1680). *Garbouge* and *gondole* are particularly interesting here because of their likely Venetian origin, in line with d'Armagnac's time spent there. *Mercantellement* (in a manner relating to commerce; 40 07 29) predates the first attestation of its base, *mercantile* in 1551.

The largest group of foreign-influence neologisms is made up of forms influenced by Italian orthography and calques or nonce borrowings from Italian which do not become established loanwords. We have seen already that d'Armagnac's orthographic choices may be influenced by the Italian counterpart of the word he is using in French, as in the example of *cahuz* and the choice of <u> in *nunce*, although there is also one attestation of

---

61 D'Armagnac, *Correspondance*, p. 58.
62 D'Armagnac, *Correspondance*, p. 11.

the more common *nonce* (40 11 24), showing variability. Italian influence can be invoked for forms such as *je me rallegre de* (I am happy that; 37 04 27), *barche* (boat; 37 07 15), *rotture* (break; 38 04 23), *papat* (papacy; 40 07 29), and *servitu* (servitude; 57 04 15), as they conform more to Italian orthography than to the corresponding French forms *je m'allègre de*, *barque*, *rupture*, *papauté*, and *servitude*. *Neutral* (neutral; 38 03 29) rather than the French *neutre* is also likely affected by Italian, perhaps with reinforcement from the French nominal form *neutralité*. According to Samaran and Lemaître, the use of *espyes* (spies; 37 07 15) here is an Italianism, based on *spia*. It is, however, also reminiscent of the Old French *espie*. Although *espie* was still attested in the eighteenth century with the form *épie*, it had been largely replaced by the thirteenth-century *espion*, itself borrowed or at least influenced by the Italian *spione*. Thus, though likely at least partially influenced by its Italian cognate, we cannot come to a definite conclusion on its origin. The case of *spade* (sword; 40 07 29) seems clearer; although the form ultimately incorporated into the language was *espadon*, Rabelais's use of *espade* is listed as an adaptation of the Italian *spada*, and the same origin can be attributed to this usage. This brings us to the question of vowel prosthesis brought up by Rodney Sampson, who argues that the addition of a prosthetic vowel in many Italianisms may be due to both the source and the method of borrowing, in that items belonging to intellectual, literary, and artistic spheres were frequently borrowed without an initial vowel, whereas military, seafaring, or trade items had the opposite tendency due to their different modes of transmission: written and oral, respectively.[63] With only a few items (*espyes* and *spade*) upon which to base our analysis, it is difficult to give a comprehensive response, except to note that one contains a prosthetic vowel and one does not, though both are terms associated with military operations borrowed through writing, thus bypassing the 'southern filter'. As we have seen, d'Armagnac almost invariably adapts foreign items to French phonology and orthography, so it may be reasonable to discard *espie* as an Old French form.[64]

In *secretesse* (secrecy; 37 07 15) and *inimicquer* (to make an enemy of; 38 04 05) we see calques of the Italian *segretezza* and *inimicare*. *Record* (memory; 54 09 03) is also likely based on the Italian given the French *souvenir*, despite the existence of the French verb *recorder*. The diplomatic term *lettres credenciales* (letter of credence; 37 07 16) is a clear calque of *lettere credenziali*, but in a later missive, d'Armagnac uses the French form, *lettres de credance* (40 11 29). A final category is of terms specific to the Italian political or military spheres: *barryzel* (a military captain, *bargello*; 36 07 31); *pregay/preguay* (the Venetian

---

63 Sampson, 'The Loss of French Prosthesis and the Problem of Italianisms'.
64 Sampson also argues that some words borrowed from northern and central dialects may have originally had a prosthetic vowel; d'Armagnac's correspondence shows that the variety of Italian he used did not have this feature, e.g. *speranza* (hope; 37 01 12).

senate, the *pregadi*; 36 09 19); and *forscizi/Foruscitz/Forussitz* (those who fled Florence after Cosmo de' Medici's coup, the *fuorisciti*; 37 01 10). Except for the last term, which is eventually borrowed into French as *forussit* (outlaw) in 1578,[65] these proper nouns have no existing equivalent, and thus we see d'Armagnac borrow and adapt the Italian term in his letters.

There are a few words with Italian counterparts which d'Armagnac uses but whose status as Italian borrowings are less clear: among these are *cadastre* (land registry; 58 01 04) and *frégatte* (frigate; 36 10 02; first attestation 1525). Both likely were borrowed from Italian to French by way of Provençal, in a similar fashion to earlier borrowings *camp* and *campagne* (camp, campaign). *Preside* (garrison, fort; 37 03 07) also has a complicated history: it is listed as a borrowing from Spanish (1556) but also an earlier attestation in 1542 in a translation of an Italian text. Both the Italian and Spanish *presidio* were originally borrowed from the Latin *praesidium*. This appearance in d'Armagnac's letters in 1537 suggests that an Italianate version was circulating before one was borrowed from Spanish, but it is extremely likely that there were multiple sources which reinforced one another. The same reinforcement argument could be applied to those words borrowed through Provençal, in that the existence of an Italian cognate reinforces its use for bilingual speakers such as d'Armagnac. Finally, words ending in -*issime* in French come from both Italian and Latin sources; compare Italianisms such as *illustrissime* (most illustrious, only attested in a speech given in Venice; 1536) with *reverendissime* (most Reverend; 36 08 22), which is listed as a Latinism first attested in 1528. It is therefore difficult to say whether the use of this suffix in *imperialissime* (highest; 38 03 29) can be attributed to the family of Latinate or Italianate words, or even to the growing number of French words using this suffix.

Overall, there are forty-two items which can be classed as either calques, nonce borrowings, or very recent foreign borrowings from Italian, Latin, and other languages. As can be seen in Table 7.2, over half of them appear for the first time in the 1530s, specifically in letters from 1536, 1537, and 1538. The rest are fairly evenly split between the next two decades (in letters from 1540, 1542, 1544, 1554, 1555, 1557, 1558, and 1559). However, d'Armagnac sent more letters in French in the 1550s than in the other two decades, so in fact the differences are more striking when adjusted to account for this, particularly in comparing the 1540s to the 1550s. The rate of the first use of foreign lexical items decreases by half from the 1530s to the 1540s, and dwindles to a very low rate in the 1550s. None are attested for the first time in the four letters written in 1560. In other words, d'Armagnac was much more likely to introduce foreign words into his vocabulary in the 1530s than in later years.

---

65 This is dated to 1559 in the work of Ronsard by Malcolm C. Smith. Smith, 'Italianisms in the Work of Ronsard'.

Table 7.2. Use of foreign-origin words by decade.

Decade	Number of calques, nonce borrowings, or very recent loanwords (first use in the corpus)	Number of letters composed in French	Foreign-origin words per letter
1530–1539	23 (54.8%)	25	0.92
1540–1549	9 (21.4%)	20	0.45
1550–1559	10 (23.8%)	119	0.08
1560	0	4	0
Total	**42**	**168**	**0.25**

Items categorized as Italian calques, nonce borrowings, or words predating attestations given in the etymological literature appear much more frequently in the 1530s. Eleven items first appear in this decade as compared to three in the 1540s and two in the 1550s. In contrast, very recent Italianisms are more balanced, with two each appearing in the 1530s and 1550s and three in the 1540s. This indicates that in fact the period in which d'Armagnac incorporated the largest number of words of Italian origin into his compositions and perhaps into his vocabulary more broadly was in 1536–1539, the period corresponding with his ambassadorship in Venice and a time when he also composed a large number of letters in Italian. This confirms a logical interpretation, that interference and borrowing occur more frequently in contexts where the speaker in question was frequently exposed to and using both of the languages in question, although speakers may continue to use already-borrowed words throughout their lifetime. In contrast to nonce borrowings and antedated uses, the use of terms which are already attested in other French texts does not serve as definite proof of bilingual transfer on the part of d'Armagnac. Although there is nothing to exclude the possibility that he independently recreated the borrowing process or even that his choice of lexical item was influenced by the existence of a close cognate in Italian, it is probable that these words entered d'Armagnac's lexicon through French.

The timing of these Italianisms is interesting from a broader perspective. Hope locates the period of most intense borrowing from the 1530s to the 1550s. However, in each of the latter two decades the number of borrowed items is about one and a half times greater than the number attested in the 1530s, which Hope calls a 'transitional decade', and many of the new items in the 1530s first appeared in Rabelais's *Pantagruel* and *Gargantua*.[66] This is not the trend we see from d'Armagnac's letters, and it highlights a difference in the ways one might approach the question of lexical borrowing. As Hope

---

66 That is, 54, 89, and 90 borrowings, respectively. Hope, *Lexical Borrowing in the Romance Languages*, p. 234.

himself notes, one issue is whether a borrowing should be dated from its first attestation or the point when it can be assumed to be used by a large number of speakers.[67] In the latter case, we are documenting words which have spread into the lexicon, but not their entry point and the circumstances surrounding their introduction, as words are very likely circulating even before their first written attestation and certainly before they are counted as widespread. It is also evident from the words appearing in d'Armagnac's correspondence that many such innovations are nonce borrowings, that is, they did not catch on. For the items which predate their first attestation in the *TLFi* or Hope's study, there is of course nothing to say that d'Armagnac was the first to use the term, only that it was in circulation earlier than we had previously thought.

We may now return to the question of scribal influence on the language of this diplomatic correspondence. The fact that d'Armagnac's secretary Philandrier wrote his French and Latin missives during his time in Venice, but not generally the Italian ones, would be expected to affect the amount of Italian appearing in the French-language texts. As the letters produced during this time do in fact show a number of Italianisms, we may speculate that this is due less to the influence of the scribe and more to d'Armagnac's lexical choices during dictation. This interpretation is strengthened by the fact that some of the Italianisms noted above appear in parts of the letter which Samaran and Lemaître have identified as being written in d'Armagnac's own hand, for example *secretesse* (not the first attestation) and *gondole* in a letter dated 10 August 1559. This is not to say that the various secretaries d'Armagnac employed had no effect as we know that these men, humanists themselves, undoubtedly influenced d'Armagnac's thinking and interests.[68] At the very least, it seems likely that the orthographic influences discussed above were the work of the scribe.

Conclusion

This study has approached cultural and linguistic contacts between French and Italian varieties through a case study of diplomatic letters. Although diplomatic communication is sometimes dismissed because of its lack of literary or stylistic interest and rigid structure, it can shed light on processes of linguistic contact and lexical borrowing as well as sociocultural questions of language choice. One of these is the choice of language for daily communication: evidence from this case shows that although Italian might have enjoyed prestige in the French court, it was not used between French speakers for diplomatic communication, as seen by the fact that the messages that d'Armagnac

---

67 Hope, *Lexical Borrowing in the Romance Languages*, p. 233.
68 D'Armagnac, *Correspondance*, p. lvi.

composed in Italian were sent almost exclusively to Italian recipients. In this sense, there is a clear sphere of use of each language for practical purposes according to location and recipient.

These diplomatic letters can also illuminate the process of lexical borrowing taking place during this period. D'Armagnac does not fit into the category of French courtiers parodied by Estienne for their overuse of Italianisms, nor does he engage in the playful adoption of multilingual resources familiar from literary genres such as macaronic verse or the work of authors like Rabelais. However, there are still traces of language contact observable within his French letters. D'Armagnac's familiarity with Latin and Italian are manifest in his French, as evidenced by the nonce borrowings used in addition to a few established loanwords. The contact effects are reliably attributable to his presence in Italy, and specifically his time in Venice in the 1530s, when he introduced on average one word of foreign origin per letter. This time period of increased contact effects on his lexicon also corresponds to a time period in which he sent numerous letters in Italian, confirming that social and linguistic integration privileges the incorporation of lexical items from one language to the other, even in conventionalized genres.

The semantic sphere and dating of these lexical items are important considerations. Firstly, as might be expected, they are overwhelmingly nouns, although a few verbs, adjectives, and prepositional phrases are also represented. Many (but certainly not all) of the items refer to military, religious, or political concepts, reinforcing the impression that these are practical or need-based borrowings, as opposed to the result of a desire to flaunt his knowledge of the Italian language. The use of religious words is to be expected given d'Armagnac's profession, and the use of military terms is logical in the context of military intervention in the Italian peninsula. It also fits in with the general trend of borrowing observed by Hope, but highlights the distinctions that should be made about different points of entry for items from different semantic fields. Hope notes that the latter half of the sixteenth century sees an uptick in 'middle class' loans associated with the commercial sphere corresponding with the decline of the court;[69] it seems clear that this type of need-based borrowing was taking place all along but that its effect is partially obscured by the large numbers of words originating in courtly and literary language.

Both the initial use of Italianisms and their establishment in the language are conditioned by the type of document in which they appear — and the conditions of production and reception of that document. Thus an examination of diplomatic correspondence, and perhaps correspondence more broadly, is more informative of the initial borrowing mechanism enacted by bilinguals than of the establishment and spread of a particular lexical borrowing into

---

[69] Hope, *Lexical Borrowing in the Romance Languages*, pp. 235–36.

monolingual use. While d'Armagnac uses a number of Italianate forms in his writing, most of them are nonce borrowings which do not come into more general use. Some of this may be due to the lexical specificity of terms like *pregay* or *barryzel*. However, it can also be attributed to the potential number of hearers who might adopt a given innovation. The audience of a diplomatic letter is much more restricted than a work of literature, and it is therefore unsurprising that a neologism first used by Rabelais might have a greater chance of becoming an established loanword. However, the predating of words like *mercantellement* (presuming the existence of the adjective from which it is derived), *preside*, the form *fanteryees* for the recent borrowing *infanterie*, or even the sculptural meaning of *bust* in the d'Armagnac letters does confirm that these words were likely in circulation in some form before they were spread via published works. In this way, these letters, and others like them sent to persons high in the French social and administrative hierarchy, may be one intermediary between the Italian varieties spoken on the peninsula and the Italianizing French authors or courtiers responsible for the eventual fixing of Italian loanwords in French.

Diplomatic correspondence is only one point of contact in the great ecosystem of interaction between French and Italian people and ideas during this century. Although this chapter has focused on the effects of Italian on French as introduced by French speakers living in Italy, one avenue for future work would be to understand the effect of non-native speakers. As Scharinger has noted, Italians living in France played a large and as-yet-understudied role in the Italianization of French.[70] A holistic view of the effects and mechanisms of contact in this period will take into account the roles played by both source and recipient language speakers — what van Coetsem terms 'borrowing' and 'imposition' respectively — in the initial innovations and their spread.[71] The same is true of the role Frenchmen played in Italy; in contact with Italians, foreigners could also conceivably have contributed to the codification of a prestige or standard variety. Though those from France arguably had less claim to 'nativeness' than speakers of other Italo-Romance varieties, the fact they were often learning the new literary variety of Italian as adults, from formal education, is in many ways similar to the profile of the Italian 'new speaker' discussed by Serra, and it is logical to believe that they too could effectuate change. In fact, previous work has shown that the variety acquired by L2 speakers is often less conservative than that of native speakers.[72] Further study of these phenomena will require us to continue to look beyond such sources as the literary work of Italianizing authors to the evidence of day-to-day communicative practices.

---

70 Scharinger, 'Les lettres de Catherine de Médicis', p. 52.
71 Van Coetsem, *Loan Phonology and the Two Transfer Types in Language Contact*.
72 Thomas, 'L'espagnol, une langue administrative?'.

Works Cited

Primary Sources

Armagnac, Georges d', *Correspondance du Cardinal Georges d'Armagnac*, ed. by Charles Samaran and Nicole Lemaître, Collection de documents inédits sur l'histoire de France, Série in-80, 41 (Paris: CTHS, 2007)

Secondary Studies

Aimerito, Francesco, 'Aspects of Legal Multilingualism in the States of Savoy', in *Medieval Multilingualism: The Francophone World and its Neighbours*, ed. by Christopher Kleinhenz and Keith Busby, Medieval Texts and Cultures of Northern Europe, 20 (Turnhout: Brepols, 2010), pp. 237–66

Amatuzzi, Antonella, 'La valeur linguistique des correspondances diplomatiques du XVIIe siècle: Le cas des lettres de René Fare de la Valbonne et de Monseigneur Albert Bailly', in *Nouvelles voies d'accès au changement linguistique*, ed. by Wendy Ayres-Bennett, Anne Carlier, Julie Glikman, Thomas M. Rainsford, Gilles Siouffi, and Carine Skupien Dekens (Paris: Classiques Garnier, 2018), pp. 55–68

Ayres-Bennett, Wendy, *A History of the French Language through Texts* (London: Routledge, 1996)

Balsamo, Jean, 'Le voyage d'Italie et la formation des élite françaises', *Renaissance and Reformation / Renaissance et Réforme*, 27.2 (2003), 9–21

Benincà, Paola, Mair Parry, and Diego Pescarini, 'The Dialects of Northern Italy', in *The Oxford Guide to the Romance Languages*, ed. by Adam Ledgeway and Martin Maiden (Oxford: Oxford University Press, 2016), pp. 185–205

Bergs, Alexander, 'Letters: A New Approach to Text Typology', *Journal of Historical Pragmatics*, 5.2 (2004), 207–27

———, 'Linguistic Fingerprints of Authors and Scribes', in *Letter Writing and Language Change*, ed. by Anita Auer, Daniel Schreier, and Richard J. Watts (Cambridge: Cambridge University Press, 2015), pp. 114–32

Bingen, Nicole, *Aux escholles d'outre-monts: Étudiants de langue française dans les universités italiennes (1480–1599). Français, Francs-Comtois, Savoyards*, Travaux d'humanisme et Renaissance, 596 (Geneva: Droz, 2018)

———, *Le Maître italien (1510–1660): Bibliographie des ouvrages d'enseignement de la langue italienne destinés au public de langue française, suivie d'un répertoire des ouvrages bilingues imprimés dans les pays de langue française*, Documenta et opuscula, 6 (Brussels: Évan Balberghe, 1987)

Boucher, Jacqueline, *Présence italienne à Lyon à la Renaissance du milieu du XVe à la fin du XVIe siècle* (Lyon: Éditions LUGD, 1994)

Brown, Joshua, 'Language History from Below: Standardization and Koineization in Renaissance Italy', *Journal of Historical Sociolinguistics*, 6.1 (2020), <https://doi.org/10.1515/jhsl-2018-0017>

———, 'Language Variation in Fifteenth-Century Milan: Evidence of Koineization in the Letters (1397–1402) of the Milanese Merchant Giovanni Da Pessano', *Italian Studies*, 68.1 (2013), 57–77

———, 'Multilingual Merchants: The Trade Network of the 14th Century Tuscan Merchant Francesco di Marco Datini', in *Merchants of Innovation: The Languages of Traders*, ed. by Esther-Miriam Wagner, Bettina Beinhoff, and Ben Outhwaite, Studies in Language Change, 15 (Berlin: De Gruyter, 2017), pp. 235–51

Brundin, Abigail, 'Vittoria Colonna and the Virgin Mary', *Modern Language Review*, 96.1 (2001), 61–81

Burke, Peter, *Languages and Communities in Early Modern Europe*, Wiles Lectures (Cambridge: University Press, 2004)

Burns, Loretta T., 'Cleric-Diplomats and the Sixteenth-Century French State', *The Historian*, 57.4 (1995), 721–32

Cella, Roberta, *I gallicismi nei testi dell'italiano antico: Dalle origini alla fine del sec. XIV* (Florence: Accademia della Crusca, 2003)

Coetsem, Frans van, *Loan Phonology and the Two Transfer Types in Language Contact*, Publications in Language Sciences, 27 (Dordrecht: Foris, 1988)

Cremona, Joseph, 'Italian-Based Lingua Francas around the Mediterranean', in *Multilingualism in Italy: Past and Present*, ed. by Anna Laura Lepschy and Arturo Tosi, Studies in Linguistics, 1 (Oxford: Legenda, 2002), pp. 24–30

Cro, Melinda A., 'Montaigne's Italian Voyage: Alterity and Linguistic Appropriation in the "Journal de Voyage"', *South Atlantic Review*, 78.3/4 (2013), 150–66

Dossena, Marina, 'The Study of Correspondence: Theoretical and Methodological Issues', in *Letter Writing in Late Modern Europe*, ed. by Marina Dossena and Gabriella Del Lungo Camiciotti (Amsterdam: John Benjamins, 2012), pp. 13–30

Dubost, Jean-François, *La France italienne: XVIe–XVIIe siècle*, Histoires (Paris: Aubier, 1997)

Elspass, Stephan, 'The Use of Private Letters and Diaries in Sociolinguistic Investigation', in *The Handbook of Historical Sociolinguistics*, ed. by Juan Manuel Hernández Campoy and Juan Camilo Conde Silvestre (Oxford: Blackwell, 2012), pp. 156–69

Fallows, David, 'French as a Courtly Language in Fifteenth-Century Italy: The Musical Evidence', *Renaissance Studies*, 3.4 (1989), 429–41

Heller, Henry, *Anti-Italianism in Sixteenth-Century France* (Toronto: University of Toronto Press, 2003)

Hope, T. E., *Lexical Borrowing in the Romance Languages: A Critical Study of Italianisms in French and Gallicisms in Italian from 1100 to 1900*, Language and Style Series, 10 (Oxford: Blackwell, 1971), vol. I

Joseph, John E., Gijsbert Rutten, and Rik Vosters, 'Dialect, Language, Nation: 50 Years On', *Language Policy*, 19.2 (2020), 161–82

Koch, Peter, and Wulf Oesterreicher, 'Langage parlé et langage écrit', in *Lexikon der romanistischen Linguistik*, ed. by Günter Holtus, Michael Metzeltin, and Christian Schmitt, vol. I (Tübingen: Niemeyer, 2001), 584–627

Lazzarini, Isabella, *Communication and Conflict: Italian Diplomacy in the Early Renaissance, 1350–1520*, Oxford Scholarship Online (Oxford: University Press, 2015)

Lodge, Anthony, 'Standardisation, koinéisation et l'historiographie du français', *Revue de Linguistique Romane*, 74 (2010), 5–25

Maiden, Martin, 'The Definition of Multilingualism in Historical Perspective', in *Multilingualism in Italy: Past and Present*, ed. by Anna Laura Lepschy and Arturo Tosi, Studies in Linguistics, 1 (Oxford: Legenda, 2002), pp. 31–46

Melani, Igor, *'Di qua' e 'di là da' monti': Sguardi italiani sulla Francia e sui francesi tra XV e XVI secolo* (Florence: Firenze University Press, 2011)

Minerva, Nadia, *Manuels, maîtres, méthodes: Repères pour l'histoire de l'enseignement du français en Italie* (Bologna: CLUEB, 1996)

Nurmi, Arja, and Päivi Pahta, 'Social Stratification and Patterns of Code-Switching in Early English Letters', *Multilingua: Journal of Cross-Cultural and Interlanguage Communication*, 23.4 (2004), 417–56

Paré, François, 'L'impact sur l'Italie des débats français sur la langue au milieu du XVIe siècle', *Renaissance and Reformation / Renaissance et Réforme*, 27.2 (2003), 53–63

Pellandra, Carla, 'Toward a Bibliography of Manuals for the Instruction of French in Italy through 1860', *Études de Linguistique Appliquée*, 78 (April–June 1990), 45–52

Picot, Emile, *Des Français que ont écrit en italien au XVIe siècle*, Revue des bibliothèques, 8 (Paris: [n.pub.], 1898)

——, *Les Italiens en France au XVIe siècle*, Memoria bibliografica, 25 (Rome: Vechiarelli, 1995)

Richardson, Brian, 'The Italian of Renaissance Elites in Italy and Europe', in *Multilingualism in Italy: Past and Present*, ed. by Anna Laura Lepschy and Arturo Tosi, Studies in Linguistics, 1 (Oxford: Legenda, 2002), pp. 5–23

Rigolot, François, 'Introduction', in Michel de Montaigne, *Journal de voyage*, ed. by François Rigolot (Paris: Presses Universitaires de France, 1992), pp. v–xxxvi

Sampson, Rodney, 'Henri Estienne and Vowel Prosthesis: A Problem in the Phonetic Adaptation of Sixteenth Century Italianisms in French', *French Studies*, 58.3 (2004), 327–41

——, 'The Loss of French Prosthesis and the Problem of Italianisms', *Forum for Modern Language Studies*, 39.4 (2003), 439–49

Scharinger, Thomas, 'Les lettres de Catherine de Médicis: Une source négligée par les historiographes de la langue française', in *Nouvelles voies d'accès au changement linguistique*, ed. by Wendy Ayres-Bennett, Anne Carlier, Julie Glikman, Thomas M. Rainsford, Gilles Siouffi, and Carine Skupien Dekens (Paris: Classiques Garnier, 2018), pp. 39–53

Schneider, Edgar W., 'Investigating Variation and Change in Written Documents', in *The Handbook of Language Variation and Change*, ed. by J. K. Chambers and Natalie Schilling-Estes, 2nd edn (Hoboken: Wiley-Blackwell, 2013), pp. 67–96

Serra, Eleonora, 'New Speaker Paradigm and Historical Sociolinguistics: Dynamics between Florentines and Learners in Early Modern Italy', *Journal of Historical Sociolinguistics*, 5.1 (2019), <https://doi.org/10.1515/jhsl-2018-0004>

Smith, Malcolm C., 'Italianisms in the Work of Ronsard', in *Mélanges de poétique et d'histoire littéraire du XVIᵉ siècle, offerts à Louis Terreaux*, ed. by Jean Balsamo, Bibliothèque Franco Simone, 23 (Paris: Champion, 1994), pp. 51–67

Thomas, Jenelle, 'L'espagnol, une langue administrative? Le multilinguisme et le français écrit des gouverneurs hispanophones de la Louisiane coloniale', in *Les français d'ici en perspective*, ed. by Davy Bigot, Denis Liakin, Robert Papen, Adel Jebali, and Mireille Tremblay (Québec: Presses de l'Université de Laval, 2020), pp. 35–50

Thomason, Sarah G., 'Social and Linguistic Factors as Predictors of Contact-Induced Change', *Journal of Language Contact*, 2.1 (2008), 42–56

TLFi: *Trésor de la Langue Française informatisé*, <https://www.atilf.fr/tlfi>, ATILF – CNRS & Université de Lorraine

Tosi, Arturo, *Language and the Grand Tour: Linguistic Experiences of Travelling in Early Modern Europe*, Cambridge Core (Cambridge: University Press, 2020)

Wal, Marijke J. van der, and Gijsbert Johan Rutten, 'Ego-Documents in a Historical-Sociolinguistic Perspective', in *Touching the Past: Studies in the Historical Sociolinguistics of Ego-Documents*, ed. by Marijke J. van der Wal and Gijsbert Johan Rutten (Amsterdam: John Benjamins, 2013), pp. 1–17

Watts, Richard J., 'Setting the Scene: Letters, Standards and Historical Sociolinguistics', in *Letter Writing and Language Change*, ed. by Anita Auer, Daniel Schreier, and Richard J. Watts (Cambridge: Cambridge University Press, 2015), pp. 1–13

Weinreich, Uriel, *Languages in Contact: Findings and Problems*, Publications of the Linguistic Circle of New York, 1 (New York: Linguistic Circle of New York, 1953)

Wind, Bartina H., *Les mots italiens introduits en français au XVIᵉ siècle* (Deventer: Kluwer, 1928)

IMMACOLATA PINTO

The Impact of Aragonese and Castilian Dominations on the Language and Literature of Sardinia

Geographical and Historical Context

For almost four centuries (1323–1713), Sardinia was part of the Kingdom of Aragon and the Crown of Castile.[1] From a sociolinguistic point of view, Castilian dominance in Sardinia (from 1479) did not give rise to the immediate replacement of Catalan with Spanish. In contrast to other parts of Italy, in Sardinia the two languages existed alongside each other for quite some time, before the slow and gradual marginalization of Catalan. The Aragonese-Castilian period was characterized by the simultaneous presence of at least five languages: Catalan, Spanish, Sardinian, Latin, and Italian. The relationships between these languages were not equal. Spanish became the dominant language from the second half of the seventeenth century onwards and the only one used, besides Latin, in the classroom during the period. Notwithstanding the prominent role of Spanish, each of the other four languages did retain some high functions within the written and spoken repertoire. It is, however, challenging to assign a specific domain of linguistic usage to a single variety.

Despite the significant documentation produced in Sardinia in the late medieval and early modern periods, a systematic comparative study has never been carried out. The current chapter aims to fill this gap by analysing some of the surviving texts, and in doing so it sheds light on the effects that the Iberian-Romance superstratum had on the development of the Sardinian language.

---

1 This article reflects some basic aspects of the PRIN 2017 (2020–2023) — 'National Project Writing Expertise as a Dynamic Sociolinguistic Force: The Emergence and Development of Italian Communities of Discourse in Late Antiquity and the Middle Ages and their Impact on Languages and Societies', coordinated by Piera Molinelli.

Immacolata Pinto (pinto@unica.it) is Associate Professor of Linguistics in the Department of Humanities, Languages, and Cultural Heritage at the University of Cagliari.

Languages and Cross-Cultural Exchanges in Renaissance Italy, ed. by Alessandra Petrocchi and Joshua Brown, LMEMS 30 (Turnhout: Brepols, 2023), pp. 239–267
BREPOLS PUBLISHERS   10.1484/M.LMEMS-EB.5.131434

I have chosen to focus on four emblematic word-formation processes (Sard. N-*eri*, (*i*)*s*-, N-*dora*, and V → N-*u*)[2] because of their morphological productivity, mostly caused by the vast number of Catalan and Spanish borrowings. An attempt is then made to elucidate the morphological analysis of contemporary Sardinian in light of the evidence provided by sources of the early modern period and by taking into account the nature of multilingualism in Sardinia, particularly code-switching and mixed-language accounts. This is a corpus-based study and the first of its kind. The selected corpus consists of the following four groups of texts: (1) texts written in Sardinian with borrowings from Latin, Catalan, Spanish, and Italian; (2) mixed works written in Spanish with some parts in Catalan or Sardinian; (3) monolingual but coeval texts written in either Latin, Spanish, Catalan, Sardinian, or Italian; and (4) texts in which contextual factors, such as users and audience, account for language choice.[3]

Between the fourteenth and eighteenth centuries CE, Sardinia was the Mediterranean region that fell for the longest time within Spain's political and cultural orbit. The Spanish dominance was not only due to political and legal factors (the granting of Sardinia as a fief to James II, king of Aragon, by Pope Boniface VIII in 1297), but also to the economic interests which the Catalans had established in Sardinian ports since the thirteenth century.[4] For entrepreneurs from Barcelona, Sardinia was a small but not insignificant piece on the economic chessboard of the Mediterranean. In the mid-fourteenth century, major events such as the agricultural crisis, the demographic collapse caused by the Black Death, and internal conflicts resulted in reinforcing the power and authority exerted by the Catalan-Aragonese Crown first and the Kingdom of Castile afterwards, following the union of the two Crowns (1479).[5] Political and military control of the countryside and surrounding villages was mainly entrusted to grandees of Catalan origin loyal to the monarchy, but from the mid-sixteenth century onwards Sardinian *letrados* (law experts) also became part of the ranks of the kingdom's bureaucracy. University education provided by Hispanic and Italian institutions (and later in Sardinia, for example the foundation of the University of Sassari in 1617 and Cagliari in 1620) helped to end the long-standing exclusion of Sardinians from government positions and, at the same time, improved the relationship between the Sardinian ruling classes and the Hispanic monarchy (the prolonged use of Spanish in Sardinia even under Savoy rule is noteworthy).[6]

---

2 N stands for noun, V stands for verb, and A stands for adjective.
3 Sanson, 'The Romance Languages in the Renaissance and After'; see also Pountain, 'Standardization'.
4 Manconi, 'Catalogna e Sardegna'; see also Manconi, 'L'ispanizzazione della Sardegna', p. 221.
5 Day, *Uomini e terre nella Sardegna coloniale*; see also Anatra, 'La Sardegna aragonese'; Ortu, 'La Sardegna nella corona di Spagna'.
6 Paulis, 'L'influsso linguistico spagnolo'; see also Manconi, 'The Kingdom of Sardinia' and Putzu, 'La posizione linguistica del sardo nel contesto mediterraneo'; Dettori, 'Superstrato piemontese'.

The wealth of documents surviving from the Aragonese-Castilian period remains, unfortunately, mainly studied by historians rather than by linguists.[7] A comparative linguistic analysis of the different types of texts written in late medieval and early modern Sardinia has never, in fact, been carried out. These texts can be subdivided into the following groups: normative texts (for instance, acts of parliament,[8] municipal statutes, and craft guild statutes), private administrative documents (notarial deeds), religious administrative documents (parish registers or the *quinque libri*, five books, relating to baptism, confirmation, marriage, death, and the state of souls[9]) and documents which alternate between a secular and a religious tone (brotherhood statutes).[10] Similarly, the literature produced in Sardinia in the early modern period has been approached by literary scholars but almost fully ignored by linguists or philologists, with a few exceptions.[11] As a result, many of the texts written in the various languages (Latin, Sardinian, Catalan, Spanish, and Italian) common in medieval and modern Sardinia are still in need of linguistic-philological analysis. Given the exceptional history of Sardinian (which served as the official language between the eleventh and fourteenth centuries), philologists and linguists have focused their attention mainly on medieval texts from the Giudicato period (from the eleventh century until 1409).[12] However, on the basis of the *DES* some linguists have analysed the lexical and morphological contribution of the Iberian-Romance superstratum in contemporary Sardinian.[13] In particular, Paulis has looked at Catalan influence in Logudorese and challenged the accepted opposition between the occurrence of Hispanisms in the north and Catalanisms in the south (e.g. Log. *feu* 'ugly' < Sp. vs. Camp. *leğğu* 'id.' < Cat.).[14]

By analysing a selected textual corpus, the goal of this chapter is to demonstrate that the high productivity of four word-formation processes

---

7   For the former, Carbonell and Manconi, eds, *I catalani in Sardegna*; see also Schena and Oliva, *La Sardegna catalana*; Manconi, *La Sardegna al tempo degli Asburgo*; Cadeddu, 'Scritture di una società plurilingue'. For the latter, a first project on notarial acts from Bosa is currently underway. See Puddu and others, *Documenti notarili sardi di Età moderna*.
8   Pirodda, *Letteratura delle regioni d'Italia*, p. 16; Ferrero Micó and Guia Marín, eds, *Corts i parlaments de la corona d'Aragó*.
9   A sort of book that reported the state of the souls of those who had confessed, taken communion, been confirmed, etc.: see Lai, 'I quinque libri', p. 195.
10 Meloni and Schena, eds, *Culti, santuari, pellegrinaggi in Sardegna e nella penisola iberica*; Schena and Meloni, *Santuari d'Italia*.
11 Paulis, 'L'espressione dilogica della trasgressione sessuale'; see also Araolla, *Rimas diversas spirituales*, ed. by Virdis.
12 Putzu, 'Il repertorio sardo tra Tardo Antico e Alto Medio Evo'; see also Loi Corvetto, 'La variazione linguistica in area sarda'; Puddu and Talamo, 'EModSar'.
13 *DES* = Wagner, *Dizionario Etimologico sardo*. Paulis, 'L'influsso linguistico spagnolo'; Pinto, *La formazione delle parole in sardo*; Pinto, 'The Influence of Loanwords on Sardinian Word Formation'.
14 Paulis, 'Le parole catalane dei dialetti sardi'. For a summary of the Catalan and Spanish superstrate, see Barbato, 'Superstrato catalano'; Virdis, 'Superstrato spagnolo'.

(henceforth WFP), namely one prefix (*(i)s-*), two suffixes (*-eri, -dora*), and a verb-to-noun conversion (V → N) in contemporary Sardinian, is largely related to four centuries of Catalan-Castilian domination.[15] The first section offers a description of the linguistic repertoire in Sardinia between the fourteenth and eighteenth centuries and a brief summary of the literature produced in the early modern period. The second section analyses the textual corpus by subdividing it into four groups, according to the four multilingual phenomena described above. The third section presents a comparison between early modern and twentieth-century Sardinian by drawing upon recent studies in contact linguistics and historical sociolinguistics.

The Linguistic Repertoire between the Fourteenth and Eighteenth Centuries

From a sociolinguistic perspective, when analysing a linguistic repertoire it is essential to examine the hierarchical relationships that exist between the different varieties present.[16] As far as early modern Sardinia is concerned, the language varieties of the period were Latin, Sardinian, Catalan, Spanish, and Italian. Some of these were mainly spoken varieties (Sardinian), while others were used in writing (Latin, Catalan, Spanish, and Italian).[17] A peculiar feature of Sardinia, which distinguishes it from the rest of the Italian peninsula, is the survival of Catalan alongside Spanish, even after the union of the two Crowns.[18] Documents in Catalan are found up until the eighteenth century, for instance the document of the Marquises of Quirra of 1738.[19] Despite their coexistence, Catalan and Spanish were used in differing settings. Unlike Spanish, Catalan was not the language of scholarship, and it was rarely used for literary purposes. Catalan was mainly employed in the administrative field, where it replaced the prestigious role previously held by Pisan and Sardinian in the Giudicato period. Sardinian, like Catalan, was never adopted as the language of instruction, neither under Aragonese-Castilian nor under Savoy rule (Italian replaced Spanish in 1764). Unlike Catalan, it was employed in literature — a fact probably revealing anti-Catalan sentiments.[20] In some

---

15 Pinto, 'Sardinian'; Pinto, 'Tra derivazione e flessione'. For further details on conversion or similar morphological processes, see Booij, Lehmann, and Mugdan, eds, *Morphology*.
16 Mattheier, 'Varietätenkonvergenz'; see also Auer, 'Dialect Levelling and the Standard Varieties in Europe'; Berruto, 'Dialect/Standard Convergence, Mixing, and Models of Language Contact'; Berruto, 'The Languages and Dialects of Italy'.
17 Paulis, 'Dinamiche linguistiche e sociali a Cagliari nel corso dei secoli'; see also Barbato, 'Superstrato catalano'; Virdis, 'Superstrato spagnolo'.
18 Krefeld, 'L'Italia spagnola'.
19 Paulis, 'L'influsso linguistico spagnolo', p. 212.
20 Sardinian was certainly used in the nationalistic struggle against the Spanish in the second half of the eighteenth century by the Savoy regime (see Dettori, 'Italiano e sardo dal Settecento al Novecento'; Pinto, 'Tra derivazione e flessione', p. 10).

circumstances relating to institutional and political contexts, Sardinian was, however, preferred to Catalan: the spoken use of Sardinian as an expression of political dissent in the parliamentary meetings of Spanish Sardinia is significant, as testified by the case of the Mayors of Sassari and Bosa in the first half of the seventeenth century.[21] Furthermore, although in the legal-administrative field Sardinian lost ground to Catalan,[22] in private writings there exist some exceptions, such as in some notarial deeds from Bosa.[23]

The prevailing use of Spanish in the literary field is striking, especially between the second half of the sixteenth and the first half of the eighteenth centuries. More than half of the surviving literary texts are written in Spanish, the others are in Latin, with only a few in Sardinian. Notably, there was an increase in the number of Spanish texts printed in Sardinia from 1566 to 1699 (from 25% to 87%) compared to a reduction in those printed in Latin (from 48% to 12%), a disappearance of those printed in Catalan (from 22% to 0%), and a constant but marginal presence of Sardinian (from 2.5% to 1%).[24] Moreover, the prestige of literary Italian contributed to the further marginalization of Sardinian and Catalan. Evidence shows that Italian was at times combined with Sardinian and Spanish; other times it was used in opposition to the dominant linguistic varieties.[25] The presence of literature in Italian private collections in Sardinia has recently called attention to the role played by Italian on the island.[26] It should be borne in mind that, notwithstanding the occurrence of medieval administrative documents in Sardinian, literary texts written in Sardinian are few and discontinuous.

On the basis of the data so far available and excluding the Giudicato period, the literature in Sardinian is spread over at least three periods: the Aragonese-Spanish period; the Savoy period; the post-unitary period (after 1861), including up until today. The Aragonese-Spanish period includes six works in Sardinian (of which five are in Logudorese and one in Campidanese) compared to twenty-one in Spanish.[27] Catalan, on the other hand, although less represented in the literary field, appears in the form of loanwords in Sardinian texts, either in particular genres (*goigs*) or in different domains (legal-administrative texts: for example, *Condaghe di Santa Chiara*;[28] statutes of craft guilds). At the beginning of the Savoy period, some authors continued to use Spanish alongside Sardinian. Following

---

21 Paulis, 'L'impiego orale del sardo come espressione di dissenso politico nelle adunanze parlamentari della Sardegna spagnola', pp. 304–05.
22 Cadeddu, 'Scritture di una società plurilingue'.
23 Puddu and others, *Documenti notarili sardi di Età moderna*.
24 Anatra, 'Editoria e pubblico in Sardegna tra Cinque e Seicento', p. 242.
25 Virdis, 'Introduzione'; Badas, 'Introduzione'.
26 Seche, *Libro e società in Sardegna tra medioevo e prima Età moderna*.
27 Pirodda, *Letteratura delle regioni d'Italia*; Marci, *In presenza di tutte le lingue del mondo*.
28 Maninchedda, 'Introduzione'.

the introduction of an anti-Spanish policy promoting the use of Sardinian alongside Italian and ad hoc restrictive norms (see the prohibition to use Spanish in 1760), the production of literary texts in Italian prevailed from the second half of the eighteenth century onwards. Consequently, the use of Sardinian in literature was once again marginalized, with the exception of popular poetry.[29]

Texts and Linguistic Varieties between the Sixteenth and Eighteenth Centuries

The purpose of this section is to provide a first account of the complex multilingualism characterizing Sardinia from the sixteenth to the eighteenth century.[30] The publication of a critical edition and a text's representativeness for each of the four categories are the main criteria adopted to select the corpus. As mentioned in the introductory section, the present corpus-based study subdivides and analyses the following four sources:
1) texts written in Sardinian (Logudorese, Campidanese) with loans from Latin, Catalan, Spanish, and Italian;
2) texts in Spanish with short sections in Sardinian and Catalan;
3) monolingual texts in either Latin or Spanish or Catalan or Sardinian or Italian;
4) texts in which language choice is determined by contextual factors, such as users and audience.

Based on the data available, I have identified four WFPs: Camp., Log. (i) s-, $-eri$, $-dora$ and the noun-to-verb conversion V-are/-ai → N-u/-a. These WFPs are of particular importance to understand the changes occurring in the Sardinian language over its development and since they were caused by the intense contact with Catalan and Spanish.[31] I have then isolated the presence of these word-formation processes in the corpus and compared the findings with those obtained by analysing some features of contemporary Sardinian.[32]

---

29 Pittalis, 'Il sardo come lingua letteraria'.
30 Barbato, 'Superstrato catalano'; see also Virdis, 'Superstrato spagnolo'; Puddu and Talamo, 'EModSar'.
31 Pinto, 'Alcune osservazioni sul prefisso in- negativo nel sardo e in area romanza'; Pinto, *La formazione delle parole in sardo*; Pinto, 'The Influence of Loanwords on Sardinian Word Formation'; Pinto, 'Tra derivazione e flessione'; Pinto, Paulis, and Putzu, 'Morphological Productivity in Medieval Sardinian'.
32 Such a perspective comes from the field of historical sociolinguistics; see Hernandez Campoy and Conde Silvestre, eds, *The Handbook of Historical Sociolinguistics*; see also Molinelli, ed., *Language and Identity in Multilingual Mediterranean Settings*.

Texts Written in Sardinian with Loans from Latin, Catalan, and Italian

This first group of texts is small in number. I have selected four of these texts, three of which are literary works: the first is a hagiographic work and the first surviving literary text written in the Logudorese dialect (Antonio Cano 1557);[33] the second, also in Logudorese, clearly follows Petrarchesque models and represents one of the few attempts by illustrious writers to elevate the Sardinian language on par with other languages of culture (Girolamo Araolla 1597);[34] the third, which is the first literary text in the Campidanese dialect, is religious in nature, with some addenda in Spanish (Friar Antonio Maria da Esterzili 1688);[35] the fourth text comes from the administrative-accounting field and is the *Condaxi Cabrevadu* (1533), written in a dialect halfway between Logudorese and Campidanese.[36] A first examination of the four texts of this subgroup shows that there is a discrete number of occurrences with the Iberian-Romance prefix *des-* (often integrated into Sardinian as *(i)s*),[37] as can be seen in the following examples:

(1) Log.
  los fetit **desligare** dae su tormentu   free them from pain[38]
  esserent **ismayados**, pro tantos   they passed out on account of the
  ispantos   many acts of intimidation[39]

  Log.-Camp.
  et sj cali si ogiat persona o personas   and if any persons commits [acts of]
  fagueren algunu **dessacatu**,   disobedience, violence[40]
  violenxia

  Camp.
  ancu marteddu e tanallas   and also hammer and pincers
  po podiriddu **isclavari**   to be able to take him down (from
                                              the cross)[41]

Although emphasis has generally been given to the prevalence of Hispanisms in works of the early modern period, the challenging task of distinguishing a Spanish from a Catalan loan has often been pointed out;[42] therefore, a Catalan influence cannot be excluded a priori. In fact, in the case of *desligare*

---

33 Cano, *Sa vitta et sa morte, et passione de sanctu Gavinu, Prothu et Januariu*, ed. by Manca.
34 Araolla, *Rimas diversas spirituales*, ed. by Virdis.
35 Frate Antonio Maria da Esterzili, *Libro de comedias*, ed. by De Martini.
36 *Il Condaxi cabrevadu*, ed. by Serra.
37 Pinto, *La formazione delle parole in sardo*, p. 155.
38 Cano, *Sa vitta et sa morte, et passione de sanctu Gavinu, Prothu et Januariu*, ed. by Manca, v. 536.
39 Cano, *Sa vitta et sa morte, et passione de sanctu Gavinu, Prothu et Januariu*, ed. by Manca, v. 982.
40 *Il Condaxi cabrevadu*, ed. by Serra, 2.18.
41 Frate Antonio Maria da Esterzili, *Libro de comedias*, ed. by De Martini, fol. 109ʳ, ll. 475–76.
42 Wagner, *Historische Wortbildungslehere des Sardischen*; Barbato, 'Superstrato catalano'; Putzu, 'History of Sardinian Lexicon'; Contini, 'Le catalan dans les parlers sardes'.

(untie/loosen) both solutions may be valid: Sp. *desligare* and Cat. *deslligar*.[43] The same holds true for *ismayados* (in a swoon, fainted) < Sp. *desmayar*, Cat. *desmaiar*.[44] On the other hand, *ispantos* (scares) can be traced back to only one of the two source languages: Sp. *espanto*.[45] The same applies to *dessacatu* (disobedience, disrespect) < Sp. *desacato*.[46] The word *isclavari* (lit. to unnail) is particularly interesting, because together with *isclavamentu* (lit. unnailing) it is still widely used in Sardinia in some rites during Easter, with reference to the deposition of Christ from the cross. These are Sardinian devotional practices that reflect a strong link with the Iberian world: compare Cat., Sp. *desclavar*, Cat. *desclavamentu*;[47] also the case of *gocius* or *gozos*, see (12) and (13) below.

In the four texts analysed in the first subgroup of our corpus, there are several occurrences of the suffix *-eri* (pl. *-eris*), as shown in the examples below:

(2) **Log.**

Si lu vides, lu tocas, e ispermentas	If you see it, you touch it, and you
Qu'est ingannosu, falsu e **mentideri**	experience it
	It is deceptive, false, and untruthful[48]
A sas lusingas suas pius non consentas	You can no longer surrender to his flattery
Qu'est atrativu, dottu **bacigleri**	As tempting as it is, learned scholar[49]
Unu de custos santos **Cavaleris**	One of these holy Knights
Ti fettas Eclesia militante	makes you a Church militant[50]

Camp.

Baxi po domu os chircari	Go, find yourself a house
ca inoxi **istrangeris**	because here there are foreigners
senoris, et **cavalleris**	gentlemen and knights
a quini non potzu faltary	whom I cannot offend[51]

It can be seen from the phenomena occurring in the two Sardinian dialects that Logudorese does not have the expected form *-ere*, but -*eri*: cf. Log. -*dore* vs Camp. -*dori* and in general Log. N-*e* vs Camp. N-*i*. In medieval Logudorese sources, the form -*eri* is already attested in loans of Pisan origin: see the following occurrences in the Sassarese Statutes of 1316, *caualleri / caualeri* (knight of the chief magistrate); *barberis / barberi* (barbers/barber).[52] It is therefore most

---

43 Manca, 'Introduzione', p. cxvi.
44 Wagner, *Dizionario Etimologico sardo*, s.v. *dismayare*; see also Manca, 'Introduzione', p. cxvi.
45 Wagner, *Dizionario Etimologico sardo*, s.v. *ispantare*; see also Manca, 'Introduzione', p. cxv.
46 Wagner, *Dizionario Etimologico sardo*, s.v. *disak(k)at(t)u)*.
47 Wagner, *Dizionario Etimologico sardo*, s.v. *kravu*.
48 Araolla, *Rimas diversas spirituales*, ed. by Virdis, I 29.
49 Araolla, *Rimas diversas spirituales*, ed. by Virdis, I 29.
50 Araolla, *Rimas diversas spirituales*, ed. by Virdis, V 82–83.
51 Frate Antonio Maria da Esterzili, *Libro de comedias*, ed. by De Martini, fol. 16ᵛ, ll. 690–93.
52 *Gli Statuti Sassaresi*, ed. by Guarnerio, bk I, chs 2, 72, 131, 151; see also Pinto, 'Tra derivazione e flessione'.

likely that the loans from subsequent Catalan, Spanish, and Italian layers were morphologically adapted and integrated into already existing forms used in both northern and southern Sardinia — a phenomenon which is evident in the lexicon used in medieval, modern, and contemporary texts. The suffix *-eri* also prevails over other suffixes of Tuscan origin which entered medieval Sardinian (*-aiu* and *-ayolu*).[53] In particular, only two occurrences of *-ayolu* were found in our corpus: *lignajolu* (woodcutter) and *piscayolos* (fishermen).[54]

The suffix *-dora* shows a most productive process to form feminine agent nouns in Sardinian, although in some ritual contexts the use of the suffix *-issa*, of Greek-Byzantine origin, can also be seen. The latter was initially used in medieval religious contexts, for example, Log. *abatissa* (abbess),[55] and subsequently found in the context of female confraternities: Camp., Log. *priorissa* (lay woman who carries out tasks within the Church, with particular regard to certain feasts, processions).[56] The suffix *-dora*, unlike *-issa*, is more common by far in contemporary Sardinian and has been replaced rarely by the competing Italian form *-trice*, probably also due to its use in denoting Mary, the Mother of Jesus:

(3) **Log.**

tue, Virgine ogni hora	and you, always Virgin
De su fattore tou sa **genitora**	the parent of your Creator[57]
Vana isperansa, sola **causadora**	Vain hope, which alone causes
Qui m'apartai da sa Regina Astrea?	my distancing from the Queen Astrea?[58]
Intercessora de sos peccadores	She who intercedes for her sinners[59]
Segnora universale, humile e pia	Universal, humble, and pious Lady
Protectora infallibile e segura	infallible and reliable Protector[60]
Sos inimigos tres conculca, e atterra	The three enemies trample and
Et **vinquidora** restes de sa Guerra	knock down And win the war[61]

Camp.

pues si lamat Maria […]	because her name is Maria […]
mama, sposa, et fila, y **emperadora**	mother, bride, daughter, and empress[62]
is unidi assa parti **binchidora**	joins the winning side[63]

---

53   Pinto, *La formazione delle parole in sardo*, p. 159; see also Pinto, 'La derivazione in sardo medievale'.
54   *Il Condaxi cabrevadu*, ed. by Serra, 2.17.
55   *Il Condaghe di San Pietro di Silki*, ed. by Soddu and Strinna.
56   Meloni and Forci, 'En nom de nostre Senyor Deus Jhesu Christ e de Madonna Santa Maria'.
57   Araolla, *Rimas diversas spirituales*, ed. by Virdis, II 20, 7–8.
58   Araolla, *Rimas diversas spirituales*, ed. by Virdis, VIII 7–8.
59   Araolla, *Rimas diversas spirituales*, ed. by Virdis, I 42.
60   Araolla, *Rimas diversas spirituales*, ed. by Virdis, II 1, 4–5.
61   Araolla, *Rimas diversas spirituales*, ed. by Virdis, I 40, 7–8.
62   Frate Antonio Maria da Esterzili, *Libro de comedias*, ed. by De Martini, fol. 2ᵛ, ll. 59–60.
63   Frate Antonio Maria da Esterzili, *Libro de comedias*, ed. by De Martini, fol. 4ʳ, l. 134.

Both -*dora* and -*eri* are part of the pan-Sardinian suffixes (with no diatopic variation) which generally have a considerable frequency in contemporary Sardinian. The suffix -*dora* is extensively present in religious songs of Iberian-Romance origin (see below, (8) and (13)).[64]

The productive continuity in Sardinian of the morphological process of conversion from verb to noun has been documented in several works.[65] Conversely, the influence of the Iberian-Romance model has been rarely investigated:

(4) Camp.

po sa quali mi agatu cun **aconortu**	for this, I have found solace once again[66]
noti qui nos fais ispantari	night that frightens us
atonitus po di pensari	speechless because we are thinking
e' prenus totu de **ispantu**	of you
	all filled with disbelief[67]

The form *aconortu* dates back to medieval Sp. *conhortar* (cf. also Old Cat. *aconhortar*), compared to contemporary Sp. *confortar*. Sometimes, the difficulty of distinguishing between Spanish and Catalan origins of some formations also extends to Italian, as in the following example:

(5) Camp.

qui a sa cumparri a'nosu po **consolu**!	you appear to us to bring us comfort![68]

In fact, the action noun *consolu* could be an Italianism, a Catalanism, or a Hispanism: compare Old It. *consolo*, Cat. *consol*, and Sp. *Consuelo*.[69]

Texts in Spanish with Short Sections in Sardinian and Catalan

The second and third categories of the corpus make up the largest group of the surviving texts of the Aragonese-Castilian period. The texts chosen as representative of the second category are Antonio Lo Frasso's pastoral novel (1573, in both prose and verse),[70] written in Spanish, with a sonnet in Sardinian and a sonnet in Catalan, and a Spanish-Sardinian Canzoniere

---

64 Bover i Font, 'I goccius nei Paesi Catalani e in Sardegna', p. 23.
65 Blasco Ferrer, *Storia linguistica della Sardegna*; Pinto, Paulis, and Putzu, 'Morphological Productivity in Medieval Sardinian'; Pinto, 'Genere e contatto linguistico'.
66 Frate Antonio Maria da Esterzili, *Libro de comedias*, ed. by De Martini, fol. 10ᵛ, l. 419.
67 Frate Antonio Maria da Esterzili, *Libro de comedias*, ed. by De Martini, fol. 26ʳ, ll. 78–80.
68 Frate Antonio Maria da Esterzili, *Libro de comedias*, ed. by De Martini, fol. 13ʳ, l. 530.
69 Wagner, *Dizionario Etimologico sardo*, s.v. *konsolare*.
70 Lo Frasso, *Los diez libros de fortuna de amor*, ed. by Murtas.

(collection of poems) from the second half of the seventeenth century, with parts in Spanish and parts in Sardinian, Logudorese, and Gallurese.[71] Below I provide some passages from these texts, subdivided according to the language and dialect used:

(6) **Sp.**
Si por suerte la noche es sin luna   If by chance the night is moonless
los **marineros** se van desmayando   the sailors lose heart[72]
que havías tú herido un **forastero**   that you have hurt a stranger[73]
porque Judas hizo el mal   because Judas did wrong
y a mí tienen **prisionero**   and I am held prisoner[74]
Don Floricio, el valiente **guerrero**   Don Floricio, the brave warrior[75]

In (6) we find the original Spanish form of the suffix *-ero*. It is somewhat surprising that Sardinian has not integrated the Spanish forms as *-eru* in accordance with its internal rules here,[76] for example, Log. *tsurru*, Camp. *čurru* (gush) < Sp. *chorro*. Note that Catalan *-er* had been integrated according to the already existing *-eri* before the integration of the Spanish form *-ero*. Recent studies in the field of contact linguistics argue that, in the case of multiple superstrate languages, these types of morphological elements generally align with the rules of integration of the first superstrate language, in this case Pisan *-ieri* > Log. *-eri*.[77]

(7) **Cat.**
Lo **mariner** qu'en golfo fortuna   The sailor who is lucky enough to
alcança   reach the bay[78]

As can be seen in example (2) above, Cat. N-*er* is integrated as Log., Camp. N-*eri*.

---

71 *Il canzoniere ispano-sardo*, ed. by Paba.
72 Lo Frasso, *Los diez libros de fortuna de amor*, ed. by Murtas, p. 37.
73 Lo Frasso, *Los diez libros de fortuna de amor*, ed. by Murtas, p. 292.
74 Lo Frasso, *Los diez libros de fortuna de amor*, ed. by Murtas, p. 307.
75 Lo Frasso, *Los diez libros de fortuna de amor*, ed. by Murtas, p. 459.
76 Wagner, 'Los elementos español y catalan en los dialectos sardos', p. 245.
77 Pinto, 'Tra derivazione e flessione', p. 14. In particular, from the perspective of contact linguistics, *-eri* can be considered a hybrid form: *-(i)* and *-er*, present both in the source languages and in the receiving language, + *-i* of Pisan origin, a typical condition of multilingual interference.
78 Lo Frasso, *Los diez libros de fortuna de amor*, ed. by Murtas, p. 602.

(8) Sp.

que una tan docta muger	that a wife so learned
muriesse **descabeçada**	should die beheaded[79]
descompassada cimera	excessive delusion[80]
son los más **descabesados**	are mostly beheaded
[...] **desgarrados**	[...] lacerated[81]
y blanco en los **desengaños**	and pure in disappointments[82]
Soberana **Emperadora**	Supreme Empress
Virgen y Madre [de] Dios	Virgin and Mother of God[83]
el anima **pecadora** [...]	the sinful soul [...]
que sea su **intercessora**	that it is she who intercedes[84]
Perdonadme, Señora	Forgive me, my Lady
[...] siendo mi **amparadora**	[...] being my protector[85]
nuestro firme y fuerte **amparo**	our firm and strong protection[86]
A un diestro **artillero**	To a skilled artilleryman[87]
El pastor más **grosero**	The rather rough shepherd[88]
Cauallero soy, senora	I am a Knight Gentleman, Lady
cauallero de Motril	Knight of Motril[89]

With respect to the suffix Sp. -*ero* > Log. -*eri*, compare *grosero* in (8) to Log. *grosseri* (uncouth person).[90] The examples in (9) also show other occurrences in Log. N-*eri*.

---

79 *Il canzoniere ispano-sardo*, ed. by Paba, p. 83.
80 *Il canzoniere ispano-sardo*, ed. by Paba, p. 103.
81 *Il canzoniere ispano-sardo*, ed. by Paba, p. 166.
82 *Il canzoniere ispano-sardo*, ed. by Paba, p. 113.
83 *Il canzoniere ispano-sardo*, ed. by Paba, p. 106.
84 *Il canzoniere ispano-sardo*, ed. by Paba, p. 106.
85 *Il canzoniere ispano-sardo*, ed. by Paba, p. 144.
86 *Il canzoniere ispano-sardo*, ed. by Paba, p. 123.
87 *Il canzoniere ispano-sardo*, ed. by Paba, p. 159.
88 *Il canzoniere ispano-sardo*, ed. by Paba, p. 229.
89 *Il canzoniere ispano-sardo*, ed. by Paba, p. 244.
90 Araolla, *Rimas diversas spirituales*, ed. by Virdis, IV 70.

(9) Log.

Penas han postu custos **conziceris** et sun a'instancia totus sos **Caualleris**	These Councillors have determined the punishments and are [here] at the request of the Knights[91]
O suprema Caliope eterna et pia de sas musas felice **inperadora** [...] de sos tristes **protetora**	O supreme Calliope eternal and pious among all the muses, happy empress [...] protector of the unfortunate[92]
o' ispietade condenas a' **disterru**	o [ruthless] life that condemns [one] to exile[93]

The form *disterru* (exile) appears alongside *disterrare* (to exile, banish) in numerous pairs, noun and verb, of Iberian-Romance origin,[94] which has contributed to strengthening the endogenous process of morphological conversion that was already frequent in medieval Sardinian, for example, Log. *kertare* (to dispute), *kertu* (dispute).[95]

(10) Gallur.

| cunu stremadu dolori mi g'unsi un certu **dismay** ma [...] **disamparadu** | a sharp pain made me feel somewhat faint[96] but [...] abandoned[97] |

Notwithstanding that Gallurese is a non-Sardinian Tuscan dialect, it shares some features with Logudorese, for example, the N-i-A compound,[98] and Campidanese, for example, the neutralization of gender in the plural definite article: Gallur. *li*; Camp. *is* vs Log. *sos, sas*.[99] In particular, *dismayu* (fainting fit) is a Hispanism that entered Gallurese through the Logudorese variant *dis-* in place of *is-*.[100] The form *disamparadu* (abandoned) is also a Hispanism: Sp. *desamparar, desamparo*;[101] compare also Sp. *amparo* in (8).

---

91 *Testi in sardo*, ed. by Deplano, p. 318.
92 *Testi in sardo*, ed. by Deplano, p. 285.
93 *Testi in sardo*, ed. by Deplano, p. 305.
94 Wagner, *Dizionario Etimologico sardo*, s.v. *disterrare*.
95 Pinto, Paulis, and Putzu, 'Morphological Productivity in Medieval Sardinian', p. 256.
96 *Testi in sardo*, ed. by Deplano, p. 293.
97 *Testi in sardo*, ed. by Deplano, p. 296.
98 Pinto, Paulis, and Putzu, 'Sardinian Adjectives with the N-i-A Structure'.
99 Loporcaro, *Gender from Latin to Romance*; Pinto, 'Tra derivazione e flessione'.
100 Wagner, *Dizionario Etimologico sardo*, s.v. *dismayare*.
101 Wagner, *Dizionario Etimologico sardo*, s.v. *amparare*.

Monolingual Texts in either Latin or Spanish or Catalan or Sardinian or Italian

There was an increase in the number of texts written exclusively in Spanish between the seventeenth and eighteenth centuries. However, in the sixteenth century some prestigious authors, such as Sigismondo Arquer (Cagliari 1530 – Toledo 1571) and Giovanni Francesco Fara (1542–1591), who both graduated in Law and Theology, wrote historical texts not only in Spanish but also in Latin. In particular, Arquer wrote the *Sardiniae brevis historia et descriptio* (1550), which provides interesting insight into the linguistic repertoire of the period, for example, the opposition between Catalan, spoken in urban areas, and Sardinian, spoken in rural areas.[102] In the sixteenth century, Girolamo Olives, a jurisconsult of Sassari who joined the Council of Aragon in 1554 as a tax lawyer, the first of the Sardinian magistrates to do so, wrote a series of comments in Latin on the *Carta de Logu*, entitled *Commentaria* and *Glosa in Cartam de Logu* (1567).[103] The *Carta de Logu* was used by the two Crowns in regulating the law of native Sardinians.[104] Pietro Delitala (Bosa c. 1550–1592) was the first Sardinian poet to use Italian in his works.[105] Like Araolla, Delitala was greatly influenced by Italian poetry, and especially by Torquato Tasso. In 1596, Delitala published a collection of poems in Italian entitled *Rime diverse*, which is probably to be interpreted as a form of resistance to Spanish power — a struggle which to some extent emerges also in his numerous brushes with the law.[106] There are also texts in Spanish, called *Relaciones*, dated between the sixteenth and eighteenth centuries, that can be considered a sort of narrative account or chronicle relating to Sardinia.[107]

The statutes are of great interest for linguists, although they have mainly been studied by historians so far. A quick glance shows that they are written in the different language varieties present in the Sardinia of the time. The statutes relating to the craft guilds provide us with interesting information both about the history of various professions and the evolution of lexicon and word formation in Sardinian, particularly in regard to agent nouns. The lexicon in the gremial statutes reflects the large presence of Catalan merchants in Sardinia: textiles, coral, silver, and artistic items; see terms such as *drapers* (cloth merchants), *corallers* (coral merchants), *argenters* (silver merchants),

---

102 Paulis, 'Le parole catalane dei dialetti sardi', p. 155.
103 Murgia, 'Un "sociolinguista" cinquecentesco'.
104 *La Carta de Logu dell'Arborea*, a legal code prepared by Judge Mariano IV, was promulgated in 1392 by his daughter Eleonora. Later, in 1421, the Catalan-Aragonese rulers extended it to the whole of Sardinia (with the exception of the Royal Cities), where it remained in force until 1827, when Carlo Felice issued the new code of *Leggi civili e criminali del Regno di Sardegna*. See Paulis and Lupinu, 'Tra Logudoro e Campidani', p. 136.
105 Pirodda, *Letteratura delle regioni d'Italia*, p. 112.
106 Badas, 'Introduzione'.
107 Paba, 'Eternizar la memoria'.

and *picapedrers* (stonecutters). Furthermore, these documents demonstrate that Sardinian corporations of the period were structured like the guilds of Barcelona. Most of the documents relating to the craft guild statutes are in Catalan, some are in Spanish, and from the second half of the eighteenth century onwards, one finds translations in Italian and more rarely in Sardinian.[108] In particular, the gremial statutes in Catalan show a high frequency of N-*er* integrated into Sardinian as N-*eri* (e.g. Cat. *draper* > Log. *drapperi*; Cat. *ferrer* > Camp. *ferreri*, etc.):

(11) **Cat.**

Item ordenen los majorals y prohomens de la dita confraria […] **sabaters** […] **pellisseres**, **sellers** […] en pena de deu lliures la mitat a sant Pere e laltra mitat al **veguer** de Caller	Thus we order that the leaders and chosen men of the brotherhood […] shoemakers […] tanners, saddlers […] pay a fine of 10 pounds, half to saint Pere and the other half to the vicar's king of Cagliari[109]
Los **ferrers** […] seran obligats […]	Smiths […] will be obliged […][110]

The statutes of guilds and brotherhoods represent an extremely interesting source for linguists. They show a close connection with the ancient popular traditions of Sardinia. In particular, the brotherhoods boast a long musical tradition inspired by religion with songs of Iberian origin (Cat. *goigs*, Sp. *gosos*, Sard. *gocius* or *gozos*), in which the suffix -*dora* occurs frequently; compare above, (8) and (9):[111]

(12) **Log.**

Goccius	Songs
De sa gloriosa **imperadora**	of the glorious empress
Sant'Elena	Saint Helen
Tui ses **rescatadora**	You are the redeemer
De sa Gruxi de Gesus	Of the cross of Jesus
De tottus is devotus tuus	Of all your devotees
Sias Elena **defensora**	May you be, Oh Helen, she who defends[112]

---

108 Manconi, 'Catalogna e Sardegna'; Di Tucci, 'Le corporazioni artigiane della Sardegna'; Loddo Canepa, 'Statuti inediti di alcuni Gremi sardi'.
109 Di Tucci, 'Le corporazioni artigiane della Sardegna', p. 78.
110 Di Tucci, 'Le corporazioni artigiane della Sardegna', p. 82.
111 The *gosos* are songs that embrace both popular and learned traditions and testify to practices that are still widespread in Sardinia. They were transmitted both orally and in written form; cf. Pinna, 'I gosos e la paraliturgia'; see also Romero Frías, 'Gòsos, gòccius … goigs'; Armangué i Herrero, 'I precedenti dei "gosos" sardi'; Macchiarella, 'Le manifestazioni musicali della devozione cristiana in Italia'; Lupinu, 'Lingua sarda e gosos'.
112 Casu and Lutzu, *Enciclopedia della Musica*, p. 61.

(13) **Cat.**
Com la nostra **protectora** As our protector
en cada temps seu estada at all times you have
siau sempre nostra advocada always been our advocate
de Vallverd nostra Senyora our Lady of Vallverd[113]

Texts in which Language Choice is Determined by Contextual Factors

Finally, in the fourth multilingual text-type of the selected corpus, language choice seems to depend largely on contextual factors, such as the social status of the subjects involved. This usage becomes particularly clear in the drafting of notarial deeds and in some dramatic texts. For example, in the case of notarial deeds, if the contracting parties belong to the clergy, the preferred language is Latin or Spanish. If the contracting parties come from a lower social class (such as farmers, shoemakers, or tailors) the act is mainly in Catalan (see the notarial acts from Masullas). However, it is interesting to note that whenever Sardinian witnesses are present, writings which are not in Sardinian are recited aloud, as reported in a document written in Catalan dating back to 1694. The following is a will that contains a legal formula: 'Testimonis per mí, testador, […] tots d'esta present vila, en presència delts quals se ha llegit lo present testament, […] en lengua sarda' (My witnesses [undersigned], testator, […] all from this town, in whose presence the present will was read, […] in the Sardinian language).[114] An intriguing example can be seen in the *Condaghe di Santa Chiara* (15th–16th centuries),[115] which contains documents in Sardinian and Catalan and/or Sardinian-Catalan. In some cases, the language seems to depend on the origin of the notary. For instance the notary Pinna writes in Sardinian, while the notary Armengol writes in Catalan.[116] This multilingual mode is also found in dramatic texts. In the comedies by the Friar of Esterzili (1688), some roles are in Logudorese, for instance the shepherds: 'o anzone immaculado | reclamado de sa zente' (O immaculate lamb | invoked by the people);[117] others in Spanish, for instance Saint Augustine: 'esso no es fundado en conscientia | siendo todo falsedad' (this is really unfounded | and all a falsehood);[118] or even Latin, which is used by Pilate: 'nos Poncius Pilatus, sacri Romany Imperij […] | Jesus Nazarenus qui se temeraria asserçione | filiu dei se predicat […]' (we Pontius Pilate, governor of the Holy Roman Empire […] | Jesus of Nazareth, who with reckless assertion | […] proclaims

---

113 Bover i Font, 'I goccius nei Paesi Catalani e in Sardegna', p. 23.
114 Pau, 'Nuovi documenti sull'uso linguistico in Sardegna nei secoli XVI–XVIII', pp. 340–44; see also Romero Frías, 'Note sulla situazione linguistica a Cagliari (Sardegna)'.
115 A collection of *contratti 'di livello'* (land lease contracts) stipulated between Oristano's Monastery of the Poor Clares and various lessees or recipients.
116 Maninchedda, 'Introduzione', p. 31.
117 Frate Antonio Maria da Esterzili, *Libro de comedias*, ed. by De Martini, fol. 19v, ll. 916–17.
118 Frate Antonio Maria da Esterzili, *Libro de comedias*, ed. by De Martini, fol. 20v, ll. 1004–05.

himself the son of God).[119] Another interesting example comes from a dramatic text written by the Sardinian-Hispanic author Juan Francisco Carmona, (a jurisconsult in Cagliari, in 1623), known for having highlighted the farcical dispute between a shepherd and a townsman, in which the former speaks Sardinian-Campidanese: 'naraidemi eite este tanta genti in compagnia | e de quali santu feist inoxi festa? | Ques biu totu sa ia e' is fenestras prenas de genti que est maravilla' (Tell me, why are so many people gathered together | and which saint are you celebrating here? | Because I see the street and the windows full of people, which is marvellous),[120] and the latter Spanish: 'A todos la atencion eo mucho extorto | pues oiran de san George los favores | y como Dios con el fue manirroto'[121] (I urge you to pay the utmost attention | because you will hear the miracles of St George | and how God was kind to him).[122]

The Effects of the Iberian-Romance Superstratum on Word Formation

As is known, exogenous morphemes are absorbed in the following circumstances: (1) a long and intense contact between two or more varieties; (2) a high number of loans demonstrating the same WFP; and (3) a genetic affinity between the different superstrate languages. All of the above conditions are reflected in the case of the contact between Sardinian, Catalan, and Spanish which thus represents the exogenous layer that has most characterized the history of the Sardinian language. Furthermore, unlike Italian, Spanish not only did not have time to replace Sardinian but was rather integrated with it, combining productively with endogenous elements: Log. *castandza* → *castandzeri* (chestnut seller) vs It. *muratore* > Log. *muradore* instead of Log. *mastru de muru* (bricklayer).[123]

As mentioned above, while medieval and contemporary Sardinian have been investigated, the Sardinian of the early modern period has not been studied in full. For each of the WFPs identified in examples (1)–(13) above, here I offer an overview of current research which shows the influential role played in the creation of a new WFP (*-eri*)[124] by the superstratum

---

119 Frate Antonio Maria da Esterzili, *Libro de comedias*, ed. by De Martini, fol. 88ʳ, ll. 2709–11.
120 Pirodda, *Letteratura delle regioni d'Italia*, p. 123.
121 From a morphological point of view, it is interesting to note the occurrence of the conservative structure N-i-A (*manirroto*), since in the Romance milieu it seems to be still productive in both Spanish and in Sardinian with the exception of southern Campidanese; see Pinto, Paulis, and Putzu, 'Sardinian Adjectives with the N-i-A Structure'.
122 Pirodda, *Letteratura delle regioni d'Italia*, p. 122; see also Bullegas, *Il teatro in Sardegna tra Cinque e Seicento*.
123 The interference of Italian was much more pervasive than that of Spanish, since alongside written literary Italian, spoken Italian played an influential role as well, especially after the second half of the twentieth century. See Dettori, 'La Sardegna', p. 934.
124 Mensching and Remberger, 'Sardinian'.

so far discussed and/or in enhancing the productivity of already existing endogenous WFPs (*(i)s-*, V → N-*u*, N-*a*, and -*dora*). Systematic studies of the first three phenomena have been carried out on both medieval and contemporary Sardinian. With regard to the fourth phenomenon, research is currently being undertaken, although some data have already been brought to light by Pinto and Wagner.[125]

On the basis of the data so far available, despite its initial Pisan origin (-*eri* < Pis. -*ieri*) the high productivity of -*eri* is largely attributable to contact with Catalan and Spanish.[126] This is mainly because the rich and continuous supply of loans from these two languages paved the way for the use of this suffix with a native Sardinian basis,[127] for example, Log. *krae* (key) → *kraeri* (guardian of the key).[128] The standardizing effect of this contact (all loans regardless of the final vowel were integrated as N-*eri*; e.g. Log., Camp. *kaltsettéri* (hosier) < Sp. *calcetero*) has contributed to making this suffix even more productive. N-*eri* is the only valid form for all dialects of Sardinian, and notably, it has not been subjected to the influence of the northern Sardinian isogloss N-*e* (vs southern Sardinian N-*i*). It is a unique case within the Sardinian word formation system: see Log. N-*ale*, N-*dore*, N-*ile* vs Camp. N-*ali*, N-*dori*.[129] Previous work has shown that -*eri* was initially present more in the area of Logudoro than in the Campidanese: *guerreri* (warrior), *leoneri* (lionkeeper), *timoneri* (helmsman), *colomberi* (pigeon breeder),[130] *medianeri* (mediator), and *dispenseri* (bestower).[131] Agent nouns in -*eri* are particularly interesting, as they denote individuals who occupy important positions of power, *veguer* (vicar of the king) and *cap conseller* (chief adviser), and who carry out the most profitable professions, for example, *coraller*, *argenter*.[132] It is clear that there were many textile merchants operating in northern Sardinia, see *drap*; compare Cat. *draper* > Log. *drapperi*.[133] Various gremial statutes record the high frequency of this suffix for names of occupations. From the point of view of contact linguistics, this context has certainly favoured the adoption of the WFP since, as it is known, derivational agent morphemes are among those

---

125   Wagner, *La vita rustica*; Wagner, *Historische Wortbildungslehere des Sardischen*; Pinto, *La formazione delle parole in sardo*.
126   A similar case can be found in the context of verbal morphology: the non-etymological forms of the Sardinian imperfect subjunctive reconstructed on Italian models and later on Iberian-Romance ones; see Pisano, 'Importanza del superstrato catalano, castigliano e italiano in alcune varietà sarde moderne'.
127   Wagner records about one hundred of them in the N-*er*, Sp. N-*ero* category, distributed throughout the Sardinian territory. Wagner, *Dizionario Etimologico sardo*.
128   Pinto, 'Sardinian', p. 2701.
129   Pinto, 'Tra derivazione e flessione', p. 12.
130   Vidal, *L'Urania sulcitana*, ed. by Bullegas.
131   Delogu Ibba, *Index libri vitae*, ed. by Marci, p. 280, ll. 71 and 75.
132   Manconi, 'Catalogna e Sardegna'; Loddo Canepa, 'Statuti inediti di alcuni Gremi sardi', p. 186.
133   Manconi, 'Catalogna e Sardegna', p. 38; Paulis, 'Le parole catalane dei dialetti sardi', p. 157.

with the highest rate of prestige.[134] Furthermore, from a functional perspective, one should also note the only variant of the exogenous -*eri* suffix in opposition to the several diatopic variants of the native rival suffix: compare Camp., Log., Nuor. -*eri* vs Camp. -*arğu*/-*raxu*, Log. -*ardzu*, Nuor. -*ariu* < Lat. *arius*.

The endogenous prefix *(i)s-* (< Lat. *dis-*, *ex-*) is the most productive in Sardinian. This high productivity is attributable to at least three factors: (1) the absence of the *in*-negative prefix of learned origin; (2) the influence of the Iberian-Romance superstratum; and (3) the high productivity of parasynthetic verbs that prefer prefixes of popular origin. A first comparison between some medieval *Condaghi* (administrative documents, 11th–14th centuries) and a later text dating to the end of the early modern period shows that the occurrences of *(i)s-* nearly tripled from 61 to 159.[135] Considering the fact that in twentieth-century Sardinian there are at least 309 neoformations,[136] it becomes clear that the four centuries of Catalan-Castilian domination have contributed to increasing the vitality of this prefix. Moreover, in Wagner's corpus it appears that the most numerous exogenous prefixes are those with *dis-/des-* or *is-*, for instance Sp. *desgarrar* > Log. *isgarrare* (to tear, rip).[137] Consequently, the data studied here in examples (1), (8), (9), and (10) above suggest the need for a systematic and comparative examination of the works of the early modern period. A study of this kind would provide a detailed account of the influence of the Iberian-Romance superstratum on Sardinian.

Action nouns obtained by conversion are particularly productive in Sardinian for several reasons, including the sociolinguistic history of Sardinian. The high productivity of this WFP can be traced back to its uninterrupted frequency, the absence of the suffix -*tione*, and the scarce presence of lexemes of learned origin. These are conditions that characterize the Romance varieties with a similar status as Sardinian, namely non-official, non-national, non-standard languages.[138] However, in this case too the data demonstrate that contact with genetically related languages (cf. Sardinian, Catalan, and Spanish) has certainly favoured the increase in the number of action nouns obtained by conversion. In this regard, with reference to the importance of structural transparency for derivational morphemes which are copied and applied to native Sardinian bases, consider, for example, the presence in contemporary Sardinian of numerous Catalan and Spanish exogenous pairs — Log. *akkabare*, *akkabu* (finish, end) < Sp. *acabar*, *acabo*; Camp. *disgaǧǧai*, *disgaǧǧu*

---

134 Matras, *Language Contact*, p. 210.
135 Pinto, 'Alcune osservazioni sul prefisso in- negativo nel sardo e in area romanza'; Pinto, 'The Influence of Loanwords on Sardinian Word Formation'; Pinto, 'Sardinian'; Pinto, 'Lessico e formazione delle parole'; Pinto, 'Word Formation in Standard Languages vs Minor Languages and Dialects'; Cossu, *La coltivazione de' Gelsi*, ed. by Marci.
136 Pinto, Paulis, and Putzu, 'Morphological Productivity in Medieval Sardinian', p. 251.
137 Wagner, *Dizionario Etimologico sardo*; Pinto, *La formazione delle parole in sardo*, pp. 155–56.
138 Rainer, 'Konvergenz- und Divergenzphänomene in der Romania'.

(untangle, ease) < Sp. *desgajar, desgaje*[139] — on which numerous Sardinian neoformations have been modelled: Camp. *skomai* (to prune, trim down) → *skomu* (branches); Log. *iskondzare* (to sprain) → Log. *iskondzu* (sprain).[140] Even today Sardinian prefers this morphological strategy over Italian N-*tione*, for example, Camp. *approvu* < It. *approvazione* (approval).[141] Consequently, the first data identified in the texts from the Aragonese-Castilian period seem once again to attribute a central role to the Iberian-Romance superstratum in the increase of the WFP V → N-*u*.

The suffixes of feminine agent nouns in non-standard Romance varieties have been little investigated. Some fundamental studies of the history of Sardinian material culture help us to glean some interesting clues. In particular, Wagner shows the prestige of the -*dora* suffix, as it is connected to activities considered to be of the highest importance, for instance spinning, weaving, and bread making: Camp., Log. *filadora* (spinner, literally the woman who spins), Camp., Log. *tessidora* (weaver, literally the woman who weaves), Log. *suigidora*, Camp. *suettora* (kneader, literally the woman who kneads bread) from Log. *suigere* (to knead) and from Camp. *suettu* (kneaded).[142] These endogenous formations replace the role played by the Italian suffix -*trice*: for example, It. *filatrice* (vs. Sard. *filadora*), *tessitrice* (vs Sard. *tessidora*), and *impastatrice* (vs. Sard. *suigidora* and *suettora*). Alongside these endogenous formations, there is a formation of Catalan origin: *levadora* (midwife).[143] Notably, -*dora* has been used within an archaic ritual dimension to indicate activities typically associated with women: for example, Camp. *abbrebadora* (sorceress, who knows magic formulas), from *brebus* (word, formula); Camp., Log. *attittadora* (woman who mourns the dead),[144] from Log. *attittiare*, Camp. *attittiai* (specifically stir up, incite; sometimes revenge).[145] The use of N / A-*dora* in the religious lexicon of Spanish and Catalan is particularly striking, as is its enduring presence in terms common to traditional Sardinian songs.[146]

---

139 Pinto, *La formazione delle parole in sardo*, p. 158.
140 Pinto, *La formazione delle parole in sardo*, p. 143.
141 Pinto, 'Genere e contatto linguistico', p. 472.
142 Wagner, *La vita rustica*, pp. 281, 287; Pinto, *La formazione delle parole in sardo*, p. 80.
143 Wagner, *La vita rustica*, p. 336.
144 Cf. 'prefica': in ancient Rome, a woman paid to be part of funeral processions and to sing songs of praise for the deceased, accompanied by cries of pain, tears, gestures of despair. The same name (or other regional names: *reputatrici, vociferatrici*, etc.) was also used among the peasant classes in some areas of southern Italy for those women who were commissioned to accompany the funeral and who took part in the rite behaving like the *preficas* of ancient days: weeping, wailing, rending their clothes and also singing traditional funeral songs; see Treccani on-line, s.v.
145 Wagner, *La vita rustica*, p. 346; Pinto, *La formazione delle parole in sardo*, p. 80.
146 Armangué i Herrero, 'I precedenti dei "gosos" sardi'; Romero Frías, 'Gòsos, gòccius … goigs'; Casu and Lutzu, *Enciclopedia della Musica*.

Conclusion

This corpus-based study has analysed a group of texts from late medieval (14th–15th-century) and early modern (16th–18th-century) Sardinia. It has demonstrated that, due to its complex history characterized by a long foreign domination, multilingualism has long been the norm in Sardinia. Language contact resulted in the establishment of a complex multilingual repertoire. Four different ways of achieving multilingualism have been identified, and these have been the main criteria chosen to subdivide the corpus. Passages from the selected corpus were examined for each of the four multilingual categories, and their analysis has yielded interesting findings. For example, the text by Araolla has not only provided useful data for the history of Sardinian derivational morphology, but it also reflects the author's intention to raise the status of Sardinian, enriching it with loans from languages of culture and higher status, such as Latin, Spanish, and Italian. The texts that are representative of the second multilingual modality clearly show the predominance of Spanish in literary works. However, in the Aragonese-Spanish phase, the number of works written in Sardinian outweighs those written in Catalan, although such works are considerably fewer than those in Spanish. As regards the third group of texts, multilingualism is visible in the relationship between a language variety and a certain genre: for example, several authors use Latin in historical texts and Spanish in historical-literary ones. It should be noted that such choices are certainly not clear-cut or definitive, and they change in accordance with the political power or cultural hegemony that a language variety expresses. Of particular interest are those texts in which language choice depends on the users and audiences involved, corresponding to the fourth group of works in our corpus. In modern Sardinian, the opposition is between Catalan, used mostly in administrative-legal writings, and Sardinian, used to report spoken speech in a variety of contexts, including statements in a notarial deed.

From a morphological point of view, the continuity of the Sardinian suffix *-eri* has been shown, although different forms of the superstratum are involved (Pis. *-ieri*, Cat. *-er*, Sp. *-ero*, and It. *-iere*). This suffix embodies the occurrence of some of the most important linguistic phenomena elaborated by scholars in the second half of the twentieth century relating to analogy, frequency, transparency, and the application of an exogenous rule to a native base. Also, the history of *-eri* is important for the linguistic concepts of degree of borrowability and copy of similar structures as developed in the fields of Romance comparative morphology, historical linguistics, and contact linguistics.[147] It can also be observed how the homologating effect of an exogenous suffix can inhibit the productivity of an endogenous suffix, especially if the latter has many diatopic variants (e.g. Camp., Log., Nuor. *-eri* vs Camp. *-arǧu/-raxu*, Log. *-ardzu*, Nuor. *-ariu*). In line with the

---

147 Matras, *Language Contact*; see also Matras and Adamou, eds, *The Routledge Handbook of Language Contact*.

most recent findings, the data show a close relationship between morphology and lexicon. In this regard, the high number of lexemes of Iberian-Romance origin with *des-* has strengthened the productivity of the Sardinian prefix *(i)s-*. On the other hand, the weak contribution of lexemes of Sardinian origin has reduced the derivative force of the competing *in-* negative prefix to zero.

Finally, this analysis can be considered as a preliminary linguistic study of medieval and early modern Sardinian sources. It is hoped that a digital archive of texts will be created to carry out intertextual analysis; comparative study with works from other Romance areas of the same periods seems to be promising.[148] In this respect, the mingled religious and secular elements found in the statutes of brotherhoods make these texts particularly worthy of linguistic attention. Such statutes reflect long-standing traditions that are still practiced in Sardinia and, most likely, have strong ties with the Iberian-Romance culture and languages.[149]

Works Cited

Abbreviations

Camp.: Campidanese
Cat.: Catalan
Gallur.: Gallurese
It.: Italian
Lat.: Latin
Log.: Logudorese
Nuor.: Nuorese
Pis.: Pisan
Sard.: Sardinian
Sp.: Spanish

Primary Sources

Araolla, Gerolamo, *Rimas diversas spirituales*, ed. by Maurizio Virdis (Cagliari: CUEC, 2006)

Bover i Font, August, 'I goccius nei Paesi Catalani e in Sardegna: Un'evoluzione parallela', *Insula*, 8 (2010), 21–34

Cano, Antonio, *Sa vitta et sa morte, et passione de sanctu Gavinu, Prothu et Januariu*, ed. by Dino Manca (Cagliari: CUEC, 2002)

Il canzoniere ispano-sardo e la letteratura in lingua spagnola nella Sardegna del Seicento, ed. by Antonina Paba (Cagliari: CUEC, 1996)

---

148 Puddu and Talamo, 'EModSar'.
149 Usai, 'Le Confraternite'; Usai, 'L'associazionismo religioso in Sardegna nei secoli xv–xvi'; Demontis, 'Le *cofradías* del Mediterraneo occidentale'.

Casu, Francesco, and Marco Lutzu, *Enciclopedia della Musica*, VII (Cagliari: l'Unione Sarda, 2012)

Il Condaghe di San Pietro di Silki, ed. by Alessandro Soddu and Giovanni Strinna (Nuoro: Ilisso, 2013)

Il Condaxi cabrevadu, ed. by Patrizia Serra (Cagliari: CUEC, 2006)

Cossu, Giuseppe, *La coltivazione de' Gelsi, e propagazione de' filugelli in Sardegna 1788–1789*, ed. by Giuseppe Marci (Cagliari: CUEC, 2002)

Delitala, Pietro, *Rime diverse*, ed. by Mauro Badas (Cagliari: CUEC, 2015)

Delogu Ibba, Giovanni, *Index libri vitae*, ed. by Giuseppe Marci (Cagliari: CUEC, 2003)

Di Tucci, Raffaele, 'Le corporazioni artigiane della Sardegna. Con Statuti inediti',[150] *Archivio Storico sardo*, 16 (1926), 33–160

Frate Antonio Maria da Esterzili, *Libro de comedias*, ed. by A. Luca De Martini (Cagliari: CUEC, 2006)

Loddo Canepa, Francesco, 'Statuti inediti di alcuni Gremi sardi', *Archivio Storico sardo*, 27 (1961), 177–442[151]

Lo Frasso, Antonio, *Los diez libros de fortuna de amor*, ed. by Antonello Murtas (Cagliari: CUEC, 2012)

Pau, Anna Rita, 'Nuovi documenti sull'uso linguistico in Sardegna nei secoli XVI–XVIII: La zona nord-orientale della diocesi di Ales', in *La Sardegna e la presenza Catalana nel Mediterraneo*, ed. by Paolo Maninchedda (Cagliari: CUEC, 1998), pp. 334–50

Pirodda, Giovanni, *Letteratura delle regioni d'Italia: Storia e testi. Sardegna* (Brescia: Editrice La Scuola, 1992)

Relaciones de sucesos sulla Sardegna (1500–1700): Repertorio e studi, ed. by Antonina Paba (Cagliari: CUEC, 2012)

Gli Statuti Sassaresi, ed. by P. E. Guarnerio, *Archivio Glottologico Italiano*, 13 (1892), 1–124

Testi in sardo, ed. by Andrea Deplano, in *Il canzoniere ispano-sardo e la letteratura in lingua spagnola nella Sardegna del Seicento*, ed. by Antonina Paba (Cagliari: CUEC, 1996), pp. 284–344

Vidal, Salvatore, *L'Urania sulcitana: Classicità e teatralità della lingua sarda*, ed. by Sergio Bullegas (Cagliari: Edizioni della Torre, 2004)

---

150 'Chapters of the Guild of Shoemakers and Tanners of Cagliari (15th–16th centuries)'. Statutes of the Guild of Blacksmiths and the like of Cagliari drawn up in 1643. Statutes of the Guild of Gardeners of Cagliari, drawn up in 1721, rectifying the chapters of 1426 and 1634. Statutes of the Guild of Masons and Carpenters of Sassari, drawn up in 1776. Statutes of the Guild of Shoemakers of Oristano, drawn up in 1721, rectifying the chapters of 1629. Statutes of the Guild of Shoemakers of Iglesias, drawn up in 1829.

151 Statutes of the Guild of Tailors of Cagliari of 1622. Statutes of the Guild of Carters of Cagliari, year 1634, with supplements from 1699. Statutes of the Guild of Coopers of Cagliari, 1638. Chapters of the Guild of Landworkers of Cagliari, 1689. Chapters of the Guild of the Cagliari Wine Unloaders, prior to 1702. Chapters of the Guild of Masons of Oristano, 1615. Chapters of the Guild of Pottery Makers of Oristano, 1692. Statute of the Grooms of Sassari, 1633. Chapters of the Guild of Masons of Sassari.

Secondary Studies

Anatra, Bruno, 'Editoria e pubblico in Sardegna tra Cinque e Seicento', in *Oralità e scrittura nel sistema letterario*, ed. by Giovanna Cerina, Cristina Lavinio, and Luisa Mulas (Rome: Bulzoni, 1982), pp. 233–43

———, 'La Sardegna aragonese: Istituzioni e società', in *Storia della Sardegna*, I, ed. by Manlio Brigaglia, Attilio Mastino, and Gian Giacomo Ortu (Rome: Laterza, 2006), pp. 151–66

Armangué i Herrero, Joan, 'I precedenti dei "gosos" sardi (metrica: secoli XVI e XVI)', *Insula*, 8 (2010), 35–74

Auer, Peter, 'Dialect Levelling and the Standard Varieties in Europe', *Folia Linguistica*, 32.1–2 (1998), 1–9

Badas, Mauro, 'Introduzione', in Pietro Delitala, *Rime diverse*, ed. by Mauro Badas (Cagliari: CUEC, 2015), pp. xi–cliii

Barbato, Marcello, 'Superstrato catalano', in *Manuale di linguistica sarda*, ed. by Eduardo Blasco Ferrer, Peter Koch, and Daniela Marzo (Berlin: De Gruyter, 2017), pp. 150–67

Berruto, Gaetano, 'Dialect/Standard Convergence, Mixing, and Models of Language Contact: The Case of Italy', in *Dialect Change: Convergence and Divergence in European Languages*, ed. by Peter Auer, Frans Hinskens, and Paul Kerswill (Cambridge: Cambridge University Press, 2005), pp. 81–97

———, 'The Languages and Dialects of Italy', in *Manual of Romance Sociolinguistics*, ed. by Wendy Ayres-Bennett and Janice Carruthers (Berlin: De Gruyter, 2018), pp. 494–525

Blasco Ferrer, Eduardo, *Storia linguistica della Sardegna* (Tübingen, Niemeyer, 1984)

Booij, G., C. Lehmann, and J. Mugdan, eds, *Morphology: An International Handbook of Inflection and Word-Formation*, 2 vols (Berlin: De Gruyter, 2000–2004)

Bullegas, Sergio, *Il teatro in Sardegna tra Cinque e Seicento* (Cagliari: Edes, 1976)

Cadeddu, Maria Eugenia, 'Scritture di una società plurilingue: Note sugli atti parlamentari sardi di epoca moderna', in *Reperti di plurilinguismo nell'Italia spagnola (sec. XVI–XVII)*, ed. by Thomas Krefeld, Wulf Oesterreicher, and Verena Schwägerl-Melchior (Berlin: De Gruyter, 2013), pp. 13–26

Carbonell, Jordi, and Francesco Manconi, eds, *I catalani in Sardegna* (Cinisello Balsamo: Silvana Editoriale, 1984)

Contini, Michel, 'Le catalan dans les parlers sardes', *Estudis Romànics*, 36 (2014), 405–21

Day, John, *Uomini e terre nella Sardegna coloniale: XII–XVIII secolo* (Turin: Einaudi, 1987)

Demontis, Luca, 'Le *cofradías* del Mediterraneo occidentale: A proposito di associazionismo medievale in Spagna e Sardegna', *Nuova Rivista Storica*, 92.1 (2008), 193–204

Dettori, Antonietta, 'Italiano e sardo dal Settecento al Novecento', in *Storia d'Italia: Le regioni d'Italia. La Sardegna*, ed. by L. Berlinguer and A. Mattone (Turin: Einaudi, 1998), pp. 1155–97

―――, 'La Sardegna', in *I dialetti italiani: Storia, struttura, uso*, ed. by Manlio Cortelazzo, Carla Marcato, Nicola De Blasi, and Gianrenzo P. Clivio (Turin: UTET, 2002), pp. 898–958

―――, 'Superstrato piemontese', in *Manuale di linguistica sarda*, ed. by Eduardo Blasco Ferrer, Peter Koch, and Daniela Marzo (Berlin: De Gruyter, 2017), pp. 184–99

Ferrero Micó, Remedios, and Lluís Guia Marín, eds, *Corts i parlaments de la corona d'Aragó* (València: Guada Impressors, 2008)

Hernandez Campoy, Juan Manuel, and Juan Camilo Conde Silvestre, eds, *The Handbook of Historical Sociolinguistics* (New York: Wiley-Blackwell, 2012)

Krefeld, Thomas, 'L'Italia spagnola — parametri di uno spazio comunicativo prenazionale', in *Reperti di plurilinguismo nell'Italia spagnola (sec. XVI–XVII)*, ed. by Thomas Krefeld, Wulf Oesterreicher, and Verena Schwägerl-Melchior (Berlin: De Gruyter, 2013), pp. 1–10

Lai, Maria Bonaria, 'I quinque libri', in *La società sarda in età spagnola*, II, ed. by Francesco Manconi (Cagliari: della Torre, 1993), pp. 190–99

Loi Corvetto, Ines, 'La variazione linguistica in area sarda', *Revista de Filología Románica*, 17 (2000), 143–56

Loporcaro, Michele, *Gender from Latin to Romance: History, Geography, Tipology* (Oxford: Oxford University Press, 2017)

Lupinu, Giovanni, 'Lingua sarda e gosos', in *Le chiese e i gosos di Bitti e Gorofai*, ed. by Raimondo Turtas and Giovanni Lupinu (Cagliari: CUEC, 2005), pp. lxxxvii–cxvii

Macchiarella, Ignazio, 'Le manifestazioni musicali della devozione cristiana in Italia', in *Enciclopedia della musica*, III, ed. by Jean-Jacques Nattiez, Margaret Bent, Rossana Dalmonte, and Mario Baroni (Turin: Einaudi, 2003), pp. 340–71

Manca, Dino, 'Introduzione', in Antonio Cano, *Sa vitta et sa morte, et passione de sanctu Gavinu, Prothu et Januariu*, ed. by Dino Manca (Cagliari: CUEC, 2002), pp. ix–cxliii

Manconi, Francesco, 'Catalogna e Sardegna: Relazioni economiche e influssi culturali fra Quattrocento e Cinquecento', in *La Sardegna e la presenza Catalana nel Mediterraneo*, ed. by Paolo Maninchedda (Cagliari: CUEC, 1998), pp. 35–54

―――, 'L'ispanizzazione della Sardegna: Un bilancio', in *Storia della Sardegna*, I, ed. by Manlio Brigaglia, Attilio Mastino, and Gian Giacomo Ortu (Rome: Laterza, 2006), pp. 221–37

―――, 'The Kingdom of Sardinia: A Province in Balance between Catalonia, Castile, and Italy', in *Spain in Italy: Politics, Society, and Religion, 1500–1700*, ed. by Thomas J. Dandelet and John A. Marino (Leiden: Brill, 2007), pp. 45–72

―――, *La Sardegna al tempo degli Asburgo: Secoli XVI–XVII* (Nuoro: Il Maestrale, 2010)

Maninchedda, Paolo, 'Introduzione', in *Il Condaghe di Santa Chiara*, ed. by Paolo Maninchedda (Oristano: S'Alvure, 1987), pp. 13–40

Marci, Giuseppe, *In presenza di tutte le lingue del mondo* (Cagliari: CUEC, 2006)

Matras, Yaron, *Language Contact* (Cambridge: Cambridge University Press, 2009)

Matras, Yaron, and Evangelia Adamou, eds, *The Routledge Handbook of Language Contact* (London: Routledge, 2021)

Mattheier, Klaus J., 'Varietätenkonvergenz: Überlegungen zu einem Baustein einer Theorie der Sprachvariation', *Sociolinguistica*, 10 (1996), 31–52

Meloni, Maria Giuseppina, and Antonio Forci, 'En nom de nostre Senyor Deus Jhesu Christ e de Madonna Santa Maria: Lo Statuto inedito di una confraternita religiosa nella Cagliari del '300', *Rivista dell'Istituto di Storia dell'Europa Mediterranea*, 10 (2013), 5–56

Meloni, Maria Giuseppina, and Olivetta Schena, eds, *Culti, santuari, pellegrinaggi in Sardegna e nella penisola iberica tra Medioevo ed Età contemporanea* (Genoa: Brigati, 2006)

Mensching, Guido, and Eva-Maria Remberger, 'Sardinian', in *The Oxford Guide to the Romance Languages*, ed. by Adam Ledgeway and Martin Maiden (Oxford: Oxford University Press, 2016), pp. 270–91

Molinelli, Piera, ed., *Language and Identity in Multilingual Mediterranean Settings: Challenges for Historical Sociolinguistics* (Berlin: De Gruyter, 2017)

Murgia, Giulia, 'Un "sociolinguista" cinquecentesco: Girolamo Olives e i suoi Commentaria et Glosa in Cartam de Logu (1567)', *Rhesis: International Journal of Linguistics, Philology and Literature*, 5.1 (2014), 79–112

Murtas, Antonello, 'Introduzione', in Antonio Lo Frasso, *Los diez libros de fortuna de amor*, ed. by Antonello Murtas (Cagliari: CUEC, 2012), pp. vii–cxx

Ortu, Gian Giacomo, 'La Sardegna nella corona di Spagna', in *Storia della Sardegna*, I, ed. by Manlio Brigaglia, Attilio Mastino, and Gian Giacomo Ortu (Rome: Laterza, 2006), pp. 167–86

Paba, Antonina, 'Eternizar la memoria: Duecento anni di *relaciones* sulla Sardegna', in *Relaciones de sucesos sulla Sardegna (1500–1700): Repertorio e studi*, ed. by Antonina Paba (Cagliari: CUEC, 2012), pp. 13–38

—— , 'Introduzione', in *Il canzoniere ispano-sardo e la letteratura in lingua spagnola nella Sardegna del Seicento*, ed. by Antonina Paba (Cagliari: CUEC, 1996), pp. 9–28

Paulis, Giulio, 'Dinamiche linguistiche e sociali a Cagliari nel corso dei secoli: Le alterne fortune di un vocativo di lunga durata', in *Repertorio plurilingue e variazione linguistica a Cagliari*, ed. by Giulio Paulis, Ignazio Putzu, and Immacolata Pinto (Milan: Franco Angeli, 2013), pp. 40–81

—— , 'L'espressione dilogica della trasgressione sessuale in un Canzoniere ispano-sardo del Seicento e in Calderón de la Barca (*albur, tahúr* e dintorni, tra semantica etimologia e testualità)', in *Etimologia fra testi e culture*, ed. by Giulio Paulis and Immacolata Pinto (Milan: Franco Angeli, 2013), pp. 106–277

—— , 'L'impiego orale del sardo come espressione di dissenso politico nelle adunanze parlamentari della Sardegna spagnola', in *Balaus annus et bonus: Studi in onore di Maurizio Virdis*, ed. by Patrizia Serra and Giulia Murgia (Florence: Cesati, 2019), pp. 295–305

—— , 'L'influsso linguistico spagnolo', in *La società sarda in età spagnola*, II, ed. by Francesco Manconi (Cagliari: della Torre, 1993), pp. 212–21

———, 'Le parole catalane dei dialetti sardi', in *I catalani in Sardegna*, ed. by Jordi Carbonell and Francesco Manconi (Cinisello Balsamo: Silvana Editoriale, 1984), pp. 155–63

Paulis, Giulio, and Giovanni Lupinu, 'Tra Logudoro e Campidani: I volgari sardi e le espressioni della cultura', in *Storia della Sardegna*, I, ed. by Manlio Brigaglia, Attilio Mastino, and Gian Giacomo Ortu (Rome: Laterza, 2006), pp. 131–39

Pinna, Antonio, 'I gosos e la paraliturgia: Un incrocio fra tradizione popolare e tradizione colta. Due casi di studio', *Insula*, 8 (2010), 101–22

Pinto, Immacolata, 'Alcune osservazioni sul prefisso in- negativo nel sardo e in area romanza', *Rivista Italiana di Dialettologia*, 28 (2004), 97–217

———, 'La derivazione in sardo medievale: Una prima analisi in prospettiva sociolinguistica', in *Modelli epistemologici, metodologie della ricerca e qualità del dato: Dalla linguistica storica alla sociolinguistica storica*, ed. by Piera Molinelli and Ignazio Putzu (Milan: Franco Angeli, 2015), pp. 264–81

———, *La formazione delle parole in sardo* (Nuoro: Ilisso, 2011)

———, 'Genere e contatto linguistico: Il caso degli italianismi N-*zione* in sardo', in *Al femminile: Scritti linguistici in onore a Cristina Vallini*, ed. by Anna De Meo, Lucia di Pace, Alberto Manco, J. Monti, and Rossella Pannain (Florence: Cesati, 2017), pp. 471–83

———, 'The Influence of Loanwords on Sardinian Word Formation', in *Morphologies in Contact*, ed. by Martine Vanhove, Thomas Stolz, Hitomi Otsuka, and Aina Urdze (Berlin: Akademie, 2012), pp. 227–45

———, 'Lessico e formazione delle parole: Sincronia', in *Manuale di linguistica sarda*, ed. by Eduardo Blasco Ferrer, Peter Koch, and Daniela Marzo (Berlin: De Gruyter, 2017), pp. 413–30

———, 'Sardinian', in *HSK-Word Formation*, IV, ed. by Peter O. Müller, Ingeborg Ohnheiser, Susan Olsen, and Franz Rainer (Berlin: De Gruyter, 2016), pp. 2693–2712

———, 'Tra derivazione e flessione: Il caso del suffisso -*éri* in sardo', *Rhesis: International Journal of Linguistics, Philology and Literature*, 9.1 (2018), 5–26

———, 'Word Formation in Standard Languages vs Minor Languages and Dialects', in *Oxford Research Encyclopedia of Linguistics*, <https://oxfordre.com/linguistics>

Pinto, Immacolata, Giulio Paulis, and Ignazio Putzu, 'Morphological Productivity in Medieval Sardinian: Sociolinguistic Correlates. Action Nouns and Adverbs of Manner', in *Language and Identity in Multilingual Mediterranean Settings: Challenges for Historical Sociolinguistics*, ed. by Piera Molinelli (Berlin: De Gruyter, 2017), pp. 245–68

———, 'Sardinian Adjectives with the N-i-A Structure', *Lingue e Linguaggio*, 11.1 (2012), 49–70

Pisano, Simone, 'Importanza del superstrato catalano, castigliano e italiano in alcune varietà sarde moderne: Aspetti lessicali, fonetici e morfosintattici', in *Le lingue d'Italia e le altre: Contatti, sostrati e superstrati nella storia linguistica della Penisola*, ed. by Lorenzo Filipponio and Christian Seidl (Milan: Franco Angeli, 2015), pp. 149–65

Pittalis, Paola, 'Il sardo come lingua letteraria', in *Manuale di linguistica sarda*, ed. by Eduardo Blasco Ferrer, Peter Koch, and Daniela Marzo (Berlin: De Gruyter, 2017), pp. 217–31

Pountain, Christopher J., 'Standardization', in *The Oxford Guide to the Romance Languages*, ed. by Adam Ledgeway and Martin Maiden (Oxford: Oxford University Press, 2016), pp. 634–43

Puddu, Nicoletta, Elena Maccioni, Giulia Murgia, and Luigi Talamo, *Documenti notarili sardi di Età moderna: Verso la creazione di un corpus* (Milan: Franco Angeli, forthcoming)

Puddu, Nicoletta, and Luigi Talamo, 'EModSar: A Corpus of Early Modern Sardinian Texts', in *Atti del IX Convegno annuale dell'Associazione per l'Informatica umanistica e la Cultura digitale (AIUCD) — La svolta inevitabile: Sfide e prospettive per l'informatica umanistica*, ed. by Cristina Marras, Marco Passarotti, Greta Franzini, and Eleonora Litta, (2020), pp. 210–15, <http://amsacta.unibo.it/6316/1/AIUCD_2020_volume_FINAL.pdf> [accessed 19 June 2020]

Putzu, Ignazio, 'History of Sardinian Lexicon', in *Oxford Research Encyclopedia of Linguistics*, <https://oxfordre.com/linguistics>

——, 'La posizione linguistica del sardo nel contesto mediterraneo', in *Neues aus der Bremer Linguistikwerkstatt*, ed. by Cornelia Stroh (Bochum: Brochmeyer, 2011), pp. 175–205

——, 'Il repertorio sardo tra Tardo Antico e Alto Medio Evo: Un breve *status quaestionis*', in *Itinerando senza confini dalla preistoria ad oggi: Scritti in ricordo di Roberto Coroneo*, ed. by Rossana Martorelli (Perugia: Morlacchi, 2015), pp. 497–518

Rainer, Franz, 'Konvergenz- und Divergenzphänomene in der Romania: Wortbildung', in *Romanische Sprachgeschichte: Ein internationales Handbuch zur Geschichte der romanischen Sprachen / Histoire linguistique de la Romania: Manuel international d'histoire linguistique de la Romania*, III, ed. by Gerhard Ernst, Martin-Dietrich Gleßgen, Christian Schmitt, and Wolfgang Schweickard (Berlin: De Gruyter, 2008), pp. 3293–3307

Romero Frías, Marina, 'Gòsos, gòccius … goigs: A própositio de una edición del Index libri vitae de Giovanni Delogu Ibba Marina', *Espéculo: Revista de estudios literarios*, 2006, <http://webs.ucm.es/info/especulo/numero33/gdelogu.html> [accessed 4 August 2020]

——, 'Note sulla situazione linguistica a Cagliari (Sardegna) nel periodo 1598–1615', in *Estudis Universitaris Catalans: Estudis de Llengua i literatura catalanes oferts a R. Aramon i Serra en el seu setantè anniversari* (Barcelona: Curial edicions catalanes, 1983), pp. 453–65

Sanson, Helena L., 'The Romance Languages in the Renaissance and After', in *The Cambridge History of the Romance Languages*, II: *Contexts*, ed. by Martin Maiden, John Charles Smith, and Adam Ledgeway (Cambridge: Cambridge University Press, 2013), pp. 237–82

Schena, Olivetta, and Maria Giuseppina Meloni, *Santuari d'Italia: Sardegna* (Cagliari: Fondazione di Sardegna, 2019)

Schena, Olivetta, and A. M. Oliva, *La Sardegna catalana* (Barcelona: Institut d'Estudis Catalans, Publicacions de la Presidencia, 2014)

Seche, Giuseppe, *Libro e società in Sardegna tra medioevo e prima Età moderna* (Florence: Olschki, 2018)

Treccani on-line, <https://www.treccani.it/vocabolario/> [accessed 10 June 2020]

Usai, Giuseppina, 'L'associazionismo religioso in Sardegna nei secoli xv–xvi', in *Corporazioni, gremi e artigianato: Tra Sardegna, Spagna e Italia nel Medioevo e nell'Età moderna*, ed. by Antonello Mattone (Cagliari: AM&D, 2000), pp. 191–203

——, 'Le Confraternite', in *La società sarda in età spagnola*, I, ed. by Francesco Manconi (Cagliari: Della Torre, 1992), pp. 156–65

Virdis, Maurizio, 'Introduzione', in Gerolamo Araolla, *Rimas diversas spirituales*, ed. by Maurizio Virdis (Cagliari: CUEC, 2006), pp. ix–clxxv

——, 'Superstrato spagnolo', in *Manuale di linguistica sarda*, ed. by Eduardo Blasco Ferrer, Peter Koch, and Daniela Marzo (Berlin: De Gruyter, 2017), pp. 168–83

Wagner, Max Leopold, *Dizionario Etimologico sardo*, ed. by Giulio Paulis (1960–1964; repr. Nuoro: Ilisso, 2008)

——, 'Los elementos español y catalan en los dialectos sardos', *Revista de Filologia Española*, 9.3 (1922), 221–65

——, *Historische Wortbildungslehere des Sardischen* (Bern: Francke, 1952)

——, *La vita rustica* [1921], ed. by Giulio Paulis (Nuoro: Ilisso, 1996)

MEGAN TIDDEMAN

Libri alienigeni

Evidence of Anglo-Italian Language Contact from the Fifteenth-Century Port of Southampton

Southampton played a key role in Anglo-Italian trade in the late 1300s and 1400s, and medieval administrative records in its city archives contain numerous instances of Italian lexical borrowings. This essay focuses on three sets of account books from the fifteenth century which contain maritime and mercantile Italianisms, most commonly of Genoese or Venetian origin. These loanwords are all found in published editions by historians but are either little-known to linguists or have never been explored in an England-specific context before. The earlier two of these sources have late Anglo-French (also known as Anglo-Norman or insular French) as their matrix language. This refers to the distinct dialect of medieval French used in huge amounts of bureaucratic and literary material in the British Isles following the Norman Conquest in 1066 and surviving — in government records — until the 1500s. The third source, which dates from fifty years later, is written in late Middle English. Taken together, these texts shed further light on the realities of medieval Anglo-Italian language contact, a phenomenon which, until recently, has been largely overlooked by scholars.[1]

Italians and Late Medieval Southampton

The busy and profitable port of Southampton dominated maritime trade on the south coast of England in the later Middle Ages.[2] It boasted several

---

1 An intriguing document containing evidence of an English scribe writing in Tuscan at the Canterbury Mint in the 1290s has recently been unearthed, showing that such contact stretches back to at least the late thirteenth century. See Cappelletti, 'Un testo in volgare italo-romanzo'.
2 See also Tiddeman, 'Southampton and the Later Medieval Textile Trade'.

> **Megan Tiddeman** (M.Tiddeman4@westminster.ac.uk) is a Research Fellow with 'The Semantics of Word Borrowing in Late Medieval English' project, led by Professor Louise Sylvester at the University of Westminster, and funded by the Leverhulme Trust.

Languages and Cross-Cultural Exchanges in Renaissance Italy, ed. by Alessandra Petrocchi and Joshua Brown, LMEMS 30 (Turnhout: Brepols, 2023), pp. 269–297
BREPOLS ❧ PUBLISHERS   10.1484/M.LMEMS-EB.5.131435

geographical advantages: a wide, deep harbour accessible to large foreign vessels, double tides, overland proximity to the capital, and a hinterland rich in wool and cloth producers. In the 1270s, the establishment of a direct sea route from Italy to England, via the Atlantic coast of Europe, opened up a new world of commercial opportunity: transport by sea cost a mere quarter of its overland equivalent.[3] Such an innovation had been made possible by 'the great outburst of maritime activity in the Italian seaports stimulated by the Crusades [...] and technical developments in shipbuilding, particularly in Genoa'.[4] The first Genoese vessel recorded in England docked in London in 1281, followed by another in Sandwich in 1287, and then a third in Southampton in 1303. Ships from Genoa were run by private merchants, whereas Venetian state galleys, captained by noblemen elected by the Senate, arrived later to English shores, with their first visit being to Southampton in 1314.[5] The Florentines — who are recorded as trading in England as early as 1223[6] — held a series of privileged yet ultimately doomed positions as Crown Bankers to Kings Edward I, II, and III, and shipped enormous quantities of English wool out of Southampton from the late 1200s.[7] Yet their export relied mainly on hiring vessels from other Italians, or from Spanish or Flemish traders. It was not until 1429 that they brought their own state fleet to Southampton, having won the port of Porto Pisano from Pisa in 1406.[8]

Imports could vary greatly depending on the Italian city state involved. The Genoese dominated the market for the chemical dye fixer alum, mined in their colonies in modern-day Turkey.[9] This was indispensable not just to the English cloth-making industry but also to tanners and painters. Visiting carracks also supplied dyes (such as woad to give blue and fustic to give yellow) and large amounts of tin. The Venetians and Tuscans were famous for a more luxurious cargo, especially sugar, spices, dried fruit, sweet wines, and lavish silks, satins, and velvets, both of native manufacture or imported

---

3   Bolton, *The Medieval English Economy*, p. 311.
4   Ruddock, *Italian Merchants*, p. 19.
5   Ruddock, *Italian Merchants*, pp. 20–22, 51–52. The most comprehensive analysis to date on the number of Italian vessels docking at medieval English ports focuses on the Genoese: Nicolini lists all extant records of 260 Genoese carracks landing in England between 1280 and 1495, including port, ship name, and patron name. His study also finds that the two main peaks in visiting Genoese maritime traffic were in the 1380s and the 1430s. See Nicolini, 'Commercio marittimo genovese', pp. 291–317.
6   Cella, 'Anglismi e francesismi', p. 191.
7   There exists a sizeable scholarly literature on the Tuscan role in Crown banking and their domination of the English wool market. The two business ventures neatly overlapped, with the former being used to pay the interest on the huge sums borrowed by the royal household. Some notable examples include Sapori, *La compagnia dei Frescobaldi*; Kaeuper, *Bankers to the Crown*; Hunt, *The Medieval Super-Companies*; Bell, Brooks, and Moore, *Accounts of the English Crown*.
8   Ruddock, *Italian Merchants*, pp. 57–58, 62; Mallett, *The Florentine Galleys*, pp. 3–20; Goldthwaite, *The Economy of Renaissance Florence*, p. 48.
9   Cf. Goldthwaite, *The Economy of Renaissance Florence*, pp. 233–34. See also Tiddeman, 'Alum'.

from the Middle East and beyond. These expensive goods, aimed at the richest of consumers, did not stay long in Southampton and were nearly all transported to London for sale.[10]

Relations between local and alien merchants were not always harmonious. The first visit of a Venetian galley to the Southampton docks in 1314 ended in a violent brawl between crew and townsfolk — Venetians avoided the port for the following two decades and still brought up the event in native sources sixty years later.[11]

However, records also survive which show the extent to which some Italians became part of the local community in the fifteenth century, both as regular visitors and as permanent residents. Alien merchants were hosted by the same locals year after year,[12] and incoming vessels (whose crews could number two hundred men) would spend weeks, or even months, in the harbour over the winter.[13] The Cattanei and Spinola families, shipowners from Genoa, established a colony in the town and feature heavily in its civic accounts.[14] The Florentine Paolo Morelli, first recorded in a Port Book in 1429 as *Paul Morell*, worked as a commission agent (handling the goods of others) and was based permanently in the port for nearly thirty years.[15] The Venetian Gabriele Corbizzi married an Englishwoman and took English citizenship. He became Steward of Southampton in the 1440s and introduced new Italian accounting methods to the role.[16] Cristoforo Ambruogi of Florence was twice elected mayor of Southampton in 1486 and 1497 (an exceptional privilege for an alien-born merchant at the time), and he also took in and trained English apprentices.[17] Furthermore, as we see in more detail below, records attest that local workers and Venetian galley crews worked together on a regular basis to source and fell timber in the New Forest and build dockside equipment from *c.* 1481 to 1522.[18]

---

10 Bradley, 'Southampton's Trading Partners'.
11 Edward II and the Doge of Venice wrote to each other several times about the 'affray'. The king tried unsuccessfully to repair relations by offering pardons and promises of future safe-conduct to the galley crews (Ruddock, *Italian Merchants*, pp. 26, 148).
12 See Bradley, *The Views of the Hosts*.
13 The logbook of galley captain Luca di Maso degli Albizzi of Florence covers the winter of 1429–1430 spent in Southampton where he was hosted by a local shipowner and dined with the mayor (Mallett, *The Florentine Galleys*, p. 262).
14 Bradley, 'Southampton's Trading Partners', p. 67.
15 Ruddock, *Italian Merchants*, pp. 98–105. See also Bradley, 'Southampton's Trading Partners', p. 72.
16 Thick, 'The Fifteenth-Century Stewards' Books', pp. 73–74; James, 'The Town of Southampton', p. 13.
17 Ruddock, *Italian Merchants*, pp. 185–86; James, 'The Town of Southampton', p. 13.
18 See Ruddock, 'The Method of Handling the Cargoes'.

The Source Texts

The Southampton Archives contain a wealth of trade records that are of great interest to historians of maritime trade in England.[19] These include the famous Oak Book from c. 1300 (with its Anglo-French copy of the laws of the sea: the Rolls of Oléron) and numerous Port Books, Stewards' Books, and Books of Remembrance from the fifteenth and early sixteenth centuries. Ruddock's meticulous study from 1951 has long been considered the definitive work on the economic life of 'one of the most cosmopolitan towns in medieval England'.[20] She analysed these manuscript sources and others (such as the Book of Fines, the Book of Oaths and Ordinances, and the Wool House Books) to track the shifting fortunes of the prosperous Italian colony in the port. Much more recently, the contents of the thirteen extant Latin-matrix Brokerage Books from 1430–1540 have been examined in detail and also made available in an online database.[21]

The loanwords discussed below come from three published editions of Southampton sources: the Port Books of 1427–1430 and 1435–1436, and the Stewards' Books of 1487–1493. Sections of the accounts dedicated to foreign trade, frequently Italian, were referred to as the *libri alienigeni*. The two earliest texts are written in a late Anglo-French matrix interspersed with numerous Latin and Middle English lexemes, forming a trilingual business 'code', typical of fifteenth-century England.[22] These sources appear in the corpus of the *Anglo-Norman Dictionary* (*AND*). Their writer is identified as Robert Florys, the town 'water-bailiff' and customs collector, who details all incoming and outgoing vessels in the harbour, the goods on board, and the various fees and taxes payable. The accounts were edited in 1913 and in 1963,[23] with both authors flagging up the unusual presence of a handful of Italianisms in the insular French text.[24] These five loanwords were revisited much later by my late doctoral supervisor and *AND* chief editor, David Trotter, in one of two articles from 2011 which highlighted the need to examine language contact

---

19 For a full idea of the extent of the Southampton Archives corpus, see James, *Southampton Sources*.
20 Ruddock, *Italian Merchants*, p. 10.
21 Hicks, *English Inland Trade*. These accounts are accessible via an online database at <http://oltrade.geodata.soton.ac.uk>.
22 For numerous studies of mixed-language record keeping in medieval England, see the work of Wright, e.g. 'Bills, Accounts, Inventories' and 'Code Intermediate Phenomena'.
23 Studer, *The Port Books of Southampton* and Foster, *The Local Port Book*, respectively.
24 These are AF *fangot* < It. *fangotto* ('a bundle of cloth') in Studer, *The Port Books of Southampton*, p. 50, and AF *cotegnate* < It. *cotognato* ('quince jam'); AF *sarme* < It. *sarma* ('a measure of capacity'); AF *sport* < It. *sporta* ('a basket'); AF *comyt* < It. *comito* ('ship's commander or overseer') in Foster, *The Local Port Book*, p. xiv. Note that Foster's suggestion that *dosses* is borrowed from Italian *dossi* ('back skins') is not convincing. The word is more likely a simple variant of Anglo-French *dos* ('back').

between medieval Italian and Anglo-French.[25] As we see below, various studies have examined French–Italian contact at great length but never in an England-specific context.

Our third source, the Stewards' Books of 1487–1494, were written in late Middle English but are not currently included in the corpora of the *Oxford English Dictionary* (*OED*) or the *Middle English Dictionary* (*MED*). These accounts were first transcribed in 1944 (again by Ruddock) and also feature in later work by Thick from the 1990s.[26] The stewardship was an important administrative and civic position, second only to the town aldermen, whose role was to oversee expenditure in the port. Crucially, the accounts reveal payments to build derricks (or cranes) on the dockside to load and unload valuable cargo. They reveal that locals and Venetian crew worked together on construction and timber cutting in nearby forests. As Ruddock stresses in a later work, the days of brawling in the port seem long forgotten:

> More positive evidence of absences of animosity on the part of the ordinary townsmen is seen in the numerous occasions when townsmen and galleymen cooperated on various jobs about the port. The captains of the galley fleet contracted with the mayor, agreeing to pay a lump sum for the necessary repairs or the hire of equipment for steeving their cargoes and the stewards' accounts of these contracts in the fifteenth century show there to be a remarkable degree of cooperation between town officials, English artisans and galleymen when need arose and profit was indicated [...]. Galley carpenters helped the local woodcutters to fell great oaks and elms at Beaulieu, Marchwood and Eling [...], local craftsman and galleymen worked together making derricks, pulleys, vices, capstans and slices for stowing freight.[27]

Examples of Italian borrowings in English-matrix texts which predate the sixteenth century, such as those in the Stewards' Books, are extraordinarily rare. The popularity of Italian Renaissance culture in English noble circles in the 1500s led to a surge of well over one hundred borrowings in the fields of architecture, music, poetry, mathematics, cuisine, and warfare: for example, *piazza, stucco, contrabass, duo, violin, stanza, tercet, algebra, romby, artichoke, bottarga, pistachio, arsenal*, and *falconet*.[28] In contrast, studies of the corpora

---

25   See Trotter, 'Death, Taxes and Property'. His other article explored language contact in the opposite direction, namely Anglo-French and Middle English borrowings in the London account book of the Gallerani of Siena: see Trotter, 'Italian Merchants in London and Paris'. These two pieces provided the inspiration for my PhD research on early Anglo-Italian contact.
26   Ruddock, 'The Method of Handling the Cargoes'; Thick, 'The Fifteenth-Century Stewards' Books'; Thick, *The Southampton Steward's Book*.
27   Ruddock, *Italian Merchants*, p. 152.
28   See Iamartino, 'La contrastività italiano-inglese', pp. 22–28; Durkin, *Borrowed Words*, pp. 370–72. For studies on the sixteenth-century craze for Italian language learning, see Lawrence, *Who the Devil Taught Thee so much Italian?* and Gallagher, *Learning Languages in Early Modern England*.

of the *OED* and the *MED* put the total of direct loans from the late 1300s to 1500 at between three and seven.[29] Furthermore, only a handful of literary Italianisms (e.g. *cornuto* 'cuckold' or *vecke* 'old woman') in the works of Chaucer, Gower, and Lydgate have so far received widespread academic attention.[30] The four Italian loanwords in the Stewards' Books are therefore of key interest to historical linguists and lexicographers.

Loanword Case Studies

This section focuses on nine borrowings linked to maritime trade in Southampton: words linked to ships and their crew, the containers of goods stowed within them, and dockside equipment. I have looked elsewhere at Italianisms specifically related to the sugar and spice trade and the luxury textile market in England.[31] Some of these words also have citations which appear in the Port Books, but these will not be included here.

As we have noted, the northern Italians were at the forefront of maritime technology in the late Middle Ages, and their lexical legacy in the fields of Continental French navigation and ship-building has long attracted scholarly attention.[32] The royal naval dockyards in Rouen known as the *Clos des Galées*, run by Genoese shipbuilders in the 1340s, provided an optimal environment for the transfer of lexis, and, as Trotter notes, it could well be here that the loanwords *comyt* (< Gen. *còmito*, 'ship's commander or overseer')[33] and *calfater* (< Gen. *calafatare*, 'to caulk')[34] began their journey into Anglo-French and,

---

29 See Dietz, 'Die frühen italienischen Lehnwörter'; Durkin, *Borrowed Words*, p. 369. Pinnavaia's survey of Italianisms in the entire *OED*2 corpus cites twenty candidates from the medieval period but does not include parallel consultation of the *AND* (Pinnavaia, *The Italian Borrowings*, pp. 269–312). On closer inspection, nearly all of these loanwords appear to have entered Middle English indirectly from Italian, via an Anglo-French intermediary, e.g. ME *celestrine* < AF *celestrin* < It. *cilestrino* ('sky-blue fabric'). Cf. Tiddeman, 'Early Anglo-Italian Contact', p. 220, and Tiddeman, 'Lexical Exchange with Italian', p. 124. These word histories remain vitally important, however, as they are still evidence of Anglo-Italian contact taking place in England.
30 It is well known that all three English authors were influenced by the great works of the Trecento, especially Dante's *Divina Commedia* and Boccaccio's *Decameron*. See, for example, Childs, 'Anglo-Italian Contacts', pp. 65–88; Hines and Yeager, *John Gower*; Mortimer, *John Lydgate's Fall of Princes*. It is believed that Chaucer was first inspired by the texts during diplomatic missions to Italy on behalf of Richard II in the 1370s: see Lerer, *The Yale Companion to Chaucer*, p. 36; Childs, 'Anglo-Italian Contacts', pp. 66–67.
31 Tiddeman, 'More Sugar and Spice' and Tiddeman, 'Lexical Exchange with Italian', respectively.
32 See Vidos, *Storia delle parole*; Hope, *Lexical Borrowing in the Romance Languages*; Fennis, *Trésor du langage des galères*; Tomasin, 'Sulla diffusione del lessico marinaresco italiano'.
33 Trotter, 'Death, Taxes and Property', p. 170. See also Hope, *Lexical Borrowing in the Romance Languages*, I, p. 35; Vidos, *Storia delle parole*, p. 331; Fennis, *Trésor du langage des galères*, p. 592.
34 Trotter, 'Oceano vox', pp. 23–24. See also Hope, *Lexical Borrowing in the Romance Languages*, I, p. 32; Vidos, *Storia delle parole*, pp. 265–66; Fennis, *Trésor du langage des galères*, pp. 450–57.

from there, into Middle English. Other Gallo-Italianisms which are attested in a bilingual naval treaty from 1246 between the city of Genoa and the French king, and which are also found in later Anglo-French material, include *poupe* (< Gen. *poppa*, 'ship's stern or poop deck'),[35] and *patron* (< Gen. / It. *patrone* / *padrone*, 'ship's captain', discussed below). *Taride* (< Gen. *tarida*, 'long, flat merchant vessel')[36] and *carrak* (< Gen. / It. *caracca*, 'large, armed merchant vessel', discussed below) first appear in French in an Italianizing crusade chronicle from the first half of the 1200s, and both, unsurprisingly, have ultimate Arabic etyma.

However, we have no extant record in insular French of many other Genoese maritime loanwords found in Continental French texts. To give just three examples: *nochier* < Gen. *nozher* ('helmsman'),[37] *proue* < Gen. *proa* ('prow, front of a ship'),[38] and *fougoun* < Gen. *fogone* ('ship's hearth').[39] Other possible maritime borrowings (such as *goundel*[40] and *timon*[41]) are hidden in

---

[35] *Powpe* appears in a citation from 1409–11 in the *AND*2 entry sub **forcastell**. See also *OED*3 sub **poop¹**; Vidos, *Storia delle parole*, pp. 543–44; Fennis, *Trésor du langage des galères*, p. 1477.
[36] Cf. Vidos, *Storia delle parole*, p. 27. Interestingly, while Genoese-derived *taride* is the dominant form in Continental French, there is only one attestation of this variant in Anglo-French — in a Crusade treatise of the Knight Hospitaller Roger de Stanegrave from 1332. The citation is found in the *AND*2 entry sub **columbé**. Most of the examples found in English documents in the 1300s (be they in Anglo-French, Middle English, or British Medieval Latin) seem to have come directly from the Venetian form of the same boat name, *taretta* (att. in Venetian in 1284, see Chizzola, *Prose e Poesie*, pp. 229–30). This dialectal variant of the loanword is not attested in the major Continental French dictionaries suggesting direct contact between insular French and Venetian in this case. See *AND*1 sub **tarette**, *MED* sub **tarette**, *OED*2 sub **tarette**, *DMLBS* sub **tarita**. Typically, in these last three dictionary entries, the word is classed as a borrowing from French, and of ultimate Arabic origin, but the role of Italian is not considered.
[37] Tomasin, 'Sulla diffusione del lessico marinaresco italiano', p. 267; Vidos, *Storia delle parole*, pp. 491–94; Fennis, *Trésor du langage des galères*, pp. 1285–86.
[38] Fennis, *Trésor du langage des galères*, p. 1496. We do have evidence of the latter term's transmission into English, of course (*OED*3 sub **prow, n. 2**, att. 1555): given the fact that *proe* entered Continental French along with technical terms such as *poupe* (referring to the opposite end of the ship) we could argue that an unattested Anglo-French intermediary existed.
[39] Tomasin, 'Sulla diffusione del lessico marinaresco italiano', p. 266.
[40] See *MED* sub **goundel**. The boat type named *goundell* / *gondell* / *gundell* appears three times in Latin customs accounts under Henries V and VI between 1417 and 1425. It could well represent a borrowing in insular French, or even in Middle English from Venetian *gondola* ('a narrow boat to transport people and goods'). There is only one isolated borrowing of the term in medieval Continental French from 1246 (Fennis, *Trésor du langage des galères*, p. 65; Vidos, *Storia delle parole*, pp. 430–34).
[41] See *MED* **timon**. The word is already attested in Anglo-French in the non-nautical sense of 'plough or cart shaft' (see *AND*1 sub **timon**), but its use to mean 'ship's rudder' in two Latin-matrix accounts from 1324 and 1392 could represent a semantic loan from Genoese *timone* in Anglo-French as it does in Continental French (see Fennis, *Trésor du langage des galères*, p. 1751).

English texts but ones written in a Latin-matrix; nevertheless, we can imagine that they were also used in the vernacular within shipping communities.

The loanwords discussed below have been divided into three subgroups based on their frequency in the historical record, ranging from the relatively common and attested outside the Southampton corpus, to hapaxes which only feature in a single Southampton source.

Common Loanwords

Our first two examples found in Southampton material are the maritime borrowings *carrak* and *patron*, both of which are widely attested in texts in England from the 1380s onwards.

AF carrak: 'a large, armed merchant vessel, with three or four masts, used especially by the Genoese and the Portuguese from the 1300s to the 1700s'. (CF *carraque*) < Gen. / It. *caracca* < Arabic *harrāqa* ('fire ship')

> *Entre le xxviij^{me} jour de august j <u>carrake</u> patron karole ytalyen* (Port Bks 82) (att. 1427–1430)[42]
>
> *Entre j <u>carrake</u> de Janne, patron Anree Spinol* (Port Bks 42) (1427–1430)[43]
>
> *Entré de .j. <u>carrake</u> donk est patron Piere Vent de Lime* (Local Port Bk 10) (1435–1436)[44]

As mentioned above, the Genoese were at the forefront of medieval shipbuilding technology and originally developed the carrack to transport even larger amounts of cargo: over three times as much as a standard medieval galley.[45] By the time Southampton officials were recording the arrival of such imposing vessels and their Italian captains into the harbour, as in the examples above, the term had been appearing in documents in England for at least half a century and in France for much longer.

Carrak / *caraque* is ultimately derived from the Arabic *harrāqa* ('fire ship'), meaning a ship equipped to throw fire at enemies at sea.[46] There is general

---

[42] Cf. *AND*2 sub **carrak**. Note that the Southampton examples are not in this entry but are found in the dictionary corpus as citations under other headwords, in this instance *AND*2 sub **Italien**.
[43] See *AND*2 sub **patron**.
[44] See *AND*2 articles sub **dunt¹**.
[45] Nicolini, 'Commercio marittimo genovese', p. 227.
[46] The role of Italian as a conduit for Arabisms into western Europe is well known, bearing testimony to a transmission route forged by the Saracen occupation of Sicily and southern Italy in the late ninth and tenth centuries and the enduring commercial contacts this created. Schweickard estimates that there are approximately two hundred loanwords of Arabic origin recorded in Italian between 1100 and 1500, found in the semantic fields of shipping, commerce, civic administration, food, furnishings, alchemy, astronomy, and mathematics (Schweickard, 'Storia interna dell'italiano', pp. 2852–53).

agreement among scholars that the term entered Continental French in the mid-1200s via an Italian intermediary, *carraca*, most likely of Genoese origin, and that its meaning shifted gradually from 'small Saracen vessel' to 'large vessel with sails'.[47] Noting the presence of *carraca* in the Latin of Genoa as early as 1157, Vidos concludes that the ship name entered Genoese (possibly via Sicily) and, from there, radiated out into Spanish, Portuguese, and French maritime lexis.[48] It is worth noting, however, that there is some controversy surrounding the first attestation of *caracca* in an Italian vernacular text, *c*. 1300, and as the *Tesoro della Lingua Italiana* (*TLIO*) points out, it is probably what is known as a 'Redi fake'.[49]

The Italo-Arabic roots of the *caraque* are nonetheless clearly represented in its earliest Continental French attestation (*que les Sarazins apelent en lor lengage karaque*), *c*. 1245, in the writings of Phillip of Novara, a northern Italian knight and jurist who travelled extensively in the Holy Land.[50] Subsequent attestations of the ship name are found in Froissart's chronicle of the Hundred Years War (*c*. 1375) in which Genoese fleets and mercenaries played a key role.[51]

The name of this large Italian merchant ship takes longer to first appear in English records, but from the 1380s onwards, citations abound in British Medieval Latin, Anglo-French, and Middle English material.[52] As noted above, the historian Nicolini has carefully catalogued over 260 landings made in Southampton, London, and Sandwich by Genoese vessels. His sources are the (nearly all) unpublished Latin-matrix Exchequer Customs Accounts and sections of the King's Remembrancer, together with Foster's and Studer's editions of the Southampton Port Books. The first reference to a Genoese *carrake* appears in an account referring to a ship named the

---

47 See Hope, *Lexical Borrowing in the Romance Languages*, I, p. 33; Vidos, *Storia delle parole*, pp. 290–91; Tomasin, 'Sulla diffusione del lessico marinaresco italiano', p. 268.
48 The author notes that the phonetic change from Arabic *h*- to Spanish *c*- is rare but that this development is normal in Sicilian: Vidos, *Storia delle parole*, pp. 290–91.
49 This refers to the rather extraordinary tale of Francesco Redi (1626–1697), a renowned scholar, scientist, and lexicographer for the Accademia della Crusca, who simply invented hundreds of 'medieval' citations and source texts to go in his dictionary entries. His academic misconduct is detailed in Volpi, 'Le falsificazione di Francesco Redi'. Due to the unreliability of the dates, the *TLIO* entry sub **caracca** suggests that the word may not be a direct Arabism in Italian but an Arabism that first entered Italian via the intermediary of Portuguese. Tomasin ('Sulla diffusione del lessico marinaresco italiano', p. 268), however, remains convinced this maritime term is an *arabismo*.
50 See *TLFi* sub **caraque** / **carraque**, *DEAF* sub **caraque**, *FEW*, XIX, p. 66b: **harraqa**. Note that the second section of this Italianizing text, a well-known crusade chronicle known as the *Gestes des Chiprois*, has traditionally been attributed to Phillip, but it has now been suggested that another author drew on his writings and incorporated them extensively into his own: see Minervini, 'Les Gestes des Chiprois'.
51 See *DMF* sub **caraque**.
52 See *DMLBS* sub **carraca**, *MED* sub **carik(e)**, and *OED*2 sub **carrack**. The earliest attestation in an English-matrix text comes from Chaucer's Summoner's Tale (*c*. 1386): *Brodder than of a carryk is the sayl*.

Saynte Marie (patrons: Paulus Spynarde and Antonius Isnarde) which left Southampton docks on 20 April 1380.[53] As Nicolini points out, the switchover from smaller Genoese merchant vessels (recorded as *naves*) to the new term, *carrak*, is clearly mirrored over a decade or so in the Southampton records.[54] The number of times the two terms appear is summarized in Table 9.1.

Table 9.1. Frequency of the terms *naves* and *carrak* in Southampton sources (1371–1384) studied by Nicolini.

1371–1372	naves 3	carrake 0
1379–1380	naves 2	carrake 1
1380–1381	naves 2	carrake 4
1383–1384	naves 0	carrake 11

The carrack was not the sole preserve of the Genoese, however, and the Venetians (as well as Iberian merchants) embraced these capacious vessels; fifty years later, in the *View of the Hosts of Alien Merchants (1440–1444)*,[55] we find numerous references to carracks in relation to merchants from Venice:

> In a <u>carak</u> the patrone Jacome Rose xxxix case sope (accounts of Sir William Estfield, host to Leonardo and Giulio Contarini, merchants of Venice) (1441–1442)[56]

> Primerment rescu en j <u>carrake</u> veignantz a Hampton en le mois de Fevere vC xlviij buttys Malvesey (accounts of Thomas Walsingham, host to Federico Corner and Carlo Contarini, merchants of Venice) (1441–1442)[57]

Some final fifteenth-century English examples are found in a set of accounts recording the sale of English wool in Tuscany on behalf of Sir William Cantelowe and his business partners, the Salviati of Florence.[58] These refer to Genoese carracks transporting the shipments out of Southampton which were captained by Antonio Doria and Maurizio Cataneo:

---

53   TNA E122/138/2, m. 1. Customs Accounts, Southampton (Nicolini, 'Commercio marittimo genovese', p. 292).
54   Nicolini, 'Commercio marittimo genovese', p. 228.
55   This collection of accounts represents an intriguing and short-lived bureaucratic attempt by the Crown to register the business dealings of all alien merchants in England, with the wealthy Venetian community being the main target of the exercise. Extant records remain from London, Southampton, and Hull. See Bradley, *The Views of the Hosts* for an English translation edition. The author's transcription of the mixed-language (Latin, Anglo-French, and Middle English) text is available online: <https://sas-space.sas.ac.uk/102/>.
56   TNA E101/128/30 return 8.
57   TNA E101/128/31 return 8.
58   For a full historical and linguistic analysis of these accounts, see Tiddeman, *The Cantelowe Accounts*.

Firste, for the costys of iiij^c lxvi pokes wolle of my mayster, Wyllyam Cantelowe, comyd to the Porte Pysane in the <u>caryke</u> of Antonio de Aurea, patrone et marchaunt of Jene (1450)[59]

The whyche Ciiij pokes was schippyd at Hamptone in the monyth of aprelle 1451 upon a <u>caryk</u> of Jene, patrone Morys Catane [...] for to be delyvered by the grace of God at Porte Pysane to Frances et Johan Salviati (1451)[60]

AF patron: 'a ship's captain or master'.
(CF *patron*) < Gen. / It. *patrone* / *padrone* < Lat. *patronus* ('patron, benefactor')

Entre .j. carrake de Janne, <u>patron</u> Anree Spinol (Port Bks 42) (att. 1427–1430)[61]

Entré de .j. carrake donk est <u>patron</u> Piere Vent de Lime (Local Port Bk 10) (1435–1436)[62]

Allso Ressewed the xxviij day of marche of the <u>patron</u> of the gayle ffranses conteryn for the styves that he ocupyed in his gayle, v li. (Southampton Steward's Book) (1487–1488)[63]

Allso ressewed of the sayde <u>patron</u> for a single pulle and a pece y-called kavaldebowk, v s. (Southampton Steward's Book) (1487–1488)[64]

Patron appears in all three of our Southampton sources, with reference to Genoese and, in later examples, to Venetian vessels. Like *carrak*, it seems to be a Gallo-Italianism which was first attested in Continental French nearly a century before it appears in 'English' documents, be they written in Middle English, Anglo-French, or British Medieval Latin. Technically speaking, we are dealing with a semantic loan rather than a loanword, that is, the specific maritime use of the term in Italian brought about the borrowing of a new meaning for a word that already existed in the recipient language(s).[65]

As the *TLIO* entry notes, it is not always possible to distinguish between the two meanings of the word ('master' vs. 'captain' of the ship) in medieval citations: the nuance can either be towards commanding the ship once it leaves

---

59   AS Serie I: 339, fol. 41^r.
60   AS Serie I: 339, fol. 5^v.
61   See *AND*2 sub **patron**.
62   See *AND*2 sub **patron**.
63   Ruddock, 'The Method of Handling the Cargoes', p. 148. Note the author's footnote here: 'Galley, Francesco Contarini patron, from Venice: compare PRO, Exchequer K.R Customs Accounts (E122/142/10)'.
64   Ruddock, 'The Method of Handling the Cargoes', p. 148. As Ruddock notes, the noun *kavaldebowk* is unidentified. Is it linked to Anglo-French variant *kivil* (see *AND*2 sub **cheville**) meaning a peg, wedge, or fastening bolt? Or is it an Italianism, perhaps linked to *cavalletto* (see *TLIO* sub **cavalletto**) meaning trestle or beam?
65   The word *patron*, attested from the late twelfth century in Anglo-French and the early fourteenth century in Middle English, already had numerous meanings, including 'patron saint', 'protector', 'design for a building', 'founder of a religious order', and 'advisor, mentor': see *AND*2 sub **patron**, *MED* sub **patroun**, and *OED*3 sub **patron**.

port or ensuring the ship is sufficiently equipped before it leaves, often as its legal owner.[66] There is also considerable semantic overlap between *patron* and another maritime Italian borrowing found in Anglo-French noted above: *comyt* ('galley commander').

Patronus is first used to mean 'ship's captain / master' in the Latin of Genoa in 1246, with Italian vernacular attestations dating from the 1280s.[67] The earlier Latin text also contains vital evidence for the adoption of *patron* into Continental French nautical terminology that has been overlooked by the major French historical dictionaries.[68] The word's history is also strangely absent from Vidos's otherwise comprehensive study of maritime terminology but is detailed in Fennis's *Trésor du langage des galères*. The author confirms that the maritime use of *patron* probably radiated out initially from Genoa but later from Cyprus, Venice, and Marseille.[69] He draws our attention to the 1246 source which is in fact a bilingual French-Latin naval charter drawn up between the French Crown and Genoa. The relevant section of the French text is also known as the *Propositions des commissaires de Louis IX*:

> li *patron* des naves et tuit li maronnier (1246)[70]
>
> [...] pour le pris desseurdit, Thomas Rapairus de Genne une, pour le pris devantdit, et doit ester *patrons* de la nave (1246)[71]

In England, the earliest extant example of *patronis* is found in a Latin Close Roll from the royal Chancery. The document grants safe conduct to the Genoese sea captains Giovanni Doria and Niccolo Bianca (also the nephew of the king's advisor, Cardinal Niccolinus Fieschi) to sail two galleys to Berwick, apparently in an attempt to conduct a clandestine meeting with Edward III:[72]

---

66 See *TLIO* sub **padrone**.
67 See *TLIO* sub **padrone**. It is worth noting in extant records, *patrone* is the less common Italian variant with Tuscan / Central *padrone* and Venetian *paron* appearing much more frequently in the *OVI* corpus.
68 There are no medieval examples in the *TLFi* or *GDC* entries sub **patron**. The *FEW*'s entry sub **patronus** (VIII, p. 25a) contains very little information about the nautical use of the term, and there is no mention of the Italian forms *padrone / patrone* or the early link to Genoese lexis, noted above by Fennis. This could be because the loanword is not discussed in Vidos (*Storia delle parole*), a key *FEW* source for Italianisms. The dictionary does list a late fourteenth-century example of French *paron* as a borrowing from Venetian, but Fennis (*Trésor du langage des galères*, p. 1365) remarks that he has been unable to find this citation. The *DEAF* entry sub **patron** has recently added a reference to Fennis's comments.
69 Fennis, *Trésor du langage des galères*, pp. 1365–67. Note that his entry also collates numerous new citations of Continental French *patron* from the fourteenth to eighteenth centuries that are not currently listed elsewhere.
70 Fennis, *Trésor du langage des galères*, p. 1365.
71 Fennis, *Trésor du langage des galères*, p. 1365.
72 These events are linked to the controversial topic of the death of Edward II and the infamous 'Fieschi letter', written by a Genoese papal envoy, which claimed that the king was not murdered in Berkeley Castle in 1327. Some scholars now believe that he did indeed escape

> Johanni Dorye et Nicholao Blaunk, _patronis_ duarum galearum nostrarum, super vadiis et expensis suis ac sociorum suorum in eisdem galeis existencium super mare de mandato nostro eundo (Cl.160m.3) (1338)[73]

Forty-two years later, we find our earliest Anglo-French example of _patron_ appearing in the Parliament Rolls and referring to the same Genoese carrack mentioned above — the _Seinte Marie_ — which docked in Southampton in 1380.

> […] _patron_ d'une carice appellé le Seinte Marie (Rot Parl¹ iii 75) (1380)[74]

Later attestations from the _Views of the Hosts of Alien Merchants_ (currently not in dictionaries) show the word in use in Anglo-French matrix accounts, referring to the captains of Venetian galleys (as we find above in the Southampton Steward Books):

> John Pattesley nadgaires mair de la citte de Loundres pur estre host a Jacomo Corner marchaunt & _patrone_ dune galey de Venise (John Welles, host to Giacomo Corner, merchant and patron of a Venetian galley and named crew) (1441–1442)[75]

In Middle English, our first citation is found in a literary source but clearly referring to a fleet of Genoese carracks:

> The erle of huntyngdon, with othir lordis..foughten with ix Carrikkis of Gene.. and..thei toke iiij grete carrikkis and her _patronys_ (Brut Corpus Cambr. 307) (c. 1400)[76]

What seems abundantly clear from all these examples from late medieval England is that _patron_ (and _carrak_ for that matter) was a technical term firmly linked to northern Italy and Italians, regardless of whether its transmission route into any one particular source involved the intermediary of Continental French or not. Indeed, its maritime use in English would remain associated with Italy specifically until the 1600s and the wider Mediterranean until the 1700s.[77]

---

and flee to Europe, meeting his son, Edward III, under the pseudonym of _William le Galeys_ ('William the Welshman') in Koblenz, on the Rhine, in 1338. The Genoese sea captains mentioned above are thought to have been contracted (and handsomely paid) by Edward III to transport his father from the Nice / Marseilles region to Cologne from where he went on to Koblenz: see Mortimer, _Medieval Intrigue_, pp. 202–05.

73 See _DMLBS_ sub **patronus**.
74 This citation is found in the _AND_2 entry sub **carrack**.
75 TNA E101/128/30 return 1.
76 See _OED_3 sub **patron**, _MED_ sub **patroun**.
77 See _OED_3 sub **patron**. For example: _These particulars,.come from Naples, brought thither by the Patron of a Felucca_ (London Gaz. No. 1066/3) (1676) / _Patron, in Navigation, a Name given in the Mediteranean, to the Person who commands the Vessel and Seamen; sometimes to the Person who steers it_ (E. Chambers, Cycl.) (1728). As the _OED_3 entry states, _patron_ remains in North American English to refer to a barge captain.

Rarer Loanwords

The next three mercantile examples are found in both Southampton Port Books, with a small number of citations also appearing in other Anglo-French, Middle English, or British Medieval Latin material. They are also all very rare in the Continental French record. In each case, the relevant Port Book sections record the cargo of incoming vessels from Venice,[78] and the additional source texts also offer clues as to the likelihood of borrowing from Italian. *Balet* and *cassel* have not been examined as potential Italianisms before. *Sport(in)* has been discussed as an instance of Anglo-Italian language contact by Trotter,[79] with new evidence in another set of accounts emerging since his article's publication.

AF balet: 'a small bale of merchandise (usually fabric, wool, or dyestuffs), wrapped up for sale and shipping'.
< It. *balletta* < *balla* < Lat. **bal(l)-* / **pall-* ('a round-shaped form')

> *vij balet, j fardelet de cere* (Port Bks 77) (1427–1430)[80]
>
> *j balet de wod* (Port Bks 31) (1427–1430)[81]
>
> *iiij. balet de paper negre, contenu xl remes* (Port Bks 78) (1427–1430)[82]
>
> *iii balet de garbelure de peper* (Local Port Bk 94) (1435–1436)[83]

The diminutive of the mercantile 'bale' seems widespread in medieval Italian: it is first attested *c.* 1277 in Tuscan before moving into Venetian in the fifteenth century where it continues to occur until the 1700s.[84] Italian merchants also used an augmentative term, *ballone*, to describe a large bale of goods.[85]

In England, based on the extant evidence, we can make a strong argument for an Italian influence on the brief appearance of Anglo-French *balet* in

---

78 Foster, *The Local Port Book*, pp. 82, 94. Page 94 of the accounts also contains two references to bales of *marmatik*, unique in the English and French record. As Foster (p. 95) footnotes, this is 'probably some kind of spice or herb', and given the source text, the name could well be an Italianism. However, I have been unable to track down a suitable Italian etymon to propose for the merchandise in question.
79 Trotter, 'Death, Taxes and Property', pp. 163–64.
80 See *AND*2 sub **balet**.
81 See *AND*2 sub **balet**.
82 This example is found in the *AND*2 entry sub **niger**.
83 This example is found under the *AND* entry sub **garbelure**. Further examples of *balet* from the Southampton Port Books can be found in *AND* entries sub **grain¹**, **ploume**, and **ailespatik**.
84 See *LEI* sub **bal(l)-** which gives the following examples: *ballette* (*e tele*) (1289, prat.), *ballette* (*di panni*) (1385, pis.), *ballette* (*d'aloe*) (1391), *ballete* (1419, venez.), *balletta* (1569, lucch.) *balette* (1760–1761, venez.). See also *TLIO* sub **balletta**, *OVI* sub **balette**, *AD* sub **ballette**, and *DEI* sub **balletta**.
85 Cf. Edler, *Glossary of Mediaeval Terms of Business*, p. 39.

the 1400s. It appears in the Port Books in reference to typical Genoese and Venetian imports such as the dyestuffs grain and woad, paper, spices, and dried fruit. The earliest Latin-matrix example is also from a fifteenth-century Southampton Port Book and refers to cloth, but it is difficult to pinpoint if the borrowing is an Anglo-Normanism or a 'direct' Italianism in this case.

> pro. iij *balett'* panni continentibus xxj pannos (Port Bk. Southampt. 84) (1440)[86]

We also find a slightly earlier insular French example of *balet* from the accounts of the Worshipful Company of Grocers. It is worth noting the close links that this London company maintained with Italian merchants[87] and the presence of other commercial Italian loanwords in both their Anglo-French and Middle English accounts which I have examined elsewhere:[88]

> Ressu in Gayn de .xvij. *balettes* curances (Grocers 218) (1432)[89]

Dictionaries offer only one late Middle English–matrix example of *balet*. The loanword appears once again twenty-one years later in the documentation of the Grocers and records the purchase of grain and woad:

> Greynes, 1 *balet*, ye C xijd ... Woode, y^e *balett* ijd. (Some Acct. Worshipful Company of Grocers, 421) (1453)[90]

It seems less likely that *balet* is borrowed from Continental French. *Ballette* is (perhaps surprisingly) very rare in the record, with just a single citation in dictionaries from the mid-1300s. This refers to small imported bales of the dyestuff madder and the dye-fixer alum (the European market for which was dominated by the Genoese, as we noted above).[91] The *Französisches etymologisches Wörterbuch* (FEW) suggests an Occitan etymon in this case, but there is no reason why Italian trade lexis could not be an equally viable option.

AF cassel: 'a chest or coffer, used to transport merchandise'.

---

[86] See *DMLBS* sub **baletta**. The other two citations in the entry are from 1443 and 1461 and also refer to ship cargoes.

[87] One of the Grocers' founding members in 1348 was the Lucchese Vivian Roger. The company was also partly managed from 1428 by Italians who trained their English apprentices: see Bradley, *The Views of the Hosts*, p. xxi; Nightingale, *A Medieval Mercantile Community*, pp. 182, 185.

[88] Examples include *belendin* ('high-quality Indian ginger'), *celestrin* ('of fabric: sky-blue colour'), *cot* ('of sugar — number of refinements through boiling'), *garbeler*, ('to sift the refuse from spices'), *net* ('remaining weight or money after deductions'), and *tare* ('weight of packaging deducted from gross'): see Tiddeman, 'Lexical Exchange with Italian', pp. 120, 124; Tiddeman, 'More Sugar and Spice', pp. 390–91, 394–400, 402–05.

[89] See *AND*2 sub **balet**.

[90] See *OED*2 sub **ballet(te)** and *MED* sub **balet**. There is one further citation from 1540, and then the term became obsolete.

[91] See *DMF* sub **ballette** and *FEW*, xv.1, p. 42a: *balla¹.

< Ven. / It. *cassella* < Lat. *capsella* ('small chest')

> j *cassel* de suchre cassen (Port Bks 110) (1427–1430)[92]
>
> j. *cassel* de gynzibre (Local Port Bk 82) (1435–1436)[93]
>
> j. *cassel* de triacle cont. .clxxiiii. boistes (Local Port Bk 94) (1435–1436)[94]

I believe that this is another rare mercantile Italianism in the Anglo-French Southampton Port Books, recording the import of coffers of sugar, ginger, and treacle.[95] This argument is strengthened by the only other record of the term in an insular French text — the Gloucester Inventory of 1397. This text contains a list of goods seized from the Duke of Gloucester, following his imprisonment by Richard II, and includes other loanwords to designate high-end satins, silks and velvets supplied to the English nobility by the Tuscans and Venetians.[96]

> un enter vestment de velvet rouge [...] ové .j. tuaille, .j. chesible, .ij. tunicles, .ij. *casels* [...] (Gloucester Inventory 296) (1397)[97]

Furthermore, we can pin down *cassel* as a Venetian loanword, as is confirmed by the *Lessico etimologico italiano* (*LEI*) and the large number of Venetian attestations in the *TLIO* corpus from c. 1275 onwards.[98]

Apart from our Anglo-French examples — to which the *Dictionnaire du Moyen Français* (*DMF*) refers its readers[99] — evidence of the lexeme in medieval French is very thin on the ground. There are three thirteenth-century literary citations of the Old French plural *cassiau*, meaning 'chests' or 'coffers', found in Godefroy.[100] I cannot find any other clear record of this medieval form in the major French dictionaries; the *FEW* has two undated examples of *cassiau*, one in its 'Unknown' section and one (meaning 'baptismal font') under the Greek etymon *cyathion* ('bowl').[101]

There is a single attestation of *cassellam* in British Medieval Latin — attested c. 1170 and glossed as 'little receptacle, basin'.[102] It seems reasonable to assume that this is not linked to Venetian *cassella* and is a 'homegrown'

---

92 See *AND*2 sub **cassen**.
93 See *AND*2 sub **cassel**.
94 See *AND*2 sub **cassel**.
95 Note that medieval treacle was a medicinal salve containing many ingredients, not the sugar syrup we know today; cf. *OED*2 sub **treacle**.
96 See, for example, the silk types *attaby* and *taffata*: Tiddeman, 'Lexical Exchange with Italian', pp. 123, 127.
97 See *AND*2 sub **cassel**.
98 See *LEI* sub **capsella**, *TLIO* sub **cassella**, *OVI* sub **cassell / e, chaxella / e, chasela, casela**.
99 See *DMF* sub **cassel**.
100 See GDF sub **cassel**.
101 See *FEW*, XXII.2, p. 32a: 'Inconnus'; *FEW*, II.2, p. 1610a: **cyathion.**
102 See *DMLBS* sub **cassella**.

Latin variant, independent of the Italianized, commercial-based usage found in the Southampton Port Books and Gloucester Inventory.

Middle English evidence is more problematic, and interestingly, the only potential record we have of *cassel* is in a culinary context. We find the plural form *casselys* in a recipe for stuffed capon from 1381:

> For to make capons in <u>casselys</u>. Nym caponys..opyn the skyn at the hevyd and blowe hem tyl the skyn ryse from the flesshe […] (Pegge Cook.Recipes (Dc 257), p. 99) (1381)[103]

The *MED* glosses the term as 'a casing' and derives it from Old French (but gives no etymon). The most modern edition of *Curye on Inglysch* (where we find the citation) simply states that '*in casselys* may mean enclosed' and does not discuss the origins of the word.[104] There appears to be no equivalent term in the medieval French cooking repertoire (or indeed in the Italian one), but it does seem likely that we are dealing with a Gallicism here. It is not clear whether the term represents a borrowing of Continental or Anglo-French *cassel* but I believe the case is still strong for arguing for direct Italian influence in the Southampton and Gloucester sources.

AF sport(in): 'a (small) basket used to transport dry goods, such as raisins, almonds, and sugar'.
< It. *sporta* / *sportino* < Lat. *spŏrta* ('basket')

> *vij <u>sport</u> de resins* (Port Bks 43) (1427–1430)[105]
>
> *i <u>sport</u> de suchre pot, val. xxs.* (Local Port Bk 66) (1435–1436)[106]
>
> *iiij <u>sport</u> ij <u>sportin</u> de almand* (Port Bks 49) (1427–1430)[107]
>
> *viii <u>sportin</u> de resin* (Local Port Bk 108) (1435–1436)[108]

Sport and its diminutive, *sportın*, are two of a handful of Italian loanwords that have already been identified in Southampton material by Foster and

---

103 See *MED* sub **cassel** (there is no *OED* entry). The second *MED* citation appears much later in a cookbook from *c.* 1475 where the recipe name is *Capon in cassolont*. A third example of the dish name, not given in the *MED*, can be found in another cookbook from *c.* 1430: *Capone in Cassolyce* (see Morris, *Liber cure cocorum*, p. 62). The origins of these terms are more opaque, but they could perhaps be linked to *cassole* ('cooking utensil, pan' — see *DEAF* / *DMF* / *GDF* sub **cassole**) or its diminutive, *cassolette* (see *TLFi* / *DMF* / *GDC* sub **cassolette**).
104 Hieatt and Butler, *Curye on Inglysch*, p. 176. The authors also note that this clever method of 'turning the capon into two' could be Arabic in origin.
105 See *AND*1 sub **sport**.
106 See *AND*1 sub **sport**.
107 See *AND*1 sub **sportin**.
108 See *AND*1 sub **sportin**.

Trotter.[109] However, further evidence of the lexeme's use can also be found in contemporary Latin customs accounts from the port of Sandwich (near Dover on the south coast), recorded in 1439–1440. In all cases, these containers appear on the cargo lists of Italian vessels and are used to transport dried fruits, nuts, and sugar:

> *De Nicholao de Pero, alienigena, pro II sportis de reyseinis, precio III s. IIII d.* (1439–1440)[110]

> *De Petro Baptisto Gryllo, alienigena, mercatore de Ianua, pro V sportis cum reyseinis, precio in toto XIII s.* (1439–1440)[111]

Looking through the corpora of the *OVI* and the Datini Archives, we can find countless examples of *sporta* from 1318 onwards, as well as its derivative, *sportello / sportella*, of which there are over one hundred attestations.[112] Surprisingly, there are no medieval Italian citations of the diminutive, *sportino*, from which the borrowing *sportin* must surely have derived. However, the name of a Florentine fruited bread known as the *sportina di Pasqua*, although not recorded until the nineteenth century, may hint at the earlier existence of the term.[113] In addition, as Trotter mentions, *isportinu* has been recorded in medieval Sardinian.[114]

Sporte and *esporte* also occur in the Continental French record, albeit rarely. The lexeme was first transmitted in the second half of the thirteenth century via the Italianizing texts *Les estoires de Venise* and *Le Livre de Marco Polo*. As the *FEW* notes, Occitan variations such as *esporta* may also have influenced later continental forms from the fifteenth century.[115]

Hapaxes in the Southampton Stewards' Books

This final section discusses four new maritime loanwords (*arigon, barkeroll, maregon, styves*) firmly linked to Venetian and Genoese technical terminology, which are currently unattested in the Middle English lexicographical record.[116]

---

109 Foster, *The Local Port Book*, p. xiv; Trotter, 'Death, Taxes and Property', p. 163.
110 TNA, E122/127/18, fol. 19ʳ, Customs Accounts, Sandwich, in Nicolini, 'Navi liguri in Inghilterra', p. 131.
111 TNA, E122/127/18, fol. 21ʳ, Customs Accounts, Sandwich, in Nicolini, 'Navi liguri in Inghilterra', p. 136.
112 See *OVI* sub **sporta**, **sportello / a** and *AD* sub **sporta**.
113 *DEI* sub **sporta**.
114 Trotter, 'Death, Taxes and Property', p. 164.
115 See *FEW*, XII, p. 213a: **sporta**.
116 The loanwords have been termed hapaxes because they only appear in this source, not because they only appear in one citation. In fact, *arigon* is attested four times, *barkeroll*, six, *maregon*, twenty-six, and *styves*, nine. There are other words in the accounts that Ruddock suggests represent Italianisms, but these seem to be, in fact, established Anglo-French vocabulary, e.g. *trave* ('beam'), see *AND*1 **travure**, *OED*3 sub **trave**; *trest* ('trestle'), see *AND*1 sub **trestre**, *OED*2 sub **trest²**, *MED* sub **trest(e)**.

They provide compelling evidence of language contact 'on the ground' in a medieval port, with English locals and alien crew collaborating on joint construction projects. The subtleties of daily language use within this speech community remain a mystery, but we can be sure that port towns and shipyards were real melting pots of maritime lexis — in this respect Southampton can be seen as a miniature *Clos des Galées*. Remnants of evidence such as the borrowings below offer proof of a technical term exchange that was almost certainly reciprocal on the ground.[117]

ME arigon: 'capstan or windlass; a horizontal wooden cylinder turned by detachable levers, used to hoist heavy weights'.
< It. *àrgano* / Ven. *àrgana* < Lat. **arganum* < Lat. *órganum* < Greek *órganon* ('tool, instrument')

> *Item payd the xvj day of Nouvembre to John Shyssh of Hyth for a elme to make a <u>arygon</u> and for the ffellyng costs and cariage to the watersyde, iiij s j d.* (1493–1494)[118]

> *Item payd the xxiiii day of Novembre to John Smale of Fally for ij elms of the on was made an <u>Arigon</u> & a Tester of the other was made an <u>arygon</u>, ix s.* (1493–1494)[119]

> *Item payd the xxiiij day of Januare to Richard Ffolewer for a pece of tymber that the Capetyn galye hadde to make an <u>Arygon</u>, iiij s.* (1493–1494)[120]

The use of these capstans is documented in Southampton sources between c. 1481 and 1522, according to the accounts' editor.[121] Some decades earlier, in his diary from 1429–1430, the state galley captain Luca di Maso degli Albizzi also regularly refers to the *argani* used at Southampton docks to unload cargo.[122]

In the *TLIO* and *OVI* corpus, the earliest attestation of *argano* is in the Florentine prose of Francesco da Barberino in 1314, followed by a Latin-matrix document from Sicily in 1348 where its use on a ship is clearly stated.[123] *Argano* as the nautical 'capstan' or more generic 'winch' or 'hoist' remains in modern Italian terminology today whereas *argana* was still recorded in dictionaries of the Venetian dialect in the nineteenth century.[124]

---

117 For discussions of Anglo-French and Middle English borrowings in the writings of Italians who lived and worked in England, see Cella, 'Anglismi e francesismi'; Trotter, 'Italian Merchants in London and Paris'; Tiddeman, 'Mercantile Multilingualism'; Tiddeman, 'Early Anglo-Italian Contact'; Tiddeman, 'Lexical Exchange with Italian'.
118 Ruddock, 'The Method of Handling the Cargoes', p. 143.
119 Ruddock, 'The Method of Handling the Cargoes', p. 143.
120 Ruddock, 'The Method of Handling the Cargoes', p. 144.
121 Ruddock, 'The Method of Handling the Cargoes', p. 140. See also Ruddock, *Italian Merchants*, pp. 152–53.
122 E.g. Mallett, *The Florentine Galleys*, p. 256.
123 *TLIO* sub **àrgano**, *OVI* sub **argana, argani**.
124 *DDV* sub **argana**.

Note that there are examples of *argan* / *arganne* in Continental French texts as early as 1279, but crucially, they were in written in Naples.¹²⁵ The borrowing did not reappear until 1526 (as *argue*), and it seems that Occitan played at least a partial role in its transmission into French, alongside Italian.¹²⁶

Finally, it is worth pointing out that before the adoption of its Italianized equivalent, *arigon*, the earlier Steward's Book uses the Middle English word, *captystayn*.¹²⁷

> Item Resseved off the sayd patron for the head of a trave and a <u>captystayn</u> that he broke (1487–1488)¹²⁸

Traditionally, it is assumed that technical loanwords are borrowed into a lexicon to 'plug' a semantic gap and express a new concept. It is interesting to consider why the steward switched to the alien term when he had a native one at his disposal — perhaps an *arigon* was built slightly differently to a *capstan* and he used the Italianized term to refer to this newer model?

ME barkeroll: 'boatman in charge of small merchant vessels, at sea and on rivers'.

< Ven. *barcharol* < It. *barca* < Lat. *barca* / **barica* ('small sailing vessel')

> Item then payd to a <u>barkroll</u> for fecchyng home of the same tymber, ij s. (1493–1494)¹²⁹

> Item then payd to ij <u>bark rollys</u> to feche asshis from Botteley their labor and exspences, v s. (1493–1494)¹³⁰

> Item then payd to a <u>barkeroll</u> to feche the seid asshis at Reedbregge, xvj d. (1493–1494)¹³¹

> Item then payd to the <u>barkeroll</u> of the galy Valier for fechyng of ashys at Boteleigh that was left behind, ii s. (1493–1494)¹³²

Barkeroll is an unequivocally Venetian borrowing found in the stewards' accounts. Ruddock footnotes *barkeroll* correctly as 'the man in charge of a small boat' but does not suggest an etymon.¹³³ In her edition, Thick glosses

---

125 Fennis, *Trésor du langage des galères*, p. 246.
126 Fennis, *Trésor du langage des galères*, p. 251. See also *TLFi* sub **argue**, *FEW*, VII, p. 409a **organum**.
127 See *OED*2 sub **capstan**, *MED* sub **capstan**.
128 Ruddock, 'The Method of Handling the Cargoes', p. 148.
129 Ruddock, 'The Method of Handling the Cargoes', p. 143.
130 Ruddock, 'The Method of Handling the Cargoes', p. 143.
131 Ruddock, 'The Method of Handling the Cargoes', p. 144.
132 Ruddock, 'The Method of Handling the Cargoes', p. 144. The editor notes that the galley is named after its patron, Battista Falier.
133 Ruddock, 'The Method of Handling the Cargoes', p. 142.

the loanword as 'bark, a small sailing vessel (Italian, *barca*)'.[134] Whilst the word is, of course, ultimately linked to *barca*, *barkeroll* is surely an adaption of *barcharol*, attested in Venice from 1312–1314 onwards.[135]

The Anglicized forms found in the Southampton accounts are by far the earliest attestations in a British text and are clearly pragmatic, technical terms. By the time the early modern Italian form, *barcaruolo*, appeared as an unmodified loanword again in 1611, it had already acquired more fanciful and exotic connotations — with the folkloric hero of the gondolier.

> *The Barcaruolo appetite His Gondola directed right Vnto a female Elfe* (T. Coryate Crudities sig. c4) (1611)[136]

Well over a century later, *barcarolle* was transmitted into French (1760s)[137] and English (1770s)[138] as a musical term meaning 'gondolier's song', entering a new semantic field but retaining its very Venetian roots.

ME maregon: 'a galley carpenter'.
< Ven. *marangóne* < It. *margone* / *mergone* ('cormorant') < *mergo* ('seabird')
< Lat. *mergus* < *mergere* ('to plunge / immerse')

> *The Maregones. Here folew^t the payementes of the galys carpenters and their men fo rmakyng of the Styvis* (1493–1494)[139]

> *In primis payd the xxiiij day of Nouembre to the maregon of the galy Capetyn and then for viij days werkmanship aboute the same Styves, v s. iiij d.* (1493–1494)[140]

> *Galy falier. Item payd the same marygon the xxvj day of Januar for vj days, iiij s.* (1493–1494)[141]

> *Item payd to the seid marigon fo rij skruys, ij s.* (1493–1494)[142]

This is by far the most prolific of the four new Italianisms in the Stewards' Books, with twenty-six attestations, and again, it has strong Venetian connections. The medieval lexeme *marangóne* had two meanings: 'cormorant' (a diving seabird) and 'ship's carpenter', with the former sense being transferred to refer figuratively to a profession which involved carrying out repairs underwater.[143] In addition, the oldest surviving bell in the famous San Marco tower in Venice

---

134   Thick, 'The Fifteenth-Century Stewards' Books', p. liii.
135   *OVI* sub **barcharol**. The Tuscan equivalent, *barcaiuolo*, is much more widely attested in the *TLIO* / *OVI* corpora from *c*. 1322 onwards; see *TLIO* sub **barcaiuolo**.
136   *OED*2 sub **barcarole** / **barcarolle**.
137   *TLFi* sub **barcarolle**.
138   *OED*2 sub **barcarole** / **barcarolle**.
139   Ruddock, 'The Method of Handling the Cargoes', p. 145.
140   Ruddock, 'The Method of Handling the Cargoes', p. 145.
141   Ruddock, 'The Method of Handling the Cargoes', p. 147.
142   Ruddock, 'The Method of Handling the Cargoes', p. 147.
143   *VTO* sub **marangóne²**.

has been nicknamed *la Marangona* since the Middle Ages, traditionally ringing twice a day to signal the start and end of work in the dockyard.[144]

The earliest citation of *marangonus* ('carpenter') appears in the Latin of Venice in 1271,[145] with the surnames *Mara[n]ghini* and *Marangone* appearing in Lucchese and Venetian sources from 1279–1302 and *c*. 1318, respectively.[146] A source not yet added to Italian dictionary corpora is the Villani company account fragment from London; here the ship's carpenter is mentioned alongside the *calafato* (or caulker) in an entry recording the export of Essex cloths from the English capital to Sicily, *c*. 1422:

> *Panni di Sex peze Cxvj mandatii a Palermo a messer Giovani Abattegli, cioè peze C leghatti in ij balle e charichi in su la ghallea gradinigha ne hostazio del <u>Maranghone</u> e Chalaffado [...] e peze xvii [sic] messi ne lo scrignio del chomitto de la detta ghallea* (Villani frammento) (*c*. 1422)[147]

Marengon is currently attested in only one medieval Continental French source. This is the 1441 treatise of Emmanuele Pioloti, addressed to the pope and detailing the religious and economic case for a crusade in Alexandria, which was translated from an original version composed in the Italian vernacular.[148]

The mention of the *maregons* and their payment in the Southampton Stewards' Books is an extremely rare example of the term's use outside Italy or, indeed in a non-Venetian writer's work. Its presence, however, is by no means surprising, especially when we consider the fact that the skilled galley carpenters were paid a higher daily rate than the local craftsman. It therefore made sense for the author to differentiate between the two groups of workers in his accounts.[149]

ME styves: 'specially constructed wooden derricks for unloading a ship's cargo'. < It. *stiva* < Gen. *stivare* ('to stow') < Lat. *stipare* ('to cram / pack')

> <u>Styves</u> *of the gales: Allso Resseved the xxviij day of marche of the patron of the gayle ffranses conteryn for the <u>styves</u> that he ocupyed in his gayle, v li.* (1487–1488)[150]

> *Item then payd the mason in Seynt Micaelles parish for pece tymber for the <u>styves</u>, xij d.* (1493–1494)[151]

---

144 *DEI* sub **marangona**, *DDV* sub **marangona**, *TLIO* sub **marangona**.
145 *DEI* sub **marangone²**.
146 *OVI* sub **Mara[n]ghini**, **Marangon**.
147 Guidi Bruscoli, 'Un frammento inedito', p. 397.
148 Cf. Fennis, *Trésor du langage des galères*, p. 108.
149 Cf. Ruddock, 'The Method of Handling the Cargoes', p. 142.
150 Ruddock, 'The Method of Handling the Cargoes', p. 148.
151 Ruddock, 'The Method of Handling the Cargoes', p. 144.

Item payd the xij day of Septembre to ij Carpenters for on day hewyng tymber at Reedbregge for the seid <u>styvis</u>, xij d. (1493–1494)[152]

Expenses and payementes of bying of tymbre and stuffes for the Galy <u>styvys</u> w^t Cariage Werkmenship and Wages of laborers as folew^t (1493–1494)[153]

Our last case study from Southampton concerns the borrowed term *styves*, used to describe the specialist equipment built on the dockside alongside visiting vessels. It is of ultimate Genoese origin, and apparently unique to the medieval English record.

According to the *Dizionario etimologico italiano* (*DEI*), the verb *stivare* ('to stow') was attested in Genoa in 1268.[154] A list of Tuscan shipping fees from 1396 offers two derivations — the nouns *stiva* ('stowing of cargo') and *stivatori* (the workers who loaded and unloaded the cargo).[155] We also find several examples of *stiva* in the Albizzi ship's log (introduced above) which describes the loading of wool at Southampton in 1430. This source is not currently found in Italian historical dictionary corpora:

Mercoledì adì 18 fu il primo dì si conta alla <u>stiva</u>, passati i x dalla nostra giunta, per lo manifesto e mettere a punto gli argani. Il dì si stivò la lana ch'esra asciutta in galee […] (Albizzi diary) (1430)[156]

The word *estive* ('cargo') does not appear until 1539 in Continental French in the ship's inventory of the *Sainte Claire*; Fennis accepts a probably Italian ultimate etymon but is also convinced that Occitan acted as an intermediary for the transmission of the loanword.[157] The relevant *FEW* entry also contains the fourteenth-century examples *estiva / stiva* from 'ancien vaudois', that is, the language of the Piemonte region of northern Italy which borders the Occitan valleys.[158]

Given the circumstances surrounding the compilation of the Southampton steward's accounts and the absence of an equivalent term in medieval French (either insular or continental), it seems certain that our *styves* are Italian in origin, albeit via an interesting process of semantic development from '(un)loading of cargo' to the 'equipment to (un)load cargo'. The verb 'to steeve' ('to stow cargo') would be reborrowed into English from French in the 1660s, before shifting again to mean 'derrick used to stow cargo' in the nineteenth century.[159]

---

152 Ruddock, 'The Method of Handling the Cargoes', p. 142.
153 Ruddock, 'The Method of Handling the Cargoes', p. 142.
154 *DEI* sub **stivare**. See also Vidos, *Storia delle parole*, p. 386.
155 *AD* sub **stiva, stivatori**.
156 Mallett, *The Florentine Galleys*, p. 278.
157 Fennis, *Trésor du langage des galères*, p. 866.
158 *FEW* (XII, p. 270ab: **stipare**). See also *TLFi* sub **estiver**.
159 See *OED2* sub **steeve²** (verb) and **steeve²** (noun). Note that the lone medieval verb *stive*, attested c. 1330 in the poem *Sir Tristem*, is puzzling but seemingly unconnected to the forms described above. See *MED* sub **stiven³**, where it is glossed as '?To install (sb. somewhere),

Conclusion

Traditional accounts of Anglo-Italian language contact focus either on the impact of the *Tre Corone* on the most famed works of late medieval English literature, or elite England's fashionable obsession with Renaissance culture in the sixteenth century. Borrowings found in the Southampton *libri alienigeni* highlight the linguistic effects of a much more pragmatic sphere of influence of Italian achievement — trade and shipping — which flourished throughout the 1400s.

The case studies above have been chosen to demonstrate the varying degrees of proximity to Italian etyma which can occur and the inherent difficulties in trying to untangle possible influences from several Romance languages, as well as from Latin.[160] Key examples have been discussed from both Anglo-French- and Middle English–matrix texts but all were written in England. Both very frequent and very rare vocabulary can prove problematic, with the former being so ubiquitous in international trading documents that it becomes impossible to track its origins,[161] and with the latter often being written off as 'scribal error'.[162] Overall, however, it is hoped that, when taken together, these loanword examples will demonstrate the sustained and varied influence northern Italian lexis exerted on the professional language of fifteenth-century Southampton.

The Stewards' Books are an exciting find for historical linguists and offer a very tangible example of language contact in action. Sadly, we can only speculate as to how locals and foreigners communicated in real life, but we can be confident that they succeeded in cooperating on an everyday basis to everyone's mutual benefit. The crew members themselves would not all have been Venetian, or even from the Italian peninsula, but most likely a mixed-nationality group used to employing some form of *lingua franca*.[163] Yet practical situations such as these, involving shared and complex tasks, must

---

place, put' and listed as of uncertain but possibly French origin. The *OED* sub **stive²** derives the word from 'Old French *estiver*', but this is mistaken: as we have seen, this verb (itself borrowed from Italian / Occitan) was not attested in French until 1539.

160 See Durkin's comments on this issue (*Borrowed Words*, p. 370) and on *mizzen* in particular (a potential Italianism but not one found in Southampton sources): 'In some cases, such as the nautical term *mizzen* (1416), the mode of transmission is entirely unclear, and there is little to rule out transmission directly from Italian, although also nothing to rule out transmission via any of several other languages [i.e. Anglo-French, Continental French, Occitan, Catalan, Spanish, or Portuguese]'.

161 Cf. the editors' comments on 'international loanwords' in Schendl and Wright, *Code-Switching in Early English*, p. 31.

162 See Bradley's comment (*The Views of the Hosts*, p. liv) on the hapax *ceta* (< *seta*, 'silk') which is found only in the Anglo-French hosting accounts of a Southampton merchant, John Bethan, recording the imports of the Florentine trader Benedetto Borromei.

163 See Kowaleski's work on language use in international maritime communities: for example, '"Alien" Encounters in the Maritime World' and 'The French of England'.

surely have facilitated the transfer of technical lexis, and this is shown by the presence of four new loanwords (two of which are distinctly Venetian) in the accounts. The evidence contained in the Stewards' Books is therefore of great lexicographical value and underscores the need to include more non-literary texts in dictionaries to attain a better view of late medieval multilingualism and of Anglo-Italian contact, in particular.

Works Cited

Abbreviations

Languages

AF = Anglo-French
CF = Continental French
Gen. = Genoese
It. = Italian
Lat. = Latin
ME = Middle English
Ven. = Venetian

Dictionaries

AND1 / AND2 = *Anglo-Norman Dictionary*, 1st / 2nd edn, <https://www.anglo-norman.net>
DDV = Boerio, Giuseppe, *Dizionario del dialetto veneziano* (Venice: Santini, 1829)
DEAF = *Dictionnaire étymologique de l'ancien français*, <http://www.deaf-page.de>
DEI = Battisti, Carlo, and Giovanni Alessio, *Dizionario etimologico italiano* (Florence: Barbèra, 1950–1957)
DMF = *Dictionnaire du Moyen Français*, <http://www.atilf.fr/dmf>
DMLBS = *Dictionary of Medieval Latin from British Sources*, ed. by Ronald Edward Latham and others (Oxford: British Academy, 1975–2013)
FEW = *Französisches etymologisches Wörterbuch: Eine Darstellung des galloromanischen Sprachsatzes*, ed. by Walther von Wartburg and others (Bonn: Zbinden, 1922–)
GDF / GDC = *Dictionnaire de l'ancienne langue française et de tous ses dialectes du IXe au XVe siècle*, ed. by Frédéric Godefroy (Paris: Vieweg, 1881–1902), *première partie* (GDF), vols I–VII / *Godefroy Complément* (GDC), vols VIII–X
LEI = *Lessico etimologico italiano*, ed. by Max Pfister, Wolfgang Schweickard, and Elton Prifti (Wiesbaden: Reichert Verlag, 1979–)
MED = *Middle English Dictionary*, <https://quod.lib.umich.edu/m/middle-english-dictionary/dictionary>
OED2 / OED3 = *Oxford English Dictionary*, 2nd / 3rd edn, <https://www.oed.com>

TLFi = *Trésor de la Langue Française informatisé*, <http://atilf.atilf.fr/tlf.htm>
TLIO = *Tesoro della Lingua Italiana delle Origini*, <http://tlio.ovi.cnr.it/TLIO/>
VTO = *Vocabolario Trecanni*, <https://www.treccani.it/vocabolario/>

Online lexical databases

AD = *Archivio Datini: corpus lemmatizzato del carteggio Datini*, <https://aspweb.ovi.cnr.it/>
OVI = *Opera del Vocabolario Italiano: Corpus OVI dell'Italiano antico*, <http://gattoweb.ovi.cnr.it>

Archives

AS = Archivio Salviati, Scuola Normale Superiore, Pisa, Italy
TNA = The National Archives, Kew, United Kingdom

Secondary Studies

Bell, Adrian R., Chris Brooks, and Tony K. Moore, *Accounts of the English Crown with the Italian Merchant Societies, 1272–1345* (London: List and Index Society, 2009)

Bolton, James, *The Medieval English Economy, 1150–1500* (London: Dent, 1980)

Bradley, Helen, 'Southampton's Trading Partners: London', in *English Inland Trade, 1430–1540: Southampton and its Region*, ed. by Michael Hicks (Oxford: Oxbow, 2015), pp. 65–80

———, *The Views of the Hosts of Alien Merchants, 1440–1444* (London: Boydell, 2012)

Cappelletti, Luigi Alessandro, 'Un testo in volgare italo-romanzo in un rotolo della zecca di Canterbury (1291–1294)', *Studi linguistici italiani*, 46 (3rd Ser., 25.2) (2020), 163–200

Cella, Roberta, 'Anglismi e francesismi nel registro della filiale di Londra di una compagnia mercantile senese (1305–1308)', in *Identità e diversità nella lingua e nella letteratura italiana: Atti del XVIII Congresso dell'A.I.S.L.L.I.*, ed. by Serge Vanvolsem and others (Florence: Cesati, 2007), pp. 189–204

Childs, Wendy, 'Anglo-Italian Contacts in the Fourteenth Century', in *Chaucer and the Italian Trecento*, ed. by Piero Boitani (Cambridge: Cambridge University Press, 1983), pp. 65–88

Chizzola, Orazio, *Prose e Poesie dei secoli XII e XIV* (Trieste: M. Quidde, 1910)

Dietz, Klaus, 'Die frühen italienischen Lehnwörter des Englischen', *Anglia: Zeitschrift für englische Philologie*, 123.4 (2006), 573–631

Durkin, Philip, *Borrowed Words: A History of Loanwords in English* (Oxford: Oxford University Press, 2014)

Edler, Florence, *Glossary of Mediaeval Terms of Business: Italian Series, 1200–1600* (Cambridge, MA: Mediaeval Academy of America, 1934)

Fennis, Jan, *Trésor du langage des galères: Dictionnaire exhaustif, avec une introduction, des dessins originaux de René Burlet et des planches de Jean-Antoine de Barras de la Penne, un relevé onomasiologique et une bibliographie* (Tübingen: Niemeyer, 1995)

Foster, Brian, *The Local Port Book of Southampton for 1435–36* (Southampton: Southampton University Press, 1963)

Gallagher, John, *Learning Languages in Early Modern England* (Oxford: Oxford University Press, 2019)

Goldthwaite, Richard, *The Economy of Renaissance Florence* (Baltimore: John Hopkins University Press, 2009)

Guidi Bruscoli, Francesco, 'Un frammento inedito di un libro di conti di Domenico Villani e compagni di Londra, 1422–24', *Storia Economica*, 13 (2010), 375–409

Hicks, Michael, *English Inland Trade, Southampton and its Region* (Oxford: Oxbow, 2015)

Hieatt, Constance B., and Sharon Butler, *Curye on Inglysch: English Culinary Manuscripts of the Fourteenth Century (Including the Forme of Cury)* (London: Early English Text Society, 1985)

Hines, John, and Robert Yeager, *John Gower, Trilingual Poet: Language, Translation and Tradition* (Cambridge: Boydell and Brewer, 2010)

Hope, Thomas Edward, *Lexical Borrowing in the Romance Languages: A Critical Study of Italianisms in French and Gallicisms in Italian from 1100 to 1900*, 2 vols, Language and Style Series, 10 (Oxford: Blackwell, 1971)

Hunt, Edwin S., *The Medieval Super-Companies: A Study of the Peruzzi Company of Florence* (Cambridge: Cambridge University Press, 1994)

Iamartino, Giovanni, 'La contrastività italiano-inglese in prospettiva storica', *Rassegna Italiana di Linguistica Applicata*, 33.2–3 (2001), 7–130

James, Tom Beaumont, *Southampton Sources, 1086–1900* (Southampton: Southampton University Press, 1983)

———, 'The Town of Southampton and its Foreign Trade, 1430–1540', in *English Inland Trade, 1430–1540: Southampton and its Region*, ed. by Michael Hicks (Oxford: Oxbow Books, 2015), pp. 11–25

Kaeuper, Richard, *Bankers to the Crown: The Riccardi of Lucca and Edward I* (Princeton: Princeton University Press, 1973)

Kowaleski, Maryanne, '"Alien" Encounters in the Maritime World of Medieval England', *Medieval Encounters*, 13 (2007), 96–121

———, 'The French of England: A Maritime lingua franca?', in *Language and Culture in Medieval Britain: The French of England, c. 1100–c. 1500*, ed. by Joyce Wogan-Browne and others (Woodbridge: York Medieval Press, 2009), pp. 103–17

Lawrence, Jason, *Who the Devil Taught Thee so much Italian? Italian Language Learning and Literary Imitation in Early Modern England* (Manchester: Manchester University Press, 2005)

Lerer, Seth, *The Yale Companion to Chaucer* (New Haven: Yale University Press, 2006)

Mallett, Michael, *The Florentine Galleys in the Fifteenth Century* (London: Oxford University Press, 1967)

Minervini, Laura, 'Les Gestes des Chiprois et la tradition historiographique de l'Orient latin', *Le Moyen Age*, 110.2 (2004), 315–25

Morris, Richard, *Liber cure cocorum: Copied and Edited from the Sloane MS 1986* (Berlin: Asher, 1862)

Mortimer, Nigel, *John Lydgate's Fall of Princes: Narrative Tragedy in its Literary and Political Context* (Oxford: Oxford University Press, 2005)

Mortimer, Ian, *Medieval Intrigue: Decoding Royal Conspiracies* (London: Continuum, 2010)

Nicolini, Angelo, 'Commercio marittimo genovese in Inghilterra nel Medioevo (1280–1495)', *Atti della Società Ligure di Storia Patria*, 47.1 (2007), 215–327

——, 'Navi liguri in Inghilterra nel Quattrocento: Il registro doganale di Sandwich per il 1439–40', *Collana storica dell'oltremare ligure*, 7 (2006), 91–251

Nightingale, Pamela, *A Medieval Mercantile Community: The Grocers' Company and the Politics & Trade of London, 1000–1485* (New Haven: Yale University Press, 1995)

Pinnavaia, Laura, *The Italian Borrowings in the 'Oxford English Dictionary': A Lexicographical, Linguistic, and Cultural Analysis* (Rome: Bulzoni, 2001)

Ruddock, Alwyn, *Italian Merchants and Shipping in Southampton, 1270–1600* (Southampton: University College, 1951)

——, 'The Method of Handling the Cargoes of Mediaeval Merchant Galleys', *Bulletin of the Institute of Historical Research*, 19 (1944), 140–48

Sapori, Armando, *La compagnia dei Frescobaldi in Inghilterra* (Florence: Leo S. Olschki, 1947)

Schendl, Herbert, and Laura Wright, *Code-Switching in Early English* (Berlin: De Gruyter, 2011)

Schweickard, Wolfgang, 'Storia interna dell'italiano: Lessico e formazione delle parole', in *Romanische Sprachgeschichte: Ein internationales Handbuch zur Geschichte der romanischen Sprachen / Histoire linguistique de la Romania: Manuel international d'histoire linguistique de la Romania*, III, ed. by Gerhard Ernst, Martin-Dietrich Gleßgen, Christian Schmitt, and Wolfgang Schweickard (Berlin: De Gruyter, 2008), pp. 2847–72

Studer, Paul, *The Port Books of Southampton or (Anglo-French) Accounts of Robert Florys, Water-Bailiff and Receiver of Petty-Customs, A.D. 1427–1430* (Southampton: Southampton Record Society, 1913)

Thick, Anne, 'The Fifteenth-Century Stewards' Books of Southampton' (unpublished doctoral thesis, King Alfred's College, University of Southampton, 1995)

——, *The Southampton Steward's Book of 1492–1493 and the Terrier of 1495* (Southampton: University of Southampton, 1996)

Tiddeman, Megan, 'Alum', in *Encyclopedia of Dress and Textiles in the British Isles, c. 450–1450*, II, ed. by Gale R. Owen Crocker, Elizabeth Coatsworth, and Maria Hayward (April 2018), <https://referenceworks.brillonline.com/browse/encyclopedia-of-medieval-dress-and-textiles> [accessed 15 September 2020]

——, *The Cantelowe Accounts: Multilingual Merchant Records from Tuscany, 1450–1451* (Oxford: Oxford University Press, 2022)

——, 'Early Anglo-Italian Contact: New Loanword Evidence from Two Mercantile Sources, 1440–1451', in *Merchants of Innovation: The Languages of*

Traders, ed. by Esther-Miriam Wagner, Bettina Beinhoff, and Ben Outhwaite (Berlin: De Gruyter, 2017), pp. 217–34

——, 'Lexical Exchange with Italian in the Textile and Wool Trades in the Thirteenth to Fifteenth Centuries', in *Medieval Clothing and Textiles*, XIV, ed. by Robin Netherton and Gale R. Owen-Crocker (Woodbridge: Boydell & Brewer, 2018), pp. 113–40

——, 'Mercantile Multilingualism: Two Examples of Anglo-Norman and Italian Contact in the Fourteenth Century', in *Present and Future in Anglo-Norman: La Recherche Actuelle et Future sur L'Anglo-Normand* (Aberystwyth: The Anglo-Norman Online Hub, 2012), pp. 91–99

——, 'More Sugar and Spice: Revisiting Medieval Italian Influence on the Mercantile Lexis of England', in *The Multilingual Origins of Standard English*, ed. by Laura Wright (Berlin: De Gruyter, 2020), pp. 381–410

——, 'Southampton and the Later Medieval Textile Trade', in *Encyclopedia of Dress and Textiles in the British Isles, c. 450–1450*, II, ed. by Gale R. Owen Crocker, Elizabeth Coatsworth, and Maria Hayward (April 2018), <https://referenceworks.brillonline.com/browse/encyclopedia-of-medieval-dress-and-textiles> [accessed 15 September 2020]

Tomasin, Lorenzo, 'Sulla diffusione del lessico marinaresco italiano', *Studi Linguistici Italiani*, 36 (2010), 263–92

Trotter, David, 'Death, Taxes and Property: Some Code-Switching Evidence from Dover, Southampton and York', in *Code-Switching in Early English*, ed. by Herbert Schendl and Laura Wright (Berlin: De Gruyter, 2011), pp. 155–89

——, 'Italian Merchants in London and Paris: Evidence of Language Contact in the Gallerani Accounts, 1305–1308', in *On Linguistic Change in French: Socio-historical Approaches. Studies in Honour of R. Anthony Lodge / Le changement linguistique en français: Aspects socio-historiques. Études en homage au professeur R. Anthony Lodge*, ed. by Dominique Lagorgette and Tim Pooley (Chambéry: Université de Savoie, 2011), pp. 209–26

——, '*Oceano vox*: You Never Know Where a Ship Comes From. On Multilingualism and Language-Mixing in Medieval Britain', in *Aspects of Multilingualism in European Language History*, ed. by Kurt Braunmüller and Gisella Ferraresi (Amsterdam: John Benjamins, 2003), pp. 15–33

Vidos, Benedek Elemér, *Storia delle parole marinaresche italiane passate in francese: Contributo storico-linguistico all'espansione della lingua nautica italiana* (Florence: Leo S. Olschki, 1939)

Volpi, Guglielmo, 'Le falsificazione di Francesco Redi nel Vocabulario della Crusca', *Atti della R. Accademia della Crusca per la lingua d'Italia: Anno academico 1915–1916*, 1917, pp. 33–136

Wright, Laura, 'Bills, Accounts, Inventories: Everyday Trilingual Activities in the Business World of Later Medieval England', in *Multilingualism in Later Medieval Britain*, ed. by David Trotter (Woodbridge: D. S. Brewer, 2000), pp. 149–56

——, 'Code Intermediate Phenomena in Medieval Mixed-Language Texts', *Language Sciences*, 24 (2002), 471–89

THOMAS SCHARINGER

The Influence of French on Sixteenth-Century Italian

It is well known that during the Renaissance the impact of French on the Italian language was considerably less strong than in the periods either side of it. This is mainly due to two factors: firstly, Spanish came to play a more important role in Italy for obvious political reasons; secondly, Italians were less open to linguistic influences from abroad, as Italian, that is, Tuscan, was considered a prestigious *lingua franca* among the elites of Renaissance Europe. In fact, it was Italian that exercised a strong influence on other European languages, especially on French, which — both in the fifteenth and sixteenth centuries — borrowed more words from Italian than vice versa. Notwithstanding that the cultural and linguistic exchanges between France and Italy were undeniably asymmetric in these centuries, they were not unidirectional.

The aim of this chapter is to shed some light on the influence of French on Italian by focusing on the sixteenth century, which has so far been neglected in linguistic research. After a brief survey of the existing literature on the mutual contacts between French and Italian, I will identify some of the contact scenarios and channels through which French might have exerted an influence on Italian. First, literary *loci* of language contact will be examined. Apart from the production of French books in the peninsula and the use of French in multilingual literary texts, translations of French texts into Italian will be looked at in more detail. Secondly, letters written by Italian ambassadors and intellectuals who spent some time in France will be analysed. A closer examination of their texts demonstrates that these migrating individuals played a more important role in introducing Gallicisms into Italian than the circulation of French books and translations did.

Thomas Scharinger (thomas.scharinger@uni-jena.de) studied English, French, and Italian Philology at Friedrich-Alexander-Universität Erlangen-Nürnberg, received his PhD in Romance Linguistics from Ludwig-Maximilians-Universität München in 2017, and is currently Assistant Professor of French and Italian Linguistics at Friedrich-Schiller-Universität Jena.

Languages and Cross-Cultural Exchanges in Renaissance Italy, ed. by Alessandra Petrocchi and Joshua Brown, LMEMS 30 (Turnhout: Brepols, 2023), pp. 299–327
BREPOLS ❧ PUBLISHERS   10.1484/M.LMEMS-EB.5.131436

Cultural and Linguistic Contact between France and Italy — A Literature Survey

The intense cultural and linguistic contacts between France and Italy have been investigated widely over the past decades.[1] Given that the two languages had been in close mutual contact since the early Middle Ages, it is not surprising that among the Romance languages, French had the most significant impact on Italian, while Italian can be considered the most important Romance donor language for French. As pointed out above, however, linguistic exchange between French and Italian was not always symmetrical. The following tables (cf. Table 10.1 and 10.2), based on Thomas E. Hope's major work on Italianisms in French and Gallicisms in Italian,[2] demonstrate that Italian was strongly influenced by French in the Middle Ages as well as in the eighteenth and nineteenth centuries, whereas in the Renaissance it was Italian that had a considerable impact on French.[3]

Table 10.1. Number of Italianisms in French per century

13th c.	14th c.	15th c.	16th c.	17th c.	18th c.	19th c.
28	59	91	462	203	106	81

Adapted from Fleischman, 'HOPE, T.E. *Lexical Borrowing in the Romance Languages*', p. 642.

Table 10.2. Number of Gallicisms in Italian per century

13th c.	14th c.	15th c.	16th c.	17th c.	18th c.	19th c.
106	94	16	72	100	270	813

Adapted from Fleischman, 'HOPE, T.E. *Lexical Borrowing in the Romance Languages*', p. 642.

Most scholars explain this asymmetry by referring to the different prestige of the two languages over the centuries.[4] While the importance of French in medieval Italy was mainly due to the spread and adaptation of literary

---

1 For the substantial body of literature on this topic, see the works cited in Morgana, 'L'influsso francese'; Bouvier, 'Französisch und Romanisch'; Lorenzetti, 'L'italiano e le lingue romanze'; Antonelli, 'Italiano e Francese'; Formisano, 'Contatti linguistici all'interno della Romània'; Trotter, 'Contacts linguistiques intraromans'; Gleßgen, 'Histoire interne du français (Europe)'; Schweickard, 'Storia interna dell'italiano'; Cella, 'Francesismi'; and Scharinger, *Mehrsprachigkeit im Frankreich der Frühen Neuzeit*, pp. 21–104.
2 Hope, *Lexical Borrowing in the Romance Languages*. This study, which consists of two volumes, is unique in that it is dedicated to both Gallicisms in Italian and Italianisms in French, and it covers a period which ranges from the Middle Ages to the nineteenth century. For a critical review of this work, see the literature cited in Scharinger, *Mehrsprachigkeit im Frankreich der Frühen Neuzeit*, p. 79 n. 105.
3 In this chapter, I use the expression *Middle Ages* to refer to the cultural period preceding the Renaissance, i.e. the late medieval period.
4 See Morgana, 'L'influsso francese', pp. 691–92; Antonelli, 'Italiano e Francese', p. 584; and Formisano, 'Contatti linguistici all'interno della Romània', p. 1763.

models from France (e.g. Franco-Italian literature and *Scuola Siciliana*),[5] the presence of the Normans and later Angevins in southern Italy,[6] and Italian traders who borrowed numerous French words during their business in France and England,[7] the significant influence of French on Italian from the seventeenth century onwards is generally associated with the growing prestige of French as *langue universelle* among European elites.[8] The scarce adoption of Gallicisms in the Renaissance period can in turn be explained by the cultural reputation of Italy and hence of Italian, which by the sixteenth century had become the most prestigious literary language in Europe and — besides Latin — the most important Western vehicular language in the Ottoman Empire.[9] Unsurprisingly, the influence of Italian on French was therefore much more intense than vice versa. In contrast to the French, who were fascinated by Italian literature and by the highly developed culture of Renaissance Italy with which they came into contact during their travels in Italy or while they were fighting in the so-called Italian Wars,[10] the Italians were conscious of their cultural supremacy and consequently less open to influences from French. All the more so because with the Spanish dominion of southern Italy, Catalan and Spanish came to play a more important role as donor languages for Italian than French.[11]

Against this background, it is not surprising that previous research on Gallicisms in Italian has so far mainly focused on the Middle Ages and on the period from the seventeenth century onwards,[12] whereas the sixteenth century has not been looked at in detail. This is not to say that studies of language contact between French and Italian in the sixteenth

---

5   On Franco-Italian literature, see Holtus, 'Plan- und Kunstsprachen auf romanischer Basis IV. Franko-Italienisch' and the literature cited therein. For information on the *Scuola Siciliana*, see e.g. Rizzo, 'Elementi francesi nella lingua dei poetici siciliani della "Magna Curia"'.
6   On the Normans, see Coluccia, 'La situazione linguistica dell'Italia meridionale al tempo di Federico II' as well as Varvaro, 'Notizie sul lessico della Sicilia medievale. I. Francesismi'. On the Angevins, see Sabatini, *Napoli angioina* and Formisano and Lee, 'Il "francese di Napoli" in opere di autori italiani dell'età angioina'.
7   See, for example, Cella, 'Prestiti nei testi mercantili toscani redatti di là dalle Alpi' and Trotter, 'Italian Merchants in London and Paris'.
8   See Dardi, *Dalla provincia all'Europa*; Matarrese, *Il settecento*, pp. 53–71; and Giovanardi, *Linguaggi scientifici e lingua comune nel Settecento*.
9   For an overview, see Baglioni, 'L'italiano fuori d'Italia' and the literature cited therein.
10 For the adaptation of literary models from Italy, see Balsamo, *Les rencontres des muses*. On the so-called *voyage d'Italie*, see Balsamo, 'Le voyage d'Italie et la formation des élites françaises'. On the Italian Wars, see Boillet and Piéjus, eds, *Les guerres d'Italie* and Fournel and Zancarini, *Les guerres d'Italie*.
11 For information on the Spanish impact on Italian, see Beccaria, *Spagnolo e spagnoli in Italia*.
12 See the seminal monographs by Bezzola, *Abbozzo di una storia dei gallicismi italiani nei primi secoli*; Cella, *I gallicismi nei testi dell'italiano antico*; and Dardi, *Dalla provincia all'Europa*. Studies on Gallicisms in Italian dialects seem to be also limited to the respective periods; see e.g. Dardi, 'Elementi francesi moderni nei dialetti italiani' and Zolli, *L'influsso francese sul veneziano del XVIII secolo*.

century are scarce in number, but they are all dedicated to Italianisms in French.[13] The findings of more recent research, however, suggest that the influence of French on Italian in the sixteenth century deserves more attention than it has received until now. Although in the following tables (cf. Table 10.3 and 10.4) data confirm the asymmetry of linguistic exchange between French and Italian in the Renaissance (497 Italianisms in French vs. 172 Gallicisms in Italian), they clearly show that the contact was not unidirectional.[14]

Table 10.3. Number of Italianisms in French per century

13th c.	14th c.	15th c.	16th c.	17th c.	18th c.	19th c.
54	69	120	497	254	434	243

Based on the *DIFIT*; cf. Stammerjohann and Seymer, 'L'italiano in Europa', p. 49.

Table 10.4. Number of Gallicisms in Italian per century

13th c.	14th c.	15th c.	16th c.	17th c.	18th c.	19th c.
201	267	64	172	215	376	1150

Based on the *GRADIT*; cf. Schweickard, 'Storia interna dell'italiano', p. 2851.

A closer look at these 172 Gallicisms in Italian reveals that a substantial part of these loans are military terms:[15] for example, *banda* < fr. *bande* (company, troop), *barricata* < fr. *barricade* (barricade), *buttasella* < fr. *boute-selle* (saddle-up, boot and saddle), *marciare* < fr. *marcher* (to march), *massacro* < fr. *massacre* (massacre), *mina* < fr. *mine* (mine), *pattuglia* < fr. *patrouille* (patrol), *picca* < fr. *pique* (pike), *trincea* (*trincera*) < fr. *tranchée* (trench). As already stated by Hope, these terms are likely to have entered Italian through French soldiers fighting in the so-called Italian Wars (1494–1559):

> The French invasions and military contacts of that turbulent first thirty years do a lot to account for the terms of warfare which stand out as a large group in this otherwise lean century-list. They are more than a quarter of the total (20 out of 72). We can detect a typical semantic pattern in them; most are in some way connected with artillery and siege warfare.[16]

---

13 See Wind, *Les mots italiens introduits en français au XVIᵉ siècle* and Sarauw, *Die Italianismen in der französischen Sprache des 16. Jahrhunderts*.
14 With respect to the same centuries, it can be observed that the numbers given in Table 10.1 and Table 10.3, and those found in Table 10.2 and Table 10.4, sometimes differ considerably. This can be easily explained. Unlike Hope, *Lexical Borrowing in the Romance Languages* (1971), both Stammerjohann and Seymer, 'L'italiano in Europa' (2007) and Schweickard, 'Storia interna dell'italiano' (2008) could rely on newer and more exhaustive dictionaries based on the findings of almost forty more years of etymological research.
15 The following examples are taken from the *GRADIT* (s.vv.).
16 Hope, *Lexical Borrowing in the Romance Languages*, I, p. 266.

In fact, it is more than plausible that these military encounters not only led to the adoption of Italianisms in French but also vice versa. Unfortunately, the consequences of the brief French presence in large parts of northern Italy in the Renaissance period have — at least to the best of my knowledge — not yet been investigated in detail from a linguistic point of view.[17]

There are numerous sixteenth-century Gallicisms in other semantic fields too. These appear to have been transmitted via other channels: *biglietto* < fr. *billet* (note, short letter), *gabinetto* < fr. *cabinet* (private room), *appuntamento* < fr. *appointement* (agreement, arrangement), *cochino* < fr. *coquin* (despicable person), and *madamigella* < fr. *mademoiselle* (mademoiselle).

In what follows, I will explore scenarios of language contact to understand how and in which types of situations French might have exerted an influence on sixteenth-century Italian. It is beyond the scope of this study to provide a comprehensive picture of Gallicisms in sixteenth-century Italian; I shall attempt instead to put forward some hypotheses for consideration and debate concerning French–Italian language contact situations and contact-induced change. It is hoped that the present findings will provide direction for future research on the topic.

Migrating Texts

It is well known that the intense impact of Italian on Renaissance French was — at least in part — due to the circulation and production of Italian books in France, the use of Italian as a literary language among French poets and intellectuals, and the numerous translations of Italian works into French. The following sections are dedicated to the question of whether comparable *loci* of language contact can be identified in Renaissance Italy.

Production and Circulation of French Books

As has been shown by several scholars, the demand for Italian books in Renaissance France was so high that Italian books were not only imported but also printed in France throughout the sixteenth century.[18] In a previous study based on data from the *USTC* (*Universal Short Title Catalogue*),[19]

---

17 The French rule in Milan (1499–1512 and 1515–1521), for instance, is investigated neither in Bongrani and Morgana, 'La Lombardia' nor in Morgana, *Storia linguistica di Milano*. On this problem, see Wilhelm, 'Regionale Sprachgeschichte als Geschichte eines mehrsprachigen Raumes'. Piedmont is the only region which has been investigated; see Marazzini, 'Piemonte e Valle d'Aosta'.
18 See the studies by Bingen, *Philausone (1500–1660)*; Bingen and Renaud, *Lectures italiennes dans les pays wallons*; Balsamo, *L'amorevolezza verso le cose Italiche*; and Baldacchini, ed., *Il libro e le sue reti*.
19 On the value of this database for historical linguistics, see Ambrosch-Baroua, *Mehrsprachigkeit im Spiegel des Buchdrucks*, p. 25 n. 48, and Scharinger, 'L'italiano fuori d'Italia im Spiegel des frühneuzeitlichen Buchdrucks', pp. 165–66.

I demonstrated that from 1501 to 1600 France even produced the largest number of Italian books printed outside of Italy.[20] As for French books printed in the 'Italian states' in the same period, the situation appears to be quite different. Although the *USTC* lists 347 editions (vs. 528 Italian editions printed in France),[21] a closer look at the places where the books were actually printed shows that only half of them were produced in the Italian peninsula. As can be seen in Table 10.5, the *USTC* also considers those places that were under 'Italian' or Sabaudian rule as belonging to the 'Italian states', irrespective of whether they were actually situated on the peninsula or not. Avignon, for instance, remained a papal enclave until the French Revolution, although the last antipope had left the city in the early fifteenth century.

Table 10.5. Number of French books printed in the 'Italian states' from 1501 to 1600 (*USTC*).

	Number of French books	Total of books (all languages, incl. Latin)
Avignon	129	213
Venezia	76	28,283
Chambéry	52	58
Torino	44	960
Roma	19	8854
Annecy	6	17
Firenze	2	5043
Milano	2	3229
Genova	1	381
Bologna	0	6377

This table contains only some of the cities listed in the *USTC*. For all Italian cities that produced French books in the sixteenth century, the reader can refer to the information given in the *USTC*.

Since the books printed in papal Avignon are likely to have been read there — or at least in other parts of France — they should not be taken into account when measuring the diffusion of French in Renaissance Italy. The same could be argued for the books printed in Chambéry and Annecy, as both Sabaudian cities belong to the Gallo-Romance area.[22] As for Turin, where French works appear to have been widely read, the data retrieved in the *USTC* is in line with what has been stated by many scholars. In fact, French played

---

20 See Scharinger, 'L'italiano fuori d'Italia im Spiegel des frühneuzeitlichen Buchdrucks', p. 170.
21 The data was collected on 1 August 2020; cf. also the bibliography at the end of this chapter.
22 Although the language used for oral communication was Franco-Provençal, French played a significant role as a written language in this area from the fourteenth century onwards (cf. Jauch, *Das Frankoprovenzalische in Italien, Frankreich und der Schweiz*, pp. 16–17, 46–47 and the literature cited therein).

an important role in Piedmont, which was due to the region's affiliation to the Duchy of Savoy as well as to its geographical proximity to France.[23]

With respect to the rest of the Italian peninsula, the number of books printed in French is rather negligible. Given that Venice was the most important printing location in Renaissance Italy,[24] it comes with little surprise that some seventy-six French books were produced there. In any case, the demand for works in other languages was more substantial (e.g. 132 Spanish books vs. 76 French books between 1501 and 1600). What is particularly striking is the scarcity of French books in cities like Florence, Milan, Bologna, and Rome — all of which were relevant printing locations (cf. the total number of books in Table 10.5).[25] This paucity appears to confirm what has been said above about the asymmetry of cultural exchange between France and Italy in the sixteenth century. While the French were fascinated by Italian literature, Italians seem to have had little interest in French books.

According to some scholars, this lack of interest in French literature was due to the scarce knowledge of the French language in Renaissance Italy.[26] Evidence from studies on historical grammars and bilingual dictionaries suggests that French did not enjoy much prestige as a foreign language among Italians. Whereas in France the first grammar for learners of Italian was printed as early as 1549 (Jean de Mesmes's *La grammaire italienne*),[27] in Italy a comparable work was not published before 1625 (Pietro Durante's *La grammatica italiana per imparare la lingua francese*).[28] A similar asymmetry can be observed with regard to bilingual dictionaries: although the first 'real' French–Italian dictionary (Jean Antoine Fenice's *Dictionnaire françois et italien*) was printed in Morges (near Geneva),[29] the title '[...] Et se vendent à Paris chez Iaques du Puys' shows that it was sold in France as well.[30] In 1603, a revised edition (Pierre Canal's *Diction[n]aire françois et italien*) was published in Paris.[31] In Italy, however, the first French–Italian dictionary, also an edition of Canal's dictionary, was printed only in 1647.[32]

---

23 The linguistic history of this area is explored by Marazzini, 'Piemonte e Valle d'Aosta', who also studies the diffusion of French books in Renaissance Piedmont.
24 According to the *USTC*, 28,283 out of 69,540 books in Renaissance Italy (1501–1600) were produced in Venice. On the significant role of Venice, see the literature cited in Ambrosch-Baroua, *Mehrsprachigkeit im Spiegel des Buchdrucks*, p. 20 n. 35.
25 On the importance of these printing locations, see also Bartoli Langeli and Infelise, 'Il libro manoscritto e la stampa', pp. 957–59.
26 See e.g. Morgana, 'L'influsso francese', pp. 691–93, and Grohovaz, 'La traduzione dal francese all'italiano nel XVI secolo', pp. 71–73.
27 Mattarucco, *Prime grammatiche d'italiano per francesi*, p. 313.
28 Colombo Timelli, 'Grammaires italiennes pour l'enseignement du français', p. 565, as well as Mormile, *L'italiano in Francia, il francese in Italia*, pp. 40–42.
29 Colombo Timelli, 'Le *Dictionnaire* de Jean Antoine Fenice', p. 9, and Mormile, *Storia dei dizionari bilingui italo-francesi*, pp. 23–25.
30 For the full title, see Nadia Minerva's presentation in Lillo, ed., *1583–2000*, pp. 1584–85.
31 See Nadia Minerva's presentation in Lillo, ed., *1583–2000*, pp. 1592–93.
32 Minerva, 'À l'aube de la lexicographie bilingue', p. 19.

Yet, despite the absence of French grammars and French–Italian dictionaries, we cannot fully exclude that French played a certain role as a foreign language in Renaissance Italy: some scholars believe that the diffusion and popularity of multilingual dictionaries and phrasebooks such as the *Solenissimo Vochabuolista* slowed the production of more significant bilingual works.[33] As they usually contained parts in French, French–Italian dictionaries might have been perceived as unnecessary. Other scholars conducted archival research in Italian libraries and found numerous copies of French–Italian dictionaries printed in sixteenth-century France. On this basis, it has been concluded that there might have been an active trade market of imported French–Italian dictionaries.[34] As Raugei's study of Gian Vincenzo Pinelli's correspondence has demonstrated, at least some erudite Italians had regularly sent French books from France.[35] Pinelli (1535–1601) received not only the latest works by contemporary French poets (e.g. Marot, Ronsard), but also several French dictionaries and grammars. Based on these grammars, he even compiled a short French grammar in Latin — probably for his own personal use.[36] It is difficult to determine whether Pinelli's keen interest in French can be considered indicative of a changing attitude towards this language among erudite Italians in the late sixteenth century, as supposed by Morgana.[37] Further studies on the holdings of family libraries in Renaissance Italy would be needed in order to ascertain a comprehensive picture of the actual circulation of French books.

Still, even if future research on the importation and circulation of French books were to show that French was learned (and read) to a larger extent, the lean production of French *oeuvres* itself remains significant, especially when compared to the printing of Spanish books. Despite the constant importation of Spanish works from Spain, Italian printers continued to produce Spanish books, including grammars and dictionaries, throughout the whole sixteenth century.[38] The scarcity of French books therefore suggests that the demand for books in this language was simply not substantial enough. All in all, French books do not appear to have been an important point of language contact in Renaissance Italy.

---

33 See Bingen and Van Passen, 'La lexicographie bilingue', pp. 3007–08. On these polyglot phrasebooks, see Rossebastiano Bart, *Antichi vocabolari plurilingui d'uso popolare*.
34 See e.g. Minerva and Pellandra, *Insegnare il francese in Italia*, pp. 12–13, and Minerva, 'À l'aube de la lexicographie bilingue', p. 19.
35 Raugei, *Un abbozzo di grammatica francese del '500*, pp. 11–44.
36 The manuscript has been edited by Anna Maria Raugei. See Raugei, *Un abbozzo di grammatica francese del '500*, pp. 65–146.
37 Morgana, 'L'influsso francese', p. 692.
38 The importation and production of Spanish books in Renaissance Italy is investigated in Ambrosch-Baroua, *Mehrsprachigkeit im Spiegel des Buchdrucks*. For further information on grammars and bilingual dictionaries in France and Italy in the sixteenth century, see Scharinger, *Mehrsprachigkeit im Frankreich der Frühen Neuzeit*, pp. 42–46.

French in Multilingual Italian Texts

Due to the prestige of Italian literature in Renaissance France, some poets and writers known as *Français italianisants* (Italianizing Frenchmen) even composed works in Italian.[39] Conversely, in sixteenth-century Italy, a corresponding use of French as a literary language cannot be observed.[40] As has been pointed out by Morgana, French played a negligible role even in multilingual comedies.[41] Spanish and Italian dialects appear to have been more influential in such texts. A closer look at the use of French by Giulio Cesare Croce (1550–1609), whose multilingual works were known extensively in the sixteenth and seventeenth centuries,[42] suggests that knowledge of French in Renaissance Italy was indeed 'ancora limitato' (still limited).[43]

> '**Alè**, villen **cucchì**'
> Me respos un frances 'Regardè a moi'
> 'Ve pandre per la gorgia **per ma foi**!'[44]

>> ('Come on, you mischievous man'
>> A Frenchman answered 'Look at me'
>> 'By my faith, I will hang you by the throat!')[45]

> 'Ch'en Frans bien puode **supè da roi**
> De grasia, guardè moi.'[46]

>> ('In France you can dine like a king
>> I beg you, look at me.')

> 'Regarde a moi che ve pre **madmoisella**
> [...]
> Se vu est **donsiella**
> **Moi son garzon**, prendem per marì.'[47]

>> ('Look at me, I beg you Mademoiselle
>> [...]
>> If you are a young woman,
>> I am a young man, take me as your husband.')

---

39 On the so-called *Français italianisants*, see Picot, *Les Français italianisants au XVIe siècle*.
40 The notorious exception of Piedmont is mentioned in Marazzini, 'Piemonte e Valle d'Aosta', pp. 6–7.
41 Morgana, 'L'influsso francese', p. 691.
42 Foresti, Marri, and Petrolini, 'L'Emilia e la Romagna', pp. 379, 384.
43 Morgana, 'L'influsso francese', p. 691.
44 *Opere di Giulio Cesare Croce, Disgratie del Zane narrate in un sonetto di diecisette linguaggi*, vv. 111–13.
45 Unless otherwise noted, all translations are my own.
46 *Opere di Giulio Cesare Croce, Le nozze del Zane in lingua bergamasca, nelle quali si vedono sedici linguaggi diversi*, vv. 139–41.
47 *Opere di Giulio Cesare Croce, Il Maridazzo della bella Brunettina. Con un sonetto sopra l'Aglio*, vv. 40–43.

As can be seen in the extracts cited above, the French used in these comedies must be considered a mixture of Italian and French. Not only do Italian and French elements appear within the same sentence (e.g. *supè da roi* and *moi son garzon*), but there are hybrid expressions too, for example, *per ma foi* (by my faith) which contains an Italian form (*per*). The quality of this macaronic French suggests that the readers (or the audience) had insufficient command of French to understand complex utterances in this language. It is interesting to note that some of the (Italianized) French words used by Croce are Gallicisms that entered Italian in the sixteenth century (e.g. *Alè* < fr. *Allez* (Come on), *cucchì* (a variant of *cochino*) < fr. *coquin* (mischievous person), *madmoisella* < fr. *mademoiselle* (mademoiselle)).[48] As these words were already more or less established in Italian, they could have facilitated the audience's understanding of the French parts. Nevertheless, they must still have been felt to be somewhat exotic. It is no coincidence that Croce placed these obvious Gallicisms into the mouths of French-speaking characters. The same could be hypothesized for *donsiella* (a variant of *donzella*) < prov. *donsela* (young woman) and *garzon(e)* < fr. *garçon* (young man). Although both words had already been introduced into Italian in the Middle Ages,[49] they seem to have remained recognizable as Gallicisms.[50]

These few examples may suffice to confirm what is generally acknowledged in the literature: the use of French in Italian literary texts seems to have been limited to short passages in multilingual works. It is by no means comparable to the extensive use of Italian by the so-called *Français italianisants*. Rather, it is a further example of the notorious asymmetry of cultural and linguistic exchange between France and Italy in the Renaissance period. Therefore, literary texts do not seem to have been an important *locus* of language contact.

Translations of French Texts into Italian

It is well known that translations of Italian texts into French were rich in Italianisms, and hence represented an important point of language contact in Renaissance France.[51] While large scholarly anthologies on works translated from Italian into French have been published,[52] translations from French into Italian are still awaiting attention. The findings in Grohovaz's 'Avvio di

---

48 First attestations: *Alè* 1572, *cochino* 1530–1533, *madamigella* 1552 (cf. *GRADIT* s.vv.).
49 According to the *GRADIT* (s.vv.), the noun *donzella* is attested before 1257, whereas *garzone* dates to 1274.
50 Some scholars argue that neither *donzella* nor *garzone* are Gallicisms (see Cella, *I gallicismi nei testi dell'italiano antico*, pp. 29–30). Even if we assume that both lexemes are vernacular Italian forms (*garzone* being introduced directly via Germanic), we cannot fully exclude that the influence of French enhanced the spread of these lexemes. In any case, Croce seems to consider them as Gallicisms.
51 See e.g. Scharinger, 'Italianismi nel lessico schermistico del francese cinquecentesco' and the literature cited therein.
52 See e.g. Balsamo, Castiglione Minischetti, and Dotoli, *Les traductions de l'italien en français*. On bilingual editions, see also Bingen, *Le Maître italien (1510–1660)*.

una catalogazione', however, suggest that the number of translations from French into Italian (c. 96) was considerably less than translations from Italian into French (c. 1566).[53] According to Grohovaz, this asymmetry can even be considered one of the most significant examples of the 'singolare squilibrio che caratterizza gli scambi culturali tra Francia e Italia nel XVI secolo' (remarkable imbalance which characterizes the cultural exchanges between France and Italy in the sixteenth century).[54] Indeed, Grohovaz's findings are in line with what has been observed above about the printing of French books and the use of French in literary texts. Notwithstanding their small number, translations of French texts could have played a certain role in the diffusion of Gallicisms, especially since many of the translations listed by Grohovaz are non-literary texts, among which one finds many treatises. As translators of technical treatises were constantly exposed to new ideas and concepts, their translations were usually rich in loanwords.

In the following, I will take a closer look at four of the translations mentioned by Grohovaz — which are all available online — in order to demonstrate that they are fruitful sources for the investigation of Gallicisms in Italian. The two passages cited below are taken from a translation of a medical text which was published in 1592:

> Io non so se per **questo i Franzesi chiamano Coccù** colui che permette alla sua moglie d'adoperar quella parte in servitio d'altri, per che à chiamarlo **Coccù** per somigliante modo di fare dell'uccello chiamato cuculio, questo sarebbe troppo grande errore, poiche il cuculio non lascia ad altro uccello di covare, & porsi nel suo nidio, anzi per il contrario lo va à porre nel nidio altrui.[55]

> (I do not know if it is for this reason that the French call *Coccù* (fr. *cocu*) [deceived husband] a man who allows his wife to use this part of her body with other men. It would be a great mistake to call such a man *Coccù* in reason of a putatively similar behaviour of a bird called cuckoo, because a cuckoo does not let other birds lay their eggs into its nest; on the contrary, it lays its eggs into the nest of others.)

---

53 The figures in brackets are taken from Balsamo, Castiglione Minischetti, and Dotoli, *Les traductions de l'italien en français*, pp. 9–12, and Grohovaz, 'La traduzione dal francese all'italiano nel XVI secolo'. Both anthologies take into consideration printed translations only. The first, however, adopts more inclusive criteria: Grohovaz only lists Italian translations of texts that were originally written in French or that were translated into French, whereas Balsamo, Castiglione Minischetti, and Dotoli do not only enumerate French translations of Italian texts or that were translated into Italian, but also French translations of Latin texts that were themselves translations of Tuscan texts. Grohovaz also catalogues forty-six French 'opuscoli' (brochures) which were translated into Italian. If these minor translations were added to the ninety-six translations mentioned above, the total of Italian translations of French texts would still be less in number than the Italian works translated into French.
54 Grohovaz, 'La traduzione dal francese all'italiano nel XVI secolo', p. 71.
55 Joubert, *La Prima Parte De Gli Errori Popolari*, trans. by Luchi, p. 134.

> E cosa di grand'importanza, che la donna si liberi felicemente del parto, considerato il pericolo, che essa, & il suo bambino passano, quando ci è qualche difficoltà. Onde con buona ragione **si chiamano sagge donne** le matrone, […], perche bisogna che sieno ben prudenti, & accorte, sopratutto quando ci sono due, ò tre figliuoli a nascere.[56]
>
>> (It is very important that a woman can give up the responsibility of the birth, considering in what danger she and her child are when there are complications. It is for a good reason that midwives are called 'wise women' […] because they must be very careful and cautious, especially when there are two or three babies to be delivered.)

Neither the borrowed noun *coccù* < fr. *cocu* (deceived husband)[57] nor the loan translation *sagge donne* < fr. *sages-femmes* (midwives) have so far been registered in studies on Gallicisms in sixteenth-century Italian.[58] It is true that the metalinguistic comments (e.g. *i Franzesi chiamano*) suggest that these words were coined by the translators, who might have used them only once (*hapax legomena*). Yet we cannot fully exclude that these Gallicisms entered Italian usage, albeit confined to the ephemeral variety of a special group: although there are no entries of *saggia donna* in the larger dictionaries (*DELI*, *GDLI*, *GRADIT*), the *GDLI* (s.v. *arguto*) cites a passage from a text by Giovan Battista Marino (1569–1625) (*sagge donne e nobili matrone*) in which *sagge donne* seems to mean 'midwives'. As for *cocu*, there is an entry in the *GRADIT* (s.v.), which considers the lexeme an exotic Gallicism not attested before 1956. Further research is needed to determine whether these Gallicisms were really used more widely in the sixteenth and seventeenth centuries. If this is the case, the occurrences in the translation could be considered first attestations of these Gallicisms in Italian. In any case, these two examples shed light on the fact that translations were an important *locus* of language contact that facilitated the introduction of Gallicisms.

Unlike *saggia donna* and *cocu*, the Gallicism *ciapperone* < fr. *chaperon* (hood, cowl) (cf. the passage cited below) is registered in the *GDLI* (s.v.),[59] which cites examples from works by Lorenzo Bellini (1643–1704). Although there are occurrences of this lexeme in medieval Italian texts,[60] it does not seem to have become well established in sixteenth-century Italian. As can be seen in the following passage, the translator felt the need to explain the word, which may have designated a very special hood worn in sixteenth-century France.

---

56 Joubert, *La Prima Parte De Gli Errori Popolari*, trans. by Luchi, p. 137.
57 Despite the translator's doubts, fr. *cocu* derives indeed from fr. *coucou* (cuckoo) (cf. *TLFi* s.v. *cocu*).
58 There are no corresponding entries in Hope, *Lexical Borrowing in the Romance Languages*.
59 No corresponding entry is found either in the *DELI* or in the *GRADIT*.
60 Cella, *I gallicismi nei testi dell'italiano antico*, pp. 24 n. 20, 114. See also Morgana, 'L'influsso francese', p. 688.

Marciava in primo luogho il Mazzieri del'Ordine, vestito di veste di raso bianco, [...], con lo scappucino (**che è ditto in Francia ciapperone**).[61]

(The Mazzieri dell'Ordine [the subaltern of the order] was marching in first place. He was wearing a vest of white satin, [...], with a special hood (which in France is called a *ciapperone*).)

In contrast to *saggia donna*, *cocu*, and *ciapperone*, the Gallicisms found in the translation of Commyne's memoirs are all well known and documented in the literature on Gallicisms in Italian.

Voi havete inteso come quelli quali il Re haveva alloggiati in quelle **trinciere** lungo il fiume di Seine, si disloggiorno [...]. La tregua no durava mai piu d'un di ò doi. [...]. Compagnie è **bande** grosse non uscivano fuor di Paris.[62]

(You have heard how those whom the king had quartered in the trenches along the Seine were dislodged [...]. The truce never lasted more than one or two days. [...] No companies or large troops left Paris.)

Loro se accaminorno diritto a Gand, dove trovorno **Madamigella** di Borgogna, e con essa il Duca di Cleves [...]. Il Vescovo di liege con parecchi altri, **personaggi** grandi vi erano per far compagnia a detta Damigella.[63]

(They walked directly to Gent, where they met Mademoiselle de Bourgogne, and with her the Duc de Clèves [...]. The Bishop of Liège and other important people were there to keep company with the above-mentioned damsel.)

The two passages demonstrate that the translation abounds with Gallicisms. Apart from numerous military terms such as *banda* < fr. *bande* (troop) and *trincera* < fr. *tranchée* (trench)[64] as well as *marciare* < fr. *marcher* (to march) and *picca* < fr. *pique* (pike),[65] there are more neutral Gallicisms too, e.g. *personaggio* < fr. *personnage* (personage) and *madamigella* < fr. *mademoiselle* (mademoiselle).[66]

A look at the corresponding entry in the *GRADIT* (s.v.) shows that the occurrences of *madamigella* in this translation — published in 1544 — must

---

61 Scève, *La Magnifica et Triumphale Entrata del Christianiss. Re di Francia*, trans. by F.M. The word *ciapperone* is used twice again in the same passage.
62 Commynes, *La Historia Famosa di Monsignor di Argenton*, trans. by Raince, fol. 32ᵛ.
63 Commynes, *La Historia Famosa di Monsignor di Argenton*, trans. by Raince, fols 202ᵛ–203ʳ.
64 For further occurrences of these lexemes, see Commynes, *La Historia Famosa di Monsignor di Argenton*, trans. by Raince, fols 14ᵛ, 28ʳ⁻ᵛ, 29ʳ⁻ᵛ, 38ᵛ, 54ʳ, 79ʳ, 153ᵛ.
65 For occurrences of these Gallicisms, see Commynes, *La Historia Famosa di Monsignor di Argenton*, trans. by Raince, fols 8ʳ, 11ʳ, 13ᵛ, 34ʳ, 49ᵛ, 75ʳ, 171ʳ. According to Cella, *I gallicismi nei testi dell'italiano antico*, pp. 478–79, *marciare* is not necessarily a Gallicism. Since the noun *marcia* < fr. *marche* is already attested in the Middle Ages, the verb *marciare* could derive from *marcia* and be an Italian formation as well.
66 For further occurrences of *personaggio* and *madamigella*, see Commynes, *La Historia Famosa di Monsignor di Argenton*, trans. by Raince, fols 12ᵛ, 23ᵛ, 40ʳ, 42ʳ, 197ʳ, 198ᵛ, 200ʳ, 227ᵛ.

be considered new first attestations of this Gallicism in Italian. The first known occurrences registered by the *GRADIT* date from 1554.[67]

Another first attestation of a known Gallicism can be found in Roseo's *Tre Libri Della Disciplina Militare*, a translation which, despite its military content, is also of some literary value.[68]

> Anticamente qualunche volta volevano levar un campo, che il trombetta del Capitan generale sonava tre volte. Al primo suono si levavan le tende […], al secondo caricavano, e al terzo ciascun […] **marciava** verso il luogo dove gli indrizzava il Generale. Al tempo nostro il primo suon della Tromba grida **buttasella**.[69]

> > (Back then, each time they had to leave the camp, the captain's trumpeter sounded the trumpet three times. At the first sound of the trumpet they packed up the tents […], at the second sound they packed their things and at the third sound […] they started to march where the general told them to. Nowadays the first sound of the trumpet means boot and saddle.)

In this translation we find again a large number of Gallicisms, which are mostly military terms, for example, *banda, picca, marciare*, and *trenciera* (a variant of *trincea*).[70] Given that the translation was published in 1550, the occurrence of *buttasella* < fr. *boute-selle* (saddle and boot) is a new first attestation of this Gallicism in Italian.[71]

As a short glimpse at these four translations has shown, translations of French texts into Italian were definitely a *locus* of language contact in Renaissance Italy. The fact that they contain both unknown Gallicisms and new first attestations of well-documented Gallicisms suggests that they too played a role in introducing and diffusing Gallicisms. In any case, they can be considered a fertile source for etymological studies on French loanwords in Italian.

Migrating Individuals

Recent research on Italianisms in sixteenth-century French has shown that Italian's influence was not only due to the circulation of Italian books, the translation of Italian texts, and the use of Italian as a literary language among French poets, but also to the presence of Italian immigrants in Renaissance

---

67 The entry in the *DELI* (s.v. *madama*) gives the same date.
68 The French original by Raymond de Fourquevaux is ascribed to Guillaume Du Bellay (cf. Grohovaz, 'La traduzione dal francese all'italiano nel XVI secolo', p. 123).
69 Fourquevaux, *Tre Libri Della Disciplina Militare*, trans. by Roseo, fol. 152^r.
70 For occurrences of these Gallicisms, see Fourquevaux, *Tre Libri Della Disciplina Militare*, trans. by Roseo, e.g. fols 6^r, 18^{r-v}, 20^r, 25^r, 29^r, 39^r, 52^r, 66^v, 73^r, 80^r, 113^r, 126^r, 137^r.
71 According to the *DELI* (s.v. *buttare*) and the *GRADIT* (s.v. *buttasella*), the first known attestation dates from 1561. Interestingly, the *LEI* (VI, 1421) registers an occurrence of the variant *buttaselle* from 1546.

France, especially in Lyons and at the French court.[72] By using both French and Italian regularly, these bilinguals played a significant role in promoting and spreading Italianisms in French.

Although less significant than the presence of the Italians in Renaissance France, that of the French in northern Italy is very likely to have had a certain linguistic impact on sixteenth-century Italian (cf. above). Since there are no available studies on the actual influence of the French soldiers who fought in the Italian Wars or of the French sovereigns of Milan, this issue cannot be dealt with in the framework of this chapter. There were other migrating individuals who could have exerted an influence on the Italian language: some Italians who had immigrated to France returned to their country of origin after they had stayed more than twenty years abroad. It is therefore more than likely that they brought with them not only new ideas, but also words from France. In addition to them, there were numerous Italian artists, ambassadors, and merchants who frequently sojourned in Renaissance France.[73] Although some of them spent just a few years in France, they too were exposed to language contact. As recent interdisciplinary historical studies on such migrating individuals worldwide have demonstrated, their role in promoting loanwords cannot be overestimated.[74] The impact of such 'agents in terms of innovation' or 'cultural brokers' on medieval Italian has been investigated by Trotter and Cella, both of whom analysed the language of merchants.[75] In the following, I will focus on migrating individuals belonging to two other groups: ambassadors and courtiers.

Italian Ambassadors in France

As pointed out above, French did not enjoy great prestige as a foreign language in Renaissance Italy. A closer look at some letters written by Tuscan ambassadors and envoys from the fifteenth and sixteenth centuries suggests that even among this group, only a few individuals had a good command of French.[76]

In a letter from 1493, the Bishop of Arezzo informs Pietro de Medici about his negotiations at the French court and admits that sometimes he could not follow the conversation because his interlocutor answered 'in francese' (in French).[77]

---

72   See Scharinger, *Mehrsprachigkeit im Frankreich der Frühen Neuzeit*, pp. 433–610, as well as Scharinger, 'Les lettres de Catherine de Médicis'.
73   See e.g. Picot, *Les Italiens en France au XVIe siècle* and Dubost, *La France italienne*.
74   See the contributions in Gialdroni and others, eds, *Migrating Words, Migrating Merchants, Migrating Law* and Wagner, Beinhoff, and Outhwaite, eds, *Merchants of Innovation*.
75   Cella, *La documentazione Gallerani-Fini nell'Archivio di Stato di Gent*; Cella, 'Prestiti nei testi mercantili toscani redatti di là dalle Alpi'; and Trotter, 'Italian Merchants in London and Paris'. The quoted phrases are from Wagner and Beinhoff, 'Merchants of Innovation', p. 5, and Cordes and Gialdroni, 'Introduction', p. 2, respectively.
76   *Négociations diplomatiques de la France avec la Toscane*, ed. by Desjardins, is still a fruitful source for the study of the language repertoire of Tuscan ambassadors at the French court.
77   *Négociations diplomatiques de la France avec la Toscane*, ed. by Desjardins, I, p. 334.

As the following passage from a letter written by Francesco Pandolfi from the French court in 1506 suggests, some Tuscan envoys had difficulty in speaking French still at the beginning of the sixteenth century.

> Il predetto uomo fece un longo discorso, [...], parlando al continuo in francese, in modo che Sua Maestà [Louis XII], nel mezzo del parlare, gli disse: 'Parlate in linguaggio vostro, che io v'intenderò meglio'.[78]
>
> (The above-mentioned man gave a long speech, [...], speaking continuously in French so that His Majesty [Louis XII] interrupted him and said: 'Speak your language, so I will understand you better'.)

This passage also demonstrates that the French king could speak — or at least understand — Italian, which can be explained by the prestige of Italian as an international vehicular language in Renaissance Europe (cf. above). Further information about the knowledge of Italian among French kings is given by the ambassador André Albertani in a letter from 1571:

> Sua Maestà [Charles IX] mi replico [...]: 'Mi so molto male di non saper parlare così bene italiano, ch'io vi possa esprimere il concetto mio'. E, replicandoli io che seguitassi di parlar francese, che l'intenderei, mi disse [...].[79]
>
> (His Majesty [Charles IX] answered me [...]: 'I am sorry that I cannot speak Italian well enough to express my thoughts to you'. And when I answered him that I could follow if he continued in French, he said: [...].)

Although Charles IX apologizes for not knowing Italian enough, he seems to understand it. In any case the Tuscan ambassador appears not to have spoken French during this private audience. The situation described by Albertani indicates that even in the second half of the sixteenth century it was not absolutely necessary for Italian ambassadors to know French perfectly at the beginning of their stay in France.[80] At least in some cases a kind of receptive bilingualism seems to have facilitated communication with French courtiers.[81]

---

78 *Négociations diplomatiques de la France avec la Toscane*, ed. by Desjardins, II, p. 186.
79 *Négociations diplomatiques de la France avec la Toscane*, ed. by Desjardins, III, p. 683.
80 The use of Italian at the French court is investigated in Scharinger, *Mehrsprachigkeit im Frankreich der Frühen Neuzeit*, pp. 327–71. See also Bingen, 'Usage et connaissance de la langue italienne dans la diplomatie française'. For a general overview of language use among Italian ambassadors in the early Renaissance, see Lazzarini, *Communication and Conflict*, pp. 239–62.
81 It should be borne in mind that, unlike the Scandinavian languages, French and Italian were not mutually intelligible in the sixteenth century. In order to understand French, an Italian had to acquire some basic knowledge by actively learning the language. The same is true for Frenchmen who wanted to speak or understand Italian. This special kind of receptive bilingualism was only possible because many French courtiers learned Italian as a foreign language in the sixteenth century.

Yet there were more gifted ambassadors too. The Venetian ambassador Girolamo Zorzi, whose letters have been edited and published only very recently,[82] claims to be fluent in French (cf. the following extracts from his letters from 1485 and 1486).

> Andai insieme cum el [...] duca a visitatione de la illustrissima madama de Bieiù [...]; e [...], volendoli narrar *latino sermone* quanto de supra ho dicto, [...] me referì i conseiri suo, che dovesse parlare *gallico sermone*, peroché la intendeva che io sapeva la lingua, né lei sapeva parlare altramente.[83]
>
> (Together with the [...] Duke I went to see the most distinguished Madame Beaujeu [...]; and [...], as I wanted to tell her in Latin about what I have mentioned above, [...] her counsellor told me to speak French, because she had heard that I could speak that language and because she did not speak any other language.)
>
> Et avanti principiasse a parlar, dise suo maestà [Charles VIII]: 'Oratore, io ve ho aldito parlar buon latin e franzoso, parlate mo italiano'.[84]
>
> (And before I started to speak, His Majesty [Charles VIII] said: 'Speaker, I have heard you speak good Latin and French, speak to me in Italian'.)

A glimpse at the language used in Zorzi's letters reveals some interesting Gallicisms. Apart from numerous occurrences of *grafier* < fr. *greffier* (a special kind of chancellor or a clerk)[85] and *balì* < fr. *bailli* (bailiff),[86] there are also some occurrences of *appuntamento* < fr. *appointement* (agreement, deal, arrangement).[87]

> Io rispondo che non posso creder che questo sia el voler del re, perché come loro sano è stà deliberato altramente et per la maestà del re mi è stà promesso molte volte la satisfaction, over far uno buono apunctamento.[88]
>
> (I answer that I cannot believe that this is the king's will, because, as you know, it has been decided otherwise and the king had promised that he would satisfy our requirements or make an alternative arrangement.)

---

82 For these eighty letters written between 1485 and 1487 and published for the first time in 2020, see *Lettere di Girolamo Zorzi*.
83 *Lettere di Girolamo Zorzi*, p. 26.
84 *Lettere di Girolamo Zorzi*, p. 65.
85 *Lettere di Girolamo Zorzi*, e.g. pp. 63–64, 65, 101. According to the editors (p. 257), *grafier* means 'chancelier' (chancellor). For other meanings of fr. *greffier*, see *TLFi* (s.v. *greffier* 1).
86 *Lettere di Girolamo Zorzi*, e.g. pp. 77, 86, 110, 175, 191.
87 *Lettere di Girolamo Zorzi*, pp. 177, 179, 191.
88 *Lettere di Girolamo Zorzi*, p. 191.

While *grafier* is hardly ever recorded in Italian dictionaries,[89] *balì* and *appuntamento* are usually treated as sixteenth-century loans.[90] The occurrences of these lexemes in Zorzi's letters, which were written between 1485 and 1487, can therefore be considered new first attestations of these Gallicisms in Italian.[91]

These findings, that is, the use of Gallicisms by Zorzi, are in line with what has already been observed by Migliorini and Zolli in letters and memoirs written by Italian ambassadors and travellers in sixteenth-century France.[92] Both scholars make a distinction between Gallicisms that remained limited to the idiolect of a certain individual (e.g. *sotto* < fr. *sot* (idiot)) and Gallicisms that became fully established in Italian at a later time (e.g. *lacchè* < fr. *laquais* (servant), *massacro* < fr. *massacre* (massacre)). Further examples are easy to find, for instance in documents written by Venetian ambassadors at the French court:[93]

> Mi rispose egli che veramente era stato avvertito di questi **volori** che non attendavano altro che noi, e che quella notte avevano alloggiato in un villaggio una lega innanzi.[94]

> (He answered me that in truth, he had been warned of these robbers who were only waiting for us and who that night had lodged in a village one mile ahead of us.)

> So bene che è stata veduta nel suo **gabinetto** a piangere più d'una volta: poi, fatta forza a se stessa, asciugatisi gli occhi, con allegra faccia si lasciava vedere nei luoghi pubblici.[95]

> (I know well that she has been seen crying in her private room more than once: then, having steeled herself, dried her eyes, and put on a happy face, she showed up in public places.)

While the noun *volori* < fr. *voleurs* (robbers) used by Girolamo Lippomano in 1577 must be considered an ephemeral borrowing which appears to have

---

89 No entry is found either in the *DELI* or in the *GRADIT*. The *GDLI* (s.v. *graffiere*) lists only one occurrence (with the meaning 'scrivano, funzionario di cancelleria' (clerk, official of a chancellery)) from a text by Pietro Giannone (1676–1748) referring to the Angevins' rule in southern Italy.

90 In the *GRADIT* (s.vv.) the first attestation of *appuntamento* dates from 1502, and that of *balì* from 1554. As for *balì*, the *Zingarelli* (s.v.) has an attestation from 1509. Cf. also the *LEI* (IV, 505).

91 In contrast to the *GRADIT*, the latest version of the *Zingarelli* (s.v. *appuntamento* 2) lists an attestation from 'av. 1471' — so even before the ones found in Zorzi's letters. As it is a *dizionario dell'uso*, it does not mention the source.

92 Migliorini, *Storia della lingua italiana*, pp. 378–80; Zolli, *Le parole straniere*, pp. 11–13.

93 Unlike Zorzi's correspondence, these documents are well known. They were edited and published already in 1838. See *Relations des ambassadeurs vénitiens sur les affaires de France*, ed. and trans. by Tommaseo.

94 *Relations des ambassadeurs vénitiens sur les affaires de France*, ed. and trans. by Tommaseo, II, pp. 286–88. The editor considers this Gallicism a 'Gallicismo barbaro' (II, p. 288 n. 1).

95 *Relations des ambassadeurs vénitiens sur les affaires de France*, ed. and trans. by Tommaseo, II, p. 156.

been used to add foreign allure to the description of his stay in France, in a text by Giovanni Correro from 1569 the term *gabinetto* < fr. *cabinet* (study, private room) can be considered one of the first occurrences of this Gallicism which was widely used in Italian from the late sixteenth century onwards.[96]

Given the numerous first occurrences of Gallicisms in the writings of these authors, it is not unlikely that ambassadors — just as merchants or other migrating individuals — played a significant role in introducing French loanwords into Italian.[97] As influential people of a high social rank, they could easily set new linguistic trends after their return to Italy. It is generally acknowledged that while code-switching requires a competence in both languages used, borrowing single words from a source language does not. Hence, even those ambassadors who had no good command of French (cf. above) could have contributed to the diffusion of Gallicisms.

Italian Courtiers at the French Court

Italians who had immigrated to France and returned to Italy after spending more than twenty years abroad could have had an even greater impact on the spread of Gallicisms than ambassadors and travellers. Although it has been shown that the use of their mother tongue remained highly vital due to Italian networks and the international prestige of Italian,[98] they sometimes borrowed French words.

A closer look at the letters written by Filippo Cavriana (1536–1606), who spent more than two decades in France as Catherine de Medici's personal physician,[99] is instructive:

> Stima egli molto il giuditio di V.E., [...], ma non si puo scordare l'offesa perché l'haver egli udito che V.E. havesse mal parlato di lui a Roma, et temendo che fosse vero, non puo metter in oblio cosi tosto lo sdegno. Anzi disse, doi giorni sono, [...] **Si vous sceussies ce qu'on m'escrit [...] de Rome de Mons. de Nevers, qu'il traitte encor avecq le pape, vous ne me parleries de luy, com[me] vous parles**. I prencipi, come V.E. sa, si senteno piu offesi dalle maledicenze altrui, che da le insidie.[100]

---

96 According to the *GRADIT* (s.v.), the first attestation dates from 1582. Note, however, that there are some earlier attestations of *gabinetto* in letters written by Italian ambassadors (cf. Migliorini, *Storia della lingua italiana*, p. 379).

97 See also Morgana, 'L'influsso francese', p. 690, who does not seem to exclude this either.

98 On the vitality of Italian as an immigrant language in sixteenth-century France, see Scharinger, *Mehrsprachigkeit im Frankreich der Frühen Neuzeit*, pp. 327–431.

99 For further information on Filippo Cavriana, see Vons, 'Les milieux médicaux à Paris vus par un médecin italien de Catherine de Médicis' and Scharinger, *Mehrsprachigkeit im Frankreich der Frühen Neuzeit*, p. 384.

100 BnF, MS fonds français 3374, fol. 48ᵛ. See also *Lettere di Filippo Cavriana*, p. 277. The spelling adopted for the transcription of Cavriana's letters in this chapter reflects the one used in the manuscripts, and may differ from the spelling used in Spigarolo's edition.

> (He greatly appreciates Your Excellence's opinion, [...] but he cannot forget this offence, because he has been told that Your Excellence has spoken ill of him in Rome, and as he fears that this could be the truth, he cannot forget this indignation so rapidly. In fact, two days ago [...] he said: 'If you knew the content of the letters about M. de Nevers I receive from Rome [...], for instance that he is still negotiating with the pope, you would not talk about him the way you are doing now'. For princes, as Your Excellence knows well, others' insinuations are worse than their noxious deeds.)

The instance of code-switching in this document from 1586 is exemplary of the numerous other switches in Cavriana's letters. It clearly shows that he had a good command of both Italian and French. What is striking, however, is that the two languages are used distinctly and for specific purposes. The parts in French are almost always citations of what has been said by French interlocutors, while the main text is in Italian. There is no language mixing, that is to say, no insertion of French elements into Italian. Despite this lack of interference with French, Cavriana regularly uses Gallicisms in Italian. Besides several occurrences of *gabinetto*,[101] *madamigella*,[102] and *lachais* (a variant of *lacchè*),[103] which can also be found in letters written by Italian ambassadors (cf. above), one finds *hardoise* < fr. *ardoise* (slate),[104] *billietto* < fr. *billet* (short notice or letter), *preudhommia* < fr. *preudhommie* (honourability, respectability),[105] and *rimarcare* < fr. *remarquer* (to remark).

> Il cavallo del conte d'Aulbigeau è stato visto dal capitan Iacopo Poiana, che bacia humilissimamente le mani a V.E., et lo trova buono et bello et ardito. [...]. È zaino et ha la testa non montonina, ma più tosto camusa, come egli **ha rimarcato**, giovine di sei a sette anni per lo piu.[106]

> (Captain Iacopo Poina, who humbly kisses Your Excellence's hands, has seen Count d'Aulbigeau's horse and finds it good, beautiful, and courageous [...]. It is of one colour only and its head is not like that of a ram, but rather flat, as he remarked. It is young. It is not older than six or seven years.)

---

101 BnF, MS fonds français 3374, fols 21ᵛ, 49ʳ, 70ʳ. BnF, MS fonds français 3974, fol. 108ʳ. See also *Lettere di Filippo Cavriana*, pp. 245, 278, 283, 311.
102 BnF, MS fonds français 3374, fols 53ʳ, 100ᵛ, 106ʳ. See also *Lettere di Filippo Cavriana*, pp. 225, 276, 288.
103 BnF, MS fonds français 3374, fols 17ʳ, 36ʳ, 44ʳ, 90ʳ. BnF, MS fonds français 3974, fol. 106ʳ. See also *Lettere di Filippo Cavriana*, pp. 228, 255, 262, 267, 281.
104 BnF, MS fonds français 3374, fol. 53ᵛ. See also *Lettere di Filippo Cavriana*, p. 289.
105 BnF, MS fonds français 3374, fols 53ʳ, 90ʳ. See also *Lettere di Filippo Cavriana*, pp. 255, 288.
106 BnF, MS fonds français 3374, fol. 50ᵛ. See also *Lettere di Filippo Cavriana*, p. 279.

> Ho havuto [lettera] di Toscana, et le mando il **billietto** che mi manda il segretario Vinta, della ricevuta delle [lettere] di V.E. che erano state smarrite per camin.[107]

> (I received a letter from Tuscany and I send you the short letter from Vinta in which he declares that he has received Your Excellence's letters which had been lost on their way to him.)

While the exotic abstract noun *preudhommia* has not yet been registered as a Gallicism in the relevant Italian dictionaries,[108] *hardoise*, *billietto*, and *rimarcare* can be considered new first attestations of *ardesia*, *biglietto*, and *rimarcare*, as the corresponding letters were written in 1586.[109] Unlike *preudhommia*, which appears to be a *hapax legomenon*, *ardesia*, *biglietto*, and *rimarcare* could have been introduced into Italian by migrating individuals like Cavriana after their return to Italy. Since there are no known attestations of *ardesia* in Italian texts before 1741,[110] this seems not to be the case for this Gallicism. As for *biglietto* and *rimarcare*, however, the occurrences in Cavriana's letters precede those found later on in Italian documents from Italy only for a short time.[111] It is therefore not unlikely that these Gallicisms were indeed brought to Italy by repatriates from France.

The spelling of most of Cavriana's Gallicisms clearly shows that the words he used were not yet established in Italian. Besides obvious cases such as <hardoise>, <preudhommie>, and <lachais>, the spelling <billietto> is noteworthy, too. As Cavriana never uses <ll> to render /ʎ/ in Italian, this spelling reveals that the word was of French origin and coined by Cavriana himself. This frequent use of Gallicisms seems to contradict what has been said above about the vitality of the Italian immigrants' mother tongue. How can it be explained that Cavriana introduces certain Gallicisms while his Italian in general does not display any interferences with French? In a previous study, I argued that most of his borrowings must be considered *cultural borrowings*.[112] In contrast to *core borrowings*, *cultural borrowings* are borrowed out of pragmatic necessity. As they usually designate new objects or ideas, there is not yet a corresponding word in

---

107 BnF, MS fonds français 3374, fol. 51ʳ. See also *Lettere di Filippo Cavriana*, p. 279.
108 No corresponding entry is found either in the *DELI*, the *GRADIT* or the *GDLI*.
109 According to both the *DELI* (s.vv.) and the *GRADIT* (s.vv.), *ardesia* is not attested before 1741, whereas *biglietto* (before 1600) and *rimarcare* (1630) are loanwords dating from the sixteenth and seventeenth century.
110 The latest version of the *Zingarelli* (s.v.) gives an attestation from 1733.
111 Since the relevant dictionaries give no precise date of the first attestation of *biglietto* ('av. 1600', i.e. in the works of Bernardo Davanzati (1529–1606), cf. note 109), the occurrence in Cavriana's letter could be parallel to the one in Davanzati's writings. Cf. also the *LEI* (VII, 1571).
112 Scharinger, *Mehrsprachigkeit im Frankreich der Frühen Neuzeit*, pp. 418–20.

the recipient language, thereby prompting the borrowing.[113] Lexemes like *preudhommia* (an ideal among French noblemen), *lachais* (a special kind of servant), and *hardoise* (a new material) can be easily identified as *cultural borrowings*, whereas others can not. Why, for instance, should *rimarcare* be a necessary loanword? This verb appears, in fact, to be a classical *core borrowing* (a synonym is *osservare* (observe, remark)). Yet even the use of such *core borrowings* does not mean that Cavriana had difficulty in finding the right word in Italian. On the contrary: according to Myers-Scotton, *core borrowings* are typical of the language of bilinguals, who sometimes make deliberate use of their bilingual repertoire. For this reason, these *core borrowings* in Cavriana's letters can by no means be considered unconscious interferences indicative of attrition.

To sum up, the sizeable number of Gallicisms in Cavriana's texts demonstrates that bilingual Italian immigrants in Renaissance France were primary channels of language contact. The fact that some of the French loanwords which became widely used in seventeenth-century Italian are attested for the first time in the writings of these migrating individuals suggests that they played an important role in promoting Gallicisms in Italian after their return to Italy.

Conclusions

The aim of this chapter was to present some plausible channels through which French might have exerted an influence on Italian in the sixteenth century. In contrast to the French influence on Italian in the Middle Ages or later in the seventeenth and eighteenth centuries, the French impact in the Renaissance has not been investigated in detail from a linguistic perspective.

A closer look at the production of French books in Italy has pointed out that French books were not a major vector of language contact. Throughout the whole sixteenth century, the number of French books produced in the peninsula (with the notorious exception of Piedmont) was negligible and by no means comparable to that of Italian books produced in Renaissance France. Even in multilingual literary texts, especially in comedies, French played a less important role than Spanish or Italian dialects. These findings are in line with what has been pointed out by many scholars: while Italian enjoyed great prestige as a literary language in sixteenth-century France, Italians were not particularly interested in French. This asymmetry of cultural exchange between France and Italy is also reflected in the lean number of translations from French. Although an exhaustive anthology of translations of French texts into Italian is not yet available, their number appears to have

---

113 On the difference between *core borrowings* and *cultural borrowings*, see Myers-Scotton, *Contact Linguistics*, p. 239.

been inferior to the inverse case. Despite their small number, translations from French must be considered an important *locus* of language contact. As has been shown, especially translations of non-literary texts (e.g. treatises) often abound with unknown Gallicisms and sometimes even contain new first attestations of known loanwords.

The exploratory study of letters and memoirs written by Italian ambassadors and courtiers who had resided in France for a long time suggests that such migrating individuals played a significant role in promoting Gallicisms after their return to Italy. Apart from exotic loans which seem to have remained confined to their idiolect, there are numerous first attestations of Gallicisms that became eventually established in Italian. The impact of such Italian repatriates should therefore not be underestimated. Their texts are a fruitful source for the study of Gallicisms in Italian and deserve more attention than they have received so far.

Works Cited

Abbreviations

DELI = Cortelazzo, Manlio, and Paolo Zolli, *Dizionario etimologico della lingua italiana*, 2nd edn (Bologna: Zanichelli, 1999)

DIFIT = Stammerjohann, Harro, and others, eds, *Dizionario di italianismi in francese, inglese, tedesco* (Florence: Accademia della Crusca, 2008)

GDLI = Battaglia, Salvatore, *Grande dizionario della lingua italiana*, 21 vols (Turin: UTET, 1961–2002) [electronic version, <https://www.gdli.it>]

GRADIT = De Mauro, Tullio, *Grande dizionario italiano dell'uso* (Turin: UTET, 2007) [electronic version, CD-ROM]

LEI = *Lessico etimologico italiano*, ed. by Max Pfister, Wolfgang Schweickard, and Elton Prifti (Wiesbaden: Reichert, 1979–)

TLFi = *Trésor de la langue française informatisé*, <http://atilf.atilf.fr/tlf.htm> [accessed 1 August 2020]

USTC = *Universal Short Title Catalogue: A Digital Bibliography of Early Modern Print Culture*, <https://www.ustc.ac.uk> [accessed 1 August 2020]

Zingarelli = Zingarelli, Nicola, *Lo Zingarelli 2020: Vocabolario della lingua italiana* (Bologna: Zanichelli, 2019) [electronic version, CD-ROM]

Manuscripts and Archival Sources

Paris, Bibliothèque nationale de France, MS fonds français 3374, <https://gallica.bnf.fr/ark:/12148/btv1b9059610x.r=3374?rk=171674;4> [accessed 1 August 2020]

Paris, Bibliothèque nationale de France, MS fonds français 3974: *Mémoires de la Ligue*, vol. I, <https://gallica.bnf.fr/ark:/12148/btv1b9059407r.r=3974ligue%20ligue?r> [accessed 1 August 2020]

Primary Sources and Databases

Commynes, Philippe de, *La Historia Famosa di Monsignor di Argenton delle Guerre et Costumi di Ludovico undecimo Re di Francia. Con la Battaglia et Morte del gran Duca di Borgogna, Tradotta à commune beneficio in lingua Italiana. Opra degna da essere letta da ogni gran Principe*, trans. by Nicolas Raince (Venice: Michele Tramezzino, 1544)

Fourquevaux, Raymond de, *Tre Libri Della Disciplina Militare: Tradotti nella lingua Italiana, Opera molto notabile*, trans. by Mambrino Roseo (Venice: Michele Tramezzino, 1550)

Joubert, Laurent, *La Prima Parte De Gli Errori Popolari Dell'Eccellentiss. Sign. Lorenzo Gioberti, Filosofo, Et Medico, Lettore nello Studio di Mompellieri. Nella quale si contiene l'Eccellenza della Medicina, [...] — Tradotta di Franzese in lingua Toscana dal Mag. M. e Alberto Luchi da Colle*, trans. by Alberto Luchi (Florence: Filippo Giunti, 1592)

Lettere di Filippo Cavriana = Filippo Cavriana: Mantovano del XVI secolo, letterato tacitista, storico e politico, ed. by Bruno Spigarolo (Mantova: Sometti, 1999)

Lettere di Girolamo Zorzi = La correspondance de Girolamo Zorzi, ambassadeur vénitien en France (1485–1488), ed. by Joël Blanchard, Giovanni Ciappelli, and Matthieu Scherman (Geneva: Droz, 2020)

Négociations diplomatiques de la France avec la Toscane: Documents recueillis par Giuseppe Canestrini, ed. by Abel Desjardins, 6 vols (Paris: Imprimerie Impériale, 1859–1886)

Opere di Giulio Cesare Croce = Trascrizione di alcune opere di GCC (v. 2.0 – gennaio 2019), <http://www.giuliocesarecroce.it/trascrizioni.html> [accessed 1 August 2020, no longer active]

Relations des ambassadeurs vénitiens sur les affaires de France au XVIe siècle, ed. and trans. by M. N. Tommaseo, 2 vols (Paris: Imprimerie Royale, 1838)

Scève, Maurice, *La Magnifica et Triumphale Entrata del Christianiss. Re di Francia Henrico secondo di questo nome, fatta nella nobile & antiqua Città di Lyone à luy & à la sua serenissima consorte Chaterina alli 2I. di Septemb. 1548. Colla particulare descritione della Comedia che fece recitare la Natione Fiorentina à richiesta di sua Maesta Christianissima*, trans. by F.M. (Lyon: Gulielmo Rouillio, 1549)

Secondary Studies

Ambrosch-Baroua, Tina, *Mehrsprachigkeit im Spiegel des Buchdrucks: Das spanische Italien im 16. und 17. Jahrhundert* (Cologne: MAP, 2015) <http://dx.doi.org/10.16994/bad> [accessed 1 August 2020]

Antonelli, Giuseppe, 'Italiano e Francese', in *La lingua nella storia d'Italia*, ed. by Luca Serianni (Florence: Società Dante Alighieri; Milan: Libri Scheiwiller, 2002), pp. 579–96

Baglioni, Daniele, 'L'italiano fuori d'Italia: Dal Medioevo all'Unità', in *Manuale di linguistica italiana*, ed. by Sergio Lubello (Berlin: De Gruyter, 2016), pp. 125–45

Baldacchini, Lorenzo, ed., *Il libro e le sue reti: La circolazione dell'edizione italiana nello spazio della francofonia (sec. XVI–XVII)* (Bologna: Bononia University Press, 2015)

Balsamo, Jean, *L'amorevolezza verso le cose Italiche: Le livre italien à Paris au XVIe siècle* (Geneva: Droz, 2015)

——, *Les rencontres des muses: Italianisme et anti-italianisme dans les Lettres françaises de la fin du XVIe siècle* (Geneva: Slatkine, 1992)

——, 'Le voyage d'Italie et la formation des élites françaises', *Renaissance and Reformation / Renaissance et Réforme*, 27.2 (2003), 9–21

Balsamo, Jean, Vito Castiglione Minischetti, and Giovanni Dotoli, *Les traductions de l'italien en français au XVIe siècle* (Fasano: Schena, 2009)

Bartoli Langeli, Attilo, and Mario Infelise, 'Il libro manoscritto e la stampa', in *L'italiano nelle regioni: Lingua nazionale e identità regionali*, ed. by Francesco Bruni (Turin: UTET, 1992), pp. 941–77

Beccaria, Gian Luigi, *Spagnolo e spagnoli in Italia: Riflessi ispanici sulla lingua italiana del Cinque e del Seicento*, Ristampa anastatica (1968; repr. Turin: Giappichelli, 1985)

Bezzola, Reto R., *Abbozzo di una storia dei gallicismi italiani nei primi secoli (750–1300): Saggio storico-linguistico* (Zürich: Seldwyla, 1924)

Bingen, Nicole, *Le Maître italien (1510–1660): Bibliographie des ouvrages d'enseignement de la langue italienne destinés au public de langue française, suivie d'un répertoire des ouvrages bilingues imprimés dans les pays de langue française*, Documenta et opuscula, 6 (Brussels: Van Balberghe, 1987)

——, *Philausone (1500–1660): Répertoire des ouvrages de langue italienne publiés dans les pays de langue française de 1500 à 1660* (Geneva: Droz, 1994)

——, 'Usage et connaissance de la langue italienne dans la diplomatie française (1490–1540)', in *Les langues étrangères en Europe: Apprentissages et pratiques (1450–1700)*, ed. by Marc Zuili and Susan Baddeley (Paris: Presses Universitaires de Paris-Sorbonne, 2012), pp. 123–56

Bingen, Nicole, and Adam Renaud, *Lectures italiennes dans les pays wallons à la première Modernité (1500–1630)* (Turnhout: Brepols, 2015)

Bingen, Nicole, and Anne-Marie Van Passen, 'La lexicographie bilingue français-italien, italien-français', in *Wörterbücher: Ein internationales Handbuch zur Lexikographie*, ed. by Franz-Josef Hausmann and others, vol. III (Berlin: De Gruyter, 1991), pp. 3007–13

Boillet, Danielle, and Marie-Françoise Piéjus, eds, *Les guerres d'Italie* (Paris: Paris III Sorbonne Nouvelle, 2002)

Bongrani, Paolo, and Silvia Morgana, 'La Lombardia', in *L'italiano nelle regioni: Lingua nazionale e identità regionali*, ed. by Francesco Bruni (Turin: UTET, 1992), pp. 84–142

Bouvier, Jean-Claude, 'Französisch und Romanisch', in *Lexikon der romanistischen Linguistik*, ed. by Günter Holtus, Michael Metzeltin, and Christian Schmitt, vol. VII (Tübingen: Niemeyer, 1998), pp. 56–67

Cella, Roberta, *La documentazione Gallerani-Fini nell'Archivio di Stato di Gent (1304–1309)* (Florence: SISMEL – Edizioni del Galluzzo, 2009)

———, 'Francesismi', in *Enciclopedia dell'italiano*, ed. by Raffaele Simone, vol. I (Rome: Treccani, 2010), pp. 520–24

———, *I gallicismi nei testi dell'italiano antico: Dalle origini alla fine del sec. XIV* (Florence: Accademia della Crusca, 2003)

———, 'Prestiti nei testi mercantili toscani redatti di là dalle Alpi: Saggio di glossario fino al 1350', *La lingua italiana: Storia, strutture, testi*, 6 (2010), 57–99

Colombo Timelli, Maria, 'Le *Dictionnaire* de Jean Antoine Fenice ou le charme discret des débuts en lexicographie bilingue', *Quaderni del CIRSIL*, 5 (2006), 9–24

———, 'Grammaires italiennes pour l'enseignement du français (1500–1700)', in *Grammaire et enseignement du français, 1500–1700*, ed. by Pierre Swiggers, Jean de Clerq, and Nico Lioce (Leuven: Peeters, 2000), pp. 565–87

Coluccia, Rosario, 'La situazione linguistica dell'Italia meridionale al tempo di Federico II', in *Scripta Mane(n)t: Studi sulla grafia dell'italiano*, ed. by Rosario Coluccia (Galatina: Congedo, 2002), pp. 7–26

Cordes, Albrecht, and Stefania Gialdroni, 'Introduction', in *Migrating Words, Migrating Merchants, Migrating Law: Trading Routes and the Development of Commercial Law*, ed. by Stefania Gialdroni and others (Leiden: Brill, 2020), pp. 1–9

Dardi, Andrea, *Dalla provincia all'Europa: L'influsso del francese sull'italiano tra il 1650 e il 1715* (Florence: Le Lettere, 1992)

———, 'Elementi francesi moderni nei dialetti italiani', in *Elementi stranieri nei dialetti italiani*, ed. by Consiglio Nazionale delle Ricerche/Centro di Studio per la Dialettologia Italiana, vol. I (Pisa: Pacini, 1986), pp. 21–35

Dubost, Jean-François, *La France italienne: XVIe–XVIIe siècle* (Paris: Aubier, 1997)

Fleischman, Suzanne, 'HOPE, T.E. *Lexical Borrowing in the Romance Languages: A Critical Study of Italianisms in French and Gallicisms in Italian from 1100–1900.* 2 vols New York: New York University Press, 1971. Pp. xiv, 1–354; iv, 355–782', *Romance Philology*, 28 (1975), 637–46

Foresti, Fabio, Fabio Marri, and Giovanni Petrolini, 'L'Emilia e la Romagna', in *L'italiano nelle regioni: Lingua nazionale e identità regionali*, ed. by Francesco Bruni (Turin: UTET, 1992), pp. 336–401

Formisano, Luciano, 'Contatti linguistici all'interno della Romània: Lingue romanze e italiano, sardo', in *Romanische Sprachgeschichte: Ein internationales Handbuch zur Geschichte der romanischen Sprachen / Histoire linguistique de la Romania: Manuel international d'histoire linguistique de la Romania*, ed. by Gerhard Ernst and others, vol. II (Berlin: De Gruyter, 2006), pp. 1758–76

Formisano, Luciano, and Charmaine Lee, 'Il "francese di Napoli" in opere di autori italiani dell'età angioina', in *Lingue e culture dell'Italia meridionale (1200–1600)*, ed. by Paolo Trovato (Rome: Bonacci, 1993), pp. 133–62

Fournel, Jean-Louis, and Jean-Claude Zancarini, *Les guerres d'Italie: Des batailles pour l'Europe* (Paris: Gallimard, 2003)

Gialdroni, Stefania, and others, eds, *Migrating Words, Migrating Merchants, Migrating Law: Trading Routes and the Development of Commercial Law* (Leiden: Brill, 2020)

Giovanardi, Claudio, *Linguaggi scientifici e lingua comune nel Settecento* (Rome: Bulzoni, 1987)

Gleßgen, Martin-Dietrich, 'Histoire interne du français (Europe): Lexique et formation des mots', in *Romanische Sprachgeschichte: Ein internationales Handbuch zur Geschichte der romanischen Sprachen / Histoire linguistique de la Romania: Manuel international d'histoire linguistique de la Romania*, ed. by Gerhard Ernst and others, vol. III (Berlin: De Gruyter, 2008), pp. 2947–73

Grohovaz, Valentina, 'La traduzione dal francese all'italiano nel XVI secolo: Avvio di una catalogazione delle opere a stampa (1501–1600)', in *La lettera e il torchio: Studi sulla produzione libraria tra XVI e XVIII secolo*, ed. by Ugo Rozzo (Udine: Forum, 2001), pp. 71–165

Holtus, Günter, 'Plan- und Kunstsprachen auf romanischer Basis IV. Franko-Italienisch', in *Lexikon der romanistischen Linguistik*, ed. by Günter Holtus, Michael Metzeltin, and Christian Schmitt, vol. VII (Tübingen: Niemeyer, 1998), pp. 705–56

Hope, T. E., *Lexical Borrowing in the Romance Languages: A Critical Study of Italianisms in French and Gallicisms in Italian from 1100 to 1900*, 2 vols, Language and Style Series, 10 (Oxford: Blackwell, 1971)

Jauch, Heike Susanne, *Das Frankoprovenzalische in Italien, Frankreich und der Schweiz: Sprachkontakt und Mehrsprachigkeit im Dreiländereck* (Bern: Lang, 2016)

Lazzarini, Isabella, *Communication and Conflict: Italian Diplomacy in the Early Renaissance, 1350–1520* (Oxford: Oxford University Press, 2015)

Lillo, Jacqueline, ed., *1583–2000: Quattro secoli di lessicografia italo-francese*, 2 vols (Bern: Lang, 2008)

Lorenzetti, Luca, 'L'italiano e le lingue romanze', in *Lexikon der romanistischen Linguistik*, ed. by Günter Holtus, Michael Metzeltin, and Christian Schmitt, vol. VII (Tübingen: Niemeyer, 1998), pp. 32–55

Marazzini, Claudio, 'Piemonte e Valle d'Aosta', in *L'italiano nelle regioni: Lingua nazionale e identità regionali*, ed. by Francesco Bruni (Turin: UTET, 1992), pp. 1–44

Matarrese, Tina, *Il settecento* (Bologna: Il Mulino, 1993)

Mattarucco, Giada, *Prime grammatiche d'italiano per francesi (secoli XVI–XVII)* (Florence: Accademia della Crusca, 2003)

Migliorini, Bruno, *Storia della lingua italiana*, 12th edn (Milan: Bompiani, 2007)

Minerva, Nadia, 'À l'aube de la lexicographie bilingue: Les dictionnaires de Pierre Canal', in *Les best-sellers de la lexicographie franco-italienne, XVIe–XXIe siècle*, ed. by Jacqueline Lillo (Rome: Carocci, 2013), pp. 19–31

Minerva, Nadia, and Carla Pellandra, *Insegnare il francese in Italia: Repertorio di manuali pubblicati dal 1625 al 1860* (Bologna: Pàtron, 1991)

Morgana, Silvia, 'L'influsso francese', in *Storia della lingua italiana*, III: *Le altre lingue*, ed. by Luca Serianni and Pietro Trifone (Turin: Einaudi, 1994), pp. 671–719

——, *Storia linguistica di Milano* (Rome: Carocci, 2012)

Mormile, Mario, *L'italiano in Francia, il francese in Italia: Storia critica delle opere grammaticali francesi in Italia ed italiane in Francia dal Rinascimento al Primo Ottocento* (Turin: Meynier, 1989)

—— , *Storia dei dizionari bilingui italo-francesi* (Fasano: Schena, 1993)

Myers-Scotton, Carol, *Contact Linguistics: Bilingual Encounters and Grammatical Outcomes* (Cambridge: Cambridge University Press, 2002)

Picot, Emile, *Les Français italianisants au XVIe siècle*, 2 vols (1906–1907; repr. New York: Franklin, 1968)

—— , *Les Italiens en France au XVIe siècle*, Ristampa anastatica dell'edizione Bordeaux 1918 (1918; repr. Rome: Vecchiarelli, 1995)

Raugei, Anna Maria, *Un abbozzo di grammatica francese del '500: Le note di Gian Vincenzo Pinelli* (Fasano: Schena; Paris: Nizet, 1984)

Rizzo, Palma Letizia, 'Elementi francesi nella lingua dei poetici siciliani della "Magna Curia"', *Bollettino del Centro studi filologici e linguistici siciliani*, 1 (1953), 115–29; 2 (1954), 93–151

Rossebastiano Bart, Alda, *Antichi vocabolari plurilingui d'uso popolare: La tradizione del 'Solenissimo Vochabuolista'* (Alessandria: Dell'Orso, 1984)

Sabatini, Francesco, *Napoli angioina: Cultura e società* (Naples: Edizioni Scientifiche Italiane, 1975)

Sarauw, Christine, *Die Italianismen in der französischen Sprache des 16. Jahrhunderts* (Borna: Noske, 1920)

Scharinger, Thomas, 'Italianismi nel lessico schermistico del francese cinquecentesco: Un'indagine sulla traduzione francese del *Nobilissimo discorso intorno il schermo di spada* di Girolamo Cavalcabò', in *Actes du XXIXe Congrès International de Linguistique et de Philologie Romanes (Copenhague, 01.–06.07.2019) Section 5*, ed. by Lene Schøsler and Juhani Härmä (Strasbourg: ÉLiPhi, 2021), pp. 735–45

—— , '*L'italiano fuori d'Italia* im Spiegel des frühneuzeitlichen Buchdrucks – Zu Marktwert und Verbreitung italienischer Drucke im Europa des 16. Jahrhunderts', in *Mehrsprachigkeit und Ökonomie*, ed. by Tina Ambrosch-Baroua, Amina Kropp, and Johannes Müller-Lancé (Munich: Open Access LMU, 2017), pp. 161–88, <https://doi.org/10.5282/ubm/epub.40524> [accessed 1 August 2020]

—— , 'Les lettres de Catherine de Médicis: Une source négligée par les historiographes de la langue française', in *Nouvelles voies d'accès au changement linguistique*, ed. by Wendy Ayres-Bennett and others (Paris: Classiques Garnier, 2018), pp. 39–53

—— , *Mehrsprachigkeit im Frankreich der Frühen Neuzeit: Zur Präsenz des Italienischen, seinem Einfluss auf das Französische und zur Diskussion um das 'françois italianizé'* (Tübingen: Narr, 2018)

Schweickard, Wolfgang, 'Storia interna dell'italiano: Lessico e formazione delle parole', in *Romanische Sprachgeschichte: Ein internationales Handbuch zur Geschichte der romanischen Sprachen / Histoire linguistique de la Romania: Manuel international d'histoire linguistique de la Romania*, ed. by Gerhard Ernst and others, vol. III (Berlin: De Gruyter, 2008), pp. 2847–72

Stammerjohann, Harro, and Gesine Seymer, 'L'italiano in Europa: Italianismi in francese, inglese e tedesco', in *Firenze e la lingua italiana fra nazione ed*

Europa: Atti del Convegno di studi, Firenze, 27–28 maggio 2004, ed. by Nicoletta Maraschio (Florence: Firenze University Press, 2007), pp. 41–55

Trotter, David, 'Contacts linguistiques intraromans: Roman et français, occitan', in *Romanische Sprachgeschichte: Ein internationales Handbuch zur Geschichte der romanischen Sprachen / Histoire linguistique de la Romania: Manuel international d'histoire linguistique de la Romania*, ed. by Gerhard Ernst and others, vol. II (Berlin: De Gruyter, 2006), pp. 1776–85

———, 'Italian Merchants in London and Paris: Evidence of Language Contact in the Gallerani Accounts, 1305–1308', in *On Linguistic Change in French: Sociohistorical Approaches. Studies in Honour of R. Anthony Lodge / Le changement linguistique en français: Aspects socio-historiques. Études en homage au professeur R. Anthony Lodge*, ed. by Timothy Pooley and Dominique Lagorgette (Chambéry: Université de Savoie, 2011), pp. 209–28

Varvaro, Alberto, 'Notizie sul lessico della Sicilia medievale. I. Francesismi', *Bollettino del Centro studi filologici e linguistici siciliani*, 12 (1973), 72–104

Vons, Jacqueline, 'Les milieux médicaux à Paris vus par un médecin italien de Catherine de Médicis', Cour de France, <http://cour-de-france.fr/article1632.html> [accessed 1 August 2020]

Wagner, Esther-Miriam, and Bettina Beinhoff, 'Merchants of Innovation: The Languages of Traders', in *Merchants of Innovation: The Languages of Traders*, ed. by Esther-Miriam Wagner, Bettina Beinhoff, and Ben Outhwaite (Berlin: De Gruyter, 2017), pp. 3–16

Wagner, Esther-Miriam, Bettina Beinhoff, and Ben Outhwaite, eds, *Merchants of Innovation: The Languages of Traders* (Berlin: De Gruyter, 2017)

Wilhelm, Raymund, 'Regionale Sprachgeschichte als Geschichte eines mehrsprachigen Raumes: Perspektiven einer Sprachgeschichte der Lombardei', in *Mit Clio im Gespräch: Romanische Sprachgeschichten und Sprachgeschichtsschreibung*, ed. by Jochen Hafner and Wulf Oesterreicher (Tübingen: Narr, 2007), pp. 77–101

Wind, Bartina H., *Les mots italiens introduits en français au XVIe siècle* (Deventer: Kluwer, 1928)

Zolli, Paolo, *L'influsso francese sul veneziano del XVIII secolo* (Venice: Istituto veneto di scienze, lettere ed arti, 1971)

———, *Le parole straniere* (Bologna: Zanichelli, 1976)

PART 3

Encounters with the East

SAMANTHA KELLY

Ethiopia and Ethiopian Languages in Renaissance Italy

Italy played a major role in Ethiopian–European contacts in the Renaissance. It was the region most commonly visited by Ethiopian ambassadors before 1500, and through the papacy, retained an important role in diplomatic exchange in the sixteenth century; it was also the primary destination of Ethiopian pilgrims throughout the period. These relations, which have been well documented, provide an opportunity to approach the question of Ethiopian languages in Italy from a social-cultural perspective, by addressing the interests that undergirded contact, the occasions and methods of knowledge transfer, and the individuals and networks involved.[1] As we shall see, before the sixteenth century and despite a long-standing interest in the Ethiopian Church, Italians evinced virtually no interest in Gəʿəz.[2] An ancient Ethiopian language attested in script from at least the first century CE, Gəʿəz was no longer used in common speech by around the eleventh century, replaced by a variety of vernacular languages including Amharic and Tigrinya, but remained the language of the Ethiopian Church, of royal chronicles and administrative documents, and indeed of virtually all Christian Ethiopian writing through the sixteenth century.[3] Without recourse to it before the Cinquecento, Italians and Ethiopians communicated rather through a many-sided vernacular multilingualism utilized by, but only occasionally remarked in, the great Italian courts and

---

1 For a similar approach to Arabic in Renaissance Italy, see Grévin, 'De Damas à Urbino'.
2 For Ethiopian terms I use the transliteration system of Uhlig and Bausi, eds, *Encyclopaedia Aethiopica*.
3 Kelly, 'Introduction', pp. 25–26. Words in Tigrinya are attested in royal documents from the twelfth century, and at least one document was written fully in Amharic, the spoken language of the ruling Solomonic dynasty and court (1270 ff.) by the fourteenth century: Derat, *L'énigme d'une dynastie sainte*, pp. 33–36, 261–63; Lusini, 'Lingua letteraria e lingua di corte', pp. 278–81.

Samantha Kelly (slkelly@history.rutgers.edu) is Professor of History at Rutgers University. A specialist of late medieval Italy and Ethiopian–European relations, she recently edited *A Companion to Medieval Ethiopia and Eritrea* (Brill, 2020).

centres of learning. This practice, which continued in the sixteenth century, included the use of an intermediate idiom, Arabic, as well as limited European acquisition of Ethiopian languages (and the reverse as well). Only among a rather small group of humanist scholars did Gəʿəz eventually attract notice. By collaborating with Ethiopian scholars in Europe, they helped produce landmarks in the burgeoning field of European 'oriental' language study: the first editions of Gəʿəz texts and scholarly studies of the Gəʿəz language. The final section of this essay will review these groundbreaking efforts, again with an eye to the cultural trends and logistical conditions surrounding them. From this social-cultural perspective, as I propose in conclusion, certain red threads can be detected that link the Renaissance to the more famous age of European study of Ethiopian language, the Seicento.

The Context: Ideas about and Contacts with Ethiopians

The earliest relatively accurate western European reports about Christian Ethiopia came out of the Holy Land in the thirteenth century, when Latin pilgrims to and historians of the region began to include Ethiopians in their thumbnail portraits of the various Christian communities to be found there. Their information was imperfect: Ethiopians were sometimes confused with Nubians or conflated with 'Jacobites' generally, and said to hail from a land (often called India, following an ancient tradition linking southern Asia with regions around the Red Sea) of uncertain location and extent.[4] Nonetheless, a much-cited account like that of Jacques de Vitry, bishop of Acre from 1216 to 1227, correctly stated that the Ethiopians were ruled by a Christian king, that their Church was ancient (indeed, according to Jacques, an apostolic foundation), that it had split from the Greek and Roman Churches at the Council of Chalcedon (451) and thereafter followed practices, including circumcision, that diverged from those of Rome.[5] Such information was enough to spark the main lines of Italian (and European) interest in Ethiopia, which developed over the course of the thirteenth and fourteenth centuries. For the papacy, the existence of an established Christian Church somewhere south of Egypt fuelled hopes of an eventual ecclesiastical union, and popes from Nicholas III on sporadically dispatched envoys in the hope of making contact.[6] The value of the Ethiopian king's political independence from Muslim domination took a bit longer to be recognized. By the early fourteenth century, when the last

---

[4] See the accounts collected in Cerulli, *Etiopi in Palestina*, I, pp. 42–61, and (for association of Ethiopia with India) 102–06, 121–22; cf. Fiaccadori, 'India as a Name of Ethiopia'.

[5] Jacques de Vitry, *Libri duo, quorum prior orientalis [...] historiae*, ed. by Moschus, pp. 144–47. For an overview of thirteenth-century clerical views, see Kelly, 'Heretics, Allies, Exemplary Christians', pp. 197–99.

[6] For the papal letters dispatched by Nicholas III (1289), John XXII (1329), and many successors, see *Lettere tra i pontefici romani e i principi etiopici*, ed. by Raineri.

Latin outpost in the Levant had fallen, proponents of a new crusade initiative were advocating a military alliance with this Christian ruler, whose strategic location south of Egypt could place critical pressure on Mamluk Egypt. Just such military aid had long been hoped for from 'Prester John', and over the course of the fourteenth century that legendary Christian ruler, once thought to reside in Asia, was increasingly identified with Ethiopia's Christian ruler, who thereby acquired the Prester's other attributes: a great army, fabulous wealth, and an increasingly idealized Christian piety.[7]

The sort of attitudes towards Ethiopia that one might find in Italy already in the early fourteenth century are reflected in the *Tractatus* of the Genoese priest Giovanni da Carignano, who claimed to have interviewed an Ethiopian embassy dispatched to 'the king of the Spains' that stopped in his native Genoa around 1310. Although Carignano identified Prester John as the Ethiopian patriarch rather than the 'emperor' himself, he stressed that the Prester was 'perfectly Christian, far greater and more powerful than the Roman pope is', but 'accepts the Roman pope as his lord [and] readily would obey him, if he could come or send his ambassadors to us'. The emperor he described as 'the most powerful lord in the world [...] more powerful than the emperor of the Western Christians', who 'continually fights against the Muslims' and who indeed had sent these envoys to offer military aid to the Spanish king in his own battles against Muslim foes.[8] This much could be considered the hopeful portrait cobbled together from the Prester legend and other European sources: an index of current opinion rather than reliable testimony to an actual encounter. Until recently, when only a short and much later citation of Carignano's now-lost text was available, the veracity of the embassy, and indeed of Carignano's text itself, was in doubt. However, the recent discovery of a work explicitly citing and paraphrasing Carignano at length, and written within a few decades of the original, not only makes clear that the *Tractatus* existed but, in its inclusion of accurate details of Ethiopian religious, epistolary, and military practice, suggests that an Ethiopian visit to Genoa may indeed have occurred.[9] If this Ethiopian party was a formal royal embassy, it was a failed one: according to the account itself it never reached the 'king of the Spains', nor is it plausible, as the text claims, that it visited the pope. Alternately, it may attest to informal contacts on Italian soil, about which there is nothing implausible. Ethiopian Christians had established diasporic communities in Egypt, Jerusalem, and probably also Cyprus by this

---

7 Latin texts originally identified Prester John as a heterodox 'Nestorian', and debates over his orthodoxy never entirely ceased: Kelly, 'Heretics, Allies, Exemplary Christians', pp. 200–204.
8 Chiesa and Bausi, 'The *Ystoria Ethyopie* in the *Cronica Universalis*', pp. 14–21, 32–33.
9 In addition to accurate statements regarding Ethiopian Christian practice, these include the ornamental heading of formal Ethiopian correspondence and the mention of a 'baboon army', surprisingly reminiscent of the royal practice of naming military regiments after animals: see Chiesa and Bausi, 'The *Ystoria Ethyopie* in the *Cronica Universalis*', pp. 30–31, 34–37.

time, from which Ethiopian pilgrims or envoys could well have reached Italian ports on board Genoese or Venetian ships plying the eastern Mediterranean, as was the case some decades later.[10]

For successful and well-attested diplomatic contacts we must await the turn of the fifteenth century, after which they became regular. The best documented embassies of the fifteenth century, almost all to Italy, are those of the Ethiopian rulers Dawit II (to Venice, 1402), Yəsḥaq (to Alfonso of Aragon in Valencia, 1427), Zärʾa Yaʿqob (to Alfonso of Aragon in Naples, 1450), and a delegation that reached Sixtus IV in Rome in 1481, during the reign of the child-ruler Ǝskəndər.[11] Also unofficial, but significant, was the Ethiopian delegation solicited by Pope Eugene IV for participation at the Council of Ferrara-Florence (1441). It comprised four monks from the Ethiopian monastery in Jerusalem, pressed into service by a papal envoy when official delegates from Ethiopia could not be obtained, whose unofficial status did not prevent them from being interviewed regarding the main conciliar aims of ecumenical union and military alliance in a new crusade.[12] In the sixteenth century, Portugal played the central diplomatic role, having taken the lead in pursuing military alliance with Ethiopia and having successfully landed its ambassadors there, but the papacy remained involved in these exchanges, sending and receiving envoys and diplomatic correspondence (for instance, in 1515, 1533, and 1544) and continuing to pursue, in varying configurations, its goal of ecclesiastical union.[13]

The Ethiopian presence represented by these embassies was supplemented by a rather regular stream of Ethiopian pilgrims to Italy. The papal archives record pilgrimage certificates, *litterae passus*, and certificates of indulgence for any who aided the pilgrims on their return voyage issued to some thirty 'Ethiopian' or 'Indian' pilgrims between 1403 and 1492. Not all of these can be definitively identified as Ethiopian Orthodox.[14] Conversely, there were likely

---

10 For a recent overview on these communities, see Kelly, 'Medieval Ethiopian Diasporas', pp. 427–37.
11 For sources and interpretations over time, see Jorga, 'Cenni sulle relazioni tra l'Abissinia e l'Europa cattolica'; Cerone, 'La politica orientale di Alfonso d'Aragona', pp. 64–87; Garretson, 'A Note on Relations between Ethiopia and the Kingdom of Aragon'; Lowe, 'Representing Africa', pp. 101–05; Ghinzoni, 'Un'ambasciata del Prete Gianni'; Marinescu, *La politique orientale d'Alfonso V d'Aragon*, pp. 18–23, 198–200; Salvadore, *The African Prester John*, pp. 24–26, 39–49, 66–70; Krebs, *Medieval Ethiopian Kingship, Craft, and Diplomacy*, pp. 17–29, 62–73, 123–32.
12 Cerulli, 'Eugenio IV e gli etiopi al Concilio di Firenze'; Tedeschi, 'Etiopi e Copti al Concilio di Firenze'; Weber, 'La bulle *Cantate Domino*'; Kelly, 'Biondo Flavio on Ethiopia'; Kelly, 'Ewosṭateans at the Council of Florence'.
13 *Lettere tra i pontefici romani e i principi etiopici*, ed. by Raineri; Martínez d'Alòs-Moner, *Envoys of a Human God*.
14 Lefevre, 'Documenti pontifici sui rapporti con l'Etiopia', pp. 21–27. The terms 'Indian' and 'Ethiopian' are both employed, sometimes together (as in 'James of India Major [...] of Ethiopia'). However, both 'Indian' and 'Ethiopian' could denote people from multiple regions: see Weber, 'Gli Etiopi a Roma nel Quattrocento', at n. 6; Spicer, 'Free Men and

other Ethiopian visitors not included in these registers. Latin references to encounters with Ethiopians in Rome in 1404 and Bologna in 1407 provide other indices of how often Ethiopian Christians might be encountered in Italy, even before they benefited from a stable residence in Rome toward the end of the Quattrocento.[15]

Such visitors thus provided numerous opportunities for Italians to indulge interests in Ethiopia that might go beyond ecumenical union and military alliance. One was certainly a general curiosity about the land and culture of Ethiopia: its flora and fauna, governmental organization, buildings, clothing, and customs. The committee that interviewed the Ethiopian delegates at the Council of Florence in 1441 (and that included two curious papal secretaries, the humanists Poggio Bracciolini and Biondo Flavio) asked a number of such questions.[16] So did the Venetian Alessandro Zorzi, who collected information from Ethiopians passing through his home city in the late 1510s and 1520s.[17] Perhaps the most famous Renaissance collection of such information was that of Francisco Álvares, chaplain to the Portuguese embassy that spent the years 1520–1526 in Ethiopia. His account of these years circulated in manuscript in Italy even before it was published under the title *Verdadera Informaçam das terras do Preste Joam das Indias* in Lisbon in 1540, and in the (somewhat different) Italian translation of Ramusio in Venice in 1550.[18]

In a number of cases, this general curiosity was accompanied or even driven by a more specific interest: in geographical knowledge. It had political import in rendering access to and military cooperation with Ethiopia more feasible, commercial potential in indicating the routes to the legendary wealth of the country, and intellectual appeal for scholars excited about the possibility of surpassing the natural-scientific knowledge of the ancients. Not surprisingly, perhaps, many Ethiopian embassies and informal visits can be associated with the production of an itinerary or map. These include the map of Carignano, mutilated even before going missing in World War II but believed to have boasted a detailed rendering of the Ethiopian region; the itinerary outlining the journey from Venice to Aksum, produced in Venice around the time of the 1402 embassy; the map drawn up, with the aid of Ethiopian ambassadors, in Valencia in 1427; the 'Egyptus Novelo', with its own detailed rendering of Ethiopia, produced in Florence in the wake of the Council of Florence; Fra Mauro's *mappamundi* of the 1440s, based on Ethiopian informants in Venice;

Women of African Ancestry', p. 85.
15 Salvadore, *The African Prester John*, pp. 54–58; Krebs, *Medieval Ethiopian Kingship, Craft, and Diplomacy*, pp. 25–29.
16 Tedeschi, 'L'Etiopia di Poggio Bracciolini'; Bouloux, 'Du nouveau au sud de l'Égypte'; Bouloux, 'Du nouveau sur la géographie de l'Éthiopie'.
17 See *Ethiopian Itineraries*, ed. by Crawford, pp. 108–93, which include much information beyond the geographical.
18 Álvares, *Verdadera Informaçam*, ed. by Beckingham and Huntingford, trans. by Adderley, with information on the textual versions at I, pp. 5–9.

and the itineraries recorded by the aforementioned Alessandro Zorzi in the 1520s.[19] Such information, as well as the lingering legend of Prester John, continued to feed the keen geographic and cartographic interest in Africa through the sixteenth century.[20]

For at least a few humanists, finally, Ethiopia sparked curiosity as a window onto antiquity. Biondo Flavio is the best witness of this curiosity in the fifteenth century. When at the Council of Florence the Ethiopian delegates affirmed their biblical ancestors (the Queen of Sheba and Queen Candace) or recalled Ethiopia's sixth-century conquest of Ḥimyar in the Yemen, Biondo could envision Ethiopia as a living vestige of that ancient past, even going so far as to prove its current military capacity by citing the size of armies credited to Ethiopia in the Bible.[21] When the delegates claimed to have 'the books of Solomon, of which they said they had more than we', Ethiopia indeed promised to offer texts from that ancient past, and from Europe's and Ethiopia's shared traditions, that the Latins had lost. Biondo was not the only Italian susceptible to such attractions. In 1459, Duke Francesco Sforza of Milan, upon encountering a visitor who claimed ties to the Ethiopian royal court, pressed him about the books of Solomon's wisdom, in the hopes of acquiring a Latin translation.[22]

The Language of Italian–Ethiopian Encounters

Francesco Sforza's interest in a Latin translation is typical of his time. Despite some clergy's keen interest in Ethiopian Christianity, despite the curiosity of humanists and bibliophiles in its ancient past and potentially revelatory ancient Judaeo-Christian texts, there seems to have been virtually no interest in the authentically ancient language through which they could be known. It was not for lack of examples. Admittedly, fifteenth-century Ethiopian embassies to Latin Europe do not seem to have carried official royal letters, the envoys instead communicating their messages orally.[23] But the delegation to Florence was an exception. Niqodemos, prior of the Ethiopian monastery in Jerusalem, had penned a letter to the pope. Like virtually all Christian Ethiopian writing

---

19 A brief survey of most is Lefevre, 'Riflessi etiopici', pp. 341–44, 351–61, 378–80; on the map of 1427, see Thomassy, 'De Guillaume Fillastre considéré comme géographe'.
20 Relaño, *The Shaping of Africa*, esp. pp. 60–66.
21 Biondo Flavio, *Historiarum ab inclinatione Romanorum quartae decadis liber secundus*, ed. by Nogara, pp. 20–21, 24, 26–27, discussed in Kelly, 'Biondo Flavio on Ethiopia', pp. 175–77.
22 Kelly, 'Biondo Flavio on Ethiopia', p. 176; on Francesco Sforza, Ghinzoni, 'Un'ambasciata del Prete Gianni', p. 149.
23 No fifteenth-century royal letters to European addressees are extant or mentioned in the sources, and Alfonso of Aragon's return letter in 1450 (edited in Cerone, 'La politica orientale di Alfonso d'Aragona', pp. 64–65) makes clear that those envoys communicated their message orally.

of the time, it was in Gəʿəz, and was translated into Latin at the council. The papal court thus had the basic elements necessary to begin to inquire into and even potentially use this language, for instance in a multilingual 'Confession of Faith' such as the council had drawn up, in 1439, for the benefit of various foreign communities. I have found no evidence that it did.[24]

Seventy years later that indifference would give way. In the meantime, another question merits exploration: if not through Gəʿəz, through what linguistic means did the many formal and informal exchanges of the fifteenth (and even fourteenth) century take place? Few occasions offer explicit information on this matter. One that does is the Council of Florence in 1441, perhaps because Biondo Flavio, who witnessed the Ethiopian delegation's oration and subsequent interview, was simultaneously writing a history and therefore took careful notes. He specified that for the principal delegate's oration (and also, presumably, the subsequent interview) two interpreters were employed, one *Arabs*, the other *Latinus*.[25] The Arabic translator has been identified as Beltramo Mignanelli, a Sienese merchant and diplomat who had learned Arabic in his frequent travels to Egypt, Syria, and other Muslim-ruled lands.[26] Mignanelli, it is safe to say, knew no Ethiopian language: his task was to translate from Arabic into Italian. The Latin translator was then employed for the benefit of the attending clerics who did not understand Italian. This means that the Ethiopian delegates spoke not in Gəʿəz or in any Ethiopian vernacular, but in Arabic. Their facility in Arabic is perfectly plausible. It is not impossible that one or more of them learned it in Ethiopia itself. The Egyptian-born metropolitans of the Ethiopian Church (and whatever companions accompanied them from Egypt) were native Arabic speakers, whose presence demanded a certain degree of multilingualism, either on the part of the metropolitans themselves, some of whom are known to have translated Arabic Christian texts into Gəʿəz, or on the part of Ethiopian interpreters who translated for them.[27] We may recall, however, that the delegates had come from the Ethiopian monastery in Jerusalem, and it is more likely that they acquired Arabic there. In Jerusalem and in Egypt (where the Ethiopians had three more diasporic monasteries), Arabic was a spoken language of the Christian population as well as the Muslim majority, and the *lingua franca*

---

24 A copy of the 1439 *Confession of Faith*, written in Greek, Hebrew, Arabic, Syriac, Armenian, and 'Tartaric', was later owned by the Florentine collector Niccolò Gaddi (1537–1591), who wrote (or had written) on the final pages his name in Arabic and Gəʿəz characters, as well as 'Jesus Christ' in Gəʿəz: an index of interest in the mid-sixteenth century, but not the fifteenth. Cerulli, 'Eugenio IV e gli etiopi al Concilio di Firenze', pp. 361–62.

25 Biondo Flavio, *Historiarum ab inclinatione Romanorum quartae decadis liber secundus*, ed. by Nogara, p. 20.

26 Grévin, 'Between Arabic and Latin', p. 157.

27 On the metropolitan Sälama as translator, see Bausi, 'Ethiopia and the Christian Ecumene', pp. 229–30; on the metropolitan using a translator, see Álvares, *Verdadera Informaçam*, ed. by Beckingham and Huntingford, trans. by Adderley, II, p. 350.

through which the Ethiopians, who often remained for years in these settlements, interacted with their neighbours. Gəʿəz manuscripts produced in these communities include marginal notes in Arabic and — perhaps more telling of Arabic's use in everyday speech — common Arabic terms transliterated into Gəʿəz script in Gəʿəz texts themselves.[28] The German pilgrim Bernhard von Breydenbach, who visited the Holy Land in 1483, confirms such a usage: while acknowledging that the Ethiopians had their own language, he also observed that they 'know the Saracen idiom and use it when they wish'.[29]

A second instance of the use of Arabic in Italian–Ethiopian exchanges comes to us indirectly. Dominican friars in Pisa wrote an account of the conversations they held with two Ethiopian pilgrims on their way from Rome to Santiago de Compostela in 1516. This account now survives only as part of a larger work published by the Dominican Serafino Razzi in 1577. The Ethiopians' testimony thus reaches us third-hand, but on the question of language there would seem to be little reason for the redactors to invent. According to this account, when around 1515 Pope Leo X wished to converse with a newly arrived Ethiopian pilgrim called 'Tommaso', the latter (who had spent a year in the Holy Land) spoke in Arabic, and his words were translated into Italian by 'Florentine merchants to the Levant who served as interpreters'.[30] The circumstances exactly match those of the Council of Florence: Ethiopians' acquisition of Arabic primarily through residence in the Levant, Italians' acquisition of Arabic primarily through commercial activity in the same region, and the use of this intermediate language for Ethiopian–Italian encounters in Italy. This second example's occurrence in the 1510s also indicates that Arabic continued to be used even after the study of Gəʿəz in Europe had begun.

The vernacular multilingualism of both Ethiopians and Italians thus made communication possible. Both groups, however, acquired Arabic through practical use in everyday exchanges, which had its drawbacks. The interview with the Ethiopian delegation at Florence, for instance, included delicate theological questions, some (like the issue of Christ's nature that had divided the churches at Chalcedon) turning on precise terminological issues. Biondo Flavio lamented the 'great inconvenience of the translator's ignorance'—a judgement confirmed by the errors in Mignanelli's Arabic translation of the bull of union drafted at the council.[31] Misunderstandings on both sides were

---

[28] For instance, BnF, MS Éth. 35, copied in Cairo, with a donation notice in Arabic at fol. 198; BAV, MS Vat. et. 25, with an inventory probably from Jerusalem including terms for clothing in transliterated Arabic at fol. 263ᵛ.

[29] Breydenbach, *Peregrinatio in Terram Sanctam*. I cite from the first (1486) edition, unfoliated. In the modern foliation of a freely accessible digitized copy at the Technische Universität Darmstadt (http://tudigit.ulb.tu-darmstadt.de/show/inc-iv-97), this is fol. 82ʳ.

[30] Razzi, *Vite dei santi e beati*, p. 294.

[31] Biondo Flavio, *Historiarum ab inclinatione Romanorum quartae decadis liber secundus*, ed. by Nogara, p. 22; Hamilton, *The Copts and the West*, pp. 54–55.

a likely result. Each side might have heard what they wished to hear.[32] The interpreters themselves might have interposed their own perspectives. Such is likely in a third case where use of an interpreter is known: the Ethiopian embassy to Pope Sixtus IV in 1481. According to eyewitnesses, the interpreter was the Ethiopians' Italian escort from Jerusalem to Rome, Giovanni Battista Brocchi. Since Brocchi had not been to Ethiopia and his acquaintance with the envoys was brief, it is highly unlikely he translated from Gəʿəz or an Ethiopian vernacular. Probably he had learned some Arabic in Jerusalem and used this as an intermediate language of communication. It is also quite possible that the message he conveyed was influenced by an Italian prior in the Holy Land who had urged the Ethiopians to visit Rome, who had sent them with an explanatory letter in which the pope placed great stock, and who had his own views on Ethiopian–European relations.[33]

The above examples were all unofficial or unplanned visits, in which Ethiopians in Italy had to deploy the skills they possessed.[34] What of official Ethiopian embassies dispatched to western Europe — did Ethiopian rulers make some provision for the linguistic difficulties their envoys were likely to face? The best evidence comes from the Aragonese records regarding the embassy to Naples in 1450, which identify three ambassadors. One, and doubtless the chief royal representative, was an Ethiopian monk named Mikaʾel. Accompanying him was an Arabic-speaking envoy, Abū ʿUmar (called 'Buamar' in the records).[35] The inclusion of an Arabic-speaking Muslim, who might have been drawn from the kingdom's Muslim subjects or recruited from foreign Muslim merchants to the kingdom, was long-standing practice in Ethiopian embassies to Islamic rulers, useful in negotiating the journey to and from Egypt or Yemen and in interpreting once there.[36] No doubt this practice was simply extended to Europe, where it served the same purpose for travel through Egypt and was potentially useful in western Europe too. The embassy to Valencia in 1427 also included a Christian Ethiopian and an 'infidel', identified by several scholars as the Persian trader al-Tabrīzī famously tried and executed in Cairo for his alleged role mediating a political alliance between Ethiopian and Latin

---

32   For some proposals in this vein at the Council of Florence, see Kelly, 'Biondo Flavio on Ethiopia'.

33   Kelly, 'Heretics, Allies, Exemplary Christians', pp. 212–13. The eyewitness source (in Ghinzoni, 'Un'ambasciata del Prete Gianni', pp. 152–53) notes the pope's 'very great faith' in the Italian prior's accompanying letter.

34   The 1481 embassy was an originally unplanned offshoot of a formal Ethiopian embassy to Cairo, though as Krebs observes (*Medieval Ethiopian Kingship, Craft, and Diplomacy*, pp. 124–29), European sources characterize it as authorized by the principal ambassador to Cairo to proceed to Rome.

35   Aragonese treasury record of 1450 naming the three ambassadors, including 'Buamar moro embaxador', reproduced in Cerone, 'La politica orientale di Alfonso d'Aragona', p. 71.

36   Loiseau, 'The Ḥaṭi and the Sultan', pp. 650–52, who also observes that 'Arabic was the only language used in diplomatic exchanges' between Christian Ethiopia and the Egyptian sultan in Cairo.

Christian powers.[37] In Valencia, where Arabic speakers were not uncommon, a Muslim interpreter may have been instrumental. In Naples, however, he was at most a back-up interpreter, for the Ethiopian ruler had also sent a native European. The Aragonese records give his name, Pietro Rombulo. His life story comes from a fellow Sicilian who interviewed him on this occasion. Born in Messina, Rombulo started travelling the world at age fifteen, got as far as Egypt, and accepted an Ethiopian envoy's invitation to accompany him from Cairo back to Ethiopia. There Rombulo remained for many years, marrying an Ethiopian wife and fathering eight children, before serving with the Ethiopian embassy to Naples as a man already in his sixties. Rombulo may well have embellished his tale, and his interlocutor certainly embellished it further, 'intercalating, substituting, and deforming' the information he received.[38] In terms of language, however, there can be little doubt that Rombulo's decades of involvement in domestic and court life in Ethiopia resulted in his acquisition of a spoken Ethiopian language, and that he translated Mikaʾel's message from this language for the benefit of Alfonso's court.

Rombulo's experience was not unique. An Italian visitor to Ethiopia in 1482–1483 reported meeting eleven Europeans at the royal court, all but two Italian; six had been there for a quarter-century. Asked why they had come, they answered that 'their intention was to find jewels and precious stones', and though the Ethiopian ruler would not let them leave, he had 'rewarded and provisioned them, each according to his station'.[39] Men like these must have reached Ethiopia already in the fourteenth century, for the Ethiopian embassy to Venice in 1402 also included an Italian: a Florentine named Antonio Bartoli. The minutes of the Venetian Senate do not record the identities of his companions, suggesting that discussions were held with or through Antonio. But he was perhaps, again, an interpreter, who translated between an Ethiopian envoy and the Venetian officials armed with his knowledge of an Ethiopian language. There is even a clue that such linguistic knowledge spread among commercially minded parties in Venice. Around the time of this embassy — certainly during the reign of King Dawit II (r. c. 1379/80–1413), who is named in the document — an itinerary from Venice to Ethiopia was drafted in Venice.[40] Originally composed in Italian but translated into Latin, it concluded with a lexicon of words and phrases useful for travellers, and perhaps especially merchants. From the 'language of Jerusalem' (that is,

---

37 On the two ambassadors, 'unus christianus et alter infidelus', see Thomassy, 'De Guillaume Fillastre considéré comme géographe', p. 148. The latter is identified al-Tabrīzī in Salvadore, *The African Prester John*, pp. 40–44; Krebs, *Medieval Ethiopian Kingship, Craft, and Diplomacy*, pp. 65–68; cf. Petry, '"Travel Patterns in the Medieval Near East" Reconsidered', pp. 170–73.

38 Lefevre, 'Riflessi etiopici', pp. 390–91.

39 His oral account was recorded in Jerusalem in 1485 by Suriano, *Trattato di Terra Santa e dell'Oriente*, ed. by Golubovich, here at p. 86.

40 Bartoli's involvement, proposed by Pigli, *Italian Civilization in Ethiopia*, pp. 9–10, is assumed by Salvadore, *The African Prester John*, pp. 26–27.

Arabic) it offered translations of such phrases as 'Where is the hostel?' and 'Where do the merchants live?'. The translations from Ethiopian languages include terms for basic provisions (bread, wine, fish, meat, linen cloth) and phrases such as 'Is this a good route?', 'Give me a good bed for God's sake', and 'How much do you want for this?'.[41]

This itinerary is the first and, to my knowledge, only textual witness of an interest in fifteenth-century Italy in acquiring a basic working vocabulary in Ethiopian vernaculars.[42] As with Arabic, it suggests that the practical multilingualism of European and Ethiopian travelers was an important vector of information exchange and feature of the linguistic landscape. Those Europeans who remained in Ethiopia played a similar role in the Ethiopian context. What information an Italian visitor to Ethiopia in the 1480s managed to gain was doubtless primarily through those compatriots who had lived there already for twenty-five years. Pero Covilhã, dispatched by the Portuguese king to Ethiopia in 1487 (and not, therefore, a merchant-adventurer, though he did share their fate), remained ever after, and served as translator for the second and more famous embassy of 1520–1526 when it reached the Ethiopian royal court.[43]

Although less central to the subject of Italian knowledge of Ethiopian languages, it is well to observe that just as Italians long resident in Ethiopia could gain good knowledge of Ethiopian vernaculars and transmit it to their fellows, Ethiopians resident in Italy could acquire and transmit knowledge of European languages too. It is possible that they did so before 1500, but thereafter it is certain. We have already met the Ethiopian pilgrim called 'Tommaso', who communicated through Arabic upon his arrival in Rome. By fall 1516, however, 'Tommaso' and his younger companion, the deacon called 'Giovanni', had been in Italy eighteen months, 'in which time they had well learned our language, and much more the young deacon [...] such that often [...] we used brother Giovanni as a translator'.[44] Similarly, Alessandro Zorzi was able to interview an Ethiopian pilgrim called 'Raphaello' in Venice in 1522 because he had 'quite good Latin from having been four years in Italy', while the pilgrim 'Tomaso' the next year also '[spoke] quite fluently'.[45] In the 1530s, the monk Yoḥannəs of Cyprus, who had lived in Europe since the age of fifteen, knew both Latin and Italian.[46] Täsfa Ṣəyon, who arrived in Rome in the mid-1530s, not only

---

41 In addition to the 'language of Jerusalem', the text provides lexicons for the 'Ethiopian language' (Amharic) and a related language 'of the Indians' — 'India' being identified here as four days distant from Šäwa in central Ethiopia — for which different theories have been proposed. See Jorga, 'Cenni sulle relazioni tra l'Abissinia e l'Europa cattolica', pp. 143–50; reproducing the text at pp. 146–50; Cohen, *Études d'éthiopien méridional*, pp. 356, 371–72; Krebs, *Medieval Ethiopian Kingship, Craft, and Diplomacy*, pp. 29–34.
42 On Mariano Vittori's brief exposition of Amharic verbs in the sixteenth century, see note 90 below.
43 Álvares, *Verdadera Informaçam*, ed. by Beckingham and Huntingford, trans. by Adderley, II, p. 350.
44 Razzi, *Vite dei santi e beati*, p. 294.
45 *Ethiopian Itineraries*, ed. by Crawford, pp. 138–39, 148–49.
46 Kelly and Nosnitsin, 'The Two Yoḥannəses', pp. 395–98, 416.

spoke but wrote Italian well enough to pen a letter to his colleague Pietro Paolo Gualtieri in 1547.[47] From late 1545 until 1548 he also studied Latin with a tutor paid by the pope in monthly instalments.[48] The apparently increased ability of Ethiopians to acquire Italian and other European languages in the sixteenth century was surely facilitated by their acquisition of a stable residence in Rome, and thus their opportunity to stay for long periods. This residence, or at least its cultic centre, was the church of Santo Stefano Maggiore, located just behind St Peter's Basilica. Exactly when Ethiopian pilgrims began to utilize the church is unknown, but they are first recorded there in 1497.[49] Data relative to the 1510s — the account of the Pisan prior discussed above, which described the community as then having thirty members and a prior of its own, as well as the testimony of Johann Potken, to which we will turn in a moment — suggest it was by then an established Ethiopian pilgrim hostel-cum-monastery along the lines of those already long in existence in the eastern Mediterranean.

The Study of Gəʿəz: Religious Debates and Indigenous Knowledge

Mention of the Ethiopian pilgrims of Santo Stefano brings us to the Gəʿəz side of our story, for they played a crucial role in inaugurating Gəʿəz language study in Europe. Most Ethiopian Christians who went on pilgrimage abroad were monks: this is why Ethiopian pilgrim hostels were also monasteries, replete with priors, regulations, and communal possessions, albeit adapted to their foreign contexts and the necessity of hosting transient visitors. Monks were Christian Ethiopia's *literati*, its principal masters and guardians of Gəʿəz, and with the establishment of Santo Stefano Rome now boasted a stable population of them — not always the same monks, of course, although some indeed stayed for years and even decades, but a continuous supply.

The onset of Europeans' Gəʿəz study required not only a supply of able teachers, but demand — interested students. As we have seen, certain stimuli (an interest in Ethiopian Christianity and its ancient texts) were present in the mid-fifteenth century without resulting in any notable inquiry into Gəʿəz language. In following decades several intertwined religious-philosophical currents charted a path towards such inquiry: a greater attention to Christian antiquity, related to reform efforts, that included study of all the biblical languages and the traditions of early Christian communities;[50] the study of non-Christian religious

---

47 First noted and edited by Guidi, 'La prima stampa del Nuovo Testamento in etiopico'.
48 Lefevre, 'Documenti e notizie su Tasfā Ṣeyon', p. 79; Romani, 'La stampa del N. T. in etiopico', pp. 490–91.
49 Rightly emphasized by Proverbio, 'Santo Stefano degli Abissini', pp. 55–56. On Santo Stefano, see also Mauro da Leonessa, *Santo Stefano Maggiore*; Delsere and Raineri, *Chiesa di S. Stefano dei Mori*; Adankpo-Labadie, 'Acceuillir et contrôler les pèlerins éthiopiens'.
50 The polyglot Bibles, such as Jimenez's (1509) and the Complutense (1520), are products of this.

traditions, not only for traditional motives of refutation and conversion but, as for Marsilio Ficino and Giovanni Pico della Mirandola, with the aim of proving their essential conformity with Christian truth;[51] and comparative linguistic study itself, including proposals of filiation (such as the Aramaic origin of Etruscan) and speculation concerning the original language of mankind.[52] These currents reached Gəʿəz in a rather roundabout way, which might be briefly summarized as follows. Among the touted linguists of the late fifteenth century was Pico's Hebrew and Arabic teacher, the Sicilian Jewish convert who went by the name Flavius Mithridates and who, like Pico later, argued in an oration before the pope in 1481 that even non-Christian religious traditions proved the truth of Christ. Among his proofs were certain hitherto unknown 'ancient Chaldean oracles', in fact invented by Mithridates and (to hide this fact) 'quoted' in an appropriately indecipherable script — that of Gəʿəz. A copy of this oration passed to the Vatican and was eventually (between 1508 and 1511) perused by the librarians, who recognized that its mysterious ancient Chaldean script was identical to that in an authentic Ethiopian codex they had since acquired but could not read. They therefore identified the latter, in the catalogue they were preparing, as 'a book in the Chaldean or Ethiopic language, and written in Chaldean characters'.[53]

It was evidently the tantalizing spectre of access to this ancient Chaldean language that prompted the first European study of Gəʿəz. On 29 October 1511 the librarians' colleague in papal service, the apostolic scriptor Johann Potken, borrowed from the Vatican this same 'Chaldean' manuscript, a psalter, now BAV, MS Vat. et. 20.[54] Around the same time — probably a few weeks or months earlier — he had approached the Ethiopian monks of Rome, heard them chant the liturgy, and 'not without difficulty learned from them that in their sacred rites they use Chaldean letters'. By whatever 'difficult' means Potken managed to communicate with the monks, it is clear that the Chaldean appellation, utterly foreign to Ethiopia, was a local invention: either Potken's suggestion, or a term Ethiopians in Rome had already heard and accepted as a foreign translation of Gəʿəz. Thus encouraged, Potken sought 'an interpreter through whom I could speak with them at more length, but finding no one in Rome [...] who was capable, I resolved to be instructed by them themselves'. This, by his report, was two years before the edition of the Gəʿəz psalter that he and his Ethiopian teacher and collaborator published (June and September 1513), thus roughly in summer or early fall 1511.[55] The Vatican psalter was borrowed

---

51 Allen, *Synoptic Art*; Bori, *Pluralità delle vie*; for the next generation, O'Malley, *Giles of Viterbo on Church and Reform*; Wilkinson, *Orientalism, Aramaic, and Kabbalah in the Catholic Reformation*.
52 Tavoni, 'Renaissance Linguistics', esp. pp. 44–59.
53 Kelly, 'The Curious Case of Ethiopic Chaldean', esp. pp. 1235–36, 1242–49.
54 BAV, MS Vat. lat. 3966 (register of loaned books), fol. 48ʳ.
55 *Psalterium Aethiopicum*, ed. by Potken and Tomas Wäldä Samu'el, fol. [1ᵛ]. The edition was foliated using Ethiopic quire signatures and numerals. I here use a continuous, Arabic-numeral foliation, starting from the frontispiece.

in October, doubtless to aid in this study, and probably inspired the decision to print an edition, for which it served as one textual basis.

For Potken Gəʿəz's prime attraction, and the theme he continually invoked, was its status as Chaldean, a very ancient language and potentially humankind's first. His short preface begins with an invocation of that primordial time: 'The human race once had a single language only, as is testified in both sacred and profane literature', before Nimrod's pride in constructing the Towel of Babel caused the divine punishment of linguistic diversity. Now Potken could offer an edition in 'this true Chaldean language (*ipsa vera lingua Chaldea*) for the delight of those who desire to know foreign languages'. Potken knew that the term 'Chaldean' was commonly used to denote one or another version of Aramaic. He countered with historical arguments: the language used by the Hebrews captive in ancient Babylon was not that of the Chaldean *literati*, while the Ethiopians, situated around the Nile and Gyon Rivers, may use different vernaculars but all still use Chaldean in their sacred rites, 'and have done so since the time of the birth of the Christian faith'. But indeed, as he elaborated in a comment at the end of the text of the psalms and biblical canticles, the language itself was much older: the Ethiopians, he claimed, 'affirm […] that Abraham and Eber and their ancestors as far back as their first parents used this Chaldean language'.[56] These various evocations — of Abraham, the Tower of Babel, and the biblical rivers said to flow from Paradise — intimated that *this* Chaldean was potentially the oldest and original language.

These prefatory and concluding comments attracted much attention, as we shall see, but they occupied only a few paragraphs. The main contribution of the edition was of course the text itself and the learning aids appended at its end. As Riccardo Contini has observed, until the mid-sixteenth century they 'represented the privileged source for the first Semiticists who interested themselves in Gəʿəz […] to compare it to the other Semitic languages then known'.[57] Unlike the Chaldean claims, which Potken attributed to the Ethiopians but which can only have originated in Europe, these features must be credited to Potken's collaboration with his tutor, Tomas Wäldä Samuʾel.[58] On a practical level, only Tomas could have supplied, through his fellow Ethiopian pilgrims, the added exemplars needed to complete the psalter text (the Vatican copy being incomplete) and to add the Song of Songs.[59] Just as important was the

---

56 *Psalterium Aethiopicum*, ed. by Potken and Tomas Wäldä Samuʾel, fol. [100ʳ].
57 Contini, 'I primordi della linguistica semitica comparata', p. 89.
58 That is, Tomas, (spiritual) son of (*wäldä*) St Samuʾel of Wäldəbba, whose role is known only thanks to a Gəʿəz colophon he included in the psalter edition itself, at fol. [100ᵛ].
59 BAV, MS Vat. et. 20 ended at the 110ᵗʰ psalm, as Potken noted when borrowing it (see note 54 above), requiring another exemplar, though as Potken observed, Ethiopian monks knew the text by heart and could recite it without a book (*Psalterium Aethiopicum*, ed. by Potken and Tomas Wäldä Samuʾel, fol. [100ʳ]). Potken also explained (fol. [106ᵛ]) that the Song of Songs was added to the edition three months after the first printing because two manuscripts containing this text had recently been obtained.

chart of the Gəʿəz syllabary printed at the end of the edition. It was not, in fact, the first such chart ever printed: Bernhard von Breydenbach had included one in his pilgrimage account of the Holy Land, published in Mainz in 1486, that offered a representation of what he claimed were the forty-seven letters of the Ethiopians' language — in fact, a random assemblage of characters of various vocal orders and their putative transliteration/pronunciation, riddled with repetition, omission, and error.[60] The syllabary of Potken and Tomas was therefore a true leap forward, offering a complete grid of the 182 most common characters of the kind still used today. Along the vertical axis were the twenty-six consonantal characters, following the traditional Ethiopian sequence;[61] the horizontal axis listed the seven vocal orders, each identified at the head of the column by its Gəʿəz name. A Roman transliteration, useful for pronunciation, accompanied each individual character. Two more charts followed: one for the four labiovelars in their five vocal orders, and one for numerals to 10,000, whose transliterated names were also provided. These charts made it possible to sound out the accompanying text and compare it to any similar text in another language, and its thoroughness and close conformity to Ethiopian norms must reflect Tomas's teaching and editorial role. It was a teaching that Potken learned well. Although later scholars ridiculed Potken's offhand comment that the language 'has no grammatical rules', this comment doubtless stemmed from Potken's 'epilinguistic' rather than 'metalinguistic' knowledge: that is, from the fact that he was not taught Gəʿəz grammar through abstract paradigms but rather through practice with actual texts.[62] There are indications that he gained good mastery through such practice.[63] If the edition still contained flaws, as later and better philologists noted, this cannot detract much from the accomplishment of creating the first text (and indeed the type to print it) ever published in Gəʿəz.[64]

---

60 To give just one example, the character ፙ, transliterated 'me', is repeated three times, and ፆ, transliterated 'mun', twice: though these transliterations are consistent (not true in other cases) and as pronunciation not inaccurate, even a casual reader could easily see that these were not five distinct *litterae* of forty-seven. Breydenbach, *Peregrinatio in Terram Sanctam*, fol. 82ʳ.

61 The characters ሰ (sä) and ሠ (śä) were, however, transposed: they had come to be pronounced identically and were often substituted for each other in writing. *Psalterium Aethiopicum*, ed. by Potken and Tomas Wäldä Samuʾel, fol. [107ʳ].

62 As astutely observed by Contini, 'I primordi della linguistica semitica comparata', p. 89.

63 Regarding the sixth order, the 1513 *Psalterium Aethiopicum* vocalized it in the chart (as 'short o') but explained in the accompanying text (fol. [108ʳ]) that it can also remain unvocalized. Potken's grasp of practice is suggested by his 1518 polyglot psalter, published in Germany, where he marked the unvocalized occurrences in the text itself with a dot: see Hopkins, review of *150 Years after Dillmann's Lexicon*, p. 599 n. 5. I thank Alessandro Bausi for this reference.

64 Hiob Ludolf noted its textual errors in his own psalter edition of 1701, cited in Lefevre, 'Giovanni Potken e la sua edizione', p. 305 n. 26, who also observes Potken's experience with typography (p. 303 n. 21).

We might say that it was Potken's Chaldean claims that attracted the criticism of fellow linguistic scholars, but it was the text he and Tomas offered that made their refutations possible.[65] Among the first and most influential ripostes came from Sebastian Münster, author of the first Aramaic grammar (*Chaldaica grammatica*, 1527). Like Potken, he opened with a historical excursus: Hebrew was 'the earlier, more sacred and more noble language', but after the Tower of Babel tongues had multiplied, becoming more diverse the greater the distance from Babylon, whence Chaldean (i.e. Aramaic, for Münster) 'is closer to Hebrew than all others'.[66] Turning then to Potken's claims, he compared a passage culled from the printed Gəʿəz psalter with the same passage in Aramaic, compiled a list of fourteen terms in Gəʿəz, Aramaic, and Hebrew, and concluded, 'you can now easily judge that this language [...] is not Chaldean [... but] a language peculiar to its people, having a certain affinity now with Hebrew, now with Chaldean, but with both a greater difference'.[67] In the Italian milieu, one can name Teseo Ambrogio degli Albonesi, who in 1539 compared more than a dozen languages in an effort to indicate a certain 'harmony' among them all. He too frequently cited the psalter edition, for instance in noting similarities between Gəʿəz and Hebrew characters, but also recorded his efforts to 'dissuade [Potken] from his error and false opinion' that Gəʿəz was Chaldean.[68] Yet in refuting Potken, these and other authors necessarily compared Gəʿəz to Aramaic, Hebrew, Syriac, and Arabic, noting their similarities as well as their differences. As Theodorus Bibliander (Theodor Buchmann) wrote in 1548, echoing the judgement of Guillaume Postel, 'Johannes Potken [...] falsely insisted, in agreement with common belief, that Ethiopian is an offshoot of Chaldean. [... However], Ethiopian is so close to Hebrew, Chaldean, and Arabic that there is rarely an utterance in one language that cannot be found in the other two languages'.[69] Already by mid-century, and partly as a result of these polemics, Gəʿəz came not only to be included in the main line of 'oriental' language study, but correctly classed in that group that would eventually be known as the Semitic language family.

A second line of interest in Gəʿəz concerned its relation not to ancient Chaldea and the origins of human language but to the early Christian Church. Although the antiquity of Ethiopian Christianity had long been known, the reform movement of the fifteenth century, which held the apostolic Church as its model and sought authentic early Christian texts to explore the nature of that primitive Church more fully, lent it a new attractiveness. As we have

---

65 For a survey of the critiques of the Chaldean appellation, see Bobzin, 'Miszellen zur Geschichte der Äthiopistik', pp. 86–92.
66 Münster, *Chaldaica grammatica*, pp. 8–9.
67 Münster, *Chaldaica grammatica*, pp. 15–17.
68 Ambrogio degli Albonesi, *Introductio in Chaldaicam linguam, Syriacam, atque Armenicam*, fols 12^r–13^v.
69 Bibliander, *De ratione communi omnium linguarum et literarum commentarius*, ed. and trans. by Amirav and Kirn, pp. 36–37.

seen, Biondo Flavio hinted in this direction in the 1440s. Potken's associates in papal service did so again in the 1510s, claiming that precisely where Ethiopian practices diverged from those of Rome they were 'redolent of the rite of the primitive Church'.[70] Such ideas were soon complicated and intensified by growing concerns about nonconformity among Protestants and *conversos*. For some Catholic authorities, all deviations from Roman norms had now to be combatted, including those of the Ethiopian Church. This was the case in Portugal from the late 1520s, where the Ethiopian ambassador Ṣägga Zäʾab was detained for some eleven years, interrogated by Bishop Diogo Ortiz and, as he recounted, subject to 'the bitter taunts of many who, setting aside all reverence, do not hesitate to defame and revile [the King of Ethiopia] and us his subjects, calling us Jews and Muslims'.[71] For others, however, Ethiopian texts could be deployed in defence of Catholicism, to prove the legitimacy of papal authority and of Catholic practices against Lutheran critique.

It was this that spurred Cardinal Marcello Cervini, close associate of Pope Paul III and one of the papal legates (effective co-presidents) of the Council of Trent, to collect information from Gəʿəz religious texts, again from the community of Santo Stefano, soon after the council opened. It doubtless took some time to find men in Rome willing and able to learn Gəʿəz and to help with translating texts. Bernardino Maffei was approached in March 1546 with no result.[72] By July 1547, relevant information was coming in. Täsfa Ṣəyon, an erudite monk from the distinguished Ethiopian monastery of Däbrä Libanos, had already developed a relationship with Pope Paul III and emerged as the principal authority in Ethiopian matters in Rome.[73] He was now working with the humanist and papal secretary Pietro Paolo Gualtieri, and together they had almost finished translating the Ethiopian ritual of the Mass. Gualtieri had also learned from his Ethiopian colleague, and reported to Cervini, that the Ethiopians possessed a text of the canons of the Council of Nicaea that contained many more articles than the twenty known in Greek and Latin. The latter offered the tantalizing possibility of hitherto lost texts of the Christian tradition, much as the Ethiopian delegates had intimated with regard to Solomonic books a century before. The main line of Cervini's interest is evident in the correspondence between him and Guglielmo Sirleto, who reported to him on the group's progress while simultaneously collecting similar data from Greek works. The Gəʿəz canons of Nicaea, Sirleto reported in July, 'include one that treats the primacy of the Roman Church, and that it be put before all others; I had the greatest pleasure in hearing this'. On 31

---

70 Paride de Grassi, *Tractatus de oratoribus*, BAV, MS Vat. lat. 12270, fol. 78ᵛ–79ʳ (ed. in Stenzig, *Botschafterzeremoniell am Papsthof*, 1, p. 237), citing the authority of his colleague Giovanni Battista Brocchi.
71 Góis, *Fides, religio, moresque Aethiopum*, pp. 76, 82–83, with quotation at p. 82.
72 Letter of Cervini to Maffei, transcribed in Lefevre, 'Documenti e notizie su Tasfā Ṣeyon', p. 80.
73 For his biography, see Salvadore and de Lorenzi, 'An Ethiopian Scholar', and bibliography.

August he was similarly pleased to report that 'the Ethiopian canon conforms with the Greek Mass, composed by St Basil, that is in commemorating the living and the dead and regarding the intercession of the saints'. Cervini, in thanking Sirleto for the Mass translation he received that month, noted that 'I read it the more willingly, since we are now treating the articles of the Mass in the council, and what to do about this material'.[74] In short, Cervini sought confirmation in Ethiopian as well as Greek texts for the antiquity and legitimacy of specific Catholic positions challenged by the Lutherans, and as an aid in formulating the response at Trent.

The texts and translations prepared for Cervini — ultimately two translations of the Ethiopian Mass ritual, and a manuscript of the Gəʿəz canons of Nicaea (that is, an excerpt of the *Senodos*, the Ethiopian collection of early conciliar canons and other canon-law texts) with a Latin table of contents and partial Latin translation — were meant for specific eyes.[75] They were, however, developed in parallel with a second project that achieved much wider circulation: a print edition of the Gəʿəz New Testament, together with the ritual of the Mass. According to one person involved, this too was the brainchild of Cervini, whose interests in 'oriental' traditions were varied and numerous.[76] Though Cervini must have authorized this project, its principal creator was Täsfa Ṣəyon, credited as editor on the edition's title page when it was published in 1548–49. In 1547, as he and Gualtieri were producing translations for Cervini, they were also working on this edition, with the aid of a growing number of others: the Ethiopians Yoḥannəs of Cyprus, Tänśəʾa Wäld, and Zäśəllase, and the Italian clerics Bernardino Sandri of Cremona and Mariano Vittori of Rieti.[77]

Like the psalter edition before it, the New Testament edition was delayed by an insufficiency of textual exemplars. Lacking any manuscript of the Pauline Epistles, as early as 1546 the Ethiopians of Santo Stefano had sought to obtain one from the Ethiopian community on Cyprus with help from well-connected European intermediaries like Pietro Bembo.[78] The first instalment of the edition indeed was published in 1548 without this text, which was added in the

---

74 The relevant passages of this correspondence, found in BAV, MSS Vat. lat. 6177 and 6178, are transcribed in Lefevre, 'Documenti e notizie su Tasfâ Ṣeyon', pp. 83–84, though I offer a longer excerpt of Sirleto's letter of 31 August (MS Vat. lat. 6177, fol. 332) to illustrate the disputed Catholic practices seeking defence.

75 In addition to the translation of the Mass prepared by Täsfa Ṣəyon and Gualtieri, a second was prepared by the Ethiopian monk Yoḥannəs of Cyprus (see Kelly and Nosnitsin, 'The Two Yoḥannəses', p. 398); the Latin-Gəʿəz manuscript excerpting the *Senodos* is now BAV, MS Vat. et. 2.

76 The claim is Mariano Vittori's: see Romani, 'La stampa del N. T. in etiopico', p. 485; Cardinali, 'Ritratto di Marcello Cervini *en orientaliste*', p. 90.

77 All were thanked in the edition, on which work was said to have proceeded for two years: *Testamentum Novum*, ed. by Täsfa Ṣəyon (= editio princeps of the Gəʿəz New Testament), fols 157ʳ, 225ʳ.

78 Raineri, 'Pietro Bembo e la prima stampa delle lettere di San Paolo in etiopico'.

second instalment of 1549. No complete text of the Acts of the Apostles was immediately at hand either, whence the Gəʿəz had to be partially reconstructed from Greek and Latin.[79] If one adds the printers' ignorance of the language and script, it is not surprising that the resulting edition contained errors, which Täsfa Ṣəyon was the first to concede.[80] It was nonetheless a second major landmark for Gəʿəz studies in Europe: custom frontispieces were added to several copies bearing coats of arms of individual recipients, including Pope Paul III, King Henri II of France, Emperor Charles V, and a number of cardinals.[81] The studies of interested linguists were doubtless further aided by the 1549 publication of Latin translations of the Ethiopian Mass and baptismal rituals, on which Täsfa Ṣəyon collaborated with Gualtieri and Sandri.[82]

In addition to the texts' own role as study aids for other scholars, the several years of intensive collaboration on these projects had provided the European collaborators with a solid education in Gəʿəz. Täsfa Ṣəyon wrote that for the translation of the baptismal ritual he had relied on the 'very keen judgment of Bernardino Sandri', a man 'proven in his knowledge of letters' and 'not ignorant of our language'.[83] As for Gualtieri, his colleague Mariano Vittori called him 'a learned and indeed very courteous man, who alone among us [Europeans] could correct errors and indicate what in a [Gəʿəz] work was to be removed or added, as no one before him among Latin men is known to have done'.[84] But Mariano Vittori himself surely rivalled him. Continuing his study with Täsfa Ṣəyon, and apparently at Gualtieri's urging, in 1552 Vittori offered the first printed grammar of Gəʿəz: the *Chaldeae seu Aethiopicae linguae institutiones*. Like other scholars of his day, Vittori commented on the origins and development of this language in relation to others. Aware of the objections to Potken's claims but also following in his footsteps (not least as a fellow student of the Ethiopian monks of Santo Stefano), he sought what might be called a compromise. Gəʿəz was not the Chaldean of ancient Babylon but, like Syriac and Arabic, was descended from it, whence all these descendant languages were also called 'Chaldean', not least by the Ethiopians themselves.[85] He thus used the term 'Chaldean' interchangeably

---

79 *Testamentum Novum*, ed. by Täsfa Ṣəyon, fol. 157ʳ.
80 As he wrote in a Gəʿəz notice in the edition's prefatory matter, 'O my fathers and brothers, do not criticize the defects of this book and its making: those who printed it had no knowledge of the script, nor we of the art of printing'. Cited from the translation in Lefevre, 'Documenti e notizie su Tasfā Ṣeyon', p. 90.
81 Raineri, 'Studi etiopici nell'età del Giovio', p. 124.
82 *Modus baptizandi*, trans. by Täsfa Ṣəyon, fol. [1ʳ] (= second page of dedicatory letter to Pope Paul III, dated 9 November 1548). Täsfa Ṣəyon credited the Mass translation to Gualtieri.
83 *Modus baptizandi*, trans. by Täsfa Ṣəyon, fol. [1ʳ].
84 Vittori, *Chaldeae seu Aethiopicae linguae institutiones*, dedicatory letter of 1552 edn, fol [6ʳ].
85 Vittori, *Chaldeae seu Aethiopicae linguae institutiones*, dedicatory letter of 1552 edn, fol [3ʳ]; proemium, fol. [8ʳ] (= p. 2 of 1630 edn). For the main text, I cite henceforth from the more widely available 1630 edition.

with 'Ethiopic' throughout his work as well as in its title, refuting but at the same time perpetuating the appellation.

Although 'known to every orientalist', Vittori's grammatical exposition itself has yet to be systematically studied.[86] From a social as well as a linguistic perspective, it might well repay further analysis, for it bears traces of the process of Vittori's instruction and the confrontation of two different approaches to the study and exposition of language. Täsfa Ṣəyon taught Vittori in the Ethiopian tradition of grammatical instruction that came to be written down, perhaps as early as the sixteenth century but certainly in the seventeenth, in treatises known as *säwasəw* ('ladder'). Their original nucleus was vocabularies in which particular lexemes and grammatical forms were explained, often (though not always) in the order of their appearance in standard religious works. This likely reflects the instructional practice of working experientially through a given text — for instance, the psalter — and explaining terms and forms as they appeared; classification and paradigms were thus also part of *säwasəw*, in their written form and without doubt in oral teaching as well.[87] Vittori's assertion of biliteral verbs, his treatment of causative and passive verbs as inflections of a base verb, and his treatment of adjectives all echo features of *säwasəw*, and suggest his effort to transmit the teaching he received.[88] At the same time, he brought his own experience with Latin to the project, imposing familiar habits and structures onto an unfamiliar tongue. His choice of the verb 'to love' (*afqärä*) as his usual example, so natural in Latin (*amo, amas*), seems a reflex of his prior experience, as does his insistence on the imperfect tense, more or less equivalent to the Latin present, as the base from which others are formed.[89] Also suggestive of his Latin background are his concern to find consistent noun endings to mark gender and number, and his desire to include verb tenses with no precise equivalent in Gəʿəz — for which tenses he substituted Amharic, thus offering a first, albeit very limited discussion of Amharic grammar.[90] Whatever the level of Vittori's own mastery of Gəʿəz,

---

86 Only a summary of its headings is offered in Fiaccadori, 'Vittori, Mariano' and Raineri, 'Studi etiopici nell'età del Giovio', pp. 128–29, to whom the quotation (p. 128) belongs.

87 Meley Mulugetta, 'Säwasəw', pp. 562–63; Moreno, 'Struttura e terminologia del Sawāsĕw', p. 13. On the experiential aspect of instruction, cf. Vittori's comment on participles that 'you can easily learn this from long reading': *Chaldeae seu Aethiopicae linguae institutiones*, p. 59.

88 Compare Vittori, *Chaldeae seu Aethiopicae linguae institutiones*, pp. 38, 48–49 (biliterals), 33–34 (causative, passive), 18, 25 (adjectives), and Moreno, 'Struttura e terminologia del Sawāsĕw', pp. 25, 28, 38, 42–44.

89 Vittori, *Chaldeae seu Aethiopicae linguae institutiones*, pp. 39, 41, 46, 51, 52–53, 54, etc. (*afqärä* as an example); 33, 41 (imperfect, which he calls 'future', as base for other tenses). In Ethiopian tradition by contrast the perfect was classified as the first conjugation, and examples usually started with it: see Moreno, 'Struttura e terminologia del Sawāsĕw', pp. 16–17, 38. Vittori himself understood that the third person masculine singular of the perfect revealed the verb root and was 'to be investigated first': *Chaldeae seu Aethiopicae linguae institutiones*, p. 37.

90 Vittori, *Chaldeae seu Aethiopicae linguae institutiones*, pp. 20–25 (noun endings), 43–46 (Amharic conjugation, including past imperfect and pluperfect).

for readers of his work his knowledge was, and still is, filtered through the complexities of communicating across different languages and from the vantage of different learning systems.

How much sixteenth-century readers did glean from Vittori's work is difficult to ascertain, for few had the chance. Although encouraged by and dedicated to Cardinal Cervini, the work must have been printed in few copies and circulated little: before its reprinting by the Propaganda Fide in 1630, it was so rare that one interested reader had to order a manuscript copy made.[91] Nor was it consulted by Angelo Canini, who relied rather on the Gəʿəz editions of 1513 and 1548–1549 for his comparative study entitled *Institutiones linguae Syriacae, Assyriacae atque Talmudicae, una cum Aethiopicae atque Arabicae collatione*. Indeed, to some extent Canini's work may have rendered Vittori's redundant, both because the broader European scholarly audience for Gəʿəz was in comparative studies like this, and because Canini's was a notable advance in the genre, offering for the first time not just lexical but morphological comparisons among the various Semitic languages.[92]

That the advances of the 1550s turned away from the religious content of Gəʿəz works to the features of the language itself was perhaps a sign of the times. In September 1549 the Council of Trent was suspended and Cervini's work with it ceased; in November the Ethiopian community's great patron, Paul III, died. The reform current willing to view Ethiopian Christianity as an orthodox ally against Lutheran heretics was on the wane in Rome: as Täsfa Ṣəyon complained already in late 1548, he and his fellow Ethiopians were now 'called by all, with one voice, impious, Nazarenes, and schismatics'.[93] Soon Täsfa Ṣəyon himself, for years the greatest champion in Rome of Ethiopian Christianity, was dead as well. Thereafter it was the Jesuits who took the lead in Ethiopian–European exchanges, launching a mission to Ethiopia in 1557 whose primary aim, under Portuguese direction and with Portuguese logistical support, was the Ethiopians' conversion to Catholic orthodoxy. The Jesuits are famous for their interest in mastering foreign languages as a vehicle for conversion, and their efforts in Ethiopia were no exception. These efforts, however, took place not in the Jesuit headquarters in Rome but in Ethiopia, and not, it appears, until the seventeenth century; many of their works, in any case, were destroyed or lost and did not make their way back to Europe.[94]

---

91 Raineri, 'Studi etiopici nell'età del Giovio', p. 129.
92 Contini, 'I primordi della linguistica semitica comparata', pp. 91–92.
93 *Modus baptizandi*, trans. by Täsfa Ṣəyon, dedicatory letter to Paul III, dated November 1548, fol. [1ʳ].
94 Martínez d'Alòs-Moner and Cohen, 'On the Roots of Ethiopic Philology'.

Conclusion: The Renaissance and the Seicento

The seventeenth century was the great age of early modern Ethiopian studies in Europe, surpassing in quantity and quality the achievements of the Renaissance. But I should like to draw attention, in conclusion, to the continuities that link the two eras, the ways in which patterns of thought and networks of exchange laid down in Renaissance Italy perdured even while they mutated, and the ways in which the scholarly achievements of the Cinquecento, imperfect as they were, helped fuel their more illustrious successors. One might note, for instance, that Santo Stefano remained an important source of linguistic (and more generally cultural) information for Athanasius Kircher, Jacob Wemmers, Johann Michael Wansleben, and Hiob Ludolf, who met his Ethiopian informant and collaborator Gorgoryos there during his brief Roman visit of 1649.[95] One might observe the continued diplomatic-religious outreach to Ethiopia not only by Catholics now (whose seventeenth-century Jesuit missions were much more successful) but also by Protestants and, perhaps more importantly for our purposes, the perduring link between religious interests and linguistic study.[96] European production of Ethiopia-related knowledge in the seventeenth century is well represented in the works published by Ludolf: a Gəʽəz grammar that remained the standard in Europe for two centuries (1661, updated and corrected in a second edition of 1702); the first printed Amharic grammar and a Latin–Amharic lexicon (1698); and a voluminous history of Ethiopia (1681), supplemented by a commentary and appendices in following years.[97] As disparaging as he was toward his (Catholic) predecessors, even Ludolf could not help but refer to those first efforts to make known in Europe the sacred language and religious traditions of Ethiopia — the edited psalter and New Testament — that the pilgrims of Santo Stefano and their European colleagues produced in Rome.

---

[95] Conti Rossini, *Storia d'Etiopia*, pp. 12–15; Kennerly, 'Ethiopian Christians in Rome', pp. 162–63; for more on Wansleben and Ludolf, see Bausi, 'Johann Michael Wansleben's Manuscripts and Texts' and Tubach, 'Hiob Ludolf und die Anfänge der Äthiopistik in Deutschland'.

[96] On the Jesuit missions, see Cohen, *The Missionary Strategies of the Jesuits*, and Martínez d'Alòs-Moner, *Envoys of a Human God*; on Protestant outreach, see the mission on which the young Wansleben was sent, discussed in Bausi, 'Johann Michael Wansleben's Manuscripts and Texts', pp. 198–99. Notions of Protestant–Ethiopian religious affinities began with Luther and Melanchthon, who met an Ethiopian deacon in the 1530s, and increased thereafter: see Paulau, *Das Andere Christentum*; Paulau, 'An Ethiopian Orthodox Monk in the Cradle of the Reformation'; Kelly, 'The Curious Case of Ethiopic Chaldean', pp. 1257-60; Belcher, *Abyssinia's Samuel Johnson*, p. 66. Some still viewed Ethiopian Christianity as conforming to and confirming Catholicism: the conversion of Wansleben to Catholicism, in part through his exposure to Ethiopian Christian texts, is one example (see Bausi, 'Johann Michael Wansleben's Manuscripts and Texts', pp. 216–17).

[97] Tubach, 'Hiob Ludolf und die Anfänge der Äthiopistik in Deutschland'.

Works Cited

Manuscripts and Archival Sources

Città del Vaticano, Biblioteca Apostolica Vaticana, MS Vat. et. 2
Città del Vaticano, Biblioteca Apostolica Vaticana, MS Vat. et. 20
Città del Vaticano, Biblioteca Apostolica Vaticana, MS Vat. et. 25
Città del Vaticano, Biblioteca Apostolica Vaticana, MS Vat. lat. 3966
Città del Vaticano, Biblioteca Apostolica Vaticana, MS Vat. lat. 6177
Città del Vaticano, Biblioteca Apostolica Vaticana, MS Vat. lat. 6178
Città del Vaticano, Biblioteca Apostolica Vaticana, MS Vat. lat. 12270
Paris, Bibliothèque nationale de France, MS Éth. 35

Primary Sources

Álvares, *Verdadera Informaçam*, ed. by Charles Fraser Beckingham and George Wynn Brereton Huntingford under the title *The Prester John of the Indies: A True Relation of the Lands of the Prester John, being the narrative of the Portuguese Embassy to Ethiopia in 1520 written by Father Francisco Alvares*, based on the translation of Lord Stanley of Adderley (1881) with editions and revisions, 2 vols (Cambridge: Cambridge University Press, 1961)

Ambrogio degli Albonesi, Teseo, *Introductio in Chaldaicam linguam, Syriacam, atque Armenicam, et decem alias linguas* (Pavia: Joannes Maria Simoneta, 1539)

Bibliander, Theodorus, *De ratione communi omnium linguarum et literarum commentarius*, ed. and trans. by Hagit Amirav and Hans-Martin Kirn, Travaux d'humanisme et Renaissance, 475 (Geneva: Droz, 2011)

Biondo Flavio (Blondius Flavius), *Historiarum ab inclinatione Romanorum quartae decadis liber secundus*, ed. by Bartolomeo Nogara, in *Scritti inediti e rari di Biondo Flavio* (Rome: Tipografia Poliglotta Vaticana, 1927), pp. 3–28 [each text is paginated afresh]

Breydenbach, Bernhard von, *Peregrinatio in Terram Sanctam* (Mainz: Erhard Reuwich, 1486), <http://tudigit.ulb.tu-darmstadt.de/show/inc-iv-97>

Ethiopian Itineraries circa 1400–1524, ed. by O. G. S. Crawford (Cambridge: Cambridge University Press, 1958)

Góis, Damião de, *Fides, religio, moresque Aethiopum sub Imperio Preciosi Ioannis* (Paris: Christian Wechel, 1541; 1st edn Louvain, 1540)

Lettere tra i pontefici romani e i principi etiopici (sec. XII–XX), ed. by Osvaldo Raineri (Vatican City: Biblioteca Apostolica Vaticana, 2003)

Jacques de Vitry (Iacobus de Vitriaco), *Libri duo, quorum prior orientalis sive Hierosolymitanae, alter occidentalis historiae nominee inscribitur*, ed. by Franciscus Moschus (1597; repr. Farnborough: Gregg, 1971)

Modus baptizandi, preces et benedictiones quibus Ecclesie Ethiopum utitur [...] Item Missa qua communiter utuntur [...] ex Lingua Chaldea sive Aethiopica in Latniam conversae, trans. by Täsfa Ṣəyon [Petrus Ethyops] (with Bernardino Sandri and Pietro Paolo Gualtieri) (Rome: Antonio Blado, 1549)

Münster, Sebastian, *Chaldaica grammatica* (Basel: Johann Froben, 1527)
Psalterium Aethiopicum, ed. by Johannes Potken and Tomas Wäldä Samuʾel (Rome: Marcellus Silber, 1513)
Razzi, Serafino, *Vite dei santi e beati cosi uomini come donne del sacro ordine dei Frati Predicatori* (Florence: Bartolomeo Sermartelli, 1577)
Suriano, Francesco, *Trattato di Terra Santa e dell'Oriente*, ed. by Girolamo Golubovich (Milan: Tipografia Editrice Artigianelli, 1900)
Testamentum Novum, cum Epistola ad Hebraeos tantum …, ed. by Täsfa Ṣəyon [Petrus Ethyops] (Rome: Valerio Dorico, 1548–1549)
Vittori, Mariano, *Chaldeae seu Aethiopicae linguae institutiones* (Rome: Valerio Dorico, 1552; 2nd edn, Rome: Sacra Congregazione di Propaganda Fide, 1630)

Secondary Studies

Adankpo-Labadie, Olivia, 'Acceuillir et contrôler les pèlerins éthiopiens à Rome: L'institution de l'hospice pontifical de Santo Stefano dei Mori au XVIᵉ siècle', *Mélanges de l'École française de Rome – Moyen Âge*, 131 (2019), 437–45
Allen, Michael, *Synoptic Art: Marsilio Ficino on the History of Platonic Interpretation* (Florence: Olschki, 1998)
Bausi, Alessandro, 'Ethiopia and the Christian Ecumene: Cultural Transmission, Translation, and Reception', in *A Companion to Medieval Ethiopia and Eritrea*, ed. by Samantha Kelly (Leiden: Brill, 2020), pp. 217–51
Bausi, Alessandro, 'Johann Michael Wansleben's Manuscripts and Texts: An Update', in *Essays in Ethiopian Manuscript Studies: Proceedings of the International Conference 'Manuscripts and Texts, Languages and Contexts: The Transmission of Knowledge in the Horn of Africa', Hamburg, 17–19 July 2014*, ed. by Alessandro Bausi and others, Supplement to Aethiopica, 4 (Wiesbaden: Harrassowitz, 2015), pp. 197–244
Belcher, Wendy, *Abyssinia's Samuel Johnson: Ethiopian Thought in the Making of an English Author* (Oxford: Oxford University Press, 2012)
Bobzin, Hartmut, 'Miszellen zur Geschichte der Äthiopistik', in *Festschrift Ewald Wagner zum 65. Geburtstag*, I: *Semitische Studien*, ed. by Wolfhart Heinrichs and Gregor Schoeler (Stuttgart: Steiner, 1994), pp. 82–101
Bori, Pier Cesare, *Pluralità delle vie: Alle origini del 'Discorso' sulla dignità umana di Pico della Mirandola* (Milan: Feltrinelli, 2000)
Bouloux, Nathalie, 'Du nouveau au sud de l'Égypte: Une ambassade éthiopienne au concile de Florence', in *La Terre: Connaissance, représentations, mésure au Moyen Âge*, ed. by P. Gautier Dalché (Turnhout: Brepols, 2013), pp. 420–28
——— , 'Du nouveau sur la géographie de l'Éthiopie: Poggio Bracciolini, Biondo Flavio et le témoignage de l'ambassade éthiopienne au concile de Ferrare-Florence', *Afriques* [online journal], Varia (2017) <https://journals.openedition.org/afriques/2008>
Cardinali, Giacomo, 'Ritratto di Marcello Cervini *en orientaliste* (con precisazioni alle vicende di *Petrus Damascenus*, Mosè di Mārdīn *ed Heliodorus Niger*)', *Bibliothèque d'Humanisme et Renaissance*, 80.1 (2018), 77–98

Cerone, Francesco, 'La politica orientale di Alfonso d'Aragona', *Archivio storico per le provincie napoletane*, 27 (1902), 3–93

Cerulli, Enrico, *Etiopi in Palestina: Storia della comunità etiopica di Gerusalemme*, 2 vols (Rome: Librera dello Stato, 1943–1947)

——, 'Eugenio IV e gli etiopi al Concilio di Firenze nel 1441', *Rendiconti della Reale Accademia nazionale dei Lincei*, 6th ser., 9 (1933), 347–68

Chiesa, Paolo, and Alessandro Bausi, 'The *Ystoria Ethyopie* in the *Cronica Universalis* of Galvaneus de la Flamma (d. c. 1345)', *Aethiopica*, 22 (2019), 7–57

Cohen, Leonardo, *The Missionary Strategies of the Jesuits in Ethiopia (1555–1632)*, Aethiopistische Forschungen, 70 (Wiesbaden: Harrassowitz, 2009)

Cohen, Marcel, *Études d'éthiopien méridional*, Collection d'ouvrages orientaux (Paris: Paul Geuthner, 1931)

Conti Rossini, Carlo, *Storia d'Etiopia. Parte prima: Dalle origini all'avento della dinastia Salomonide* (Bergamo: Istituto italiano d'arte grafiche, 1928)

Contini, Riccardo, 'I primordi della linguistica semitica comparata nell'Europa rinascimentale: Le *Institutiones* di Angelo Canini (1554)', in *Circolazioni culturali nel Mediterraneo antico*, ed. by Paolo Filigheddu (Cagliari: Antonio M. Corda, 1994), pp. 85–97

Delsere, Ilaria, and Osvaldo Raineri, *Chiesa di S. Stefano dei Mori: Vicende edilizie e personaggi* (Vatican City: Edizioni Capitolo Vaticano, 2015)

Derat, Marie-Laure, *L'énigme d'une dynastie sainte et usurpatrice dans le royaume chrétien d'Éthiopie du XIe au XIIIe siècle*, Hagologia, 14 (Turnhout: Brepols, 2018)

Fiaccadori, Gianfranco, 'India as a Name of Ethiopia', in *Encyclopaedia Aethiopica*, vol. III, ed. by Siegbert Uhlig (Wiesbaden: Harrassowitz, 2007), pp. 145–47

——, 'Vittori, Mariano', in *Encyclopaedia Aethiopica*, vol. V, ed. by Alessandro Bausi and Siegbert Uhlig (Wiesbaden: Harrassowitz, 2014), pp. 546–47

Garretson, Peter, 'A Note on Relations between Ethiopia and the Kingdom of Aragon in the Fifteenth Century', *Rassegna di studi etiopici*, 37 (1993), 37–44

Ghinzoni, Pietro, 'Un'ambasciata del Prete Gianni a Roma nel 1481', *Archivio storico lombardo*, 6 (1889), 145–54

Grévin, Benoît, 'Between Arabic and Latin in Late Medieval and Renaissance Italy', in *Latin and Arabic: Entangled Histories*, ed. by Daniel G. König, Heidelberg Studies on Transculturality, 5 (Heidelberg: Heidelberg University Publishing, 2019), pp. 145–77

——, 'De Damas à Urbino: Les savoirs linguistiques arabes dans l'Italie renaissante (1370–1520)', *Annales: Histoire, Sciences Sociales*, 70.3 (2015), 607–35

Guidi, Ignazio, 'La prima stampa del Nuovo Testamento in etiopico fatta in Roma nel 1548–49', *Archivio della Reale società romana di storia patria*, 9 (1886), 273–78

Hamilton, Alastair, *The Copts and the West, 1439–1822* (Oxford: Oxford University Press, 2006)

Hopkins, Simon, review of *150 Years after Dillmann's Lexicon: Perspectives and Challenges of Geez Studies*, ed. by Alessandro Bausi and Eugenia Sokolinski, *Bibliotheca Orientalis*, 75.5–6 (2018), 596–604

Jorga, Nicola, 'Cenni sulle relazioni tra l'Abissinia e l'Europa cattolica nei secoli XIV–XV, con un itinerario inedito del secolo XV', in *Centenario della nascita di*

Michele Amari, ed. by Giuseppe Salvo Cozzo, 2 vols (Palermo: Virzi, 1910), I, pp. 139–50

Kelly, Samantha, 'Biondo Flavio on Ethiopia: Processes of Knowledge Production in the Renaissance', in *The Routledge History of the Renaissance*, ed. by William Caferro (London: Routledge, 2017), pp. 167–82

——, 'The Curious Case of Ethiopic Chaldean: Fraud, Philology, and Cultural (Mis)Understanding in European Conceptions of Ethiopia', *Renaissance Quarterly*, 68 (2015), 1227–64

——, 'Ewosṭateans at the Council of Florence (1441): Diplomatic Implications between Ethiopia, Europe, Jerusalem and Cairo', *Afriques* [online journal], Varia (2016), <https://journals.openedition.org/afriques/1858>

——, 'Heretics, Allies, Exemplary Christians: Latin Views of Ethiopian Orthodox in the Late Middle Ages', in *Late Medieval Heresy: New Perspectives*, ed. by Michael D. Bailey and Sean L. Field, Heresy and Inquisition in the Middle Ages, 5 (Woodbridge: York Medieval Press in association with Boydell & Brewer, 2018), pp. 195–214

——, 'Introduction', in *A Companion to Medieval Ethiopia and Eritrea*, ed. by Samantha Kelly (Leiden: Brill, 2020), pp. 1–30

——, 'Medieval Ethiopian Diasporas', in *A Companion to Medieval Ethiopia and Eritrea*, ed. by Samantha Kelly (Leiden: Brill, 2020), pp. 425–53

Kelly, Samantha, and Denis Nosnitsin, 'The Two Yoḥannəses of Santo Stefano degli Abissini, Rome: Reconstructing Biography and Cross-Cultural Encounter through Manuscript Evidence', *Manuscript Studies*, 2.2 (2017), 392–426

Kennerly, Sam, 'Ethiopian Christians in Rome, c. 1400–c. 1700', in *A Companion to Religious Minorities in Early Modern Rome*, ed. by Emily Michelson and Matthew Coneys Wainwright (Leiden: Brill, 2021), pp. 142–68

Krebs, Verena, *Medieval Ethiopian Kingship, Craft, and Diplomacy with Latin Europe* (Basingstoke: Palgrave Macmillan, 2021)

Lefevre, Renato, 'Documenti e notizie su Tasfā Ṣeyon e la sua attività romana nel sec. XVI', *Rassegna di studi etiopici*, 24 (1969–1970), 74–133

——, 'Documenti pontifici sui rapporti con l'Etiopia nei secoli XV e XVI', *Rassegna di studi etiopici*, 5 (1946), 17–41

——, 'Giovanni Potken e la sua edizione romana del Salterio in etiopico (1513)', *La Bibliofilía*, 68 (1966), 289–308

——, 'Riflessi etiopici nella cultura europea del medioevo e del Rinascimento', *Annali Lateranensi*, 9 (1945), 331–444

Loiseau, Julien, 'The Ḥaṭī and the Sultan: Letters and Embassies from Abysssinia to the Mamluk Court', in *Mamlūk Cairo, a Crossroads for Embassies*, ed. by Frédéric Bauden and Malika Dekkiche (Leiden: Brill, 2019), pp. 638–57

Lowe, Kate, 'Representing Africa: Ambassadors and Princes from Christian Africa to Renaissance Italy and Portugal, 1402–1668', *Transactions of the Royal Historical Society*, 17 (2007), 101–28

Lusini, Gianfrancesco, 'Lingua letteraria e lingua di corte: Diglossia e insegnamento tradizionale in Etiopia fra Tardo Antico e Medio Evo', *Aion: Sezione di filologia e letteratura classica*, 41 (2019), 274–84

Marinescu, Constantin, *La politique orientale d'Alfonso V d'Aragon, Roi de Naples (1416-1458)* (Barcelona: Institut d'Estudis Catalans, 1994)

Martínez d'Alòs-Moner, Andreu, *Envoys of a Human God: The Jesuit Mission to Ethiopia, 1557-1632* (Leiden: Brill, 2015)

Martínez d'Alòs-Moner, Andreu, and Leonardo Cohen, 'On the Roots of Ethiopic Philology and a Bilingual Letter from the Jesuit Mission Period', in *Manuscripts and Texts, Languages and Contexts*, ed. by Alessandro Bausi, Alessandro Gori, and Denis Nosnitsin (Wiesbaden: Harrassowitz, 2015), pp. 181-97

Mauro da Leonessa, *Santo Stefano Maggiore degli Abissini e le relazioni romano-etiopiche* (Vatican City: Tipografia Poliglotta Vaticana, 1929)

Meley Mulugetta, 'Säwasəw', in *Encyclopaedia Aethiopica*, vol. IV, ed. by Siegbert Uhlig and Alessandro Bausi (Wiesbaden: Harrassowitz, 2010), pp. 562-64

Moreno, Martino Mario, 'Struttura e terminologia del Sawāsĕw', *Rassegna di studi etiopici*, 8 (1949), 12-62

O'Malley, John, *Giles of Viterbo on Church and Reform: A Study in Renaissance Thought* (Leiden: Brill, 1968)

Paulau, Stanislau, *Das Andere Christentum: Zur transkonfessionalen Verflechtunggeschichte von äthiopischer Orthodoxie und europäischen Protestantismus* (Göttingen: Vandenhoeck & Ruprecht, 2021)

——, 'An Ethiopian Orthodox Monk in the Cradle of the Reformation: *Abba* Mikaʾel, Martin Luther, and the Unity of the Church', in *Ethiopian Orthodox Christianity in a Global Context: Entanglements and Disconnections*, ed. by Stanislau Paulau and Martin Tamcke (Leiden: Brill, 2022), pp. 81-109

Petry, Carl F., '"Travel Patterns in the Medieval Near East" Reconsidered: Contrasting Trajectories, Interconnected Networks', in *Everything Is on the Move: The Mamluk Empire as a Node in (Trans-)Regional Networks*, ed. by Stephan Conermann, Mamluk Studies, 7 (Göttingen: V&R Unipress, 2014), pp. 165-79

Pigli, Mario, *Italian Civilization in Ethiopia* (London: Dante Alighieri Society, 1936)

Proverbio, Delio Vania, 'Santo Stefano degli Abissini: Una breve rivisitazione', *La parola del passato: Rivista di studi antichi*, 66 (2011), 50-68

Raineri, Osvaldo, 'Pietro Bembo e la prima stampa delle lettere di San Paolo in etiopico', *Rendiconti dell'Accademia Nazionale dei Lincei, Classe di scienze morali, storiche e filologiche*, 8th ser., 35 (1980), 395-98

——, 'Studi etiopici nell'età del Giovio', in *Atti del Convegno Paolo Giovio: Il Rinascimento e la memoria (Como, 3-5 giugno 1983)*, Raccolta storica, 17 (Como: Società a Villa Gallia, 1985), pp. 117-31

Relaño, Francesc, *The Shaping of Africa: Cosmographic Discourse and Cartographic Science in Late Medieval and Early Modern Europe* (London: Routledge, 2002)

Romani, Valentino, 'La stampa del N. T. in etiopico (1548-1549): Figure e temi del Cinquecento romano', in *Studi di biblioteconomia e storia del libro in onore di Francesco Barberi* (Rome: Associazione italiana biblioteche, 1976), pp. 481-98

Salvadore, Matteo, *The African Prester John and the Birth of Ethiopian-European Relations, 1402-1555* (New York: Routledge, 2017)

Salvadore, Matteo, and James de Lorenzi, 'An Ethiopian Scholar in Tridentine Rome: Täsfa Ṣeyon and the Birth of Orientalism', *Itinerario*, 45 (2021), 17-46

Spicer, Joaneath, 'Free Men and Women of African Ancestry in Renaissance Europe', in *Revealing the African Presence in Renaissance Europe*, ed. by Joaneath Spicer (Baltimore: Walters Art Museum, 2012), pp. 81–97

Stenzig, Philipp, *Botschafterzeremoniell am Papsthof der Renaissance: Der 'Tractatus de oratoribus' des Paris de Grassi — Edition und Kommentar*, 2 vols (Frankfurt am Main: Peter Lang, 2013)

Tavoni, Mirko, 'Renaissance Linguistics: Western Europe', in *History of Linguistics*, III: *Renaissance and Early Modern Linguistics*, ed. by Giulio Lepschy (London: Routledge, 2014), pp. 1–108

Tedeschi, Salvatore, 'Etiopi e Copti al Concilio di Firenze', *Annuarium Historiae Conciliorum*, 21 (1989), 380–407

——, 'L'Etiopia di Poggio Bracciolini', *Africa: Rivista trimestrale di studi e documentazione dell'Istituto italiano per l'Africa e l'Oriente*, 48 (1993), 333–58

Thomassy, Raymond, 'De Guillaume Fillastre considéré comme géographe à propos d'un manuscrit de la Géographie de Ptolomée', *Bulletin de la Société de Géographie [de Paris]*, 2nd ser., 17 (1842), 144–55

Tubach, Jürgen, 'Hiob Ludolf und die Anfänge der Äthiopistik in Deutschland', in *Von Hiob Ludolf bis Enrico Cerulli: Halle/S. 3.–5. Oktober 1996. Akten der 2. Tagung der Orbis -Aethiopicus-Gesellschaft zur Erhaltung und Förderung der äthiopischen Kultur*, ed. by Piotr O. Scholz, Biblioteca nubia et aethiopica, 8 (Warsaw: Zas Pan, 2001), pp. 1–47

Uhlig, Siegbert, and Alessandro Bausi, eds, *Encyclopaedia Aethiopica*, 5 vols (Wiesbaden: Harrassowitz, 2003–2014)

Weber, Benjamin, 'La bulle *Cantate Domino* (2 février 1442) et les enjeux éthiopiens du concile de Florence', *Mélanges de l'École française de Rome – Moyen Âge*, 122 (2010), 441–49

——, 'Gli Etiopi a Roma nel Quattrocento: Ambasciatori politici, negoziatori religiosi o pellegrini?', *Mélanges de l'École française de Rome – Moyen Âge*, 125 (2013), <https://journals.openedition.org/mefrm/1036>

Wilkinson, Robert J., *Orientalism, Aramaic, and Kabbalah in the Catholic Reformation: The First Printing of the Syriac New Testament*, Studies in the History of Christian Traditions, 137 (Leiden: Brill, 2007)

HAN LAMERS

Ascanio Persio and the 'Greekness' of Italian*

The classicist Bernard Knox once wrote that, during the Renaissance, 'Greek was the instrument of change and disturbance in the religious as well as in the cultural sphere' and in later periods continued to play its role of 'intellectual gadfly'.[1] The Renaissance rediscovery of ancient Greek language and literature — Platonism, the Greek Gospels, the Hellenistic novel, and so much more — encouraged people to abandon well-trodden paths and explore new ones. One of those new paths that lastingly changed Europe's cultural landscape was the further emancipation of the vernaculars from the dominance of Latin. The role that Greek played in this process is, perhaps, better known for sixteenth-century France than for any other time and place; Renaissance Italy has received less attention in this regard than it deserves. Scholars have explored humanist Hellenism and the *questione della lingua* largely in isolation, even though the importance of Greek in the Italian language question has incidentally been acknowledged in the scholarship.[2] Carlo Dionisotti, for instance, emphasized

---

* This article was made possible by the generous financial support of the Department of Philosophy, Classics, and the History of Art and Ideas at the University of Oslo. I am also grateful to Stefan Derouck and other staff of the University Library of Leuven for providing me with scans of the relevant literature I could not get my hands on due to COVID-19 restrictions, as well as to Marjolein van Zuylen for her advice on the sometimes difficult, 'baroque-ish' Italian text of the *Discorso*. Many thanks also to Chris Turner-Neal for his advice on English style and idiom, as well as to this volume's attentive editors.

1 Knox, *The Oldest Dead White European Males*, p. 18.
2 See, e.g., Dionisotti, *Gli umanisti e il volgare*, pp. 2–3, 51; Dionisotti, 'Per una storia delle dottrine linguistiche', p. 19; Dionisotti, 'Girolamo Claricio', p. 165; Lepschy, 'The Classical Languages and Italian', pp. 31–32; Tavoni, 'Renaissance Linguistics', pp. 46, 50–51; Trapp, 'The Conformity of Greek with the Vernacular', pp. 11–12. The discussion was resumed more recently in Caruso and Laird, 'Introduction', p. 8.

> **Han Lamers** (han.lamers@ifikk.uio.no) is Professor of Classics at the Department of Philosophy, Classics, and the History of Art and Ideas at the University of Oslo. His research focuses on scholarly, cultural, and ideological receptions of the classical heritage in early modern and modern Europe.

Languages and Cross-Cultural Exchanges in Renaissance Italy, ed. by Alessandra Petrocchi and Joshua Brown, LMEMS 30 (Turnhout: Brepols, 2023), pp. 359–388

that the study of Greek encouraged some humanists to embrace the vernacular, and he observed elsewhere that the transition from Latin to Italian would not even have been possible without the mediation of Greek.[3] 'The entrance of Greek into the humanist system', Mirko Tavoni further explained, 'opened up some space for the recognition of the vernacular and its variants by breaking the monopoly of Latin as the language of culture'.[4]

This chapter obviously cannot complete our still imperfect understanding of the connection between Greek humanism and Italian vernacular culture, but it will perhaps enable us to see the link in better light. The relationship can be studied from at least three different perspectives, which have not always been neatly distinguished, as they sometimes overlap. First, we can explore how individual humanists, through their study of Greek letters, opened up to the vernacular tongues and eventually embraced them as languages in their own right. Secondly, we can examine how they deployed their knowledge of the categories of Greek grammar to describe and understand the specificities of their native languages. Thirdly, we can look at how they enhanced the cultural status of their languages by identifying affinities with the sounds, expressions, and structures of ancient Greek. This chapter takes the latter approach.

To this end, the present chapter will unpack a notable argument about the 'Greekness' of Italian which Ascanio Persio formulated in his *Discorso intorno alla conformità della lingua italiana con le più nobili antiche lingue, & principalmente con la greca* (*Discourse on the Conformity of the Italian Language with the Most Noble Ancient Languages, and Greek in Particular*), first published in 1592. Persio's case reminds us that the emancipation of the vernacular by no means implied an uncontested consensus about what form the vernacular should take.[5] It shows that ancient Greek continued to play its role in discussions about the vernaculars also after the main battles for their acceptance had been won. Ascanio proposed the creation of a standard variety of written Italian that would incorporate speech varieties different from the dominant Tuscan. He also wanted to reaffirm the superiority of a newly modelled, common Italian over the other emerging languages of culture in Europe by enhancing the 'Greekness' of its lexicon, syntax, phonetics, and phraseology. In addition to exploring Persio's argument with a special interest in the role of Greek, this chapter shows how his argument both responded to European debates over the cultural significance of the vernaculars and creatively intervened in the Italian language question. After introducing the author and his project in the following section, I will discuss his notion of the conformity of Italian with Greek both as an intellectual endeavour and as a cultural project of language

---

3 See Dionisotti, 'Girolamo Claricio', p. 165, and Dionisotti, *Gli umanisti e il volgare*, pp. 2–3, 51. For a milder formulation, see also Dionisotti, 'Per una storia delle dottrine linguistiche', p. 19.
4 Tavoni, 'Renaissance Linguistics', p. 46.
5 See the perceptive criticism in Burke, *Languages and Communities in Early Modern Europe*, pp. 61–65.

reform, set against the background of Hellenizing tendencies both in Italy and elsewhere in Europe.

Ascanio Persio and his *Discorso* (1592)

Not much is known about the life of Ascanio Persio (1554–1610).[6] Born in Matera in the southern Italian region of Basilicata, Persio went to the humanist school of his maternal uncle Lorenzo Goffredo and afterwards studied logic and philosophy at the convent of Saint Francis of Assisi in his native town. Having completed his education in Matera, Persio probably travelled to Naples with his brother Antonio, and to Rome and Venice, before he settled in Padua for further studies in Greek, Latin, and philosophy (with Giacomo Zabarella). When the chair of Greek at the University of Bologna became vacant due to the death of Pompilio Amaseo, Persio applied for the position and obtained it in 1586. After receiving an additional degree in philosophy in 1589, he was appointed as the city's *publicus interpres* of Aristotle; in this capacity, he was allowed to teach on the Greek text of the philosopher's work.[7] In addition to his well-received teaching activities, he found time to write essays and treatises on philosophical subjects, especially logic.[8]

Besides his philosophical interests, Ascanio Persio also cultivated a vivid interest in the Greek language. Most notably, he compiled a lexicon of the first book of the *Iliad*, published by Grazio Lodi Garisendi in 1597. It contained a Greek–Latin and a Latin–Greek wordlist with glosses. His Homeric lexicon enjoyed particular popularity. It was partly reprinted by the German historian and classicist Martin Kraus (Crusius) and later in its entirety by the Florentine philologist, theologian, and bibliophile Alessandro Politi.[9] Persio also worked on a Greek grammar, which remained unfinished,[10] and he wrote literary and historical works. Some of them are written in his humanist version of ancient Greek. In addition to some scattered Greek poems and letters,[11] he authored

---

6 On Ascanio Persio and his work, see Pignatti, 'Persio, Ascanio', with the sources and scholarship cited there (some additional work is cited in the footnotes below). The most extensive treatment of Persio and his family is Padula and Motta, *Antonio e Ascanio Persio*, esp. pp. 65–79. Apart from the works listed in Pignatti's overview, the anonymous work *La Pazzia* (variously dated) has sometimes also been attributed to Ascanio Persio (on this matter, see Figorilli, 'Elogi paradossali', p. 266 n. 78, with the literature cited there).
7 See the official document cited in Padula and Motta, *Antonio e Ascanio Persio*, p. 66.
8 See the annotated list of publications in Padula and Motta, *Antonio e Ascanio Persio*, pp. 75–79.
9 Persio, *Indicis in Homeri poemata*. Crusius, *Commentationes*, fols N2^r–O6^v (only the Greek–Latin list, reduced), and Politi, *Commentarii*, pp. xli–lxvii. Reviewing Politi's edition, Archibald Bower still referred to Persio's lists as 'famous' (Bower, *Historia Litteraria*, p. 25).
10 Padula and Motta, *Antonio e Ascanio Persio*, p. 79.
11 Two Greek distichs on the death of Pierre Pithou (d. 1596) are printed in Pontani, 'Il greco di Gianfrancesco Mussato', p. 158; another small poem was included in *Tempio*, ed. by Segni, p. 202; an epigram to Ippolita Paleotti (d. 1581) and a short letter are preserved in Città del

a remarkable trilingual prose work in Greek, Latin, and Italian narrating the history of the famous icon of the Holy Virgin, reportedly painted by Saint Luke and preserved in the Sanctuary of the Madonna di San Luca on the top of the Colle della Guardia, to Bologna's south-west.[12]

If Persio is remembered today, it is mainly for the work under discussion here. The treatise has an unusual printing history. It was first published in Venice in 1592 by Giovanni Battista Ciotti. In that same year, Persio himself published a corrected edition, this time in Bologna with Giovanni Rossi, and dedicated it to his benefactor Bonifacio Caetani.[13] The Bolognese edition was reprinted in 1874 by the Calabrese historian and philosopher Francesco Fiorentino, in 1985 by the Romanist Tristano Bolelli, and then again, with Fiorentino's preface, by Mauro Padula and Camilla Motta in 1991.[14] Apart from Bolelli's important and pioneering work, detailed studies on the *Discorso* are lacking, even though it has by no means gone unnoticed in scholarship.[15] An edition of the treatise with a full and up-to-date linguistic commentary and an English translation is still a serious desideratum. In what follows, I will cite and refer to the Bolognese edition of 1592, as this is the only edition the author saw through the presses.

As Persio himself explained, his work on the *Discorso* was part of a long-standing project to map and chart similarities between Italian and other languages, especially the ancient and 'noble' ones, that is, Aramaic, Hebrew, Greek, and Latin. He planned a larger volume on these 'etymologies', which he, however,

---

Vaticano, Biblioteca Apostolica Vaticana, MS Vat. lat. 3435, fols 63^r and 64^r. Paleotti wrote Greek herself: although her verses are regarded as lost (Stevenson, *Women Latin Poets*, p. 524), a letter survives in the Archivio Isolani in Bologna, MS F 30.99.18. CN 58 (according to Kristeller, *Iter Italicum*, p. 506).

12 Persio's history was part of a miscellaneous collection of Greek, Latin, and Italian poems, which formed part of a campaign to keep the icon in Bologna after the pope had claimed it for Rome. Persio brought together the contributors to the book, which Giulio Segni edited. The Greek text is printed in Persio, *Componimenti*, fols O^r–Y8^v. The Latin version was reprinted in Garnefelt, ed., *Vita*, pp. 132–70. On the collection, see Callegari and McHugh, '"Se fossimo tante meretrici"', pp. 35–37, and Pontani, 'Il greco di Gianfrancesco Mussato', pp. 159–61. On its historical context, see Callegari and McHugh, 'Playing Papal Politics'.

13 Persio, *Discorso*, pp. 5–7. On Persio and Caetani, see Padula and Motta, *Antonio e Ascanio Persio*, p. 76.

14 Padula and Motta, *Antonio e Ascanio Persio*, pp. 83–124 (with Fiorentino's preface on pp. 125–39).

15 See especially Bolelli, 'Ascanio Persio linguista', reprinted as a self-standing booklet (Bolelli, *Ascanio Persio linguista*), as a chapter in Bolelli, *Leopardi linguista*, pp. 53–81, and again in Padula and Motta, *Antonio e Ascanio Persio*, pp. 143–66. On various aspects of Persio's linguistic thought, see also Bolelli, 'Di vocali latine'; Bolelli, 'Principi di linguistica generale', pp. 96–98; De Blasi, *L'italiano in Basilicata*, pp. 69–71; D'Ovidio, *Le Correzioni*, pp. 176–77; Droixhe, 'On the Origins of Historical Linguistics', pp. 18–19; Padula and Motta, *Antonio e Ascanio Persio*, pp. 141–66; Pignatti, *Etimologia e proverbio*, pp. 119–30; Sorrento, *Benedetto Varchi*, pp. 72–79; Tavoni, 'On the Renaissance Idea that Latin Derives from Greek', p. 227; Tavoni, 'Renaissance Linguistics', pp. 50–51.

left unfinished.[16] The *Discorso* served to give a first rough outline of the project, focusing on the conformity of Italian with Greek (for Persio's view of 'Italian' and 'Greek' I refer to my discussion below).[17] In earlier scholarship, Persio's treatise has sometimes been understood as an argument for the idea that Italian originated in Greek. This is, however, an unfortunate (and persistent) misrepresentation of his actual thesis.[18] The author himself recognized that Italian — even in its linguistic diversity — was predominantly Latin, not Greek. Persio looked at the language as a 'corpo misto' ('blended body') of diverse influences displaying similarities with various other languages.[19] As we shall see, Persio's *conformità* did not rely on crude assumptions about the origin of the vernacular but on a subtle understanding of the different ways in which different languages can show various similarities.

Additionally, the *Discorso* provided the outlines of Persio's ambitious plan to reform the language of Italy's 'publiche scritture' ('public writings'), that is, the written language of the educated inhabitants of the peninsula.[20] This work contributed to the then ongoing debate concerning the standardization of the written vernacular. While by the end of the sixteenth century, the battle for the vernacular against Latin had been won, many thorny questions remained. Should the model for the common language, for instance, be exclusively Tuscan? And if so, what kind of Tuscan should serve as a standard: contemporary parlance or the literary language of the Florentine classics of the Trecento? Some disagreed with the primacy of Tuscan in the first place. What about the other Italian varieties? Should they be given a place in a common written language? And if so, how? In conjunction with these disputes, there was the lesser question of foreign influence on Italian, especially of French and Spanish, heard in some of the peninsula's foreign-ruled areas. Persio's *Discorso* directly responded to most of these issues, which are together known as the *questione della lingua* — a 'struggle for the standard'.[21]

---

16 Persio, *Discorso*, pp. 10–11. Parts of Ascanio's notes remain in manuscript in the Biblioteca Ambrosiana in Milan (MS R. 109 sup.). Bolelli published some of Persio's notes from this manuscript (Bolelli, 'Un inedito').
17 Persio, *Discorso*, p. 11.
18 See, in particular, Gröber, *Grundriss der romanischen Philologie*, p. 15 (confusing Ascanio and Antonio Persio); Pisani, *L'etimologia*, p. 35; Renzi, *Introduzione alla filologia romanza*, p. 29. Tristano Bolelli repeatedly criticized this position: Bolelli, 'Ascanio Persio linguista', pp. 7–12; Bolelli, 'Di vocali latine', p. 298; Bolelli, 'Principi di linguistica generale', pp. 96–97. A notably early exception to the misunderstanding is D'Ovidio, *Le Correzioni*, p. 177 (see also Flamini, *Il Cinquecento*, pp. 138, 475). The idea still resonates in recent literature: see, e.g., Brincat, 'Da Ascoli a Gusmani', p. 93, citing Persio as a proponent of the idea that Italian originated in Greek, and Swiggers, 'Les études linguistiques romanes', p. 19 n. 14, listing him together with Guillaume Budé, Joachim Périon, Léon Trippault, and Agnolo Monosini as advocates of 'la thèse de l'origine grecque'.
19 Persio, *Discorso*, p. 37.
20 Persio, *Discorso*, p. 49.
21 Burke, *Languages and Communities in Early Modern Europe*, p. 63 (with discussion of the phenomenon from a Europe-wide perspective on pp. 89–110). For overviews of the Italian language question in the sixteenth century, see Antonelli and Ravesi, 'La questione della

In this struggle, two sets of conflicting positions stand out: (1) Tuscanist positions, promoting Tuscan as the gold standard, versus approaches stressing the importance of other varieties, and (2) archaizing arguments, favouring Trecento literature as an ideal, versus anti-archaic stances advocating different forms of more recent varieties.[22] The *questione* was eventually settled in favour of Tuscanism by the 1525 publication of Pietro Bembo's *Prose della volgar lingua*. Around the time Persio was writing, a consensus in favour of archaizing Tuscanism (esp. Florentine) had been established, and the Accademia della Crusca in Florence (est. 1583) had started working on an Italian lexicon that would cement Tuscanist aspirations.[23] As we shall see in more detail below, Persio positioned himself in the debate by embracing the primacy of Tuscan for the *lingua commune*,[24] while also advancing the argument that, under specific conditions, it should be possible to use non-Tuscan words and expressions as well — which he regarded as an antidote to what he saw as excessive borrowing from French and Spanish. For Persio, an important criterion for admission to the written vernacular was an expression's conformity with an ancient, noble language.

Although the *questione della lingua* was an Italian affair, it did not unfold in a vacuum. In the sixteenth century, discussions of the vernaculars raged all over Europe. The question of how written languages should be shaped — from syntax to orthography — went hand in hand with the need to assert their existence and identities against both Latin and other, competing vernaculars.[25] Intellectuals — often humanists — sought to establish distinctive places for their native vernaculars in the linguistic landscape of Europe. They did so in various ways, but they shared a common strategy of 'nobilizing' their vernacular by showing its privileged connection with an ancient language. As antiquity implied nobility, and priority inferred superiority, the older the language the better for its cultural status. The matrix languages included Aramaic, Hebrew, Greek, and Latin but also then-largely unattested languages such as 'Gaulish' and 'Etruscan' (sometimes identified with Aramaic). Ancient Greek played a particularly important role in the expansion of the vernaculars both in Italy and elsewhere. In France and the German lands, in particular, humanists worked

---

lingua'; Campanelli, 'Languages', pp. 153–63; Daniele, 'Sviluppo della critica', pp. 1523–39; Hall, *The Italian 'Questione della lingua'*; Labande-Jeanroy, *La question de la langue*, passim; Vitale, *La questione della lingua*, pp. 22–63.

22 These viewpoints were not entirely monolithic: there was considerable discussion even within the opposing camps. Within the archaizing camp, for example, there was debate about what should be included under the rubric of Trecento literature and what not (Antonelli and Ravesi, 'La questione della lingua', p. 744).

23 Daniele, 'Sviluppo della critica', p. 1524. By the end of the century, the main criticism of archaizing Tuscanism seems to have come from the Sienese camp criticizing its overemphasis on Florentine (Antonelli and Ravesi, 'La questione della lingua', p. 744).

24 Persio, *Discorso*, p. 48.

25 For a critical and wide-ranging overview of the competition between the European vernaculars, see Burke, *Languages and Communities in Early Modern Europe*, pp. 61–88.

hard to show the Greek features of their native languages. Such attempts went hand in hand with cultural myths about the Greek origins of French and German (or even the vernacular roots of ancient Greek), the invention of Greek etymologies, and proposals for Hellenizing spelling reforms. In order to understand Persio's contribution on its own terms and in the context of wider debates, the next section will first introduce the imagined 'Greekness' of the vernacular in Renaissance Italy and sixteenth-century Europe before analysing the argument of the *Discorso* itself — and especially its notion of *conformità*.

Imagined Greekness in Sixteenth-Century Europe

Ascanio Persio's attempt to 'Hellenize' Italian does not stand alone in sixteenth-century Europe, and yet his *Discorso* represents a unique thought experiment in the Italian context. The French connection — and hence the European dimension — of Persio's argument is immediately apparent from the key term of the title of his treatise: *conformità* ('conformity'). This term had been put on the map in French by the philologist and printer Henri Estienne (Stephanus). Estienne used the term *conformité* to denote similarities between ancient Greek and French, which he explained in a treatise entitled *Traicté de la conformité du langage françois avec le grec* (*Treatise on the Conformity of the French Language with Greek*), first published in 1565 and reprinted, with revisions, in 1569.[26] In his view, French had lost its characteristic *accointance* ('relationship') with Greek, mainly due to Italian and Spanish influences, which were most apparent in the language of the court. Striving to promote French as a language of culture superior to all the other vernaculars, Estienne aspired to restore its connection with ancient Greek.[27] He discussed the conformity of French with Greek in three sections. These deal, in order, with the eight parts of speech (omitting interjections and adding the articles that Latin

---

26 For the intellectual and cultural background of Estienne, see, e.g., Boudou, *Mars et les muses*, pp. 21–62, and references there. On the various aspects of his ideas on language and the role of ancient Greek in particular, see Adamou, 'Le rôle de l'imaginaire linguistique'; Boudou, 'La place de la mémoire'; Cerquiglini, *Une langue orpheline*, pp. 43–51; Clément, *Henri Estienne et son oeuvre française*, pp. 277–304 and passim; Demaizière, 'Deux aspects de l'idéal linguistique'; Demaizière, 'Les réflexions étymologiques'; Steinfeld and Pescarini, 'Pleins feux sur l'ellipse en étymologie'; Trudeau, 'La mémoire de la langue'; Trudeau, *Les inventeurs du bon usage*, pp. 116–40. On the role of proverbs, see Boudou, 'Proverbes et formules gnomiques', pp. 166–71, and Pineaux, 'La formule proverbiale', pp. 87–88, 92–93.

27 Estienne, *Traicté* (1569 edn), fol. *v^r. On Estienne's views on Italian and French, see Clément, *Henri Estienne et son oeuvre française*, pp. 305–62; Cowling, 'Henri Estienne'; Shangler, 'The Language of Identity'; Swiggers, 'Le français et l'italien en lice'. For Estienne, 'French' coincides with the spoken language of Paris, including the vernaculars of Orléans, Tours, Bourges, and Chartres (Swiggers, 'Le français et l'italien en lice', p. 73).

lacks), phraseology (fixed word combinations and set phrases, including some grammatical anomalies), and etymology (with an alphabetical wordlist).[28]

The title of Persio's treatise clearly echoes Estienne's work. His prominent use of the term *conformità* in the title suggests that he wanted to present his own project as an Italian response to Estienne's. Although Persio did not mention his French colleague by name, he paraphrased and challenged 'the French' several times in his *Discorso* and showed awareness of their approach, even though his interest in the Greekness of Italian probably predated his reading of the French humanists.[29] Modern scholars have sometimes referred to the Hellenizing attitude of the French as *celt'-hellénisme*.[30] Hellenizing attitudes were also found in other parts of Europe. Estienne himself, for instance, replied to the claims of the Dutch humanist Hadrianus Junius, who had pointed out the Greekness of Dutch (contesting previous French claims).[31] German scholars, too, emphasized the Greekness of their language in their attempts to nobilize it.[32] They singled out, in addition to etymologies, a range of similarities with ancient Greek, including correspondences in sound and prosody, tense categories, and word classes.[33] Estienne takes a special place

---

28 The similarities between French and Greek did not lead Estienne to conclude that French descended from Greek (see Trudeau, 'La mémoire de la langue', p. 19, and Swiggers, 'Le français et l'italien en lice', p. 74 n. 2). It would be misleading, therefore, to bring his argument under the rubric of 'word genealogies' designed to demonstrate that French was derived from ancient Greek (as did Berrong, 'Genealogies and the Search for an Origin', pp. 75–76).

29 Bolelli, 'Ascanio Persio linguista', p. 8. Bolelli assumed additional influence of Joachim Périon, Charles Bovelles, and Guillaume Postel (Bolelli, 'Ascanio Persio linguista', pp. 7–8). Estienne's influence is also recognized in Daniele, 'Sviluppo della critica', p. 1536; Pignatti, *Etimologia e proverbio*, pp. 121, 125–26; Richardson, 'Renaissance Linguistics in Italy', pp. 153–54; Sorrento, *Benedetto Varchi*, pp. 72–73. Tavoni seems to be more reticent in this regard, without further explanation (Tavoni, 'Renaissance Linguistics', pp. 50–51). For Persio's response to French positions, see Persio, *Discorso*, pp. 9–10. Some of Persio's contemporaries also took issue with French etymology in general (e.g. Benedetto Varchi: Sorrento, *Benedetto Varchi*; Ward, 'Benedetto Varchi as Etymologist', p. 246) or Estienne's treatise in particular (e.g. Bernardo Davanzati: Daniele, 'Sviluppo della critica', p. 1523).

30 The term is after the title of Léon Trippault's dictionary of Greek–French etymologies (1581). It is slightly misleading insofar as it suggests a coherent and consistent set of ideas regarding the Greek origin of French. The ways in which individual scholars construed the privileged relationship between French and Greek varied greatly from case to case and was moreover contested. On this Hellenizing movement in early modern France, see Courouau, 'Les apologies', pp. 46–48; Lamers, 'Wil de echte Griek opstaan?', pp. 102–16; Tavoni, 'Renaissance Linguistics', pp. 51–53, with the references there. Interestingly, the conformity of French with Greek remained present in the French educational curriculum until well into the nineteenth century (Savatovsky, 'Contact de langues et enseignement du grec ancien', pp. 34, 40–43).

31 On Junius's pioneering role, see Van Hal, 'A Man of Eight Hearts', pp. 198–205.

32 See Van Hal, 'Bevoorrechte betrekkingen tussen Germaans en Grieks', pp. 428–29.

33 A systematic treatment of the wider phenomenon is still lacking, but I am planning to publish a more extensive study elsewhere. For some Europe-wide treatments of 'vernacular Greekness', see Tavoni, 'Renaissance Linguistics', passim; Trapp, 'The Conformity of Greek

in this 'Hellenizing' discourse in France and Europe more broadly as he was the first to discuss the similarities between Greek and a vernacular in such detail in a self-standing treatise. As we shall see, Persio holds a similar position in the Italian context.

What about Italian Greekness? Comparisons with ancient Greek played a notable role in the discussion and promotion of Tuscan, in particular. Tuscanists sometimes cited similarities between the two in order to describe and/or promote their language ('describing' and 'promoting' are not easy to distinguish here: the very fact that Tuscan could be described in terms of Greek was in itself already proof of its excellence). This is the approach we find — with different emphases — in the work of Benedetto Varchi, Vincenzio Maria Borghini, and Orazio Lombardelli, to name just three. Notwithstanding their different positions on the language question, some parts of their work show methodological overlaps with Persio. Varchi's approach, for example, was not limited to etymology but extended to include also morphosyntactic resemblances. Varchi was moreover interested in similarities not only with Greek but with other languages as well (in his case, Hebrew, Latin, and Provençal).[34] These and other methodological correspondences merit a detailed discussion elsewhere. Advocates of dialects other than Tuscan, too, sometimes relied on Greek parallels to promote their languages, yet it would seem they did so less extensively.[35]

Critics of Tuscanism could cite the dialects of ancient Greece as a positive model for more pluriformity in Italian. They usually singled out copiousness and variation of expression as positive qualities that Greek and Italian shared, or should share. As early as 1496, the Venetian printer Aldo Manuzio observed that, in contrast to Latin, Italian shared with ancient Greek its dialectical copiousness — an observation suggesting an appreciation of the Italian dialects, which Aldo, however, did not develop

---

with the Vernacular'; Van Hal, *Moedertalen en taalmoeders*, pp. 415–17; Lamers, 'Wil de echte Griek opstaan?'.

34 On Varchi, see Sorrento, *Benedetto Varchi*. For more recent literature, see the bibliography in Vallance, *Les grammairiens italiens*, p. 692, with the important addition of Ward, 'Benedetto Varchi as Etymologist'.

35 See, for example, Pontico Virunio on Venetian (*Erotemata Guarini*, ed. by Virunio, fols 46ᵛ–47ʳ and 97ʳ, with Tramontana, *Pontico Virunio*, pp. 119–20, and Van Rooy, *Greece's Labyrinth of Language*, pp. 122–23) and Giulio Cesare Capaccio on Neapolitan (Capaccio, *Il forastiero*, pp. 19–22 with Lazzarini, 'Ancora sui rapporti tra letteratura dialettale riflessa e toscano', p. 169, and Stenhouse, 'The Greekness of Greek Inscriptions', pp. 315–18). While Naples's history as a Greek colony was well known, Virunio suggested that some Greek features in Venetian were due to the long-standing Venetian presence in Greece. On Virunio's views, see, apart from Tavoni, 'On the Renaissance Idea that Latin Derives from Greek', pp. 221–22 (with Tramontana, *Pontico Virunio*, p. 119 n. 3), also Van Rooy, *Greece's Labyrinth of Language*, pp. 21–22, and Tramontana, *Pontico Virunio*, pp. 113–34.

further.³⁶ Baldassare Castiglione, on the other hand, cited the Greek dialects in support of an outspoken, anti-Tuscan argument: he favoured a common Italian language drawn from the vernaculars of Italy's main cities, chiefly their courtly elites.³⁷ More radically, Persio's close contemporary Scipione Bargagli argued for a pluralistic and inclusive approach to Italy's speech varieties, not restricted to the courts. For him, the example of the Greek world proved that it was possible for different groups of one language community to speak and write in an orderly fashion in consonance with their own natural parlances.³⁸ The idea of a fifth Greek variety (*koine*) that would have sprung from the four main dialects of ancient Greece also suggested a model for those who advocated the creation of a common Italian language that would assimilate the qualities of several or even all Italian vernaculars.³⁹ These few examples show that different parallels between Greek and Italian could be cited in support of different positions in the debate.⁴⁰

Persio holds a distinctive place in this intellectual landscape. He did not cite parallels with Greek to set one dialect over all the others but used them instead as a means of promoting words and expressions from several different dialects to the status of Tuscan terms. A somewhat similar approach, at least at first sight, is foreshadowed in a curious passage from the encyclopaedia of Raffaele Maffei, published in 1506. Arguing that words are not random and have meaningful origins, Maffei claimed that even vernacular words derive their authority both from Latin and from ancient Greek. To illustrate his point, he cited around twenty Greek etymologies for words used in the dialects of Rome, Tuscany, and what he called 'Italia Transpadana' (i.e. roughly, the region of Italy surrounded by the Alps in the north and west, the Adriatic in the east, and Lucca in the south). He understood these words as the historical residues of cultural contacts with the ancient Greeks who, as his etymologies evidenced, had once inhabited large parts of the peninsula. Maffei, however, confined his brief note to a few word etymologies and did not turn his observations into a programme of language reform.⁴¹ In this respect, too, Persio's work is different. Before him, discussions of Greek–Italian parallels had usually been confined

---

36 On Aldo Manuzio's comment from his preface to his *Thesaurus cornucopiae et horti Adonidis*, see Trapp, 'The Conformity of Greek with the Vernacular', pp. 11–12, with Caruso and Laird, 'Introduction', pp. 7–8, offering an English translation of the passage.
37 Trapp, 'The Conformity of Greek with the Vernacular', p. 12.
38 See Daniele, 'Sviluppo della critica', pp. 1533–34, with the references there.
39 Campanelli, 'Languages', pp. 158–59.
40 For a discussion of the role of the Greek dialects in early modern debates over the vernaculars more generally, see also Van Rooy, *Greece's Labyrinth of Language*, pp. 122–43.
41 Maffei, *Commentariorum rerum urbanorum liber primus*, fol. CCCCXXXVʳ. On Maffei, see Dionisotti, *Gli umanisti e il volgare*, pp. 49–53, quoting the relevant passage in full, and Trapp, 'The Conformity of Greek with the Vernacular', pp. 11–12 (interpreting Maffei's remark as an exhortation to use expressions from the southern dialects, in particular).

to cursory remarks in letters, commentaries, prefaces, and treatises on language and history. To the best of my current knowledge, Persio was the first Italian humanist who produced a standalone discussion of the similarities between Italian and Greek that spelled out their implications for the language question.[42]

In view of Persio's own roots in the former Magna Graecia, his special interest in the Greekness of Italian is perhaps not too surprising.[43] The area had seen an almost continuous Greek presence from the first Greek colonizers in the eighth century BC onwards. This Greek presence, in conjunction with the long-standing connections with the Greek world and Byzantium, profoundly shaped the region's cultural and linguistic orientation. Humanists, antiquarians, and local historians promptly emphasized the Greek heritage in the region's monuments, its history, and its idioms. It gave their area a distinctive cultural identity which even predated the arrival of the Romans and their language.[44] Persio, too, showed particular interest in the Greek heritage of his native region around Matera and the traces of Greek in the Romance *idiomi* of Magna Graecia. He was deeply aware that, even in his own time, 'there are quite a few hamlets and fortified towns on Italy's Ionian coasts where people speak Greek, albeit corrupted Greek, as is the case in Greece itself'.[45] But by no means did Persio promote a form of linguistic *campanilismo*. He was interested in the Greekness of all of the peninsula's dialects, not only the southern, profoundly Hellenized ones.

In order to understand Persio's project better and in more detail, we will now unpack his argument in the *Discorso*. How did Persio analyse the conformity of Italian with Greek? What kinds of similarity did he describe? How did he account for them, and how did he deploy them in his argument for language reform? The answers to these questions will enable us both to appreciate Persio's project on its own terms and to situate his *Discorso* in the ongoing debate over the Italian language.

---

42 Note should be taken of the work of Bartolomeo Benvoglienti of Siena (d. 1486) which falls, however, outside the scope of the language question. Benvoglienti not only analysed the classical languages on a par with the vernaculars but also demonstrated that ancient Greek and Italian shared features that classical Latin lacked. He further suggested that such correspondences should be explained on the basis of a common matrix language rather than a relationship of direct dependence of Italian on Greek. On Benvoglienti, see Coseriu and Meisterfeld, *Geschichte der romanischen Sprachwissenschaft*, pp. 182–91. His treatise was edited with commentary by Tavoni, *Il discorso linguistico* (to be consulted in conjunction with Tavoni, 'On the Renaissance Idea that Latin Derives from Greek', pp. 210–17).

43 Sorrento, *Benedetto Varchi*, p. 74.

44 On southern Italian antiquarians and their emphasis on the Greek antiquity of their region, see, e.g., Stenhouse, 'The Greekness of Greek Inscriptions', esp. pp. 315–19, with the references there. On Sicilian *grecità* in local historiography, see also Pietrasanta, 'La Sicilia graeca'. On Greekness in early modern Puglia and Calabria, see the testimonies collected in Pellegrini, 'Il dialetto greco-calabro di Bova', pp. 19–25.

45 Persio, *Discorso*, p. 9.

The Conformity of Italian with Greek

Unlike Henri Estienne, Persio prefaced his discussion of Greek and Italian with a concise theoretical statement in which he explained his views on language in general. If we want to understand the idea of *conformità*, we need to consider these basic views. Persio saw language as an explication (*spiegamento*) in either sound (*voce*) or in writing (*iscrittura*) of concepts (*concetti*) of the human intellect. In his view, the human intellect receives simple concepts from the senses (*senso*) and then combines them into more complex constellations, forging composite concepts. Simple concepts are represented in language by words (*parole* or *semplice parlare*), while composite concepts are represented by speech (*il parlare* or *composto parlare*: this is what the Latins call *oratio*). These two elements — *parole* and *parlare* — are the constitutive elements of language.[46] As languages generally differ and converge in these two respects, Persio's discussion of the conformity of Italian with Greek focuses on words and the ways they are joined together to form compounds or phrases. Just as Estienne had done before him, he thus decidedly abandoned the overemphasis on word derivation and etymology in the study of language similarity in order to embrace a more comprehensive approach to the similarities between, in his case, Greek and Italian.

The Parameters of 'Conformità'

What does this more comprehensive approach look like? In order to structure his discussion of the conformity of Italian with Greek, Persio explicitly distinguished between four principal linguistic levels, which cannot be easily identified with modern linguistic categories but should be understood on their own terms:

1. Words as parts of speech (*il parlare*), that is, in terms of word classes (noun, verb, etc.), roughly corresponding to modern notions of grammar. This includes a discussion of the perceived similarities between the ways in which specific word classes (mainly articles and personal pronouns) are used in both Italian and Greek.
2. Words as combinations of a certain number of letters or sounds (*lettere*) with specific qualities, that is, a word's *propria materia* ('proper substance') and *corpo* ('body'). This includes a discussion of etymology, which concerns, in this context, the ways in which Greek words have been 'incorporated' into Italian.

---

46 Persio, *Discorso*, pp. 12–13, 63. Persio's distinctions in these pages clearly echo Aristotle's three operations of the intellect, as understood by Thomas Aquinas and the tradition following him, i.e. (1) apprehending simple concepts (definition), (2) combining simple concepts to form propositions (predication), and (3) arranging propositions in deductive chains (syllogizing) (the formulation follows Pini, 'Reading Aristotle's *Categories*', p. 157). Persio excluded the third operation as irrelevant to his discussion (Persio, *Discorso*, p. 13).

3. Words as bearing a *particolare impronto* ('specific imprint') distinguishing them from other words; Persio calls this feature a word's *forma* ('form') or *conio* ('minting mark'). He explained it more clearly elsewhere in his treatise: 'by *form* we mean some sort of formation, derivation, and composition of words', that is, word formation.[47] This includes a discussion of the ways in which prefixes and suffixes are used in both Italian and Greek, as well as of the ways in which words may be truncated or shortened.
4. Words as signs (*segni*) of concepts, that is, in terms of their meaning (*significato*). In Persio's account, this concerned both word semantics and the ways in which words are joined together in set phrases and fixed expressions (i.e. phraseology).[48]

Persio discussed the conformity of Italian with ancient Greek on all four of these language levels. By 'Italian' (*lingua italiana*) he meant the Romance varieties (*idiomi*) spoken in the Italian peninsula that had come to his attention (apart from Tuscan or Florentine, Persio also cited examples from the dialects spoken in Bologna, Venice, Treviso, Ancona, Naples, and what he called 'Magna Graecia': the area of modern Campania, Apulia, Basilicata, Calabria, and Sicily).[49] For Persio, 'Greek' (*greco*) primarily meant ancient Greek in its principal regional varieties (and including New Testament Greek), but he also cited the living language of his own time, especially as it survived in southern Italy, in Calabria and Apulia. Whereas Persio distinguished between 'dead' ancient Greek and 'corrupted' living Greek, the modern language also served as a reference point for him.[50]

Persio did not neatly define what he understood by the term *conformità*. Instead, he used various terms to denote the similarities between Greek and Italian without defining them clearly (these include *parentela, conuenienza, somiglianza, riscontri*, and *simulitudine*).[51] This aligns with the humanist inclination to use a varied vocabulary that reflects — rather than reduces — the complexity of the subject under discussion.[52] In order to get a better idea of how Persio understood the conformity of his language with Greek, we therefore need to look in greater detail at some of the examples he discussed under the four rubrics mentioned above. The *Discorso* does not offer a full and systematic treatment of the subject; Persio cherry-picked his examples and discussed them rather loosely.

---

47 Persio, *Discorso*, p. 38.
48 Persio, *Discorso*, p. 13.
49 Persio, *Discorso*, pp. 10, 19, 20–24, 52–53, 56. On the use of *italiano* and *lingua italiana*, see also Vallance, *Les grammairiens italiens*, p. 61 (with n. 59).
50 Persio, *Discorso*, p. 9. For a modern scholarly overview of Greek elements in Italian, see Crifò, 'Popular Lexicon of Greek Origin'.
51 See, e.g., Persio, *Discorso*, pp. 55, 56, 59, 61, 63.
52 The problematics of early modern language terminology are also emphasized in Van Hal, *Moedertalen en taalmoeders*, pp. 466–71, offering a useful overview of some of the most central terms used to express different relationships between languages.

(1) On the level of the words as parts of discourse, Persio singled out the use of the articles, the pronouns, and some particles for discussion. In his opinion, Italian uses its pronouns in a flexible manner comparable to Greek. He explains, for example, how both Italian and Greek can place pronouns both before and after the verb (compare, e.g., Gr. τὴν ἔδωκε (*tēn edōke*) = It. *la diede* 'he gave her/it' with Gr. ἔδωκε τήν (*edōke tēn*) = It. *diedela* 'he gave her/it'), and how possessive enclisis in Italian corresponded to the use of the genitive personal pronoun in Greek (see below). He also discussed Italian 'particles' for which he saw parallels in Greek. For example, he linked the pronominal augment syllable *-ne* used in some Italian dialects for emphasis (as in *mene, tune,* and *tene,* cited by Persio) with Greek.[53] Persio here seems to have had in mind the Greek enclitic particle -γε (*ge*), used for emphasis in the personal pronouns ἔγωγε (*egōge*), ἔμοιγε (*emoige*), and less commonly also in τύγε (*tuge*).

(2) In addition to the use of the articles, pronouns, and particles, Persio discussed the ways in which many Italian words can be traced to ancient Greek. His etymologies are usually based on the permutation, subtraction, or addition of letters, without adhering to strict and explicit rules.[54] Persio cited words from different dialects and paid particular attention to the language of his own region around Matera. Specifically, he discussed words that others had considered barbarian, for which he revealed their Greek origin (e.g. *panaiare* 'merchant' from Gr. πανήγυρις, *panēgyris,* 'general' and *stregnare* 'to joke lasciviously' from Gr. στρηνιᾶν, *strēnian,* 'to wax wanton'). He showed a particular interest in Italian words that, according to him, could be traced directly to Greek words, without the mediation of Latin. Additionally, he offered some etymologies from Latin as well as from Aramaic and Hebrew.[55]

(3) Additionally, Persio sensed conformity between Greek and Italian in the ways in which both languages build words. For example, he cited the Italian augmentatives ending in *-óne* and *-áccio*. In Persio's view, these words 'represent' (*rappresentano*) Greek words ending in *-on* and in *-ax*. Even

---

53 The usage of the augment syllable *-ne* is attested in Logudorese-Nuorese Sardinian (*mene, tene*) and in central and southern Italian dialects (*mene, tene,* and *sene* appear, with local variations, in Tuscany, Umbria, Lazio, the Marche, Abruzzo, Naples, Calabria, Sicily, and Salento). While usually confined to oblique forms, the augment has in many areas been extended to the subject pronouns (e.g. *tune* in Castro dei Volsci). See Operstein, 'A New Look at an Old Problem', pp. 235–36, with the references there.

54 For a full discussion of Persio's etymologies, see Bolelli, 'Ascanio Persio linguista', pp. 13–19. See also the assessment by De Blasi, *L'italiano in Basilicata*, pp. 69–71. Persio has been praised for his etymologies in particular: Christian Joseph Jagemann even reckoned him among the greatest Italian etymologists of the Renaissance (Jagemann, *Anfangsgründe vom Bau und Bildung*, pp. vii–viii).

55 On Persio's Aramaic and Hebrew etymologies, in particular, see Bolelli, 'Ascanio Persio linguista', p. 15, with Pignatti, *Etimologia e proverbio*, pp. 124–25. From the twenty Italian words Ascanio traced to Aramaic (19) and Hebrew (1), only ten actually are of Semitic (Arabic, not Aramaic) origin.

though the Greek endings -*on* and -*ax* do not represent augmentatives, Persio considered words with these endings 'of not dissimilar meaning (*forza*) and nature' and 'corresponding [with the Italian words] both in their ending and in their meaning'.[56] Thus he compared It. *riccone/ricconaccio* ('immensely wealthy man') with Gr. πλούταξ (*ploutax*, 'rich fool') and *giovenone/giovenaccio* ('young, inexperienced boy') with νέαξ (*neax* = νεανίας, *neanias*, 'young boy'). He moreover compared the ways in which Italian derives adjectives and nouns. Just as Greek derives πολεμίζειν (*polemizein*, 'wage war') from πόλεμος (*polemos*, 'war'), so Italians derive *padrigno* from *padre*, according to 'the Greek proportion (*proportione*) and rule they call "Analogy"'. Similarly, Persio argued, Italians derived the verb *guerreggiare* from the noun *guerra* the same way the Greeks derived their πόλεμος (*polemos*, 'war') from πολεμίζειν (*polemizein*, 'wage war').[57] Composite words are also put together 'according to Greek usage', Persio claimed, citing among other examples the prefix *dis-* as an equivalent to Greek *alpha privans* to indicate negation (compare, e.g., It. *disordine* with Gr. ἀταξία, *ataxia*, 'disorder') and the Italian preposition *fra-*, sometimes used as a prefix to verbs, with the Greek preposition παρα- (*para*) used in the same way (compare, e.g., It. *fraintendere*, 'misconstrue', with Gr. παρακούειν, *parakouein*, 'misunderstand').[58]

(4) Finally, Persio discussed words in their capacity of 'signs' or 'portraits' of concepts. As to word semantics, he discerned similarity (*parentela*) between the ways in which Greek and Italian distribute meaning. In addition to individual words with almost identical ranges of meaning in the two languages, Persio also saw similar semantic pairs in Greek and Italian. For example, he paralleled the Italian pair *disciplina* ('education') and *gastigo* ('correction') with the Greek pair παιδεία (*paideia*, 'education') and κόλασις (*kolasis*, 'correction'), *huomo* ('man') and *maschio* ('male') with ἄνθρωπος (*anthrōpos*, 'man') and ἄρσην (*arsēn*, 'male'), and *sangue* ('blood') and *parentela* ('kinship') with αἷμα (*haima*, 'blood') and συγγένεια (*syngeneia*, 'kinship').[59] Under this rubric, Persio further discussed the use of adjectives as substantives and the ways in which words are joined together to create more or less fixed expressions.[60]

These examples show how, in Persio's analysis, Greek and Italian can be variously similar on all four of the above-mentioned levels. Conformity is discernible in phonetic, semantic, and syntactic resemblances between Italian and Greek. Persio looked at correspondences in letters and sounds as similarities in 'substance' (*materia*) or 'body' (*corpo*), while he regarded semantic and syntactic affinities as similarities in 'meaning' (*significato*) or 'invention' (*invention*).[61] The above-mentioned examples also raise the question

---

56 Persio, *Discorso*, p. 39.
57 Persio, *Discorso*, pp. 39–40.
58 Persio, *Discorso*, pp. 40–41.
59 Persio, *Discorso*, pp. 43–44.
60 Persio, *Discorso*, pp. 44–45.
61 Persio, *Discorso*, pp. 16, 20, 68.

of how all these correspondences should be explained. Are they imitations or borrowings from ancient Greek? Are they the residues of the long-standing Greek presence on the Italian peninsula, or do they result from the common and, perhaps, universal ways in which human beings translate their thoughts into language? Persio's own words suggest different answers.

Persio himself remained slightly vague about the origins of the similarities he dissected. As we have seen, he mentioned obvious cases of imitation and adoption, both direct and indirect, both ancient and more recent, often via Latin and sometimes also carrying the imprint of Hebrew (which he regarded as 'the universal mother of all').[62] He also mentioned the influence of the Greek presence on the language spoken in southern Italy in particular. At the same time, however, he emphasized that the ancient presence of Greek in Italy could not account for all the correspondences between Greek and Italian.[63] Some of them could not be sufficiently explained from borrowing, imitation, or some form of 'inheritance', but nor were they random. Persio suggested the possibility that words and phrases in different languages can have common properties as their production is 'somehow guided by the nature of concepts' of which speech (*parlare*) and words (*parole*) are, after all, 'portraits' or 'images' or 'signs'.[64] To put it differently, the ways in which different populations articulate similar concepts in different languages can produce similar linguistic structures and sometimes even similar words. This means that languages spoken by faraway and mutually unknown nations can, in principle, show striking commonalities. As to Greek and Italian, Persio suggested that the majority of the similarities between them should be explained this way.[65]

Persio's *conformità* thus relied on at least two different implicit assumptions about the origins of similarity between languages. On the first assumption, Italian and Greek show similarities because of historical causes such as borrowing, imitation, and language contact. On the second, they have shared features by common 'invention', that is, similarities may result from the fact that — in Persio's own terms — complex concepts can be voiced in different languages by joining different words together in similar ways. In Persio's treatment, these two assumptions do not mutually exclude each other but are rather mutually supportive. In this respect, Persio's notion of *conformità* shows some resemblance to Estienne's *conformité* which, as Danielle Trudeau has argued, relied on a similar combination of both active imitation of the Greek language and otherwise unspecified mental dispositions which the French (or their ancestors) shared with the ancient Greeks.[66]

---

62 Persio, *Discorso*, p. 64.
63 Persio, *Discorso*, p. 68.
64 Persio, *Discorso*, p. 63.
65 Persio, *Discorso*, pp. 63–64.
66 See Trudeau, 'La mémoire de la langue', p. 21, and Droixhe, *Linguistique et l'appel de l'histoire*, p. 99.

Persio's Language Reform

As Persio himself noted, however, his main purpose was to show — not to explain — the similarities between Italian and Greek in order to demonstrate the linguistic excellence of Italian, especially compared to other European languages. On the other hand, he insisted that he did not want to make Italian 'entirely Greek', as he believed the French tried to do with their language.[67] To the French he replied that they exaggerated the Greek element in their language, that their etymologies were often wrong or far-fetched, whereas the conformity of Italian with Greek was more thorough and more natural given the long-standing Greek presence on the peninsula, which the French could not boast.[68] But his *Discorso* was first and foremost an address to his fellow Italians. If anything, French patriotism should inspire them to make better claims for the conformity of their own language with Greek.[69] He thus advised his compatriots to appreciate their own 'goods' (*beni*) and to look at their own local idioms for suitable expressions instead of parading posh foreign words. He specifically criticized the use of French and Spanish loanwords and also regarded Latinisms — and especially Latin neologisms — as 'foreign' expressions to be shunned as much as French and Spanish.[70] To facilitate his project, Persio planned the publication of a dictionary that could then serve as a standard reference point for Italian usage, a 'thesoro della nostra lingua vniuersale' ('thesaurus of our universal language'), perhaps in tacit emulation of the project that had just been launched by the Florentine Accademia della Crusca.[71] His project thus required sustained lexicographical fieldwork, and Persio confirmed that he himself had dwelled in many cities and areas taking notes, in addition to relying on reports of friends and colleagues on their *lingua materna* (meaning their specific dialects or *idiomi*).[72]

In order to understand the parameters of selection underlying Persio's language reform, let us consider an example of a word that, in his view, qualified for admission to common Italian. This concerns the Neapolitan verb *incegnare*, which means, in Persio's wording, 'to put almost any thing in use for the very first time'. Thus, in Neapolitan Italian, one can *incegnare* a bottle of wine (if not opened before), a piece of clothing (not previously worn), or an instrument (when used for the

---

[67] Persio, *Discorso*, p. 36.
[68] Similar criticism of the French is found in Varchi's work: Sorrento, *Benedetto Varchi*, p. 34.
[69] For Persio's responses to the French, see Persio, *Discorso*, pp. 9–10, 18, 29–35, 36.
[70] Persio, *Discorso*, p. 49. Persio specifically criticized the inclination of some writers of his time to introduce extravagant Latinizing expressions into Italian. This tendency was also satirized in Camillo Scroffa's *Cantici di Fidenzio* (1562), which Persio mentioned, and which was itself written in a morphosyntactical mix of Latin and Italian and affected Latinisms. On this poem, see Hartmann, *I Cantici di Fidenzio di Camillo Scroffa*.
[71] Persio, *Discorso*, p. 50.
[72] Persio, *Discorso*, p. 50.

first time).⁷³ In Persio's opinion, there was no Tuscan equivalent to this usage (others later objected that there was).⁷⁴ Moreover, the word showed conformity with an ancient language, as its origin was Latin or, rather, Greek *di corpo* (in substance). Specifically, Persio traced the word to the Latin verb *encaeniare* ('to inaugurate'), for which he cited Augustine. The Church Father had related the late Latin noun *encaenium* ('feast of dedication') and its companion verb *encaeniare* to the Greek adjective καινός (*kainos*, 'new').⁷⁵ Thus, under the double condition of having a unique meaning not yet available in Tuscan and showing conformity with Latin and ultimately Greek, *incegnare* could be admitted to common Italian.

In addition to the fieldwork of collecting non-Tuscan expressions, then, Persio's reform project also entailed a critical assessment of these expressions' cultural status. This status for him depended on (1) their expressive added value compared to Tuscan and (2) their phonetic, semantic, or syntactic conformity with a noble language, preferably ancient Greek. In some cases, his linguistic assessments resulted in 'rehabilitating' expressions that others had previously excluded from standard written Italian. For example, Persio argued in favour of the use of enclitic possessives of the kind he found used frequently in his native region, including *fratemo* (instead of *il frate mio*), *figlioto* (instead of *il figlio tuo*), and *signorso* (instead of *il signor suo*). These formations were rejected as vulgarisms by Pietro Bembo in his epoch-making *Prose della volgar lingua* (1525), which set the standard for Tuscanism on the basis of fourteenth-century classics (mainly Boccaccio and Petrarch). Even though Boccaccio had incidentally used enclitic possessives, Bembo regarded them as undesirable departures from the norm; 'perhaps too licentious', 'a lowly expression', 'only used by the crowd', he judged.⁷⁶ Persio, by contrast, did not consider them to be a violation of a norm but a sign of nobility. Without explicitly mentioning Bembo, he argued that this type of enclitic possessive was comparable to what was found 'if not [in] ancient Greek then at least [in] the [Greek] language that is still spoken today, and that is spoken in Italy itself'.⁷⁷

---

73 Persio, *Discorso*, p. 48. See also the discussions of Bolelli, 'Ascanio Persio linguista', p. 22, and De Blasi, 'Napoli', pp. 319–20. For the word's etymology, see Mayer-Lübke, *Romanisches Etymologisches Wörterbuch*, p. 255, no 2867. In early modern sources, the word is registered in Capaccio's *Il forastiero* among Neapolitan words (Capaccio, *Il forastiero*, p. 20; cf. Zambaldi, *Le parole greche*, p. 25 n. 1, and Lupoli, *Juris ecclesiastici praelectiones*, pp. 290–91, with note a).
74 Ménage, *Le origini della lingua italiana*, p. 278 s.v. 'Incegnare, incignare' (cf. Bargagli, *Il Turamino ouuero del parlare*, pp. 64–65). For later judgements, see also D'Ovidio, *Le Correzioni*, p. 177, and the extensive discussion in Viani, *Dizionario*, pp. 471–73.
75 Augustine on Jn 4. 9. On the Latin *encaenium* (*encaenia*) and *encaeniare*, see Du Cange, *Glossarium*, p. 263, and Niermeyer, *Mediae latinitatis lexicon*, p. 375 s.v. Compare also the Greek verb ἐγκαινίζειν in Heb. 9. 19 and 10. 20, not mentioned by Persio.
76 Bembo, *Prose*, ed. by Vela, p. 105. Bembo regarded them as the result of subtracting the middle vowel from *mio*, *tuo*, and *suo*.
77 Persio, *Discorso*, pp. 15–16. A recent study on the use of enclitic possessives in southern Italian dialects is Fahrnbach, 'Variation in Enclitic Possessive Constructions'. For a tentative typology, see also D'Alessandro and Migliori, 'Sui possessivi'.

Specifically, he saw the construction paralleled in Greek formulations with a noun and a possessive pronoun, such as σύντροφός μου (*syntrophos mou*, 'my companion'). For Persio, then, phrasings such as *compagnomo* resonated with the ancient Greek more brilliantly than the more standard Tuscan phrasing *il compagno mio*. Unlike the verb *incegnare*, which he regarded as a Latin or Greek word in 'substance' (*corpo*), possessive enclisis for Persio exemplified a Greekish construction by 'invention'. This distinction is important to understand the language aestheticism informing Persio's project.

The language aestheticism of Persio's *Discorso* implicitly favours the ancient resonance of living language. In sharp contrast to Latinizing tendencies in literature, infusing Italian with learned and sophisticated Latinisms, Persio favoured Greek and Latin words that had been incorporated into Italian 'da principio', that is, in an often unspecified, remote past.[78] For him, therefore, superior words and expressions were those whose ancient tradition of use in the Italian peninsula made them seem to belong almost 'naturally' to Italy's linguistic fabric. Even better, however, were Italian forms of expression that resonated with Greek without having been borrowed or imitated from Greek. Persio explained this with an interesting simile from the arts: just as we value writers and artists who create directly from their own imagination more highly than poets who slavishly imitate their predecessors or painters who only create after models, so it is also better to speak a language 'shaped by ourselves without relying on an example' than to speak a language which has been moulded after the image of another one.[79] Contrary to what sometimes has been suggested, then, Persio's language reform did not merely rely on excavating the historical strata of Greek in Italian, as found in his native region and elsewhere on the peninsula. Structural similarities between Greek and Italian stood as a tribute to his people's ability to spontaneously formulate a language that resembled one of the most beautiful languages the world had ever seen. The Italians were able to follow the 'gentile vsanza Greca' ('gentle Greek usage') intuitively without compromising the natural character (*naturalità*) of their own language.[80] Persio's predilection for such 'spontaneous' correspondences may also explain his relative lack of interest in a Hellenizing orthography to mark Italian expressions with traces of their alleged ancient roots as we find, for instance, in the work of Estienne.[81]

Persio thus carved out a distinctive position for himself in the debates surrounding the *questione della lingua*, as explained above. According to Carlo Caruso and Andrew Laird, 'the advocates of conformity [of Italian with Greek]

---

78 Persio, *Discorso*, p. 49.
79 Persio, *Discorso*, pp. 63–64.
80 See Persio's discussion of the habit of using adjectives in place of substantives (*Discorso*, p. 50).
81 On this feature of Estienne's language aestheticism, see Trudeau, 'La mémoire de la langue', p. 17.

militated for an anti-archaic and anti-Tuscan ideal of language', but Persio's argument offers an interesting, alternative position.[82]

First of all, he was neither a defender of 'pure Tuscan' nor an advocate of anti-Tuscanism. As we have seen, he embraced the primacy of Tuscan while arguing that it should be enriched with words from other regions. Secondly, we cannot qualify his position as 'anti-archaizing' without some qualification. Persio favoured 'ancient Italian',[83] but was not an advocate of conventional archaism. He could be qualified as an 'archaist' in the sense that he valued the ancient resonance of living language: expressions that showed conformity with ancient Greek, in particular, met with his approval. The matrix of his archaism then was not so much Trecento Florentine literature — as in conventional Tuscan archaism — as it was Greek and, by extension, other noble languages with roots in antiquity. Persio's approach can thus be seen as a response to the reproach of anarchy often hurled at more 'eclectic theories' of Italian: while he affirmed the established primacy of Tuscan, he made the admission of non-Tuscan words and expressions in Italy's main written language strictly conditional upon their conformity with Greek.[84]

Additionally, the way Persio used Greek as a standard of excellence for Italian is notable. The preceding discussion has shown how far his approach moved beyond occasional word genealogies cited in support of this or that vernacular or the almost clichéd references to Greek dialect diversity as a model for the Italian linguistic landscape. With a subtle sense for similarities between languages, Persio traced and discussed various forms of conformity on multiple linguistic levels. This makes his project fairly unique in the Italian context. After his work, the project of Agnolo Monosini probably comes closest in scope, albeit from a very different (more classically archaizing-Tuscanist) viewpoint. In 1604, Monosini published an extensive treatment of the correspondences between Greek and the dialect of Tuscany and the Maremma area in order to show the excellence of Florentine, yet his discussion was not as wide-ranging as Persio's and largely restricted to proverbs and phraseology.[85]

Concluding Remarks

In the Italian context, then, Persio holds a position similar to Estienne's with regard to French in the sense that he, too, brought previously scattered ideas together in an orchestrated attempt to show the 'Greekness' of the vernacular.

---

82 Caruso and Laird, 'Introduction', pp. 9–10. Compare also the case of Agnolo Monosini (note 85 below), who combined the conformity of Tuscan with Greek with Tuscanism. Cf. Larotonda, 'Ascanio Persio', suggesting an anti-Tuscan position in Persio's work.
83 Persio, *Discorso*, p. 49.
84 On criticism of 'eclectic theories', see Campanelli, 'Languages', pp. 158–59.
85 On Monosini's project, see Pignatti, *Etimologia e proverbio*, with bibliography (and an interesting comparison with Persio's approach on pp. 119–30).

At the same time, the similarities should not blind us to at least one significant difference between their cultural projects.[86] Whereas Persio shared Estienne's purist rejection of foreign influence, the French Hellenist wanted to 'return' to an original Frenchness that had been lost due to the influence of, mainly, Italian and Spanish. Persio's project, on the other hand, does not strive to recreate a lost, purer form of Italian but to *create* an Italian vernacular that united the best features of the *lingua italiana* in all its varieties spoken on the peninsula. As we have seen, this is not tantamount to saying that Persio advocated a 'popular' or 'demotic' (let alone 'democratic') kind of common Italian. His project was just differently purist and differently selective.

Against this backdrop, it would be interesting to study how Persio put his own linguistic ideals into practice in his literary work in the vernacular such as in his *Corona d'Arrigo III* (1574) and his history of the icon of St Luke, mentioned above.[87] Moreover, Persio's position with respect to his immediate predecessors and contemporaries in Italy would merit further exploration. His theorization of the vernacular reveals some interesting correspondences with the work of, among others, Benedetto Varchi, who was also sceptical about the role of etymology in establishing the provenance of words and, like Persio, emphasized the multiple influences that had shaped the vernacular rather than looking for one single origin. Reading Persio's work side by side with that of his Italian predecessors and contemporaries would enable us not only to better understand his methodological innovations but also to define his exact position in the more eclectic, liberal camp of the 'struggle for the standard'.

Even though Persio's project met with some acclaim, it was never seriously taken further on its own terms.[88] His *Discorso* was used, on the other hand, as a source by others, from his own time well into the nineteenth century, usually without consideration of its original content and context. Orazio Lombardelli, for example, mined it as a source for similarities between Tuscan and Greek,[89] while later scholars also went through it looking for

---

86 Compare Daniele, 'Sviluppo della critica', p. 1536, and Tavoni, 'Renaissance Linguistics', p. 51.
87 Persio's literary work remains understudied. On his *Corona*, see Sacchi, 'Esperienze minori della mimesi', pp. 1068–69.
88 Apostolo Zeno showed interest in Persio's projected dictionary. See Zeno's comment in Fontanini, *Biblioteca dell'eloquenza italiana*, p. 37 n. 2 (cf. Napoli-Signorelli, *Vicende*, pp. 246–47). Prospero Viani expressed overall agreement with Persio on the use of dialectal forms in a Tuscan-based common language. See Viani, *Dizionario*, pp. 473–74. He cited Persio's *Discorso* several times with approval and admiration, singling out the treatise in his extensive list of Italian vocabularies, adding between brackets: 'osservabil discorso' (Viani, *Dizionario*, p. xliii).
89 Lombardelli, *I fonti toscani*, pp. 43–44. On Lombardelli, see Daniele, 'Sviluppo della critica', pp. 1532–33, with the references there. For some other traces of Persio's early reception, see also notes 85 and 88 above. Ménage also used Persio's *Discorso* in his *Dictionaire étymologique*.

traces of Greek in Italy's southern dialects.⁹⁰ Although Persio's proposals for reform were not universally adopted, the interest in the conformity of the European languages with Greek, which his *Discorso* reflects, persisted. Among the most notable later examples of vernacular Greekness are, in addition to Monosini's work, Otto Reitz's *Belga graecissans* of 1730 — taking up the argument for Dutch by way of a belated response to Estienne's criticism of Junius, mentioned above — as well as Gotthold Ephraim Lessing's recently rediscovered manuscript on the affinities of German with Greek, which he started in 1759 and left unfinished at his death in 1781.⁹¹

As we have come to think of ancient Hellas as a shared European heritage, it might come as a surprise to find that, during the early modern period, Hellenism was also used as a source of vernacular, regional, or 'national' distinctiveness and even superiority. The question 'Who is more Greek?' seems to capture the cultural dynamics of those years better than the oft-cited adage 'We are all Greeks' of modern Philhellenism. A comprehensive comparative treatment of the different roles Greek played in the expansion of different vernacular cultures, and the group identities they were made to sustain, is still needed to understand the variations and implications of this Europe-wide phenomenon. Even if it remains to be seen to what extent Persio's work eventually influenced the debates elsewhere in Europe, his work definitely merits a place in this history of European Greekness.

Works Cited

Primary Sources

Bargagli, Scipione, *Il Turamino ouuero del parlare, e dello scriuer sanese* (Siena: per Matteo Florimi, in Banchi, 1602)

Bembo, Pietro, *Prose della volgar lingua: L'editio princeps del 1525 riscontrata con l'autografo Vaticano Latino 3210*, ed. by Claudio Vela (Bologna: CLUEB, 2001)

Capaccio, Giulio Cesare, *Il forastiero: Dialogi* (In Napoli: Per Gio. Domenico Roncagliolo, 1634)

Crusius, Martinus, *Commentationes, in I. lib. Iliad. Homeri, grammaticae, rhetoricae, poeticae, historicae, philosophicae: insertus est suis locis Graecus Homeri textus cum versione Argentinae edita, & jam paulum interpolata; accessit etiam index omnium vocum [...] ex indice Ascanii Persii Romae edito desumtus* ([Heidelberg]: Typis Gotthardi Voegelini, 1612)

---

90 E.g. Pellegrini, 'Il dialetto greco-calabro di Bova', p. 21, and Festa, 'Il dialetto di Matera', pp. 131–33. Persio is sometimes also cited in more recent dialectological studies as, e.g., in Bekakos, 'Panaiere e Pan(n)aiero', pp. 31–32.

91 On Reitz's project, see in particular Van Hal, 'Bevoorrechte betrekkingen tussen Germaans en Grieks', with the references there. For Lessing's treatise, see Lessing, *Von der Aehnlichkeit*, ed. by Dehrmann and Weber.

Erotemata Guarini cum multis additamentis, et cum commentariis Latinis, ed. by Pontico Virunio (Ferrariae: per me Ioannem Mazochum, 1509)

Estienne, Henri, *Traicté de la conformité du language françois avec le grec, Divisé en trois livres, dont les deux premiers traictent des manieres de parler conformes: le troisieme contient plusieurs mots françois, les uns pris du grec entierement, les autres en partie: c'est à dire, en ayans retenu quelques lettres par lesquelles on peut remarquer leur etymologie. Avec une preface remonstrant quelque partie du desordre et abus qui se commet aujourd'huy en l'usage de la langue françoise. En ce traicté sont descouverts quelques secrets tant de la langue grecque que de la françoise ...* ([Geneva]: Henri Estienne, 1565)

——, *Traicté de la conformité du langage françois avec le grec, Divisé en trois livres, dont les deux premiers traictent des manieres de parler conformes: le troisieme contient plusieurs mots françois, les uns pris du grec entierement, les autres en partie: c'est à dire, en ayans retenu quelques lettres par lesquelles on peut remarquer leur etymologie. Avec une preface remonstrant quelque partie du desordre et abus qui se commet aujourd'huy en l'usage de la langue françoise. En ce traicté sont descouverts quelques secrets tant de la langue grecque que de la françoise ...* (Paris: Jaques du Puis, 1569)

Fontanini, Giusto, *Biblioteca dell'eloquenza italiana [...] con le annotazioni del signor Apostolo Zeno ...*, 2 vols (Venezia: Presso Giambatista Pasquali, 1753)

Garnefelt, Georg, ed., *Vita B. M. Nicolai Albergati Carthusiani, Episcopi Bononiensis [...] Accessit etiam testimonii loco Historia de imagine B. M. Virginis, a S. Luca depicta, et in Monte Guardiae prope Bononiam miraculis corsucante, auctore Ascanio Persio* (Coloniae Agrippinae: Apud Ioannem Kinchium, sub Monocerote, 1618); note that Ascanio's treatise has a separate title page on p. 132, dated independently: *Sacrae imaginis Deiparae Virginis, quae in Monte Guardiae Bononiae adiacente, in S. Lucae opificis sui Templo asservatur, Historia: Ascanio Persio, auctore* (Coloniae Agrippinae: Apud Ioannem Kinchium, sub Monocerote, 1619)

Lessing, Gotthold Ephraim, *Von der Aehnlichkeit der Griechischen und Deutschen Sprache*, ed. by Mark-Georg Dehrmann and Jutta Weber (Göttingen: V & R Unipress, 2016)

Lombardelli, Orazio, *I fonti toscani d'Orazio Lombardelli senese, accademico vmoroso* (In Firenze: Appresso Giorgio Marescotti, 1598)

Lupoli, Vincenzo, *Juris ecclesiastici praelectiones ...* (Neapoli: Ex Officina Michaelis Morelli, 1777), III

Maffei, Raffaele, *Commentariorum rerum urbanorum liber primus* (Romae: per Ioannem Besicken Alemanum, 1506)

Ménage, Gilles, *Dictionaire étymologique ou Origines de la langue françoise [...] Nouvelle édition revue et augmentée par l'Auteur* (Paris: Chez Jean Anisson, 1694)

——, *Le origini della lingua italiana ...* (In Geneva: Appresso Giovani Antonio Chouët, 1685)

Monosini, Angelo, *Angeli Monosinii Floris Italicae linguae libri novem ...* (Venetiis: Apud Jo. Guerilium, 1604)

Napoli-Signorelli, Pietro, *Vicende della coltura nelle Due Sicilie* ... , vol. IV (In Napoli: Presso Vincenzo Flauto, 1785)

Persio, Ascanio, *Componimenti poetici volgari, latini et greci di diversi, sopra la s. imagine della beata Vergine dipinta da san Luca la quale si serba nel monte della Guardia presso Bologna, con la sua historia in dette tre lingue scritta da Ascanio Persii* (Bononiae: Apud Victorium Benatium, 1601)

———, *Discorso d'Ascanio Persio intorno alla conformità della lingua italiana con le più nobili antiche lingue, & principalmente con la greca. Nuouamente corretto dall'originale dell'Auttore. All'illustriss. Signore, il signor Bonifacio Caetano* (In Venetia et ristampato in Bologna: per Giouanni Rossi, 1592)

———, *Discorso del s. Ascanio Persio intorno alla conformità della lingua italiana con le più nobili antiche lingue, & principalmente con la greca* (In Venetia: Appresso Gio. Battista Ciotti, al segno della Minerua, 1592)

———, *Discorso di Ascanio Persio intorno alla conformità della lingua italiana con le più nobili antiche lingue e principalmente con la greca*, ed. by Francesco Fiorentino (Naples: Morano, 1874)

———, *Discorso intorno alla conformità della lingua italiana con le più nobili antiche lingue & principalmente con la greca*, ed. by Tristano Bolelli (Pisa: Giardini, 1985)

———, *Indicis in Homeri poemata, quae exstant omnia, graecolatini, et latinograeci, qui scholiorum fere vicem explere possit, ab Ascanio Persio diligentissime constructi, specimen (videlicet in primum Iliados vterque index) a Gratio Lodio Garisendum editum* (Bononiae: Apud Haeredes Io. Rossij, 1597)

Politi, Alessandro, *Eustathii* [...] *Commentarii in Homeri Iliadem*, 2 vols (Florentiae: Apud Bernardum Paperinium, 1730), vol. I

Tempio all'illustrissimo et reverendissimo signor Cinthio Aldobrandini ... , ed. by Giulio Segni (In Bologna: Presso gli heredi di Giovanni Rossi, 1600)

Trippault, Léon, *Celt'hellenisme, ou Etymologic des mots francois tirez du Græc. Plus: preuues en general de la descente de nostre langue* (Orléans: Par Eloy Gibier, 1581)

Secondary Studies

Adamou, Evangelia, 'Le rôle de l'imaginaire linguistique dans la néologie scientifique à base grecque en français', *La Linguistique*, 39.1 (2003), 97–108

Antonelli, Giuseppe, and Marcello Ravesi, 'La questione della lingua nel Cinquecento', in *Atlante della letteratura italiana*, ed. by Amedeo De Vincentiis, Sergio Luzzatto, Gabriele Pedullà, Erminia Irace, and Domenico Scarpa, 3 vols (Turin: Einaudi, 2010–2012), I, pp. 739–49

Bekakos, Sotirios, 'Panaiere e Pan(n)aiero e i suoi reflessi in Puglia e Basilicata', *Thalassia Salentina*, 32 (2009), 29–51

Berrong, Richard M., 'Genealogies and the Search for an Origin in the "Oeuvres" of Rabelais', *South Atlantic Bulletin*, 42.4 (1977), 75–83

Bolelli, Tristano, *Ascanio Persio linguista e il suo discorso (1592)* (Pisa: Pacini Mariotti, 1967)

——, 'Ascanio Persio linguista e il suo discorso (1592)', *L'Italia dialettale*, 30 (1967), 1–28

——, 'Di vocali latine e di Ascanio Persio', *L'Italia dialettale*, 40 (1977), 297–99

——, 'Un inedito di Ascanio Persio', in *Scritti in onore di Giuliano Bonfante*, ed. by Giuliano Bonfante (Brescia: Paideia, 1976), I, pp. 65–72

——, *Leopardi linguista ed altri saggi* (Messina: G. D'Anna, 1982)

——, 'Principi di linguistica generale in autori del Cinquecento italiano', *Studi e Saggi Linguistici*, 28 (1988), 81–100

Boudou, Bénédicte, *Mars et les muses dans l'Apologie pour Hérodote d'Henri Estienne* (Geneva: Librairie Droz, 2000)

——, 'La place de la mémoire dans la composition chez Henri Estienne', *Nouvelle Revue du XVIe Siècle*, 20.2 (2002), 57–72

——, 'Proverbes et formules gnomiques chez Henri Estienne: De l'histoire à la poésie', *Seizième Siècle*, 1 (2005), 161–74

Bower, Archibald, *Historia Litteraria: Or, An Exact and Early Account of the Most Valuable Books Published in the Several Parts of Europe [...]*, vol. II (London: Printed for N. Prevost, 1731)

Brincat, Giuseppe, 'Da Ascoli a Gusmani: La stratigrafia linguistica con particolare riferimento ai movimenti demografici', in *Dialoghi sulle lingue e sul linguaggio*, ed. by Nicola Grandi (Bologna: Pàtron, 2011), pp. 93–100

Burke, Peter, *Languages and Communities in Early Modern Europe* (Cambridge: Cambridge University Press, 2004)

Callegari, Danielle, and Shannon McHugh, 'Playing Papal Politics: Senatorial and Monastic Allies in Early Modern Bologna', *Renaissance Studies*, 32.4 (2018), 602–18

——, '"Se fossimo tante meretrici": The Rhetoric of Resistance in Diodata Malvasia's Convent Narrative', *Italian Studies*, 66.1 (2011), 21–39

Campanelli, Maurizio, 'Languages', in *The Cambridge Companion to the Italian Renaissance*, ed. by Michael Wyatt (Cambridge: Cambridge University Press, 2014), pp. 139–63

Caruso, Carlo, and Andrew Laird, 'Introduction: The Italian Classical Tradition, Language and Literary History', in *Italy and the Classical Tradition: Language, Thought and Poetry, 1300–1600*, ed. by Carlo Caruso and Andrew Laird (London: Bloomsbury, 2013), pp. 1–28

Cerquiglini, Bernard, *Une langue orpheline* (Paris: Les Éditions de Minuit, 2007)

Clément, Louis, *Henri Estienne et son oeuvre française (étude d'histoire littéraire et de philologie)* (Geneva: Slatkine Reprints, 1967)

Coseriu, Eugenio, and Reinhard Meisterfeld, *Geschichte der romanischen Sprachwissenschaft*, vol. I (Tubingen: Gunter Narr Verlag, 2003)

Courouau, Jean-François, 'Les apologies de la langue française (XVIe siècle) et de la langue occitane (XVIe–XVIIe siècles): Naissance d'une double mythographie', *Nouvelle Revue du XVIe Siècle*, 21.2 (2003), 35–51

Cowling, David, 'Henri Estienne pourfendeur de l'emprunt linguistique franco-italien', *Le Moyen Français*, 60–61 (2007), 165–73

Crifò, Francesco, 'Popular Lexicon of Greek Origin in Italian Varieties', in 'Language Contact in the Mediterranean in the Middle Ages and in Early Modern Times (with special focus on loanword lexicography)', ed. by Francesco Crifò, Elton Prifti, and Wolfgang Schweickard, thematic part of *Lexicographica: International Annual for Lexicography*, 33 (2018), 95–120

D'Alessandro, Roberta, and Laura Migliori, 'Sui possessivi (enclitici) nelle varietà italo-romanze meridionali non estreme', in *Di tutti i colori: Studi linguistici per Maria Grossmann*, ed. by Roberta D'Alessandro, Gabriele Iannàccaro, Diana Passino, and Anna M. Thornton (Utrecht: Utrecht University Press, 2017), pp. 55–71

D'Ovidio, Francesco, *Le Correzioni ai Promessi Sposi e la questione della lingua* (Naples: Luigi Pierro, 1895)

Daniele, Antonio, 'Sviluppo della critica', in *Storia letteraria d'Italia: Il Cinquecento*, ed. by Giovanni Da Pozzo, 3 vols (Florence: Vallardi, 2007), III, pp. 1523–58

De Blasi, Nicola, *L'italiano in Basilicata: Una storia della lingua dal Medioevo a oggi* (Potenza: Il Salice, 1994)

———, 'Napoli', in *Città italiane, storie di lingue e culture*, ed. by Pietro Trifone (Rome: Carocci, 2015), pp. 305–54

Demaizière, Colette, 'Deux aspects de l'idéal linguistique d'Henri Estienne: Hellénisme et parisianisme', in *Henri Estienne: Actes du Colloque organisé à l'Université de Paris-Sorbonne le 12 mars 1987, par le Centre V.-L. Saulnier* (Paris: École normale supérieure de jeunes filles, 1988), pp. 63–75

———, 'Les réflexions étymologiques d'Henri Estienne de la *Conformité*, 1565, aux *Hypomneses*, 1582', in *Discours étymologiques*, ed. by Jean-Pierre Chambon and Georges Lüdi (Tübingen: Niemeyer, 1991), pp. 201–10

Dionisotti, Carlo, 'Girolamo Claricio', in *Scritti di storia della letteratura italiana*, 5 vols (1964; repr. Rome: Storia e letteratura, 2009), II, pp. 141–71

———, 'Per una storia delle dottrine linguistiche del Rinascimento', *Filosofia*, 21 (1970), 15–24

———, *Gli umanisti e il volgare fra Quattro- e Cinquecento* (Florence: Le Monnier, 1968)

Droixhe, Daniel, *Linguistique et l'appel de l'histoire (1600–1800): Rationalisme et révolutions positivistes* (Geneva: Librairie Droz, 1978)

———, 'On the Origins of Historical Linguistics: Materials and Proposals for the Italian Case', in *Historical Roots of Linguistic Theories*, ed. by Lia Formigari and Daniele Gambarara (Amsterdam: Benjamins, 1995), pp. 11–30

Du Cange, Charles, *Glossarium mediae et infimae Latinitatis [...] Editio noua aucta pluribus uerbis aliorum scriptorum*, vol. III (Niort: Favre, 1883)

Fahrnbach, Eugenia, 'Variation in Enclitic Possessive Constructions in Southern Italian Dialects: A Syntactic Analysis' (unpublished doctoral thesis, Johann Wolfgang Goethe-Universität, 2019)

Festa, Giovanni Battista, 'Il dialetto di Matera', *Zeitschrift für romanische Philologie*, 38.2 (1917), 129–62

Figorilli, Maria Cristina, 'Elogi paradossali nelle "Lettere facete e piacevoli" (1561–1575)', *Italianistica: Rivista di letteratura italiana*, 32.2 (2003), 247–73

Flamini, Francesco, *Il Cinquecento* (Milan: Vallardi, 1898)

Gröber, Gustav, *Grundriss der romanischen Philologie*, vol. I (Strassburg: Karl J. Trübner, 1888)

Hall, Robert J., *The Italian 'Questione della lingua': An Interpretative Essay* (Chapel Hill: University of North Carolina, 1942)

Hartmann, Katharina, *I Cantici di Fidenzio di Camillo Scroffa e la pluralità dei mondi: Il canone classico, l'eredità del Petrarca e la tradizione giocosa* (Bonn: Bonn University Press, 2013)

Jagemann, Christian Joseph, *Anfangsgründe vom Bau und Bildung der Wörter der Italienischen Sprache, wie sie in ächt Toskanischer Mundart gesprochen u. geschrieben wird* (Leipzig: Siegfried Lebrecht Crusius, 1800)

Knox, Bernard, *The Oldest Dead White European Males and Other Reflections on the Classics* (New York: W. W. Norton, 1993)

Kristeller, Paul Oskar, *Iter Italicum: A Finding List of Uncatalogued or Incompletely Catalogued Humanistic Manuscripts of the Renaissance in Italian and Other Libraries*, vol. V (Leiden: Brill, 1990)

Labande-Jeanroy, Thérèse, *La question de la langue en Italie de Baretti a Manzoni: L'unité linguistique dans les théories et les faits* (Paris: Champion, 1925)

Lamers, Han, 'Wil de echte Griek opstaan? Verwantschap en vereenzelviging met de oude Grieken in vroegmodern Europa' [Imagined Greekness: Identifications with the Ancient Greeks in Early Modern Europe], *Tetradio: Tijdschrift van het Griekenlandcentrum*, 26 (2017), 101–29

Larotonda, Lucano, 'Ascanio Persio', in *Riprendiamoci la storia: Dizionario dei Lucani* (Milan: Electa, 2012), pp. 416–17

Lazzarini, Andrea, 'Ancora sui rapporti tra letteratura dialettale riflessa e toscano: Una dedicatoria di G. C. Cortese a G. B. Basile', *Studi secenteschi*, 56 (2016), 159–83

Lepschy, Giulio, 'The Classical Languages and Italian: Some Questions of Grammar and Rhetoric', in *Italy and the Classical Tradition: Language, Thought and Poetry, 1300–1600*, ed. by Carlo Caruso and Andrew Laird (London: Bloomsbury, 2013), pp. 29–40

Mayer-Lubke, Wilhelm, *Romanisches Etymologisches Wörterbuch*, 3rd edn (Heidelberg: Carl Winter, 1935)

Niermeyer, Jan Frederik, *Mediae Latinitatis lexicon minus* (Leiden: Brill, 1956)

Operstein, Natalie, 'A New Look at an Old Problem: On the Origin of the Pronominal Augment -NE', *Romance Notes*, 52.2 (2012), 235–42

Padula, Mauro, and Camilla Motta, *Antonio e Ascanio Persio: Il filosofo e il filologo* (Matera: Amministrazione provinciale, 1991)

Pellegrini, Astorre, 'Il dialetto greco-calabro di Bova', *Rivista di filologia e di istruzione classica*, 2 (1874), 13–25

Pietrasanta, Daniela, 'La Sicilia graeca e Diodoro da P. Ranzano a T. Fazello', *Mediterraneo antico: Economie, società, culture*, 6.2 (2003), 697–720

Pignatti, Franco, *Etimologia e proverbio nell'Italia del XVII secolo: Agnolo Monosini e i Floris Italicae linguae libri novem* (Manziana (Rome): Vecchiarelli, 2010)

——, 'Persio, Ascanio', in *Dizionario biografico degli Italiani*, vol. LXXXII (Rome: Istituto dell'Enciclopedia Italiana, 2005), <http://www.treccani.it/enciclopedia/ascanio-persio_%28Dizionario-Biografico%29/>

Pineaux, Jacques, 'La formule proverbiale dans *La Précellence*', in *Henri Estienne: Actes du Colloque organisé à l'Université de Paris-Sorbonne le 12 mars 1987, par le Centre V.-L. Saulnier* (Paris: École normale supérieure de jeunes filles, 1988), pp. 85–97

Pini, Giorgio, 'Reading Aristotle's *Categories* as an Introduction to Logic: Later Medieval Discussions about its Place in the Aristotelian Corpus', in *Medieval Commentaries on Aristotle's Categories*, ed. by Lloyd A. Newton (Leiden: Brill, 2008), pp. 145–81

Pisani, Vittore, *L'etimologia: Storia – questioni – metodo* (Turin: Rosenberg & Sellier, 1947)

Pontani, Filippo Maria, 'Il greco di Gianfrancesco Mussato, peritoso umanista', *Rivista di studi bizantini e slavi*, 1 (1981), 131–65

Renzi, Lorenzo, *Introduzione alla filologia romanza* (Bologna: Il Mulino, 1976)

Richardson, Brian, 'Renaissance Linguistics in Italy', in *Concise History of the Language Sciences: From the Sumerians to the Cognitivists*, ed. by E. F. K. Koerner and R. E. Asher (New York: Pergamon, 1995), pp. 152–56

Sacchi, Guido, 'Esperienze minori della mimesi', in *Storia letteraria d'Italia: Il Cinquecento*, ed. by Giovanni Da Pozzo, 3 vols (Florence: Vallardi, 2007), II, pp. 1036–1126

Savatovsky, Dan, 'Contact de langues et enseignement du grec ancien: Revisiter le colinguisme', *Langue Française*, 167 (2010), 31–47

Shangler, Nicholas, 'The Language of Identity: Henri Estienne's Anti-Italian Polemics', *Journal of the Early Book Society for the Study of Manuscripts and Printing History*, 18 (2015), 103–35

Sorrento, Luigi, *Benedetto Varchi e gli etimologisti francesi del suo secolo* (Milan: Bietti e Reggiani, 1921)

Steinfeld, Nadine, and Sandrine Pescarini, 'Pleins feux sur l'ellipse en étymologie: Un fait linguistique et un outil métalinguistique. Premier volet: Étude historique et épistémologique de l'ellipse', *Neuphilologische Mitteilungen*, 114.2 (2013), 237–68

Stenhouse, William, 'The Greekness of Greek Inscriptions: Ancient Inscriptions in Early Modern Scholarship', in *Receptions of Hellenism in Early Modern Europe, 15th–17th Centuries*, ed. by Han Lamers and Natasha Constantinidou (Leiden: Brill, 2020), pp. 307–24

Stevenson, Jane, *Women Latin Poets: Language, Gender, and Authority, from Antiquity to the Eighteenth Century* (Oxford: Oxford University Press, 2005)

Swiggers, Pierre, 'Les études linguistiques romanes des origines jusqu'au début du XIXe siècle: Les "prémices" de la romanistique', in *Manuel des langues romanes*, ed. by Andre Klump, Johannes Kramer, and Aline Willems (Berlin: De Gruyter, 2014), pp. 13–42

——, 'Le français et l'italien en lice: L'examen comparatif de leurs qualités chez Henri Estienne', *Synergies Italie*, 5 (2009), 69–76

Tavoni, Mirko, *Il discorso linguistico di Bartolomeo Benvoglienti*, Biblioteca degli studi mediolatini e volgari, 3 (Pisa: Pacini, 1975)

——, 'On the Renaissance Idea that Latin Derives from Greek', *Annali della Scuola Normale Superiore di Pisa: Classe di Lettere e Filosofia*, 16.1 (1986), 205–38

——, 'Renaissance Linguistics: Western Europe', in *History of Linguistics*, III: *Renaissance and Early Modern Linguistics*, ed. by Giulio Lepschy (Londen: Routledge, 1998), pp. 1–108

Tramontana, Alessandra, *Pontico Virunio tra storia, mito e letteratura* (Messina: Centro internazionale di studi umanistici, Università degli studi di Messina, 2017)

Trapp, J. B., 'The Conformity of Greek with the Vernacular: The History of a Renaissance Theory of Languages', in *Essays on the Renaissance and the Classical Tradition* (Aldershot: Variorum, 1990), I, pp. 8–21

Trudeau, Danielle, *Les inventeurs du bon usage* (Paris: Les Éditions de Minuit, 1992)

——, 'La mémoire de la langue: Apologie pour Henri Estienne', *Tangence*, 87 (2008), 11–30

Vallance, Laurent, *Les grammairiens italiens face à leur langue (15e–16e s.)* (Berlin: De Gruyter, 2019)

Van Hal, Toon, 'Bevoorrechte betrekkingen tussen Germaans en Grieks: Wilhelm Otto Reitz' *Belga graecissans* (1730)' [Privileged Relations between Germanic and Greek in Wilhelm Otto Reitz's *Belga graecissans* (1730)], *Leuvense Bijdragen: Tijdschrift voor Germaanse Filologie*, 99–100 (2016), 427–43

——, 'A Man of Eight Hearts: Hadrianus Junius and Sixteenth-Century Plurilinguism', in *The Kaleidoscopic Scholarship of Hadrianus Junius (1511–1575): Northern Humanism at the Dawn of the Dutch Golden Age*, ed. by Dirk van Miert (Leiden: Brill, 2011), pp. 188–213

——, *Moedertalen en taalmoeders: Het vroegmoderne taalvergelijkende onderzoek in de Lage Landen* [Mother Tongues and Language Mothers: Comparative Language Research in the Early Modern Low Countries] (Brussels: Koninklijke Vlaamse Academie van België voor Wetenschappen en Kunsten, 2010)

Van Rooy, Raf, *Greece's Labyrinth of Language: A Study in the Early Modern Discovery of Dialect Diversity* (Berlin: Berlin Language Science Press, 2020)

Viani, Prospero, *Dizionario di pretesi francesismi e di pretese voci e forme erronee della lingua italiana* (Naples: Per Francesco Rossi-Romano, 1860)

Vitale, Maurizio, *La questione della lingua*, 4th edn (Palermo: Palumbo, 1967)

Ward, Michael T., 'Benedetto Varchi as Etymologist', *Historiographia Linguistica*, 16.3 (1989), 235–56

Zambaldi, Francesco, *Le parole greche dell'uso italiano*, 2nd edn (Turin: Ditta G. B. Paravia e Comp., 1883)

FABRIZIO LELLI

Hebrew Literature in Italy (1300–1600)

The contacts between Hebrew and Italian literature from the fourteenth to the seventeenth centuries have not undergone a thorough academic analysis until recently, and mainly only among specialists in Jewish studies. The vast Hebrew production of the Italian Jews (for the most part still unpublished) is often considered by scholars as poorly related to Italian literature; yet the various Hebrew *corpora* composed in the Mediterranean peninsula show many affinities, in terms of both style and content, with the contemporary works written in the various Italian vernaculars, and the contacts between the two productions are numerous and much more significant than might be expected. In most cases, Jewish Italian authors were able to use Hebrew and Romance languages for their scripts. When we consider the relative numerical significance of the Jewish population in northern and central Italy, we cannot but assume that this social minority was necessarily influenced by the main intellectual trends of the majority. However, in spite of the weight of the cultural majority, Italian Jewish communities developed specific linguistic and stylistic patterns that allowed them to follow in the footsteps of their own internal traditions, while borrowing elements from the outside.

In this chapter, I will shed light on the main parallels between the Hebrew productions of the Italian Jews and those of their non-Jewish contemporaries. I shall first focus on the linguistic contacts between the two communities, and then survey four main study-cases, one for each of the centuries taken into account in this essay. I will mainly deal with authors who were active in northern and central Italy. Due to its paucity — all the more so when compared to the much larger production of the tenth–thirteenth centuries — the Hebrew

Fabrizio Lelli (fabrizio.lelli@uniroma1.it) taught Hebrew language and literature at the University of Salento (Lecce, Italy) in the years 2001–2022 and is now teaching at the University of Rome 'La Sapienza'. His research activity focuses mainly on the philosophical and mystical literature of late medieval and early modern Italian Jewish authors, on the memory of Jewish refugees hosted in the United Nations DP transit camps, which were operative in Southern Italy after WWII, and on late medieval and contemporary Hebrew belles-lettres.

Languages and Cross-Cultural Exchanges in Renaissance Italy, ed. by Alessandra Petrocchi and Joshua Brown, LMEMS 30 (Turnhout: Brepols, 2023), pp. 389–410
BREPOLS PUBLISHERS   10.1484/M.LMEMS-EB.5.131439

literature composed in the south of the peninsula between the fourteenth and the fifteenth centuries will be only sporadically mentioned.[1]

Hebrew–Italian Linguistic Contact: A General Overview

The influence of Hebrew on standard literary Italian is scant and mainly consists of loanwords related to the Bible and the linguistic field of the Jewish-Christian religion.[2] However, Italian dialects witness a variety of words and idiomatic expressions borrowed over the centuries from Hebrew and other Judaeo-languages.[3] For the broadly scattered Italian Jewish communities, vernacular languages were more easily understandable than Hebrew, which was mainly confined to school education, erudition, and liturgy. This functional bilingualism did have a significant gender component: women could usually read the Hebrew alphabet better than Latin, but their knowledge of the Hebrew language was poorer than it was of men. This phenomenon may well explain the significant number of literary texts (including biblical and liturgical) which circulated in the local vernaculars, but which were written in Hebrew characters (so-called ancient Judaeo-Italian, not to be confused with modern and contemporary Judaeo-Italian dialects).[4] An extensive Judaeo-Italian literature flourished in the Middle Ages, especially in southern Italy, though the original texts underwent thorough linguistic modifications,

---

1 The Hebrew production of southern Italian communities was relevant until the twelfth century; see Tamani, *La letteratura ebraica medievale*, pp. 155–79. After the decadence of Jewish academies in the south during the thirteenth century, their partial renaissance is documented from the mid-fourteenth century, as well as a more intense activity of Jewish scholars, and especially of translators of philosophical texts, at the Anjou court in Naples, who mainly conveyed Provençal intellectual trends into the Kingdom of Sicily: see Sirat, *Les traducteurs juifs*. Over the fifteenth century, the Neapolitan State hosted a great number of Jewish exiles from the Iberian peninsula and Provence (see Ferorelli, *Gli ebrei nell'Italia meridionale*). They were sought as partners in intellectual cooperation by both Jews and Christians, on a local and international level, and their mediating role was significant in the transfer of Iberian scientific productions to the Italian peninsula. See, e.g., Busi and Campanini, 'Marco Lippomano and Crescas Meir'; Stein Kokin, 'Isaac ha-Kohen's Letter to Marco Lippomano'; Lelli, 'Una compilazione medica ebraica'. The significant number of fifteenth-century Hebrew codices — especially from Naples, Apulia, and Sicily — that have been recently rediscovered in major eastern European libraries attest to the extraordinary vitality of local Jewish communities, the use of different languages alongside Hebrew, and of diverse writing patterns inspired by the most various regions of the diaspora. See Tamani, 'Manoscritti e libri'; David, 'I manoscritti ebraici'; Lelli, 'Una compilazione medica ebraica'. From the end of the fifteenth century, the numerous and rather large communities of the Kingdom of Sicily progressively left the area, under the subsequent strokes of the anti-Jewish policy of the Spanish Crown.
2 Aprile and Lelli, 'La sezione degli ebraismi', pp. 460–65.
3 See Aprile, *Grammatica storica*.
4 See Friedmann, *Italian Texts in Hebrew Characters*; Mayer Modena, 'The Spoken Languages of the Jews of Italy'; Aprile, *Grammatica storica*.

due to the exposure to other dialects or languages of the written (and oral) material that accompanied the Jews in their migrations.[5]

Since Hebrew was understood at least by cultured Jews, it was probably used over the centuries and up to the modern era also for oral communication. Jewish education still makes the knowledge of Hebrew and Aramaic necessary for attending liturgical services in the synagogues, as well as for prayer. Hebrew was (and still is) a *lingua franca* that allowed members of different communities in various parts of the diaspora to communicate with one another. For instance, from Nicholas of Otranto's (*c.* 1155–1235) *Diàlexis katà Iudàion* (*Dialogue against the Jews*),[6] written in Greek just before 1220, we understand that the learned Jews of southern Apulia spoke in Hebrew with each other.[7] In his 1489 *Epistle to his Brother*, 'Ovadyah of Bertinoro (*c.* 1455–*c.* 1516), born in central Italy, wrote that, while in Jerusalem,

"ואני דורש לקהל פעמים בחדש, בבית הכנסת, בלשון הקודש, כי רובם מבינים בלשון הקודש... ומשבחים ומהללים את דרשותי"

> (I preach to the congregation twice a month in the synagogue in the holy language, since most people here understand it [...] they praise my sermons and congratulate me on account of them.)[8]

Like many of his Italian coreligionists, 'Ovadyah was travelling to the Near East for both commercial and religious purposes. He could communicate in Hebrew with Jewish interlocutors of more or less distant regions. Not only was he a learned rabbi, able to preach an entire sermon in Hebrew, but his audience could understand his words, certainly pronounced with a central Italian accent.

Thus, the Jewish component of Italian society could speak Hebrew on specific occasions: furthermore, they used the language of the place where they resided and the languages of the places of their previous residence (or of their family's previous residence).[9] Extant letter collections, along with the rich tradition of juridical *responsa*,[10] provide a better understanding of the Hebrew language used in Italy. The authors of these two *corpora* mainly resorted to a biblical prose, interwoven to a large extent with Rabbinic Hebrew and Aramaic

---

5 On the southern Judaeo-Italian legacy in northern Italian dialects, see Cuomo, 'Il giudeo-italiano e le vicende linguistiche'; Sermoneta, 'La cultura linguistica e letteraria'; Aprile, 'Tracce linguistiche'. See also the case of the Judaeo-Italian dialect spoken in the island of Corfu: Lelli, 'Liturgia, lingue e manifestazioni letterarie e artistiche'.
6 Nicholas of Otranto, *Nektarìu [...] diàlexis katà Iudàion*, ed. by Chronz, p. 121.
7 Schiano, 'Libri nel conflitto', p. 136.
8 'Ovadyah of Bertinoro, *From Italy to Jerusalem*, ed. by Hartom and David, p. 87 (my translation).
9 As pointed out by Boksenboim, 'the Italian Jewish Community had no equal in the use of Hebrew'. *Letters of Jews in Italy*, ed. by Boksenboim, p. vi.
10 See *Letters of Jews in Italy*, ed. by Boksenboim; on *responsa*, see, e.g., David, 'Jewish Intellectual Life'.

phrasing, and interspersed with Romance words. Many morphosyntactic calques from Romance languages can be observed.

Between the fourteenth and the sixteenth centuries, a period of intense Jewish mobility, northern and central Italian Jews, depending on the origins of their families, were fluent in French, or German, Catalan, Spanish, Portuguese, or their Judaeo-variants, while southern Italian Jews could express themselves also in Greek or Arabic. A very significant phenomenon of minorities is the tendency of migrants to maintain linguistic traits of previously spoken languages for longer periods than other migrants sharing closer cultural and linguistic affinities with the majority culture of their destination.[11]

It should not surprise us that the first documented evidence of the written usage of a vernacular language in southern Apulia is a commercial correspondence between Sabatino (Shabbetay) Russo, a Jewish merchant from Copertino (near Lecce), and Biagio Dolfin, his Venetian non-Jewish colleague. This exchange of letters, which dates to the years 1392–1414, was redacted in the *lingua franca* of the two partners, an Italian which, in the case of the Jewish interlocutor, was influenced by Salentine traits.[12]

The large usage of Italian words within Hebrew texts composed by Italian Jews is generally explained by pointing out the lack of technical lexica in medieval Hebrew. For specific usages, such as the language of commerce, navigation, philosophy, natural sciences, medicine, etc., Jews were forced to adopt terms from the surrounding languages, all the more so since their jobs most often relied on their knowledge of several languages and their abilities as cultural mediators.[13]

The coexisting trend of composing high-standard Hebrew productions destined for a more cultured audience, and Italian texts in Hebrew characters aimed at a less scholarly public, may be explained by assuming the existence of similar intellectual hierarchies in Italian Jewish and non-Jewish societies. However, while the largest part of non-Jewish society was illiterate, Jewish communities provided all their members with at least the most basic competencies in reading and writing. This literacy also depended on the harsher social-class distinction in non-Jewish society (where culture was mainly accessible only to the wealthiest), whereas the larger middle-class component within Jewish society made literacy a necessary skill for virtually all of its members, who — unlike Christians — were often obliged to be at the same time traders, doctors, and teachers.

From the end of the fifteenth century new specialized figures of intellectuals started appearing in Italian Jewish society, as much as they did among contemporary Christians.[14] Printing was certainly a crucial factor for the

---

11 Arnold, *Spracharkaden*, p. 142.
12 The correspondence has been published by Stussi, 'Antichi testi salentini in volgare'.
13 For instance, Ilana Wartenberg is carrying out an analysis of the Judaeo-Italian lexicon of mathematics. See also Wartenberg, *The Epistle of the Number by Ibn al-Aḥdab*.
14 See Lelli, 'Biography and Autobiography'.

dissemination of Hebrew literature. Venetian printing houses, though in the hands of Christians, hired Jewish scholars for editing and publishing an incredibly rich array of texts, ranging from Hebrew grammars, the Scripture and biblical exegesis, the Talmud and rabbinical literature, to Kabbalah and juridical *responsa*.[15] The diffusion of lexical works in print provides some evidence of this phenomenon. Paralleling the non-Hebrew glossaries of biblical names based on Jerome's lexicon, new vocabularies became common among Jews, such as David de' Pomis's (1524–1594) *Ẓemaḥ David* (David's Scion), a trilingual Hebrew, Latin, and Italian dictionary (Venice, 1587), intended to foster intellectual collaboration between Jewish and Christian scholars, or Jacob Zahalon's (1630–1693) *Ozar Hayyim* (Treasure of Life) on medicine (Venice, 1683).[16]

The feeling of religious uncertainty that characterized the Jewish society of the Counter-Reformation period led to separating the fields of investigation that Jews had shared until then with non-Jews.[17] More traditional subjects were to be debated within the religious community boundaries, whereas 'external' topics could be discussed with non-Jews in the local languages and outside of the community. This is why treatises composed by Jewish intellectuals on the most central concerns of non-Jewish society took the shapes and languages of the contemporary non-Hebrew productions. This process was fostered by the participation of Italian Jewish scholars in non-Jewish academies.[18] A case in point of this major change in the Italian Jewish intellectual identity is Simone Luzzatto's (1583–1663) Italian treatise *Socrate, overo dell'humano sapere*, published in Venice in 1651.[19]

After this introduction, I will focus on the activity of specific authors, each one representing a different period of time. First, I take Immanuel of Rome into account, then Yohanan Alemanno, Abraham Farissol, and finally Leon Modena. In my opinion, these intellectuals are the best examples of the dynamics of exchange between scholars belonging to different religious milieus within Italian society. In the concluding section, I attempt to demonstrate that the circulation of cultural motifs and literary texts between the two communities was not a univocal process: while non-Jews sought Hebrew authorities for their speculation, Jews absorbed and adapted the main literary genres and intellectual themes from the surrounding majority. In other words, the interest in their own legacy that they managed to arouse in non-Jewish colleagues triggered both cultural development and a higher self-perception within the Italian Jewish communities.

---

15 See Tamani, 'L'attività tipografica a Venezia'.
16 See Bartolucci, '"Hebraeus sempre fidus"'; Ruderman, *Jewish Thought and Scientific Discovery*, p. 187.
17 Kaufmann, 'Elia Menahem Chalfan'.
18 On Jews and modern academies, see Veltri and Chajes, *Oltre le mura del ghetto*.
19 See Luzzatto, *Socrates*, ed. and trans. by Veltri and Torbidoni.

Immanuel ben Solomon of Rome (Fourteenth Century)

Immanuel ben Solomon of Rome (aka Immanuel Romano, Immanuel ha-Romi, or Manoello Giudeo, c. 1261–c. 1335), one of the greatest Hebrew poets of all times, travelled around all central and northern Italy. His life and works have often been compared to those of most renowned Italian scholars of his time such as Dante Alighieri (1265–1321), who, according to some scholars, would have been a sort of mentor to Immanuel, following an encounter that might have taken place in Verona.[20] While there is no documentary evidence of such a direct connection between them, we know of Immanuel's familiarity with at least two non-Jewish poets of his time, Bosone da Gubbio (d. c. 1349) and Cino da Pistoia (1270–1336), who were among Dante's closest friends. The parallel established by critics between the greatest poet of Hebrew literature in Italy and the greatest poet of Italian literature stresses the significant intellectual weight of Jewish communities in Italian intellectual society. Despite this sort of 'nationalist' pride (Immanuel's work became especially influential at the time of the renaissance of modern Hebrew literature in the contemporary Land of Israel, at exactly the same time as the late nineteenth-century reappraisal of Dante in unified Italy), the analogies between the two medieval intellectuals are striking. What transpires from their works is the sharing of the same intellectual categories. However, if Dante almost certainly had no direct knowledge of Hebrew, Immanuel, like all his contemporaneous coreligionists, did express himself in a variety of Italian dialects, besides being at ease with the most literary productive layers of Hebrew. Is it possible that Hebrew for Immanuel was tantamount to Latin for Dante? For both authors those were the languages of their own distinct liturgies and the basic tools for their literary, philosophical, and scientific education. However, Immanuel, being a philosopher and a scientist, could read Latin texts, whereas Dante depended on Latin or Italian translations for accessing Hebrew literature (basically the Bible, though he might have been familiar with other post-biblical Hebrew productions).[21] Moreover, Dante wrote his best-known poem, the *Divine Comedy*, in Italian, whereas the most significant poetic production of Immanuel, his *Mahbarot 'Immanu'el* (literally: Immanuel's Compositions), was written in Hebrew.[22] In addition to this 'higher' production, we possess a significant collection of Italian poems by Immanuel that belie the most common stylistic trends and contents of contemporary central Italian poetic milieus, with a more prominent interest in the so-called 'comic-realistic' vein.[23] Political, social, and religious issues are tackled in the Italian poetry of Immanuel,

---

20 Cassuto, *Dante e Manoello*; Fasani, *Il Fiore e il Detto d'amore*.
21 See Lelli, 'Dante e la mistica ebraica'.
22 The *Mahbarot* were first published in Brescia: Gershom Soncino, 1491. The most recent edition of the Hebrew text is 'Immanu'el ha-Romi, *The Cantos*, ed. by Jarden.
23 Immanuel's Italian poems have been published by Marti, 'Immanuele Romano'. See also Alfie, 'Immanuel of Rome'.

alongside the more central topic of love, which dominates his *Mahbarot*. This is a collection of twenty-eight framework tales shaped after literary models originating in the Arabic *maqama* genre and circulated via Jewish medieval Spain. Immanuel's most direct model is Judah al-Harizi's (1165–1225) *Sefer Tahkemoni* (The Book of the Wise). Like Harizi, Immanuel composed his work in rhymed Hebrew prose, interspersed with metrical poems (following the *prosimetrium* technique of classical origin that became popular also in medieval Romance literatures and was employed, e.g., in Dante's *Vita Nova*): it is in the *Mahbarot* that we find the first instance of Hebrew sonnets.[24] Like his Judaeo-Arab sources, Immanuel decided to insert various narratives within a framework that centres upon two protagonists whose function is that of binding the different stories together. This structure, which is reminiscent of Giovanni Boccaccio's (1313–1375) *Decameron*, might have been inspired by the two protagonists of the underworld voyage of Dante's *Comedy*. The close relation between Immanuel's narrator-protagonist (seemingly the poet himself) and his assistant, the so-called *sar* ('prince'), triggers an intense dialogue that peruses the most common issues at stake in contemporary poetics. Many topics of the *Mahbarot* are directly borrowed from their Spanish Hebrew models, although the third, sixteenth, and seventeenth chapters show affinities with Dante's *Vita Nova*. Ladies that are worthy of praise are both 'gazelles', according to Arab-Jewish Spanish poetry, and 'angels', according to 'stilnovo' patterns. In order to describe the symptoms and effects of love, Immanuel drew upon traditional scientific-medical literature of Arabic origin that circulated all over western Europe, and followed in the footsteps of both the 'stilnovo' and the 'realistic' contemporary schools.[25]

The reading of a few verses of the best-known third *Mahberet* may offer a glimpse of the intertwining of different conceptual traditions and Immanuel's close connection with Dante's *Vita Nova*:

"אם תחפץ לראות היעלה ותפארתה עד אשר תעבר / ולבי כאש תבער יער/ ורעיוני אחזו שער / וישבתי פתח השער / זהר יפעתה... ואשמורות קדמתי ל כל החושקים עת /קול המלה כקול מחנה / עוד מעט והנה / אם היא כלילת יפי כאשר יאמרו ממנה /היפה ואראנה יפה / והנה חברת גבירות ובתוכם נערה / ואשא עיני ואראה את המראה היקרה / וקם כל העם והשתחוו /בואה יקוו ויפגעו בנו מלאכי אורה" /כלבנה וכחמה ברה

(If you wish to see the gazelle so fair | lo, she goes every day to her house of prayer: | get up before-times and see her radiance there [...] I rose well before and sat by the door | with my thoughts in a daze | and my heart all ablaze | till the lady arrived to see if her beauty is the way he described. | And lo! | A murmur began to swell through the crowd | as all the lovers this beauty had wowed | stood

---

24 See Bregman, *The Golden Way*, pp. 25–83.
25 See Brener, 'Stealing Wisdom'; Brener, 'The Scroll of Love'.

before her and bowed. | And I lifted mine eyes and beheld the sight | of a group of ladies, and a young girl as bright | as the moon and as fair as the sun: an angel of light!)[26]

The intertwining of motifs, both in style and contents, drawn from different cultural traditions but ultimately modelled after the Bible, may parallel the similar attitude displayed by Dante in his *Comedy*. We may wonder whether such a choice for Immanuel can be held as apologetic (i.e. motivated by his willingness to stress the superiority of Jewish over non-Jewish culture), or the fruit of the contemporary intellectual milieus. Seen from the viewpoint of the Hebrew literary tradition, which often condemned Immanuel's works for his overly lascivious contents, the latter explanation seems to be more correct.

The past adventures of the two wandering protagonists become exemplary for their present and future lives. The importance of memory and rhetoric for providing the readers with models of morality is a further parallel to Dante's poetics. Immanuel's Hebrew language is extraordinarily rich: his lexicon is biblical, but references to post-biblical literature are frequent. The outstanding linguistic talent of the poet is striking, as he is able to draw upon a biblical verse to hint at a situation or concept that opposes the biblical model (sometimes charged with ironic tones). Immanuel's *Mahbarot*, along with his Italian poetic production (and we should not forget his philosophical and exegetic treatises), attests to the author's deep knowledge and admiration of contemporary intellectual trends and to his ability to use a variety of Eastern and Western sources — both ancient and contemporaneous — and to reshape them according to his intents.

At the turn of the fifteenth century and once again in central Italy, another scientist-poet, Moses ben Isaac of Rieti (1388–c. 1460), was the first to introduce in his *Miqdash Me'at* (The Little Temple) a new metre, based on Dante's successful *terza rima* (a flow of interlocking three-line strophes).[27] The theme of the underworld voyage had already been borrowed by Immanuel Romano in his last *Mahberet*.[28] In his poem, Moses of Rieti resorts to a sequence of ten-syllable verses in which a mobile *shewa* was considered a full vowel.[29] Due to the major circulation of hendecasyllable poems in Renaissance Italy (usually modelled after Francesco Petrarca's (1304–1374) sonnets), the pattern introduced by Rieti was adopted and used for more than a century by Italian Jewish authors, although it started losing ground from the beginning of

---

26 'Immanu'el ha-Romi, *The Cantos*, ed. by Jarden, p. 47; English translation by Brener, 'The Scroll of Love', p. 154.

27 The entire issue of *Prooftexts* 23 (1992), edited by Alessandro Guetta, was devoted to an analysis of Moses of Rieti's *Miqdash me'at*. See Bregman, 'A Note on the Style and Prosody'.

28 Immanuel's twenty-eighth chapter is a rhymed-prose version of a journey through the underworld that has the separate title *Ha-tofet we-ha-'eden* (Hell and Paradise) and is the only *Mahberet* that does not contain lyrical inserts.

29 *Shewa* or *Shwa* is a vowel sign that indicates, in the standard biblical Hebrew text, either a phoneme /ə/ or the complete absence of a vowel (Ø).

the sixteenth century, when the quantitative-syllabic system that had been created by Immanuel was revived.[30] A special emphasis was attributed at the turn of the sixteenth century to *terza rima* poems that were debating the nature of women and of love, according to the same patterns that had been followed by Immanuel of Rome and Moses of Rieti: the Hebrew 'tenzone' (poetic argument) between Avigdor of Fano, Abraham of Montepulciano, and Elijah Hayyim of Genazzano (all of them flourished at the very end of the fifteenth century) centres on the unending struggle between spiritual and earthly love and parodies the 'stilnovo' poetry. Like Immanuel's sonnets, *terza rima* was in use in Italy until its revival in the late eighteenth and early twentieth centuries (in the fifteenth and sixteenth centuries mainly in poems for mourning the dead).[31]

Although deeply indebted — especially in terms of lexicon — to the liturgical poetry of the early Middle Ages, Rieti relied much more than his precursor Immanuel on the Italian tradition represented by Dante. His vocabulary includes all the lexical layers of medieval Hebrew.[32]

Yohanan ben Isaac Alemanno (Fifteenth Century)

The revival of philological interest in classical Latin and Greek, which took place in Italy during the fifteenth and sixteenth centuries, triggered an extensive reappraisal of the language of the Scriptures among non-Jews. Biblical Hebrew became an essential basis for Christian curricula of learning, giving rise to an extraordinary exchange of grammatical information between Jewish and non-Jewish scholars. The latter aimed to learn Hebrew by resorting to linguistic categories traditional in Jewish education; to this end, they hired Jews, and the latter decided to rework a new linguistic literature, which was also grounded in humanist sources. In the fifteenth and sixteenth centuries, the Christian–Jewish intellectual encounter triggered the production of Hebrew grammars composed for non-Jewish students.[33] As time went by, Jewish teachers were more frequently replaced by converts. The inception of the printing industry allowed the dissemination of these educational instruments and an ever-growing quest for Jewish or convert teachers.[34]

This phenomenon led to the emergence of major works of encyclopaedic erudition, whose intellectual foundation was humanist rhetoric.[35] These

---

30 Bregman, 'A Note on the Style and Prosody', p. 23.
31 See Steinschneider, 'Zur Frauenliteratur'; Lelli, 'Jews, Humanists, and the Reappraisal of Pagan Wisdom', pp. 59–66.
32 Bregman, 'A Note on the Style and Prosody', p. 24.
33 See, for instance, Abraham De Balmes's (*c.* 1460–*c.* 1523) *Miqne Avram / Peculium Abrae* (Abram's Property), published in a bilingual Hebrew-Latin edition (Venice: Bomberg, 1523).
34 See Lelli, 'Italy: Pre-Modern Period'.
35 Alemanno, *Hay ha-'olamim*, ed. by Lelli.

writings were composed in highly refined biblical Hebrew (although the medieval scientific and philosophical lexica influenced by both Arabic and Latin terminologies played a decisive role in them) and targeted the scholarly community or the students of local academies. Among the major figures who inspired later generations of Jewish intellectuals, Judah Messer Leon (c. 1420–1498) deserves a special mention. Messer Leon headed an important itinerant *yeshivah* (a Jewish educational institution),[36] which was attended by most of the late fifteenth- and early sixteenth-century Italian intellectuals who cooperated with non-Jews in the search for the *Hebraica Veritas* (Hebrew Truth), the pristine and most authoritative truth enclosed in the Hebrew Scripture.[37] Among them, Yohanan ben Isaac Alemanno (c. 1435–c. 1506) played a significant role in the circulation of humanist patterns in Jewish education: his encyclopaedic treatises are worthy of mention for their adoption of sources drawn from the most diverse cultural traditions. Alemanno was probably born in Mantua, but moved early in his life to Florence, where he received his first education. He then studied at Messer Leon's *yeshivah*. Once back in Florence, he became the tutor of the sons of the wealthiest Tuscan fifteenth-century Jewish banker, Yehiel ben Samuel of Pisa (d. 1492).[38] Alemanno, who probably spoke a variety of northern Italian,[39] made massive use of Italian and Latin words in Hebrew characters when discussing specific disciplines in his treatises. However, the language of his intellectual production was mainly shaped after biblical Hebrew patterns: such use may parallel the revival of classical Latin among humanists. In the rhetorical introductions to his didactic writings, Alemanno stresses the need for contemporary Jewish students to draw upon a 'common' Hebrew language, free from medieval asperities, to be shared by a universal network of Jewish scholars.[40] Alemanno motivates his profound concern with rhetoric by drawing upon the attitudes of the contemporaneous Florentines, who have a keen interest in the ancient art of persuasion. In the introduction to his *Commentary on Song of Songs* (*Hesheq Shelomoh*, Solomon's Yearning[41]), the author singles out the virtues of the Florentines, thus establishing that

חמישית לה הלא היא המדה לא נהיתה לגוי מיום הוסדה חכמת ההלצה אשר ידעו
ואשר יבינו בה להפיק רצון איש ואיש בהמשל וסימן לאמת כל אחד עם רעהו וגבר
על עמיתו את אשר בלבבו ולהפיקו אל רצונו.

---

36 Messer Leon wandered from place to place, and so did his *yeshivah* with him over four decades (c. 1455–1495). Having started in Ancona, Messer Leon's school subsequently moved to Padua, Bologna, Mantua, and Naples.
37 See Judah Messer Leon, *The Book of the Honeycomb's Flow (Sefer Nophet Zuphim)*, ed. by Rabinowitz.
38 On Alemanno's life, see an up-to-date bibliography in Idel, *La Cabbalà in Italia*, p. 216.
39 See Sermoneta, *Un glossario filosofico*.
40 See Alemanno, *Hay ha-'olamim*, ed. by Lelli, pp. 65–67.
41 On which see Lesley, 'The "Song of Solomon's Ascents" by Yohanan Alemanno'.

(the fifth is a virtue that no other people [more than the Florentines] valued to such an extent since the origin of rhetoric; indeed [the Florentines] learn this discipline and practice it to bend men's will by means of examples and specific syllogisms and get the better of their fellows, [by moving] what is hidden in their hearts and orienting the will of their interlocutors to their own.)[42]

Alemanno's *Commentary* is built as a humanist praise of King Solomon, the alleged author of the biblical Song of Songs. In order to motivate his concern with the classical biographic genre, the author confesses that he greatly envied the nations who write huge treatises about a single man.[43] Parallel to the reception of stylistic patterns from non-Hebrew literatures is the phenomenon of the Hebrew translations of Latin or Italian texts, be they literary, philosophical, or scientific. This trend gathered momentum in the fifteenth century, when Jewish scholars, hired by non-Jewish humanists for their competence in Hebrew, inserted their own translations of extensive quotes from external sources into texts received from their cultural legacy. In other words, they adapted their own Hebrew renderings of non-Hebrew literatures to texts that they would later translate into Latin or Italian, upon request of their non-Jewish colleagues. For instance, Alemanno inserts quotes from non-Hebrew works into his own writings, after turning them to Hebrew, as in the case of John Mandeville's fourteenth-century *Travels*. In order to 'Judaize' those texts, the information that does not interest him is crossed out and what is more significant in his eyes is stressed.[44] Like many of his contemporaneous coreligionists, Alemanno appropriated the non-Jewish literary legacy, creating a parallel to the appropriation adopted by Christian humanists of Hebrew traditional lore.

Abraham ben Mordekhai Farissol (Sixteenth Century)

Alemanno was one of the closest assistants of Giovanni Pico della Mirandola (1463–1494) and other Christian humanists who, in their passionate search for universal knowledge, turned to illustrious Jewish and convert intellectuals to explore the secret subjects allegedly hidden in Hebrew literature and thought. Figures such as Alemanno, the Cretan Elijah Delmedigo (1458–1493), or the Sicilian convert Flavius Mithridates (*c.* 1450–*c.* 1489) played a major role in the creation of new intellectual Latin and Italian Jewish *corpora* that they made available for their non-Jewish patrons. These writings would become extremely influential in shaping the intellectual categories of western European

---

42 Text in Perles, 'Les savants juifs à Florence', p. 254 (my translation).
43 See Lesley, 'The "Song of Solomon's Ascents" by Yohanan Alemanno', p. 53.
44 See Lelli, 'La version hébraïque abrégée des *Voyages*'.

modern thought.[45] A very significant case of the appropriation of Italian scientific literature for a Jewish audience is Abraham Farissol's (1452–c. 1528) geographic treatise *Sefer Orhot 'Olam* (The Book of the Paths of the World), the earliest Hebrew book to contain a sketch of the 'new continent', America.[46] Composed in Ferrara in 1524, this work became a best-seller, especially after its first Venetian printed edition (1587).[47] Like many of his cultured predecessors, Farissol meant to collect scientific data from non-Hebrew literature and translate them into Hebrew in order to create a sort of compendium of knowledge that was otherwise only accessible in print in other languages. His main source was an Italian work entitled *Paesi novamente retrovati et novo mondo da Alberico Vesputio intitulato* (*Newly Discovered Countries and New World called after Alberico i.e. Amerigo Vespucci*). This was an Italian anthology of travel accounts, first published in Vicenza in 1507 (reprinted in Venice, 1521) by an Italian professor of sciences who worked in the Venetian area, Fracanzo (or Francesco Antonio) da Montalboddo (15th–16th century). Farissol translated into Hebrew full sections of Montalboddo's work.

Farissol targets his work to the upper Jewish intellectual elite. In his opening words, he warns readers against the *meshalim*, that is, the fictional literature or *belles lettres* that he describes as mainly consisting of

שירות באהבה זמה ובספרי מלחמות קדומות אשר... לא היו ולא נבראו אלא למשל

(songs of lascivious love and books of ancient wars that [...] never took place and were forged only as fictional literature.)[48]

Born in Avignon, Farissol, who had studied with Judah Messer Leon, lived most of his life in Ferrara, where he enjoyed the vibrant cosmopolitan society of the time of Ludovico Ariosto (1474–1533). Versions of Ariosto's chivalric poem *Orlando Furioso* were produced in Hebrew and in several Judaeo-languages.[49] Many lists of books attest to the presence of the *Furioso* in private collections of northern Italian Jews.[50] At the end of the sixteenth century, one of the most important Italian rabbis of the early modern era, the Venetian Leon Modena (1571–1648), translated the first and twenty-eighth cantos of the *Furioso* into Hebrew. The chivalric genre was otherwise influential on the literary models of sixteenth-century Jewish society, as it was often adapted to the biblical narrative, especially among Italian Ashkenazi Jews. We still have lengthy poems on the

---

45 Idel, *La Cabbalà in Italia*, pp. 188–200.
46 The drawing appears in all the extant manuscript copies of Farissol's work and also in its printed editions. See, e.g., Philadelphia, University of Pennsylvania Libraries, MS LJS 499, fol. 32ᵛ; Farissol, *Itinera mundi*, ed. and trans. by Hyde, p. 34.
47 On Abraham Farissol, see Ruderman, *The World of a Renaissance Jew*.
48 Farissol, *Itinera mundi*, ed. and trans. by Hyde, p. 1 (my translation).
49 See Minervini, 'Una versione giudeo-spagnola'.
50 See the lists of books owned by Mantuan Jews at the end of the sixteenth century that reveal the extraordinary circulation of the *Orlando Furioso* in their collections: Baruchson-Arbib, *La culture livresque des juifs*, pp. 163–82.

Books of Kings, and a poetic version of the Books of Samuel dating to the end of the fifteenth century. These epic poems merged motifs from non-Jewish sources with rabbinical texts, which made them more authoritative.[51] The German-born Elijah Levita (1469–1549) — best known for his intellectual collaboration in Italy with non-Jews, especially Cardinal Egidio Antonini da Viterbo (1469–1532) — adapted two chivalric stories, *Buovo d'Antona* and *Paris and Vienna*, into Yiddish. The first was titled *Bovo-Buch* and dates to the first decade of the sixteenth century, making it one of the oldest monuments of Yiddish literature;[52] the second, *Pariz un Wiene*, composed around 1530, is based on an Italian version of a tale of chivalry from the thirteenth century.[53] The beginnings of Yiddish literature can be correctly located in northern Italy, from where they started circulating in print all over Europe. These might have been the *meshalim* mentioned by Farissol in his introduction. The printing industry allowed wider audiences to become accustomed with works and subjects that were not part of traditional education, and this aroused anxiety, all the more so within Italian Jewish society.

Since its inception, the printing industry was much cherished by Jewish scholars, who cooperated with the most prestigious printers, be they Jewish or Christian.[54] Venice was developing an impressive production of Hebrew printed books, and Farissol's *Commentary on Job* was published in Venice by Daniel Bomberg in 1517 in the first *Biblia rabbinica* edition.[55] Farissol was lucky enough to see his manuscript production published in print while he was still alive. In his 'itinerant' *yeshivah*, Messer Leon had taught many Jewish students Aristotelian philosophy, rhetoric, and other topics that constituted the core of the Italian humanist curriculum. Messer Leon highlights the significant role played by the natural sciences in Jewish education in his masterwork, *Sefer Nofet Zufim* (The Book of the Honeycomb's Flow).[56] In other words, the intellectual reception of Italian Jewish Renaissance scholars was subject to the condition that the new literary and scientific attitudes be concordant with biblical and post-biblical traditional Jewish lore. Just as Messer Leon had rediscovered classical rhetoric in the Hebrew Scripture, so Farissol wanted to match the interest of his contemporaries in geographical discoveries with the Jewish traditional interpretation of the Bible. His goal was to demonstrate that Hebrew Scripture was the treasured source of all possible knowledge and information. It is in this vein that, in the introduction to his geographic treatise, Farissol exclaims:

---

51 Bikard, 'Elia Levita's Yiddish Works'.
52 Bikard, 'Elia Levita's Yiddish Works', p. 33.
53 Bikard, 'Elia Levita's Yiddish Works'.
54 On the beginning of Hebrew print in Italy, see Amram, *The Makers of Hebrew Books in Italy*.
55 Farissol's commentary was published again in the second 1524–1525 edition.
56 Judah Messer Leon, *The Book of the Honeycomb's Flow (Sefer Nophet Zuphim)*, ed. by Rabinowitz, pp. 144–45.

וצא ולמד כמה החכימה התורה האלהית והרחיבה נפשה במקומות הצריכים להגיד הגבולים והשוכנים בישובים... ורבים בספר בראשית בהגדת כל תולדות העמים וגבולותיהם במושבותיהם... מאלה בספר יהושע"

(Try now to understand how wise is the divine *Torah* and the breadth of its description of places that we need to know in order to derive [information on their] borders and on the residents of those lands [...] [as it is evident] from the book of *Genesis*, [or information on] the history of the generations of the populations and their borders in their countries [...] and many of these things [can be found] in the book of *Joshua*.)[57]

This is why modern readers should not be surprised by Farissol's descriptions of actual places and people along with the location of the 'נהר סבטיון' (River Sabbatyon or Sambatyon) and the Ten Lost Tribes of ancient Israel, or the Garden of Eden.[58] Farissol's first aim is that of drawing inspiration from the Bible, as appears from the choice of the title. Indeed, *Orhot 'Olam* or 'paths of the world' is a quotation from the Book of Job (22. 15), where the Hebrew phrase is endowed with a profoundly different meaning than what we would expect. In the standardized English version of the Bible the verse (הַאֹרַח עוֹלָם תִּשְׁמוֹר אֲשֶׁר דָּרְכוּ מְתֵי־אָוֶן) is rendered: 'Will you keep to the old path that the wicked have trod?' Thus, the *orhot 'olam* of Job are certainly not 'the ways of the [New] World', the itineraries a modern traveller should follow, nor are they the paths of wickedness (as in Job), but are rather those of the valued tradition that should not be abandoned, even in new worlds. Despite the major change produced by the recent geographic discoveries, men should keep faithful to the word of the Lord.

Like many of his cultured predecessors and followers working in Italy, Farissol meant to collect scientific data and translate them into Hebrew in order to create a sort of compendium of material that was widely accessible in other languages. Like Alemanno, Farissol wanted to build a Jewish intellectual legacy that asserted the Jewish identitarian belonging to Renaissance culture. It is not surprising that Farissol's book enjoyed wide circulation for many generations.[59]

Leon Modena (Seventeenth Century)

As noted above, Venice developed an impressive production of Hebrew printed books. The peak of the intellectual exchanges between the Venetian Jews and

---

57 Farissol, *Itinera mundi*, ed. and trans. by Hyde, p. 3.
58 See Farissol, *Itinera mundi*, ed. and trans. by Hyde, chaps 25 and 30.
59 The *Iggeret*, first published in Venice in 1586, was republished in Oxford in 1691 with a Latin translation by Thomas Hyde (*Itinera mundi*).

the non-Jewish local society was reached at the beginning of the seventeenth century, when the multicultural local Jewish community was headed by the outstanding personality of Leon Modena (Judah Aryeh ben Isaac of Modena, 1571–1648), one of the most significant Italian rabbis of all times.[60] Modena well represents the ideal universal learned man of the Renaissance Italian tradition. He occupied himself with every literary genre, extensively writing poetry in both Hebrew and Italian, composing the first modern Hebrew autobiography,[61] and being a talented preacher and playwright. Leon published in Italian one of the very first modern ethnographic works on Jewish customs and rituals, *Historia de gli riti Hebraici* (Venice, 1637). This work became a best-seller and was translated into many languages. As seen above, in Modena's time, the Venetian ghetto was a place of encounter, where Christians could attend Jewish ceremonies and hear rabbis preach and where even a cultured Jewish lady, Sara Copio Sullam (1592–1641), could discuss philosophical issues in the local vernacular and exchange mannerist sonnets in Petrarchan Italian with non-Jewish intellectuals.[62] Modena, who took advantage of the development of the Hebrew printing industry in Venice, published many of his works. His variegated poems, composed for holy or profane goals, and dedicated to both Jews and non-Jews, belie the contemporary trends of Baroque Italian poetry. His poetic production includes a well-known Hebrew elegy, composed in 1584 in memory of a contemporary rabbi, whose verses can be read in both Hebrew and Italian. The opening is 'קינה שמור אוי מה כי פס אוצר בו' (*Qinah shemor, oi meh ke-pas ozer bo* — literally meaning 'Behold the elegy, the one who kept a treasure in himself passed away', though it can be understood from a phonetic Italian reading 'Chi nasce mor, ohimè che pass'acerbo', He who is born is destined to death, alas what a sorrowful step!). In addition to authoring the already mentioned partial translation of Ludovico Ariosto's *Orlando Furioso*, Modena was responsible for the Hebrew version of the thirteenth-century moral collection entitled *Fiore di virtù* (Flower of virtue or of virtues). This work enjoyed a unique appreciation on a popular level. The central topic of the opposition of virtues and vices that it contains in association with the characters of animals made it into a sort of widely circulated moral handbook. During the fifteenth and the sixteenth centuries it was translated into several European languages, and many were the printed versions of the *Fiore di virtù* that came out of the Italian presses. While the Greek version of the work was being prepared in Venice, Leon Modena adapted it to Hebrew and printed it at the press of Daniele Zanetti in 1600. Modena's translation was entitled *Zemah Zadiq* (The Scion of the Righteous). The Venetian rabbi did not sign his work but hinted at himself in various places. As in many other cases of Hebrew renderings of Latin or Italian best-sellers produced in the

---

60 On Modena, see Malkiel, ed., *The Lion Shall Roar*.
61 See Modena, *The Autobiography*, trans. by Cohen.
62 See Copia Sulam, *Jewish Poet and Intellectual*, ed. and trans. by Harrán.

late Middle Ages or the Renaissance period, translators adapted the original texts to the interests of the local Jewish communities and often eliminated any textual references to habits other than those common among Jews, while stressing instead these aspects that were best suited to Judaism. As in the case of Immanuel Romano's renderings of Dante's *Comedy* or Alemanno's rendering of Mandeville's *Travels*, Modena's translation made use of biblical and rabbinic traditions to demonstrate that Jewish literary ability should be deemed tantamount to the non-Jewish one. The justification purported by Alemanno for borrowing the biographic genre from non-Jews was possibly held valid by all the above-mentioned authors for composing all sorts of writings dealing with 'external sciences' — though many more significant Jewish Italian authors should also be included in this list, such as David, the son of Judah Messer Leon (c. 1460–c. 1526), Azaryah de' Rossi (1513–1574), Judah Moscato (c. 1530–c. 1593), and Abraham Portaleone (1542–1612). They all devoted a significant segment of their production to the Hebrew adaptation of the most significant contributions of the intellectual agenda of the 'nations'. In this perspective, the role of Jewish literati, philosophers, and scientists in medieval and early modern Italy was primarily that of intellectual mediators, of scholars who were able to convey the legacy of their past to non-Jews and to adapt other sources of knowledge to the needs of their coreligionists.[63] To define them properly, the formula chosen by Modena in the introduction to the *Zemah Zadiq* chimes well: there he refers to himself as a *mehabber ma'atiq*, an 'author-translator', one who is able to trans-create a text to make it suitable for his own audience.[64]

The more exclusivist trends of the ghetto culture gave rise to a religious poetry that developed especially within Jewish confraternities: these had spread throughout the Italian Jewish communities starting from the late sixteenth century. In their biblical and rabbinic lexicon, liturgical hymns relied on the classical tradition of the early medieval *piyyutim* (religious poems), though they most often employed overtly contemporary Kabbalistic formulas, while borrowing strophic structures also from contemporary Italian and Spanish poetry.[65] By and large, Italian Jewish poets followed in the footpaths of Immanuel of Rome and Moses of Rieti, thus giving rise to a synthesis of stylistic and lexical patterns that flourished in the works of Joseph Zarfati (d. 1527), Leone de' Sommi (1525–1592), Samuel Archivolti (1516–1611), Leon Modena, and Jacob (1615–1667) and Immanuel Frances (c. 1618–1703) and reached their peak in the seventeenth-century 'mannerism' of Moses Zacuto (c. 1625–1697).[66] Zarfati, Sommo, Modena, and Zacuto were also playwrights who adapted traditional Jewish genres to Renaissance Italian theatre. While

---

63   See Ruderman and Veltri, eds, *Cultural Intermediaries*.
64   See Weinberg, 'Leon Modena and the *Fiore di virtù*'.
65   See Andreatta, *Poesia religiosa ebraica*.
66   See Bregman, 'Shifting Trends'.

tragedies, comedies, and other dramatic forms inspired by the revival of classical theatre were composed and performed in Italian by Jewish authors for both a Jewish and a non-Jewish audience, more traditional Jewish theatrical productions, such as the *Purimspielen*,[67] were now reinterpreted, in both Hebrew and the local Judaeo-languages, to suit the new stylistic standards current among non-Jews.[68] Leone de' Sommi from Mantua based a play of his own on Ariosto's comedy *Lena*. Leone's comedy, written in Hebrew, is titled *Zahut Bediquta de-Qiddushin*: the title is an Aramaic formula, 'A Stylish Farce on Engagement / Betrothal'. This was the first Hebrew comedy that adapted the contemporary revived classical theatre to the *Purimspiel* genre.[69] The growing involvement of Jews in staging activities during the fifteenth and sixteenth centuries brought them wide renown as actors and impresarios, even outside of their communities, and led to the establishment of Jewish dramatic societies.[70] Jews also resorted to the tragic genre to take biblical episodes onto stage. For these productions they used both Hebrew and Italian.[71] The participation of non-Jews in theatrical performances staged by Jews is a well-documented phenomenon in northern Italy.[72]

Concluding Remarks

Far from being unrelated to non-Hebrew literature, the wide Hebrew production of Italian Jews must be acknowledged as part and parcel of the Italian cultural heritage. Over the centuries Italian Jews continued to adhere to the same patterns of cultural exchange with the majority, which have characterized Judaism since Antiquity. Their intellectual receptivity was subject to the condition that 'external' literary or scientific trends be concordant with biblical and post-biblical Jewish lore. This well-tested dynamic of the cultural integration of non-Jewish elements by Jewish society allowed the latter to adapt their own heritage to the most outstanding achievements of their neighbours, and at the same time gave them the opportunity to draw on those same features that represented the common arena of intellectual exchange with the others, without blame by religious authorities. By borrowing 'external' styles and contents and by adapting them to Hebrew productions,

---

67 *Purimspiel* performances (farces to be staged on the occasion of the *Purim* festival) seem to have been staged already in the twelfth century, when the humorous parody of the biblical Book of Esther started to enjoy popularity in Italy: see Davidson, *Parody in Jewish Literature*, pp. 123–25, 264–65.
68 See Busi, *La istoria de Purim*.
69 The Hebrew text was published in Leone de' Sommi, *Zahut Bediquta de-Qiddushin*, ed. by Schirmann; English version in Leone de' Sommi, *A Comedy of Betrothal*, trans. by Golding.
70 See Roth, *History of Jews in Venice*, p. 200.
71 See Piattelli, '"Ester"'.
72 See Roth, *History of Jews in Venice*, p. 199.

they supplemented their 'internal' literary creativity, shaped after biblical and post-biblical models, and made it consonant to the intellectual agenda of their non-Jewish contemporaries. Analogous were the patterns of integration of Hebrew and non-Hebrew languages among Italian Jews. Likewise, the general trend of Italian Jewish communities to translate into Hebrew (or into any local Judaeo-language) the best-sellers of the majority not only aimed at the broader circulation of those productions among Jews, but also boosted their own identity: Italian Jews could feel proud for observing their own traditions while sharing the same legacy of their non-Jewish neighbours, at times even showing them that the most prestigious disciplines held in esteem among non-Jews actually derived from Judaism.[73]

Works Cited

Primary Sources

Alemanno, Yohanan, *Hay ha-'olamim (L'immortale). Parte I: La Retorica*, ed. by Fabrizio Lelli (Florence: Leo S. Olschki, 1995)

Copia Sulam, Sarra, *Jewish Poet and Intellectual in Seventeenth-Century Venice*, ed. and trans. by Don Harrán (Chicago: University of Chicago Press, 2009)

Farissol, Abraham, *Iggeret 'orhot 'olam id est Itinera mundi, sic dicta nempe Cosmographia autore Abrahamo Peritsol*, ed. and trans. by Thomas Hyde (Oxford: E Theatro Sheldoniano, 1691)

'Immanu'el ha-Romi, *The Cantos of Immanuel of Rome (Mahberot 'Immanu'el Ha-Romi)*, ed. by Dov Jarden, 2 vols (Jerusalem: Mossad Bialik, 1957)

Judah Messer Leon, *The Book of the Honeycomb's Flow (Sefer Nophet Zuphim) by Judah Messer Leon*, ed. by Isaac Rabinowitz (Ithaca, NY: Cornell University Press, 1983)

Leone de' Sommi, *Zahut Bediquta de-Qiddushin*, ed. by Jefim Schirmann (Yerushalayim: Tarshish, 1946)

Leone de' Sommi, Ebreo, *A Comedy of Betrothal (Tsahoth B'dihutha D'Kiddushin)*, trans. by Alfred S. Golding (Ottawa: Dovehouse Editions, 1988)

Letters of Jews in Italy: Selected Letters from the Sixteenth Century, ed. by Yacov Boksenboim (Jerusalem: Ben Zvi Institute and Hebrew University, 1994)

Luzzatto, Simone, *Socrates, Or On Human Knowledge*, ed. and trans. by Giuseppe Veltri and Michela Torbidoni (Berlin: De Gruyter, 2019)

Marti, Mario, 'Immanuele Romano', in *I poeti giocosi al tempo di Dante*, ed. by Mario Marti (Milan: Rizzoli, 1956), pp. 315–27

Modena, Leon, *The Autobiography of a Seventeenth-Century Venetian Rabbi: Leon Modena's Life of Judah*, trans. by Mark Cohen (Princeton: Princeton University Press, 1988)

---

73 On the 'theft' of Jewish wisdom by non-Jews, see Veltri, *Alienated Wisdom*.

Nicholas of Otranto, *Nektarìu, igumènou tis mònis Kasulòn (Nikolàu Ydruntinù) diàlexis katà Iudàion*, ed. by Michael Chronz (Athens: Metropolis of Thebes; Levadeia: Byzantine Monastery Hosios Loukas, 2009)

'Ovadyah of Bertinoro, *From Italy to Jerusalem: The Letters of Rabbi Ovadiah of Bertinoro from the Land of Israel*, ed. by Menahem Hartom and Abraham David (Ramat-Gan: Bar Ilan University, 1997)

Secondary Studies

Alfie, Fabian, 'Immanuel of Rome, Alias Manoello Giudeo: The Poetics of Jewish Identity in Fourteenth-Century Italy', *Italica*, 75 (1998), 307–29

Amram, David W., *The Makers of Hebrew Books in Italy: Being Chapters in the History of the Hebrew Printing Press* (Philadelphia: Greenstone, 1909)

Andreatta, Michela, *Poesia religiosa ebraica di età barocca: L'innario della confraternita 'Šomerim la-boqer' (Mantova 1612)* (Padua: Studio Editoriale Gordini, 2007)

Aprile, Marcello, *Grammatica storica delle parlate giudeo-italiane* (Galatina: Congedo, 2012)

———, 'Tracce linguistiche degli ebrei nell'Italia meridionale', in *Gli ebrei nel Salento (secoli IX–XVI)*, ed. by Fabrizio Lelli (Galatina: Congedo, 2013), pp. 407–12

Aprile, Marcello, and Fabrizio Lelli, 'La sezione degli ebraismi nel Lessico Etimologico Italiano (LEI)', *Revue de Linguistique Romane*, 69 (2004), 453–73

Arnold, Rafael, *Spracharkaden: Die Sprache der sephardischen Juden in Italien im 16. und 17. Jahrhundert* (Heidelberg: C. Winter Verlag, 2006)

Bartolucci, Guido, '"Hebraeus sempre fidus": David de' Pomis e l'apologia dell'ebraismo tra volgare e latino', in *Umanesimo e cultura ebraica nel Rinascimento italiano*, ed. by Stefano U. Baldassarri and Fabrizio Lelli (Florence: Angelo Pontecorboli, 2016), pp. 59–89

Baruchson-Arbib, Shifra, *La culture livresque des juifs d'Italie à la fin de la Renaissance* (Paris: CNRS, 2001)

Bikard, Arnaud, 'Elia Levita's Yiddish Works: Echoes of the Italian Renaissance in the Poetical Creation of a Jewish Humanist', in *'Jewish Migration: Voices of the Diaspora'*, ed. by Raniero Spelman, Monica Jansen, and Silvia Gaiga, special issue, *Italianistica Ultraiectina*, 7 (2012), 32–39

Bregman, Dvora, 'A Note on the Style and Prosody of *Miqdash me'at*', *Prooftexts*, 23 (2003), 18–24

———, *Shevil hazahav* (Jerusalem: Ben-Zvi Institute; Beer Sheva: Ben-Gurion University Press, 1995); English translation: *The Golden Way* (Tempe: Arizona University Press, 2006)

———, 'Shifting Trends in the Style of Hebrew Italian Poetry', *Tarbiz*, 61 (1991), 505–27 [in Hebrew]

Brener, Ann, 'The Scroll of Love by Immanuel of Rome: A Hebrew Parody of Dante's *Vita Nova*', *Prooftexts*, 32 (2012), 149–75

———, 'Stealing Wisdom: A Story of Books (and Book-Thieves) from Immanuel of Rome's *Mahbarot*', *Prooftexts*, 28 (2008), 1–27

Busi, Giulio, *La istoria de Purim io ve racconto … : Il Libro di Ester secondo un Rabbino Emiliano del Cinquecento* (Rimini: Luisè Editore, 1987)

Busi, Giulio, and Saverio Campanini, 'Marco Lippomano and Crescas Meir: A Humanistic Dispute in Hebrew', in *Una manna buona per Mantova — Man tov le Man Tovah: Studi in onore di Vittore Colorni per il suo 92° compleanno*, ed. by Mauro Perani (Florence: Cadmo, 2004), pp. 169–202

Cassuto, Umberto, *Dante e Manoello* (Florence, 1921)

Cuomo, Luisa, 'Il giudeo-italiano e le vicende linguistiche degli ebrei d'Italia', in *Italia Judaica: Atti del I convegno internazionale* (Rome: Istituto Poligrafico dello Stato, 1983), pp. 427–54

David, Abraham, 'Jewish Intellectual Life at the Turn-of-the-Sixteenth-Century Kingdom of Naples according to Hebrew Sources', *Materia Giudaica*, 11.1 (2006), 143–51

——, 'I manoscritti ebraici come fonti storiche dell'ebraismo salentino quattrocentesco', in *Gli ebrei nel Salento (secoli IX–XVI)*, ed. by Fabrizio Lelli (Galatina: Congedo, 2013), pp. 257–71

Davidson, Israel, *Parody in Jewish Literature* (New York: Columbia University Press, 1907)

Fasani, Remo, *Il Fiore e il Detto d'amore: Attribuiti a Immanuel Romano* (Ravenna: Angelo Longo, 2008)

Ferorelli, Nicola, *Gli ebrei nell'Italia meridionale dall'età romana al secolo XVIII*, ed. by Filena Patroni Griffi (Naples: Dick Person, 1990)

Friedmann, Alan, *Italian Texts in Hebrew Characters: Problems of Interpretation* (Wiesbaden: Otto Harassowitz, 1972)

Idel, Moshe, *La Cabbalà in Italia (1280–1510)*, ed. by Fabrizio Lelli (Florence: Giuntina, 2007)

Kaufmann, David, 'Elia Menahem Chalfan on Jews Teaching Hebrew to Non-Jews', *Jewish Quarterly Review*, o.s., 9 (1896), 500–508

Lelli, Fabrizio, 'Biography and Autobiography in Yohanan Alemanno's Literary Perception', in *Cultural Intermediaries: Jewish Intellectuals in Early Modern Italy*, ed. by David B. Ruderman and Giuseppe Veltri (Philadelphia: University of Pennsylvania Press, 2004), pp. 25–38

——, 'Una compilazione medica ebraica del XV secolo: Il manoscritto St Peterburg RGB EVR II A 11', *Rudiae: Ricerche sul mondo classico*, n.s., 3 (2017), 253–70

——, 'Dante e la mistica ebraica', *Lectura Dantis Lupiensis*, 6 (2017), 23–34

——, 'Italy: Pre-Modern Period (1500–1700)', in *Encyclopedia of Hebrew Language and Linguistics*, ed. by Geoffrey Khan (Leiden: Brill, 2013), II, pp. 374–78

——, 'Jews, Humanists, and the Reappraisal of Pagan Wisdom, Associated with the Conception of *Dignitas Hominis*', in *Hebraica Veritas? Christian Hebraists and the Study of Judaism in Early Modern Europe*, ed. by Allison P. Coudert and Jeffrey S. Shoulson (Philadelphia: University of Pennsylvania Press, 2004), pp. 49–70

———, 'Liturgia, lingue e manifestazioni letterarie e artistiche degli ebrei di Corfù', in *Evraikì: Una diaspora mediterranea da Corfù a Trieste*, ed. by Tullia Catalan and others (Trieste: La Mongolfiera Libri, 2013), pp. 31–58

———, 'La version hébraïque abrégée des *Voyages* de Jean de Mandeville, réalisée par Yohanan Alemanno', in *Le masque de l'écriture: Philosophie et traduction de la Renaissance aux Lumières*, ed. by Charles Le Blanc and Luisa Simonutti (Geneva: Droz, 2014), pp. 169–86

Lesley, Arthur M., 'The "Song of Solomon's Ascents" by Yohanan Alemanno: Love and Human Perfection according to a Jewish Associate of Giovanni Pico della Mirandola' (unpublished doctoral dissertation, University of California – Berkeley, 1976)

Malkiel, David, ed., *The Lion Shall Roar: Leon Modena and his World* (Jerusalem: Hebrew University – Ben-Zvi Institute, 2003)

Mayer Modena, Maria Luisa, 'The Spoken Languages of the Jews of Italy: How Far Back?', in *The Jews of Italy: Memory and Identity*, ed. by Bernard D. Cooperman and Barbara Garvin (Bethesda: University Press of Maryland, 2000), pp. 307–16

Minervini, Laura, 'Una versione giudeo-spagnola dell'*Orlando furioso*', *Annali di Ca' Foscari*, 32–33 (1993), 35–45

Perles, Joseph, 'Les savants juifs à Florence à l'époque de Laurent de Médicis', *Revue des études juives*, 12 (1892), 243–57

Piattelli, Angelo A., '"Ester": L'unico dramma di Leon da Modena giunto fino a noi', *La Rassegna Mensile di Israel*, 34.3 (1968), 163–72

Roth, Cecil, *History of Jews in Venice* (Philadelphia: Jewish Publication Society of America, 1930)

Ruderman, David B., *Jewish Thought and Scientific Discovery in Early Modern Europe* (New Haven: Yale University Press, 1995)

———, *The World of a Renaissance Jew: The Life and Thought of Abraham ben Mordecai Farissol* (Cincinnati: Hebrew Union College Press, 1981)

Ruderman, David B., and Giuseppe Veltri, eds, *Cultural Intermediaries: Jewish Intellectuals in Early Modern Italy* (Philadelphia: University of Pennsylvania Press, 2004)

Schiano, Claudio, 'Libri nel conflitto: Gli scritti di polemica antigiudaica nelle comunità italogreche medievali', in *Ketav, Sefer, Miktav: La cultura ebraica scritta tra Basilicata e Puglia*, ed. by Mariapina Mascolo (Bari: Di Pagina, 2014), pp. 135–47

Sermoneta, Giuseppe, 'La cultura linguistica e letteraria: I testi giudeo-pugliesi', in *Gli ebrei nell'Italia meridionale peninsulare dalle origini al 1541*, ed. by Cosimo Damiano Fonseca and others (Galatina: Congedo, 1996), pp. 161–68

———, *Un glossario filosofico ebraico-italiano del XIII secolo* (Florence: Leo S. Olschki, 1969)

Sirat, Colette, *Les traducteurs juifs à la cour des rois de Naples et de Sicile* (Paris: Éditions du CNRS, 1989)

Stein Kokin, Daniel, 'Isaac ha-Kohen's Letter to Marco Lippomano: Jewish-Christian Exchange and Arabic Learning in Renaissance Italy', *Jewish Quarterly Review*, 104 (2014), 192–233

Steinschneider, Moritz, 'Zur Frauenliteratur', *Israelitische Letterbode*, 12 (1888), 49–95

Stussi, Alfredo, 'Antichi testi salentini in volgare', *Studi di filologia italiana*, 23 (1965), 191–224

Tamani, Giuliano, 'L'attività tipografica a Venezia fra il 1516 e il 1627', in *Venezia ebraica*, ed. by Umberto Fortis (Rome: Carucci, 1982), pp. 85–97

———, *La letteratura ebraica medievale (secoli X–XVIII)* (Brescia: Morcelliana, 2004)

———, 'Manoscritti e libri', in *Gli ebrei nell'Italia meridionale peninsulare dalle origini al 1541*, ed. by Cosimo Damiano Fonseca and others (Galatina: Congedo, 1996), pp. 225–40

Veltri, Giuseppe, *Alienated Wisdom: Enquiry into Jewish Philosophy and Scepticism* (Berlin: De Gruyter, 2018)

Veltri, Giuseppe, and Evelien Chajes, *Oltre le mura del ghetto: Accademie, scetticismo e tolleranza nella Venezia barocca* (Palermo: New Digital Press, 2016)

Wartenberg, Ilana, *The Epistle of the Number by Ibn al-Aḥdab: The Transmission of Arabic Mathematics to Hebrew Circles in Medieval Sicily* (Piscataway, NJ: Gorgias Press, 2015)

Weinberg, Joanna, 'Leon Modena and the *Fiore di virtù*', in *The Lion Shall Roar: Leon Modena and his World*, ed. by David Malkiel (Jerusalem: Hebrew University – Ben-Zvi Institute, 2003), pp. 137–57

CAROLINA STROMBOLI

Language Contacts and Contact Languages in Renaissance Naples

From the moresche *to* Lo cunto de li cunti

During the Spanish domination in the sixteenth and seventeenth centuries, Naples was one of the most populated cities in Europe. Capital of the Spanish Viceroyalty in southern Italy, Naples was a multicultural and multilingual city where Italian (that is to say the form of Tuscan based principally on Florentine which became the literary language of Italy), Neapolitan and other Italo-Romance varieties, the Spanish of the ruling class, and other foreign languages existed side by side. In Renaissance Naples, there was a rich and varied production of theatrical and musical genres in Neapolitan, such as songs, lyrics, farces, and street theatre performances. In the first half of the seventeenth century, Neapolitan literature thrived with the works of the writers Giovan Battista Basile and Giulio Cesare Cortese, who for the first time used Neapolitan in texts not intended for the stage.

This essay analyses literary evidence to investigate the presence in Renaissance Naples of a contact language similar in some respects to the coeval so-called Mediterranean *lingua franca*. This latter variety commonly refers to a Romance-based language characterized by a restricted lexicon and simplified grammar, and documented in the Mediterranean basin from the sixteenth to the nineteenth century. It was used by the Arabs, Turks, Greeks, and other populations from Northern Africa and the eastern Mediterranean areas to communicate with people from western Europe. Some scholars dispute the very existence of such a language, yet important traces which attest its presence can be found in Italian texts since the Renaissance.[1]

---

[1] According to some scholars, traces of *lingua franca* are found in the following literary texts: the poem *Contrasto della Zerbitana* (end of the thirteenth century–beginning of the fourteenth century); a sonnet by Luigi Pulci against Marsilio Ficino (c. 1473); the *Villancico* by Juan de Encina (c. 1520); the play *La Zingana* by Gigio Artemio Giancarli (1542); the play *La Sultana* by Giovambattista Andreini (1622); the plays *Le Sicilien* (1667) and *Le bourgeois gentilhomme* (1670) by Molière; the play *L'impresario delle Smirne* by Carlo Goldoni (1774).

Carolina Stromboli (cstromboli@unisa.it) is Associate Professor of Italian Linguistics and Italian Dialectology at the University of Salerno.

The goal of this essay is to bring to light some aspects of a well-established Neapolitan tradition in the representation of black slaves and their language which starts with the *moresche*, a genre of Neapolitan musical poetry that developed in the sixteenth century. In this poetry, black slave characters speak a sort of 'distorted' Neapolitan, rich in onomatopoeias and (seemingly) nonsense words. In the following paragraphs, I survey selected passages from sixteenth- and seventeenth-century Neapolitan literary and theatrical texts in which black slave characters appear, and I describe the language used therein. In the first section, I shall focus on the language used by a black female slave character in two stories of *Lo cunto de li cunti*, a collection of fairy tales written in Neapolitan dialect and Baroque style by Giovan Battista Basile. The second section highlights literary traces of the dance called *catubba* and street performances named *luciate*: in both, the main character is the black slave Lucia, whose linguistic repertoire is similar to the one employed by the slave in *Lo cunto*. In the third section, I shall discuss Neapolitan *moresche*. The last section is dedicated to an analysis of the term *bernaguallà*, which is a hallmark of the language used by Neapolitan black people and which occurs in all texts presented here.

The Language of the Black Slave in *Lo cunto de li cunti*

Lo cunto de li cunti (henceforth *Cunto*, 1634–1636) is a fairy tale collection written in Neapolitan dialect and Baroque style by the Neapolitan writer Giovan Battista Basile (Naples, 1570/72–1632). It is structured around a frame story, in which fifty fairy tales (called *cunti* in Neapolitan, from *cuntare* 'to relate, tell') are related over the course of five days. The *Cunto*, which was considered by Benedetto Croce 'il più bel libro italiano barocco' (the most beautiful Italian baroque book), represents the first literary collection of fairy tales in Europe: it includes the first written versions of famous fairy tales by Basile, such as Cinderella (the tale *La gatta Cennerentola* in the *Cunto*), Puss in Boots (*Cagliuso*),[2] Sleeping Beauty (*Sole Luna e Talia*), Rapunzel (*Petrosinella*), and several others. The *Cunto* offers a realistic representation of the Neapolitan of the sixteenth century in all its diaphasic and diastratic varieties, and also gives brief examples of other languages, such as Italian,

---

The bibliography on *lingua franca* is very large; the reader can refer to some of the secondary sources mentioned in the Works Cited. See, for instance, the works by Minervini ('La lingua franca mediterranea', 'Lingua franca (italiano come)', and 'La lingua franca mediterranea fra realtà storica e finzione letteraria'), Cifoletti (*La lingua franca barbaresca*), Venier (*La corrente di Humboldt*), and Baglioni ('Attestazioni precinquecentesche della lingua franca?').

2 A previous version of this fairy tale was written by the Italian writer Giovan Francesco Straparola (the tale *Costantino Fortunato*, in the collection of tales *Le piacevoli notti*, 1550–1553).

Latin, Spanish,³ and so-called foreigner talk (the simplified language usually used by foreigners). Here I shall focus on the language spoken by the character of the black female slave. Two stories, namely the frame story and the ninth tale of the fifth day, include this character, called Lucia in the frame story. In the first story, she steals a princess's future husband; in the second story, she steals a fairy's future husband, who is also a prince; in the end, Lucia is unmasked and cruelly punished. I would argue that the language spoken by the slave could be described as a literary Neapolitan version of *lingua franca*.⁴

In the *Cunto* there are sixteen lines pronounced by the slave, six in the frame story and ten in the ninth tale of the fifth day. The first five passages (see below, passages 1-5) have the same syntactic structure: *si* or *se no* 'if not' + a sentence with the verb in the infinitive, followed by the sentence *mi punia a ventre dare e Giorgetiello mazzoccare* (I will punch myself in the belly and kill Giorgetiello); here the pregnant slave threatens her husband-prince to kill the unborn child if he is not able to meet her request. Sentence 5 is particularly significant because it sets the whole narrative mechanism of the *Cunto* in motion: the pregnant slave asks her husband to tell her some tales, and the prince hires ten expert female storytellers, who tell her ten *cunti* (tales) a day. Example 6 has a slightly different syntactic structure, with two infinitives with imperative meaning at the beginning of the sentence, followed by *si no* and then the usual sentence *mi punia a ventre dare, e Giorgetiello mazzoccare*:⁵

1) Se fenestra no levare, mi punia a ventre dare e Giorgetiello mazzoccare.⁶

(I Introd. 31)

2) Si no avere chella piccinossa che cantare, mi punia a ventre dare e Georgetiello mazzoccare.⁷

(I Introd. 35)

---

3 See, for example, the Italian verses 'Tre volte cadde ed a la terza giacque' (III 5 53), by Annibal Caro, *Eneide* [Italian translation], IV 1061, c. 1566, or 'Ite sveglianno [svegliando] gli occhi col corno' (I Introd. 11), by Giovan Battista Guarino, *Pastor fido*, I 1 3–4, 1590. There are several Latin expressions, some of which are corrupted, coming from medical or legal language. In addition to the many Spanish loanwords, there is also a whole sentence in Spanish: 'La muccia chella es causa de despriezzo [la mucha aquella es causa de desprecho]' (II Egl. 284).
4 Cf. Minervini, 'La lingua franca mediterranea fra realtà storica e finzione letteraria', p. 384, and Stromboli, 'Il plurilinguismo de *Lo cunto de li cunti*' and 'Contatti linguistici e lingua franca a Napoli'.
5 The quotations of *Lo cunto de li cunti* are taken from the edition by Stromboli.
6 If you do not move away from the window, I will punch myself in the belly and kill Giorgetiello.
7 If I do not have that little thing that sings, I will punch myself in the belly and kill Giorgetiello.

3) Si chella voccola no pigliare, mi punia a ventre dare e Georgetiello mazzoccare.[8]

(*1 Introd. 38*)

4) Si pipata no accattare, mi punia a ventre dare e Giorgetiello mazzoccare.[9]

(*1 Introd. 41*)

5) Si no venire gente e cunte cuntare, mi punia a ventre dare e Giorgetiello mazzoccare.[10]

(*1 Introd. 46*)

6) Stare zitta, appilare, si no punia a ventre dare, e Giorgietiello mazzoccare.[11]

(*v 10 13*)

In tale v 9, the lines pronounced by the black slave are more varied (see below, passages 7–16). Here the slave is sent three times to fetch water from a fountain; she sees the image of a beautiful white woman reflected in the water, whom she thinks to be herself. The third time she realizes that the beautiful face is that of a fairy hidden in a tree, and she tries hard to deceive the fairy and take her place:

7) Che bedere, Lucia sfortunata cossì bella stare? E patrona mannare acqua a pilliare, e mi sta cosa comportata, o Lucia sportonata.[12]

(*v 9 37*)

8) Iuta a fontanella, tozzata a preta lancella.[13]

(*v 9 37*)

9) Mi no stare schiava mossuta, mi no stare pernaguallà, culo gnamme gnamme, pocca stare accossì bella e portare a fontana varrile.[14]

(*v 9 39*)

10) Aseno passato, varrile tozzato, 'n terra cascato e tutto sfrecoliato.[15]

(*v 9 40*)

---

8 If you do not take that hen, I will punch myself in the belly and kill Giorgetiello.
9 If you do not buy that doll, I will punch myself in the belly and kill Giorgetiello.
10 If people do not come to tell tales, I will punch myself in the belly and kill Giorgetiello.
11 Shut up, shut your mouth, if not, I will punch myself in the belly and kill Giorgetiello.
12 What do I see? Is the unfortunate Lucia so beautiful? And the mistress sends her to fetch the water, and I do it, oh unfortunate Lucia.
13 I went to the fountain, the jug was hit.
14 I am not a slave with a big mouth, I am not a slave *pernaguallà*, arse *gnamme gnamme*, because I am so beautiful and I carry the jug to the fountain.
15 The donkey passed, the jug was hit, fell to the ground and broke completely.

11) Mi stare marfussa, s'acqua pigliare, meglio è maritare a Giorgia mia; no stare bellezza chesta da fare morta arraggiata, e servire patrona scorrucciata.[16]

(v 9 43)

12) Tu stare causa che mi bastonata, ma non curare.[17]

(v 9 45)

13) Che fare loco susa, bella feliola?[18]

(v 9 45)

14) Pocca aspettare marito, lassare venire 'ncoppa e pettenare capo e fare chiù bella.[19]

(v 9 47)

15) No maravegliara, prencepa mia, ca stare ucciahè fatata, anno facce ianca, anno cula nigra.[20]

(v 9 52)

16) Meritare abbrosciare e porvere da coppa castiello iettare.[21]

(v 9 64)

The lines of the black slave represent literary stereotypes of foreigner talk.[22] In the *Cunto* there is also an example of foreigner talk used by a white girl: in tale III 2, the main character Penta asks a black male slave to cut her hands off and speaks in a way which reproduces the way slaves usually speak:

17) Alì mio, tagliare mano meie, volere fare bella secreta e deventare chiù ianca.[23]

(III 2 16)

---

16 I am crazy if I fetch the water, it is better to marry my Giorgio: with this beauty I cannot die angry and serve a bad mistress.
17 You are the reason I was beaten, but never mind.
18 What are you doing up there, beautiful girl?
19 Since you are waiting for your husband, let me come up and comb your hair and make you more beautiful.
20 Don't wonder, my prince, because I am cursed: one year white face, one year black arse.
21 She deserves to be burnt and the ashes should be thrown from the top of the castle.
22 The expression *foreigner talk* indicates the simplified way in which we speak to foreign interlocutors who are supposed not to know our language sufficiently. Many of the linguistic features in the black slave's language (generalized use of infinitive and of past participle, *mi* as subject, lack of definite article) are well documented in modern Italian foreigner talk. The bibliography on *foreigner talk* is large, starting from Ferguson, 'Absence of Copula and the Notion of Simplicity'. As for Italian foreigner talk, see, for instance, Bernini, 'Foreigner Talk', and the bibliographical references provided there.
23 My Alì, cut my hands, I will do something beautiful and secret and become whiter.

The last example of a similar language is in a passage which is not directly connected to the black slaves:

> 18) Ed essa restata a trivoliare a la fenestra, passaie pe disgrazia da chella casa na vecchiarella che, sentennose allancare da la famme, le cercaie quarche refrisco. A la quale la negrecata giovane respose: 'O bona femmena mia, *Dio sapere core*, ca sto 'n potere de no zifierno'.[24]
>
> *(I 5 27–28)*

In (18), the poor girl Porziella, forced by her father to marry an ogre, uses the sentence *Dio sapere core* ('God knows the heart'), an expression which is also found in other Neapolitan contemporary literary texts, such as the poem *La Rosa* by Giulio Cesare Cortese (1621), the Neapolitan translation of the *Gerusalemme liberata* by Gabriele Fasano (1689), and the eighteenth-century poem *Le bbinte rotole de lo Valanzone* by Nunziante Pagano. Fasano considers *Dio sapere core* as a typical expression used by black slaves in Naples. The note by Fasano, which explains 'dimandato uno schiavo se amasse il padrone, rispose: *Dio sapere core*',[25] suggests that the expression might not have been completely straightforward to everybody, despite the fact that it was still in use in Naples in the second half of the seventeenth century.

In the following linguistic analysis of examples 1–18, I try to show that the main features of the black slave's language in the *Cunto* are the same as found in texts of *lingua franca*. At the orthographic level, we note the tendency of final vowels in verbs, nouns, and adjectives to become *-a* (see *maravegliara* instead of *maravigliare* 'to wonder' and *cula nigra* rather than *culo nigro* 'black arse').[26] This use has implications for nominal morphology: *prencepa mia* 'my prince' and *Giorgia mia* 'my Giorgio' are masculine, whereas one would expect a final *-a* to denote the feminine gender. Some important morphological features are the invariant use of the infinitive for verbs in all persons and tenses (e.g. *cuntare* 'to tell', *dare* 'to give', *mazzoccare* 'to kill', *portare* 'to bring', and so forth), the use of the past participle as invariant past tense (*passato* 'passed', *tozzato* 'hit', *cascato* 'fallen', *sfrecoliato* 'broken'), the dative *mi* as a subject pronoun (instead of *io* 'I'), the lack of definite articles, and so forth. There is also a case of prepositional direct object (*meglio è maritare a Giorgia mia*, with the preposition *a* before the direct object),[27] but this feature is typical

---

24 She was complaining at the window, when by chance an old woman passed by that house and, feeling faint from hunger, asked her something to eat. And the poor young girl answered: 'My good woman, God knows the heart, but I am in the power of a monster'.
25 Fasano, *Lo Tasso napoletano*, p. 799 (a slave, who was asked if he loved his master, replied: God knows the heart).
26 See also the insult *cula pertosata* 'broken arse', that the mistress addresses to the slave (example 22, below).
27 This structure, documented in old Neapolitan texts and in literary texts of the seventeenth century, although not widely, is scarcely present in the *Cunto*, where it occurs mainly with proper names.

of Neapolitan and other southern dialects (and occurs in Spanish as well), while in texts in *lingua franca*, for example in the Venetian play *La Zingana* by Giancarli (1542), we usually find it with the preposition *per*, not *a*. At the syntactic level, one can observe that the word order (S)OV is prevalent. There are few subordinate clauses (introduced by the conjunctions *si* 'if', *ca/che* 'that', *pocca* 'because'), and in passage 15 there is a nominal sentence (*anno facce ianca, anno cula nigra* 'one year white face, one year black arse').

From a lexical point of view, in the passages from the *Cunto* (1–18) the verb *stare* always replaces *essere* 'to be', and we find some peculiar terms, such as the uncommon *pernagualla* (which I will discuss later) and the nonsense words *gnamme* (both occurring in passage 9) and *ucciahe* (passage 15). The only Arabic loanword is *marfussa* 'crazy, strange' (passage 11), from Arabic *marfūḍ* 'despised, cast out': this borrowed term, also documented in Spanish from the thirteenth century (cf. DCECH, s.v. *malfuz* 'renegato, traidor' ('renegade, traitor')), was introduced into Italian with adapted spelling and pronunciation. It took the masculine form *malfusso* which is attested, for instance, in the mock-heroic poem *Morgante* by Luigi Pulci (*c.* 1480) and in Neapolitan literary texts since 1491.[28] Notably, it also occurs in another passage of the *Cunto* not referring to the slave.[29] The word is found in some texts in *lingua franca*, such as the *Villancico* by Juan Del Encina (1520) (v. 29: 'taybos non *marfuzes* rruynes')[30] and the Venetian play *La Zingana* by Giancarli (1542) (III 415: 'no star si no 'l gente bestial, *marfus*, cattiba').[31]

Almost all features mentioned here are also found in the texts in *lingua franca* cited in note 1: some characteristics include the final vowel -*a*, object pronouns used as subject (like *mi*), the lack of definite articles, and above all the simplification of the verbal system and the invariant use of the infinitive. Basile was probably influenced by plays where characters who use the *lingua franca* occur (for example the above-mentioned play *La Zingana*), and especially by the theatrical representations of black slaves in the Iberian area (see, for

---

28 Cf. Cardona, 'L'elemento orientale nel *Morgante* e nel *Ciriffo*', p. 98. The first Neapolitan occurrence is in the chronicle *Le Effemeridi delle cose fatte per il duca di Calabria*, by Leostello, where the word is the proper name of a black man ('un negro chiamato Malfusso'); cf. Sabatini, Coluccia, and Lupis, 'Prospettive meridionali nella lessicografia storica italiana', p. 151. In the description of the same event in the coeval *Cronaca* by Ferraiolo (1494–1498), the name of the black man was changed to *Fellusso*, probably because *Malfusso* would have been seen as uncommon in Naples at the end of the fifteenth century. However, the word was often used in the Neapolitan literary texts of the seventeenth and eighteenth centuries, by authors like Giulio Cesare Cortese, Andrea Perrucci, Nicola Stigliola, and Nicola Capasso.
29 'Lo prencepe, se primmo steva *marfusso* de lo boffettone, mo se 'nzorfaie per vederese renfacciata la 'ngnoranzia soia' (v 6 17; If the prince was first angry because of the slap, then he became angrier because he saw his ignorance held against him).
30 Cf. Minervini, 'La lingua franca mediterranea', p. 282.
31 Minervini, 'La lingua franca mediterranea', p. 283.

example, the plays of Lope de Vega and other contemporary Spanish authors).[32] It is most likely, however, that Basile drew on a local Neapolitan repertoire of black slaves' representation: references to black slaves and examples of their language are, in fact, found in other previous and contemporary Neapolitan literary texts, as we shall see in the following sections.

Dances and the *luciate*

In the *Cunto* there are references to the Moorish dance called *catubba* or *Lucia canazza* which, according to literary and iconographic evidence, must have been very popular in Naples at the beginning of the seventeenth century.[33] The main character of this dance was a black female slave, conventionally called Lucia. The word *catubba* is probably an onomatopoeia referring to the sound of the music, and it often appears in the phrase *tubba catubba*. As for the form *canazza*, it consists of the word *cana* 'female dog' + the pejorative suffix *-azza*. *Cane* was an insult for infidels, such as Muslims (usually Moors and Turks), but it was also employed as an affectionate female nickname (not necessarily black). This use, as Ferrari Barassi claims, often occurs in sixteenth- and seventeenth-century love poetry, especially in Neapolitan texts:[34] the terms *cane/cana* and *canazza* are found in many lyrics and *villanelle*, like the one that Basile quotes in the *Muse napolitane*[35] (*Calliope*, v. 195: 'canazza perra, nata Mbarvaria', where both the Neapolitan *canazza* and the Spanish *perra* mean 'bitch'). In a sonnet which mocks the poetic genre of the *mattinata* (a morning serenade) and which is contained in the Neapolitan poem *La tiorba a taccone* (1648) by Felippo Sgruttendio de Scafato,[36] we find the onomatopoeic phrase *tubba catubba* and the series of affectionate nicknames *cana, canazza*, and the diminutive form *canella*, addressed to a woman looking out the window:

> 19) 'Canta, io diciette, ca Cecca mia bella,
> Stace affacciata mo: videla vì?
> Cana, cornuta canazza, canella!'
> Muchio aprije canna, e dicette accossì:

---

32 In Spain there was a rich tradition representing black slaves, whose *hablas de negros* (black people's language) had linguistic features quite similar to those of the *Cunto* (cf. Lawrance, 'Black Africans in Renaissance Spanish Literature'; Camus Bergareche, 'Lingua franca y lengua de moros'; Weber de Kurlat, 'El tipo del negro en el teatro de Lope de Vega').
33 Cf. Lombardi, *Danze e buone maniere*, pp. 94–99.
34 Cf. Ferrari Barassi, 'La tradizione della moresca', p. 43.
35 The work *Le muse napoletane* (1635) is a collection of nine eclogues, written in Neapolitan by Basile.
36 This name is a pseudonym. The identification of the author is not yet certain; cf. Fulco, 'La letteratura dialettale napoletana'.

> '*Tubba catubba, la tubba tubbella,*
> *Tubba tubbella, e lo chichirichì*.'[37]
>
> (*Tiorba*, I, XLV, *Matinata a Cecca*, vv. 9–14)[38]

The Neapolitan term *tiorba* refers to a musical string instrument (English 'theorbo'), and therefore the poem *La tiorba a taccone* (henceforth *Tiorba*), which mocks Petrarchist lyric poetry, is divided into ten parts, named *corde* 'strings'. The ninth 'string' is dedicated to the dance *catubba*; in example 20 there are two stanzas of the accompanying song: the text suggests a whirling dance, full of jumps and turns. As for the language, note, in particular, in addition to the already discussed affectionate nickname *canella*, the seemingly nonsense words, like *pernaguallà* (again), *cotognì*, *'ngritta*, *cuccorasà*, *cucherecù* (which sounds like a rooster, see also *chichirichì* in 19), and the phrase *bona me sa*:

> 20) O Lucia, ah Lucia,
> Lucia, Lucia mia!
> Cotognì, cotognì, cotognì!
> Vide chest'arma ca scola, ca squaglia,
> tiente, ca passo, sautanno, na quaglia!
> Cucherecù,
> Sauta mo su!
> Vecco ca sauto, ca torno, ca roto,
> Vì ca mme voto:
> Sauta Lucia, ca zompo io da ccà!
> Uh, che te scuosse, e pernovallà![39]
> [...]
> O Lucia, ah Lucia,
> Lucia, Lucia mia,
> Cocozza de vino bona me sa!
> Vide, canella, ca tutto me scolo,
> Tiente, ca corro, ca roto, ca volo!
> Cucherecù,
> Rota mo su!
> Vecco ca roto, ca corro, ca giro,
> Vì ca sospiro:

---

[37] Sing, I said that my beautiful Cecca looks out the window now, can you see her? *Cana*, cuckquean, *canazza*, *canella*! Muchio opened his mouth and said: *Tubba catubba, tubba tubbella, tubba tubbella*, and *chichirichì*.

[38] The *Tiorba a taccone* is edited by Malato, in Cortese, *Opere poetiche*.

[39] '[O Lucia, ah Lucia, Lucia, my Lucia! *Cotognì, cotognì, cotognì!*] See this soul how it quivers and quakes, watch how I jump more than a quail. *Cuccurucu*, jump up high. Here I am leaping, twisting, wheeling, watch how I turn. Jump up, Lucia, I'm leaping over here! Uh how you shake yourself, *pernovallà*!' (Otter, 'The Neapolitan *moresche*', p. 167, n. 52; the translation of the first line is my own).

> Rota, Lucia, ca scompo mo ccà!
> 'Ngritta, ca 'ngritta, e cuccarasà!⁴⁰
>
> (*Tiorba*, IX, IV, vv. 118–47)

In the same part of this poem, the *catubba* is also mentioned in a passage about entertainment, dances, and games of Carnival, but in this case children (*piccerille*) dance it. The dance is accompanied, as usual, by cries such as *vucciahè*, *cierne Lucia*, and *pernovallà*:

> 21) Lo bede' da piccerille
> Chella rota che se fa:
> Uno canta, e cchiù de mille
> Fanno po': 'Pernovallà'.
> [...]
> Lo bedere pe na via
> Na catubba che gusto è!
> Uno fa: 'Cierne Lucia',
> N'auto dice: 'Vucce hè'.⁴¹
>
> (*Tiorba*, IX, II, vv. 129–38)

The phrase *cierne Lucia*, which literally means 'twist Lucia', is used as an insult in a passage of the *Cunto* where the mistress speaks to the slave (passage 22). The verb *cernere* occurs also in another passage, where the slave Lucia is twisting not while dancing but in fear, because she understood that her deception is about to be discovered (passage 23):

> 22) Curre, scapizzate, schiava pezzente, gammagrillo, cula pertosata! Curre, né fare siamma siamma, né *cierne-Locia*, e portame mo chesta chiena d'acqua!⁴²
>
> (*Cunto*, V 9 42)

> 23) Ma Lucia fece veramente da Lucia, *cernennose* tutta mentre se cuntava sto cunto.⁴³
>
> (*Cunto*, V 10 4)

---

40 Oh Lucia, ah Lucia, Lucia, my Lucia, pumpkin of wine, how good it is! See, *canella*, how I drink it all, watch how I run, I turn, I fly! *Cucherecù*, now turn! Here I am twisting, running, turning, watch how I sigh: twist, Lucia, and now I stop here: *'ngritta ca 'ngritta* and *cuccarasà*.
41 Seeing children that do a cartwheel: one sings, more than one thousand say: *Pernovallà*. [...] To see a *catubba* in the street is a pleasure; one says: *Cierne Lucia*; another one says: *Vucce hè*.
42 Run, fall, poor slave, cricket leg, broken arse! Run, don't do *siamma siamma* or *cierne-Locia*, and bring me this jug full of water.
43 But Lucia really acted like Lucia, twisting while this story was told.

Returning to the *catubba*, the series of engravings called *I balli di Sfessania*, made in 1621–1622 by French printmaker Jacques Callot, offers an important iconographic reference to this dance: these engravings depict scenes with black slaves dancing in the streets, although the first printing shows a theatre stage with a curtain. The prints contain names and captions which are typically Moorish, like *Lucia, Lucia mia, Cucurogna, Pernovalla/Bernovalla, cucurucu, che buona mi sa*, and 'suggest, once again, acrobatic display and grotesque movements as well as a strong percussive element (as the onomatopoetic name *tubba catubba* implies), and the dramatic setting of a *serenata*'.[44]

In his work *Ritratto o modello delle grandezze, delizie e meraviglie della nobilissima città di Napoli* (1588; written in Tuscan, not in Neapolitan), which gives a great deal of information about the customs and the culture of Renaissance Naples, the writer Giovan Battista Del Tufo described the *catubba* as a whirling dance starring a black female slave (passage 24). Del Tufo does not provide details about the language of the song which accompanies the dance, but he uses the name *Lucia* and the term *berna gualà*, a variant spelling of the *pernaguallà/pervovallà* present in Basile, in the *Tiorba*, and in Callot's engravings:

24) e simili persone
    col tamburello o con lo colascione,
    sentendo in giro chi da là e da qua:
    Lucia mia, berna gualà!
    [...]
    Move in giro le man, natiche e piedi,
    battendo e piedi e man sempre ad un suono;
    curva il petto su 'l ventre, e allor tu vedi
    con grazia il ballator gir sempre a tuono.[45]

(Del Tufo, *Ritratto, ragionamento quarto*, vv. 646–53)

The *catubba* dance was probably at the centre of the Neapolitan street performances called *luciate*, whose main character was, once again, the slave Lucia. We know little about the *luciate*, but evidence shows that the characters speak a simplified Neapolitan, very similar to that of the black slave in the *Cunto*: see, for example, the following passage taken from a certain *Luciata nuova* (1628),[46] where we find linguistic features like the invariant use of the infinitive, the

---

44 Cf. Otter, 'The Neapolitan *moresche*', p. 148.
45 And similar people, with a tambourine and a *colascione* [another musical instrument, similar to the mandolin], hearing from here and there: my Lucia, *berna gualà*! [...] She moves her hands, her buttocks, her feet, beating her feet and hands at the same time; she lowers her chest to her belly, and then you can see that the dancer turns with grace.
46 The full title is: *La Luciata nuova. Posta in luce dal Rovinato Pover'Huono, a compiacenza de' Virtuosi* (Terni: Guerrieri, 1628); the author is unknown. This *luciata* is now edited by Rak, 'Una moresca per Lucia'; see also Rak, *Napoli gentile*, pp. 130–31, and Rak, 'La schiava mora che balla', pp. 323–24.

lack of the article, the pronoun *mi* used as subject, the verb *stare* instead of *essere*, and the word *berna valà* (variant spelling of *bernaguallà/pernaguallà*):

> 25) E mi chiamata Lucia musuta
> che havere quattro namorati,
> tutti quanti stare barbuti,
> tutti quanti stare agarbati,
> ma mi tutti fatti cornuti,
> solo à uno contentato,
> hora che tutti fare la festa
> perché auta la libertà
> mi bolere poco balare
> e tutti fare consolati,
> sonare tutta chissa iornata,
> tutti ballare la cu cu ru bà
> a a berna valà
> a a berna valà.[47]

(from La Luciata nuova, 1628)

Another *luciata* was written around 1628 by Francesco Manelli. We also know of another version composed by a certain Fasolo and entitled *Il Carro di Madama Lucia*, which is based on the same text but with some variations, one stanza less, and with a different musical score. This *luciata*, characterized by a complicated textual history, has been studied and edited by Ferrari Barassi. As this scholar explains, it is a short, partly dialectal song with two dialoguing characters, Lucia and Cola (or Coviello), as well as a third anonymous voice that joins the other two in the final trio of each verse.[48] The dialogue does not show the simplified language of the slaves, but an alternation between Italian and Neapolitan. Interestingly, one finds some words and expressions typical of the slaves' language, such as *che buono me sa, cagna Lucia*,[49] the affectionate nickname *cagna* (which recalls the form *canazza*), the term *bernavalà*, the *incipit* with the words *O sportunata* (which recalls the expression *Lucia sfortunata* and *o Lucia sportonata*, see passage 7 from the *Cunto*). In passage 26 we read the last four verses of the first stanza of the *luciata*, in passage 27 the final stanza, where both characters sing together (the text is taken from the version by Fasolo, the variations in square brackets from the version by Manelli):

---

47 My name is *Lucia* with the big mouth, and I have four lovers, they are all bearded, they are all polite, but I have betrayed them all, I have satisfied only one, now that everyone is celebrating, because they became free, I want to dance a little, and to please everyone, to play all day, everyone dances the *cu cu ru bà, a a berna valà, a a berna valà*.
48 Cf. Ferrari Barassi, '"La Luciata" di Francesco Manelli', p. 231.
49 *Cagna Lucia* is in the version by Fasolo, in the text by Manelli we find *cangia Lucia*, which is probably a *lectio facilior* (cf. Ferrari Barassi, '"La Luciata" di Francesco Manelli', p. 220).

26) Non fugge cervo [fuie ciervo] né vola lo viento [vento]
come fa Cola per [pe] chillo tormiento [tormento],
per chilla [chella] faccia che morte mi dà,
e cagna [cangia] Lucia, la biernovalà [bernovalà].⁵⁰
27) Io chiù non chiango, né vivo scontiento [scontento],
tutto di [de] gioia schiattare mi sento [siento],
per chilla [pe chella] faccia che vita mi [me] dà,
e viva Lucia, la biernovalà [bernavalà].⁵¹

The Literary Genre of the *moresche*

The figure of Lucia has existed in Neapolitan folk and musical traditions at least since 1555 (the year of publication of the *Secondo Libro delle Muse a tre voci. Canzoni moresche di diversi autori*, edited by Antonio Barré). Lucia was the main character of the Neapolitan *moresche*, Moorish songs portraying Africans. The *moresca* was a comic musical genre, born as a representation of the battles between Moors and Christians and widespread in the Mediterranean area during the Renaissance.⁵² Here we focus on the Neapolitan version of this genre and on its language.

The Neapolitan *moresche* had little in common with the European *moresche*, which portrayed battles. They were more closely connected to the *villanelle* or *canzoni villanesche*, a genre of Neapolitan music poetry, which represented a reaction against the madrigal, and often also a parody. As for the metre, a *villanella* 'is essentially a strambotto (or ottava rima) transformed by the addition of a refrain after each hendecasyllabic couplet'.⁵³ The surviving Neapolitan *moresche* number just a dozen, some of which were set to music by several composers, like the famous Flemish musician Roland de Lassus (1532–1594).⁵⁴ As Salvatore explains, these songs constitute a single cycle based on two main characters: the female slave *Lucia* and her suitor *Giorgio* (spelled *Giorgia*), plus some other minor characters. In most *moresche*, Giorgio sings a morning serenade (called *mattinata*) to Lucia, asking her to look out the window, but she rudely rejects him, and the two end up arguing and insulting

---

50 No deer flees nor the wind flies, like Cola does in torment, thanks to that face that gives me death, bitch Lucia, the *bernovalà*.
51 I cry no longer, I don't live unhappy, I feel like I am dying of joy, thanks to that face that gives me life, hooray for Lucia, the *biernovalà*.
52 Cf. Lorenzetti, *La moresca nell'area mediterranea*.
53 Cf. Cardamone and Corsi, 'The *canzone villanesca* and Comic Culture', p. 59.
54 The Neapolitan *moresche* have been performed even recently: there is, for example, a version of the *moresca Catalina* played by Teresa De Sio; a version of *O Lucia miau miau* is in the play *Gatta Cenerentola*, by Roberto De Simone; and in 2018 the album *Moresche e altre invenzioni* was published: it includes the *moresche* of Roland de Lassus and other songs arranged and played by a choir named, not by chance, *Burnogualà*, directed by Neapolitan composer and musician Maria Pia De Vito.

each other. The *moresca Chichilichi*, as Otter writes, 'is a bit more ambitious in its dramatic action: it shows Lucia and the other character Martino in bed together, with Lucia complaining bitterly that Martino has slept all night and ignored her; in the end he makes it up to her'.[55] Besides Martino, other songs also include *Carcioffola-Cristoforo*, and another female character, named Patalena 'Maddalena', appears in another *moresca*. Therefore there are, in total, three male musicians and three female slaves, 'ma traspare anche, sullo sfondo, un'intera comunità di loro pari, spesso definiti esplicitamente "gente negra"'[56] (but there is also, in the background, an entire community of their peers, often explicitly called 'black people'). Most of the slaves purchased in the Kingdom of Naples in the sixteenth century came from the area of South Sudan (or from other areas of South Saharan Africa, such as Chad, Niger, or Nigeria), through the Libyan and Mediterranean route. As Boccadamo claims,[57] the slaves were mostly Muslims, but many converted to Christianity, often out of opportunism, not conviction. The *moresche* shed a light on the daily life, customs, and culture of this composite black community of slaves and freedmen.

As for the musical aspect, Ferrari Barassi notes that the *moresche*, like the Neapolitan *villanelle*, have features such as the alternation of three voices, repeated chords, and consecutive fifths, but unlike the *villanelle*, they have neither stanzas nor refrains and binary and ternary metres freely alternate.[58] The singing is often accompanied by vocal imitations of instrumental music (*tambililili, tronc, tron, tirintron*, and so forth), and 'just as often, the text collapses in nonsense, in apparent imitation of "incomprehensible" African speech. One *moresca* (*Ala lapia*) consists virtually entirely of such material, and Massimo Troiano's "A lan fan fan" makes liberal use of it'.[59]

According to some scholars,[60] the Neapolitan *moresche* lampooned other music genres, such as the *villanelle* or the *mattinate*, and were performed by Neapolitan and white performers, who imitated and mocked the customs and the language of the African slaves living in Naples. In particular, according to Cardamone, the *moresche* 'are likely to have originated in artistic collectives comprised of musicians with a flair for comedic routines, bringing to mind Lasso (whose familiarity with the broad tradition of Italian comedy is well known) and the Dentices, who had doubled as singing actors in comedies

---

55 Cf. Otter, 'The Neapolitan *moresche*', p. 146.
56 Salvatore, 'Parodie realistiche', pp. 99–100.
57 See Boccadamo, *Napoli e l'Islam* and Boccadamo, 'A Napoli'. About slavery in Spain, cf. Blumenthal, *Enemies and Familiars*.
58 Cf. Ferrari Barassi, 'La tradizione della moresca', p. 38.
59 Cf. Otter, 'The Neapolitan *moresche*', p. 166.
60 Cf. for instance Ferrari Barassi, 'La tradizione della moresca', Otter, 'The Neapolitan *moresche*', and Salvatore, 'Ritratti sonori'.

staged at the Prince of Salerno's palace'.[61] In any case, the language is an unusual form of spoken Neapolitan or, as Ferrari Barassi writes, 'un curioso linguaggio, basato su un dialetto napoletano alquanto storpiato e intriso di onomatopee e di parole di un gergo incomprensibile, di pretesa origine africana'[62] (a curious language, based on a rather distorted Neapolitan dialect, full of onomatopoeia and words of an incomprehensible jargon of alleged African origin). This language is similar to that used by the female slave Lucia in the *Cunto* and in the *luciate*, but with more onomatopoeia and several seemingly nonsense words, among which the aforementioned *bernaguallà*. This language can be seen in examples 28–30, taken from the *moresche* of Lassus:[63]

28) Chichilichi cucurucu,
 - Uh, scontienta: uh, beschina,
 uh sportunata me Lucia!
 Non siente, Martina,
 galla cantare? -
 - Lassa cantà, possa clepare! -[64]

(*Chichilichi*)

29) Hai, Lucia, bona cosa io dice a tia:
 che patrona fatta franca,
 Et vò bella maritare;
 Giorgia tua, a vò pigliare,
 tutta negra v'invitare,
 nott'e giorno vonno sonare
 tambililili.[65]

(*Hai Lucia*)

30) Catalina, apra finestra,
 se voi senta Giorgia cantara;
 se tu sent'a me sonara
 passa tutta fantanasia
 fate priega, core mia.

---

61 Cf. Cardamone, 'The Salon as Marketplace in the 1550s', p. 88. As for the chronology of the *moresche*, see Salvatore, 'Il contributo della lingua kanuri'.
62 Ferrari Barassi, 'La tradizione della moresca', p. 55.
63 Passage 27 is quoted from Ferrari Barassi, 'La tradizione della moresca', p. 39; examples 28 and 29 are taken from the website De Liederen Wonderhoorn, http://www.liederennederlandsvertaald.nl/index-lassus.html. As for Lassus, see Bergquist, *Orlando di Lasso Studies* and Tomasin, *Europa romanza*, pp. 193–223.
64 *Chichilichi cucurucu*, oh unhappy, oh poor, oh unlucky me Lucia! Don't you hear, Martino, the cocks singing? — Let them sing, I can die!.
65 Ay Lucia, I say a good thing to you: the mistress made me free, and I want to marry your Giorgio, and invite all the black people, they want to play night and day, *tambililili*.

Non volere scorrucciare,
perché Giorgia vol cantare
per passare fantanasia.
Spetta loco e non par tutta
quant'accordo quissa liuta,
tronc, tron, tirintron.[66]

(Catalina)

Passages 28–30 confirm the impression of 'napoletano storpiato' (distorted Neapolitan) mentioned by Ferrari Barassi in her analysis. We can recognize certain linguistic features, some of which have already been found in the *Cunto*: at the orthographic level, the use of final *-a* also in masculine words (*Martina* 'Martino', *Giorgia tua* 'Giorgio tuo', *core mia* 'cuore mio'), consonant exchanges (*r > l* in *clepare* 'crepare' and *m > b* in *beschina* 'meschina'), the presence of the metaphonetic diphthong *-ie-* in *priega* and *scontienta*,[67] and at the morphosyntactic level, the lack of definite article and a simplified verbal system.

As Otter writes, 'the language of the *moresche* suggests strongly that there was an "African-Neapolitan" that was recognizable to contemporaries, and that it resembled, as one might expect, the contact languages spoken in the Iberian Peninsula and its colonies'.[68] It could be argued that the Neapolitan *moresche*, in terms of both content and language, are related to the coeval *moresche* of the Iberian area and their *hablas de negros* (black people's languages). Some of the above-mentioned linguistic features, such as the consonant exchanges, the uncertain realization of grammatical gender, and the invariant use of the infinitive, are also characteristic of the language used in the Spanish texts. Both Otter and Salvatore refer to a Spanish piece (*Gelofe, Mandinga*) from the beginning of the sixteenth century by Rodrigo de Reinosa, which stages a lively dialogue full of insults, closely resembling the Neapolitan *moresche*.[69] For example, the refrain *Canta, Giorgia, canta* strongly recalls the Spanish *Canta Jorgico canta* where, 'besides the identity of the name and the exact replication of the refrain, there is also a strong similarity of scene [...]. The parallels, muffled but surely too strong for sheer coincidence, may well

---

66 Catalina, open the window, if you want to hear Giorgio singing; if you want to hear me playing, [...]. I don't want to get angry, because Giorgio wants to sing [...]. Wait there and don't go away, while I tune this lute, *tronc tron tirintron*. I do not provide a translation of the verses *passa tutta fantanasia* | *fate priega core mia* and *per passare fantanasia* because they are unclear. The word *fantasia* (and its variants), with different meanings, is typical of the texts in *lingua franca* (cf., in particular, Cifoletti, *La lingua franca barbaresca*, pp. 66–69).
67 The metaphonetic diphtong is caused by the presence of a final *-i* or *-u*; therefore it cannot occur in words ending with *-a*.
68 Otter, 'The Neapolitan *moresche*', p. 152.
69 Cf. Salvatore, 'Ritratti sonori', pp. 236–49. See also Lawrance, 'Black Africans in Renaissance Spanish Literature'.

point to a general familiarity with the Spanish piece rather than a direct translation'.[70] In this text, however, few African forms occur, whereas in the *moresche* from Renaissance Naples there is, as Salvatore writes, 'a treasure chest of African speech in written form'.[71] According to this scholar, the Africans in the *moresche* indeed speak 'an Afro-Neapolitan pidgin that combines the mispronounced local dialect with authentic African words and sentences'.[72] Salvatore argues that many of the seemingly incomprehensible words, like *calia, biscania, celum,* and so on, are in Kanuri, an Afro-Nilotic language still spoken in the area of Lake Chad among today's Nigeria, southern Libya, Chad, and Niger, where the Bornu Empire extended at that time, and where a flourishing activity of black slave trade was developed. The slaves, who arrived there from other areas of central and southern Africa, followed a trans-Saharan route to the shores of the Mediterranean and southern Italy. It is likely that in the *moresche*, words and sentences of the African languages coexisted and became mixed with Neapolitan. However, some of the word etymologies suggested by Salvatore seem a little forced.[73] The issue surely deserves further investigation.

The Term *pernaguallà/bernaguallà*

A particularly interesting word present in the *moresche*, the *luciate*, the *Ritratto* by Del Tufo, the engravings by Callot, the *Cunto*, and the *Tiorba* is *bernaguallà* or *pernaguallà* (also in other similar spellings), which could be considered as a hallmark of the language used by Neapolitan black people. In the *Cunto*, this term seems to mean 'black' or 'Moor'. I have already quoted the sentence *mi no stare pernaguallà* 'I am not a black slave' (repeated here as passage 31), but the word also occurs in the frame story in the metaphorical phrase *mettere la varda a bernaguallà*, literally 'to put the harness in the style of the Moors'. This means that the prince has been subdued by his slave-wife (passage 32):

31) Mi no stare schiava mossuta, mi no stare *pernaguallà*, culo gnamme gnamme, pocca stare accossì bella, e portare a fontana varrile.[74]

(V 9 39)

---

70 Otter, 'The Neapolitan *moresche*', p. 149. The name *Jorge* for the black slave is widely used in the Spanish tradition. The use of the name *Giorgio* in the Neapolitan texts depends on the Spanish influence.
71 Cf. Salvatore, '"Celum calia"', p. 154.
72 Salvatore, '"Celum calia"', p. 151.
73 However, according to the scholar Cyffer, an expert in African languages, a few words used in the *moresche* (e.g. *cilim* 'black' or *calia* 'slave') may actually be Kanuri (cf. Cyffer, 'Il kanuri').
74 I am not a slave with a big mouth, I am not a slave *pernaguallà*, arse *gnamme gnamme*, because I am so beautiful and I carry the jug to the fountain.

32) Lo prencepe, che s'aveva fatto mettere la varda a *bernagualla*, mannaie subeto a Zoza se nce lo voleva vennere.[75]

(*I Introd.* 35)

Neapolitan dictionaries explain that the word *bernagualla* means 'female slave' or 'Turkish female slave', not necessarily black (but in the *Cunto* the slave is surely black):

bernagualla 'turca, negra, mora'

(Turkish woman, black woman, Moorish woman);

pernovalla 'ritornello di una qualche canzone carnevalesca'

(refrain of a carnival song).[76]

bernagualla 'schiava turca' (la voce può avere rifer. al lat. *verna* 'schiavo', *vernalitas* 'procacità, scurrilità di servi')

(Turkish female slave (the word may refer to the Latin *verna* 'slave', *vernalitas* 'scurrility of servants')).[77]

The twentieth-century Neapolitan composer and musician Roberto De Simone, in his Italian translation of the *Cunto*, writes that *pernagualla* was 'un motto caricaturale che veniva rivolto al personaggio di Lucia [...] e prima che venisse linguisticamente corrotto e assumesse un significato derisorio, questo termine, con ogni probabilità, era mutuato dall'espressione orientale "testimonianza di Allah" o anche "mezzaluna di Dio"'[78] (a caricatural motto, refer[ring] to the character of Lucia, and before it was linguistically corrupted and assumed a derisory meaning, this term was probably borrowed from the eastern expression 'witness of Allah' or also 'star and crescent of God'). However, he does not specify his sources for his conclusion nor the Arabic expressions from which he believes the term originated.

Ferrari Barassi argues that the word *bernagualla* and its variants are connected to the Empire of Burno: a certain king of Burno is consistently mentioned in the Neapolitan *moresca* called the *Bataglia moresca del re Burno contro la gente iancha* (1546) by Flemish composer Anselmo Reulx. In this battle, black people fight and win against white people (*nigra | vinciuta | ianca faiuta* 'blacks won, whites fled', below):

33) Ai bischania gualla gualla
   bernagualla gia cala gia nigra
   vinciuta

---

75 The prince, who had been put on the harness *à la bernagualla*, immediately sent someone to ask Zoza if she would sell it to him.
76 Rocco, *Vocabolario del dialetto napolitano*, s.v.
77 D'Ascoli, *Nuovo vocabolario dialettale napoletano*, s.v.
78 De Simone, *Il Cunto de li cunti di Giambattista Basile*, p. 933, n. 1.

iancha faiuta
ca cu na gua ca cu na gua
viva viva gente negra
viva viva viva viva Re burno
viva viva viva Re burno
viva viva Re burno.[79]

(Bataglia moresca)

The name *Burno* also occurs many times in the *moresca Su genta burno*, whereas the word *pernaguallà* appears in other *moresche* with different spellings. For instance:[80]

34) Allala, pia calia,
siamo *bernagualà*!

(Allala, pia calia)

35) Allah cura chi de cua,
siamo *bernagualà*!

(Canta Giorgia)

36) *Burnoguala*, scaba canaza!
ziche, lizi dinridindina,
zocolo, zocolo
che della *burnoguala* siamo.

(Lucia celu)

37) T'haver fatta zorfanata,
Bernaguallà!

(A la lappia)[81]

According to Salvatore, the term is a noun composed by a first part which follows the proper name *Burno* (note that one of the variants is *burnoguala*, used in the *moresca Lucia celu*, see passage 36 above), and a second part which corresponds to the Arabic interjection *wa-llah!* 'for Allah!' (today used in oaths). The word originally constituted 'una orgogliosa esclamazione identitaria'[82] (a proud exclamation linked to the speaker's identity). As shown in passages 34–37, the *moresche* often

---

79 It is difficult to translate this passage, due to onomatopoeia and unclear words. I explain just the meaning of the following expressions: *viva re Burno* 'hurrah for King Burno', *nigra | vinciuta | ianca faiuta* 'blacks won, whites fled'.
80 I do not translate these examples, which are taken from Ferrari Barassi, 'La tradizione della moresca'.
81 In her work 'La tradizione della moresca', pp. 41–42, Ferrari Barassi gives the first modern complete transcription of this *moresca* by Grammatio Metallo.
82 Cf. Salvatore, 'Parodie realistiche', p. 116; cf. also Salvatore, 'Il contributo della lingua kanuri'.

Primary Sources

Basile, Giovan Battista, *Lo cunto de li cunti* [1634–1636], ed. by Carolina Stromboli (Rome: Salerno Editrice, 2013)

——, *Le Muse napolitane: Egloghe* [1635], ed. by Olga Silvana Casale (Rome: Benincasa, 1989)

Cortese, Giulio Cesare, *Opere poetiche*, ed. by Enrico Malato (Rome: Edizioni dell'Ateneo, 1967)

——, *La Rosa. Favola* [1621], ed. by Andrea Lazzarini (Pisa: Pacini Fazzi, 2018)

Del Tufo, Giovan Battista, *Ritratto o modello delle grandezze, delizie e maraviglie della nobilissima città di Napoli* [1588], ed. by Olga Silvana Casale and Maria Teresa Colotti (Rome: Salerno Editrice, 2007)

De Simone, Roberto, *Il Cunto de li cunti di Giambattista Basile nella riscrittura di Roberto de Simone* (Turin: Einaudi, 2002)

Fasano, Gabriele, *Lo Tasso napoletano* [1689], ed. by Aniello Fratta (Rome: Benincasa, 1983)

Ferraiolo, *Cronaca* [1494–1498], ed. by Rosario Coluccia (Florence: Accademia della Crusca, 1987)

Secondary Studies

Baglioni, Daniele, 'Attestazioni precinquecentesche della lingua franca? Pochi dati e molti problemi', in *Migrazioni della lingua: Nuovi studi sull'italiano fuori d'Italia*, ed. by Francesca Malagnini (Florence: Cesati, 2018), pp. 69–91

Bergquist, Peter, ed., *Orlando di Lasso Studies* (Cambridge: Cambridge University Press, 1999)

Bernini, Giuliano, 'Foreigner Talk', *Enciclopedia dell'Italiano* (2010), <https://www.treccani.it/enciclopedia/foreigner-talk_%28Enciclopedia-dell%27Italiano%29/>

Blumenthal, Debra, *Enemies and Familiars: Slavery and Fifteenth-Century Valencia* (Ithaca, NY: Cornell University Press, 2009)

Boccadamo, Giuliana, 'A Napoli: "Mori negri" fra Cinque e Seicento', in *Il chiaro e lo scuro*, ed. by Gianfranco Salvatore (Lecce: Argo, 2021), pp. 143–56

——, *Napoli e l'Islam: Storie di musulmani, schiavi e rinnegati in età moderna* (Naples: D'Auria, 2010)

Camus Bergareche, Bruno, 'Lingua franca y lengua de moros', *Revista de Filología Española*, 73 (1993), 417–26

Cardamone, Donna G., 'The Salon as Marketplace in the 1550s: Patrons and Collectors of Lasso's Secular Music', in *Orlando di Lasso Studies*, ed. by Peter Bergquist (Cambridge: Cambridge University Press, 1999), pp. 64–90

Cardamone, Donna G., and Cesare Corsi, 'The *canzone villanesca* and Comic Culture: The Genesis and Evolution of a Mixed Genre (1537–1557)', *Early Music History*, 25 (2006), 59–104

Cardona, Giorgio R., 'L'elemento orientale nel *Morgante* e nel *Ciriffo*', *Lingua Nostra*, 30 (1969), 95–101

Cifoletti, Guido, *La lingua franca barbaresca* (Rome: Il Calamo, 2004)
Cyffer, Norbert, 'Il kanuri: Una lingua in costante cambiamento storico e sociale', in *Il chiaro e lo scuro*, ed. by Gianfranco Salvatore (Lecce: Argo, 2021), pp. 355–62
D'Ascoli, Francesco, *Nuovo vocabolario dialettale napoletano* (Naples: Gallina, 1993)
Ferguson, Charles A., 'Absence of Copula and the Notion of Simplicity', in *Pidginization and Creolization of Languages*, ed. by Dell Hymes (Cambridge: Cambridge University Press, 1971), pp. 141–50
Ferrari Barassi, Elena, '"La Luciata" di Francesco Manelli: Considerazioni su una perduta stampa della Biblioteca Municipale di Breslavia, l'esemplare di un manoscritto berlinese e un componimento del "Fasolo"', in *Secondo Incontro con la musica italiana e polacca: Musica strumentale e vocale strumentale dal Rinascimento al Barocco (Bologna, 29–30 September 1970)* (Bologna: AMIS, 1974), pp. 211–42
——, 'La tradizione della moresca e uno sconosciuto ballo del Cinque- Seicento', in *La moresca nell'area mediterranea*, ed. by Roberto Lorenzetti (Bologna: Forni, 1991), pp. 37–60
Fulco, Giorgio, 'La letteratura dialettale napoletana: Giulio Cesare Cortese, Giovan Battista Basile, Pompeo Sarnelli', in *Storia della letteratura italiana*, IV: *La fine del Cinquecento e il Seicento*, ed. by Enrico Malato (Rome: Salerno Editrice, 1998), pp. 813–67
Lawrance, Jeremy, 'Black Africans in Renaissance Spanish Literature', in *Black Africans in Renaissance Europe*, ed. by Thomas F. Earle and Kate J. Lowe (Cambridge: Cambridge University Press, 2005), pp. 70–93
Lombardi, Carmela, *Danza e buone maniere nella società dell'antico regime* (Arezzo: Mediateca del Barocco, 2000)
Lorenzetti, Roberto, ed., *La moresca nell'area mediterranea* (Bologna: Forni, 1991)
Minervini, Laura, 'Lingua franca (italiano come)', *Enciclopedia dell'italiano* (2010), <https://www.treccani.it/enciclopedia/lingua-franca-italiano-come_%28Enciclopedia-dell%27Italiano%29/>
——, 'La lingua franca mediterranea: Plurilinguismo, mistilinguismo, pidginizzazione sulle coste del Mediterraneo tra tardo Medioevo e prima Età Moderna', *Medioevo Romanzo*, 30 (1996), 231–301
——, 'La lingua franca mediterranea fra realtà storica e finzione letteraria', in *I dialetti e il mare*, ed. by Gianna Marcato (Padova: Unipress, 1997), pp. 379–86
Otter, Monika, 'The Neapolitan *moresche*: Impersonation and Othering', *Mediaevalia*, 31 (2010), 143–69
Rak, Michele, 'Una moresca per Lucia (*La Luciata nuova*)', in *Il chiaro e lo scuro*, ed. by Gianfranco Salvatore (Lecce: Argo, 2021), pp. 461–74
——, *Napoli gentile: La letteratura in 'lingua napoletana' nella cultura barocca, 1596–1632* (Bologna: Il Mulino, 1994)
——, 'La schiava mora che balla: Da Salomè fino a Lucia Canazza e a Josephine Baker', in *Il chiaro e lo scuro*, ed. by Gianfranco Salvatore (Lecce: Argo, 2021), pp. 307–35

Rocco, Emmanuele, *Vocabolario del dialetto napolitano* [1891], ed. by Antonio Vinciguerra (Florence: Accademia della Crusca, 2018)

Sabatini, Francesco, Rosario Coluccia, and Antonio Lupis, 'Prospettive meridionali nella lessicografia storica italiana', in *Parallela: Atti del secondo Convegno italo-austriaco (Roma, 1–4 febbraio 1982)*, ed. by Maurizio Dardano and others (Tübingen: Narr, 1983), pp. 146–69

Salvatore, Gianfranco, '"Celum calia": African Speech and Afro-European Dance in a 16th Century Song Cycle from Naples', *Palaver*, 7.2 (2018), 151–72

——, 'Il contributo della lingua kanuri alla storia delle canzoni moresche', in *Il chiaro e lo scuro*, ed. by Gianfranco Salvatore (Lecce: Argo, 2021), pp. 363–419

——, 'Parodie realistiche: Africanismi, fraternità e sentimenti identitari nelle canzoni moresche del Cinquecento', *Kronos*, 14 (2012), 97–130

——, 'Ritratti sonori: Musica, lingua, vita e socialità afroeuropea dal teatro iberico alle canzoni moresche', in *Il chiaro e lo scuro*, ed. by Gianfranco Salvatore (Lecce: Argo, 2021), pp. 159–306

Stromboli, Carolina, 'Contatti linguistici e lingua franca a Napoli tra Cinque- e Seicento: Dalle *moresche* a *Lo cunto de li cunti*', in *Grado, la lingua del mare, l'Atlante Linguistico Mediterraneo*, ed. by Carla Marcato (Alessandria: Edizioni dell'Orso, 2021), pp. 187–204

——, 'Il plurilinguismo de *Lo cunto de li cunti*: Il caso della lingua franca', in *La variazione nell'italiano e nella sua storia: Varietà e varianti linguistiche e testuali*, ed. by Patricia Bianchi and others (Florence: Cesati, 2012), pp. 201–09

Tomasin, Lorenzo, *Europa romanza: Sette storie linguistiche* (Turin: Einaudi, 2021)

Venier, Federica, *La corrente di Humboldt: Una lettura di 'La lingua franca' di Hugo Schuchardt* (Rome: Carocci, 2012)

Weber de Kurlat, Frida, 'El tipo del negro en el teatro de Lope de Vega: Tradición y creatión', *Nueva Rivista de Filología Hispánica*, 19.2 (1970), 695–704